Accounting History

Accounting History

Some British Contributions

Edited by

R. H. Parker and B. S. Yamey

CLARENDON PRESS · OXFORD

1994

Oxford University Press, Walton Street, Oxford OX2 6DP

Oxford New York Toronto
Delhi Bombay Calcutta Madras Karachi
Kuala Lumpur Singapore Hong Kong Tokyo
Nairobi Dar es Salaam Cape Town
Melbourne Auckland Madrid
and associated companies in
Berlin Ibadan

Oxford is a trade mark of Oxford University Press

Published in the United States
by Oxford University Press Inc., New York

© R. H. Parker and B. S. Yamey 1994

British Library Cataloguing in Publication Data
Data available
ISBN 0-19-828886-7

Library of Congress Cataloging in Publication Data
Data available
ISBN 0-19-828886-7

1 3 5 7 9 10 8 6 4 2

Set by Hope Services (Abingdon) Ltd.
Printed in Great Britain
on acid-free paper by
Biddles Ltd., Guildford and King's Lynn

CONTENTS

LIST OF CONTRIBUTORS

W. T. Baxter is Professor Emeritus of Accounting, London School of Economics and Political Science.

S. Burchell is European Adviser, Special Engineering Contractors Group, London.

C. D. B. Clubb is Lecturer in Accounting, Imperial College, London.

T. E. Cooke is Professor of Accounting, University of Exeter, and Visiting Professor at the Free University Amsterdam, the Netherlands.

J. R. Edwards is Professor of Accounting, Cardiff Business School.

D. A. R. Forrester is Lecturer in Accounting, University of Strathclyde.

J. Freear is Professor of Accounting and Finance, University of New Hampshire.

J. J. Glynn is Professor of Financial Management, Canterbury Business School at the University of Kent.

P. D. A. Harvey is Professor Emeritus of Medieval History, University of Durham.

A. G. Hopwood is Ernst & Young Professor of International Accounting and Financial Management, London School of Economics and Political Science.

P. Hudson is Reader in Economic History, University of Liverpool.

R. H. Jones is Professor of Public Sector Accounting, University of Birmingham.

G. A. Lee is Senior Lecturer in Accounting (retired), University of Nottingham.

T. A. Lee is Hugh Culverhouse Professor of Accounting, University of Alabama.

R. H. Macve is Julian Hodge Professor of Accounting, University of Wales, Aberystwyth.

S. Marriner is an Honorary Fellow (formerly Reader) in Economic History, University of Liverpool.

M. J. Mepham was Professor of Accounting, Heriot-Watt University.

M. J. Mumford is Senior Lecturer in Accounting and Finance, University of Lancaster.

C. J. Napier is Senior Lecturer in Accounting, London School of Economics and Political Science.

R. Newell was formerly a Fellow of Nuffield College, Oxford.

C. W. Nobes is Coopers & Lybrand Professor of Accounting, University of

Reading.

C. W. Noke is Senior Lecturer in Accounting, London School of Economics and Political Science.

R. H. Parker is Professor of Accounting, University of Exeter, and Professorial Research Fellow, Institute of Chartered Accountants of Scotland.

D. A. Postles is Research Fellow in English Local History, University of Leicester.

D. W. Rathbone is Reader in Ancient History, King's College London.

B. S. Yamey is Professor Emeritus of Economics, London School of Economics and Political Science.

ACKNOWLEDGEMENT

The editors would like to acknowledge the generous financial support of the ICAEW Research Board.

INTRODUCTION

R. H. Parker and B. S. Yamey

I

Authors of books on bookkeeping and accounts in earlier centuries sometimes included short passages on the historical development of their subject.
The earliest British example is James Peele. In his *Pathe Waye to Perfectnes*
(London, 1569) he observed that the double entry bookkeeping system, then
known as the Italian system, was 'both auncient and famous', and 'hath bene
and is frequented, by divers nacions, and chiefly by suche as have bene and
be the most auncient and famous Merchauntes . . .'. In 1801, Dr Patrick
Kelly, a well-known mathematician and astronomer, wrote in his *Elements of
Book-keeping* that 'the origin of Book-keeping, like that of most useful arts, is
involved in great obscurity': he nevertheless offered his thoughts on the subject at some length. It is fair to say that most published observations on the
history of accounting, in all languages, up to (say) about 1875, were based on
abstract speculation on the origins and subsequent development of bookkeeping rather than on the study of surviving records. This was true not only
of the contributions of authors who wrote treatises on bookkeeping and
accounts but also of those of historians of commerce such as Anderson
(1764) and Macpherson (1805).

The first book in any language devoted exclusively to the history of bookkeeping was Benjamin Franklin Foster's *Origins and Progress of Book-keeping . . . ,*
published in London in 1852. It is a slim volume. The author was an
American who lived for some time in London and built up a fine collection
of early books on bookkeeping which apparently was lost when he returned
to the United States. The text of the book is disappointing, being a collection
of material drawn from other books, sometimes without acknowledgement of
source. It is followed by a bibliography of books published since 1543, based
almost entirely on his own collection.

Beresford Worthington's *Professional Accountants: An Historical Sketch* (London,
1895) is a more substantial work, on the restricted subject indicated in its
title. The first major book in English appeared ten years later: Richard

Brown, *A History of Accounting and Accountants* (Edinburgh, 1905). This book was published for the Chartered Accountants of Scotland in celebration of the fiftieth anniversary of the incorporation of accountants in Scotland. It was edited by Brown, a Scottish CA, and its contents range widely in time, place, and subject-matter. Perhaps of most lasting interest are the three chapters by J. Row Fogo CA on the history of bookkeeping. For many decades these chapters were regarded by foreign scholars as authoritative especially on early books in English on bookkeeping and accounts.

In 1912 *A Short History of Accountants and Accountancy* by Arthur H. Woolf, a barrister of the Inner Temple, was published in London by Gee & Co (Publishers) Ltd., a major publisher of books on accounting and the weekly *Accountant*. In fact, the book appeared originally as a series of articles in that journal. It is a useful, short survey of published material on accounting in bygone centuries, from ancient Egypt to the early modern period, followed by a quick review of early books on bookkeeping, a brief chapter on the history of auditing, and a few chapters on the 'rise and progress of professional accountants'. A much more substantial and original book appeared in 1930. It was published in Glasgow after the death of its author, David Murray. *Chapters in the History of Bookkeeping Accountancy & Commercial Arithmetic* is a mine of information, reflecting a long period of meticulous study of a variety of source materials, including early newspapers. The first 120 pages are perhaps the most useful part, dealing with 'bookkeeping and accountancy in Scotland in the seventeenth and eighteenth centuries'. But the remainder of the book of some 500 pages is also full of detailed information on a diversity of subjects. The following year H. J. Eldridge's *The Evolution of the Science of Bookkeeping* was published. This book is based on a series of illustrated lectures given by the author. It is unpretentious, and the lectures must have kept the interest of their audiences. A revised edition was published in 1954.

This short account of books on the history of accounting by British authors before the Second World War must include two further items. The first is Pietro Crivelli's English translation of Luca Pacioli's *tractatus* on double-entry bookkeeping in his *Summa de arithmetica . . .* of 1494. It was published in 1924 by the Institute of Book-keepers. It is a serviceable translation of a difficult text—difficult mainly because of peculiarities of expression and language in the original, and errors in the printing. The second is volume two of the *Library Catalogue* published by The Institute of Chartered Accountants in England and Wales in 1937. Cosmo Gordon, a classical scholar and bibliographer, spent much of his working life as librarian at the Institute. He devoted special care to the Institute's outstanding collection of books on bookkeeping. Gordon was responsible for the compilation of the published Catalogue. Earlier, in 1911, he had compiled the 'Bibliography' appended to Woolf's text; and in 1914 he had read a paper (later published), to the Bibliographical Society in London on books on bookkeeping up to 1600. The 1937 volume of the *Library Catalogue* contains a Chronological List of books from 1494 (Pacioli) to 1937. The entries are for the books in the Institute's Library, with bibliographical collations on books up to 1800.

Cosmo Gordon was active in acquiring early books for the Library. He encouraged members of the Institute and others interested in the subject to use the splendid collection, unsurpassed for its riches anywhere in the world. He was also active, with Ronald S. Edwards, in the establishment and running of the Accounting Research Association in London in the 1930s. During its short life it published three papers on the history of accounting (two of which were also published in the *Accountant*). Ronald Edwards was the author of the most substantial of these, a study (1937) of French contributions to cost accounting in the nineteenth century. He also wrote a series of articles in the *Accountant* (1937) on English contributions to cost accounting. Unfortunately, the demands of his many other interests caused Edwards after the war to discontinue his fruitful and innovative enquiries into the history of accounting.

Pieter Kats, a Dutchman who spent several years in business in London, deserves a place in any survey of British contributions to the study of accounting history before the Second World War. He had a passionate interest in the history of accounting, notably the early centuries of double-entry bookkeeping. He had a deep knowledge of the early treatises in English and Dutch, and wrote several journal articles, the most important, in Dutch, being on the influence of Dutch treatises on the English literature in the sixteenth and seventeenth centuries (in the *Maandblad voor het boekhouden*, 1925).

In all, before 1939 the British contributions to the study of the history of accounting were quite impressive. They did not, however, include studies that could compare with the best works of Continental scholars. There was nothing of the quality and range of the historical chapters in Fabio Besta's *La ragioneria* (3 vols., 1909), notably his account of early journals and ledgers he had examined in various archives in Italy. There was similarly nothing like Balduin Penndorf's systematic survey of early German archival material and of books on bookkeeping in German up to around 1650 (*Geschichte der Buchhaltung in Deutschland*, Leipzig, 1913). The books published in the Low Countries up to 1800 were given detailed attention in two volumes respectively by Pieter de Waal (*De leer van het boekhouden in de Nederlanden tijdens de zestiende eeuw*, Roermond, 1927) and Onko ten Have (*De leer van het boekhouden tijdens de zeventiende en achttiende eeuw*, Delft, 1934); these comprehensive and meticulous studies did not have counterparts in respect of the books published in English. No British author attempted an ambitious history of accounting such as the American A. C. Littleton's *Accounting Evolution to 1900* (New York, 1933). It was only Ronald Edwards whose work on the history of cost accounting was ahead of that of scholars elsewhere.

Accounting records often serve as source materials for historians, some of whom become very expert in accounting techniques. Work in this category by British authors before the Second World War includes Lamond's edition in 1890 of *Walter of Henley's Husbandry*; Hughes, Crump, and Johnson's edition in 1902 of the *Dialogus de Scaccario*; the publications of the Pipe Roll Society; and several articles and chapters on, and transcriptions of, English medieval exchequer and manorial accounts, including a series of articles (mainly in *Archaeologia*, 1911, 1925) on tallies by Sir Hilary Jenkinson. For a later period, G. E. Fussell edited in 1936 *Robert Loder's Farm Accounts 1610–1620*, a source used by accounting historians after the Second World War.

II

Not surprisingly, little was published on accounting history during the war, although mention may be made of Yamey's first paper in the area (in *The Accountant*, 1940) and Baxter's study of the *House of Hancock* (Cambridge, Mass., 1945), a business history which made excellent and pioneering use of account books as a source of historical data. Shortly after the end of the Second World War, Cosmo Gordon—back at the Institute's Library after wartime work—called a meeting of people known to be interested in the history of accounting. A gathering of four proposed an ambitious survey of the early literature. Nothing came of it.

In fact, after the war interest in accounting history did not revive significantly until the mid-1950s. By coincidence several works on professional accountancy were published in 1954. The Institute of Chartered Accountants of Scotland, the Association of Certified and Corporate Accountants, and Cooper Brothers & Co. published volumes, written from the inside, to celebrate their centenaries (ICAS, Coopers) or half-centenary (ACCA). A more critical and wider view of the profession was taken in the same year by Nicholas Stacey in his *English Accountancy: A Study in Social and Economic History, 1800–1954*. In 1956 Littleton and Yamey's *Studies in the*

History of Accounting brought together twenty-four articles on accounting from the Ancient World to the nineteenth century. Of the articles written by British authors particular mention may be made of Geoffrey de Ste. Croix's 'Greek and Roman Accounting' and Harold Edey and Prot Panitpakdi's 'British Company Accounting and the Law 1844–1900'. The compilation of Littleton and Yamey was suggested by Baxter and modelled on Baxter's *Studies in Accounting* (1950) and Solomons' *Studies in Costing* (1952). *Studies in Accounting* had reprinted Yamey's 1949 *Economic History Review* paper on 'Scientific Book-keeping and the Rise of Capitalism'. This criticized the 'Sombart thesis' of the connection between double entry and capitalism, an argument taken up and discussed by several later authors in both the UK and the USA. *Studies in Costing* included Solomons' 'The Historical Development of Costing', which pointed out, *inter alia*, that there was 'remarkably little in modern costing which our fathers did not know about. What can be fairly claimed for the last four decades, however, is that great strides have been made in converting ideas into widely adopted practices', a point taken up much later by the Americans Johnson and Kaplan in their highly influential book *Relevance Lost: The Rise and Fall of Management Accounting* (1987).

A notable feature of *Studies in the History of Accounting* was that of its twenty-four contributors only two (Baxter and Edey, both of the London School of Economics) were British academic accountants. The scarcity of academic accountants in the UK and the dominance of LSE persisted until the late 1960s. During this period LSE authors continued to contribute to the literature of accounting history. For example, Yamey and Edey collaborated with Hugh Thomson (Gordon's successor as librarian of the ICAEW) to produce *Accounting in England and Scotland: 1543–1800* (1963). Histories of professional accountancy bodies continued to be written from the inside: Garrett's *History of the Society of Incorporated Accountants 1885–1957* (1961) and Howitt's *The History of the Institute of Chartered Accountants in England and Wales 1880–1965 and of its Founder Accountancy Bodies 1870–1880* (1966) both falling within this category.

Meanwhile mainstream historians continued to grapple with accounting records. Charles Johnson produced a new edition and translation of the *Dialogus de Scaccario* in 1950 (a new edition with corrections appeared in 1983). E. Stone in 'Profit-and-Loss Accountancy at Norwich Cathedral', *Transactions of the Royal Historical Society* (1962), argued that some manorial accounts were concerned with profitability as well as stewardship. Chapter 6 of Pollard's *The Genesis of Modern Management* (1965) was a notable if controversial contribution to the history of management accounting. Livock edited the

City Chamberlains' Accounts in the Sixteenth and Seventeenth Centuries for the Bristol Record Society in 1966.

Writing on accounting history began to increase in quantity as the number of UK university teachers of accounting and academic accounting journals increased, although *Accounting Research*, published from 1948 to 1958 with the support of the Society of Incorporated Accountants, proved to be a false dawn because it closed down when the Society was merged with the three Chartered Institutes. For a brief period, until the establishment of the (US) *Journal of Accounting Research* in 1963 and (Australian) *Abacus* in 1965, the (US) *Accounting Review* became once again the world's only English language academic accounting journal. *Accounting Research* was revived as *Accounting and Business Research* in 1970. The new journals were, initially at least, sympathetic to accounting history research. Later, specialized accounting history journals appeared. *Accounting History* was published by the Accounting History Society in the UK intermittently between 1976 and 1986. A more successful launch was the (US) Academy of Accounting Historian's *Accounting Historians Journal.* In the UK, *Accounting, Business and Financial History* was established in 1990.

During the last quarter-century research into accounting history has not only grown in quantity but diversified into new areas. One factor which has made this possible has been the much easier availability of many primary and secondary sources in the reprint collections of the Arno Press and Garland Publishing of New York. All accounting historians, British as much as American, are indebted to Richard Brief for his initiative and effectiveness as editor of these collections. Many British authors have contributed to them. Numerous bibliographies have appeared, including the English Institute's *Historical Accounting Literature* (1975) and Parker's collection of *Bibliographies for Accounting Historians* (1980). A second factor has been the influence of new ideas from sociology and other disciplines which has produced what its practitioners call a 'new accounting history'. This is a literature of varied merit, which has produced some papers of high quality, for example Macve and Hoskins's 'Accounting and the Examination: A Genealogy of Disciplinary Power' (*Accounting, Organizations and Society*, 1986), which fruitfully applies Foucault's concept of *savoir-pouvoir* to accounting.

III

In choosing what to include in the present volume we have restricted ourselves to papers published since the Second World War. Indeed, the earliest paper included dates from 1965 and most of our material comes from the 1980s. Any division of the field is to some extent arbitrary. Combining chronology and theme, we have adopted the following classification: the ancient world; before double entry; double entry; corporate accounting; local government accounting; cost and management accounting; accounting theory; accounting in context. We have sought to demonstrate the great variety of the accounting history literature. By selecting only a single paper from each contributor, we have tried to give some impression of the number and range of scholars who have been working in the general field.

The continuing significance of de Ste. Croix's 1956 paper on Greek and Roman accounting has already been referred to. Macve's (1985) paper reprinted here discusses in detail the contributions made by other writers during the next thirty years. He finds little to question or extend de Ste. Croix's conclusions. More recently Rathbone has published a major study of economic rationalism and rural society in third century AD Roman Egypt. A revised version of his chapter on the accounts contained in the Heroninos archive is reprinted here.

Accounting in Europe (including Britain) before the coming of double entry has attracted the attention as much of medieval historians as of academic accountants, perhaps because of the 'barriers to entry' presented by language and palaeography. Dorothea Oschinsky, who contributed a paper to *Studies in Accounting History* in 1956, edited in 1971 *Walter of Henley and Other Treatises on Estate Management and Accounting*. A detailed review of this book by P. D. A. Harvey appeared in the *Agricultural History Review* in 1972. Harvey's own work includes his edition of the *Manorial Records of Cuxham, Oxfordshire* (1976). Harvey is represented in the present volume by the chapter on 'Accounts' in his *Manorial Records* (1984). Studies of particular aspects of manorial accounting are represented here by the work of Postles (1986) (a medieval historian) on the perception and measurement of profit (a successor to Stone's article) and of Nokes (1991) (an academic accountant) on the *excessus* balance.

Contemporary to British exchequer and manorial accounting were the early accounting records of Italian merchants and bankers. The oldest surviving European account book, a Florentine bank ledger of 1211, is the subject of a paper by Geoffrey Lee (1972). Medieval accountants did not use the same writing materials and calculating aids as later accountants. Their use of tally sticks and checkerboards is comprehensively discussed in Baxter's (1989) paper which brings together and advances our knowledge of these tools of reckoning and accounting.

The origins and development of double entry have remained a favourite area of research for British accounting historians. Geoffrey Lee's 'The Development of Italian Bookkeeping 1211–1300' (*Abacus*, 1973) and 'The Coming of Age of Double Entry: The Giovanni Farolfi Ledger of 1299–1300' (*Accounting Historians Journal*, 1977) are valuable additions to the research surveyed by de Roover in his contribution to the 1956 *Studies in the History of Accounting*. This area is represented in this volume by work by Nobes (1982) on the Gallerani account book (kept by the London branch of an Italian firm), Yamey (1993) on Italian practice in balancing and closing the ledger, and the late Michael Mepham (1988) on the development of accounting in Scotland in the eighteenth century, when a country which had previously been a laggard in accounting development became one of the leaders.

Another favoured area has been the development of corporate accounting: perhaps because Britain was one of the leaders in the nineteenth century and the records are readily available to British scholars. J. R. Edwards and his collaborators have done much useful work in this area and made much primary material more readily available. Many of the largest companies were in transport. The present volume reprints work by Forrester (1980) on canal accounts, Glynn (1984) on railway accounts, and Napier (1990) on shipping accounts.

The public sector has received relatively little attention from British accounting historians. This is consistent with the relative neglect of the public sector in most British university accounting courses but clearly does not reflect the importance of the public sector to the British economy past or present or even the availability of data. Two exceptions, the first of which is reprinted in the present volume, are Jones's (1985) paper on 'Accounting in English Local Government from the Middle Ages to *c.*1835' (the date of the Municipal Corporations Act) and Livock's paper on 'The Accounts of the Corporation of Bristol', *Journal of Accounting Research* (Spring 1965).

The history of cost and management accounting has recently attracted increasing attention from British as well as American and Australian accounting historians as emphasis has switched from the textbooks to practices and from cost techniques to cost management. A vigorous debate is in progress to which the Edwards and Newell (1991) paper reprinted here is both a contribution and an interim summing up. This is a debate where the different perspective of the economic historian has much to offer as is well demonstrated in the papers by Hudson on 'Some Aspects of Nineteenth-Century Accounting Development in the West Riding Textile Industry' and Marriner (1980) on 'The Ministry of Munitions 1915–1919 and Government

Accounting Procedures'. Freear's paper (1970) shows how ideas of relevant costs for decision-making can be traced back to the seventeenth century.

Neglected by British accounting historians but certainly not by British academic accountants in recent decades is accounting theory. The neglect of history may have contributed to the recycling of ideas which is rightly emphasized by Lee in his paper reprinted here on 'The Early Debate on Financial and Physical Capital' (1983). Also reprinted is Mumford's prescient 'The End of a Familiar Inflation Accounting Cycle' (1979). Tweedie and Whittington's *The Debate on Inflation Accounting* (1984) is a major book-length contribution to this area.

Academic accountants in recent years have placed much emphasis on looking at accounting in its various contexts and have brought into accounting history concerns not previously considered. One of the earliest contributors to this area was Hopwood, whose work includes a 1985 paper (written in collaboration with Burchell and Clubb) in which the history of value-added statements is analysed not from the point of view of accounting technique but as an illustration of social context. Jones's book *Accountancy and the British Economy: The Evolution of Ernst and Whinney, 1840–1980* (1985) is the history of a professional firm written from the point of view of a business historian. In their paper 'Gender and the Construction of the Professional Accountants', *Accounting, Organizations and Society* (August 1993), Kirkham and Loft approach professionalization from the point of gender to explore aspects of the history of the accountancy profession largely neglected by the writers of more traditional professional history, whether accounting or business historians. These different approaches are a good example of how historians of accounting, like all historians, write history in the light of their own experiences and their own conceptions of what is important and interesting.

Most accounting historians agree that the history of accounting needs to be explained in cultural as well as economic terms. This is perhaps most obviously so when accounting is 'imported' and 'exported' across national boundaries. In the two final papers in this volume, Parker (1989) explores the import and export of accounting techniques, institutions, and concepts from a British perspective, and Cooke (1991) approaches the evolution of financial reporting in Japan from a 'shame culture perspective'.

IV

More accounting history is currently being written in Britain than ever before—by 'traditional' accounting historians, by 'new' accounting historians, and by mainstream historians who do not regard themselves as accounting historians. These groups are probably not as aware of each other as they profitably might be. This book is aimed at all three groups in the hope that each will gain knowledge of the value of the others' contributions. More generally, we hope that our diversified selection of twenty-three recent papers will serve both to stimulate the demand for studies in the history of accounting and also to enhance their supply.

THE ANCIENT WORLD

I · ACCOUNTING ON A LARGE ESTATE IN ROMAN EGYPT

D. Rathbone

INTRODUCTION

This chapter is a slightly adapted version of the chapter on accounting in my study of the Heroninos archive and the Appianus estate.[1] Apart from minor changes made for the sake of clarity, I have weeded out discussion of technical textual matters which does not contribute directly to an understanding of the accounts, and I have added an introduction and some Concluding Remarks to give some essential background information. I hope that these alterations will have made the piece comprehensible in itself, although anyone who wishes to understand better the nature and the system of management of the estate which produced these accounts will need to consult the book.

The Heroninos archive is the usual name for a group of over a thousand documents, found in the ruins of the ancient village of Theadelphia, of which almost half have now been published.[2] The archive includes letters, accounts,

---

[1] D. W. Rathbone, *Economic Rationalism and Rural Society in Third-Century A.D. Egypt: The Heroninos Archive and the Appianus Estate* (Cambridge, 1991), ch. 8: 'The accounts' (the 'Concluding Remarks' appended below are drawn from pp. 400–3 of the book). Permission to adapt the chapter has kindly been granted by the Cambridge University Press and the Faculty of Classics of the University of Cambridge.

[2] A preliminary checklist of the archive is given in Rathbone, *Economic Rationalism*, Appendix IA. The abbreviations used for publications of papyri (e.g. *P. Flor.* II, *SB* XVI) are explained in J. F. Oates, R. S. Bagnall, W. H. Willis, and K. A. Worp, *Checklist of Editions of Greek Papyri and Ostraca* (3rd edn., *Bulletin of the American Society of Papyrologists*, suppl. 4, 1985). Note, however, that *P. Prag. Varcl* II are what the *Checklist* describes as 'P. Prag . . . a new series' (texts reprinted as *SB* VI 9406 to 9415. 32), and that my *P. Prag.* I denotes ed. R. Pintaudi et al., *Papyri Graecae Wessely Pragenses* (*Papyrologica Florentina* XVI, Florence, 1988). Note too that *Text* I and 2 are accounts pieced together from separately published fragments in Rathbone, *Economic Rationalism*, 424–63.

Few of the documents have been translated into English. Accounts: *Text* I, the only published complete draft monthly account of Heroninos, and *Text* 2 are translated in Rathbone, loc. cit.; A. C. Johnson, *Roman Egypt to the Reign of Diocletian* (ed. T. Frank, *An Economic Survey of Ancient Rome*, vol. ii, Baltimore, 1936), nos. 114 and 116–18 are translations of *P. Lond.* III 1226 recto, *P. Flor.* III 321 and 322, and *P. Lond.* III 1170 verso. Letters: see Rathbone, *Economic Rationalism*, passim; Johnson, *Roman Egypt*, nos. 119–20; *P. Ryl.* II 236–40; *Select Papyri* (Loeb series), I 140–6.

and receipts, which were all written in Greek and most on papyrus. Almost all the texts date from the middle decades of the third century AD and relate to the running of a large private estate, which I call the 'Appianus estate' after Aurelius Appianus, a city councillor of Alexandria, who was its owner until his death in AD 258/9, when the estate passed to his daughter Aurelia Appiana Diodora alias Posidonia.[3] The estate lay in the Fayum area of Egypt, a semi-oasis leading off to the west of the Nile valley some 60 kilometres south of Cairo. It consisted of scattered small fields, vineyards, and orchards, which were grouped into managerial 'units' called *phrontides* (literally 'concerns'); these 'units' were centred on and named after particular villages, in which the estate often also owned residential and other property. Each unit (*phrontis*) was run by a permanent 'manager', normally called a *phrontistes*. The archive of documents is named after Heroninos, who was for nineteen years (AD 249 to 268) manager of the unit of the Appianus estate centred on the village of Theadelphia, because he was the addressee of most of the extant letters and he drafted most of the extant accounts. It seems that the archive as we have it is a random assortment from Heroninos' papers as thrown out by his son Heronas, who succeeded him as *phrontistes* of Theadelphia. As a result, we have to view the Appianus estate through the keyhole of the unit at Theadelphia, but we do catch sight of other areas.

  The Appianus estate had a central administration which was located in the city of Arsinoe, the regional capital, and was run mainly by local town councillors who worked part-time for Appianus under the supervision of a 'general manager' called Alypios. About half the letters to Heroninos came from members of this central administration; the other half came from fellow *phrontistai* of other nearby units. An important figure here is Eirenaios, manager of the *phrontis* of Euhemeria, a village adjacent to Theadelphia, because a number of his draft accounts have survived among the papers of Heroninos, probably because Heroninos took them on his appointment as *phrontistes* of Theadelphia to use as models for his own accounts. It should also be noted

  Note that when documents are quoted, roundbrackets are used to mark the expansion of a word abbreviated in the original Greek text, and square brackets to mark a modern restoration of a word or part of a word now missing or unreadable in the ancient text.

  As regards the money and measures used on the estate (and the abbreviations I use for them), the main unit of monetary account was the 'drachma' (dr.), which was equivalent to seven 'obols' (ob.); to give an idea of its worth, 2 dr. 2 ob. was the most common daily wage for an agricultural labourer on the estate, and 4 dr. for heavy work and for craftsmen. Land was measured by the 'aroura' (ar.), equivalent to around 0.275 ha.; the main dry measure was the 'artaba' (art.), equivalent to almost 40 litres; the main wet measure was the 'monochoron' (mon.), roughly equivalent to 7 litres.

[3] Appianus died between June 258 and October 259, as now emerges from H. Harrauer and P. J. Sijpesteijn, 'Das Todesjahr des Aurelius Appianus, des Großgrundbesitzers im Fayum', *Zeitschrift für Papyrologie und Epigrafik*, 94 (1992), 123–7; cf. Rathbone, *Economic Rationalism*, 44–51.

that *phrontistai* could work for more than one large estate simultaneously, and one important draft account of Heroninos relates to his temporary management of the unit based at Theadelphia of the estate of Herakleides, who was himself one of the central administrators of the Appianus estate. Furthermore, on the margins of the Heroninos archive proper, there survive a number of accounts from other contemporaneous large estates in the same region, some of which had links with the Appianus estate, which can be used for comparison with or to complement the accounts surviving from the Appianus estate itself.

Although a certain proportion of the produce of the Appianus estate was consumed by its owners, managers, and staff, the primary aim was not self-sufficiency—for example, the estate never produced enough hay for its needs—but the production of marketable surpluses, mainly of olives (for oil) and wine. Different *phrontides* specialized in different crops: Theadelphia, for example, was primarily a wine-producing unit, Euhemeria an olive-producing unit. The estate had a centrally directed transport system—using asses, oxen, and camels—for farmwork (ploughing and cartage) on the units and for moving crops from one unit to another or to Arsinoe, whether for internal consumption or external sale. This transport network, which permitted rapid circulation of the letters (instructions, orders and receipts) essential to the centralized management of the estate and also the sharing of resources (such as tools) between the units, was in itself the prime economy of scale achieved by the central administration. It made it possible for the marketing of all produce to be controlled by the central administration, which instructed *phrontistai* when and where to send their main surpluses, and fixed the price for these and also small local sales. The *phrontistai* were thus essentially the local 'production managers' of a structurally unified and centrally directed economic enterprise.

The Appianus estate leased out buildings, utilities (such as presses) and some fields, but most of its land was worked directly, and the main responsibility of the *phrontistai* was to organize the labour-force and supervise its work. There were two types of permanent labourers: *oiketai*, who were lifelong dependants of the estate, and received accommodation, their subsistence (basically a monthly ration of wheat) and a small cash allowance for clothing, and *metrematiaioi*, individuals who contracted to work for the estate for a set number of years, and received their subsistence and a monthly cash salary, of which the rate varied considerably, probably according to whether or not the estate also provided the *metrematiaios* with accommodation or paid his personal tax dues for him. Casual labourers were employed when necessary, normally for a daily wage in cash, but extra labour was sometimes also recruited through contractors of various types, such as *karponai* ('crop-buyers'), men who 'bought' a share of the produce of, for instance, a particular vineyard, for which they 'paid' by contracting to provide labour for the harvesting and pressing. Labour was therefore paid for both in cash and in kind, but most payments were made in cash or at least recorded in cash terms—payments made in kind could be recorded as 'sales' of produce and set against the cash payment theoretically due.

The economy of the estate was essentially monetized, and so, it seems, was the surrounding rural economy. Indeed various systems of credit were in use which multiplied the effect of the circulating coinage. Large payments to or by the estate for sales or purchases were often routed through banks as paper transactions, and the estate kept its own individual accounts for all of its permanent and some of its casual labourers, to which their cash salaries or wages were credited, and against which the price of items purchased from the estate and cash 'withdrawals' were debited. The relatively sophisticated structure of the Appianus estate, with its central management and transport system, its interest in the production of marketable surpluses, and the monetization of its own and the surrounding economy, encourage us to look for a certain level of sophistication in its accounts.

THE ACCOUNTS

(a) Introduction

The accounts of the Heroninos archive are not only invaluable sources of information for the nature and running of the Appianus and related estates, but are also of considerable historical importance in themselves. The system of accounting on the Appianus estate, as reconstructed here, is the most sophisticated presently known from the Graeco-Roman world, and it seems, although clinching proof is as yet lacking, that it was used to measure the monetary profitability of each unit of the estate. These conclusions run counter to the conventional picture of accounting in the ancient world, for which I cannot better the neat formulation of Finley: 'Graeco-Roman book-keeping was exceedingly rudimentary, essentially restricted to a listing of receipts and expenditures, from which it was impossible to determine the profitability or otherwise of any single activity in a polyculture.'[4] Its purpose

---

[4] M. I. Finley, *The Ancient Economy* (2nd edn., London, 1985), 181 (in his 'Further Thoughts').

was just to act as a check against carelessness or dishonesty on the part of subordinates. The studies of ancient accounting on which Finley relied were those of Mickwitz and de Ste. Croix, but behind his statement there also looms the whole academic tradition of taking the form of accounts as a direct reflection of, if not as a major or even the whole explanation for, the level of sophistication of economic thought and organization in the society which produced them. For Finley and others the simplicity of ancient accounts reflects the alleged simplicity of Greek and Roman economic thought and practice.[5]

The subject is complex, and is but one small corner of the much wider debate between historians, theoreticians, and practitioners of accountancy as to whether developments in accounting practices have been and are either preconditions for advances in economic thought and organization, or *post factum* attempts to analyze the workings of independently developing economic structures, attempts motivated largely by the interests of joint-stock investors or of fiscal authorities; indeed there is some dispute about the extent to which even sophisticated modern accounts can in themselves provide a useful basis for decisions on future managerial or investment policy.[6] As regards economic history, the 'Sombart' thesis that the development of double-entry accounting was a precondition for the emergence of capitalism, because it first permitted sufficiently accurate calculation of profitability for economically rational decision-making about future investment, has met with serious challenges. The alternative view, which seems to be gaining the edge in the debate, holds that the economic rationalism of modern capitalism has been exaggerated, that complex accounting systems are often of dubious value for anything more than checking the accuracy of the records, and that simpler accounting systems were and are quite adequate for economically rational management of relatively uncomplicated economic enterprises.[7] Simple

---

[5] G. Mickwitz, 'Economic Rationalism in Graeco-Roman Agriculture', *English Historical Review*, 52 (1937), 577–89; G. E. M. de Ste. Croix, 'Greek and Roman Accounting', in A. C. Littleton and B. S. Yamey (eds.), *Studies in the History of Accounting* (London, 1956), 14–74; see also R. P. Duncan-Jones, *The Economy of the Roman Empire, Quantitative Studies* (2nd edn., Cambridge, 1982), 39–59.

[6] R. H. Macve, 'Some Glosses on Ste. Croix's "Greek and Roman Accounting"', in P. A. Cartledge and F. D. Harvey (eds.), *Crux: Essays in Greek History Presented to G. E. M. de Ste Croix on his 75th Birthday* (Exeter, 1985), 233–64, provides a very helpful introduction to this debate with extensive bibliographical references in his notes.

[7] See Macve, n. 6 above. Particularly readable and interesting contributions include: B. S. Yamey, 'Introduction', in Littleton and Yamey, *History of Accounting*, 1–13; id., 'Accounting and the Rise of Capitalism: Further Notes on a Theme by Sombart', *Journal of Accounting Research*, 2 (1964), 117–36; S. M. Jack, 'An Historical Defence of Single Entry Book-keeping', *Abacus*, 2 (1966), 137–58; also, for a somewhat different approach, A. Carandini, 'Columella's Vineyard and the Rationality of the Roman Economy', *Opus*, 2 (1983), 177–204.

accounts do not necessarily indicate a simple economic mentality. Before comparing Greek and Roman accounts with any ideal of modern practice, their appropriateness to and efficacy in the context of the enterprises which produced them should be examined.

The simplicity of Greek and Roman accounting procedures, according to previous studies, is evident from the following features. Not only was double entry unknown, but so were separate balancing columns of income and expenditure. The typical account followed a day-by-day format. Receipts and disbursements of cash and of produce were frequently listed in chronological order, all in the same column. Similar minor payments or receipts were not aggregated into single summary entries, and there was little or no grouping of items according to type. Corresponding entries (e.g. quantity of wheat disbursed, cash received from its sale) are not found, and accounts were self-contained and did not form interlocking sets. There was no attempt to cost internal consumption or transfers of produce and other resources, or to distinguish capital from income, and hence there was no possibility of calculating net profitability.

Since the accounts of the Heroninos archive exhibit many of the organizational features which are supposed not to have existed in ancient accounts, it should be said in fairness to Mickwitz that few of them had been published when he wrote, and even by the date of de Ste. Croix's article there was little historical awareness of the archive. None the less, Mickwitz did cite the then known accounts of the Heroninos archive as evidence that Roman accounting was no more sophisticated than that of the early Ptolemaic period (i.e. in third-century BC Egypt), a misjudgement partly due to the tendency found also in other studies to look at individual surviving accounts in isolation rather than considering whether they might be just one fragment of a system of accounts in which they had a specific and restricted function. Of course the general problem with the papyrological evidence from Egypt is that many texts are of uncertain provenance and date, and do not obviously belong to a particular group of documents. The accounts of the Heroninos archive thus form an especially fruitful field of study because they do come from a known and relatively well-documented context and can be studied as an ensemble.

Texts from the Heroninos archive which fall under the general heading of 'accounts' can be divided into different categories. The most obvious, because of their standard format, are the drafts of the monthly accounts submitted by *phrontistai* to the owners of the Appianus estate. Then there is a variety of accounts or records which were drawn up by the *phrontistai* for their own use. Some of these, such as the day-by-day lists of disbursements of wine or of payments made, may be termed 'primary' records. Others are syntheses of information taken from the primary records, some as intermediate steps towards the drafting of their monthly accounts, others, such as the records of employees' individual accounts with the estate, to meet particular managerial needs of the *phrontistai* themselves. Another category hardly deserves the name 'accounts', and comprises odd jottings made as reminders or in the course of calculations by *phrontistai*. Lastly, there are some fragments of various types of accounts which seem to have been kept by the central administration of the estate.

What emerges is a quite sophisticated system of accounting, in which accounts of various types were drafted by different people for different specific purposes. Because the accounts do interlock, the survival of the various types opens the door to a much sounder understanding of the nature and purpose of each type of account. Unfortunately the provenance of the archive means that the various accounts kept by the central administration are barely represented. The nature of some of them, which were the lynch-pin of the total system of accounting of the estate, has to be conjectured by extrapolation from the accounts of the *phrontistai* and hints in other texts. Finally, the fragments of comparable accounts from the other related estates serve to reinforce the suspicion that if the system of accounting on the Appianus estate is the most sophisticated yet known from the Graeco-Roman world, this may only be because its surviving accounts can and have been studied as a coherent group. Similar and even more sophisticated systems are probably lurking unrecognized in the papyri.

(b) The monthly accounts of the *phrontistai*

A task which must have occupied a considerable part of the time of the *phrontistai* of the Appianus estate was the recording of the employment of men and draught animals on their *phrontides* and of all transactions in cash and produce, and the synthesis of these records into monthly accounts for submission to the owner of the estate. There survive and have been published parts—mostly small fragments—of eight or nine monthly accounts drafted by Eirenaios as *phrontistes* of Euhemeria and of fifteen drafted by Heroninos as *phrontistes* of Theadelphia.[8] Clearly these fragments all come from rough drafts, rather than

[8] Eirenaios: *P. Prag. Varcl* II 1 (Feb. 247); Ia (Mar. 247); Ib (Apr.? 247); Ic (Mar./Apr.? 247); *P. Flor.* III 322 (Apr. 248); *P. Flor.* I p. 27 (June 248?); *P. Prag. Varcl.* II 13 (*c.*247–9?); 16(?) and 20 (dates unknown). Heroninos: *P. Prag. Varcl* II 2 (Sept. 250); 9 (May 251?); *Text* 2 (Nov. 251 or 252); *P. Prag. Varcl* 11 (251 or 252); 14 (winter 251/2); 8 (Mar.? 252?); 4 (Apr. 252?); *SB* XVI 12381 (early summer? 252?); *Text* I recto (June 253); *P. Lond.* III 1226 recto (Sept. 254); *P. Prag. Varcl* II 7 (*c.*253–9?);

from the copies submitted to the central administration of the estate in Arsinoe. Those of Eirenaios were written on the verso (back) of old rolls of papyrus, while Heroninos used both sides of the papyrus, sometimes for accounts of quite different date. Most of the fragments are written in a barely legible cursive script, with frequent cancellations and incomplete entries. They must all have come from Theadelphia, which means that they had been thrown away. No examples of the final fair copies of the monthly accounts submitted to the owners of the Appianus estate are extant. Some fragments, however, of final submitted accounts survive from other estates which had links with the Appianus estate because they were later torn up and reused for letters by the central administrators of the Appianus estate, and these accounts were much more carefully laid out and written.[9]

Although these 'monthly' accounts each cover one Egyptian month, they were not drawn up each month but drafted in groups, probably all together at the end of each Egyptian year. The best evidence for this comes from *P. Lond.* III 1170 verso, a set of accounts relating to the Egyptian year 258/9 drafted by a certain Lucretius in the name of Heroninos as *pronooumenos* (manager) of the unit at Theadelphia of the Herakleides estate (Herakleides was a local landowner who was also a central administrator of the Appianus estate). Lucretius took an old roll, already used on its recto (front), unrolled it partially and wrote on the verso (back) in what are now cols. 7–13 more or less complete drafts of the monthly accounts for Hathyr and Choiak (November and December 258), presumably based on his notes on another piece of papyrus. Unrolling the rest of the papyrus and beginning at its left edge, he then recorded cash income and expenditure for Tybi (January 259) in col. 1 and the workdays of the permanent staff lost in that month at the top of col. 2 (ll. 45–52). In col. 3 he then listed, in rather confused fashion, cash income and expenditure for Mecheir to Pachon (February to May 259), and in the first half of col. 4 (ll. 129–41) workdays lost in those months. Immediately after this (l. 142 on), he wrote out a chronological list of disbursements of wine from Tybi (January) through to mid-Pauni (June); running out of space after col. 6, he continued this list in the lower part of col. 2 (ll. 53–84), and may have then continued it, perhaps up to Mecheir (August), the final month of the Egyptian year, in the now illegible and unpublished cols. 14–16. The text reveals much about the process of composition of monthly accounts

P. Flor. III 321 (Mar. 254–9); *P. Prag. Varcl* II 6 (Dec. 260); 12 (249–62); *SB* XVI 12380 verso (Jan.? 250–68). The heading only of a draft account of Heroninos for Oct. 259 has now also been published (n. 3 above).

[9] See the plates of *P. Laur.* I 11 recto and 14 (Posidonios estate), 15 (unknown estate), and IV 174 recto (Dios estate).

through intermediate syntheses by *phrontistai* of their primary records, a topic to which we will return in the next section. The important point to note here is that in this case the process of synthesis was certainly being carried out as one operation for the accounts of the six months from Tybi to Pauni (January to June), and shortly if not immediately after production of draft accounts for Hathyr and Choiak (November and December); this set of 'monthly' accounts thus seems to have been produced in one go at the end of the year.

There are indications that the same practice was followed on the Appianus estate. In his draft account for Thoth (September) 250, Heroninos accidentally included some expenditure on casual labour which had actually occurred in Phaophi (October); he then bracketed this, presumably with the intention of transferring it to the account for Phaophi.[10] It appears, furthermore, that the final fair copies of the monthly accounts were written out on a single roll of papyrus which contained all the accounts of one *phrontis* for the whole Egyptian year, and these rolls can only have been written out and submitted after the end of the year to which the constituent monthly accounts related. The evidence for this is the numbering sometimes found in the draft monthly accounts. In *P. Prag. Varcl* II 1 and *P. Flor.* III 322, his draft accounts for February 247 and April 248 respectively, Eirenaios numbered the columns consecutively. Since the extant part of *P. Prag. Varcl* II 1 begins with col. 93 and *P. Flor.* III 322 begins with col. 115, it is clear that this numbering related to the columns of more than one monthly account. Common sense suggests that col. 1 will in both cases have been the first month of the Egyptian year, and the average number of columns which this implies for the accounts of the previous months is very plausible, if we assume that Eirenaios appended to each of his main monthly accounts a monthly 'record of hay' like those drafted by Heroninos (see further below).

The extant draft monthly accounts of Heroninos do not have numbered columns, but he may have added the numbering only when he wrote out his final fair versions. Two of Heroninos' draft accounts, however, show that the rolls of monthly accounts for each Egyptian year were numbered consecutively according to the year of tenure of the *phrontistes* submitting them. Heroninos' first year as *phrontistes* of Theadelphia was 249/50: *P. Prag. Varcl* II

---

[10] *P. Prag. Varcl* II 2. 14–23; for the bracketing see Varcl's note. Heroninos then jotted at the bottom of col. 1 'Thoth 328 dr., of which Phaophi 252 dr.' (read by P. J. Sijpesteijn, *Chronique d'Égypte*, 55 (1980), 171 n. 1), which shows that the entries in ll. 17–23 totalling 252 dr. belonged to Phaophi. In *P. Prag. Varcl* II 1. 238–40, his account for Feb. (Mecheir) 247, Eirenaios made an adjustment to correct an error he had made in his account for Dec. (Choiak). This suggests that in this case the processes of drafting and of writing out the fair copies were being carried out in tandem: presumably the correction had to be made retrospectively in the account for Mecheir because the fair copies for Choiak and Tybi had already been penned.

2, his draft account for September (Thoth) 250, is headed 'roll 2', and *P. Lond.* III 1226 recto, his account for September 254, is headed 'roll 6'.[11] No example of this is yet known from Eirenaios' accounts for the simple reason that none of them are accounts for Thoth, the first month of the year, at the top of which the roll number would have been written, but presumably this consecutive numbering of rolls and of the columns within them was standard practice on the Appianus estate.

Turning now to the format of these draft monthly accounts, those of Eirenaios bore the explanatory heading: 'To Aurelius Appianus former-*exegetes* and *bouleutes* of the most glorious city of the Alexandrians and however he is styled, from Aurelius Eirenaios *phrontistes* of Euhemeria: account of receipts and disbursements of the month "x" of the present year "y", namely . . .'. Each account then began with a record of cash (*logos argurikos*). The first part of this listed items of income. Next came the record of expenditure, which was split into three sections: first, a record, arranged plot by plot (i.e. by individual fields, olive groves, etc.), of the permanent staff and casual hired labour employed on specified tasks, noting the wages paid to the hired labourers; second, a list of the cash salaries (*opsonia*) due to the individually named members of the permanent staff; third, expenditure on taxes and other miscellaneous items. Finally, total expenditure was deducted from total income to produce the balance to be carried forward to the next month. There then followed the records for each type of produce, in the fullest extant example comprising wheat, barley, beans, vetch, hay-seed, lentils, vegetable-seed, vegetable oil, wine, sour wine, and hides. In each case the record began with a statement of the stock brought forward from the previous month, then listed, in two separate sections, receipts and disbursements made in the month of the account, and ended with the remainder to be carried forward to the next month. The records of wheat and of vegetable oil included within this format individually listed disbursements of the monthly allowances (*opsonia*) due to the permanent staff; the wheat record also contained a subsection detailing how many loaves were made and their disbursement. In the one fragment of Eirenaios' accounts which continues this far, the records of produce were followed by a summary record of the employment (*apergasia*) of the permanent staff working full-time at Euhemeria, then by a list of tools, and then, as it happened in this case, by a 'village account' (*logos komes*), a self-contained record of expenditure made on behalf of the estate-run tax collectivity at

---

[11] See further Rathbone, *Economic Rationalism*, 421–2.

Euhemeria in respect of the previous year or so; the papyrus then breaks off.[12]

The extant draft monthly accounts of Heroninos followed a broadly similar format. The introductory heading was identical in form. The record of cash (*logos argurikos*) began with a similar record of income, but expenditure was recorded in three differently organized sections: first, the list of cash *opsonia* due to the individually named permanent staff; second, the payments for papyrus and taxes; third, not separated, the wages paid to casual hired labourers and other miscellaneous expenditure. Finally, as in Eirenaios' accounts, the balance of cash to be carried forward to the next account was calculated.[13] There then followed identical records for each type of produce. Heroninos too began with the records of wheat (including lists of individual *opsonia*) and of barley, and ended with those of vegetable oil, wine, and sour wine; between these items, the extant accounts variously record transactions in hay-seed, vegetables, lentils, vetch, and chickling-seed. The only extant complete draft account of Heroninos (*Text* I recto) ended with lists of equipment—jars, axles, hides, and tools, and a record of the animals on the holding.

Separately from his main monthly accounts Heroninos also drew up monthly records of hay, which at the same time functioned as a 'record of work' (*apergasia*) of the draught animals.[14] Like the records of other produce, these too listed receipts and disbursements and calculated the balance to be carried forward to the next month. These records, however, mainly consisted of a day-by-day list of issues of hay to the asses which were based on or were visiting the *phrontis*, with a description of what they had been doing; the issues to the cattle and ass-foals, on the other hand, were given as aggregate figures for the month at the end of the record. Although there are no extant examples of records of hay drafted by Eirenaios, it can be inferred, as we have seen, from the column numbers on his extant draft accounts that he did draw up and append to each main monthly account a record of this type.

[12] For a detailed presentation of the contents of the extant fragments of the monthly accounts of Eirenaios and of Heroninos, see Rathbone, *Economic Rationalism*, 342–5 (Table 17).

[13] No figures, incidentally, for the cash balance brought forward from the previous month survive in *Text* I recto, *Text* 2, *P. Lond.* III 1226 recto (unless this was the point of Heroninos' marginal note by I. 12, added by P. J. Sijpesteijn, *Aegyptus*, 68 (1988), 74) or *P. Prag. Varcl* II 2. In the cases of *P. Lond.* III 1226 recto and *P. Prag. Varcl* II 2, both for Thoth, receipts and expenditure might have been equalized in the preceding Mesore (the last month of the Egyptian year), leaving no balance to be brought forward; alternatively, if the figure was a deficit, it would probably have appeared at the missing conclusion to their cash section (as in *P. Prag. Varcl* II 4. 87; 6. 53; 8. 32). It is, however, quite possible that Heroninos often only inserted these figures in his final fair copies after he had drafted in rough a set of monthly accounts for the whole year.

[14] *Text* I verso I–I13; *Text* I verso I14–88; *P. Laur.* IV 174 verso; *SB* XVI 12382 verso. See further Rathbone, *Economic Rationalism*, 267–9, 277–8.

Some of the differences between the accounts of Eirenaios and Heroninos reflect different practices on their *phrontides*. Because there was an estate-run tax collectivity at Euhemeria but not one at Theadelphia, Eirenaios periodically had to draft and append to one of his main monthly accounts a 'village account', whereas Heroninos had far more individual tax payments to *komarchai* (village officials) to record in each monthly account. Because the permanent staff at Theadelphia did not receive a ration of oil as part of their remuneration in the period of the extant accounts, there are no lists of *opsonia* in Heroninos' records of vegetable oil. Another difference which is simply insignificant is the varying order, even within Heroninos' accounts, of the records of crops which came between the fixed termini of the records of barley and those of vegetable oil. Other differences can be attributed to the fact that the accounts are only rough drafts. Eirenaios' reversed order for loaves and wheat *opsonia* in *P. Prag. Varcl* II 1. 66–124, and Heroninos' postponement of his record of loaves in *P. Prag. Varcl* II 6. 107–24 were clearly just mistakes which would have been rectified in the final fair copies. The same is probably true of Heroninos' apparent mixing of taxes and wages in *Text 2.* 31–48 and *P. Prag. Varcl* II 9. 3–37, though since, as we will shortly see, these drafts date to a period when he was modifying his manner of recording wages, these 'mistakes' may reflect a process of experimentation. When we compare *P. Prag. Varcl* II 1 with *Text 1* recto, the fullest extant monthly accounts of the two *phrontistai*, the former apparently lacks the lists of jars, of axles and of livestock, while the latter apparently lacks the record of work. Eirenaios, however, may well have only added these lists, which could easily have been kept separately, when he wrote out his final fair copy. Heroninos too may well have composed his record of work separately for inclusion at the final stage, a difference of procedure perhaps linked to his revised method of recording wages.

Essentially the monthly accounts of Eirenaios and Heroninos follow the same format. Presumably it was standard for all the *phrontistai* of the Appianus estate, and when Heroninos was appointed *phrontistes* of Theadelphia he borrowed some draft accounts of Eirenaios to use as exemplars, thus accidentally saving them for posterity. There are, however, hints that the system was not inflexible, in that Heroninos appears to have made some improvements to the standard format. The first and minor one is that whereas Eirenaios recorded loaves as a subsection within his record of wheat, Heroninos made his record of loaves a separate one, thereby rendering his record of wheat neater and clearer. The more important change affected the recording of wages paid to casual labourers. The practice of Eirenaios, most clearly evident in *P. Flor.* III

322, was as follows. The first part of his record of expenditure dealt in turn with each plot of his *phrontis*—fields (*kleroi*), olive-groves, and so on—on which work had been done in that month. Each part had its own subsection, headed by its name, in which Eirenaios gave single aggregate entries for each type of labourer doing the same job. In entries for wage labourers he recorded the total due as wages, but he also recorded the number of days worked by his own permanent staff, who were salaried and received no wages, and quantified the work done either by the area of land or the resulting produce. Lastly he totalled the wages paid and the number of days worked by the permanent staff on the plot. To illustrate this I give a translation (with some figures restored *exempli gratia*) of the subsection in *P. Flor.* III 322. 35–49.

> Field (*kleros*) of Crown Land, Seventy-Arourai locality:
>> Bundling hay on the 5 ar. which were (recorded as) mown in
>>> the previous account, 8,800 bundles at the rate
>>> of 9 dr. per ar., 4[5] dr.
>> Transporting hay, [x asses(?).]
>> Loading (them), 21 [*oiketai* and *metrematiaioi*.]
>> Accompanying (them), [17(?) men at 2 dr. 2 ob.(?), 39] dr.
>> Stacking (it), [29(?) *oiketai* and *metrematiaioi*.]
>> Harvesting 8 ar., 32 *epoikiotai* through the men
>>> from Kleopatras and Myronos at 2 dr. 6 ob., 91 dr. 3 ob.
>> Tying up sheaves, 4 *oiketai* and *metrematiaioi*, 33 loads.
>> [?] mowing 2 ar., 12 *oiketai* and *metrematiaioi*, 12 loads.
> Total for the *kleros*: 175 dr. 3 ob.,
>>>> [6]6(?) *oiketai* and *metrematiaioi*.

It seems that in his first couple of years as *phrontistes* of Theadelphia Heroninos used much the same format, but with one major modification. In *P. Prag. Varcl* II 2 of September 250, his earliest extant draft monthly account, the record of expenditure begins with the section for wages paid, organized so that each separate plot of arable land and vineyard was dealt with in turn. Heroninos, however, did not record in these subsections the labour done by the permanent staff on his *phrontis*. Subsequently, certainly by the time he came to draft his monthly accounts for 252/3 and possibly already in 251/2 (depending on the date of *Text 2* and the other accounts of *c*.252), he decided to make further modifications. First, the wages paid to agricultural labourers were no longer recorded as the first section of expenditure, but were put after the sections dealing with cash *opsonia* and taxes, and thus were joined with the wages and prices paid to carpenters and other craftsmen and other miscellaneous expenditure. Secondly, instead of grouping payments primarily by locality, Heroninos now tended to group them primarily according to the type of job done with separate sub-entries for each locality. In *SB* XVI 12381, for example, the extant entries form the following subsections: wages for mowing and bundling hay in various fields, wages for harvesting barley in two fields (cancelled), wages to a carpenter for work in various vineyards, wages for harvesting leguminous crops, miscellaneous purchases, wages for storing hay, and payments to another carpenter for items made. A similar organization of entries is evident in *Text* I recto, again not perfectly done, but clear enough to be seen as a deliberately new format.

It could, I suppose, be argued that the format found for recording wages in Heroninos' later accounts had always been the standard one used on the estate, and that the plot-by-plot format was only an intermediate stage in the compilation of the final copies of the monthly accounts from the primary records of the *phrontistai*. This is not, however, very likely, because it does not explain the repositioning of the section for wages within the record of expenditure. Furthermore, since we seem to be able to trace the development of the change in Heroninos' draft accounts, it is probable that the change was his own idea, although presumably he had to persuade the central administration that it was an acceptable improvement; whether they then made other *phrontistai* adopt this revised format we cannot tell.

The revised format was an improvement because it had greater clarity and concision. It made sense to group together the wages for agricultural labouring and the wages and other sums paid to carpenters and the like because these were all in the end similar costs of production. The work done by the permanent staff was not really relevant in a section about cash expenditure, and was repeated anyway, in summary form, in the 'record of work' (see *P. Prag. Varcl* II I. 245–70). Eirenaios' accounts in this respect gave the central administration more information about the deployment and productivity of labour on his *phrontis*, but arguably in a detail that was unnecessary. Efficient management of production was the job of the *phrontistes*; failure on his part would have been evident from small crops and high total figures for expenditure. The information presented in accounts drafted according to Heroninos' revised format was sufficient to allow anyone interested to check, far more quickly than was possible with the old format, how much outside labour Heroninos had employed in total in that month, on what tasks and at what rates of pay, from which it would soon have been apparent whether his employment of outside labour had in general been reasonable or not. Similarly, the record of work in itself gave sufficient indication of whether the permanent staff had been usefully employed or not.

Even before the change of format, however, the monthly accounts of the Appianus estate exhibited relatively sophisticated features, mostly relating to the fact that they were monthly summaries of transactions which synthesized and compressed information from primary records to make it more immediately comprehensible. Cash and the different types of produce each had their own section, subdivided into receipts and disbursements, so there was no mixing of different types of transaction. Transactions were normally not listed individually or chronologically, but merged into single entries according to type. An obvious exception is the record of hay, which did retain day-by-day entries, but this was for the particular reason that it also functioned as a record of the employment of the estate's draught animals, and the extra detailed information was needed by the central administration, which is also why it was submitted as a separate appendix to the main monthly account.

Another exception, which probably represents persistence of older practice, is the individual listing of the recipients of *opsonia*; these payments could perhaps have been aggregated anonymously, although there were the problems that the staff did not all receive the same rate of remuneration and there were odd temporary changes in personnel. Other individual payments were recorded as such, like those to carpenters, simply because they were one-off payments. However, the anonymous aggregating of, in particular, payments to casual labourers was a great aid to concision and clarity, and was enabled, as were the summary entries in the records of work by the permanent staff, by the concept of using '*ergates*' ('labourer') or any similar noun denoting a working entity (e.g. '*oiketes*', '*epoikiotes*', 'ass') to mean in effect 'man/day' (or 'animal/day'). The record of work, for instance, in *P. Prag. Varcl* II 1. 245–70 begins: 'Record of work of the *oiketai* and *metrematiaioi*, 14 in number over the (days) from 1 to 30, making a total of 420 man/days (*ergatai*), according to locality as follows . . .' Thus primary records of odd numbers of men working for a different number of days on the same task could be synthesized into single entries (e.g. 4 men for 2 days plus 3 for 5 days makes 23 man/days).

Because the transactions involving cash and each type of produce were grouped in separate sections, corresponding entries are found for transactions which crossed categories. The most common cases concern sales or purchases of produce, which had corresponding entries in the record of cash and the record of the appropriate type of produce for, respectively, the receipt or disbursement of the cash and the disbursement or receipt of the produce. This applied equally, despite its separateness, to the record of hay: *Text* I recto 79–80, for instance, records expenditure of 800 dr. on a purchase of hay, and *Text* I verso 4 receipt of the hay purchased. Other examples of corresponding entries occur in *P. Prag. Varcl* II I. 171, 176, where Eirenaios recorded disbursement of I art. vegetable seed for making oil in his record of vegetable seed and receipt of the I metron of oil made from it in his record of oil, and in *P. Prag. Varcl* II 6. 83, 108, where Heroninos recorded disbursement of I art. wheat for making bread in his record of wheat and receipt of the 44 double-loaves made from it in his record of loaves. It should also be noted that entries for receipts and disbursements of produce were also aggregated where possible: the prime example is that Eirenaios and Heroninos recorded almost all sales of produce as single figures for the month, with no specification of the individual purchasers.[15]

On a bigger scale the monthly accounts of each *phrontistes* formed a continuous interlocking chain in that each record of cash and of produce ended with a balance to be carried forward to the account for the next month, and began with a statement of the balance brought forward from the account for the previous month. Some other entries reveal consciousness of the existence of a cumulative series of accounts. In *P. Flor.* III 322. 36–7 (quoted above) Eirenaios entered wages for bundling hay on 5 ar. 'which were (recorded as) mown in the previous account', and in *P. Prag. Varcl* II I. 238–40 he deducted 2 mon. from his total of sour wine in stock to compensate for an error made in his account for the previous December. The system, furthermore, of each *phrontistes* putting his accounts for each year on a new roll which he numbered according to the year of his tenure, and then numbering the columns within each roll consecutively, provided a cumulative 'volume' and 'page' numeration which could have facilitated subsequent consultation of these accounts.

The last, and important, point to note is that the monthly accounts of the *phrontistai* had close links with other secondary accounts (discussed in the next section) drawn up by them for their own use rather than for submission to the central administration. The most significant of these were probably the individual accounts kept for each of the permanent staff (and some of the casual labourers) on each *phrontis*, to which their cash salaries (and wages) were credited, rather than being paid on the spot, and against which were debited the price of any produce purchased from the estate, sundry other charges, and actual cash 'withdrawals' made by the employees. The monthly accounts, on the other hand, recorded what had theoretically been paid to each employee each month rather than what he had actually received, and similarly many other recorded payments and disbursements had been credit

---

[15] See further Rathbone, *Economic Rationalism*, 284–6, 314–15.

transactions or were completed only some time after the transaction was recorded as having taken place. Only the other secondary accounts kept by the *phrontistai* revealed, for example, how much cash, and when, had actually been paid to these employees and what was still owing to them. The implications of this practice for the estate's system of accounting as a whole will be discussed in section (*e*) below. The technical point of procedure to be noted here is that because the *phrontistai* kept these other secondary accounts which told them what the actual state of affairs was, they were able in their monthly accounts to record all transactions in the month when they had theoretically taken place. Hence anyone examining these accounts would have found all transactions recorded in their proper historical context in terms of the agricultural activity or need to which they related. The monthly pattern of expenditure recorded in the monthly accounts thus reflected the historical incurring of costs rather than the *post factum* cash flow.

The monthly accounts submitted by the *phrontistai* of the Appianus estate were therefore fairly compressed and sophisticated syntheses of primary information about the monetary and other transactions and the work carried out on each *phrontis* in each month, whose format can be shown to have undergone some refinement in the period covered by our documentation. They formed an interlocking series in themselves, and were also linked with other secondary accounts kept by the *phrontistai*. Before turning to look at the primary records and these other secondary accounts, and then at the use perhaps made of the monthly accounts by the central administration of the estate, there follows a brief examination of the few monthly accounts of *phrontistai* which survive from other estates related to the Appianus estate, in order to compare their format and content.

The nature of *P. Lond.* III 1170 verso, a papyrus which contains drafts in various stages of completion of a set of monthly accounts for the Theadelphian *phrontis* of the Herakleides estate in a year when it was being managed by Heroninos, has already been discussed above. The most complete drafts, those for November and December 258 in cols. 7–13, show close similarities to the accounts of the Appianus estate. Both have a similar introductory heading, and then a section recording cash income and expenditure. Next comes a record of work done by the permanent staff on the unit, analogous to that in *P. Prag. Varcl* II 1. 245–70. This is followed by a record of receipts (only stock in hand, as it happens) and disbursements of wine, and then by a day-by-day record of the employment of asses on the unit and a summary record of the employment of its yoke of oxen.

The lack of records for any other produce apart from wine is surprising, especially since l. 433 records a receipt of cash from the sale of 2 art. wheat, and this raises the suspicion that these drafts were far from complete. It is therefore possible that the records of the employment of asses were also meant to function as records of hay, but that the disbursements had not yet been added to them—a simple mechanical task of entering 10 bundles of hay per ass at the unit each day. Some aggregating of information into single entries is evident, above all in the records of work, but the process was far from complete in other sections. The receipts of cash, for example, in ll. 429–34 included three separate dated entries for sums received from the steward (*epitropos*) Horion (no entries for cash expenditure are legible), and the disbursements of wine are still listed as individual dated issues although they have been grouped and totalled for each separate recipient. On the other hand it is clear that receipts and disbursements of cash and of wine were totalled each month to produce a balance which was carried forward to the account for the next month, so these monthly accounts must also have formed a cumulative interlocking series.[16] Since Herakleides was an adminis-trator (*oikonomos*) of the Appianus estate, and some of his managers (Heroninos, Horion) were also employees of Appianus, we would expect the accounts on his estate to have been similar, and I conclude that they were and that the apparent differences are merely due to the incompleteness of these drafts.

We have fragments of two accounts submitted by *phrontistai* which certainly come from the estate of Posidonios (the father-in-law of Appianus), and of another three which probably relate to that estate.[17] Though basically similar to the accounts of the Appianus estate, they exhibit one significant difference. The main similarities are their monthly format, the use of separate sections for records of cash and each type of produce, and within these sections the separate listing first of receipts and then of disbursements, and the calculation of the balance to be carried forward to the account for the next month. The accounts therefore formed an interlocking series, and one of them, *P. Laur.* I 11 recto, shows that the columns were numbered consecutively for each year's set of accounts. The records of cash expenditure aggregate payments of wages to casual labourers doing the same task. A slight difference is the pay-ment of a standard daily wage of 12 ob., so that in *P. Laur.* I 11 recto the *phrontistes* gave up recording the total wages for each entry after ll. A14–17

---

[16] See ll. 272, 318, 372–4, 429, 467–8, and 516 (this last is probably the balance in cash to be carried forward from Choiak).

[17] Certain: *P. Flor.* I 100 (recording wheat and barley); *P. Laur.* I 11 recto (cash). Probable: *P. Laur.* I 14 (cash and wheat) and 17 (a dry crop and wine); *P. Prag. Varcl* II 15 (cash).

and in l. B15 calculated a single total for all labouring done that month. Another slight difference is that few recipients of cash *opsonion* appear in these accounts, presumably because there were few salaried permanent staff on the units to which they relate.

The main difference is that normal practice on the Posidonios estate was apparently to draw up separate monthly accounts for cash on the one hand and produce on the other. Admittedly *P. Laur.* I 14 includes sections both for cash and for wheat, but it is not certainly from the Posidonios estate; if it is, then this practice was not absolutely uniform, or there may have been a change. The clearest evidence comes from *P. Flor.* I 100 which, after the introductory heading, launches straight into the record of wheat, followed by that for barley. In contrast *P. Laur.* I 11 recto is a record of cash income and expenditure for February of an uncertain year, of which the initial column is numbered '20'. This implies an average length of under four columns for the accounts of the previous five months. Since the account for February ends at the bottom of col. 21, it is probably a fragment from a roll which contained the monthly records of cash alone submitted by this *phrontistes* to Posidonios' daughter Demetria. It is, incidentally, not possible to argue that these accounts are incomplete drafts, for they seem to be fragments of the final fair copies submitted by the *phrontistai*, which were subsequently torn up and reused on the back for letters by the central administration of the Appianus estate. Although they were submitted on separate rolls, the records of cash apparently still had entries which corresponded to entries in the records of produce, such as the entry in *P. Laur.* I 11 recto, A10–11 recording receipt of 240 dr. from the sale of 20 art. wheat, which presumably figured as a disbursement in the record of wheat for the same month.

The only fragment of an account from the Dios estate, *P. Laur.* IV 174 recto, breaks off almost immediately after the introductory heading, so nothing can be said about its format. *P. Mich.* XI 620 from the estate of Titanianus (another contemporary large landowner in the Fayum) contains a record of the leasing out of rooms over the half-year March to August 239, and also parts of draft monthly accounts for August, November, and December 239 and January 240 which were written on the recto and verso of the papyrus by Alkimedon, the manager of Titanianus' *phrontis* at Theadelphia. Probably Alkimedon submitted these monthly accounts in fair copy in one go at the end of the year. Although the drafts on this papyrus fall across two Egyptian years (238/9 and 239/40), those for 238/9 are on the recto while those for 239/40 are on the verso; furthermore the draft for November 239 is dated 2 December 239 and that for December is dated 1

January 240 (ll. 201–2, 257–8). It seems that Alkimedon did a first draft of each monthly account at the end of each month, but only completed them and produced the fair copy at a later date, probably the end of the year.

Essentially Alkimedon's monthly accounts are structured like those of the Appianus and the Posidonios estates. They have similar introductory headings, separate sections for cash and each type of produce, with separate listing of receipts and disbursements and calculation of the balance to be carried forward to the account for the next month, and work records for the three asses based on the unit.[18] The many omissions and inconsistencies, such as the lack of any record of cash income for August and December 239 or of cash income and expenditure for January 240, and the haphazard order of the records of produce, merely indicate that these texts were very preliminary drafts. As on the Appianus estate, the records of cash and produce were presented together in the same account. The entries recording payment of wages to casual labourers are aggregated, but—at least in this draft form—give more detail about the jobs done than is found in Heroninos' accounts. The only significant difference, however, from the monthly accounts of the Appianus estate, is that there were separate records of hay and of the work done by the asses based on the unit, inevitably with some overlapping information, rather than a record of work for all animals based on and from outside the unit which also noted the issues of hay. This will have made it more difficult to examine the overall deployment of the estate's draught animals, and the different practice of the Appianus estate was presumably developed in response to the particular interest of its administration in efficient management of its transport resources.

On the whole, therefore, the evidence available suggests that the estates related to the Appianus estate employed very similar systems of accounting, at least in terms of the format and content of the monthly accounts which their *phrontistai* were required to submit. The accounts of the Appianus estate show some signs of development, but they were not unique either in concept or in format. It would be interesting to try to assess the diffusion and to trace the development of accounts of this type, but this is an enterprise which would far exceed the bounds of this study.[19]

---

[18]   Headings: ll. 122–9; 203–10; 259–64. Records of cash: ll. 130–56. Records of wheat: ll. 157–69; 211–15; 265–77. Of lentils: ll. 170–9; 247–8. Of hay: ll. 216–27; 278–96. Of wine: ll. 180–91, 198–200(?); 228–42. Of sour wine: ll. 243–6; 297–305. Of reeds: ll. 306–22. Of cords: ll. 323–6. Work-records of asses: ll. 192–7; 249–56.

[19]   See, however, the 'Concluding Remarks' below.

(c) Other accounts of the *phrontistai*

The draft monthly accounts of Eirenaios and Heroninos do not record in full detail every operation and transaction which took place on their *phrontides*, but are a synthesis and distillation of this potential total information. Other texts exemplify the various types of working accounts which were kept by the *phrontistai*. These can be divided broadly into 'primary' and 'secondary' records, and the latter category can be subdivided into compilations of information for the use of the *phrontistes* himself and those undertaken as an intermediate step in the production of the monthly accounts. The main distinguishing marks of these working records are that they normally dealt with only one subject, and often recorded each transaction individually naming the person or persons involved, and listing them in chronological order. Since the monthly accounts were actually drawn up and submitted at the end of each Egyptian year, it is not surprising to find that the working records frequently covered operations and transactions over a period of several months, and sometimes from one Egyptian year into the next. The main limit to their length seems to have been the size of the piece of papyrus used, for all these working records, being for the use of the *phrontistai* rather than for submission to the owner, were written on scraps from old rolls of papyrus.

The largest group of extant working records relates to the production and distribution of wine. *P. Prag.* I 116, to begin with, is a checklist in the hand of Heronas, Heroninos' son (and, after 268, his successor as *phrontistes* of Theadelphia), listing some of the Theadelphian vineyards in order of the days in August 252 on which the grapes from them were pressed. *SB* XIV 12054 is a much fuller chronologically ordered account of part of the vintage at Theadelphia on 4–11 August 253, and *SB* XVI 12380 recto is a fragment of a similar account. The entries for each day record how many baskets of grapes from each *ktema* (vineyard) were pressed, the bonuses given out of this to the various workers and other issues set against their wages, the share taken in the case of some *ktemata* by *karponai* (labour contractors), and the final net yield to the estate. The last two columns of *SB* XIV 12054 show Heroninos excerpting and summarizing the information to be transferred to his monthly account—the net yields from individual vineyards or groups of vineyards, and the quantities received by the *karponai* as their shares; the jars issued as free bonuses and in lieu of cash wages were also presumably totalled and transferred. A minor point of interest is that the blank entries in ll. 62 and 99 suggest that Heroninos computed the gross yields for each vineyard retrospectively from his totals for disbursements, a neat way of ensuring that no unaccountable losses would appear in his records!

At the end of the (probably incomplete) account of the vintage in *SB* XVI 12380 recto Heroninos began to keep another kind of record in which he first listed some quantities of wine in reused foreign jars which he had presumably received from another unit of the estate, and then, just as the papyrus breaks off, their disbursement. The jotting in *P. Laur.* III 98A similarly lists some small quantities of wine received from seven Theadelphian vineyards, and then, in a second hand, records various disbursements made over a number of days. These records belong to a larger group, of which the clearest examples are *P. Laur.* III 99, of Eirenaios, and *SB* XIV 11555, in the hand of Heronas, both headed 'account of disbursements (of wine)'. In the accounts of this type the *phrontistai* recorded disbursements of wine to other units and to named individuals, normally in a day-by-day format, and sometimes after a section recording receipts of wine from elsewhere.

Some of these accounts do look like primary records. *P. Prag. Varcl* II 21, for instance, is a day-by-day account of Heroninos recording issues of wine made on the account of the central administrative assistant Pontikos over the period 10 August to 5 October 250, on the back of which, published as *P. Prag. Varcl* I 1, he was at the same time keeping a running receipt for deliveries of wine from August 250 to February 251 to Tryphon, the then *phrontistes* of Philoteris. Others, however, were clearly not primary records. *P. Flor.* I 76, an account in the hand of Heronas, is a long list of undated small disbursements of wine to individuals which includes, in two separate groups, the disbursements recorded in the extant part of *SB* VI 9472, another account in Heronas' hand, which itself first records the receipt on consecutive days of a number of consignments of wine from Talei, and then undated disbursements of this wine.[20] *P. Flor.* I 76 thus seems to have been a conflation of information from a number of accounts like *SB* VI 9472, which each apparently dealt with the wine from a particular source, and was probably a stage towards consolidation of the disbursements into the type of anonymous aggregate figures found in the monthly accounts. We may also note that an alternative or subsequent stage in this process is represented by the records of wine in *P. Lond.* III 1170 verso, a set of preliminary drafts of monthly accounts for the Herakleides estate (discussed in the previous section), in which the disbursements, though still dated, had been grouped under the name of each recipient.

---

[20] Correspondences between *SB* VI 9472 and *P. Flor.* I 76 are: ll. 9–12 certainly = 1–4; 13–14 probably = 5–6; 15 possibly = 36–7; 16–17 certainly = 38–41.

Even accounts like *SB* VI 9472, however, or indeed *P. Laur*. III 99 and *SB* XIV 11555, since they tend to separate receipts and large-scale and small-scale disbursements, and often appear to have been written out in one go, were probably secondary compilations from the scattered primary information of odd jottings and of the letters ordering and acknowledging transfers and disbursements of wine which constitute a large part of the Heroninos archive. Probably most of these accounts are the product of a gradual and fairly unsystematized process of compiling and distilling the information into the format required by the monthly accounts. Indeed there is a puzzling lacuna which suggests that not all stages of the procedure are represented in the extant documentation. None of these accounts contain any recognizable indication of whether the *phrontistes* had merely transferred the wine, or disbursed it gratis, or sold it for cash or set it against the recipient's wages or salary. *P. Laur*. III 99 and *SB* XIV 11555, accounts of Eirenaios and Heronas respectively, both record a mixture of transfers to other units, of presumably free issues to visiting administrators and local officials, and of disbursements to estate employees and outsiders, some of which must have been set against pay while others must have been cash sales. Sales to estate employees could have been noted immediately in their individual accounts with the estate, but unless we suppose that the *phrontistai* could simply remember the details in the other cases, this information must have been recorded somehow somewhere else.

There are only three extant examples of working records kept by *phrontistai* for other crops, *P. Laur*. I 35 verso, *P. Prag. Varcl* II 19 and *SB* XVI 12526. 9–29. All three are similar accounts, of either Eirenaios or Heroninos, which start with a dated list of receipts of wheat from the harvests of particular named fields, specified in *P. Prag. Varcl* II 19 as being among those 'worked by ourselves'. In *P. Laur*. I 35 verso and *P. Prag. Varcl* II 19 there follow some more dated receipts from named individuals, probably lessees of other plots of land. *P. Prag. Varcl* II 19 continues with a dated list of disbursements to named individuals, and *SB* XVI 12526 with a dated list of quantities 'forwarded' elsewhere. These accounts are very similar in format to some of the working accounts of wine, especially *P. Laur*. III 98A and *SB* XVI 12380 recto (see above), and support the reasonable guess that the same sorts of working accounts were drafted for other crops as for wine, and that the information in them was condensed in the same way to produce the relevant sections in the monthly accounts of the *phrontistai*.

Turning now to the recording of the employment and remuneration of labour, we have a fine example of an indubitably primary record in a probably contemporary waxed wooden diptych from an unidentifiable large estate in the area around Karanis (north-eastern Fayum), which records the employment of labourers at the harvests of various crops.[21] The men employed were individually named in a day-by-day format under general rubrics which gave the locality and the nature of their work; the author sometimes also noted the quantities of crops produced from the threshing. The plot-by-plot sections dealing with labour in the records of cash expenditure in Eirenaios' draft monthly accounts, of which an example has been quoted above, followed basically the same format, except that the total number of man/days spent on each job was given and not the name of each labourer, and that the rates of pay and totals due were added. So although there is no reason to suppose that the diptych comes from the Appianus estate, it is very likely that its *phrontistai* too kept primary records of this type. Heroninos, as we have seen, later developed a more concise way of presenting this information in his monthly accounts, but he must still have kept similar primary records and transferred the data to papyrus in an intermediate format perhaps not unlike that of Eirenaios' final versions. The work done by the permanent staff on each *phrontis* must have been synthesized separately to produce the records of work like those found in *P. Prag. Varcl* II 1 (of Eirenaios) and *P. Lond.* III 1170 verso (Herakleides estate); days lost through illness, liturgic (i.e. public) duties, and so on, must also have been noted and totalled.

As regards the salaries due to the permanent staff on the estate and the manner in which they were paid and recorded, an account which has been described but not published shows that Eirenaios kept together on one roll individual accounts for each permanent estate employee attached to his unit, to which he credited each month the cash salary due to them, and against which he debited any actual cash payments made to them, and charges for estate wine sold to them and for dues such as the *isophorion* (a collective fiscal charge) and the bath-levy; periodically he totalled the amount due to them as salary and any other credits, totalled the debits, and noted the resulting sum which the estate owed them or they owed it. The monthly payment of their wheat ration to them was also noted in these accounts.[22] Meanwhile, as we have seen, in his monthly accounts, Eirenaios recorded the cash salaries as if they had been paid every month in cash. The wages due to casual labourers

[21] A. E. R. Boak, 'An Overseer's Daybook from the Fayoum', *Journal of Hellenic Studies*, 41 (1921), 217–21 (with plates).

[22] See J. Bingen, 'Les comptes dans les archives d'Héroninos', *Chronique d'Égypte*, 26 (1951), 378–85 (with a different interpretation from mine); cf. Rathbone, *Economic Rationalism*, 112–14, 124–6.

were probably computed and recorded when they were paid at the end of each job, which was probably also when the information kept on waxed tablets like the Karanis diptych was transferred to papyrus. Although the monthly accounts record all wages as if paid at the time in cash, we know that wages earned by relatives of a permanent employee could be credited to the account with the estate of that employee, and *P. Laur.* III 99. iii. 8–20 and *SB* XVI 12526. 1–8 show that Eirenaios also kept similar individual accounts for some casual labourers, to which their relatives' wages could also be credited. Sometimes casual labourers too bought estate produce and had its price set against their wages, and *PSI* VII 811, a text perhaps from the Appianus estate, illustrates the kind of record a *phrontistes* might have kept of the arrangement: it lists the number of man/days' work done on three fields (*kleroi*) in Phaophi, multiplies the total by the wage of 2 dr. 6 ob., making 200 dr., and deducts 144 dr. for the price of twelve jars of wine, and 16 dr. which was paid in cash through a certain Ploution; the remaining 40 dr. were presumably still owing to the labourers.

The remaining extant working records of *phrontistai* all concern cash payments. *P. Flor.* III 375 verso is an account of Eirenaios which records in chronological order payments apparently due or made to members of the tax collectivity at Euhemeria as remuneration for their discharge of liturgic (i.e. public) functions on behalf of the collectivity. These payments would later have been totalled and recorded as an item in the 'village account', contributing to the total expenditure of the collectivity which was then divided to produce the per caput charge called the *isophorion*.[23] *SB* XIV 11556 is an account in the hand of Heronas which seems to record actual payments in cash, ranging from 4 dr. to 72 dr., to various estate employees; the only payment for which a reason is given is that of 40 dr. to Eudaimon, perhaps the *paralemptes* (a central administrator, in charge of central stocks of produce), 'towards the price of wheat', and the rest were probably 'withdrawals' of cash to be debited against the employees' individual accounts with the estate. This short text is the nearest we have to anything resembling part of a 'cash-book' of a *phrontistes*. Otherwise there is Heroninos' jotting of some unexplained sums in *P. Prag.* I 114 recto B, and two short and obscure 'village accounts' written by Heroninos or Heronas in *SB* XIV 11557 and *P. Laur.* III 98B. Other accounts of cash which come from the Appianus or a related estate and which may have been drawn up by a *phrontistes*, though they may derive from the central administration, are *P. Prag.* I 94, a brief account of expenditure on an

---

[23] See further Rathbone, *Economic Rationalism*, 121–3.

oil-press, and *SB* I 4424, a fragment of an account probably of miscellaneous expenditure. The relative lack of working records of cash receipts and payments is rather surprising. It may be a fluke of survival or publication, but another possibility is that these records were kept more carefully and were not thrown out with the other papyri. However, despite the lacunae in the surviving sample, enough is preserved to illustrate how the monthly accounts of the *phrontistai* were a structured, selective, and compressed synthesis of information drawn from a mass of primary and secondary working records.

(d) The accounts of the central administration

Because the Heroninos archive comes from an outlying *phrontis* of the Appianus estate there is little evidence for the accounts kept by the central administration of the estate. A few of the letters sent out by members of the central administration were written on the verso (back) of strips of papyrus which had held an account on their recto (front), but it is not certain that all these accounts, of which only small fragments survive, had been drawn up by the central administration rather than submitted to it, and some of them may have come from other related estates, like that of Posidonios, whose papers had passed into the hands of Appianus' administrators.

Some of the accounts which apparently came from the central administration of the Appianus estate are accounts of affairs which were managed centrally. Some record must have been kept of the expenditure incurred in the upkeep of Appianus' house and household in Arsinoe. A possible example of this, although it does not certainly come from the estate, is *SB* XIV 11633, a fragment of an account apparently of payments to various individuals, including a scribe and two cooks. On the recto of two letters to Heroninos, one from Alypios and one from Herakleides, are two fragments of an account, republished as *SB* VI 9365, recording expenses incurred on one or more ships' voyages between Alexandria and the Fayum which were shared equally between the person for whom the account was drawn up and another unknown party. From the recto of two letters of the same day from Alypios to Heroninos there has been reconstituted a column of an account which records day by day the wages paid to shipwrights and sawyers building a ship, and the full account probably dealt with the simultaneous construction of a number of ships.[24] If these accounts do relate to the affairs of Appianus or

---

[24] See now L. Casson, 'Documentary Evidence for Graeco-Roman Shipbuilding (P. Flor. I 69)', *Bulletin of the American Society of Papyrologists* 27 (1990), 15–19, though he thinks only one ship was under construction—*contra* Rathbone, *Economic Rationalism*, 366 n. 33.

Posidonios, they are a valuable indication of direct investment by these large landowners in mercantile activities.

Other accounts will have related to aspects of the running of the Appianus estate which were under the direct control of the central administration. Although *P. Mich.* XI 620 shows that on the Titanianus estate the renting out of accommodation at Theadelphia was accounted for by the *phrontistes* there, on the Appianus and probably the Posidonios estates, leases and similar contracts were all managed by the central administration which must therefore have kept accounts for them. In *P. Flor.* III 340 we have a fragment of a rentbook, probably from the Posidonios estate, which lists village by village the various properties leased out in them—the fragment includes houses, a mill, an empty space by a bath-house, and plots of grainland—and the rents in cash or wheat received in that year. The rents from flocks of sheep and goats were a different business and were probably recorded separately.[25]

There are three texts which record financial dealings of the central administrations of these estates. *P. Laur.* III 98C, a fragment on the recto of an account of Heroninos, is a chronological account, perhaps from the Philoxenos estate (a Philoxenos married Appianus' daughter), of receipts of fairly large sums of cash, ranging from 44 dr. to 1,192 dr. The payers include Sabinus the chief shepherd, a wine-seller (*oinopoles*) and a *karpones* ('cropbuyer'), so the account probably recorded the income from sales of various produce. *BGU* XIII 2356, an 'account with reference to Serenion' probably from the central administration of the Appianus estate, records income attributed to a Serenion of at least 10,000 or 40,000 dr., from which sums were deducted in respect of purchases of wine; he was probably a wine-seller who also had other financial dealings with the estate. Lastly, there is the puzzling *P. Laur.* I 11 verso, written in a hand similar to that of Heroninos on the back of part of a monthly account submitted by a *phrontistes* of the Posidonios estate. It is not clear whether it is an account of income or of expenditure or of both, but since the sums are quite large, and since two transactions totalling 571 dr. 2 ob. involved legionaries and another two totalling 759 dr. 4 ob. concerned the sale or purchase of horses, it was probably an account of the central administration rather than of a *phrontistes*.

A member of the central administration of the Appianus estate, probably the man in charge of the draught animals (*epiktenites*) or a deputy, must have kept a combined monthly record of hay and of the employment of draught animals based at or visiting Arsinoe similar to those kept by each *phrontistes* for

---

[25] For the centralized arrangement and supervision of leases and similar contracts on the Appianus estate, see Rathbone, *Economic Rationalism*, ch. 5.

his unit. Two fragments of similar accounts for camels survive—*P. Flor.* III 364, which almost certainly comes from the Appianus estate, and *SB* XVI 13062, which may come from the estate. The *epiktenites* or some other central administrator probably also collated the information from the monthly records of hay submitted by the *phrontistai* to produce an overall summary of the deployment and use of the estate's transport resources in the course of the preceding Egyptian year.[26] This raises the more general question of the use made by the central administration of the monthly accounts submitted annually by the *phrontistai*, a question for which there is no direct evidence. In the next section, however, it will be suggested that individual accounts for each *phrontis*, similar in concept to those kept for each permanent estate employee by the *phrontistai*, may have been kept by the central administration, in which the value of produce and other items exported from a *phrontis* was credited to its account while it was debited with the value of produce or other items which it received from other units. This suggestion is prompted by consideration of the function of the monthly accounts of the *phrontistai* within the total accounting system of the estate which is the topic of the next section.

(e) The rationale of the accounting system

The aim of this section is to try to understand the rationale behind the accounting system of the Appianus estate, and in particular that of the monthly accounts of the *phrontistai*: why were they drawn up in the way which they were, and of what use could they have been to the owner and administrators of the estate? Inevitably any suggested answers will be rather speculative because the restricted provenance of our evidence means that we have no direct evidence for the use made of the accounts. It is only possible to show what could and what could not have been done with them. In the general context of study of the economic and agrarian history of the classical world, as outlined in section (*a*) above, the question which many historians may regard as the most important is whether the estate calculated the monetary profitability of its operations and the extent to which the accounts helped it to make economically rational decisions about future activities. My conclusions are that, although direct evidence is lacking, monetary profitability probably was calculated, but that the main purpose of the accounting system was to provide a check on the efficiency of production on the *phrontides* as measured in monetary terms. The accounts did contain much useful informa-

---

[26] See further ibid. 276–8.

tion for an analysis of profitability if—and here we are in the unknown—the owner and administrators had wished to carry out such an analysis. Their concern, however, seems to have been far more with the one crucial element of profitability which the estate was most able to influence, namely the costs of production, and here there is reason to believe that the accounts were intended to be an aid to the maintenance and improvement of the cost-effectiveness of production in the future.

The easiest point of entry is the nature of the records of produce in the monthly accounts submitted each year by the *phrontistai*. They are, as has been seen, much neater than previous views about Graeco-Roman accounting might have led us to expect, with separate sections for receipts and disbursements, entries grouped by type, not by date, and sometimes consolidated, and a remainder calculated and carried forward to the account for the next month. In essence, however, they were straightforward accounts of stock. As a general rule, all transactions were recorded under the month in which they had theoretically occurred, even if completion of them had in practice been delayed. However, it was usually only the cash side of transactions which was delayed, and it seems that receipts and disbursements of produce normally did occur in the month under which they were recorded. The sole semi-exception comes from *Text* I recto 174–9, Heroninos' draft monthly account for June 253, in which he brought forward a 'deficit' of vegetable oil from the account of the previous month which he then increased by further disbursements. The disbursements, however, may not have been delayed but may have been made from another source which Heroninos later had to repay with estate oil.[27] That the figure given for the stock of each type of produce in hand at the end of each month was meant to represent the actual position is confirmed by the record in *P. Prag. Varcl* II 1. 213–18 of a stock-taking of wine at Euhemeria in February 247 by a central administrator, who downgraded some wine to the category of sour wine and wrote off some other jars as completely spoilt. The *phrontistai*, this implies, were not allowed to write off losses themselves, and their actual stocks of produce were meant to match the figures in their monthly accounts.

Clearly one of the main functions of these records of produce was to provide a check against carelessness or dishonesty on the part of the *phrontistai*, a perfectly rational aim in itself. In this connection we may note that *phrontistai* were only responsible for accounting for produce when it was under their

[27] The only other 'deficit' (i.e. occurrence of the word *prosophiletai*) of produce in the extant monthly accounts comes in *P. Prag. Varcl* II 1. 238, but this was only an adjustment to correct an arithmetic error Eirenaios had made in a previous account.

direct control. Much of the wheat, for example, grown at Theadelphia was stored soon after the harvest in the local public granary; it seems then to have become the responsibility of the central administration of the estate, and no record of its fate appears in Heroninos' monthly accounts.[28] Similarly, when produce was transferred to another manager or administrator of the estate for him to sell to provide himself with cash, Heroninos just recorded the transfer as a disbursement and did not record any details of its sale, a point which will be returned to shortly.

The most interesting section in the monthly accounts of the *phrontistai* is the record of cash (*logos argurikos*). Clearly it was the most important in the eyes of the estate too, for it came at the head of the monthly accounts of the Appianus, Herakleides, and Titanianus estates, and apparently was presented separately from the records of kind on the Posidonios estate. In origin, pre-sumably, it functioned or was meant to function just like the record of any crop, recording actual receipts and disbursements of cash in each month. However, the extensive use of credit arrangements by the Appianus estate meant that in practice its nature and function had become rather more com-plex. It has already been shown that although all receipts and payments were recorded under the month in which they had theoretically taken place, only some had actually been completed as cash transactions in that month, while others were made in cash but at a later date and yet others were made by credit transfers. I should, incidentally, make clear at this point that my use of the terms 'credit' and 'debit' does not refer to the usage of double entry.

If we start by looking at the items listed as receipts or income (*lemma*) in the monthly records of cash of Eirenaios and Heroninos, it is clear that some do represent actual receipts of cash. These include the sums drawn from the local bank or provided by the central administration, and the payments diverted to *phrontistai* of cash rents due from the lessees of flocks, bath-houses, and so on. But patently these items were not income in the sense of cash earnings by the *phrontis* from its agricultural activities, and indeed the with-drawals from the bank were not really income at all. The other items, that is sums received from the sale of produce, do on the whole represent genuine earnings of the *phrontis*, although it should be noted that the produce sold had sometimes been transferred from another unit. Another complication is that the single aggregate totals recorded for the quantity of each type of produce sold include sales for immediate cash payment, sales for which payment was made by a transfer of credit between the bank account of the purchaser and

---

[28] See Rathbone, *Economic Rationalism*, 310–11.

that of the estate, and sales to estate employees in which the price was set against the cash salaries or wages due to them. Much of the produce of each *phrontis*, furthermore, was transferred to other units of the estate without its value being recorded as an item of income or a credit in the record of cash of that *phrontis*. Thus the subsection in the record of cash detailing *lemma* recorded neither only actual 'receipts' of cash nor only or the whole of the 'income' theoretically earned by the *phrontis*. Instead it recorded the 'assets' which had been 'realized' in that month to cover expenditure, with no differentiation of them according to source (whether 'borrowings' from outside or 'earnings') or according to form (cash or credit).

Turning to the subsection detailing disbursements or expenditure (*analoma*), we find a similar lack of differentiation between payments made in cash, such as some wages and payments for goods to outsiders, the larger payments to outsiders made by credit transfers through banks, and the crediting of the wages and salaries of estate employees to their individual accounts with the estate. Here, however, there is almost no problem about the grounds for these payments: almost all the expenditure recorded was incurred directly in the running of the *phrontis* and, conversely, almost no conceivable cost associated with its running was omitted. There are, admittedly, a number of items which appear to be or may be exceptions to this general claim. Heroninos, for example, sometimes paid for items such as ploughs and water-wheels which were sent to other units of the estate, and he and Eirenaios paid the salaries of various central employees (wood-guards, carters and so on) and administrative staff (such as Pontikos and Heroninos himself when he had been *epiktenites*). Some expenditure was not recorded in monetary terms, notably the estate-produced rations in kind issued to estate staff and animals, and the wine given to *karponai* (crop-buyers) as their remuneration for providing labour for some of the vineyards.

Various explanations can be suggested for these apparent exceptions, and they affect only the degree of completeness in the recording of the running costs of each *phrontis* in monetary terms. This question of accuracy will be discussed in more detail below, but it is worth noting here that the assignment of centrally employed staff to the payrolls of different *phrontides* was in effect a way, even if a somewhat crude one, of apportioning the cost of the central services they provided—which we could call the estate's general 'overheads'—among the units which all made use of them. It also bears repetition that even when workers had on the face of it taken estate produce in lieu of cash wages or salary, these transactions were always reckoned and recorded in monetary terms. It is therefore fair to conclude that the subsection detailing *analoma* in the monthly record of cash was meant to present in monetary form the total (significant) costs of production for that month on the *phrontis*. And obviously it would have been easy to add up the figures to produce the total costs of production for the year.

Before discussing further the accuracy and the usefulness of this way of recording the finances of each *phrontis*, it is necessary to consider the relationship between the 'income' and the 'expenditure' recorded in the monthly records of cash, which leads into the question of whether and how monetary profitability was calculated. At the end of each record of cash the *phrontistes* totalled 'income' and 'expenditure' and calculated the balance to be carried forward to the account for the next month. As we can now appreciate, this monthly balance in no sense indicated the monetary profit or loss made by the *phrontis* in that month, but instead showed whether or not sufficient assets had been realized to meet the expenditure incurred. In fact the balance was not infrequently a 'deficit', because many of the labour costs theoretically incurred in any month were credited to the employees and paid later at infrequent intervals, while normally, we may presume, only sufficient assets were realized to meet the expenditure actually made in the month. The running balance was therefore just an accounting device of no real external significance, with the exception of the balance for Mesore, the last month of the Egyptian year. Over the year the total value of assets realized should have more or less matched the total recorded expenditure. If far too few or too many assets had been realized at any point in the year, the *phrontistes* would have realized this long before he came to draw up his accounts for the year, for he must in any case have kept running working records of his actual stock of cash and of the credit in the estate's account in the local bank. Indeed it is worth noting that the record of 'cash' (*logos argurikos*) in the monthly accounts was not really suited to checking the accuracy or probity of a *phrontistes'* dealings in cash, and it may be that the administration required him to keep a separate cash book for possible inspection, which may explain why no example of this kind of record was thrown out and preserved with the rest of the Heroninos archive.

The monthly accounts of the *phrontistai* did not in themselves enable calculation of the monthly or annual monetary profit made by each *phrontis*. They could not, because although they gave an analytic account of one of the two main elements which determined the level of profit, that is the costs of production, they did not record the other, that is all of (and nothing other than) the income earned by each *phrontis* from the sale of its surplus produce. Only the central administrators of the estate, who directed all sales of produce, can have had available all the information necessary to draw up accounts which showed profit. Although it is not possible to prove that they did, it can be demonstrated that it would have been fairly easy for them to have done this using only accounting techniques and concepts already attested in the accounts of the *phrontistai*, and there are some hints in other texts from the Heroninos archive that the central administration did draw up accounts of this type.

The main assumptions which I make in proposing this hypothetical reconstruction are that, as with the accounts of the *phrontistai*, these central accounts were drawn up at the end of each Egyptian year, that they recorded income from produce sold under the date (that is year) of its sale rather than the date of its harvest, and, most important of all, that the central administration kept records of the cash derived from the sales of all produce which had been exported from each *phrontis*. The primary evidence for such records could have consisted of copies of the letters to do with transfers of produce sent out by the central administration, and accounts like *BGU* XIII 2356 and *P. Laur.* III 98C (discussed in the previous section) which seem to be records of sales of wine to outsiders. In the case of sales by other *phrontistai* the central administration fixed the price at which the produce was to be sold, while in all other cases it itself received the cash from the sale; thus it should have known the income from each sale.

Whether it was a continuous or a periodic process, this information could easily have been transferred to a running account for each *phrontis*, divided into items of 'credit' and 'debit'. The items of credit would have had to comprise the cash value of all the produce exported from the *phrontis* to other units of the estate, whether for consumption or sale by the recipient. The items of debit would have had to include the value of all produce imported into the *phrontis* and sold there (that is, excepting produce merely in transit), and all sums of cash drawn by the *phrontis* from the estate's bank account or sent to it by the central administration. The balance of these items, which should normally have been a hefty credit, would then have had to be added to the final cash balance given in the *phrontistes'* account for Mesore to give the total profit or loss made by the *phrontis* for that year. The proposed possible system of accounting is represented schematically in Table I.I.

For greater accuracy in calculating the final profit of a *phrontis* the central administrator might also have added as a debit the value of stocks of produce held at the beginning of the year, and as a credit the value of stocks at the end of the year. Since the level of stocks each month was recorded in the accounts submitted by the *phrontistai*, and since the estate fixed a monthly price for each type of produce, it would have been possible to do this. It was probably not

Table 1.1 *Possible profit accounting system on the Appianus estate*

	Monthly accounts of *phrontistes*	Yearly accounts of central administration
Credit	Cash from local sales of local produce Cash from local sales of imported produce Cash from central administration or bank, diverted rent payments	Cash from sales of exported produce
Debit	All expenditure of the *phrontis* (running costs)	Value of imported produce Cash sent directly or via bank, diverted rent payments
Balance	Showed credit/debit remaining from assets realized against running costs (running total to final balance in Mesore)	Showed credit/debit resulting from sales to and purchases/borrowings from parties outside the *phrontis* (totalled yearly)
Profit	Reached by combining the above two balances	

done, however, simply because it was not worth the bother, granted that the value of the stock at the end of any year will normally have been much the same as at the end of the previous year—when stocks were low prices were probably normally high and vice versa. Some other items which could have been included are objects like ploughs or water-wheels paid for by the *phrontis* where they were made but sent to another unit; the cost of them could have been credited to the supplying *phrontis* and debited against the account of the receiving unit.

It would thus have been quite simple for the central administration to have drawn up a profit account of this type for each *phrontis*. We know that the information needed to do this was recorded anyway, and we may assume that the management was capable of drawing up these hypothetical accounts because they would have been essentially the same in concept and format to the individual accounts which we know that the *phrontistai* kept for each of their permanent staff and some casual labourers too. But the crucial question is whether such profit accounts were kept. It should first be said that since the surviving accounts from the central administration are so few, it is not significant that they do not include one of this type; equally, it is no argument against their existence that the published correspondence of the estate contains no obvious direct reference to them. There are, however, a couple of references in the Heroninos archive which make more sense if such accounts did exist.

In *P. Flor.* II 123 and 124, two letters of the same day, Alypios ordered Heroninos to send 100 mon. wine each to the *phrontistai* Horion and Palas, with the identical phrasing 'a hundred monochora of wine, for which he will render account, the monochoron being reckoned to him at sixteen drachmai'. Since they and not Heroninos were going to sell this wine and thus, as is stated ('for which he will render account'), would be responsible for recording receipt of the proceeds in their monthly accounts, the last phrase ('the monochoron being reckoned to him . . .') must mean that the *phrontides* of Horion and Palas were going to be debited by Alypios with the value of the wine, that is 1,600 dr. each. We may compare *P. Flor.* II 254, in which Syros instructed Heroninos to hand over some wine to a *karpones* who had already made part-payment for it, 'the mon. being reckoned to him at the current price of the vineyard'. Presumably the value set on the wine transferred to Horion and Palas was of interest to Heroninos, and he was told it, because his *phrontis* was going to be credited with it. An obscurer and tantalizing reference comes from the lacunose beginning of the record of cash in *P. Laur.* I 11 recto, a monthly account submitted by a *phrontistes* of the Posidonios estate. This appears to read: '[Receipts: remainder] brought forward through Heronas *cheiristes* to be [(entered?) into the] record rendered [extern]ally(?), in respect of [(name?)] from Bacchias(?), 80 dr.'[29] The meaning of the entry is far from clear, but possibly, since a central administrator (a *cheiristes*, 'amanuensis') was involved, 'the record rendered externally' denoted the central account for the *phrontis* in which these 80 dr. were to be entered as a debit.

Whether or not this entry in *P. Laur.* I 11 recto is relevant, the evidence of *P. Flor.* II 123 and 124 encourages me to believe that a central account for each *phrontis* was kept, and to go one step further and consider why it was the central administrators of the Appianus estate rather than the *phrontistai* who kept the accounts which could have shown the monetary profitability of each *phrontis*; this question in any case leads back to examination of the usefulness of the monthly accounts of the *phrontistai*. There may have been a problem of accounting technique, namely devising a format which would have distinguished between expenditure on the running costs of their *phrontis*, which was what their records of cash were designed to present, and debits in respect of produce imported into their *phrontis* for the sale to cover expenditure. But this

---

[29] Following the corrections and supplements to ll. A7–9 proposed by G. M. Parássoglou in *P. Laur.* III, p. 15. Admittedly interpretation of the description of the 'record' (*graphe*) as 'rendered [extern]ally' is far from certain, but a 'record' distinct from the monthly account (*logos*) of the *phrontistes* seems to have been meant, and we may compare *P. Flor.* I 100. 11, 27, also from the Posidonios estate, which record disbursements of wheat 'for making bread to be (issued) externally', that is outside the *phrontis*.

would not have been insuperable, and the main reason was almost certainly managerial, that is the principle and practice that *phrontistai* accounted only for transactions and activities for which they were personally and directly responsible. The *phrontistai* were responsible for the production on their units, and hence they had to account for its costs. The profit made by each *phrontis*, however, depended equally if not more on the prices at which its surplus produce had been sold, and since the marketing of all produce was centrally directed, it followed that accounting for it was the responsibility of the central administration, to whom was therefore left the drawing up of the profit accounts. It may be noted that a similar division of accounting responsibility was used by innovative nineteenth-century industrial concerns such as the Lyman Textile Mills Corporation in New England, in which production accounts were drawn up in each factory and submitted to the 'home office' where the general financial records were kept.[30]

So how accurate and useful were the monthly accounts submitted by the *phrontistai*? The figures in Heroninos' records of kind, to begin with, could easily have been collated by the owner or a central administrator to produce a summary record of how much of each crop had been produced at Theadelphia and how much had come from other units or outside purchases, and how much had been sold by Heroninos, or disbursed gratis or transferred to other units of the estate. The procedure, if repeated for a number of *phrontides*, would have revealed an overall pattern of production and distribution which could have prompted or assisted decisions about, for example, increasing or decreasing the production of particular crops at particular *phrontides*. Although no direct evidence for this kind of analysis is found in the Heroninos archive, a hint that the idea was not unknown in Roman Egypt comes from *CPR* VII 8, an account of AD 159/60, 182/3, or 214/15, of the production and use in vineyards and sale of surplus reeds on imperial properties in various Arsinoite villages, which in some places totals figures for the past twenty and more years.[31]

The records of hay and of the employment of draught animals, it may be added, were open to the same type of analysis, and in this case there is considerable subsidiary evidence to suggest that the estate was consciously trying

---

[30] Compare also the case of the Carnegie steelworks. For both see H. T. Johnson and R. S. Kaplan, *Relevance Lost: The Rise and Fall of Management Accounting* (Boston, 1987), ch. 2.

[31] I agree with J. Gascou, *Chronique d'Égypte*, 54 (1979), 337, that the reference in l. 41 to the 'patrimonial procurator' (*ousiakos epitropos*) strongly suggests that these properties were imperial domains (though *phrontistai* and *prostatai* are found on private estates too). As the editor admits, the account has no obvious fiscal purpose; the one reference to a landowner (l. 43) is very dubious, and the other named persons are probably managers or tenants, not private landowners.

to keep its expenditure on transport costs as low as possible by efficient deployment of its resources.[32] So too the monthly records of the work done by the permanent labourers on each *phrontis* were well suited to retrospective analysis. A general indication of the management's attitude here comes from the use in the Heroninos archive of the adjective '*argos*' ('idle') and its cognates, whose meaning had become extended in the Roman period to include 'out of use' of equipment or 'unable to work' of people.[33] In several letters, such as *P. Flor.* II 176, Appianus and his administrators show concern that asses and oxen should not 'be idle', perhaps better translated as 'waste time', which included being given a light load; in *P. Flor.* II 262 an irrigated garden with a broken water-wheel was also described as 'being idle'. In *P. Prag. Varcl* II I. 36–8 Eirenaios recorded payment of another man to discharge a liturgic (i.e. public) function in place of an estate employee 'so that his time should not be wasted'. In *P. Lond.* III 1170 verso and *P. Mich.* XI 620, accounts from the Herakleides and the Titanianus estates, not only were asses and oxen doing nothing described as 'idle', but so were unleased rooms and a tower in one of Titanianus' barrack-blocks, while the records of the employment of Herakleides' permanent staff count as 'time wasted' days on which staff were sick, were sent to Arsinoe or fed animals. It seems reasonable to suppose that men with this mentality, with its concern for productive employment of resources, would have scrutinized the accounts of the *phrontistai* to check on the efficiency of their deployment of labour and draught animals. And we know that someone at some stage had planned and instituted the centralized transport system of the estate to improve the efficiency of usage of transport resources.

One further point to note about the records of produce is that the extant draft monthly accounts have no sections for minor fruit such as dates or figs or for vegetables such as garlic and capers, although we know that they were consumed and, in some cases, produced on the estate. A partial explanation may be that the orchards and gardens which produced them were leased out, but the main reason is probably that production was small-scale and for domestic consumption, and a rational decision had been taken that it was simply not worth the time and effort to keep records of these crops. This selectivity about what to record is a useful indication that the management of the Appianus estate was not obsessed with checking fraud or animated by bureaucratic pedantry, but pragmatically restricted accounting to the types of produce which were of greatest economic importance to the estate.

---

[32] See Rathbone, *Economic Rationalism*, 266–78.
[33] T. Reekmans, '*Argos* and its derivatives in the papyri', *Chronique d'Égypte* 60 (1985), 275–91.

A similar explanation may be suggested for produce and other items whose disbursement was recorded in the monthly accounts of the *phrontistai* without a monetary value being assigned to it. I exclude here exports of produce and items such as ploughs to other units of the estate whose monetary value should have been credited to the *phrontis*—and, as I believe, was credited to it, albeit in a separate centrally kept account. Instead I mean here internal disbursements which should have counted towards the total costs of production of the *phrontis*, like the rations in kind issued to estate staff and animals, the seed for sowing and the wine given to *karponai* in respect of their provision of labour for some of the vineyards. In the case of the rations and the seed, the estate's practice of fixing centrally each month the price at which each type of produce was to be sold meant that the monetary value of these disbursements could have been computed retrospectively, had anyone desired to do so. Since, however, these were all regular and inescapable items of expenditure, largely if not wholly met from domestic production, the decision had probably been taken that it was not worth the bother of assigning them a monetary value. The value of the wine given to the *karponai* could also have been computed retrospectively. Although it could have been included in the record of cash in the form of a sale of so many jars of wine and of a cash payment of that amount to the *karponai*, this was probably not done because it was not expenditure for which the *phrontistes* was personally responsible. The question of whether and how the management of the estate could have established the relative financial merits of leasing as against direct working of vineyards and other land will be returned to shortly.

A rather different problem is the assignment to the payrolls of the *phrontides* of estate staff such as grooms, wood-guards, and carters, who were in fact employed centrally and only rarely worked on the *phrontis* which paid their salaries (*opsonia*), and also of some junior central administrators such as Pontikos and Heroninos himself when he was *epiktenites*. This may have been a rather crude mechanism for apportioning between the *phrontides* the costs of the central services provided by these men, but it does not seem to have been very fair. The *phrontis* at Theadelphia had to support one and a half times as many central employees as did the *phrontis* at Euhemeria, which will have artificially exaggerated its recorded costs of production.[34] One possible explanation for this practice may be that it simply derived from an earlier situa-

---

[34] See Rathbone, *Economic Rationalism*, 103–6. Note that *P. Prag. Varcl* II 6 suggests that by Dec. 260 more actual labourers and fewer central staff were on the Theadelphian payroll; this could possibly have been done to make the distribution of central costs fairer, but it may have occurred for quite different reasons.

tion, presumably the norm on smaller estates which had few or no central staff, in which the ass-drivers and the like had worked for most of their time on the unit which maintained them. Probably, however, the main reason for the practice was that, in the earlier period of our documentation at least, the rates of remuneration of permanent staff varied between *phrontides*, and employees were assigned to units according to the rate of remuneration which the estate had agreed to pay them. In most cases, furthermore, employees seem to have been assigned to the unit at their village of origin, and the fact that the central ass-drivers paid from Theadelphia all went there to celebrate the agricultural festival of the Amesysia suggests that the unit was perceived to be their 'home'.[35] Central employees were, therefore, probably assigned to the payrolls of different *phrontides* primarily for reasons other than to spread the cost of their services fairly. It is conceivable that the central administration totalled annually the cash *opsonia* paid to these employees, and charged the central account of each *phrontis* with a share of the total while also crediting it with the *opsonia* it had actually paid. On the other hand it may have been felt that the distribution of these costs achieved by the spread of staff, though not completely equitable, was adequate for practical purposes in the context of the analytical use which could have been made of the monthly accounts of the *phrontistai*, the final question to which I now turn.

The primary purpose of these accounts, to sum up the preceding discussion, was to provide a month-by-month record of the total significant costs of production, presented in monetary form, incurred on each *phrontis*, with summary details of how these costs had been incurred. They also recorded all receipts and disbursements of the main types of produce which had been made in each month, and gave a running total for the level of stocks. In a sort of appendix there was recorded the employment of all the draught animals which had worked at or visited the *phrontis*. Uses which could have been made of the records of produce and of the employment of animals have already been discussed: the focus here is on the record of expenditure. The owner or any member of the central administration could have seen by glancing at the beginning of each monthly account what the total recorded costs of production had been. If he had thought them significantly higher (or lower) than expected, he had the information available to analyse why. For example, he could have checked whether and why the *phrontistes* had employed a particularly large number of casual labourers or had paid them unusually high wages, or whether he had bought surprisingly large quantities of supplies from out-

---

[35] See Rathbone, *Economic Rationalism*, 106–47, 268–70.

side and, if so, whether this was because his own stocks were abnormally low, and so on.

Of course spotting abnormalities implies the existence of some standard for judgement, and the simplest suggestion is that the total of expenditure in a particular month of the past year could have been compared against the figures for the same month in previous years, since on the whole the same agricultural operations will have been carried out at the same time each year. This would explain why the accounts of the *phrontistai* from the Appianus and related estates never give the precise day on which expenditure was incurred, but why expenditure was always recorded in the month in which it had been incurred even if some payments were not in fact made until much later. It may be noted that if expenditure was compared against previous totals, the number of central employees paid by the *phrontis* and the quantity of produce disbursed to staff and animals, as long as the amounts did not fluctuate greatly, will not have been of much significance. It cannot be proved that analyses of this type were carried out, but the recording of most of the costs of production in cash terms and the rigorous attribution of these costs to the month in which they were incurred are, to my mind, strong hints that the format of the monthly accounts had been deliberately designed to facilitate investigation of the financial efficiency with which each *phrontistes* was running his *phrontis*.

The recording and totalling of the costs of production carried out by the *phrontistai* was half of the procedure necessary for calculation of the monetary profitability of each *phrontis*. If, as has been suggested, the procedure was completed by the central administration of the estate, it would have been possible, in theory, to compare the return from one *phrontis* against that from another, and thus also, by comparing largely wine-producing *phrontides* against mainly wheat-producing units, to gain some idea of the relative profitability of different crops. This is the kind of analysis which Mickwitz and others have proposed or assumed to be the basis of economically rational management of an agricultural enterprise. I doubt, however, whether the management of the Appianus estate would have made or put much faith in such calculations, and with good reason.

Especially in the context of the ancient world, precise desktop calculations of the theoretical profitability of different crops were unnecessary, and could have been quite misleading for planning purposes, because landowners were severely constricted by the relative difficulty of transport, which limited both the availability of labour and their access to markets. There was no point in separate detailed accounting and comparison of all the costs associated with, for instance, viticulture and wheat production, because whether or not it was economically rational to increase production of one at the expense of the other will have depended mainly on several other factors which would not appear even in double-entry accounts, such as the suitability of the land, the availability of the necessary labour and skills, and the capacity of the market to absorb increased quantities of wine or wheat without a fall in prices.[36] Normally ancient landowners will have had very little room for manœuvre in adjusting the proportions of the various crops they grew because, apart from the rare and truly exceptional developments like the foundation of Alexandria, or the Roman conquest of the Celtic West or annexation of Egypt, which opened up major new areas of demand or sources of supply, the demand for and production of agricultural goods and the mechanisms of supply remained broadly stable over a long period. The 'fast bucks' to be made came in the unpredictable bouts of crop failure and food shortage when prices could become so inflated as to make calculations of profit meaningless.

The area in which ancient landowners did have significant room for manœuvre, and where the extent to which their decisions were economically rational may more usefully be judged, was the organization of production: decisions, for example, about how intensively to cultivate particular crops, whether to aim for quantity or quality in production, about how to arrange the recruitment and deployment of labour, whether to lease out land or to exploit it directly, and about how to organize the distribution and marketing of produce. Although such decisions will also have been influenced by factors which did not appear in any account, there is much here that an economically rational landowner could have gleaned from accounts of the right type, which essentially means accounts of the monetary costs of production which allowed at least the main expenditure on separate activities to be calculated.

In the particular case of the Appianus estate we can show that, apparently by deliberate decision, the viticulture practised was intensive whereas less effort was devoted to arable crops, that most land was worked directly though some was leased out and the labour for some vineyards was provided by *karponai*, and that the estate had developed its own centralized transport system and controlled closely the distribution and marketing of its produce. We are not in a position to judge whether these had been the right decisions, nor can we know for sure whether they were based on analysis of past accounts. In the case of the use of *karponai*, for example, it is fairly clear that Heroninos' monthly accounts did not present total figures which immediately

[36] Similar points are made by Macve, n. 6 above, 247–54.

made plain the relative costs of using *karponai* as against direct exploitation; none the less, the basic information for calculating this—the employment of the permanent staff and the payments to casual labourers in the directly worked vineyards, the yields from each vineyard and the shares taken by the *karponai* and the value of the wine—was all there in his monthly accounts had anyone wished to collate it.[37]

In the end conclusions are based more on impression than proof. Without doubt the monthly accounts submitted by the *phrontistai* of the Appianus and related estates are the most sophisticated accounts so far recognized from classical antiquity. They almost certainly provided a very useful check on the efficiency, measured in monetary terms, with which each *phrontistes* was managing production on his unit. They contained much data which could have been used as the basis for making economically rational decisions about future activities and practices. Whether they were used for these purposes cannot be proved, but the presentation of the information in a logically structured format which facilitated its analysis and the more general evidence for the attitudes and practices of the management of the Appianus estate imply that its accounting system was designed and used as an aid to economically rational management of the estate.

CONCLUDING REMARKS

It bears repetition that measuring cash profitability was and is not the only, or necessarily the best, way of evaluating the performance of a productive enterprise, and it should not be taken as an indispensable element of economic rationality. To my mind the interest of the Appianus estate in rigorous control of its costs of production, as attested in the extant draft monthly accounts of the *phrontistai*, in itself indicates a high level of economic rationality in its management. An interesting comparison is Andrew Carnegie's method of managing his steelworks, which was to concentrate almost obsessively on measuring, analysing, and reducing the costs of production at each mill. As the authors of a recent study conclude: 'Carnegie's success depended upon good information about direct operating costs. For that, accounting systems mattered. For the rest, faith and intuition sufficed.' The same might

---

[37] Of course any rational decisions about making more or less use of *karponai* would have also had to consider whether the estate could itself have recruited directly the labour which they were contracted to provide, and whether it could have found an alternative outlet for the wine with which it paid them.

be said about the Appianus estate, which could perhaps be put in the category of 'multiprocess, hierarchical, managed enterprises', with a geographically distinct central office and production units and a need to cost internal transfers, which the same authors assume emerged only in the nineteenth century.[38]

New evidence may sharpen and refine our picture of the management of the Appianus estate. Already, however, it stands out as a unique example of economic rationalism in ancient landownership, which raises the question of whether it is the exception which proves the rule, or whether this is the accidental result of the survival of the uniquely rich evidence for it. Certainly the quantity and variety of documentation are important factors for the simple reason that isolated documents, and especially isolated accounts, are often very difficult to interpret. Without the monthly accounts of the *phrontistai*, for example, their working accounts would suggest to us that the Appianus estate used a very basic and limited system of accounting. Without the working accounts, and particularly the individual accounts of the employees with the estate, we could never have realized how the monthly accounts were constructed, what they showed, and their implications for the economic sophistication of the management of the estate.

A large subject awaiting treatment is examination of all the accounts and internal correspondence known from large private estates in Roman Egypt. Few other estates may provide even the range of evidence which we have for the Appianus estate, but its system of management and accounting at least provides a model against which other scattered accounts and letters can be evaluated. As we have seen, there are great similarities between its accounts and those surviving from the Posidonios, the Herakleides, and the Dios estates, which all had links with the Appianus estate, and comparable accounts survive from the Titanianus estate and from other apparently unconnected large estates of the third century AD.[39] A study of all estate accounts from Roman Egypt might be able to trace a chronological development. I know of no similarly sophisticated accounts from the first century AD, but in the second century the accounts of the archive of Laches in several ways prefigure those of the Appianus estate, and some developments may have drawn on the accounting practices of the Roman army.[40]

[38] Johnson and Kaplan, *Relevance Lost*, 6–7, 34.

[39] The clearest examples are: *BGU* I 14, AD 255, Memphite nome (translated as Johnson, *Roman Egypt*, no. 115); *P. Bad.* II 26, AD 292/3, Hermopolite; *P. Erl.* 101, AD 269, Oxyrhynchite; *P. Mich.* XV 721 and *SB* XIV 12203, both III/IV AD, provenance unknown.

[40] For example, the long first-century account, republished with a commentary by A. Swiderek, *La propriété foncière privée dans l'Égypte de Vespasien et sa technique agricole d'après P. Lond. 131 recto* (Wrocław, 1960)—recto and verso translated by Johnson, *Roman Egypt*, nos. 104–5—consists of repetitive and unsynthesized daily entries. For the accounts of Laches' family see W. S. Bagnall, *The Archive of Laches: Prosperous Farmers of*

It is possible, though not beyond doubt, that a 'decline' in the sophistication of estate accounts took place from the fourth century AD onwards, perhaps partly, to begin with, as a result of the constant serious depreciation of the currency which will have made monetized accounts more difficult to keep and to use afterwards. The evidence of fourth-century accounts is arguably equivocal, but the accounts of large estates in Byzantine Egypt, notably those of the Flavii Apiones, were apparently no more than unintegrated records of rents or taxes received or due and of expenditure made.[41] Nevertheless, whether or not we are ever able to trace analogous developments in other areas of the Roman empire, we may have to admit that economic behaviour was not uniformly 'primitive' in the classical world. In various times and places it may have reached levels of sophisticated rationality which are hard if not impossible to parallel from the early medieval period, and from which a 'decline' must therefore be posited. Economic rationalism is not necessarily the result of a progressive evolution; it may equally well be a historically discontinuous phenomenon.

the Fayum in the Second Century (Diss. Duke Univ., 1974). The individual accounts kept on the Appianus estate for each of its permanent staff may owe something to the individual accounts of pay, and of deductions against it, kept for soldiers in the Roman army—some examples in R. O. Fink, *Roman Military Records on Papyrus* (Cleveland, 1971), nos. 68–73.

[41] *P. Lips.* 97 (AD 338, Hermonthis) and *P. Lond.* I 125 recto (probably from the same estate) have monthly records of produce like the accounts of the Appianus estate, but no record of cash (*logos argurikos*). Possibly the record of cash was kept separately, as had been the case on the Posidonios estate, but since the staff received double rations in kind by the standards of the Appianus estate, they may not have received any cash. For the accounts of the Flavii Apiones see E. G. Hardy, *The Large Estates of Byzantine Egypt* (New York, 1931), and J. Gascou, 'Les grands domaines, la cité et l'état en Egypte byzantine', *Travaux et mémoires*, 9 (1985), 1–90.

R. H. Macve

I. INTRODUCTION

Geoffrey de Ste. Croix's paper on 'Greek and Roman Accounting' (hencefor-ward GRA) was published nearly thirty years ago.[1] It remains the classic treatment of this subject. Its main ('very low key') theme is a demonstration, by detailed examination of the extant evidence, that there is no support for the frequently held belief that the technique of 'double-entry bookkeeping'[2] was in use in the ancient Greek and Roman world. This conclusion has been of great importance for the history of accounting and there has been no sub-sequent successful contradiction of it.[3] The earliest documented use of 'double entry' is still believed to be in the thirteenth century AD.[4] From the point of view of the ancient historian, one might suppose that the last word had been said on this matter.

In the last thirty years or so, however, there has been a great expansion and development of the academic study of accounting[5] and of the study of the

First published in *History of Political Thought* (1985). I am very glad to have this opportunity to pay tribute to Geoffrey de Ste. Croix, who was the first to suggest that I might find an interest in the academic side of accounting. In preparing this chapter I have been helped greatly by the advice and criticisms of colleagues in various Departments at UCW, Aberystwyth, and also of Richard Duncan-Jones, Harold Edey, Keith Hoskin, Christopher Noke, Bob Parker, Dominic Rathbone, John Rea, Kenneth White, and Basil Yamey. Above all I am grateful for the help I have received from the editors of this volume. For the errors and deficiencies that remain I have only myself to blame.

[1] In A. C. Littleton and B. S. Yamey (eds.), *Studies in the History of Accounting* (London, 1956), 14–74.

[2] The method is explained in any introductory accounting text, e.g. H. C. Edey, *Introduction to Accounting* (London, 4th edn., 1978), ch. 2.

[3] For unsuccessful attempts see Appendix.

[4] Material on early examples of double entry is discussed in e.g. R. de Roover, 'The Development of Accounting Prior to Luca Pacioli', in Littleton and Yamey, *Stud. Hist. Accounting*, 114–74.

[5] In 1956 there were only two full-time chairs of Accounting in UK universities (see R. Parker, 'Room at the Top for More Academic Accountants', *Times Higher Education Supplement*, 17 Jan. 1975). Now there are some forty-six (see e.g. *British Accounting Review, Research Register 1984* (London)). There has been a much longer tradition of accounting studies in North American universities, but there has been continuing expansion there too.

history of accounting in medieval and modern times. The purpose of this paper is to offer some glosses on the original conclusions of GRA, and on some of the related explanations and subordinate themes, in the light of current views about accounting. In particular, I deal with the use of accounting in relation to taxation (section 2) and 'managerial economics'—the planning and control of business activities (section 3). I then look in section 4 at the role of 'double-entry' bookkeeping and, in an appendix, I review some later work that either criticizes or ignores the conclusions of GRA.[6]

2. TAXATION

One way in which knowledge about ancient accounting practice may be of significance to the ancient historian is illustrated by the following recent passage in which de Ste. Croix discusses the basis of ancient taxation:[7]

A conclusive argument against any assessment in terms of money income is provided by the extremely primitive nature of ancient accounting, which was incapable of distinguishing properly between what is nowadays kept apart as 'capital' and 'income', let alone enabling a merchant or even a landowner to arrive at a concept of 'net profit', without which the taxation of money income is unthinkable. There seems to have been no really efficient method of accounting, by double or even single entry, before the thirteenth century.

The same argument has been used elsewhere.[8] The 'primitive' nature of ancient accounts refers both to their content and to their form. GRA demonstrated that the content of accounts comprised 'receipts and payments' (not 'income'). As regards their form, they show no evidence of 'double entry' and scarcely any systematic interrelationship of accounts. While some tabulation and grouping of items often appear in summary accounts, many accounts are in the form of mere chronological narratives with receipts and payments intermingled.

Certainly, accounts were used to keep track of movements in other assets as well as of receipts and payments of money: for example, the σιτικοὶ λόγοι

---

[6] There is little point in attempting to distinguish Greek from Roman accounting for most of the discussion. As GRA showed, there is negligible development until the Middle Ages, so that generally one may freely cite evidence across both time and place.

[7] G. E. M. de Ste. Croix, *The Class Struggle in the Ancient Greek World* (London, 1981), (henceforward *CSAGW*), 114.

[8] E.g. in G. E. M. de Ste. Croix, review of R. Thomsen, *Eisphora*, in *Classical Review*, NS 16 (1966), 90–3; and in A. H. M. Jones. 'Taxation in Antiquity' in P. A. Brunt (ed.), *The Roman Economy: Studies in Ancient Economic and Administrative History* (Oxford, 1974), 151–85, at 175.

('grain accounts') of Zenon's or Appianus' Egyptian estates recorded receipts and issues of grain in the manner of a modern stores record.[9] But these records were all in physical terms, and without conversion of them all to some common measurement unit, such as money, there could not be that interlinking of the recorded movements in various different assets and liabilities that is a key feature of the double-entry system, nor could there be any calculation of income. Indeed, as the discussion in GRA makes clear (e.g. pp. 24, 32), the money receipts and payments accounts (ἀργυρικοὶ λόγοι) were themselves mainly intended to be the physical account of one particular asset—coins—kept largely to check on subordinates and to prevent fraud and misappropriations. All movements were typically recorded in the minutest detail to demonstrate (and facilitate checks on) the honesty of the responsible cashier, rather than with a view to forming an overall picture of 'where the money came from and where it went' which might be of some economic or management interest (as is shown by the 'statement of sources and applications of funds' included in a company's annual report today).[10]

However, it seems unlikely that it was the state of ancient accounting that made taxation of money income in antiquity 'unthinkable'. As I will argue further in section 4, one does not need double-entry accounts to be able to

---

[9] Zenon's accounts (3rd century BC) are described in GRA, 31–2, and in G. Mickwitz, 'Economic Rationalism in Graeco-Roman Agriculture', *English Hist. Rev.* (1937), 577–89, at 578–81. See also E. Grier, *Accounting in the Zenon Papyri* (New York, 1934); for the background see M. Rostovtzeff, *A Large Estate in Egypt in the Third Century BC: A Study in Economic History* (Madison, Wis., 1922). Appianus' accounts (3rd century AD), the 'Heroninos archive', are described by Mickwitz, at 581–3. Many of the papyri referred to there appear in translation in A. C. Johnson, *Roman Egypt to the Reign of Diocletian* (vol. ii of *An Economic Survey of Ancient Rome*), ed. T. Frank (Baltimore, 1936), at 174–228. There are similar records for wine and other produce, besides wheat. Calculations accounting for man-days worked (who was sick, etc.) or how e.g. the donkeys were employed appear too (e.g. *P. London* 1170 = Johnson, *Roman Egypt*, 224–6). For a similar description of farm accounts from the 2nd century BC (to be kept by the overseer, *vilicus*, himself a slave: cf. *CSAGW* 145, 181–2, 505–6, 563–4), see also Cato, *De Agricultura*, 2.5, and 5.3 (and GRA 44–5).

[10] However, many papyri are still unpublished. Dominic Rathbone of King's College, London, who has researched the estate accounts in the Heroninos archive, has informed me that greater interrelationship of entries between cash and produce accounts can be found than was suggested by Mickwitz, and that cash accounts include notional monetary amounts for disbursements of produce (e.g. in lieu of wages). This suggests that some attempt is being made to track the financial performance of the estate beyond merely keeping a record of cash movements. One needs to distinguish carefully the summary statements from the detailed working accounts.

Note also that the interpretation even of well-known papyri may not always be obvious. See e.g. the translation of *P. Lond.* 1171 (1st century BC) in Johnson, *Roman Egypt*, 176. This 'cash' account records an accumulating deficit (ὑπερδαπανῶι) on the estate's working totalling more than 1 silver talent. How can one 'hold' (or spot check) such a deficit of cash? In arriving at the final deficit there has been offset an amount of 430 drachmae 2 obols in respect of the value of 430 1/3 *artabai* of wheat. Was this wheat sold, or is the figure a notional valuation of wheat remaining in store (as the editors of the papyrus, Kenyon and Bell, took it to be)?

calculate income. Moreover the history of income tax in the UK illustrates that 'distinguishing properly' between 'capital' and 'income' has been an evolutionary process, and indeed it has often been the existence of the tax that has provided the spur to develop and refine these concepts in accounting.[11] Any notion of income basically requires an idea of the amount by which the recipient has become 'better off', i.e. by which his original 'capital' has increased. But what this logically implies has taken time to work out.

To take one example, although income tax was first imposed (as a 'temporary measure') in 1799, 'depreciation' of plant and machinery was not statutorily recognized as a legitimate charge for taxation purposes until 1878. Before then, the taxable income from a factory's machinery might include (depending on the Commissioners' attitude) an amount that should have been regarded as a return *of* capital (the depreciation of the original capital) rather than a return *on* capital. Indeed, taxpayers' complaints about the inadequacy of the amounts allowed continued into the twentieth century and depreciation of the factory building itself was not recognized until 1945.[12]

Even today, the 'depreciation' that may be deducted is still limited to those items where the income tax legislation has specifically provided for 'capital allowances', so that no deduction is allowed in respect of expenditure on other 'capital' items (such as goodwill or company formation costs) that are just as essential for the carrying on of a profitable business as is expenditure on machinery, vehicles etc. Many other anomalies remain (e.g. in relation to costs of borrowing money and in the highly confused area of distinguishing 'income' from 'capital gains').[13]

Why has Parliament had such difficulty in producing rational income tax legislation, and the courts in interpreting it? Tax rules are of course not designed primarily to implement some particular conceptual scheme, but rather to achieve certain aims of economic and fiscal policy. Nevertheless at the root of the difficulties has been the inability of accountants and economists to define satisfactorily the concepts of 'income' and 'capital', so that there are in practice a wide variety of 'accounting policies' from which business managements may choose when reporting their profits.

The controversies about income measurement in accounting practice may be classified broadly as of two kinds:

[11] See e.g. S. A. Zeff, 'Towards a Fundamental Rethinking . . .', in D. L. Jensen (ed.), *The Impact of Rule-Making on Intermediate Financial Accounting Textbooks* (Columbus, Oh., 1982), 33–51, at 36.

[12] B. E. V. Sabine, *A History of Income Tax* (London, 1966), 120–1, 150, 203.

[13] See e.g. Richard H. Macve, 'Accounting for Long-term Loans', in B. Carsberg and S. Dev (eds.), *External Financial Reporting* (London, 1984), 90–108.

1. What assets (and liabilities) should be included in measuring capital and how should they be valued? The prevailing valuation convention is 'historical cost' (although this is itself a term of considerable ambiguity) but there are also many other valuation systems that could be used (e.g. based on current buying prices or current selling prices).
2. How much of the change between the net assets (i.e. assets less liabilities) at the beginning and end of the period should be regarded as 'income'? Should one exclude amounts attributable to inflation; or to changes in interest rates; or that have not yet been 'realized' (itself a term of the accountant's art)?

Many of the practical difficulties arise because uncertainty about the future produces uncertainty about the extent to which capital has depreciated or been enhanced in a period.[14] Economists too[15] have explored the conceptual difficulties, and many have argued that they are so great that the present income and capital gains taxes (and their equivalent for companies, the 'corporation tax') should be abandoned in favour of alternatives, such as expenditure and wealth taxes, and greater substitution of indirect for direct taxes.[16] Correspondingly, many academic accountants have suggested abandoning attempts to measure income or 'profit'.[17]

To summarize, the UK income tax 'works' *despite* the fact that the courts and accountants have been unable clearly to define the concepts of 'capital' and 'income'. It works because a number of conventions (some more logical than others) have been established in the course of the development of accounting practice and in tax legislation, judicial interpretation, and Inland

[14] See e.g. H. C. Edey, 'The Nature of Profit', *Accounting and Business Research*, 1 (1970), 50–5, and Richard H. Macve, *A Conceptual Framework for Financial Accounting and Reporting* (London, 1981), 25–32.

[15] Such as J. R. Hicks, *Value and Capital* (Oxford, 2nd edn., 1946), ch. 14; and F. W. Paish, 'Capital Value and Income', *Economica*, 7 (1940), 416–18.

[16] See e.g. N. Kaldor, 'The Concept of Income in Economic Theory', in R. H. Parker and G. C. Harcourt (eds.), *Readings in the Concept and Measurement of Income* (Cambridge, 1969), 161–82, and J. E. Meade (chairman), *The Structure and Reform of Direct Taxation* (The Institute for Fiscal Studies, London, 1978). In the last decade the 'taxable profits' of UK trading and manufacturing businesses had been moving much closer to their cash flow ('receipts and payments') than to the 'profits' that they reported in their annual accounts, as a result of the increased capital allowances (up to 100% in the year of purchase for expenditure on equipment etc.) and of the system of 'stock relief', which were introduced in the 1970s to help *inter alia* with the effects of inflation. However, changes in the Finance Acts 1981 and 1984 have halted this trend. For professional firms, it has always been the custom to use a 'cash basis' of accounting for tax purposes rather than the normal 'income' or 'profit' basis.

[17] See e.g. D. Solomons, 'Economic and Accounting Concepts of Income', *Accounting Review*, 36 (1961), 374–83; and T. A. Lee, 'Cash Flow Accounting and Corporate Financial Reporting', in M. Bromwich and A. Hopwood (eds.), *Essays in British Accounting Research* (London, 1981), 63–78.

Revenue practice. These conventions have, however, come under increasing attack in recent years, especially as tax rates have risen.

I would therefore suggest that if the ancient Greeks or Romans had decided to tax 'income' rather than 'capital', then those involved in assessment and collection of direct taxes would have begun to work out something and developed conventions to meet the need. This does not of course weaken de Ste. Croix's argument that because we find no evidence of any attempt to calculate something that might be called 'income' in routine ancient accounting, there cannot in fact have been any 'income tax'. *Why* no attempt was made to tax income is a harder question, but it seems unlikely that the state of ancient accounting was a significant inhibiting factor.

It is perhaps helpful to remember that, in broad terms, taxes on capital and taxes on income may be regarded as alternative approaches to taxing the same thing.[18] One may also tax gross incomes rather than net incomes. It is indeed true that two individuals with the same gross incomes (e.g. from sales or rents received) may have different net incomes (e.g. because of different production costs or maintenance and depreciation costs, given the different assets and other factors of production employed) and that this is recognized in our income tax system by attempting to arrive at amounts for their net incomes on which to levy the tax. Nevertheless one can, in a more rough and ready way, tax gross incomes at a lower rate to achieve broadly similar results.

For example, by having different rates on the gross incomes from different activities (e.g. different types of agriculture) one may be able to make a broad allowance for the likely differences in net incomes. In some cases (e.g. rents from land where all the maintenance costs are to be borne by the lessee) gross income equals net income. If one further allows that payment of tax may be in kind as well as in money, then in that sense the taxes paid in antiquity as a percentage of agricultural produce were 'income taxes', and there was no need to try and calculate money income.

Since the main form of wealth and income in antiquity was agricultural, direct taxes based on capital values, on areas of land, on individuals' lives and

---

[18] The value of capital is a function of the income it is expected to produce. In a theoretically simple economy, if capital earns 10% p.a., levying an annual tax on capital of 5% comes to the same thing as levying a 50% tax on income (if one makes no allowance for the fluctuations of economic life). With similar oversimplification, if workers earn an average wage of £10,000 a year, levying income tax at 30% comes to the same thing as a poll tax of £3,000 (especially if one is not concerned about notions of progressive taxation). Such capital taxes were levied in antiquity, although *eisphora* (and, initially, *tributum*) was only levied when emergency demanded, not on a regular annual basis (*CSAGW* 234; Jones, 'Taxation', 154–5, 164). Another 'occasional' capital tax, the inheritance tax (*vicesima hereditatium*) was first imposed by Augustus and was extremely unpopular (*CSAGW* 362, 454–5).

on percentages of produce perhaps served well enough for su
industrial economy.[19] There was not a sufficient number of 'ordin
earning wage or business incomes of sufficient size to be worth t
these by attempting any more sophisticated measurement. Moreov
objective of achieving 'equity' between taxpayers that probably provides most
support for modern attempts to tax income, as well as giving rise to the complexity of the basis of assessment. In the light of the often arbitrary and
brutal methods of collection employed in antiquity (*CSAGW* 497–502),
equity was scarcely a significant factor.[20]

3. BUSINESS MANAGEMENT—ECONOMIC PLANNING AND CONTROL

Modern 'management accounting' is widely regarded as having an important
role in assisting large scale businesses, not only in the orderly administration
and control of their affairs, but also in decision-making on such questions as
'Which activities are most profitable? Where should we expand, and where
contract? How should we reward the managers of different activities for their
achievements?' and so on.

The major wealth producing activity in the Graeco-Roman world was
agriculture (*CSAGW* 120–33). In GRA (pp. 37–8) de Ste. Croix took up the
arguments of Mickwitz (n. 9 above) and observed:

It was hardly possible for a large Roman landowner who went in for different kinds
of agricultural activity to tell which kinds paid best, because his inadequate accounting system did not permit separate costing.

Again:

It is not surprising to find that the Roman agricultural writers never think of advising
a man who is buying a farm to examine the vendor's accounts . . . It would be impossible for the ancient landowner to estimate in advance, or even calculate in retrospect,

---

[19] Under UK income tax, farmers were originally assessed by reference to the rental value of their land
'on the assumption that farmers did not keep books', and only gradually did the option of being assessed
on their profits become the rule (Sabine, *History of Income Tax*, 35, 117–18, 126, 213–14).

[20] Two taxes on businesses—the *cheironaxia* in Roman Egypt (see e.g. S. L. Wallace, *Taxation in Egypt
from Augustus to Diocletian* (London, 1938), 191–213) and the *chrysargyron* (or *collatio lustralis*) imposed by
Constantine in the early fourth century AD (*CSAGW* 272) seem to have been collected in the form of
'license fees' for carrying on the trade. The *cheironaxia* were levied at different rates on different trades
which 'suggests that they were related to average profits of the trades or crafts' (A. H. M. Jones, 'Taxation',
175, n. 119 (by Brunt))—though individuals in a given trade all paid the same whatever their actual
income turned out to be.

from the material contained in his accounts, the profitability of making capital improvements.

Other historians have followed Mickwitz and de Ste. Croix and used this accounting evidence to emphasize the lack of 'economic rationality' in farm investment and as an important factor in explaining the lack of technical progress in Roman farming.[21] But, as in the case of income tax, one must ask whether it was lack of developments in accounting technique which inhibited economic rationality or whether there are other reasons why the information needed for rational decisions does not appear in the accounts that have survived. Again, it is helpful to look at much later developments to gain an insight into the situation in antiquity.

It is clear that the lack of double-entry bookkeeping should have been no hindrance. The technical reasons will be discussed further in section 4 below, but for evidence one can look at farm accounts from the Middle Ages and early modern times. One example is provided by the accounts of Norwich Cathedral Priory during the thirteenth and fourteenth centuries. Medieval estate accounts recorded receipts and issues of cash and of produce in essentially the same way as estate accounts, like those of Zenon or Appianus, in Graeco-Roman times. Their primary purpose was to control the accountable officials.[22] But the Norwich accounts also show concern with the profitability of the estate and, in particular, with the profitability of managing the land directly (demesne husbandry) as against farming it out on lease. Appended to the foot of the accounts are statements giving the profit (*proficuum* or *profectus*) of the manors (arrived at by including e.g. the value of produce despatched to the priory or to other manors and allowing e.g. for expenditure on improvements) and of the arable husbandry (*wainagium*), arrived at by deducting from the profit of the manor those items (e.g. for rent, the manorial court, the mill, wool and livestock) that relate to other activities.[23]

---

[21] e.g. M. I. Finley, *The Ancient Economy* (London, 1973; repr. with corrections 1975), 110; K. D. White, *Roman Farming* (London, 1970), 454 with P. A. Brunt's review, *Journal of Roman Studies*, 62 (1972), 153–8, at 155.

[22] For the similarity in objectives of ancient and medieval estate accounting see e.g. O. ten Have, *The History of Accountancy*, trans A. van Seventer (Palo Alto, 1976), 23, and B. S. Yamey, 'Some Topics in the History of Financial Accounting', in W. T. Baxter and S. Davidson (eds.), *Studies in Accounting* (3rd edn., London, 1977), 11–34, at 11–12. On medieval estates the control aspect was enhanced by the emphasis on the role of the auditors. The final audited account contained not merely the receipts and payments that had occurred but those that the auditors considered should have occurred (e.g. by reference to standard yields of land and livestock), thus often revealing the reeve or bailiff as owing his lord more than the balances he was showing as due. See C. Noke, 'Accounting for Bailiffship in Thirteenth Century England', *Accounting and Business Research*, 42 (1981), 137–51; and J. S. Drew, 'Manorial Accounts of St. Swithun's Priory, Winchester', *English Hist. Rev.* 62 (1947), 20–41.

[23] See E. Stone, 'Profit-and-Loss Accountancy at Norwich Cathedral Priory', *Transactions of the Royal Hist.*

Thus no particular form of accounting was required in order to be able to make such calculations. Another important piece of evidence is provided by the seventeenth-century farm accounts of Robert Loder.[24] These are not detailed day-to-day accounts, but annual summaries. They retain the primitive form of narrative paragraphs, often without money columns and using mainly Roman numerals. They are none the less sophisticated computations of the profitability of the various enterprises of the farm (and often of what profits might have been, had some different course of action been pursued). They include recognition of notional interest on capital employed; of what are the 'relevant' costs for particular appraisals; and even of depreciation (of horses). We do not know what day-to-day accounting records Loder may have kept but they could not have incorporated these kinds of cost calculations which are specific to the circumstances of each decision. While we have nothing similar from antiquity, it is not safe to argue from silence. As Yamey has pointed out,[25] such calculations, by their nature, are generally less likely to have survived than the formal records of actual transactions for which people were held accountable.

There is however that notorious example from antiquity, Columella's calculation of the profitability of viticulture (*De re rustica*, 3.3.7–15), which has been held up as showing that the Romans (and by implication the Greeks[26]) were actually misled by the form and content of their accounts into making economically irrational decisions. Columella's basic calculation goes as follows:

Soc. 5th series, 12 (1962), 25–48; Noke, 'Accounting for Bailiffship'; B. S. Yamey, 'Accounting and the Rise of Capitalism', *J. of Accounting Research*, 2 (1964), 117–36, at 131 n. 31; and S. M. Jack, 'An Historical Defence of Single Entry Book-keeping', *Abacus*, 2 (1966), 137–58, at 154–7. 13th- and 14th-cent. writers were able to recognize, at least implicitly, the effect of depreciation on investment choices—e.g. in comparing horses and oxen they recognized that a horse's carcass was worth little, while an ox could be fattened for meat (*Walter of Henley and other Treatises on Estate Management and Accounting*, ed. D. Oschinsky (Oxford, 1971), 160–4). Again, in comparing alternative methods of farming they could make allowance for 'opportunity costs' (ibid. 305 and Noke, 'Accounting for Bailiffship', 148).

[24] See *Robert Loder's Farm Accounts 1610–1620*, ed. G. E. Fussell, Camden 3rd Series, 53 (London, 1936); Yamey, 'Accounting and the Rise of Capitalism', 131–2 nn. 32–4, 'Some Topics', 14–15, and 'Addendum to "Accounting and the Rise of Capitalism"' in *Business History, Selected Readings*, ed. K. A. Tucker (London, 1977), 340–6, section (2); and J. Freear, 'Robert Loder, Jacobean Management Accountant', *Abacus*, 6 (1970), 25–38.

[25] B. S. Yamey, 'Business Accounts', in T. C. Barker, R. H. Campbell, *et al.*, *Business History* (Historical Assoc., Helps for Students of History No. 59) (London, 1960), 30–6 at 36. Loder's accounts were of course for his own personal use. The first example of the publishing of systematic calculations of the profitability of different agricultural enterprises in Britain was Arthur Young, *A Course of Experimental Agriculture* (London, 1770; Dublin, 1771); cf. n. 53 below.

[26] The Roman agronomists owed much to their Greek predecessors (see e.g. CSAGW 234–5 and White, *Roman Farming*, ch. 1).

	HS [*sestertii*]
Cost of land	7,000
Cost of slave vine-dresser	8,000
Cost of preparation	14,000
Total	29,000

To this, Columella adds 6 per cent interest (i.e. HS 1,740 p.a.) for the first two years while the vines mature (i.e. HS 3,480) to give a total sum of HS 32,480 which he then compares with a loan at 6 per cent. The loan would bring in HS 1,950 each year; the vineyard (on his initial conservative calculation of HS 2,100 p.a. for sale of produce) brings in HS 150 more, and is therefore a better investment (although no explicit allowance is made for the difference in the risks that might be associated with the two forms of investment).

The trouble is of course that, unlike the interest on the loan with which he compares it (3.3.9), the annual income from the vineyard will not go on for ever.[27] Both the vines and the slave vine-dresser (*vinitor*) have a limited useful life.[28] Why does Columella ignore their depreciation (or 'amortization') as well as some other relevant costs? Mickwitz argued that it was because the practice of reckoning depreciation and other non-cash costs did not appear in Graeco-Roman estate accounting. GRA takes up this argument. Columella 'ignores the amortisation of the vine-dresser, the cost of maintaining him, and of fertilisation, the hiring of casual labour, and all other current expenses. It is interesting to find that the items which Columella ignores are just those which the ancient accounting system ignored.'[29] On this view, which has been echoed by other historians,[30] the accounts were not constructed to work out the profits properly and therefore 'capitalists' (like Columella here) could not work out the profitability of their planned ventures properly.

---

[27] Or, equivalently, at the end of their life the assets initially purchased cannot be sold for the HS 32,480 originally invested, whereas the capital of the loan would be repaid.

[28] So, for the purposes of n. 27 above, they would be worthless at the end of that life. It is also questionable how much of its original value the land would retain given that it would no longer be suitable for viticulture (R. P. Duncan-Jones, *The Economy of the Roman Empire: Quantitative Studies* (Cambridge, 2nd edn., 1982), 43 n. 1).

[29] GRA 38; cf. Mickwitz, 'Economic Rationalism', 585–6: 'It is very remarkable indeed, that Columella, who obviously tries to make a most conservative estimate, entirely overlooks items which no modern farmer could possibly fail to take into consideration. Hitherto no satisfactory explanation of his reasons for doing this has been found. After having studied the evidence of the papyri, however, we find no difficulty in understanding his mistakes. If Columella's accounting was of the same type as that employed on Apollonius' estate he had no means of ascertaining the above-mentioned expenses.' ('Apollonius' estate' is that in the Zenon papyri (GRA 31–2).)

[30] e.g. Finley, *Ancient Economy*, 116–17.

There are however a number of reasons for doubting this conclusion. The evidence from the Middle Ages and later (when the routine estate accounting was still as 'primitive') that people were not prevented from working out profitability has already been mentioned. The other factors that need to be considered are:

1. It seems unlikely that Columella was in fact basing his example in any systematic way on his accounts (pp. 67–70).
2. Even today when it is natural to consult accounts for this purpose, the conventions generally employed in preparing accounts do not produce figures that necessarily accord with the concepts required in rational planning. Indeed, without care in interpretation modern accounts too may be seriously misleading, and one often needs to keep distinct the concepts of accounting and those of economic decision-making [pp. 71–5].
3. The lack of development of systematic, formalized approaches to economic decision-making was probably due mainly to the limited opportunities and choices that were generally available in antiquity [pp. 75–7].

To take these in turn:

1. At first sight, it is tempting to agree with Mickwitz that Columella must have omitted the depreciation because the estate accounts of his time would not have included it. This could also explain why maintenance of the slaves is omitted—most of this would be provided in kind in the form of food, clothes, and lodging, and thus there would be no cash entry in the accounts of the estate.[31] The same would apply to fertilization: the manure would be provided by the estate's own animals. So if Columella was referring to his accounts to check the items relating to viticulture these would be missing from the cash records.

However, it seems doubtful that Columella was referring to his accounts. The most comprehensive criticism of his calculations has been provided by Duncan-Jones[32] who has reworked Columella's figures and set out his own estimates of the yields available from Roman viticulture. There are two main aspects of this criticism: the first that Columella ignores certain costs that should have been included (and thus overstates the profitability of the enterprise), the second that his estimates for the items he does include are careless or inaccurate, suggesting that his data are to be mistrusted.

---

[31] With the exception of *peculium*, if there was any (Duncan-Jones, *Economy*, 42 n. 4).
[32] Ibid. 39–59, 376–8.

In the light of Duncan-Jones's calculations, among the items that Columella omitted are items that *would* have appeared in the accounts, such as purchase of ancillary land and slaves and the cost of farm buildings and equipment. Why were these omitted? It is of course possible that Columella just did not think about ancillary land and slaves (as his seven-*iugera* plot for the vineyard is itself probably an artificial unit chosen for the purposes of calculation on the assumption of one *vinitor* per seven *iugera*[33]). The omission of costs of buildings and equipment could also reflect the fact that no cash payment might be required, e.g. if they could have been constructed out of materials available on the land and by the owner's other slaves (although this seems less likely to be the general case). Nor does Columella include any sundry expenditure on equipment (such as the purchase and lining of baskets and wine jars)—but perhaps they would be produced on the estate too.[34] One should however question more seriously the omission from annual costs of the hire of extra labour to cope with the peak of work at harvest-time— hire of labour for the vintage being perhaps the most common form of payment in antiquity for outside agricultural labour[35]—which should have been recorded in the accounts.

If it is argued that all these omitted costs reflect the fact that a large, self-sufficient estate, worked by slaves, would not have to buy in any of them for cash, it becomes that much harder to explain why Columella allows HS 14,000 for the cost of preparing the vineyard, providing the vine-props etc.[36] Indeed a major shortcoming in the calculations is the lack of explanation of the assumptions on which the figures have been based.[37] Moreover, even for the items which Columella does include and for which he gives the money payments or receipts involved (such as cost of land, vines and preparation,

---

[33] *Rust.* 3.3.8; see e.g. Duncan-Jones, *Economy*, 42 n. 5; and C. A. Yeo, 'The Economics of Roman and American Slavery', *Finanzarchiv*, 13 (1952), 445–85, at 477.

[34] Cf. Cato's list of the equipment (including the *vilicus* and other slaves) needed for a vineyard (*Agr.* 11). For some payments for sundries see e.g. *BGU* 14 (3rd century AD): Johnson, *Roman Egypt*, 218); cf. *P. Oxy.* XVI no. 1911, 181–93 (6th cent. AD). Contrast Yeo, 'Economics', 455.

[35] However, *CSAGW* 593 n. 59 does point out that references to hired workers are conspicuously rare in Columella's writings. With sufficient variety of vines or of other activities on the estate the other slaves may again have been able to cope (Yeo, 'Economics', 461; cf. 465).

[36] Elsewhere (3.3.5; 4.30.1) Columella implies that good planning can reduce, if not eliminate, the need to go outside the estate to purchase the 'dowry' for the vines. Although this dowry might be taken to include all the equipment etc. (*instrumentum*) necessary for the vineyard, in his calculation Columella specifically refers only to props and withes (3.3.8). It is not entirely clear why even the land for the vineyard would have to be purchased if the owner already had a sufficiently large estate.

[37] A common failing of modern accounting practice too (see Richard H. Macve, *Quaere Verum vel Recte Numerare*, Inaugural Lecture 1979 (The University College of Wales, Aberystwyth, 1980)).

and the sales of wine and nursery plants), the amounts he gives are hard to reconcile with other evidence about prices and costs at that period.[38]

It therefore seems unlikely that Columella was referring to his accounts in any systematic way. Nevertheless, it might be argued that *if* Columella had looked at his accounts, he could perhaps have provided better estimates for the items for which cash would have been paid or received, but would still have been constrained by the lack of any concept of recording depreciation, or transfers in kind between different uses, from working out the true profitability of viticulture. But if this were so, from where did Columella get the idea of including the interest forgone in the first two years in arriving at the total cost of his investment outlay? This interest is notional; no cash payment would have appeared in his accounts (nor would this item normally appear in modern accounting practice). Including it is a sophisticated way of handling his decision-making problem.[39] In fact his whole analysis between 'initial capital outlay' and 'annual return' would not be mirrored by any such analysis of the payments and receipts in the accounting records themselves.

Columella's figures, therefore, cannot be viewed as reflecting in any simple way what he would have found in his accounts if he had looked. The explanation for his poor calculations must rather be that he did not really give the matter a great deal of thought. He was convinced in his own mind that viticulture was profitable and he perhaps wanted some figures to present a rationalization for this belief.[40]

[38] For example, Duncan-Jones (*Economy*, 54) concludes his discussion of the preparation costs: 'This appears to be another case where Columella has chosen a convenient round figure without considering its plausibility in detail', and starts his general conclusions (p. 55): 'Although the omissions and distortions partly reflect the shortcomings of ancient accounting practice, Columella also appears to have been careless in his choice of figures with which to show the potentialities of wine investment. Documenting his own experience in detail would probably have been easier than looking for typical figures, and it would no doubt have been more valuable to the historian.'

[39] Although, strictly, Columella should have compounded the interest (which would give HS 3,584, i.e. an additional 6% in the second year on the first year's HS 1,740), the difference is immaterial and his method reflects in a fairly sophisticated way the 'opportunity cost' of tying up the money for two years with no return. This delay (together with the later inclusion of non-annual sales of nursery plants) seriously complicates any calculation of profitability based on accounting profits and Columella's approach here is in fact even more sophisticated than modern accounting practice (which normally only charges any interest actually paid). As Yeo, 'Economics', 473, and Duncan-Jones, *Economy*, 39 n. 2, point out, the treatment of interest has caused some confusion in estimating profitability (e.g. White, *Roman Farming*, 269). The return on an investment is best calculated before deducting any interest (as whether interest is paid is an accident of financing policy). But in deciding whether to make the investment one still needs to ask (as Columella does) whether the return is better than the interest one could get elsewhere—i.e. whether it is as profitable as the alternatives that are available—and, if the capital has to be borrowed, whether the return is high enough to cover the rate of interest that will have to be paid.

[40] Note that while Mickwitz argues ('Economic Rationalism', 585) that Columella was wrong, and viticulture was really unprofitable (i.e. his accounts may have misled him), Duncan-Jones (*Economy*, 59) concludes that viticulture was indeed profitable but that Columella's own financial rationalization is not convincing. Yeo, 'Economics', 476, also argues that viticulture was profitable at this time.

Was his aim, as an advocate, to make his argument persuasive by initially presenting 'the worst case' (i.e. with a low annual revenue of only HS 2,100, and with a high initial cost for the slave etc.), rather than, as a scientist, to set out by careful calculation the range of possible outcomes? If someone had argued with him about depreciation, he might have justifiably countered with: 'Well, it's not easy to be sure how long the slave and the vineyard will be productive, but I have built in high prices for these to compensate.'[41] Anyway, having made his debating point with the 'worst case', he is more concerned with what he regards as more 'realistic' cases, i.e. with an annual revenue three times as great, and then further supplemented by large revenues from sale of nursery plants.[42] He now has ample margin in his cost calculations and can therefore treat these recalculations of revenue in only a very casual fashion.[43]

Much of this can only be speculation (especially as Columella does not set out his own assumptions clearly), but there is more than enough to doubt that Mickwitz's explanation is the most plausible. Mickwitz himself observes: 'On the whole, Columella seems not to have troubled much about calculations of the kind just described. Usually he presents no evidence when giving his opinion about economic matters.'[44]

In the light of the medieval examples from Norwich and elsewhere, and of Loder's accounts, I doubt whether any of the 'omissions and distortions' in Columella's calculation can safely be attributed to the 'shortcomings of ancient accounting practice'.[45] We should not conclude that the state of ancient accounting would have systematically misled people into making irrational decisions.

---

[41] As Duncan-Jones shows (*Economy*, 53–4), it is difficult to justify half the sum for initial outlay on these items.

[42] 3.3.10–13. Columella says his initial calculation of revenue of HS 2,100 p.a. assumes vines of the worst sort which he would root out.

[43] Using 'internal rate of return' calculations (see n. 49 below) I calculate the returns implied by Columella's own data to be 6.4% for his initial case; just over 16% when the revenue is increased to HS 6,300 p.a.; and just over 20% (not 34% as given by Duncan-Jones, *Economy*, 44 and Finley, *Ancient Economy*, 117) when the sale of nursery plants is included too. If one then reckons vines to have a working life of only thirty years and a *vinitor* of twenty years, the returns become just under 5%; nearly 16%; and just under 20% respectively. With a life for a *vinitor* of only ten years they are reduced to approximately 3%; 15% and 19% respectively, so at the higher revenue levels depreciation has only a small effect.

[44] 'Economic Rationalism', 586. Finley, *Ancient Economy*, 117 concludes it was 'a merely perfunctory desk exercise'. Given the ancient agronomists' poor showing in the use of any statistics (e.g. productivity measures—see Duncan-Jones, *Economy*, Appendix 2, pp. 327–33) one can hardly expect their financial statistics to be any better. This does not imply that farmers were unable in practice either to organize the work of their estates or to estimate the profitability of alternative investments.

2. If ancient accounting is excused the blame for Columella's own poor show-ing as *homo economicus* (or *diligens ratiocinator* (3.3.7)), it nevertheless remains true that we lack evidence from antiquity of accounts being used to assist rational planning. Would not the development of some systematic approach that showed the return on investment and the profitability of different activities have been of economic benefit? The issues here are controversial and com-plex, but may be approached from two directions:

1. How does modern accounting practice assist rational decision-making?
2. What freedom of economic choice did the ancient farmer have?

The second of these questions I discuss in (3) below. As regards the first, modern business accounting practice (including farm accounting) certainly attempts to indicate the profitability of business firms and of their individual activities or enterprises. Problems arise, however, both in calculating the over-all profitability of a firm (or a farm) and in analysing that profitability over its different enterprises. Recall the discussion in section 2 above. The same problems that have prevented the development of clear concepts of 'capital' and 'income' for tax purposes have also plagued accountants in searching for satisfactory measures of business performance. To take one example, while it is now normal practice to make a systematic annual charge for depreciation of long-lived assets, there is no way of proving that the correct charge has been made. How long will the assets last? On what pattern is their value exhausted over their useful life? If inflation raises values, should depreciation still be charged and, if so, how much?[46] It is impossible to determine analyti-cally how well the rule-of-thumb methods conventionally employed measure depreciation, or which method is best, except in certain special cases.[47]

When one tries to analyse the profitability of different enterprises in a

---

[46] See e.g. W. T. Baxter, *Depreciation* (London, 1971).

[47] See W. Beaver, *Financial Reporting: An Accounting Revolution* (Englewood Cliffs, NJ, 1981), 75–83. Because of the variety of methods that companies may use in reporting their profits, considerable caution is needed in interpreting the figures when estimating rates of profit earned by different companies, or at dif-ferent times, or in ranking the profitability of different activities—e.g. for the purposes of economic his-tory. Haydn Jones, 'A Nineteenth-Century Welsh Iron Company', *Accounting History*, 3/1 (1978), 22–40 describes the variations in an individual company's practices; cf. G. Whittington, 'On the Use of the Accounting Rate of Return in Empirical Research', *Accounting and Business Research*, 35 (1979), 201–8; and F. M. Fisher and J. J. McGowan. 'On the Misuse of Accounting Rates of Return to Infer Monopoly Profits', *American Economic Review* (1983), 82–97.

For a recent exposition for employees of how accounts may be used as a weapon in the 'class struggle' (based on the premiss that managements will seek to choose accounting methods that depress reported profits in order to resist wage claims), see C. Hird, *Challenging the Figures: A Guide to Company Finance and Accounts* (London, 1983). There are of course also incentives to choose methods that increase reported profits (e.g. to attract capital). The empirical evidence is surveyed in R. W. Holthausen and R. W. Leftwich, 'The Economic Consequences of Accounting Choice', *J. of Accounting and Economics*, 5 (1983), 77–117.

business, further problems arise. There is generally no unique way in which common costs (e.g. the rent of a factory; the running costs of a farm tractor) may be allocated to the different activities; while some methods may be more plausible than others, they are all to some extent arbitrary.[48] In assessing the usefulness of the resulting figure on an enterprise's profit or loss one needs to understand what allocation methods have been employed.

The difficulties are highlighted when one specifically asks how such analyses can assist decision-making. The kernel of the problem is how far the accounts can reflect the relevant costs and revenues that need to be appraised for a rational decision to be taken. The decision-maker is concerned about the costs and benefits to come in the future, while the accounts record past costs and revenues—how good a guide are these? The decision-maker is often concerned about marginal costs and revenues (how will costs and revenues be altered by his decision?); but the accounts record and allocate all costs and revenues and so give averages based on the present level of production.

There are therefore dangers in using the profits and losses shown by modern accounts, whether for appraising capital investment opportunities, or for choosing between different activities, without examining carefully the bases on which the figures have been arrived at. In the case of capital investment decisions, estimates of the rate of return based on accounting profits (arrived at by allowing for depreciation, etc.) may differ widely from the 'true yield' (or 'internal rate of return'). It may be safer to bypass the accounting calculations and use straightforward estimates of future cash payments and receipts over the life of the investment.[49]

---

[48] See A. L. Thomas, 'Allocation: The Fallacy and the Theorists', in Baxter and Davidson, *Studies in Accounting*, 182–94. For an example of medieval cost accounting, where a merchant computes his costs per sack of wool, see E. B. Fryde, 'The Wool Accounts of William de la Pole', St Anthony's Hall Publications, 25 (1964), 3–31 (repr. as ch. 9 in E. B. Fryde, *Studies in Medieval Trade and Finance* (London, 1983)).

[49] e.g. suppose Columella had invested his HS 29,000, and a revenue of HS 6,300 could be earned for 30 years (starting in the first year for simplicity). Suppose at the end of 30 years, vineyard and slave would be exhausted and worthless. If we charge 'depreciation' of HS 29,000 ÷ 30 = HS 967 each year, the net profit is HS 5,333 p.a., and the accounting rate of return ('ARR') of HS 5,333 ÷ 29,000 appears to be 18.4%. In fact, the internal rate of return ('IRR') (found by asking at what rate of interest is the prospect of receiving HS 6,300 a year for 30 years worth an investment of HS 29,000) is between 21% and 22%, i.e. about 3% higher. Generally, where an asset's services are equal each year, conventional 'straight-line' depreciation itself needs to be adjusted for the interest factor to give charges that are lower initially and higher later (Baxter, *Depreciation*, ch. 8). The shorter the life, or the higher the interest rate, the more severe is the effect: e.g. for a 10-year life 'straight-line' depreciation of HS 2,900 would give annual profit of HS 3,400 and an ARR of only 11.7%. The IRR would still be between 17% and 18%, i.e. about 6% higher. When considering e.g. the depreciation of slaves, shorter rather than longer lives seem more likely (*CSAGW* 232–3 with 587 n. 9).

In choosing between investments, even IRR can mislead. Modern theory recommends the calculation of 'net present value' ('NPV') by discounting the future cash flows associated with the investment at an

Some of the grosser dangers of allocating overall results between different activities may be avoided by adopting the method variously known as the 'contribution' approach (or 'direct costing') in a factory context, or the 'gross margin' approach in the farming context. This deducts shared fixed costs only in arriving at the overall profit or loss of the business or farm, and does not attempt to allocate them to individual enterprises.[50] For example, if there is little choice, at least in the short run, about how many workers are employed, then it may be positively misleading to attempt to 'charge' their labour to the individual enterprises on which they work. This could suggest that an enterprise was 'unprofitable', whereas in fact, if it was excluded, the same amount of labour would have to be paid, but out of a smaller gross margin. Similar considerations apply to the 'depreciation' of specialist buildings and machinery that are already owned and are to be kept anyway (because of the difficulty of removal, for example, or for lack of a good second-hand market). The opportunity cost of using such 'fixed' factors (for which charges will still normally appear in the overall accounts) is zero.[51]

How useful are such gross margin calculations to a farmer? This depends largely on the number of constraints facing him. The need to choose only arises because of some limit, e.g. on land available. If this were the only constraint, the farmer might indeed want to choose the type of production yielding the highest gross margin (e.g. just corn growing). However, there are likely to be other constraints: over-intensity of production of some crops may encourage diseases and parasites; it may be necessary to rotate the use of the land; the timing of the harvests may impose demands on the labour-force at certain seasons that cannot be met beyond a certain level even with the addition of hired labour; and so forth.

reflect appropriate rate of interest (to the alternatives available and the risks involved). See e.g. M. Bromwich, *The Economics of Capital Budgeting* (London, 1979).

[50] Suppose a farmer has a choice between grazing cattle, growing corn and growing vines on his land. A modern agricultural management text (e.g. F. Sturrock, *Farm Accounting and Management* (London, 7th edn., 1982), 103–12, 119–24) would recommend calculations of the following kind: (1) Estimate the revenue per hectare from each kind of activity (i.e. basically the units of physical produce multiplied by the sales price per unit). (2) Estimate those costs directly variable with production, e.g. fodder purchased for the cattle; seed and fertilizer purchased for the arable production; fertilizer purchased and casual labour hired for the vineyard. (3) On the basis of these calculations, estimate the 'gross margin' per hectare from each activity and choose the activity yielding the largest gross margin. Such calculations are in principle identical to those nowadays recommended in commercial and industrial financial management texts for choosing which products to concentrate on, at least in the short term.

[51] This situation may often have applied to the slave-gangs owned on an estate, at least in the short term. If one is feeding them and not inclined to dispose of them, one may as well keep them employed as idle. See also Yeo, 'Economics', 477–8. For further discussion see J. Arnold and A. Hope, *Accounting for Management Decisions* (London, 1983); J. R. Gould, 'Opportunity Cost', in H. C. Edey and B. S. Yamey (eds.) *Debits, Credits, Finance and Profits* (London, 1974), 91–107.

Again, one has to allow for other interdependencies between the various enterprises, such as feeding of crops to livestock; the use of manures from livestock on the arable land; and the consumption of produce by the farmer's family and his workers in lieu of money income. Where supplies are readily available from good markets, there is little problem in allowing for these factors—e.g. the home-grown grain consumed by livestock or humans can be 'charged' at market prices and added to the revenue from corn growing. But where markets are thin, not only will the pricing of such transfers be fairly arbitrary, but there may anyway be little effective freedom of choice in what to produce.

As the constraints are increased, the problem becomes one of finding the best mixture of activities, which is much more complicated than merely ranking gross margins. In fact in such a situation there is generally no way of analysing the best solution. Even today one basically has to adopt 'trial and error' (although mathematical programming techniques, such as 'linear programming' ('LP')[52] are now available which can speed the identification of the 'optimal' solution).

Thus it is clear that any attempt to prepare accounts of individual farm enterprises in such a way as to guide rational decisions is a sophisticated undertaking, requiring considerable effort. Often the identification of the relevant revenues and costs cannot be handled in a routine manner but is specific to the problem in hand. It is perhaps hardly surprising that the examples of profitability calculations that have survived from medieval and later times reveal several inconsistencies, short-cuts, illogicalities, and mistakes.[53]

[52] LP formulates as a set of simultaneous equations and inequalities the relevant costs and revenues of the various enterprises, and the various constraints, that face the decision-maker. While the problem generally has to be solved by iteration (i.e. repeated trial and error), the major theoretical achievement has been to identify 'minimum effort' trials that always move closer to the optimal solution. With the aid of a computer the remaining effort of calculation becomes trivial. However, as there is generally no way of analysing the best solution, there is thus generally no way in which a Roman agronomist could have analysed what the 'best' choice was in a situation of multiple constraints. Indeed it is only in the latest edition of Sturrock's textbook, *Farm Accounting*, 164–79, that LP has replaced more traditional 'rule of thumb' calculations.

[53] e.g. the Norwich monks often used 'standard' valuations for produce that differed from prevailing market prices. The usefulness of the figures they produced was also limited in other ways (see Stone, 'Profit-and-Loss Accountancy', and Noke, 'Accounting for Bailiffship').

Robert Loder also faced some difficulties. For example, having calculated his profits for 1610 onwards, he realized on 26 Jan. 1619 (Fussell, *Loder's Accounts*, 66–7) that, having taken credit in his profits for the value of manure produced (e.g. ibid. 60), he had forgotten to allow for the cost of the manure used on his land, and so now calculated the amount that he should have been deducting from his profits for this. (The monks of Norwich also had some difficulty with accounting for manure (Stone, 'Profit-and-Loss Accountancy', 29 n. 6).)

Arthur Young, the 18th-cent. agriculturalist (whose secretary in his last years was a Mr St. Croix) discusses in his 'introductory explanations', at pp. xxvii–xxxi of his *Experimental Agriculture*, some of his difficulties in arriving at meaningful figures for the costs and profits of individual agricultural experiments (cf. n. 25

So even for the modern farmer the agricultural textbooks have some difficulty in justifying the keeping of detailed accounts of the conventional kind.
Major incentives to the preparation of accounts showing the overall 'profit'
or 'loss' of a modern farm are the requirements of the Inland Revenue, as well
as of lending bankers, and (in the case of farms organized as, or owned by,
limited companies) of the Companies Acts for the preparation of accounts
for the absentee owners—the shareholders. Given these present-day requirements, it may be economical for modern farmers to make further internal use
of the basic data and analyse the profits and losses so calculated over the separate 'enterprises' of the farm, just as the data are often analysed into 'cost
accounts' for the different areas of industrial businesses. Such analyses may be
better than nothing, and may at least be useful as giving *prima-facie* indications
of where further investigation and analysis is needed. However, without the
need to prepare the overall account of profitability for the Inland Revenue
etc., the advantages of troubling to prepare the analysed accounts may be
hardly worth the bother.[54] If the farmer is closely involved with day-to-day
management he may well get an adequate feel for how things are going without elaborate records.[55]

3. In appraising the evidence for 'rationality' in decision-making in antiquity
it is also instructive to compare the choices available to the ancient farmer
and to the modern farmer. The former clearly had far more restricted opportunities. The modern Western farmer operates in a market economy, where
he hires labour, buys and operates expensive machinery, and pays for costly
inputs such as feeding stuffs, veterinary charges, medicines, seeds, fertilizers,
weedkillers, insecticides, etc. These inputs (and in particular the availability
of sophisticated machinery, of chemicals and of disease-resistant strains)
have freed him of many ancient restrictions and made available to him an

---

above). He later became so disenchanted with this work that 'he did his best to suppress it by buying up
and destroying all the copies he could lay hands on' (*Arthur Young and his Times*, ed. G. E. Mingay (London,
1975), 4; cf. *The Autobiography of Arthur Young*, ed. M. Betham-Edwards (London, 1898), 30).

[54] The benefits to farmers of keeping accurate modern accounts are argued in the textbooks (e.g.
Sturrock, *Farm Accounting*, ch. I) to be: (*a*) to facilitate the preparation of the annual accounts, especially
for the Inland Revenue, (*b*) to monitor cash flow during the year, and (*c*) to assist understanding of what
is happening to the business as a basis for control and planning of changes and developments. But (*a*) is a
modern, external requirement, and as late as 1948, when the Budget finally required all farms to be taxed
as businesses, 'the Opposition reminded the House of farmers' inability to keep accounts' (Sabine, *Hist. of
Income Tax*, 214). The need for control over dishonesty etc. under (*b*) and (*c*) can be achieved as effectively
by the kind of accounts kept on a Graeco-Roman estate. Control over inefficiency can be achieved largely
in physical terms, e.g. by 'standard yield' calculations. (For some difficulties of control, as illustrated by
the medieval English manors but often still met today, see Noke, 'Accounting for Bailiffship' (n. 22
above).)

[55] See also Jack, 'Historical Defence', 139, 157–8.

unprecedented range of choice in terms of relative profitability.[56] He also enjoys government (or EEC) subsidies and guaranteed prices for some of his output and despatches it to distant markets.

By comparison the ancient farmer faced many more constraints and had far fewer opportunities. He also spent less money and sold less of his output. The tools and equipment available to him were much simpler and a far smaller proportion of his costs.[57] Once he had purchased his slaves they were largely a fixed cost and to some extent self-replacing (cf. note 67 below). Mixed farming was essential. If there was no livestock in the mixture the farmer may have had to obtain manure from outside—not easy before the development of chemical fertilizers. If there was no corn grown, the farmer may have needed to purchase grain to feed his livestock. If there was not an adequate mixture of produce for human consumption, then food, clothing, fuel, etc. for those who depended on the farm would have to be purchased. The amount he could sell was limited by transport difficulties. The ideal of self-sufficiency was largely an economic necessity.[58]

The important aspect of this much greater number of constraints is that, even if one can imagine some such decision aid as 'linear programming' having been available to the ancient farmer, it seems unlikely that it could have been of much use to him. The more constraints there are in a problem, the more one is compelled towards adopting the only feasible solution, rather than the best of a number of feasible solutions.[59] If the ancient farmer was largely compelled to adopt a certain mixture of farming, what would have been the point of his trying to estimate the profitability of the individual enterprises on his farm?

The case for doing so would of course have been stronger for those estate owners who, in addition to the basic mixture of crops and livestock, grew cash crops for sale—those near large towns, or those who marketed wine and

---

[56] *CSAGW* 210 raises the question of the social and ecological costs of modern 'agribusiness'.

[57] K. D. White, *Greek and Roman Technology* (London, 1984), 58–72.

[58] Cato, *Agr.* 2.7. Sturrock, *Farm Accounting*, notes (pp. 247–8) that in developing countries where farms are remote from markets, farmers 'tend to be self-sufficient in case a drought or other misfortune makes food scarce and expensive, and they are unable to buy any when they need it. On large farms near towns, farmers sell more and buy most of the food they require. In planning holdings, the farmer's wishes must however be respected and provision made for growing a variety of vegetables and fruits'. For an almost identical discussion of the 'ideal' of self-sufficiency on a Roman farm, see Duncan-Jones, *Economy*, 37–8. The ideal applied to large estates as well as small holdings (and a large landowner might own many small estates: Brunt, review of White (n. 21 above), 156; Finley, *Ancient Economy*, 109) and would have applied to Greek as well as Roman farms.

[59] Thus LP has only acquired real potential for handling farming decisions since rotational restrictions have largely ceased to be required. See Sturrock, *Farm Accounting*, 177–8. It is doubtful whether Roman farmers had even reached the stage of enjoying the benefit of rotations (rather than being compelled to fallow the land: Brunt, review of White, 156–8).

olive oil which were more easily transported.[60] It is perhaps strange that even these grander owners did not show more interest in articulating rational approaches to their investment in cash crops—as has been seen, Columella, writing for this audience, made a poor showing. But even here choice may have been fairly limited (i.e. either vines or olives),[61] and fine calculations (given the uncertainties involved) may have been of little use. One has more-over to remember that the owners of these estates were 'gentlemen' landowners who considered too deep an involvement in the economic management of their estates beneath them.[62]

On balance the combination of limited opportunities, multiple constraints and cultural preferences would seem to have provided little incentive for ancient farmers to develop more analytical approaches to decision-making. But whatever the verdict on their 'economic rationality', it seems clear that the lack of modern accounting techniques would not, in itself, have misled them or prevented them from making sensible decisions.

As has been shown, the question of whether people are misled by accounts is still topical. Plans should be made in terms of future cash flows, internal rates of return and net present values (see note 49 above), even though accounts are still kept that calculate 'profit' or 'income' according to tradi-tional conventions. While it would be theoretically possible to recast the accounts so that they do reflect the kind of economic thinking that goes into the rational appraisal of ventures,[63] in practice this is generally not done. Consequently, the argument still arises as to whether investors and business managers are misled by modern accounting figures into making incorrect deci-sions.[64] Even if one were persuaded that this is a real danger today, one crucial difference between the modern and the ancient situations is that nowadays the accounts are published and received by a whole variety of people separated

[60] Cato, *Agr.* I.3, recommends purchasing a farm near a town or with good transport communications. See also Yeo, 'Economics', 453.

[61] C. A. Yeo, 'The Development of the Roman Plantation and Marketing of Farm Products', *Finanzarchiv*, 13 (1952), 321–42, and 'Economics' (both summarized at 'Economics', 483–5) gives a vivid description of the economics of large-scale wine and olive production, using slaves, and points out (e.g. 478) the inbuilt tendency to monoculture of the cash crop resulting from the inflexibility in the skills of the large-scale labour-force.

[62] Brunt, review of White, 154–5; *CSAGW*, 129–33.

[63] This would generally be an extremely subjective procedure: R. S. Edwards, 'The Nature & Measurement of Income', *Accountant* (July–Oct. 1938), revised and reprinted in Baxter and Davidson, *Studies in Accounting* 96–140; cf. B. V. Carsberg and S. P. Lumby, *The Evaluation of Financial Performance in the Water Industry* (London, 1983).

[64] Evidence that modern managers make little use of the theoretically best approaches to formulating decisions is reviewed in B. V. Carsberg and A. Hope, *Business Investment Decisions under Inflation* (London, 1976), 40–65; and by D. J. Cooper, 'Rationality and Investment Appraisal', *Accounting and Business Research*, 19 (1975), 198–202.

from those who manage and control the activities of a business, and it is more plausible that their reactions to what appears in the accounts (especially as these are described as 'profits' and 'losses') may constrain management decisions.[65] On an ancient estate, with an individual owner to oversee the decisions, and where the accounts did not purport to show any more than movements of cash and kind, any dependence or fixation on the accounting figures in forming ideas about profitability seems much less likely.

Finally, I must also consider briefly the argument recently advanced by Carandini,[66] that Columella's calculation, far from misleading him, does in fact express properly the relevant factors that it was rational for him to consider, given the structure of the ancient economy. The economy, as Carandini describes it, was 'bi-sectorial', comprising both the 'natural', mainly self-sufficient economy, remote from markets and tending to polyculture, and the 'monetary' economy, in which monoculture of cash crops was directed towards realizing a surplus in the market-place. In such an economic structure, Carandini argues, it was 'rational' to treat the inputs and outputs of the natural sector as essentially a given, costless infrastructure for the activities in the market sector; and in calculating 'profitability' it only made sense to count the cost of inputs which had to be purchased for money and to take credit for the money inflows from the market sales. Furthermore, the ancient accounting system properly reflected this bi-sectorial nature of the economy: items in the monetary sector appear in the money accounts while those in the natural sector do not.

While I agree with many aspects of this description of the ancient economy, nevertheless Carandini's arguments appear to me once more to link too closely the nature of accounting practice and the degree of rationality in decision-taking. First, I cannot see that it would have been rational in making a decision about profitability in the monetary sector (such as Columella attempted) always to ignore the 'opportunity cost' of using resources from the natural sector (e.g. land, buildings, tools, slaves, and the basic mix of produce on an estate). While in some circumstances there might be little or no choice about how to use these resources, so that they had no opportunity cost, in other circumstances they might either be used for the production of alternative cash crops to the crop under consideration; or they might be

---

[65] If top managers in turn expect their subordinates to produce results that will score highly under these conventions, and evaluate their performance on these criteria, then there may be serious distortion of decision-making (P. Prakash and A. Rappaport, 'Information Inductance and its Significance for Accounting', *Accounting, Organizations and Society*, 2 (1977), 29–38).

[66] A. Carandini, 'Columella's Vineyard and the Rationality of the Roman Economy', *Opus*, 2 (1983), 177–204.

exploited more effectively in the production of outputs or saving of inputs in the natural sector, thereby freeing additional resources for increased production in the monetary sector.[67]

While, as I have already argued, it would often have been difficult if not impossible to quantify formally the value or cost of resources where market opportunities and prices were not available, this does not mean that allowance could not be made for them in decision-taking. Many non-monetary factors still have to be weighed up in making financial decisions even in economies such as our own. The important thing is to be clear about what has been included and what has been omitted in the formally quantified calculations—and as I have already shown Columella does not make explicit the assumptions behind his choice of what costs he includes.

Second, whatever the verdict on how 'rational' decisions should have been taken in the ancient economy, it is clear that ancient accounts in fact classify items into monetary and non-monetary in a way that does not neatly correspond with Carandini's sectors of the economy. The criterion for the accounts is whether or not money has actually changed hands; until then the wine produced for sale in the monetary sector would be accounted for purely in physical terms, in the same way as, say, corn produced in and for the natural sector.[68] As GRA showed, the overriding accounting objective was control over the honesty of those handling the cash and other assets, not the calculation of profitability. Given the usual form of ancient accounts the landowner could only form an up-to-date idea of the profitability of his cash-crop enterprise by estimating, *inter alia*, how much the physical quantity of produce in hand could be sold for.[69] I therefore again conclude that one

---

[67] Carandini appears to miss the first of these points when he discusses the marketing of 'wine' versus 'wheat', ibid. 192–3. He has difficulty with the second when, for example, he discusses the depreciation of slaves. He uses the argument (e.g. at p. 194) that, once purchased, they will be maintained out of the produce of the estate, and reproduce and train their successors at no monetary cost. He concludes that in the case of the slaves (as with the vines) 'the economic and extra-economic become confused'; that 'Columella did not dwell on this, to avoid complications for his readers'; and (p. 198) that the slave vine-dressers lie between the two sectors in 'a dark traditional fog which hides fringes of the rational area which we define as capital'. Yeo, 'Economics', 477 would also excuse Columella's omission of depreciation on the grounds that it would be effectively met out of the cost of maintaining the slaves and so was included in the current operating expenses. But Columella omitted all the current operating expenses too.

[68] Cf. Carandini, ibid. 200–1. See also n. 10 above and text attached (but if the accountant of *P. Lond.* 1171 was valuing his wheat in store it would appear to belong to the 'natural sector', as it was being used for seed and feeding livestock).

[69] Carandini also defends Columella's accounting by attacking the arguments in Duncan-Jones, *Economy*, that Columella's prices are unrealistic. I will merely point out: (*a*) that Carandini does not appear to be aware of Duncan-Jones's reply to earlier criticisms, given in *Economy*, 2nd. edn., 376–8 and (*b*) that poor use of economic statistics is in keeping with ancient writers' poor showing in using any statistics (see n. 44 above).

must avoid looking for too much significance in the form of ancient account-ing. Ancient accounts cannot be regarded (as they appear to be by Carandini) as exemplars of the form that rational decision-taking should have assumed in an economic system like that of the ancient world.

4. THE ROLE OF 'DOUBLE-ENTRY' BOOKKEEPING

It was of great significance for the history of accounting that GRA demon-strated that the Greeks and Romans did not develop double-entry bookkeep-ing. But what did they miss as a result?[70] The most familiar products of the system today are the 'profit and loss account' and 'balance sheet'—the state-ments that purport to give the 'income' and the 'capital' of a business. Ignoring for the moment the doubts expressed in sections 2 and 3 above, let us suppose that the Greeks and Romans had wanted calculations of their business income and capital. It is important to realize that the use of the double-entry system is neither necessary nor sufficient for this purpose, though it may often be very convenient. The arguments have been set out clearly by Yamey (see note 23).

Essentially one can calculate income for a period without any transactions records at all by taking an opening and closing 'inventory', i.e. valuation of assets and liabilities. The change in net assets for the period (after adjusting for any new capital subscribed during the period, or any withdrawals of funds by the owner, e.g. for consumption) represents the income of the period. At the other extreme one can of course record all changes in all assets and liabili-ties in double-entry transactions records, and then the system produces a bal-ance sheet and profit and loss account without any need for taking an inventory.

In practice, various mixtures of both approaches are used. In a simple busi-ness one may record merely cash transactions and then adjust at the end of the accounting period for changes in other assets and liabilities. Even in the most sophisticated systems, which routinely record all regular transactions, special adjustments are made at the end of an accounting period for certain other changes in assets and liabilities (e.g. the outstanding debts are reviewed

---

[70] Goethe has Werner say 'It is among the finest inventions of the human mind': 'Welche Vorteile gewährt die doppelte Buchhaltung dem Kaufmanne! Es ist eine der schönsten Erfindungen des men-schlichen Geistes, und ein jeder gute Haushalter sollte sie in seiner Wirtschaft einführen' (*Wilhelm Meisters Lehrjahre*, i. 10). But Werner is an anti-hero. More will agree with Drew, 'Manorial Accounts', 25: 'book-keeping is at the best of times a subject which few people find attractive'.

and adjustments made to 'write off' and make provision against those now thought unlikely to be collected). The full advantage of the system is, however, realized when as much as possible is included in the routine transaction records; for then the system provides the list of 'expected' closing balances of assets and liabilities against which an independent check can be made by means of a physical inspection of the actual assets and liabilities at the end of the period. It is, indeed, the fact that much of the information in the system is 'redundant' that is one of its most valuable features—it provides some independent corroboration of the accuracy and completeness of the closing inventory.

The detailed recording of transactions in all assets and liabilities does also make it easy to analyse the *components* of the total income for the year (e.g. it makes a difference whether a net income of £200 results from £400 sales, £100 cost of goods sold, and £100 depreciation, or from £800 sales, £400 cost of goods sold, and £200 depreciation, and so on); but even this *can* be done by a suitable analysis of receipts and payments together with the opening and closing adjustments.[71]

Not only is double entry not necessary (though highly convenient) for the calculation of income, it is not sufficient. As discussed in section 2 above, determining income requires deciding how the assets are to be valued, and how much of the change in their values is to be counted as 'income'. The double-entry method itself imposes no restriction on these choices and the history of accounting shows that a variety of valuation methods have been employed in preparing accounts.[72] Similarly, those who now argue for alternative approaches to the current 'historical cost' and 'realization' conventions (see above) have no difficulty in showing how their proposals can be incorporated into the double-entry framework.[73]

Above all, the historical evidence[74] makes it clear that many medieval merchants who used double entry (often regarded as the standard-bearers of

---

[71] As summarized in e.g. Sturrock, *Farm Accounting*, ch. 7. Cf. J. O. Winjum, 'Accounting and the Rise of Capitalism', *Journal of Accounting Research*, 9 (1971), 333–50 at 338–9, who doubts whether this approach is practicable. But even modern farm management textbooks hesitate to recommend the use of double entry except on large farms. A system of basic cash recording, with analysis to different 'enterprises' by means of analysis columns across the page of the cash book, may be quite adequate (although the introduction of micro-computers is likely to make use of double entry much more widespread, albeit without necessarily requiring any understanding of it by the computer user). Thus Sturrock makes no mention of double-entry bookkeeping until it is mentioned in the context of micro-computers (p. 277); cf. M. F. Warren, *Financial Management for Farmers* (London, 1982), 88.

[72] e.g. Yamey, 'Some Topics', 23–5.

[73] e.g. E. O. Edwards and P. W. Bell, *The Theory and Measurement of Business Income* (Berkeley, Calif., 1961).

[74] e.g. in Yamey, 'Accounting and the Rise of Capitalism' and 'Some Topics'.

'economic rationality') did not do so in order to calculate their profits. Whether this was because they were well aware from personal contact of 'how things were going', or whether it was because they appreciated at an early stage the inherent limitations of any attempt at *ex post facto* calculations of profitability, or whether it was a mixture of both these factors, one cannot say.

It may be that double entry was valued for its inbuilt checks which help to indicate when errors have occurred. Inaccuracies in ancient accounts are well documented in GRA.[75] But, as Yamey has pointed out,[76] there are plenty of errors to be found in extant double-entry ledgers which have often been 'written off' uninvestigated. The system was perhaps valued more because it was a fairly small extension of the interrelated cash and personal accounts that an economy trading on credit needed to keep; because it was often convenient (though not essential) for keeping track of the shares of the partners in business adventures; and because it enabled the recording of absolutely every transaction, as well as all the 'housekeeping' work in balancing the books etc., to be reduced to a rule of one simple form ('debit account A and credit account B').[77] This made possible the division of labour between several clerks who could each do their part (e.g. all the debits or all the credits, or a particular block of accounts), without any need to understand the whole picture, while at the same time 'automatically' producing a comprehensive picture as the joint output of their several labours.

In recent years, the rule has proved to be ideal for programming computers to perform. We should, however, perhaps not expect to be able completely to explain the development of a technology and assess its value.[78] Was the development of double-entry bookkeeping more or less surprising, and more or less useful, than that of the wheelbarrow (also introduced to the West in the thirteenth century (*CSAGW*, 38))? Whatever its virtues in the eyes of

[75] Indeed the inscription (*IG* II² 1672), of which line 1 and parts of lines 114–37 are set out in GRA at p. 25, is itself inaccurate. The change in the balances held at the beginning and end of the prytany is a decrease of 10 drachmae and 1⅚ obols. But total receipts are 850 drachmae and total expenses are 950 drachmae and 1⅚ obols—a decrease of 100 drachmae and 1⅚ obols. Geoffrey de Ste. Croix has confirmed to me that the restorations made to the text of the inscription are the necessary ones. An error must have been made in totalling the detailed expenditure—this cannot now be checked as some of these lines are missing from the inscription.

[76] Yamey, 'Some Topics', 20–1.

[77] When 'balancing the books', account B is the same account as A.

[78] Compare e.g. M. T. Clanchy, *From Memory to Written Record: England 1066–1307* (London, 1979), on the development of literacy in England after the Norman conquest. For the problems of explaining the history of accounting, see B. S. Yamey, 'Some Reflections on the Writing of a General History of Accounting', *Accounting and Business Research*, 42 (1981), 127–35. The issues are explored further in K. W. Hoskin and R. H. Macve, 'Accounting and the Examination: A Genealogy of Disciplinary Power', *Accounting, Organizations & Society*, 11/2 (1986), 105–36.

those who adopted and developed it, its history, together with the arguments mentioned above, make it extremely unlikely that double-entry bookkeeping can be regarded as having been 'crucial' to the development of entrepreneurial capitalism (the so-called 'Sombart' thesis),[79] although in modern times (the era of 'managerial capitalism') it has acquired a significant role in facilitating the co-ordination and control of large commercial organizations.[80]

There seems, therefore, no reason to suppose that the lack of double-entry bookkeeping prevented the Greeks and Romans from calculating the profitability of past activities or of future alternatives, had they felt the need to do so.

5. CONCLUSIONS

There is little to suggest that we need to revise fundamentally the view of the nature of Greek and Roman accounting given by de Ste. Croix nearly thirty years ago. Historians of accounting have been able to rely gratefully on his demonstration that the Greeks and Romans did not have double-entry bookkeeping.[81] De Ste. Croix has however suggested, in relation to taxation and to business planning, that Graeco-Roman civilization was unable to carry out certain economic activities which are a feature of modern societies partly because its accounting technology was inadequate. For the reasons given in sections 2 and 3 above, this seems to put too great a weight on the role of accounting. It is also clear (see section 4) that the technological advance that came in the thirteenth century AD—the introduction of double-entry bookkeeping—did not, of itself, mark a development in the concept of 'profitability', whether for taxation purposes, or for economic planning of business activities.

In interpreting the role of accounting in the ancient world as compared with our own, it is necessary to keep distinct the functions of: (1) estimating the profitability of alternative possibilities, (2) keeping continuous accounts

[79] B. S. Yamey, 'Scientific Book-keeping and the Rise of Capitalism', *Econ. Hist. Review*, 2nd series I (1949), 99–113, and 'Accounting and the Rise of Capitalism'; Winjum, 'Accounting and the Rise of Capitalism'; K. S. Most, 'Sombart's Propositions Revisited', *Accounting Review*, 47 (1972), 722–34.

[80] See, e.g. H. T. Johnson, 'Management Accounting in an Early Integrated Industrial', *Business Hist. Review*, 49 (1975), 184–204, and 'Management Accounting in an Early Multidivisional Organization', *Business Hist. Rev.* 52 (1978), 490–517. There were of course large organizations in antiquity, in particular the army, the civil service, and the Church. But these were not primarily organized for, and their success was not judged by, creation of economic surplus (*CSAGW*, 491–3, 495–7).

[81] e.g. O. ten Have, *History of Accountancy*, II, 22–9. Cf. the literature I discuss in the Appendix.

of past transactions in such a way as to show the sources of profits achieved in the past, and (3) using double-entry bookkeeping as the method for recording the past events. Although much modern accounting practice combines tasks (2) and (3), its attempts to integrate these with task (1) (e.g. in the sophisticated 'management accounting and information systems' of large-scale businesses) have, by the nature of things, proved less successful.

The extent to which the Greeks and Romans would in fact have derived benefit from the development of systematic approaches to task (1), given the limited opportunities and severe constraints they faced in their agriculture, seems to me to be slight. But even had they wanted to do it, they would not necessarily have needed any systematic approach to task (2) to enable them to do so (cf. the calculations made at medieval Norwich). Had they wanted to tackle task (2) systematically, they would not have needed, or necessarily benefited from, double-entry bookkeeping in doing so (as e.g. Robert Loder's accounts show: see above).

It is therefore more likely to have been because they saw no need to tax income that we find nothing resembling modern calculations of 'income' in their accounts; and because they had limited opportunity to benefit from calculation of the profitability of alternative actions that we find no systematic profit calculations. It was not because they had not developed the modern methods of accounting for profit and loss. As de Ste. Croix put it himself in GRA (p. 34): 'We must not belittle the intelligence of the Greeks and Romans because they did not try to do what the nature of their economic system made it unnecessary for them to attempt.'

APPENDIX   CRITICISMS AND IGNORANCE OF GRA

Relatively little has been written on Greek and Roman accounting since GRA, but two writers have been directly or indirectly critical of what I have called its 'main theme'.[1]

[1] Two conference papers (A. Castagnoli, 'La ragioneria nel mondo romano' and V. P. Filios, 'The Transition of Systematic Accounting from Ancient to Byzantine Greece') in the proceedings of *Quarto Congresso Internaz. di Storia della Ragioneria* (Univ. of Pisa, Aug. 1984), do little more than resurrect the statements of Melis and Voigt on Roman accounting, even though these were refuted in GRA, 41–3 and 66–7. A more balanced discussion is given by P. Jouanique, 'Le "Codex Accepti et Expensi" chez Cicéron', *Revue hist. de droit français et étranger*, 46 (1968), 5–31. R. Robert, 'Roman Accounting', *Accountant*, 137 (1957), 157–8 is a sensible précis of GRA. M. E. Glautier, 'Roman Accounting', *Internat. J. of Accounting*, 8/2 (1973), 59–74, 'without attempting too rigorous an analysis' (p. 59) generally follows GRA and Mickwitz in regard to private accounting.

K. S. Most[2] seems concerned, not to demonstrate that the Romans did have double-entry bookkeeping, but to argue that GRA has not shown, beyond all reasonable doubt, that they did not. The evidence he adduces is: (I) a fragment from an incompletely preserved speech of Cicero[3] and (2) a papyrus from Karanis in Egypt.[4] However, Most's own discussion makes it clear that there is precious little in the Cicero fragment to indicate any system of double-entry bookkeeping.[5] He makes slightly more of a plea with the Karanis papyrus ('strongly suggestive of a primitive journal', p. 26), but ignores the relevant discussion in GRA (p. 36) which points out that the extract illustrated there is one of the 'best' portions of the account, which elsewhere includes 'many independent items which appear in one column only, without our being able to connect them with any particular entries in the other column'. While GRA's arguments here were directed primarily at refuting the idea that the papyrus could be a 'ledger account' in a double-entry system, they are as telling against its being a 'journal' for such a system.

Costouros[6] examines the litigation relating to the estates bequeathed by Diodotos (Lysias XXXII) and by Demosthenes' father (Dem. XXVII), and appears to find in these evidence for the view that 'accounts were properly kept and the results were summarized per month, per year, or for the full period' and that accounts 'were kept in a systematic manner so that the financial position and the results of operations could be properly measured and accounted for. Furthermore, that the concepts of capital versus income were kept separate and that asset valuation was directly related to the proper determination of both income and capital' (p. 5).

Costouros does not refer to GRA, but his conclusions put precisely the kind of modern interpretation on ancient practice that GRA was at pains to remove. What the orators were really having to do was to try to make a convincing case, using whatever records were available of original assets, various receipts and payments, and other relevant evidence, for how much should be reckoned as the value of the inheritances they were claiming. It is misleading to give the impression that they could do this by consulting records of the estates' 'income' and adding it to the opening 'capital' to get the closing 'capital' (from which legitimate expenditures on the beneficiaries must be deducted).[7] Moreover, the cases were clearly only brought because the 'executors' had

---

[2] In 'The Accounts of Ancient Rome', Working Paper No. 3 (1974), in E. N. Coffman (ed.), *Working Paper Series Volume 1* (Acad. of Accounting Historians, Richmond, Va., 1979), 22–41.

[3] Niebuhr's fragment of Cicero, *Pro M. Fonteio*. The text is translated and reproduced (but with some errors) in the Appendix to Most's paper. Compare e.g. N. H. Watts's translation in the Loeb series (London etc., 1955).

[4] *P. Goodsp. Cair.* 30 (2nd cent. AD). An extract is set out in GRA, at 36, from which Most reproduces it at 25. GRA describes it as 'the high-water-mark of ancient book-keeping'. Further extracts are given in Johnson, *Roman Egypt*, 212–13.

[5] See also his 'How wrong was Sombart?', *Accounting Historians J.* 3 (1976), 22–8.

[6] G. J. Costouros, 'Early Greek Accounting on Estates', Working Paper No. 21 (1976), in E. N. Coffman (ed.), *Working Paper Series Volume 2* (Acad. of Accounting Historians, Richmond, Va., 1979), 1–6.

[7] It is a truism to point out (as Costouros does, p. 2) that if we accept the orators' figures for opening and closing capital values, and allow for the withdrawals, we can calculate the 'income' of the estates; but that does not mean that that was what the orators were interested in. The main reason nowadays (apart from

failed to keep up the estates—systematic records were precisely what were lacking (e.g. in Demosthenes' case, because his father had surely been concealing his wealth to avoid liability for taxation),[8] and the claims made by the plaintiffs made the most of this, with as much exaggeration as they thought they might get away with.[9]

In another paper Costouros[10] discusses the accounting methods of Greek banks and concludes 'most banks kept daybooks, in which all transactions were entered as they were incurred (the journal), and ledgers, which showed how the account of each individual client stood'. But, while there are several descriptions, especially in speeches by or conventionally attributed to Demosthenes, of how individual banking transactions were recorded, there does not appear to be any direct statement of how, if at all, an individual customer's deposits and/or borrowings were summarized.

When Lycon of Heraclea set off on his voyage to Libya he 'reckoned up' ($\delta\iota\alpha\lambda o$-$\gamma\iota\sigma\acute{\alpha}\mu\epsilon\nu o\varsigma$) with Pasion the banker in the presence of witnesses to establish how much was (as we would put it) standing to the credit of his account and an entry was then made in the accounting records as if this amount were a new deposit.[11] When Apollodoros was suing Timotheos for the amount he owed Pasion's bank, although we can work out the total he was supposed to owe as 4,438 drachmae and 2 obols, in the speech it is the individual loans that are discussed in turn. Furthermore, Apollodoros claims that his father Pasion wrote out and left for him a list of the debts he was owed, and also, when he was terminally ill, discussed the details of the individual loans with him and his brother.[12] If anything, these descriptions suggest that Pasion's bank did not have readily available from day to day the running balances of each customer's 'account', as a modern bank would, even though to us it would seem a priori that such summaries would have been of great practical convenience. Once again we must avoid the tendency to read back into the limited evidence available our presuppositions from modern practice.[13]

---

taxation) for distinguishing 'income' and 'capital' in inherited estates is because of the need to distinguish what accrues to the 'life-tenant' and what to the 'remainderman' (see J. Flower, 'A Note on Capital and Income' in Edey and Yamey, *Debits, Credits, etc*, 85–90).

[8] See J. K. Davies, *Athenian Propertied Families 600–300 BC* (Oxford, 1971), 126–33, 151–4, who gives examples of the 'weasel words' Demosthenes uses to create the desired impression. (Comparisons with Davies's careful calculations indicate several errors in Costouros' figures.)

[9] See also de Ste. Croix, 'Demosthenes' $\tau\acute{\iota}\mu\eta\mu\alpha$ and the Athenian Eisphora in the Fourth Century BC', *Class et Med.* 14 (1953), 30–70, 53–6, 62. Demosthenes' estate is also of interest because Finley, *Ancient Economy*, 116, uses it as an illustration of the failure of the ancient world to understand the concept of depreciation and the idea of business assets as separate from personal assets. However, as Yamey, 'Some Reflections', 134 n. 45, points out, the same accounting treatment can be found in many businessmen's ledgers of early modern times.

[10] Costouros, 'Development of Banking and Related Book-keeping Techniques in Ancient Greece', *Internat. J. of Accounting*, 7/2 (1973), 75–81. These conclusions repeat those of G. M. Calhoun, *The Business Life of Ancient Athens* (Chicago, 1926; New York, 1968), 98.

[11] [Dem.] LII 3–6; see also GRA 27–9.

[12] Dem. XLIX 6–32, 44 ff., with Costouros, 'Banking', 80; Dem. XLIX 42.

[13] Above all one must avoid suggesting that the memoranda ($\acute{\nu}\pi o\mu\nu\acute{\eta}\mu\alpha\tau\alpha$) of individual transactions that we are told banks kept ([Dem.] XLIX 5. 8. 30), and any customer accounts that we might *suppose* that they kept, were equivalent to a modern (or Renaissance) bank's 'journal' and 'ledger accounts'. These terms

These apparent rebuttals of GRA are thus of little validity and less consequence.[14]

inevitably carry anachronistic connotations of systematized double-entry bookkeeping (cf. Costouros, 'Banking', 80–1; Calhoun, *Business Life*, 98).

[14] Most, 'Accounts', 24–5 also criticizes GRA as 'singularly deficient where modern accounting is concerned' for saying (at p. 26, cf. 34–5) that the 'concept of "petty cash", in the modern sense, which can be spent up to a certain limit without the necessity for detailed accounting by the person concerned, never really established itself as a regular feature of ancient accounts . . .' However, GRA's point of substance is valid although the words 'miscellaneous (or 'sundry') expenditure', rather than 'petty cash', might capture it better.

BEFORE DOUBLE ENTRY

3 · MANORIAL ACCOUNTS

P. D. A. Harvey

INTRODUCTION

The manorial account is a product of demesne farming and it is no coincidence that it appears during the first decade of the thirteenth century, just when this method of estate management was being generally adopted. If the landlord entrusted his manor to a local official who was answerable to him for all moneys received or spent, all the corn and livestock, there would clearly have to be a regular reckoning to show what resources remained in hand and how much cash was due from the official to the lord or vice versa. It is this regular reckoning that the manorial account records: its aim was to show the state of account between the lord and his official, to show how much was owing to one or the other once every transaction had been allowed for.

But although demesne farming depended on a regular reckoning of this sort, this did not have to take the form of a written account. There is every indication that until the mid-thirteenth century it was unusual to set down in writing the details of accounts; they would be presented by the local official and examined—audited, that is, heard—by the lord or his representative entirely by word of mouth, with no other aids than counters for the calculations, tally-sticks as vouchers, and perhaps a few brief notes as memoranda. The estates from which we do have manorial accounts in the first half of the thirteenth century were mostly very large ones indeed: the two earliest are Canterbury Cathedral Priory (1207–8) and the bishopric of Winchester (1208–9), and others include the bishopric of Worcester, Ramsey Abbey, and the honour of Gloucester.[1] It may not be coincidence that several were

First published as 'Accounts', ch. 3 of the author's *Manorial Records* (1984).

[1] *Interdict Documents*, ed. Patricia M. Barnes and W. R. Powell, Pipe Roll Soc. New Ser. 34 (1960), 69–80 (roll of manorial receipts from Canterbury Cathedral Priory); *The Pipe Roll of the Bishopric of Winchester, 1208–9*, ed. H. Hall (London, 1903); Bodl. Worcestershire Rolls 4; PRO SC6/875/6 (Broughton, Hunts.: manor of Ramsey Abbey), SC6/1109/6–11 (honour of Gloucester).

centred on the Winchester area, among them smaller estates such as Southwick Priory (Hampshire).[2] We have hardly any surviving accounts of this period from small estates elsewhere, though Little Dunmow Priory (Essex) provides an example.[3] Probably not even all large estates produced written manorial accounts before the mid-thirteenth century: they seem to have been just beginning at Westminster Abbey in the 1250s and at Durham Cathedral Priory in the 1270s.[4] But from the 1250s onwards the idea seems to have spread very fast, especially in the 1270s and 1280s. The second statute of Westminster in 1285, in setting up a form of action against defaulting bailiffs, assumes that there will be written accounts and by the end of the century they were a normal technique of estate management everywhere, on every type of estate; we find them being produced even for the lord who held only a single manor. Moreover their use continued: they may have taken their origin in demesne farming, but they outlasted it, and we still find manorial accounts in the sixteenth century even though all an estate's manors had long been leased. In looking at manorial accounting in detail it is convenient to look separately at each of three phases of development: each has its own techniques and its own particular problems for the historian. But these three phases correspond only very broadly to chronological periods—there is a good deal of overlap between them, for one estate might continue old-fashioned practices long after new forms had come in elsewhere.

By and large a manorial account will exist only in a single copy and will take the form of a roll. Sometimes, as we shall see, both a draft and a final version of an account survive, and sometimes what we have are enrolled accounts: the accounts for all of an estate's manors in a particular year are copied on to a single big roll. Historians sometimes call these enrolled accounts pipe rolls, but they were not so called by contemporaries, and the phrase is misleading for they differ in many respects from the real Pipe Rolls, the annual accounts of the sheriffs and others at the royal Exchequer. It is unusual to find manorial accounts copied into books though it did occasionally happen, as at Bolton Abbey (Yorkshire) where a single volume contained all the manorial accounts from 1286 to 1325,[5] or at Canterbury Cathedral Priory, where the accounts of local officials and farmers were entered in a series of registers from the mid-fifteenth century onwards.[6] In enrolled or other copied accounts mistakes in copying sometimes produce mistakes in

---

[2] Muniments of Winchester College, 14484.

[3] Essex Record Office, D DM Q2.

[4] To judge, that is, from the forms of the earliest accounts still surviving in each archive.

[5] Chatsworth House (Derbs.), MS 73A (described by I. Kershaw, *Bolton Priory: The Economy of a Northern Monastery 1286–1325* (London, 1973), 2–3).

the arithmetic, but in the accounts that were actually used for the audit mistakes seldom occur: too much depended on the accuracy of the figures and too many people were concerned to check them for errors to go unnoticed.

Very occasionally a collection of manorial accounts will include an imaginary account, a specimen that a clerk would use as a guide; this may not be recognized at first sight, for though it may have been copied from one of the standard specimen accounts that were in circulation it could well have had names of places and people altered to fit the particular estate.[7] These specimens were only one of various contemporary aids to manorial accounting which tell us a good deal about the aims and methods of those concerned. We have some rules or treatises for auditors, telling them what to look for on the account, what points to check, what malpractices to guard against. But most of these aids were meant for the clerks who wrote the accounts and who came to be almost the professional advisers of the officials, intermediaries between them and the auditors. Besides treatises on writing accounts and simple models for the clerk to follow there were more elaborate specimen accounts with interspersed rules and comments. The most remarkable surviving formulary comes from Beaulieu Abbey (Hampshire): the accounts of a single year, 1269–70, for all the abbey's officials who handled money, were copied into a large volume with rules and comments interspersed (those from one group of the abbey's manors were also copied into a second book for local use).[8] This seems to have been meant as a once-for-all written version of accounts that would normally be presented orally, serving as a standard and guide for the auditors.

The Beaulieu Abbey formulary was for a particular estate only, but most guides to manorial accounting were meant for general use. This helps to explain the extraordinary uniformity of these accounts. In looking at successive phases of manorial accounting we shall be noticing idiosyncrasies and variations of one sort or another, but these occur within the context of a standard pattern that was everywhere the same, from the thirteenth century to the sixteenth. How it originated is not entirely clear—it is already well developed in our earliest examples from Canterbury Cathedral Priory and the bishopric of Winchester—but there are some signs that it may have grown out of the inventories drawn up when the lease of a manor came to an end. The manorial account nearly always covers a single year, usually from Michaelmas (29 September) to Michaelmas; and it is always a charge–discharge account. It

---

[7] e.g. BL. Add. MS 45896, probably adapted on copying for the estates of the Harcourt family.

[8] BL Add. MS 48978, published as *The Account-book of Beaulieu Abbey*, ed. S. F. Hockey, Camden Soc. 4th Ser. 16 (1975); Bodl. MS Barlow 49.

lists first the charge, the money the official has to answer for—any sum he still owed from the previous year, what he received (or ought to have received) from rents, from sale of produce, from payments imposed on the manorial court, and so on—and gives the total. It then lists all the occasions of the official's paying out money: purchases of corn or livestock, hire of labour, building repairs, and the other expenses of running the demesne, and also any cash handed over to the lord or his representative. This is the discharge, showing what the official has done with the money listed in the charge, and it too is totalled. The balance, the difference between the two totals, is then entered, this being the amount that the official owes the lord or (if the outgoings have exceeded the income) vice versa.

```
CASH Charge
       TOTAL
     Discharge
       TOTAL
       BALANCE

CORN For each type of corn in turn:
     Charge
       TOTAL
     Discharge
       TOTAL
       BALANCE

STOCK For each type of live or dead stock in turn:
     Charge
       TOTAL
     Discharge
       TOTAL
       BALANCE

POSSIBLE FURTHER SECTIONS
       LABOUR SERVICES due and performed
       LAND  available and how used
       IMPLEMENTS remaining at end of year
```

Figure 3.1 Scheme of a manorial account

The formal scheme of a manorial account is set out in Figure 3.1. Nearly all cover corn as well as cash; most deal with livestock too, and many account for other things as well. For each type of corn or livestock, for every other item on the account, there was an individual charge–discharge account on the same principle as for cash. The amounts of wheat (or barley or other corn) harvested, bought or otherwise acquired would be listed and totalled, then the amounts sown as seed, sold, delivered to the lord or otherwise accounted for; the difference between the two totals would be the amount remaining in the

granary. Similarly with livestock; but here matters were a little more complicated. Animals grew up: if we have separate paragraphs for pigs and for
piglets, last year's piglets have somehow to become this year's pigs.
Sometimes they were simply slipped into the pigs account: the charge would
begin 'He answers for 5 pigs remaining and for 7 remaining as piglets on the
last account', and the piglets account would cover only those born or bought
during the current year. Often it was done more elaborately: the piglets
account would begin 'He answers for 7 remaining' and its discharge section
would include the entry 'Added to the pigs, 7', while the charge section of the
pigs account would say 'Added from the piglets, 7'. We thus find the same
seven piglets occurring in more than one paragraph of the account. This
could well become quite complicated. It became normal to have separate
accounts for calves, for year-old cattle, for two-year-olds and for each of the
three classes of adult, bulls, cows, and oxen. A calf born on the manor and
kept there would thus join the appropriate class of adult stock only on its
third successive annual transfer in the accounts. The same system of moving
items from one paragraph to another of the same account might be applied to
other things besides livestock: we quite often, for instance, find quantities of
corn being transferred, by entries in the discharge section of the accounts for,
say, barley and oats, to an account for the mixed corn which was used to pay
the wages of the manorial servants. All of which is a good deal simpler in
practice than it may sound. Probably the best introduction to the workings of
the manorial account is to compare accounts from two or more successive
years from some fairly straightforward published series, such as those from
Sevenhampton (Wiltshire) for 1275–88 or from Cuxham (Oxfordshire) for
1288–99 (see the select texts listed at the end of this chapter).

It must already be clear that the annual account for a single manor may
contain an enormous amount of detailed information; and that this information is presented in such a way that the entire account is directed to the single
aim of establishing the state of affairs between the local official and his
lord—how much was owed in cash, and what remained on the manor in
corn, livestock, and other goods at the end of the accounting year. To show
what profits the manor had brought the lord in the course of the year was no
part of the account's ostensible purpose; we have seen how it brackets
together in the cash discharge both the running costs of the manor and the
money that was handed over to the lord from the year's takings. At the same
time the account unquestionably gives enough information for the manor's
profitability to be worked out, and it is clear that manorial accounts were
used for this from a very early date. The earliest of the general audit (*assisa*

scaccarii) rolls from Canterbury Cathedral Priory in 1225 concludes the summary account of each manor in demesne with the amount of profit, and there is a note of the profit on the earliest of any surviving accounts for an individual manor, for Froyle (Hampshire) in about 1233.[9] It may well be that one reason why written accounts came into use was that manorial profits could be calculated from them, something that could not be done if accounts were presented orally. These profits would be the lord's net gain from the manor each year, taking into account the running costs and the value of produce delivered to his household, and sometimes distinguishing between the profits of demesne agriculture and the profits of the manor overall. Dr E. Stone, in a study of great interest, has shown that on the Norwich Cathedral Priory estates the figures for profit were reached by calculations of some subtlety and that in the early fourteenth century these figures were being used to decide whether to lease manors out or keep them in demesne.[10] It is not often that we can reconstruct the calculations of profit, even where we have the final figure that was reached; there are normally too many imponderables in the way of allowances for produce sent to the lord's household or for items bought on the manor for use elsewhere, or even for depreciation of stock. But, however the figure was arrived at, it can be of great interest to know how much profit a manor's lord believed that it brought him in the course of the year. Only a minority of surviving manorial accounts enter the amount of profit, but it is a substantial minority, and the information can easily be overlooked, partly because it may be entered at the extreme end of the cash account, often well beyond the rest of the writing, partly because of the variety of words used for profit: *clarum, comodum, valor, waynagium*, as well as the more obvious *profectus* or *proficuum*.

PHASE I

The first phase of manorial accounts covers those from the first half of the thirteenth century, when few estates used accounts, along with later accounts on some estates where the characteristic early forms were only slowly superseded. Its most striking feature is that the accounts were produced by the estate's central organization. Often what we have are enrolled accounts for all its manors, whether compiled at a single operation (as at Peterborough

---

[9] D. & C. Canterbury, Assisa Scaccarii Roll I; BL Add. Roll 17468.

[10] E. Stone, 'Profit-and-loss Accountancy at Norwich Cathedral Priory', *Transactions of the Royal Historical Society*, 5th Ser. 12 (1962), 25–48.

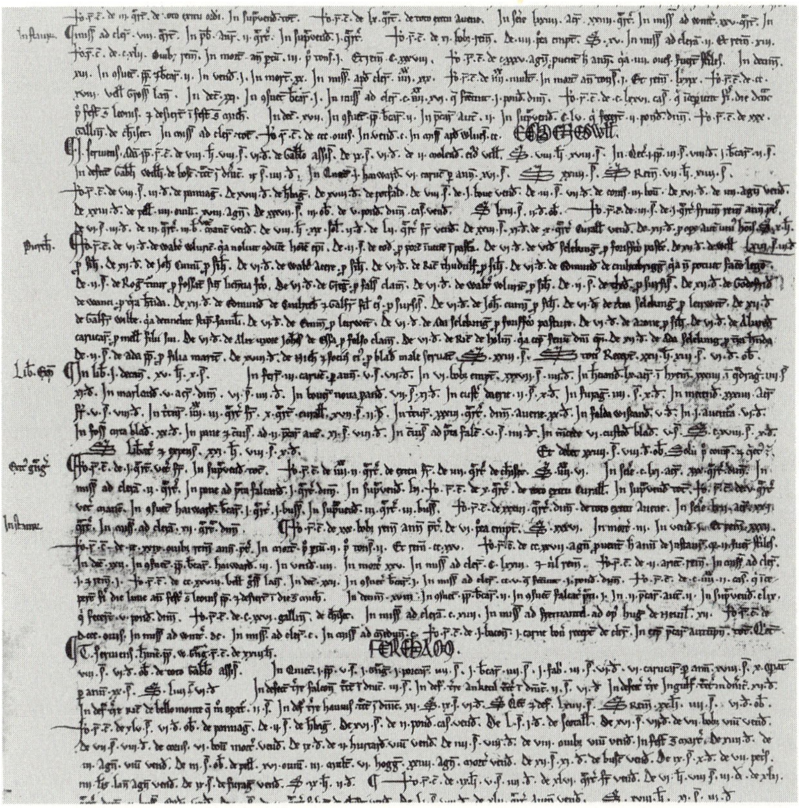

Plate 3.1 Phase I account: Itchingswell (Hants: bishop of Winchester), 1210–11. Hampshire Record Office, Eccl. 2/159270B. Printed in *Winch. Pipe Roll 1210–11*, 104–6.

Note: This is entered on a roll of the year's accounts for all the bishop of Winchester's manors; above is the end of the account for Ashmansworth and below is the start of the account for Fareham (both Hants), all obvious fair copies and written at a single operation.

Abbey) or a few manors at a time as the audit proceeded (as on the Bec Abbey estates).[11] By far the most notable series of these enrolled accounts is from the bishop of Winchester's estates (see Plate 3.1); they survive for most years from 1208–9 down to 1611 (in books, not rolls, from the mid-fifteenth century onwards), a historical source of great importance which has

[11] Peterborough: Northants Record Office, Fitzwilliam (Milton) MSS 233, 2388, 2389 (accounts of 1301–2, 1309–11), and others. Bec: muniments of King's College, Cambridge, Ministers' accounts before the time of the College (accounts of 1283–4).

already been extensively used but which still has much more to reveal.[12] On at least two estates early enrolled accounts give way to separate accounts for individual manors, perhaps developed from the draft accounts that must have been used to compile the enrolments: at Winchester Cathedral Priory probably in the 1250s, at Crowland Abbey (Lincolnshire) between 1315 and 1319.[13] But the individual accounts, just like the enrolments, were compiled by the estate's central administration and record the state of affairs as agreed at the end of the audit.

It is important to bear this in mind when using Phase 1 accounts: they are agreed accounts, agreed that is to the satisfaction of the lord of the manor. The expenses they record, for instance, may not be the actual amounts spent, but simply the amounts the lord was prepared to allow to his official. In accounts of Phase 2 we get a far closer insight into the process of auditing and we see the year's transactions from the viewpoint of the local official as well as of the lord; accounts of Phase 1 show us the viewpoint of the lord alone.

However, what we do occasionally see in manorial accounts of Phase 1, and in no others, is the close association of manorial and household accounts. The general audit rolls of Canterbury Cathedral Priory from the 1220s onwards include accounts of the sacrist, cellarer, and other non-manorial officers; at Peterborough Abbey in the early fourteenth century, accounts of the pig-keeper and the bakery were enrolled along with the manorial accounts.[14] Half of the specimen accounts from Beaulieu Abbey in 1269–70 are for officers and other workers around the monastery itself, not on the estates. All this is a useful reminder that manorial accounts give only half the financial picture; they show us the income-producing side of the organization of which the other half, the expending side, was the household. It is dangerously easy for the manorial historian to forget that this other side of his finances was of no less importance to the solvency of the medieval lord, whether lay, episcopal, or monastic.

One characteristic of Phase 1 accounts is a certain variety between one estate and another. This may be in purely external features. Thus the enrolled accounts from the Bec Abbey estates put the cash accounts for all the manors on the front of the roll, the corn accounts on the dorse, instead of (as in enrolled accounts elsewhere) placing the corn account for each manor imme-

---

[12] Hampshire Record Office, Eccles. 2/159270–159444, 1555827–155942.

[13] After the enrolled accounts of (respectively) 1247–8, 1314–15, the next accounts to survive are for single manors (Alton Priors, etc., 1260–1; Oakington, 1319–20) which demonstrably were once in annual files each covering the whole estate (D. & C. Winchester; muniments of Queens' College, Cambridge, now deposited in Cambridge University Library).

[14] D. & C. Canterbury, Assisa Scaccarii rolls; Northants Record Office, Fitzwilliam (Milton) MSS 233, 2388, 2389.

diately after its cash account. But variations also occur in the internal arrangements of the account. A very persistent example is in accounts from estates centred on the Winchester area and also, interestingly, in those from Peterborough Abbey. Here, as elsewhere, the amounts due from tenants' rents were one of the first items in the charge section of the cash account; but they were then followed by entries of rents that could not be collected for one reason or another (from a vacant holding, for instance, or where the tenant was excused payment through working as a manorial servant), and a balance was drawn to show the net receipts from rents as the effective amount the official was to answer for. On other estates these missing rents (defects of rent: *defectus reddituum*) would form an entirely separate entry in the discharge section of the account. The final balance of the account would be the same, but it would be reached by a slightly different route.

Whatever the minor variations in Phase I accounts, they all reflect the contemporary pattern of estate management. This was the early period of demesne farming, when a hierarchy of supervisors kept watch on all the doings of the local officials. On some estates (as those of the archbishop of Canterbury or of both the bishop and the cathedral priory at Winchester) accounts were presented jointly by both the manor's own reeve and the bailiff who had oversight of two or three manors, and they thus begin 'A. reeve and B. bailiff render account . . .';[15] but in the final balance the verb is in the singular—'And he owes . . .' (*Et debet . . .*)—because it was the reeve alone who carried the financial responsibility. There was a general tendency not to leave money in the reeve's hands: the lord's representative would come to collect the proceeds soon after each quarter-day when the tenants paid rent, and both cash and corn accounts were often closed at the end of the year so that no corn would be left in the granary and no money owing would be carried forward into the next year's account. It may have been to make this easier that Ramsey Abbey had an accounting year that ended at Michaelmas (29 September) for cash but at Lammas (I August) for corn.[16]

Particularly interesting in Phase I accounts are the changes we see in the course of time, changes that nearly always tended towards greater detail and greater uniformity. Livestock, for instance, came normally to be included in a manorial account instead of often being either omitted altogether (as on the Bec Abbey estates) or covered by a simple inventory (as at Crowland Abbey). More and more detail was included in the cash accounts, which rapidly developed a

---

[15] J. S. Drew, 'Manorial Accounts of St. Swithun's Priory, Winchester', *English Historical Review*, 62 (1947), 26–7; *Winch. Pipe Roll 1210–11*, p. xx; cf. for the archbishopric of Canterbury BL Add. MS 29794.
[16] BL Add. Roll 39669.

system of subdivisions. In many of the earliest accounts, the cash is entered simply in two paragraphs, one for the charge, one for the discharge, though particular items might be distinguished with special marginal headings (as the bishopric of Winchester always did for the profits of manorial courts: *purchasia*). As time went on more and more items would be hived off into special paragraphs of this sort, so that eventually both charge and discharge sections consisted of a whole series of separate paragraphs, each with its own heading and total. In each of the two sections there would be a hard core of miscellaneous items that could not be hived off in this way, each forming a paragraph on its own with a heading that had once belonged to the entire section: issues of the manor (*exitus manerii*), formerly the whole charge section, were now simply the miscellaneous receipts, necessary expenses (*expense necessarie*), formerly the whole discharge, were now the petty expenses alone.[17] Other changes tended towards rationalization. Instead of, for example, having separate paragraphs for corn that came from multure (toll from mills) or for chickens received from the rent known as churchscot, these would be included in the general paragraphs for the appropriate type of corn or poultry. An ever more rigorous logic was applied to the account—to the division between charge and discharge and to the classification of the various items of account.

PHASE 2

We can thus see developing in the first phase of manorial accounting the uniformity that is one of the features of Phase 2. This uniformity is the more striking in view of the rapid proliferation of manorial accounts: Phase 2 broadly covers the hundred years from the mid- or late thirteenth century, when written accounts became an almost universal feature of English estate management. Yet everywhere—whether the estate was large or small, whether it was lay or ecclesiastical, whether its centre was at one end of the country or the other—these accounts closely follow a single pattern, both in external form and in the methods of accountancy. The account will be for a single manor. On the inside, or front, of the roll is the cash account, divided into its many paragraphs, and on the outside, or dorse, are the accounts for the various types first of corn and then of stock. There were conventions, closely observed, about the order of items within this framework. Thus the cash

---

[17] In successive accounts between *c*.1233 and 1263 from Froyle (Hants), a manor of St Mary's Abbey, Winchester, we can clearly see this process occurring (BL Add. Rolls 13338, 13339, 17457–17478; Hampshire Record Office, Winchester City records LI I/I).

charge always begins with arrears carried forward from the previous account, followed by the tenants' rents; in the cash discharge the paragraphs for the running costs of ploughs and carts are always near the beginning; the corn accounts always deal with wheat, rye, barley, and oats in that order; and in the livestock accounts horses are always entered before cattle, cattle before sheep. Where a manorial account of Phase 2 differs from the standard form, this nearly always reflects some peculiarity of the manor itself—it might be purely a dairy-farm, for instance, or a group of rent-paying town houses—not a variation in accounting style peculiar to a particular region or estate. This uniformity, together with the division of the whole account into headed paragraphs, is extremely helpful to the historian who, with a little experience, can often find the information he needs from no more than a moment's glance, even though the account itself may be long and complex. Some idea of the length and detail of an early fourteenth-century account is given by Figure 3.2, which sets out a typical list of paragraph headings.

Despite this uniformity, another characteristic of Phase 2 accounts is that they were locally produced. Instead of enrolled accounts or accounts for individual manors written up after the audit by the estate's central administration, what we have are accounts written for the local officials before the audit by clerks of their own choosing. The account would be presented at the audit as the basis of the official's claim; often his clerk would be there to help him make his case. Any changes imposed by the auditors would be entered on the account, sometimes by the local clerk but more often by the auditors' own clerk, and the auditors would then take the account to be kept in the estate's central records; further small additions might be made to it, such as a note of the manor's profit for the year. This means that a Phase 2 account shows what happened at the audit; we see what the local official claimed, what was queried or disallowed by the auditors and very often why, for revealing notes and comments may be added to explain the alterations made on the account—'In future so much will not be allowed', 'In future the number of acres of each sort of corn should be entered' (in the costs of reaping), 'This has been sworn to at the audit', and so on. It is usually quite easy to tell what was originally written on the account and what was added at the audit; even when the local clerk entered the auditors' alterations so that they are in the same hand as the rest, the difference in ink or simply what is written makes it clear what are the additions. The result is that a Phase 2 account is virtually a dialogue, a debate between local official and auditors, not a statement from a single viewpoint like a Phase 1 account. This adds greatly to its interest and historical value.

CASH CHARGE
  Arrears
  Assessed rents
  Rents of mills
  Sale of corn
  Sale of malt
  Sale of stock
  Issues of the manor
  Sale of cheese
  Profits of the court
  Forinsec receipts
  Sales at the audit
  (*Vendicio super compotum*)

CASH DISCHARGE
  Allowances of rent
  Costs of ploughs
  Costs of carts
  Necessary expenses
  Costs of mills
  Purchase of corn
  Purchase of stock
  Costs of mowing, hoeing
  Harvest expenses
  Labourers' wages
  Lord's expenses
  Visitors' expenses
  Forinsec expenses

CORN
  Wheat
  Small-corn of wheat
  Barley
  Dredge
  White peas
  Grey peas
  Vetch
  Oats
  Malt of wheat
  Other malt
  Mixed corn for wages

STOCK
  Cart-horses
  Plough-horses
  Bulls
  Oxen
  Cows
  Bullocks
  Heifers
  2-year-old cattle
  1-year-old cattle
  Calves
  Rams
  Wethers
  Ewes
  2-year-old wethers
  2-year-old ewes
  1-year-old sheep
  Lambs
  Pigs
  Piglets
  Geese
  Capons
  Cocks and hens
  Chicks
  Ducks
  Eggs
  Doves
  Sides of bacon
  Cheese
  Milk
  Hides
  Wool
  Lambs' wool
  Woolfells

LABOUR SERVICES
  Winter ploughworks
  Autumn ploughworks
  Harvest works
  Carrying services
  Miscellaneous winter works
  Miscellaneous summer works

Figure 3.2 Headings of a typical early fourteenth-century manorial account

Note: This is the end of the cash charge account and the start of the cash discharge. Some totals and the whole of the 'Sales at the audit' paragraph have been added at the audit by the auditor's clerk; the difference in the handwriting is clear.

When the account was first drawn up the clerk would normally leave blanks in the cash account for the individual paragraph totals and for the grand totals of charge and discharge and the final balance; sometimes he entered provisional figures as a guide to the auditors, but they would be written very small to one side or even with a system of dots instead of normal figures. This meant that the auditors could alter the cash account without difficulty: they could add or increase entries of amounts received, or they could strike out or reduce the amounts claimed as expenses, all without having to cross out and rewrite totals already written in. It was otherwise on the dorse, in the corn and stock accounts. Here the totals and balances remaining could hardly be changed on audit for they recorded the actual state of affairs on the manor: the amount of barley remaining in the granary, the number of lambs in the fold, of hens in the yard, and so on. Accordingly they were fully filled in on the account when it was first written out, before the audit. If the auditors refused to pass any entry on the corn or stock account they would cross it out or alter it just as on the cash account, but because the balance remaining could not be changed they would add an extra entry to the relevant discharge paragraph, recording a sale 'at the audit' (*super compotum*) corresponding to what had been disallowed. If, say, the account claimed that 4 quarters 7 bushels of oats had been sown as seed and the auditors held that 4 quarters was the most that should have been used, the entry in the oats discharge would be altered and a further entry of 7 bushels 'sold at the audit' added at the end of the paragraph; there would be no need to change the paragraph total or balance. At the same time the auditors would usually put a 3-shaped sign in the margin opposite their 'sold at the audit' entry; when they had finished going through the corn and stock accounts it was easy to spot all these entries of fictitious sales, and a new paragraph of 'Sales at the audit' (*Vendiciones super compotum*) would be added to the cash charge on the front of the roll so that the value of all these disallowed items of corn and stock would be charged against the official as part of the cash reckoning (see Plate 3.2). This, again, is much more easily seen in operation than described; study of an original Phase 2 account on which the entries made by the auditors' clerk can be clearly distinguished will show very simply how the system of fictitious sales worked. It does not appear on the earliest Phase 2 accounts, but was in general use by the early fourteenth century. It was not understood by historians until J. S. Drew's exposition in 1947 from the accounts of Winchester Cathedral Priory.[18]

---

[18] Drew, n. 15 above, 30.

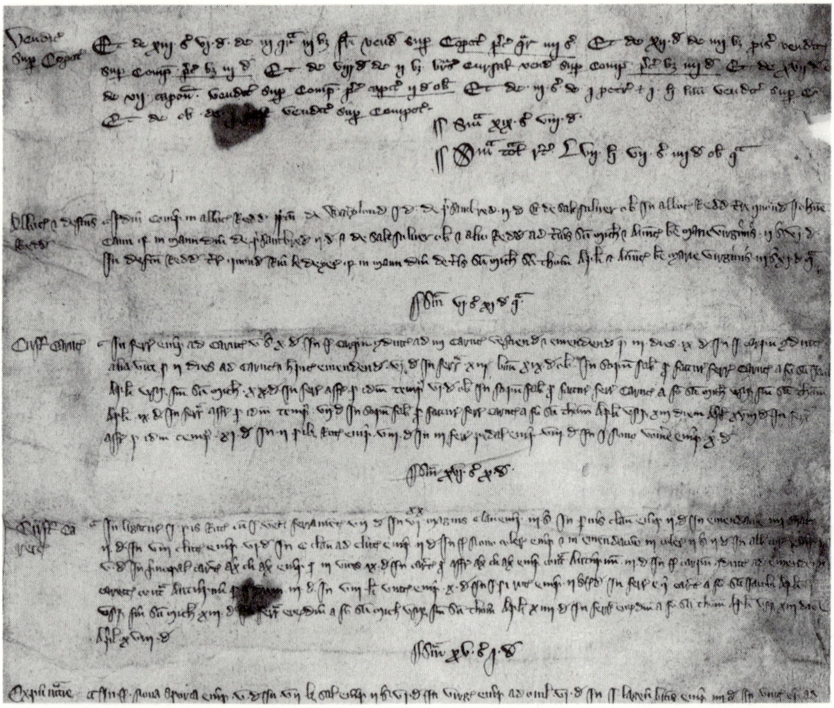

Plate 3.2 Phase 2 account: Cuxham (Oxon.: Merton College), 1348–9. Muniments of Merton College, Oxford, 5875, m. 2. Printed in *Cuxham Man. Recs.*, 449–50.
Note: This is the end of the cash charge account and the start of the cash discharge. Some totals and the whole of the 'Sales at the audit' paragraph have been added at the audit by the auditor's clerk; the difference in the handwriting is clear.

From these same accounts Drew described another sort of entry that is widely found, the entry of minimum or fixed returns (*responsiones*) for particular items of corn or livestock.[19] In some Phase 2 accounts (not, usually, before the fourteenth century) we find a marginal note added at the audit beside the account for each type of corn to show how the yield from the harvest compared with the amount of seed sown: 'He returns a fourfold yield, but for 3 bushels' (*Respondet ad quartum granum minus iii bussellos*) for instance. At first these entries seem to have been simply for information, recording the actual yield achieved, but soon they were being used to extract a minimum yield: if the

[19] Ibid. 41. But the significance of the simple notes of yield was known earlier—e.g. Frances G. Davenport, *The Economic Development of a Norfolk Manor 1086–1565* (Cambridge, 1906), 29–31.

actual yield fell below what was required or expected an entry for the missing amount would be added to the charge paragraph of the account for that type of corn 'so that he may return a fourfold yield' (*ut respondeat ad quartum granum*), and another entry would be added to the discharge paragraph recording the same amount as a fictitious sale, a sale at the audit, to be charged against the official on the cash account. The same system would be applied to livestock if the number of eggs per hen or the number of piglets per sow was thought insufficient. Eventually on some estates the required minimum yield became a fixed yield: provided the official answered for this predetermined amount, any extra he achieved by good luck or good management was his to keep, so that year after year we find on the accounts precisely the same return for particular items of corn or livestock.[20] The accounts have, in fact, ceased to record actual manorial production; yet there is nothing on the individual account to show this, and we can discover what has happened only if we see the accounts for a whole series of years. The historian forgets at his peril that the purpose of a manorial account was to establish the state of reckoning between lord and local official: we should never take for granted that it records what really happened on the manor.

Here we see changes in the manorial account reflecting changes in estate management: the predetermined fixed yield for corn or livestock was a first step towards leasing the entire manor, replacing the local official, the reeve or bailiff, with a lessee farmer. Other changes in manorial accounts in the course of Phase 2 continued the developments of the first phase: accounts became ever longer and fuller as the hierarchy of supervisors to watch the local official was replaced by ever more detailed and searching scrutiny at the audit. Throughout the account more and more information is given: the number of acres sown with each type of corn for instance, or the actual dates when corn was sold at a particular price. Often the trend is most obvious in the stock account: further paragraphs provide a formal account of an increasing range of live and dead stock—hay, turves, hurdles, peacocks' feathers, roof-tiles, brass bowls, and table-cloths are only examples of the enormous variety of items separately accounted for on one or other manor in the mid-fourteenth century. There could be further additions. Sometimes we find a works account, its charge being the labour services due on the demesne and its discharge showing how they were used; we even find the fictitious sale being used to charge the reeve for works that had not been performed. Sometimes there are separate accounts for week-works, harvest works, and other types of

---

[20] Winchester Cathedral Priory went even further and nearly every manor that kept pigs, geese, or hens accounted for 60 piglets, 28 goslings, 60 chicks, and 300 eggs as each year's issue, irrespective of the number of adult stock of the manor (Drew, n. 15 above, 39).

service. And very occasionally there is a land account, showing how the demesne arable and meadows had been used during the year.[21]

When a new reeve or bailiff took office one would expect him to start with a clean slate, so that the only debts he owed on his first account were those incurred in the single year's business. But it became increasingly common for the lord of the manor to saddle him with any outstanding debts of his predecessor, so that his first account could open with an entry of arrears. This meant only that it was the new official's job to collect the money that was owing; the lord and his auditors did not lose sight of who the real debtor was, and at the end of the account there will commonly be a note to say how much was due from the present official, how much from his predecessor. Where an office changed hands frequently this note might divide the debt between several successive holders. This method of bringing forward the former officials' debts had become the general practice by the time the third phase of manorial accounting began.[22]

PHASE 3

Phase 3 of manorial accounting belongs to the period, from the mid-fourteenth century onwards, when leasing manors was becoming once again the usual way of running an estate, and its most characteristic features result directly from this change. Above all, the uniformity that marked the second phase disappeared. Where a manor continued to be run in demesne, its accounts followed the same pattern as before. But when it was leased there was bound to be a change. The lessee farmer might present an annual written account just as the reeve or bailiff had done (in fact he seems normally to have done so) but he had much less to account to the landlord for: normally no corn or livestock, no money apart from the amount of his annual farm and no expenses beyond perhaps some building repairs. The result might be a very short document indeed—short and relatively uninformative, as the landlord and his auditors had ceased to take an interest in the minute detail that gives the accounts of manors in demesne such great historical value. Sometimes, indeed, the farmer's account was not only short but scrappy and informal; some cover more than one year.[23] But often it retained the formal

[21] As at Oakington (Cambs.) in 1361–2 (F. M. Page, *The Estates of Crowland Abbey* (Cambridge, 1934), 279).

[22] It can be seen in operation in successive collectors' accounts at Oakington from 1347 to 1351 (Page, *Crowland*, 266–71).

[23] e.g. farmers' accounts for Cuxham (Oxon.) from 1395 on, in the muniments of Merton College, Oxford, 5888–97.

structure of a Phase 2 account, simply adapted to serve for a lessee farmer. One reason for this variety was the lack of any generally accepted form or models for the clerks who drew up lessees' accounts; we have specimen accounts from the fifteenth century, but they are simply copies of the form used for manors in demesne,[24] and how this was adapted for manors at farm was entirely a matter of individual choice or local tradition. But besides this the many different forms and conditions of manorial leases were bound to produce greater variety of manorial account than in Phase 2, just because there was greater variety between one manor and another in what had to be accounted for.

Nor was it only the lessee who rendered account when a manor was set to farm. As we have seen, the lord normally excluded from the lease at least the rents of the local tenants and the profits of the manorial court, and he would appoint a collector on the manor to gather them in for him. This collector would render an annual account, so that we may have two separate accounts each year from the same manor. Sometimes the farmer and the collector presented a single joint account.[25] Occasionally a collector was appointed even when demesne farming was continued or (as could happen) restored on a particular manor; in this case the reeve or bailiff accounted for everything that would be leased if the manor were set to farm, the collector for everything else.[26] A further complication arises in nomenclature: the lessee was sometimes referred to not as farmer but as reeve or bailiff, as though he were the local official in charge of a manor in demesne. The significance of a Phase 3 account—just who is accounting for what—can be understood only by approaching it with an open, flexible mind; it is far harder than with earlier manorial accounts to know what to expect from a simple catalogue entry or description.

Despite all the variety of form and content, the basic structure of a charge–discharge account remained, but we see continuing developments in its detailed layout. These particularly affected the end of the cash account (and the cash account was, of course, normally the entire account when the manor was at farm). We find in accounts of Phase 2 that after the auditors had completed their work and entered the final balance the official would successfully plead against particular disallowances they had made, and a note of this would be added with a new balance. Sometimes this process would be

---

[24] *Walter of Henley and Other Treatises on Estate Management and Accounting*, ed. D. Oschinsky (Oxford, 1971), 247, 249–52.

[25] As at Urchfont (Wilts.) in 1463–4, where the stock-keeper also shared the account (BL Add. Roll 66603). Sometimes farmer and collector were the same person, as at Down Hatherley (Gloucs.) in 1464–5 (BL Add. Charter 74143).

formalized by setting out a special paragraph of 'Petitions for allowance' (*Petitiones allocancie*) after the first balance. In Phase 3 accounts we find this developed still further, with the first balance followed by very long notes, usually set out with the first line rather short, starting quite close to the right-hand edge of the membrane, then with each successive line starting further out to the left, producing a nearly triangular pattern (see Plate 3.3). Several successive new balances might be struck, and in a short account of a lessee or collector these notes may well be longer than everything preceding them. It seems as if it was after the audit had produced its first formal bal-

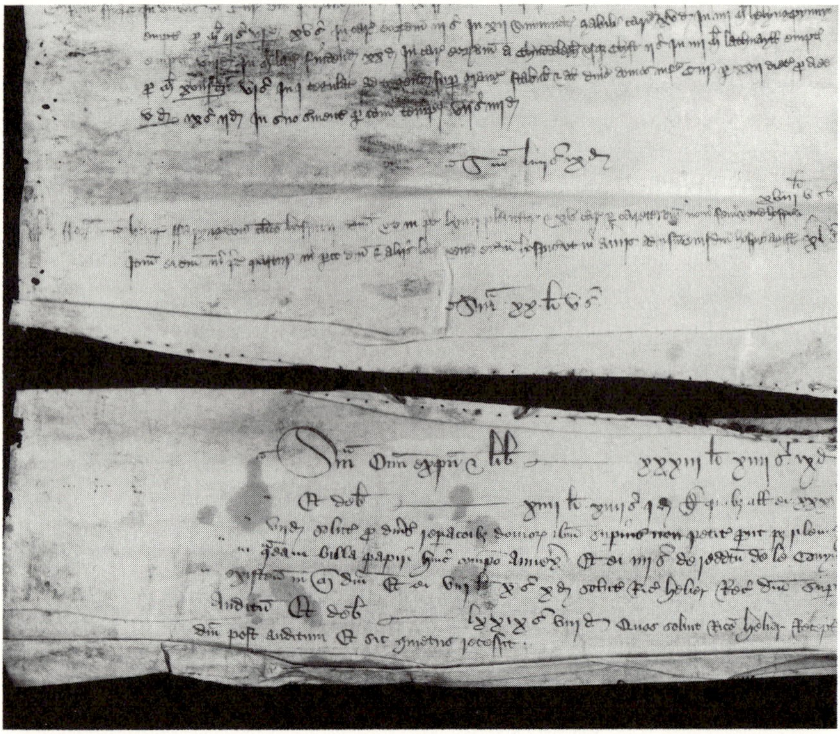

Plate 3.3 Phase 3 account: Bishop's Clyst (Devon: Bishop of Exeter), 1428–9. Devon Record Office, W.1258.G.3(4). Printed in N. W. Alcock, 'An East Devon Manor in the Later Middle Ages', *Report and Transactions of the Devonshire Association*, 105 (1973), 182.

Note: This is the end of the cash discharge account, with its total and balance on a separate membrane, formerly sewn on but now detached. As usual, in the notes following the balance (here notes of payments) each successive line starts further to the left.

ance that the real business of investigation and discussion began. It meant that a substantial part of the account lay outside the formal structure, marking a further move towards variety, away from the uniformity of the Phase 2 account.

Sometimes, like some other late medieval records, the manorial account became over-formalized, so that its layout and contents owed more to precedent than to current fact. Thus the traditional pattern might be adhered to so far that the account for a manor at farm included headings that could apply only if it were in demesne, 'Nothing' (*Nichil*) being entered after each.[27] Or within the individual paragraphs items might be included because they appeared on previous accounts or a rental, even though this year there was nothing to enter against them. Thus on the account for the countess of Devon's manor of Tiverton in 1511–12 the paragraph of minor receipts contains twenty-four items of which all but four are negative ones: 'Of certain items there nothing has been sold this year by the said accounting official. He does not answer for old oaks or cropping of oaks . . .' and so on.[28] This formalization may be carried to the point where it is not just quaint but misleading. Mr T. B. Pugh shows how in accounts for Stow, near Newport (Monmouthshire), we find the mistress (*concubina*) of Master William Cady, who was himself alive in 1424, paying 2*s.* a year for a cottage and one acre in 1446—and still in 1522. The name of the tenant would be entered on the account from the latest rental, which by then was a hundred years out of date.[29] We must always be on our guard against this sort of quirk; as Dr C. Dyer has put it, 'Reading fifteenth-century manorial accounts is an exercise in distinguishing between theory and reality'.[30]

Most of our manorial accounts of Phase 3 were drawn up locally to present to the audit, and like Phase 2 accounts they show us the auditors' alterations and comments. But more often than in the second phase we find accounts that are obvious fair copies made after audit,[31] and it is not uncommon in the late Middle Ages to find manorial accounts for an entire estate enrolled after audit as a record for its central administration.[32] On a few estates, like

[27] As at Reedham (Norf.) in 1444–5 (BL Add. Roll 26863).

[28] BL Add. Roll 64823.

[29] *The Marcher Lordships of South Wales 1415–1536: Selected Documents*, ed. T. B. Pugh (Cardiff Board of Celtic Studies, History and Law Series, 20, 1963), 162.

[30] C. Dyer, *Lords and Peasants in a Changing Society: The Estates of the Bishopric of Worcester, 680–1540* (Cambridge, 1980), 162.

[31] As at Ashey (I. of Wight) in 1535–6 (BL Add. Roll 74601).

[32] To take two examples on different scales, the enrolled estate accounts from Taunton Priory in 1437–9 (BL Add. Rolls 16333, 25873) and from the bishopric of Lincoln in 1509–10 (Lincolnshire Archives Office, diocesan records, BP accounts 8).

the bishop of Winchester's, we know that this represents a long-continued tradition from the first phase of manorial accounting, and on other estates too it may be mere chance that has preserved only late survivors of lengthy series. But the pattern of survival suggests strongly that in some cases at least we have a reversion to the practice of enrolment which many estates had abandoned in the late thirteenth or early fourteenth century.

THE CENTRAL ORGANIZATION: RECEIVERS' ACCOUNTS AND VALORS

Throughout this chapter we have been discussing manorial accounts from the viewpoint of the user, the historian. We have been looking at the details of the year's financial transactions on the individual manor, the reckoning of account between the manorial lord and the man on the spot—whether reeve or farmer, official or lessee—wherever we could find them: in accounts drawn up before audit, in fair copies made afterwards, in enrolments made by the estate's central administration. We have seen that they conform to a single pattern of arrangement, which develops and changes over the years but which is common to original draft, fair copy, and enrolment alike. But it is important to bear in mind that to the medieval estate administrator—and thus to the archivist—what we have lumped together in this way as 'manorial accounts' comprised several different sorts of document, which will have played a variety of roles in the organizations that brought them into being. In comparing the locally produced accounts of Phase 2 with the centrally enrolled accounts of Phase I we are not, archivally speaking, comparing like with like. The financial transactions of the individual manor will often have acquired the permanence of the written word at some higher level of the estate organization.

On a large medieval estate there were generally three levels of financial responsibility: the manorial official or lessee, the local receiver who collected money from the manors in a particular area, and the receiver-general who channelled the money from the local receivers to the lord and his household. Smaller estates would have a simpler organization, and in any case there was some variety in the officials' titles, in the division of responsibilities and in the detailed administrative machinery—all of which affected the style of the accounts presented at each level. What part was played in this supra-manorial structure by the varying forms of manorial account—original draft, fair copy, or enrolment—is often far from clear, and probably differed significantly from one estate to another. There have been quite a number of studies of the financial structure of particular medieval estates,[33] but still more knowledge here would assist our full understanding of the records and of the information we draw from them. From a number of estates in the fourteenth and fifteenth centuries we have substantial series of receivers' accounts, accounts which give us no more than summaries of the receipts from individual manors. Mr T. B. Pugh's edition of the individual manorial accounts and receiver's account for the duke of Buckingham's lordship of Newport in 1447–8 displays very clearly the typical relationship between the two levels of account in the late Middle Ages (see the select texts listed at the end of this chapter).[34]

However summary the details on a receiver's account, it may provide useful information about the individual manors if manorial accounts are lacking. So too may the valor. This sets out the income and expenses of an estate in more or less summary form but sometimes showing how much each manor could be expected to provide each year. A detailed valor will tell us a good deal about what was happening on each manor, with its entries for the leases of mills, hiring out of pasture, sales of timber, losses of rent for want of tenants and so on. The valor was not an account—indeed it might be seen as a form of survey— but it was based directly on the manorial and receivers' accounts and some lords had one compiled every year as a current guide to their financial resources. The formal valor first appears in the second half of the fourteenth century, but it can be compared with the summarized accounts for an entire estate that we sometimes find in the thirteenth century, and, indeed, with enrolled or filed copies of manorial accounts, which may well have served the same purpose.

SUBSIDIARY RECORDS OF ACCOUNT

We now pass from the highest level of the estate's financial administration to the lowest, to the ephemeral records that were used in drawing up the manorial account. They must usually have been thrown away once their immediate purpose was served but occasionally we find some kept along with the accounts themselves. They must have varied to some extent from one estate to another; all we can do here is to mention briefly those most likely to be encountered.

[33] Most recently P. H. W. Booth, *The Financial Administration of the Lordship and County of Chester 1272–1377*, Chetham Soc. 3rd Ser. 28 (1981).

[34] PRO DL29/354/5837 is an unpublished file of six local accounts and one receiver's account for the duchy of Lancaster's barony of Embleton (Northumb.), 1367–8, which likewise demonstrates both simply and neatly the relationship between the two levels of account.

Draft accounts of some sort must have been used to compile all the enrolled accounts of Phase 1, though we hardly ever have both the original and the enrolment. Here, of course, calling the original a draft may be open to question: the individual accounts which were used to compile the enrolments for the bishopric of Winchester and which survive in substantial series from the mid-fourteenth century on are carefully written accounts of Phase 2 pattern. But we occasionally find that a Phase 2 account exists in both draft and fair copy; the draft will often give slightly more detail than the fair copy, it may show signs of having been drawn up in successive stages in the course of the year, and, in consequence, the contents of each paragraph may be less well ordered.

Views of account sometimes served as draft accounts. The view was an inspection of the financial state of the manor made by the auditors about half-way through the year. We find so few references to these views in manorial records that we may wonder whether they really were made as regularly as was urged by the thirteenth-century treatises on estate management. When they were held, they may often have been conducted orally without a written record; but sometimes the current state of account was written out in a document that has survived. At its most formal, the view of account is a short version of the full annual account and it may show the same process of auditing; it may even contain fictitious sales ('sold at the view': *in vendicione super visum*).[35]

Particulars of account normally survive only if they are physically attached to the account itself. Often no more than tiny scraps of parchment or paper, they set out the full details of items (usually among the cash expenses) that are entered in the account only as a single total; this was information which the auditors might call for but which would overweight the relevant paragraph if put in the account itself. Expenses over the harvest period, lists of tenants and their rents, costs of putting up a new building, are among the many items that might be covered in this way.

Lists of estreats were certainly a normal part of manorial administration but have very seldom survived. They are the lists of fines and amercements imposed in the manorial court, and would be given to the local official so that he could collect the money from the people concerned. Where they have been attached to an account they presumably served as particulars of account for the profits of the court.[36]

---

[35] As at Syleham (Suff.) in 1273–4 (PRO SC6/751/7).

[36] As at Maidstone (Kent) in 1296–7, 1299–1300 (Lambeth Palace Library, London, estate documents, rolls 657, 658).

Indentures with the local official were also very common; a simple note in two parts, indented along the division, often took the place of a wooden tally-stick as a receipt or voucher that he would keep as evidence of a particular payment or delivery of produce. Occasionally indentures of this sort survive by serving as particulars of account, but mostly, like the tallies, they would be thrown away once they had been produced and checked at the audit. More formal indentures survive more often, but may not have been so much a part of normal practice. Among them are indentures of account, drawn up at the end of the audit and listing the cash debts, corn, and livestock that the official took over at the start of the new financial year; and indentures, similarly listing the manorial stock, that would be drawn up between a new local official and either his predecessor or the lord of the manor.

SELECT TEXTS

J. Z. Titow, *English Rural Society, 1200–1350* (London, 1969), 106–36. Phase 1 and Phase 2 enrolled accounts for Downton (Wilts.), 1208–9 and 1324–5. English translation.

The Pipe Roll of the Bishopric of Winchester 1210–1211, ed. N. R. Holt (Manchester, 1964), Phase 1 enrolled accounts. Latin text.

F. Page, *The Estates of Crowland Abbey* (Cambridge, 1934), 174–279. Phase 1 enrolled accounts for the whole estate, 1258–9, and select accounts for Cottenham, Dry Drayton and Oakington (Cambs.), 1267–1362, showing development from Phase 1 through Phase 2 to Phase 3. Latin text.

Accounts and Surveys of the Wiltshire Lands of Adam de Stratton, ed. M. W. Farr (1959), 31–233. Phase 2 accounts, with drafts, view and particulars of account for Sevenhampton (Wilts.), 1269–88. Latin text.

Manorial Records of Cuxham, Oxfordshire, c.1200–1359, ed. P. D. A. Harvey (London, 1976), 117–606. Phase 2 accounts, 1276, 1288–99, 1317–19, 1327–30, 1346–59, and subsidiary records of accounts, 1272–1355. Latin text.

Ministers' Accounts of the Manor of Petworth 1347–1353, ed. L. F. Salzman, Sussex Record Soc. 55 (1955). Phase 2 accounts. English translation.

N. W. Alcock, 'An East Devon Manor in the Later Middle Ages', *Report and Transactions of the Devonshire Association*, 102 (1970), 176–85; 105 (1973), 178–90. Phase 2 account, 1398–9, and Phase 3 accounts, 1428–9 and (in three versions) 1524–5. Latin text.

The Marcher Lordships of South Wales 1415–1536: Select Documents, ed. T. B. Pugh (Cardiff, 1963), 184–236. Phase 3 accounts, with receiver's account and summarized 'declaration of account' and valor, for the manors, etc., of the lordship of Newport (Monm.), 1447–8. Latin or (for the declaration of account) original English text.

The Grey of Ruthin Valor, ed. R. I. Jack (Sydney, 1965), Valor of the English lands of
the earl of Kent from accounts of 1467–8. Original English text.

Percy Bailiffs' Rolls of the Fifteenth Century, ed. J. C. Hodgson, Surtees Soc. 134 (1921).
Phase 3 enrolled accounts for the earldom of Northumberland, 1471–2. Latin
text.

Bolton Priory Rentals and Ministers' Accounts, 1473–1539, ed. I. Kershaw (1970), 25–61.
Accounts of local officials, based on rentals, 1538–9. English translation.

FURTHER READING

An important pioneer work based on manorial records that discusses helpfully the detailed contents of the various paragraphs of the manorial account
is by A. Elizabeth Levett, 'The Black Death on the Estates of the See of
Winchester', in *Oxf. Studies*, 5 (1916), 13–67. N. Denholm-Young, *Seignorial
Administration in England* (London, 1937), looking at thirteenth-century lay
estates, clearly shows the place of manorial accounts and audit in the overall
organization of estate and household. Two later studies that are basic to our
understanding of the use and purpose of manorial accounts are J. S. Drew,
'Manorial Accounts of St. Swithun's Priory, Winchester', *English Historical
Review*, 62 (1947), 20–41, and E. Stone, 'Profit-and-loss Accountancy at
Norwich Cathedral Priory', *Transactions of the Royal Historical Society*, 5th Ser. 12
(1962), 25–48. A detailed discussion of the development of Phase 2
accounts, of how they were drawn up and of the subsidiary accounting
records that were used, is in the introduction of *Cuxham Man. Recs.* 12–71,
while *Marcher Lordships*, 153–83, provides an important discussion of the local
accounts, receivers' accounts, and valors of the lordship of Newport (Monm.)
in the fifteenth century, an analysis that is of general relevance to late
medieval manorial and other estate accounts. A more general discussion of
receivers' accounts and valors is in C. D. Ross and T. B. Pugh, 'Materials for
the Study of Baronial Incomes in Fifteenth-century England', *Economic History
Review*, 2nd Ser. 6 (1953–4), 190–4; valors are also discussed in the introduction to *Ruthin Valor*, 8–9. Treatises on manorial accounting (including the
anonymous treatise on husbandry, which originated in auditors' rules) are
fully listed and discussed, and some texts printed, by Dorothea Oschinsky in
Walter of Henley, 200–57, 417–75.

POSTSCRIPT

One point that needs correction in this survey of manorial accounting is in its third paragraph: T. H. Mayberry shows in his guide to *Estate Records of the Bishops of Winchester in the Hampshire Record Office* (Hampshire Record Office, 1988), 5, that at Winchester, and presumably elsewhere too, enrolled estate accounts were in fact known as pipes in the Middle Ages: to call them pipe rolls is not a historians' whim. In the preceding paragraph, the suggestion that written manorial accounts were not used at Durham Cathedral Priory until the 1270s is called in question by A. J. Piper's discovery of a fragment of an accounting document that must date from before 1244: 'Evidence of Accounting and Local Estate Services at Durham, *c*.1240', *Archives*, 20 (1992), 36–9.

Other recent work on the early development of manorial accounting includes, notably, Marjorie Chibnall's edition, with introduction, of newly discovered documents, 'Computus Rolls of the English Lands of the Abbey of Bec (1272–1289)', *Camden Miscellany Vol. XXIX* (Camden Fourth Series, 34; 1987), 1–196, which demonstrates further that important early accounts may still come to light, and the article by E. J. King, 'Estate Management and the Reform Movement', *England in the Thirteenth Century*, ed. W. M. Ormrod (Stamford, 1991), 1–14, which includes a 1248 record of estate finance from Peterborough Abbey. Further work is in preparation, by N. C. Vincent and by myself, on the origin of the manorial account; and, more generally, long-term work on the Winchester pipe rolls projected by Hampshire County Council will certainly throw new light on many aspects of medieval estate accounts. Particularly interesting work on late-medieval accounts is by D. Postles, 'The Oseney Abbey Flock', *Oxoniensia*, 49 (1984), 141–52, who prints a 1476–7 account of the sheep organized and maintained centrally on a monastic estate after most of the manorial demesnes had been leased out.

Manorial accounts are concerned with lords' acquisition of funds and with the relevant capital expenditure. How they spent their profits was recorded in their household accounts, of which far fewer survive. They have at last been given the scholarly attention they deserve in important work by C. M. Woolgar, *Household Accounts from Medieval England* (British Academy, Records of Social and Economic History, NS 17, 18 (1992–3)), which analyses the form and development of these documents and prints specimen accounts from twenty-eight households, dating from the late twelfth century to the late fifteenth. This complements, on a much larger scale, the brief guide to manorial accounting given here.

4 · THE PERCEPTION OF PROFIT BEFORE THE LEASING OF DEMESNES

D. Postles

One of the critical questions of the agrarian economy of the thirteenth and fourteenth centuries, is the performance of the seigneurial economy. From the late twelfth century, lords had begun to resume their demesnes in hand, to exploit them directly, rather than to continue to lease them to *firmarii*.[1] Direct exploitation persisted into the later fourteenth century, when there was a return in many cases to the leasing of demesnes.[2] The inducement to lords to engage in direct exploitation is therefore a central issue. Research into particular estates has attempted to face this issue. In many cases, however, the performance of the properties has had to be reconstructed. Reflections on 'profit' have necessarily comprised retrospective analyses—the historian's interpretation of 'profitability'.[3] For want of other information, this approach is entirely valid. An equally helpful method may be to try to recognize the lords' own perceptions of how well their property was paying. As long ago as 1965, P. D. A. Harvey wrote perceptively: 'But, however reached, the figures

First published in *Agricultural History Review* (1986).
I am indebted to the British Academy for their assistance with a small research grant, which allowed me to undertake some of the research for the paper. For permission to use their archives, I am grateful to: The Queen's College, Oxford; the Warden and Fellows of Merton College, Oxford; the Dean and Chapter of Lichfield; His Grace, the Duke of Devonshire; Winchester College; Christ Church, Oxford; and the Dean and Chapter of Westminster Abbey. Above all, I am grateful to their respective archivists for enabling my research, in particular: Dr J. R. L. Highfield, Mr J. Burgass, Mrs J. Hampartumian, Mr N. MacMichael, Mrs E. Nixon, Mr J. M. Kaye, and the staff of the Bodleian Library. Without committing them to the inadequacies of the paper, I must record my gratitude for advice at various times from: Dr E. King, Professor P. D. A. Harvey, Dr J. Z. Titow, Miss B. F. Harvey, Dr C. C. Dyer, and Dr H. S. A. Fox.

[1] P. D. A. Harvey, 'The Pipe Rolls and the Adoption of Demesne Farming in England', *Econ. Hist. Rev.* 2nd ser. 27 (1974), 345–69.

[2] R. A. Lomas, 'The Priory of Durham and its Demesnes in the Fourteenth and Fifteenth Centuries', *Econ. Hist. Rev.* 2nd ser. 31 (1978), 339–53, suggests this tendency was not absolute.

[3] For example, recently, M. Mate, 'Profit and Productivity on the Estates of Isabella de Forz (1260–92)'. *Econ. Hist. Rev.* 2nd ser. 33 (1980), 326–34; and, in the past, for example, Frances Davenport, *The Economic Development of a Norfolk Manor* (London, 1967), 43–4.

are of value as showing what the College itself considered to be its profit from Cuxham.'[4] He was referring to the memorandum of the profit of the manor entered on the foot of the face of the manorial accounts of Cuxham. Perhaps only a minority of lords—or their auditors—added these statements of profit to the manorial accounts.[5] The purpose of this chapter is to assess these memoranda from a small number of lesser and medium-sized estates, to attempt to show the lords' perception of the profitability of their properties.

The principles behind these *proficua* calculations were cogently explained by Eric Stone some twenty years ago.[6] He revealed the two calculations which might be introduced: the *proficuum manerii* and the more sophisticated *proficuum ganagii (wainagii) et stauri*. This chapter is basically concerned with the *proficuum manerii* and its variants. Some attempt will be made to assess the nature of the calculation, building on Stone's research; to review the data from the selected estates, within the context of the various properties; and finally to draw some further conclusions about attitudes to the calculations.

I

The *proficuum manerii* was designed, in Dr Stone's phrase, to answer the question: 'how well is our property paying?' The objective was to assess the level of current profitability. The memorandum recording the statement would often be quite summary: *Proficuum manerii hoc anno xliiij.li. vij.s. iij.d.*[7] According to Professor Harvey, the memorandum is 'the last significant stage in the compilation of the manorial account', and 'perhaps the most interesting addition to account rolls at Stage 3'.[8] The memoranda collected together here derive from the estates of several lesser or medium-sized lordships: the estates of Merton College; God's House (Southampton); the Bishopric of Lichfield; Southwick Priory (Austin Canons); and Bolton Priory (Austin Canons). The memoranda are often very cryptic, and in many cases the brevity of the entries makes it impossible to rework the nature of the calculation which lay behind the bare statement. It may be that the principles—as explained in the treatises from a few estates[9]—varied only little from one estate to the next, with the

[4] P. D. A. Harvey, *A Medieval Oxfordshire Village* (Oxford, 1965), 97.

[5] P. D. A. Harvey *Manorial Records of Cuxham, Oxfordshire*, Historical Manuscripts Commission, JP 23 (1976), 56–7.

[6] E. Stone, 'Profit-and-Loss Accountancy at Norwich Cathedral Priory', *Transactions of the Royal Historical Society*, 5th series, 12 (1962), 25–48.

[7] Leicestershire Record Office DG9/1954 (Beaumanor, Leics.).

significant exception of whether or not the balance of the account was included in the calculation.[10]

Nevertheless, the memoranda do sometimes reveal something of the nature of the calculation. Principally, they divulge that productive investment would be added towards 'profit' or noted. For example, there is the reference to 40*s.* for the new building at Gussage (God's House) in 1312–13, the costs of the new grange (1311–12) and new house (1313–14) at Werrore with Cosham (God's House), and the new grange at Hickley (God's House) in 1296–7. Similarly, at Hickley, marling was noted in 1295–6. In that same year, ditching contributed to profit on the grange of Bolton Priory at Cononley. Improvements were also included to profit on the estates of Oseney Abbey, although not consistently. In this respect, the memoranda reflect that lords were conscious of the value of investment in their estates, even if the general level of investment was low.[11] Equally, foreign expenses were credited to profit or noted. In the Hickley memoranda, the value of hay and forage sent for the stock at Southampton in 1301–6, is consistently noted. Similarly, hay bought at Gussage in 1308–9 for the lord's horses, was valued towards profit. At Werrore with Cosham, the keep of members of the convent was recorded in two years (1313–14 and 1314–15). The rationale behind this action was presumably that the value of these commodities would otherwise have accrued to profit, had it not been consumed in an extraneous expense. Conversely, foreign receipts were deducted or noted, as the three quarters of wheat received at Cononley for seed from the tithes of Carlton in 1295–6. The great question mark about these aspects—investment, foreign expenses, foreign receipts—is how consistently they were applied.

The calculations of Bolton, Beaulieu, and Oseney allow a more detailed insight into the principles behind the calculation. The main components of the calculation were the liveries of cash to the household *and* the value of grain and stock delivered to the household or to other manors on intermanorial livery.

A further calculation—of unknown provenance, but mid-fourteenth-century—is slightly more refined than Bolton (*c*.1296), Oseney (*c*.1280), and Beaulieu (*c*.1269–70). The sophistication of this calculation rests in the inclusion of grain remaining in the granary and the issue of livestock during the year, and the deduction of arrears. The latter especially was not consid-

---

[10]   E. Stone, 'Profit-and-Loss Accountancy . . .', 29.

[11]   R. H. Hilton, 'Rent and Capital Formation in Feudal Society', repr. in *The English Peasantry in the Later Middle Ages* (Oxford, 1975), 174–214; J. Z. Titow, *English Rural Society, 1200–1350* (London, 1969), 49–50; M. M. Postan, 'Investment in Medieval Agriculture', *Journal of Economic History*, 27 (1967), 576–87.

ered in many other calculations. The author of this formulary, however, recognized that there were other possibilities: *Tamen aliqui discreti habent alium modum extrahendi verum valorem manerii.* Indeed, the author suggested other methods, including checking the current account with the extent and with accounts of previous years, as well as rules of thumb (such as grain yielding to the fourth grain for break-even, and the necessity of making £10 profit on every carucate tilled in the paragraph *De valore terre regula*).

A less refined effort was made a century earlier on the estates of Eynsham Abbey, before the Beaulieu, Bolton, and Oseney calculations. For the manors of Stoke, Charlbury and Mickleton, the Abbey noted the issue of grain each year between 1256 and 1259. A standard price was then applied to each grain: 4s. per qtr. of wheat; 2s. 6d. per qtr. of mixtil; 2s. per qtr. of barley; 1s. 6d. per qtr. of *tramesium*; 1s. per qtr. of oats but only 8d. per qtr. at Mickleton; and 2s. per qtr. of beans. An average was then calculated from the four years to provide the annual figure for profit with some of the costs of collection deducted: *Summa denariorum iiii libre xv solidi et sic subtractis de illa summa xxiiii solidos [sic] pro conduccione et locacione hominum et carectarum et remanent lxxi solidi.*[12]

Undoubtedly, however, the Oseney, Beaulieu, and Bolton calculations represented the most widespread form of the application. The significance of the basic tenets of the calculation was that they recognized the value of the supply of the household as much as the proceeds from the commercial sale of produce, an important consideration on many lesser and medium-sized estates.

Two further problems should be considered before moving on to address the data. The first problem concerns the terminology, and relates to the use of the terms *valor* and *proficuum* (*profectus*). During the fourteenth, and especially in the late fourteenth, century, some baronial and episcopal estates introduced the calculation called the *valor*. This *valor* occurred in two forms: a *valor* for each manor appended at the foot of each manorial account; a central *valor* for the entire estate, compiled from the individual returns. Professor Davies, in an important article, suggested that these later *valores* were related closely to the decision to lease demesnes, in contrast with earlier profit calculations which had been produced for demesnes being directly exploited. The later *valores* thus comprised liveries of cash, mainly rents and farm (*firma*), whilst the *proficuum* was concerned with wider agricultural activity.

[12] H. E. Salter (ed.), *The Cartulary of the Abbey of Eynsham*, I, Oxford Historical Society 49 (1906–7), 8–9; Salter, *The Cartulary of Oseney Abbey*, VI, Oxford Historical Society, 101 (1936), 184–207; Dom. S. F. Hockey, *The Account Book of Beaulieu Abbey*, Camden Society, 4th series, 16 (1975), *passim*; D. Oschinsky (ed.), *Walter of Henley and Other Treatises on Estate Management and Accountancy* (Oxford, 1971), 470–1 (*Valor manerii*); for Bolton Priory, see Appendix 4.4.

Theoretically, the *proficuum* was concerned with current profitability; by the time of the *valor* a decision had been made irrevocably in favour of leasing.

The difference, however, was not quite so absolute. Some of the calculations of the early fourteenth century were called *valeur* or *valor*. The first Merton memoranda occur as *valet manerium*, and some of the God's House statements appear initially as *manerium valet*. On the Lichfield accounts, the statement is interchangeably *valet hoc anno* and *proficuum* in the late thirteenth and early fourteenth centuries. The Stubbington accounts in the thirteenth and fourteenth centuries have consistently *valet (hoc anno) manerium*, and in 1351–2, when the demesne was still in hand, *valor*. On the estates of Westminster Abbey, the term *valor* was used in the early fourteenth century for manors where the demesne was still in hand, as well as in the later fourteenth century for demesnes then at farm. At Hickley, moreover, the term *valet* was used when the profit calculation was reintroduced transiently in 1383–4, the demesne being then still in hand, although it had previously been leased. Other *valores* which were introduced in the later fourteenth century, applied to demesnes still in hand in the 'Indian Summer' of the 1380s and 1390s. The *Valor* of the Worcester episcopal estates was initiated in 1391, when some demesnes (e.g. Bibury) were still in hand, and the *valor* included separate elements for grain, stock, wool, and 'the manor', similar to the Clare *valor* of sixty years previously. Ramsey Abbey embarked on a similar exercise as some demesnes recovered in the 1380s. The manor of Elvethall, which was held by Durham Cathedral Priory, was maintained in hand through to the sixteenth century, as a home farm for which a *clarus valor* was calculated between 1443 and 1514. One of the most remarkable examples of *valores* being employed for demesnes still in hand, was the Catesby *status maneriorum* of 1385–6, deriving from a small lay estate.[13]

A general tendency can therefore be observed. In the late thirteenth and early fourteenth centuries, a profit calculation would probably be designated *proficuum* or *profectus*, but the terms *valor* or *valet* would also be used. This is not unusual since the same terms (*valet* especially) had been used in other contexts

[13] R. R. Davies, 'Baronial Accounts, Incomes and Arrears in the later Middle Ages', *Econ. Hist. Rev.* 2nd ser, 21 (1968), 211–29; C. D. Ross and T. B. Pugh, 'Materials for the Study of Baronial Incomes in the Fifteenth Century', *Econ. Hist. Rev.* 2nd ser, 6 (1953), 185–94; C. C. Dyer, *Lords and Peasants in a Changing Society* (Cambridge, 1980), 147, 162, and 178–9; R. A. Lomas, 'A Northern Farm at the End of the Middle Ages', *Northern History*, 18 (1982), 49; for Westminster Abbey, for example, Westminster Abbey Muniments 15339 (*Valor manerii* for Launton, Oxon., 1330–1, the demesne being in hand), 20277–8 (*Valor rectorie* and *Valor manerii* of Oakham, co. Rutland, 1358–60, Oakham including the rectorial glebe, but the demesne being at farm); Jean Birrell, 'The *Status Maneriorum* of John Catesby, 1385 and 1386', in R. Bearman (ed.), *Miscellany I*, Dugdale Society, 31 (1977), 15–28. Dr C. C. Dyer kindly informed me of the last item.

previously, for example in Domesday Book, and even instead of a *summa* in some extents of manors. By contrast, most calculations in the later fourteenth century would fall under the rubric of *valor*—whether the demesnes were still in hand or, more often now, placed at farm. The change of emphasis in the use of the terms had coincided with a shift in the economic climate. By this time, the climate had altered so radically that many *valores* simply comprised cash liveries from manors now leased, although some still related to demesnes in hand. The increase in the use of *valores* in the 1380s and 1390s—the 'Indian Summer'—may have reflected a genuine effort of lords to assess again their policy towards leasing or direct exploitation at this critical juncture.

Some lords had attempted to address this important question at an earlier time, by comparing the manorial account with the extent of the manor to assess the level of profit. In this case, the extent would represent the expected return on the property and its husbandry *vis-à-vis* the actual amount achieved by reworking the account. Certain examples of this method have been discovered on the estates of the Bishopric of Worcester in the 1290s, and the Abbey of St Alban's in the fourteenth century. The officials of the bishop of Ely may also have employed the concept, as the balance of one of the accounts for Wisbech Barton is qualified: *Item debet ut Gaigneria respondeat ad extentam Liiij. li. ix.s. vij.d.* This alternative may have been more widespread than is yet known, but the *proficuum manerii* was undoubtedly the most favoured method, and it is to this calculation that the chapter returns.[14]

II

The estates selected here for comparison are not the larger Benedictine houses, but rather a collection of medium-sized and lesser estates. Several of the larger Benedictine houses are known to have introduced a *proficuum* calculation: Canterbury Cathedral Priory, Norwich Cathedral Priory, Crowland Abbey, the Abbot of Westminster for the abbatial *mensa*, the monks of Westminster, the Abbey of Bury St Edmund's, for example.[15] (See Table

---

[14] M. Hollings (ed.), *The Red Book of Worcester*, Worcs Historical Society, 1934–50, Part 2, *passim*; Stone, 'Profit-and-Loss Accountancy . . .', 34 and 46; Cambridge University Library Ely Diocesan Records D8/1/4 (Wisbech Barton, 1319–20); D. Oschinsky, *Walter of Henley*, 312–13 (Walter, c21).

[15] Stone, 'Profit-and-Loss Accountancy . . .', *passim* (Norwich and Canterbury Cathedral Priories); Frances Page, *The Estates of Crowland Abbey* (Cambridge, 1934), 240, 249, and 256; B. F. Harvey, *Documents Illustrating the Rule of Walter de Wenlok, Abbot of Westminster, 1283–1307*, Camden Society, 4th series, 2 (1965), 242 n.; Bodleian Library MS Suffolk Roll 21, m. 7 face (*Profectus* of the manor of Mildenhall, Abbey of Bury St Edmunds); J. A. Raftis, *The Estates of Ramsey Abbey* (Toronto, 1957), 262–3.

4.4.) Although significant and interesting, these great religious houses are not entirely representative. The very fact that lords of smaller estates had adopted the calculation is equally important, suggesting a far wider use of the *proficuum manerii*. Merton College introduced the calculation virtually from the foundation of the College, in the 1270s. God's House had established the statement by the time of the first extant manorial accounts from its estates, in 1293–4. Oseney Abbey had a centrally enrolled calculation by *c*.1280, although the earliest extant accounts for its estates only slightly antedate the central account. Bolton Priory had a calculation by 1295–6, the accounts in the Bolton *compotus* volume surviving from 1286. The Beaulieu memoranda, occurring in the account-book, survive for *c*.1269–70, as also the Stubbington ones survive from *c*.1268, although the earliest extant Stubbington accounts antedate the calculation by some twenty years. Some tentative points emerge: first, the increase of interest in the 1280s and 1290s, at a time when direct demesne exploitation had reached a mature level, such that even the lords of lesser estates realized a need to assess more precisely the performance of their properties; secondly, the central enrolment of some of the accounts with their *proficuum* data—Bolton (although enrolment of the accounts preceded the *proficuum*), the Merton *kalendarium* (inconsistently), the Oseney centrally enrolled account, the Beaulieu account-book, and the first account for Southampton on which are collected together the *proficua* for all the properties of God's House.

To place the *proficuum* data in context, the estates and their varied manors and granges will be summarily described. Whereas the estates of the large Benedictine houses comprised a high proportion of large 'classical' manors, the composition of the estates selected here varied greatly, including medium-sized 'classical' manors, small manors and granges. The use of each manor or grange also varied: there was a high level of sales of produce from some, whilst others acted more as suppliers of the household. The *proficuum manerii* was applied to all of them, regardless of their function. Despite these diverse functions and nature, the general picture was 'profitability', but with varying levels and ranges.

The estates of Merton College have been the subject of considerable research.[16] Analysis is concentrated here on several important manors:

---

[16] Mrs E. C. Lowry, 'The Administration of the Estates of Merton College in the Fourteenth Century', University of Oxford D.Phil. thesis, 1933, being Bodleian Library MS D.Phil c 70, relates mainly to the College's manor of Gamlingay, co. Cambs.; Harvey, *Medieval Oxfordshire Village*, for Cuxham; C. Howell, *Land, Family and Inheritance in Transition: Kibworth Harcourt, 1280–1700* (Cambridge, 1983); T. H. Aston also describes the estates in J. L. Catto (ed.), *The History of the University of Oxford, The Early Oxford Schools* (Oxford, 1984).

Cuxham, Holywell, Ibstone, Cheddington, and Malden. Holywell was a rectorial manor on the perimeter of the borough of Oxford, described in one schedule as *in manerio de Haliwelle in suburbio Oxon'*. This manor also included the smaller property at Wolvercote, from which tithe receipts were important, and for which separate accounts were rendered from *c.*1332. The manor of Holywell supported no sheep, but it was intensively cultivated with the purchase of large quantities of manure.[17] The garden was also intensively cultivated, particularly the raising of madder and hemp. Despite its proximity to the college, Holywell was not exploited as a home farm. Large quantities of grain were sold, even carted as far as Wallingford and Reading, possibly for trans-shipment to London. The following figures in Table 4.1 from sample years reflect the extent of the sale of grain. The cash receipt from sales of grain in 1296–7 comprised £25 0s. 3½d. for wheat, £13 2s. 8½d. for barley, and £2 16s. 0½d. for beans and peas. In 1300–1, the sale of grain amounted to £32 17s. 8¾d. The main deficiency continued to be oats, which were not produced on the manor until 1300–1. Consequently, 22 qrs. 1 bu. of oats were purchased in 1296–7, 35 qrs. in 1299–1300, with a further 30 qrs. 3 bu. received by inter-manorial livery in 1299–1300, offsetting some of the sales of grain. In 1300–1, the demesne issue only accounted for 7 qrs. of the total grange issue of 27 qrs. 6 bu. 3 pecks, and the account included: *Minute expense. Et dati ij garcionibus querentibus auenam apud Cukesham ij d.* In 1299–1300, the account revealed a similar story: *Et dati vij hominibus querentibus Auene* [*sic*]

Table 4.1 *Grain sales from Holywell*

	Issues	Sales
1296–7		
wheat	142 qrs. 6 bu.	114 qrs. 6 bu.
rye	21 qrs. 1 bu.	2 qrs. 2 bu.
barley	200 qrs. 2½ bu.	88 qrs. 5 bu.
legumes	38 qrs. 7 bu.	21 qrs. 1 bu.
1299–1300		
wheat	85½ qrs.	23 qrs.
barley	108 qrs.	50 qrs.
legumes	27 qrs. 5 bu.	10 qrs. 1 bu.

[17] M(erton College) M(uniments) 4493 (inventory or schedule of stock, 1331); MM 4484, 4495, and 4497 have very detailed accounts of extensive manuring and planting in the garden, but most of the Holywell accounts have similar expenses.

apud Farendon' cum vij Equis viij d. ob. et ibidem pernoctauerunt.[18] The manor, despite the deficiency of oats, was exploited by Merton as a commercial unit, with a relatively high level of investment, particularly in manuring. Its proximity to a local urban market may have influenced the decision to manage it in this way, although grain was also sold farther afield. The range of profit for the manor consequently fluctuated between £21 and £49, perhaps second only to Cuxham amongst the College's manors.

The demesne under seed at Ibstone, in Buckinghamshire, varied from 192½ acres to 240 acres between 1279/80 and 1300/1. Production of grain was concentrated on oats, mixtil, and wheat, with the oats and mixtil being virtually all consumed on the manor. The wheat was produced for sale, as in 1284–5, when 33 qrs. from the demesne issue of 44 qrs. was sold. In 1279–80, 49½ qrs. ½ bu. had been sold from the total issue of 70 qrs. ½ bu., although only 8 qrs. of mixtil (total issue 78 qrs. 2½ bu.) and 11½ qrs. oats (total issue 134 qrs.) had been sold. Ibstone thus comprised a medium-sized demesne, not intensively exploited for the market, but producing some quantities of wheat for sale. The level of *proficuum* ranged accordingly from £8 to £13.

The demesne of the College's manor of Cheddington in Buckinghamshire fluctuated between 120 and 163½ sown acres between 1297–8 and 1304–5, the principal crops being wheat, dredge, and legumes, although by 1311 pure barley began to replace dredge. Only small quantities of oats were produced. Considerable amounts of wheat and dredge/barley were sown: in 1311–12, 33 qrs. wheat and 56 qrs. 5 bu. barley; in 1313–14, 42½ qrs. wheat and 73 qrs. 7 bu. barley. Sample figures for receipts from sales are given below (Table 4.2), although the receipt from the sales of grain plummeted to only £8 7s. 7¾d. in 1315–16. As the table reveals, sales of wool also contributed highly to receipts. Cheddington was therefore a medium-sized demesne, smaller than Ibstone, but with a range of profit of £9 to £27 compared with the range of £8–13 at Ibstone.

Malden, situated in Surrey, was the most remote of the college's demesnes; it was the largest in the Surrey group of manors which included also Farleigh and Leatherhead, studied by Miss Briggs.[19] Malden was a further medium-sized demesne, with a range of profit from £1 to £29, similar to Cheddington, but with a lower bottom range.

The estates of God's House (the Hospital of St Julian) were more disparate, comprising the large 'classical' manor of Gussage, the grange at

---

[18] MM 4476–7.

[19] H. M. Briggs (ed.), *Surrey Manorial Accounts*, Surrey Record Society, 15 (1935).

Table 4.2. *Sales of produce at Cheddington*

	Grain	Wool
1302–3	£10 5s. 5¾d.	£1 4s. 0d.
1304–5	£22 16s. 0½d.	£4 8s. 8d.
1310–11	£15 17s. 2¼d.	£3 4s. 0d.
1311–12	£19 3s. 4¼d.	£4 3s. 3d.
1313–14	£23 5s. 9d.	£4 5s. 0d.
1314–15	£16 0s. 9¼d.	£4 0s. 0d.

Hickley, the small manor of Werrore with Cosham, and the property at Southampton. Of these properties, Gussage (Dorset) was the largest agricultural concern. The sown acreage at the end of the thirteenth century varied from 208 to 259½ acres, producing wheat, barley and oats as the principal crops, of which wheat and barley were largely sold. In the late thirteenth century, between 39 per cent and 66 per cent of the gross issue of wheat was sold; the proportion of barley which was sold attained 64 per cent of the gross issue in 1293–4, although none was sold when the yield fell in 1295–6. Occasionally, the sale of oats was also high. Consequently, the sale of grain accounted for as much as 77 per cent of receipts in 1295–6, 72 per cent in 1293–4, 56 per cent in 1294–5, and 47 per cent in 1297–8. Gussage, having much in common with the large 'classical' manor, had an equivalent range of profit, extending from £24 to £48.

Hickley, by contrast, had a grange-type economy. Its sown acreage in the later thirteenth century probably reached about 130 acres, and was still a carucate in 1362. The composition of crop production altered radically in the early fourteenth century. In the same way, although the grange had functioned initially in the early 1290s as an appendage of Southampton, it later became more an independent unit, although still relying on foreign receipts of cash in many years from Southampton. From c.1311, the grange developed its own flock, rather than simply being a transhumance pasture for the Southampton flock. Sales of grain were not important, except in uncharacteristic windfall years: £7 8s. 3½d. in 1299–1300, £28 3s. 7½d. in 1300–1, £2 14s. 7½d. in 1302–3. Discounting four years of loss, the *proficuum* ranged from £1 to £16.[20]

[20] e.g. Bodleian Library Queen's College Rolls 181 and 182; *De exitu stauri non respondet hic quia irrotulatur in compoto Hamton'*; *De stauro non respondet hic quia in compoto Hampton'*. In the same accounts, the foreign receipts from Southampton were £28 6s. 6d. in a total receipt of £30 0s. 6d. and more than £32 in a total receipt of £34 plus. Queen's Roll 230 is a *status manerii* describing the demesne in tillage as one carucate (1362).

Although a manorial type of property, with some customary tenants, Werrore with Cosham (Isle of Wight) was hardly a more impressive concern. The accounts do not state the acreage sown, but some impression of the size of the demesne can be obtained from figures for the demesne issue of grain. The manor also supported a small flock of sheep, but a very low level. The range of profit was higher than at Hickley, with minimum and maximum of £5 and £31.

Southampton was a totally different kind of operation. The demesne was not particularly large, producing in 1305–6, for example, 32 qrs. 2 bu. of wheat, 6 qrs. 7 bu. of rye, 27 qrs. 6 bu. of barley, 2 qrs. of beans, 3 qrs. 6 bu. of peas, 6½ bu. of vetches, 6 qrs. 2 bu. of dredge, and 13 qrs. 6 bu. of oats. The yields in 1311–12 were comparable: 35½ qrs. of wheat, 10 qrs. 3 bu. of curall, 5 qrs. 3 bu. of rye, 38 qrs. of barley, 9 qrs. 6 bu. of beans, 12 qrs. of peas, I qr. of vetch, 7 qrs. 7 bu. of dredge, and 15 qrs. 7 bu. of oats. More important for the economy of Southampton, however, was the high level of receipts from rents, usually in excess of £40. With these rents as its nucleus, the *proficuum* attained the range of £43 to £65, exceeding the level at the large 'classical' manor at Gussage.

The estate of God's House thus comprised very diverse properties, even though it was small and compact geographically. Much the same is true for the estate of the bishop of Lichfield, where the manors were of varying size and composition. Cannock, Rugeley, and Lichfield had no demesne in hand, Lichfield, moreover, being a borough. The sown acreage at Chadshunt amounted to 293 acres; at Itchington in various years about 221, 233, and 330 acres; at Stanton a mere 77 acres. The sale of grain from Chadshunt realized £36 1s. 7½d. in 1306–7; from Stanton only £7 13s. 10d. in 1314–15; from Berkswich £3 16s. 0d. in 1312–13; and from Wirksworth £29 15s. 2½d. in 1304–5 (but conversely the purchase of grain, mainly 62 qrs. 1½ bu. of oats, cost £14 2s. 7½d. there). The immense sheep flock on the Peak manor of Wirksworth yielded 999 fleeces, whilst Berkswich produced 294 fleeces. The episcopal estate thus comprised a wide variety of types of property, from the very large manors of Wirksworth and Chadshunt, to the small demesnes of Berkswich and Stanton, where the income from sales of produce was minimal in comparison with the large revenue at Wirksworth and Chadshunt. Further contrast was provided by the manors of Lichfield, Cannock, and Rugeley, where there was no demesne agriculture. The *proficuum* figures varied as greatly. Unfortunately, the sporadic survival of the Lichfield accounts prevents any analysis of the changes of the *proficuum* over a period of years on any one manor. There survives only one account for each of Berkswich,

Wirksworth, Chadshunt, Cannock, and Stanton; two accounts for each of Lichfield, Rugeley, and Turvin; and three for Itchington.

The estate of Bolton Priory has been admirably described by Kershaw.[21] Bolton relied mainly on granges, mostly with smallish demesnes, marked by a strong concentration on the production of oats, and, from the end of the thirteenth century, large sheep flocks. The exceptionally large granges were the home farm at Bolton, and Kildwick and Holmpton. The *proficuum* from the majority of the granges never exceeded £10, but the level at Bolton ranged from £28 to £175, Kildwick £7 to £34, and Holmpton £16 to £34. Receipts from tithes may have been an important element in some of the *proficua*.

Receipts from tithes were certainly contributory to the profit of Stubbington (Hampshire), a grange of Southwick Priory. The sown acreage of the demesne at Stubbington exceeded 150 acres in 1319–20 (152½ acres) and 1330–1 (151 acres), but was usually below this level. Substantial quantities of grain were delivered to Southwick, Stubbington acting somewhat as a home farm. Such a brief résumé of the estates which form the basis of this study, has necessarily been cursory, but will hopefully provide the context for the comments below on the figures of the *proficua*, and also help to relate the size and range of profit to the size and nature of the properties.

III

The statements of the *proficua* present a certain number of problems. The genuineness of some of the figures raises some doubts. The Lichfield figures, for example, are often rounded figures. On the other hand, figures from the other estates are not rounded, which suggests that a very real calculation had been made.

The Lichfield calculations were also undertaken for manors where the demesne was not in hand or where there was no demesne, such as Lichfield, Cannock, and Rugeley. Westminster Abbey similarly produced its memoranda for manors where the demesne was at farm as well as for demesnes in hand. By contrast, Merton College does not seem to have been concerned to assess profit where there was no demesne in hand. The college's manor of Barkby had no demesne, the reeve accounting continuously from 1285–6 simply for the *redditus assise*, fines and perquisites, and expenses. None of his

---

[21] I. Kershaw, *Bolton Priory* (Oxford, 1973).

Table 4.3 *The range of profit* (£)

(Figures are rounded)	
Holywell	21–49
Ibstone	8–13
Cheddington	9–27
Malden	under 1–29
Gussage	24–48
Hickley	1–16 (excluding losses)
Werrore	5–31
Southampton	43–65
Bolton	28–175
Kildwick	7–34
Holmpton	16–34
Stubbington	69–119 (but only 13 in 1351–2)

accounts contains a memorandum of the *proficuum*.[22] In the light of later *valores*, produced for estates after the leasing of demesnes, the college's attitude might seem less committed. Given the simplicity of the accounts of the reeve of Barkby, however, the Warden and Fellows may have needed no further refinement to assess the performance of the property.

The commitment of the college to the *proficuum manerii*, however, was probably less than wholehearted. The ambivalence is demonstrated by the infrequency with which the statement is recorded on the original accounts. These accounts include the memoranda most diligently in the decade 1295–1305, but before and after these years, the memoranda appear only inconsistently. Mrs Lowry, moreover, found only three statements in the accounts for the college's manor of Gamlingay in Cambridgeshire. Denholm-Young revealed the same inconsistency on the Bigod accounts, only some thirty-five of some three hundred containing *proficua*.[23] The accounts from manors of God's House record the *proficuum* consistently from 1293–4, but a decision seems to have been taken *c.*1318–19 to discontinue the calculation.[24] The demesnes, however, continued to be kept in hand, although Hickley was probably farmed for a short period in the late 1360s and Gussage in the 1380s.[25] The transience of the *proficuum* is illustrated well by its use by Oseney Abbey. Abbot William de Sutton (1267–84) was responsible for a centrally enrolled

[22] MM 6483–548: manorial accounts of Barkby, 1285–1486.

[23] Lowry, thesis, pp. 164–6; N. Denholm-Young, *Seignorial Administration in England* (Oxford, 1937), 120–30.

[24] The *responsio* on fleeces and dairy produce was also discontinued simultaneously. For the *responsio*, see J. S. Drew, 'Manorial Accounts of St Swithun's Priory, Winchester', *English Historical Review*, 62 (1947), 20–41.

[25] Bodleian Library Queen's Rolls 35–38.

account of *c.*1280, which abstracted and engrossed the manorial and obedientiar accounts, including the *proficua* of the manors. Only one original manorial account thereafter contains a *proficuum*, that for Forest Hill in 1302–3 recording a profit of £4 16s. 6d. Nothing further is heard of the *proficuum* except for a self-styled *proficuum* on a very much later account for Watlington: *Proficuum. Item petit Allocationes de viij carectis straminis liberatis domino Nicholao de la Bech.*[26]

The possibility of loss on the transactions of the manor occurs in the memoranda from some manors. Several of the granges of Beaulieu Abbey performed poorly to record a loss in 1269–70. In the early fourteenth century, the demesnes of Darley Abbey were recording a total loss of £60.[27] Hickley recorded losses in four years. The losses may have been associated with the susceptibility of some grange-type properties, where the absence of customary labour incurred higher costs of production, combined with the susceptibility of husbandry and no stable income from rents of assize. As a result, a large foreign receipt of cash would be necessary to bail out the grange. For example, Hickley produced a loss in 1295–6 and 1296–7, when foreign receipts from Southampton amounted to £28 6s. 6d. and more than £32 respectively.

The disparate nature of the data makes it difficult to assess trends over time. Kershaw remarked upon the dramatic inflation of the profit of the properties of Bolton Priory in 1309 and 1315–16. Bolton employed the current actual price of grain in its calculation rather than a notional price. Consequently, three years of dearth, poor yields, and the high price of grain, resulted in high profit. Since virtually all the grain was required for internal consumption, Kershaw concluded that 'as realistic estimates the profit calculations are therefore meaningless in these cases'.[28] A slightly different perception, perhaps that of the canons, is that, had the demesne been leased, the canons would have been obliged to spend that amount of cash on the open market to purchase grain for its consumption. In which case, the figures for profit still represented the value of the manors and the demesnes to the house. The profit accurately reflected the importance of the supply of the household. Indeed, had the demesnes been farmed out at a fixed farm, and the price of grain been enhanced so dramatically, the canons would have been

---

[26] H. E. Salter (ed.), *The Cartulary of Oseney Abbey*, VI, Oxford Historical Society, 101 (1936), 184–207; D. Postles, 'The Manorial Accounts of Oseney Abbey', *Archives*, 14 (1979), 75–80; Bodleian Library d d Christ Church Oseney Roll 23 (Forest Hill); Bodleian Library d d Christ Church Oseney Roll 63 (Watlington).

[27] Dom. S. F. Hockey, *The Account Book of Beaulieu Abbey*, Camden Society, 4th series, 16 (1975), 113, 120, 136, 145, 151, 157, and 163; Stone, 'Profit-and-Loss Accountancy . . .', 42, for losses on wainage; R. R. Darlington, *The Cartulary of Darley Abbey*, I. Kendal (1945), 34.

[28] Kershaw, *Bolton Priory*, 46, and id., 'The Great Famine and Agrarian Crisis in England, 1315–1322', in R. H. Hilton (ed.), *Peasants, Knights and Heretics* (Cambridge, 1976), 85–132.

well out of pocket by having to purchase their grain. In some sense, therefore, the canons may have concluded from this lesson the advantages at that time of keeping with direct exploitation.

The effect of the years 1315–17 is also demonstrated by the *proficua* at Southampton, Cuxham, and Hickley. Profit was inflated also at Cheddington, Gussage, and Werrore with Cosham in 1308–11. Years of higher profits occurred at Malden in 1301–5 and 1322–3; Cheddington 1337–8 and 1343–5; Gussage 1293–4 and 1295–6; Werrore 1298–9; Hickley 1299–1302 and 1307–8. The fluctuations may have been generated internally on some manors. At Hickley, for example, the level of sales of grain was affected by grain lying unthreshed in one year and sold in the following. There seems to be a general correlation, however, between the levels of profit and the levels of prices and dearth, although the effect would have been influenced by which type of grain predominated on each property.[29] The difficulties of 1315–17, however, may have persuaded God's House to abandon the calculation of profit and simply renew its commitment for direct demesne exploitation.

The manor of Ibstone may be illuminating in this respect, since it may reflect a harder relationship between the *proficuum* and the leasing of demesnes. The memorandum recorded that in 1299–1300, no profit was made. In the following year (1300–1), the recorded profit was £7 17s 11¾d. From 1303–4, the manor was placed at farm, with the *firmarii* continuing to submit accounts to Merton. The first *firmarius*, William de Mersham, the former serjeant (*serviens*), paid a farm of £10; his successor from 1313, Master William de Alburwyk, held the manor for an increased farm of £10 13s. 4d. The *firmarii*, however, deducted their expenses from the full farm, with the result that the final farm to the College approximated to the *proficuum* in several previous years. For example, the actual farm after deductions in 1319–20, represented by the balance of the account of the *firmarius*, was £7 5s. 7d.[30] The manor may also have been placed at farm in 1286–7 and 1293–4, and certainly the stock in the account for 1293–4 is described as received *de firmariis*. Then, as in 1303, the College may have based its assessment of the farm of the manor on its experience of the *proficuum*. Indeed, Kershaw has suggested that Bolton Priory may also have related the farm of leased properties to the recent profit calculation.[31] These examples, however, seem to be fairly iso-

[29] H. E. Hallam, 'The Climate of Eastern England 1250–1350', *Ag. Hist. Rev.* 32 (1984), 124–32, esp. 131–2.

[30] MM 5077, m 7.

[31] MM 5062; Kershaw, *Bolton Priory*, 46–7.

lated. In most other instances where the *proficuum* was calculated, no experiment was made with the leasing of properties.

The role of rents of assize in the calculation deserves some mention. Holmes remarked that the general stability of the Clare *valores* between 1329–30 and 1338–9, was largely imparted by the large element of rents, which comprised 35 to 50 per cent of the constituents of the calculation.[32] A suspicion must remain, however, that the profit founded on rents of assize was misleading, because of the persistence of arrears of rent. Southampton is an excellent example. Here, the major contribution of rents ensured a consistent level of the profit. Even so, the arrears of rent at Southampton attained £59 13s. 2¾d. in 1303–4, had been £55 9s. 10¼d. in 1302–3, and expanded to £68 5s. 4½d. in 1305–6. The extent of arrears was still £44 14s. 11d. in 1311–12, virtually the equivalent of the annual rental. There is no evidence that God's House took arrears into account in calculating profit, and this weakness continued to detract from *valores* in the late fourteenth and fifteenth centuries on many estates.

Table 4.4. *The adoption of profit calculations on some estates*

Canterbury Cathedral Priory	From c.1225
St Mary's Abbey, Winchester	From c.1233–4
Westminster Abbey (conventual)	From 1267–8
Norwich Cathedral Priory	From c.1268
Southwick Priory	From c.1268
Beaulieu Abbey	c.1269–70
Beaumanor, Leics.	1277–8
Bigod estates	Late thirteenth century
Oseney Abbey	c.1280
Merton College	From 1281–2
Westminster Abbey (abbatial)	By 1292
God's House, Southampton	From 1293–4
Bolton Priory	From 1295–6
Lichfield episcopal estate	From 1304–5
Abbey of Bury St Edmunds	By 1323
Clare estates	1329–30 and 1338–9
Darley Abbey	Early fourteenth century

References will be found in the text, except the following:
Westminster Abbey (conventual) – Westminster Abbey Muniments 15286;
St Mary's Abbey, Winchester – P. D. A. Harvey, *Manorial Records of Cuxham*, 15.

[32] G. A. Holmes, *The Estates of the Higher Nobility in Fourteenth-Century England* (Cambridge, 1957), 89, 108–9 and 143–7, the quotation from p. 189.

IV

The overall impression of the statements of profit is that, in the perception of the lords, even the smallest demesne or grange was of some value in the late thirteenth and early fourteenth centuries, although losses were also recorded on some types of property. This profitability extended to manors which produced simply for internal consumption as well as those properties which operated for the supply of the market. The attempts by lords to assess profit thus fully recognized the contribution of the supply of the household. The profitability of manors, however, fluctuated widely in the course of a few years, and the range of profit was often very wide. The element of rent might provide a stabilizing influence, but could be an ambivalence given the often high level of arrears. The commitment to the calculation also looks suspect on some estates. The zenith of its use may have been limited to the 1290s and first two decades of the fourteenth century. The attempt to monitor current profitability may have been no more than an intellectual exercise, of a transient nature. Managers, however, are always trying to refine their systems of analysis, even if some of their methods do not last the test of time. Certainly, the adoption of the calculation of the *proficuum manerii* extended beyond the largest estates.

APPENDIX 4.1   MERTON COLLEGE MANORS

Ibstone MM5053–5089	£	s.	d.	Holywell MM4466–4507	£	s.	d.	Malden MM4633–4662	£	s.	d.	Cheddington MM5529–5599	£	s.	d.
1279–80[a]	8	17	10½	1296–7	44	18	7¾	1281	20	0	0	1298–9	10	17	10¾
1296–7	12	0	9¾	1297–8	20	17	7½	1296–7	12	5	6	1300–1	13	9	2½
1297–8[b]	7	13	1¼	1298–9	45	15	1½	1300–1		16	4	1302–3	9	3	5
1298–9[b]	9	13	4¾	1299–1300	34	2	10½	1301–2	24	17	10	1304–5	13	15	6¾
1299–1300	0	0	0[c]	1300–1	28	0	0	1302–3	29	2	3¼	1310–11[f]	27	6	8
1300–1	7	17	11¾	1303–4	40	11	1¾	1303–4	28	17	9½	1314–15	18	3	5½
				1304–5[d]	48	14	2½	1304–5	28	6	6¼	1321–2	11	12	0½
								1316–17	15	11	7½	1323–4	18	18	4¾
								1320–1	?30	7	0	1336–7	8	17	4
								1322–3[e]	?45	8	6¼	1337–8	21	9	9
												1343–4	24	12	8
												1344–5[g]	20	0	0

*For Cuxham, P. D. A. Harvey, *A Medieval Oxfordshire Village* (Oxford, 1965), 95, Table IX.

[a] *Et valet manerium de Ybeston' de claro cum redditu assise et consuetudinibus . . . In subsequent years, the term is *profectus*.

[b] Separate *profectus* for the mill in these years.

[c] *Memorandum quod nichil de profectu isto anno set a nobis capet lx.s. preter certum redditum illius manerii.*

[d] Term is *profectus* throughout, but *profectus ecclesie* (i.e. the rectory manor) in 1300–1. There are no statements in 1287–8, 1295–6, and in the extant accounts from 1308 to 1346.

[e] *Valet manerium* in 1281–2, but *profectus* thereafter. No statements in 1271–2, 1278–80, 1285–7, 1292–3, 1298–1300, 1308–9, 1311–12, 1313–14, 1317–18, 1321–2, 1329–30, 1334–5. Figures in 1320–1 and 1322–3 are cancelled.

[f] *Profectus huius anni in hoc rotulo et rotulo annexo [sic] xlj marcas xxj.d.* (i.e. two years).

[g] No statement in 1297–8, 1311–13, 1315–16, 1317–21, 1322–3, 1325–6, 1328–9, 1332–5, 1339–40, 1341–3, 1345–6, 1347–8, 1349–50, and subsequent years.

APPENDIX 4.2   GOD'S HOUSE MANORS

Southampton R265–284				Gussage R1–39				Werrore/Cosham R236–256				Hickley R181–230			
	£	s.	d.		£	s.	d.		£	s.	d.		£	s.	d.
1296–7	42	16	5	1293–4	45	16	0¼	1293–4[f]	4	17	9	1295–6	−14	3	4½[h]
1300–1	46	9	4½	1294–5	36	9	3¼	1294–5[f]	10	7	10	1296–7[a]	−3	14	4[h]
1305–6[b]	54	6	10	1295–6	47	5	9¾	1295–6	9	7	2	1299–1300	8	7	6
1306–7	58	11	11	1296–7[a]	34	0	11	1296–7[i]	10	0	0	1300–1	8	4	0¾
1311–12	56	2	4	1297–8	30	3	8¾	1297–8	8	16	10½	1301–2	13	3	4
1314–15	65	10	0	1299–1300	29	1	8½	1298–9	24	3	2	1302–3	2	6	2
1317–18[c]	62	0	0	1300–1	29	15	5½	1301–2	12	13	6¼	1303–4	5	12	9
				1305–6	32	5	5½	1302–3	12	2	11	1304–5	1	4	1
				1308–9	47	16	6	1303–4	10	19	0	1305–6	1	7	2
				1309–10	43	10	0	1309–10	16	13	4	1306–7	2	1	2½
				1310–11	47	4	8	1310–11	31	3	0	1307–8	11	8	8¾
				1311–12	33	16	8	1311–12	11	18	3	1308–9	2	15	6
				1312–13[d]	30	0	0	1312–13	5	2	0	1309–10	4	0	7
				1312–13	33	15	3	1313–14	13	4	3	1310–11	−1	11	0[b]
				1318–19[e]	24	0	0	1314–15	12	10	2	1311–12	−1	14	4[h]
								1315–16[g]	15	0	0	1312–13	4	2	0
								t Edw II	21	11	2	1313–14	2	13	3
												1315–16	15	12	4
												1316–17	1	16	0
												1317–18[i]	2	6	8

R: Bodleian Library Queen's College Rolls.

[a] The Southampton account for this year includes statements for all the manors of the House, giving the profit from the whole estate as £83 3s. 0d.: *Et sic valent de claro iiij^xx iij. li. iij.s.*

[b] A separate figure is given for the wainage for this year: *Et sic valet Waynagium Ciiij.s. vj.d.*

[c] No statements in 1298–1300, 1302–5, 1308–9, and after 1317–18.

[d] Two accounts dated 6–7 Edw II.

[e] No statements in 1304–5, 1307–8, and after 1318–19.

[f] In 1293–5 *Manerium valet*, but *proficuum* thereafter.

[g] No accounts extant in 1316–18; no statements in 1318–19 and thereafter.

[h] Losses in 1295–7: *Waynagium consumsit*; and in 1310–12 *Manerium consumit.*

[i] No statement in 1298–9 and after 1317–18, but in 1383–4 *Valet hoc anno xlij.s.j.d.*

APPENDIX 4.3. LICHFIELD EPISCOPAL MANORS. *PROFICUA* STATEMENTS

Berkswich	1312–13	Valet hoc anno ixli. xs.	£9	10s.	0d.
Wirksworth	1304–5	Proficuum istius manerii hoc anno xiij li. xvs.	£13	15s.	0d.
Chadshunt	1306–7	Valet hoc anno Liiij li.	£54	0s.	0d.
Itchington	1309–10	Valet hoc anno xxij li. xs.	£22	10s.	0d.
Itchington	1310–11	Valet hoc anno xxxvj li.	£36	0s.	0d.
Itchington	1305–6	Valet hoc anno xxxli.	£30	0s.	0d.
Cannock	1308–9	Valet hoc anno xvj li. vjs. iiijd. per Ricardum prepositum	£16	6s.	4d.
Lichfield	1308–9	Valethoc anno Lxxviij li. vs. xd. ob.	£78	5s.	10½d.[a]
Lichfield	1312–13	Valet hoc anno Lxviij li. xiijs. iiijd.	£68	13s.	4d.[a]
Rugeley	1310–11	Valet hoc anno xviij li. cum lxvjs. de minera ferri unde respondetur in compoto de Longedon'	£18	0s.	0d.
Rugeley	1313–14	Valet hoc anno cum incremento reddituum annorum precedentium xvij li.	£17	0s.	0d.
Stanton	1314–15	Summa valoris vij li. xs.	£7	10s.	0d.
Turvin	1304–5	Proficuum istius manerii ix li.	£9	0s.	0d.
Turvin	1308–9	Valet xij li. iijs. iiijd.	£12	3s.	4d.

Source: Lichfield Joint Record Office D. & C. Muniments NI–N28.

a Cf. Jane Isaac, 'Two Medieval Accounts for the Town of Lichfield', *Transactions of the South Staffordshire Archaeological and Historical Society,* 17 (1975–6), 59–67.

APPENDIX 4.4 BOLTON PRIORY *CLARUM DE MANERIIS*

	Cononley	Rither	How	Ingthorpe	Malham	Riddings
1295–6	2–13–5	3–7–11½[1]				
1296–7	4–2–4	5–8–11[2]				
1297–8	2–12–9		0[3]	0[4]	4–19–0	3–10–10
1298–9	5–4–0		4–14–4	0[5]	4–16–3	6–18–4
1299–1300	0[7]		3–0–7	3–8–7	6–2–7	5–18–0
1300–1[8]						
1301–2[8]						
1302–3[8]						
1303–4[8]						
1304–5[8]						
1305–6		8–0–8¼	2–1–7½	3–14–6	3–19–9	6–8–9½
1306–7		6–9–5	2–7–7		5–13–8½	5–12–11½
1307–8		3–3–3	17–1		5–10–1¾	6–19–1
1308–9		8–18–2½	11–5½[10]	2–18–4	7–11–5½	9–9–4½
1309–10		12–9–4½	6–12–0	1–12–9[12]	8–17–8	14–6–11
1310–11		7–2–2	4–17–10	2–5–4[15]	4–19–2[16]	5–14–2
1311–12		7–5–8¾[20]	3–4–4	3–8–10½[21]	4–3–0¾	4–17–1½
1312–13		1–1–1¼[26]	18–0	0[27]	3–5–6	1–6–0½
1313–14		4–14–6½	3½	0[33]	1–12–0	18–10
1314–15		3–18–11	3–16–7	8–1[37]	2–7–5	1–4–11
1315–16	0[39]	10–0–0[40]	5–8	0[41]	12–2–5	1–8–6[42]
1316–17	8–6–0½[44]	10–0–0[45]	8–19–0[46]	13–12–8½[47]	19–3–7	4–16–4
1317–18	0	10–0–0[52]	0	0[53]	2–11–8	10–0–4
1318–19[8]						
1320–1[8]						
1321–2					14–12–5½	
1322–3		6–0–0[55]			12–6–1	
1323–4[8]						
1324–5[8]						

Source: Chatsworth MS 73A

[1] preter fenum in expensis equorum.

[2] preter fenum.

[3] How respondit de nichilo [sic] hoc anno.

[4] Unkethorp nichil reddidit domi hoc anno quia totum clarum ibidem deputatur ad manerium instaurandum.

[5] Unkethorp. Unkethorp nichil Respondit de claro hoc anno.

[6] Kildewik. De claro de Kildewik non fit mencio hoc anno quia non fuit in manu prioris.

[7] Conedley. De Conedley nichil hoc anno quia terre dominice dimmituntur ad firmam.

[8] No *clarum* statement this year.

[9] Et sciendum quod semen omnimodi bladi non subtractur.

[10] resumit hoc anno.

[11] De manerio de Halton ignoratur hoc anno quia compotus inde rite[?] non potuit fieri pro morte fratris I. conuersi.

[12] preter sustentacionem omnium.

[13] preter sustentacionem omnium.

[14] in parte.

[15] feno [sic] pro bidentibus.

[16] dum taxat excepto.

[17] Kyldewyk' nichil hoc anno quia bladum fuit domino Rogero.

[18] Angrum respondit de claro cum Boulton ut supra quia per carucatorem de Boulton fuit aratum et seminatum.

[19] Holmeton. Respondit de claro in parte xxiij.li. vj.s. viij.d. Et non plus hoc anno quia residuum in edificiis ibidem.

Stead	Halton	Kildwick	Bolton	Angrum	Holmpton	Appletreewick
4–19–9						
5–4–10	12–10–0	0[6]				
3–13–4		3–4–11½				
2–11–3	18–14–1½		42–13–1½	6–12–0		
2–16–8	12–18–7		61–15–6	7–11–1½		
3–0–1	16–0–6		117–3–5½[9]	4–16–0		
4–16–9	?[11]		78–17–2	14–17–8		
6–14–5½	1–0–0[13]		164–2–1	4–4–1	34–10–0[14]	
4–15–4	19–8–0	0[17]	67–4–10	—[18]	23–6–8[19]	
3–2–11	17–15–8[22]	7–2–2[23]	28–8–9¼[24]	—[25]	16–13–4	2–14–8
1–7–0	0[28]	0[29]	88–0–3[30]	—[31]	—[32]	1–9–4½
2–0–11	3–5–0	0[34]	67–17–3	—[35]	—[36]	5–2–2
13–0	2–11–5½[38]	7–9–2	62–10–4	11–18–3	31–17–11½	3–11–10
4–15–2	4–5–0	33–19–10	175–4–11	2–15–5[43]	19–15–10	10–9–4
4–15–3	?[48]	22–4–9½	130–18–8½	—[49]	—[50]	9–10–0[51]
1–19–4	0	20–4–11½[54]	109–17–0	0	32–11–2	5–14–2
		8–11–9½	77–16–8			
55		9–0–0	96–6–11¾			

[20] cum Lxj.s. vij.d. ob. de arreragiis Thome forestarii ibidem. Et non plus quia non vendebantur nisi ix acras dim. prati et residuum ad manerium in feno ad vendendum.

[21] preter sustentacionem omnium.

[22] preter sustentacionem omnium.

[23] preter sustentacionem diversorum animalium.

[24] Et non plus quia pars frumenti remanet in garbis.

[25] With Bolton.

[26] excepto feno.

[27] Unckethorp respondit de claro de nichil hoc anno.

[28] Halton respondit de claro de nichil propter mortem conuersi.

[29] Kyldewyk respondit de claro de nichil preter de feno et cariagio forinseco.

[30] preter cariagium.

[31] With Bolton.

[32] MS blank.

[33] Unckethorp Respondit de nichil hoc anno.

[34] Kyldwyk de nichil preter fenum.

[35] With Bolton.

[36] MS blank.

[37] Unckethorp Respondit de claro de nichil set resumpsit viij.s.j.d.

[38] Halton Respondit de claro de nichil set resumpsit Lj.s. v.d. ob.

[39] Condeley respondit de claro de nichil hoc anno.

[40] Ryth' respondit de claro per conuencionem de x.li.

[41] Unckthorp respondit de claro de nichil hoc anno.

[42] Ryddyngs respondit de claro de nichil set resumit xxviij.s. vj.d.

[43] Angrum respondit de claro de nichil set resumit Lv.s. v.d.

[44] Conedley respondit de claro de nichil set resumpsit in blado et denariis viij.li. vj.s. ob.

[45] Ryth' respondit de claro per conuencionem de x.li.

[46] But some grain sent to Halton and Angrum.

[47] Unckthorp respondit de claro de nichil set resumpsit xiij.li. xij.s. viij.d. ob.

[48] Halton respondit de claro de nichil set resumpsit in denariis blado liberacione et roba seruientis . . . (figure illegible).

[49] MS blank.

[50] MS blank.

[51] respondit de claro per conuencionem ix.li. x.s.

[52] ex conuencione.

[53] nichil set multum resumpsit.

[54] preter vij.li. xviij.d. solutos pro factura unius noue grangie.

[55] Rither and Stead conjointly £6.

NB From 1305–6, the Priory began to give a *Summa* of the profit of all granges, as follows:
1305–6 £94 13s. 10½d; 1306–7 left blank. 1308–9 left blank; 1309–10 left blank; 1310–11 £139 13s. 6d; 1312–13 left blank; 1313–14 £85 11s. 0d.
In 1310–11, 1311–12, 1312–13, 1313–14, 1316–17, the statement is qualified by the following:
De semine vero nec de conduccione nec de valore terre non fit mencio (fos. 237ᵛ, 264ᵛ, 297ᵛ, 325ᵛ, 394ᵛ).

The *Clarum* for 1295–6 and 1296–7 for Cononley and Rither is elaborated in some detail, and reflects the principles of the calculation.

1295–6. (Cononley) Memorandum quod manerium de Conedley Respondit hoc anno de xiij quarteriis auene precium quarterii ijs. vjd. Et de Ls. in denariis. Et de vjs. jd. in fossis factis in diuersis locis. De quibus subtrauntur xxxvs. pro iij quarteriis dim. frumenti receptis de decima de Carleton ad semen. Et sic respondit manerium hoc anno de claro de Liijs. vd.

(Rither) Memorandum quod manerium de Conodley [sic] respondit hoc anno de xij quarteriis dim. auene precium quarterii xxd. Et de xlvijs. jd. ob. in denariis liberatis.

Summa Lxvijs. xjd. ob. Preter fenum in expensis equorum.

1296–7. Clarum de maneriis.

Rither. Memorandum quod manerium de Rithert respondit hoc anno de claro De xj quarteriis frumenti precium quarterii iiijs. viijd. Et de vj bus. siliginis precium bus. vjd. Et de viij quarteriis auene precium quarterii xxd. Et de xxxixs. xjd. in denariis.

Summa de claro Cviijs. xjd. preter fenum.

Conodley. Manerium de Conodley respondit hoc anno de claro De vj quarteriis frumenti precium quarterii ijs. viijd. Et de iiij quarteriis dim. siliginis precium quarterii iijs. iiijd. Et de xij quarteriis auene precium quarterii xviijd. Et de xx plaustratis feni precium plaustrate vjd. Et de xvijs. iiijd. in denariis liberatis.

Summa iiij l.i. ijs. iiijd

.Until 1299–1300, the *Clarum* included a full list of the constituents and deductions. From 1300–5, there is no *Clarum* section. When the *Clarum* reappears in 1305–6, it is a simple statement, omitting the constituents, such as:

Manerium de Boulton Respondit de Claro hoc anno de xlij li. xiijs. jd. ob. (fo. 125^r).

The single exception is Holmpton from 1314–17 (fos. 354^v, 374^v, 394^r). The *Clarum* was omitted completely in 1318–19, 1320–1, 1323–4, and 1324–5.

Source: Chatsworth MS 73A, fos. 27^r, 31^v–32^r.

APPENDIX 4.5 STUBBINGTON FIGURES. MANOR OF SOUTHWICK PRIORY

1268	Valet hoc anno manerium in omnimodis exitibus deductis necessariis expensis iiij^{xx}iiij libras vij s jd qua. Cum tota decima infra pontem.	?1281	Et valet in hoc anno iiij^{xx}xiiij li. ixd. ob.
		1287–8	Valet hoc anno manerium de Stubinton' deductis expensis necessariis Lxviij libras xviijs. ixd. ob.
1268–9	Et valet hoc anno manerium deductis expensis necessariis in omnimodis expensis cum tota Decima infra Portesbrig' C libras vs viijd ob.	1319–20	Et valet manerium hoc anno Lxxix li. vs. jd.
		1330–1	Et valet manerium hoc anno Cxix li. vs.
		1344–5	Et valet manerium hoc anno Lxxij li. viijs. Ideo minus pro defectu bladi hoc anno.
1270	Et valet hoc anno manerium deductis omnimodis expensis necessariis cum omnimodis Exitibus* C et vij libras ij sol. iijd. ob. *expensis necessariis cancelled, Exitibus superscript.	1351–2	Valor hoc anno xx marce. Ideo minus causa pestilencie.
		c.1405	Valor huius manerii hoc anno cum decimis personatus. Lxxix. li. xiijs. vjd.

(This broken series of accounts runs from c.1247 to the early fifteenth century. The survival of the earliest accounts, c.1247 to 1268, is quite fair, but the *valor* does not appear on the accounts until 1268. The series thereafter is very sporadic.)

Source: Winchester College Muniments 15376–87.

POSTSCRIPT

One of the questions which was insufficiently explored in the article of 1986 concerned the technique of comparing accounts with the extent, mainly because of lack of good evidence, except for the estates of the Bishopric of Worcester. A further avenue of research might be through any 'status maneriorum' which includes a note of the 'proficuum'. Such documents seem to be rare, but it may be that they can reveal more about the process of calculating 'profit'. The statement of 'profit' was added at the foot of the manorial rolls of the Lichfield estates, but it is now evident that, at least in some years, these peremptory statements were collected together in a centralized 'status maneriorum', of which one of 1279–81 or 1313–15 (printed below) survives. The 'status' consisted simply of the *valor* (or calculation of 'profit') from the manorial account and a memorandum recording the grain remaining in the barns. This 'status' confirms the particular central interest in the calculation of 'profit' in the late thirteenth century on medium-sized estates, extending to central enrolment of the 'profit'.

Lichfield Joint Record Office SSI

Status maneriorum de Pychcheford Hammelacy Stokelacy Oldebury et Tassele

Pychchef' De eodem manerio computatur per Reginaldum prepositum a festo sancti Michaelis anno regni Regis E viij usque festum sancti Michaelis anno regni regis eiusdem nono Et valet manerium hoc anno .xxij. li.

Blada istius manerii remanent integraliter in garbis scilicet de frumento et siligine per estimacionem .L. quarteria Et de auena .Lxx. quarteria

Stoke lacy De eodem manerio computatur per Ricardum prepositum de anno regni Edwardi viij Et valet manerium hoc anno .xix. li.

Blada ibidem existencia in garbis vix sufficientia pro liberacionibus et semine istius manerii et de hamme

Hamme De eodem manerio computatur per Philippum Balliuum de anno regni Edwardi viij Et valet manerium hoc anno .vj. li. xv.s.

[mld]

Oldebury   De anno Regis Edwardi septimo computatur per Willelmum de Dune seruientem   Et valet manerium hoc anno .vij. li. x.s.

De anno Regis Edwardi viij computatur per eundem   Et valet manerium hoc anno .vj. li. xiij. s. iiij.d.   Sunt ibidem per estimacionem de frumento .xxx. quarteria de Auena .xl. quarteria De ordeo .vj. quarteria De pisis et vescis .x. quarteria

Stretton   De eodem manerio computatur per Thomam de Pesale seruientem de anno Regis E viij   Et valet manerium hoc anno .Cij.s. Et de .x. li. xix. s. iij.d. de blado vendito

5 · AGENCY AND THE *EXCESSUS* BALANCE IN MANORIAL ACCOUNTS

C. Noke

THE BALANCE OF A MANORIAL ACCOUNT

A common occurrence at the bottom of the account rolls of thirteenth and fourteenth century manors was an *arreragia* (or *remanencia*) balance where the sum of the charge exceeded that of the discharge. It measured the indebtedness of the accounting official to his lord. Common though it was, the exact composition and precise meaning of the balance are none the less not always clear. It may have comprised cash in the hands of the accountant, debts due but not yet received by the accountant (e.g. for rent or commuted labour services), balances brought forward from previous accounts or accountants, or some combination of these (Denholm-Young 1937: 127; Davies 1968). It is not clear, either, whether any special significance can be attached to those forms of account following the Winchester model where the accounting official pays over the balance at or shortly after the audit or before the next account is heard, and is given his acquittance, or to those following the Westminster model where the *arreragia* are carried forward and entered into the following year's charge (Oschinsky 1971: 215; Noke 1981: 143). Yet more puzzling, however, as Postles (1981: 105) has pointed out, is the *excessus* balance, where the sum of the discharge exceeds that of the charge, for this raises the question—as Postles puts it—'How can the outgoings be held to have exceeded the income? Surely it was impossible for the accounting official to have spent more than he received.'

Some of the best known treatises on estate management and accounting which were in circulation at the time do not appear to provide for this

First published in *Accounting and Business Research* (1991). The author is grateful to P. D. A. Harvey, Michael Bromwich, Christopher Napier, and an anonymous referee for their helpful comments.

possibility. Walter of Henley, for example, considers only the *arreragia* balance when he instructs:

And if any arrerages happen upon the finall accompt let it be quickelye levyed. And if thaccomptant name any parson which oweth that arrerage then take youe the name of that man, for often tymes it chaunceth that the servauntes and reeves be the debtors theimselves and yet do make other men the debtors which neyther can nor ought to paye it. And this they doe to cover theire unfaythfulnesse withall. (*c*. 110, in Oschinsky 1971: 341)

The author of the anonymous *Husbandry* also begins his section on the account with the stipulation: 'One owes first for the arrears, if there are any' (c. 37, in Oschinsky 1971: 432) with no corresponding instruction regarding an *excessus* carried forward. And while the account rolls of the Exchequer occasionally show that the sheriff '*habet de superplus*' the *Dialogus de Scaccario* gives no indication as to what should take place when this occurred (Johnson 1950: p. xlvi).

However, rule 4 of the *Regule compoti* of the Account Book of Beaulieu Abbey (believed by Hockey to date from 1269–70) (Hockey 1975) recognizes the possibility of the *excessus* when it explains how it arises and how it should be treated in subsequent accounts:

Excessus est quando aliquis plus expendit quam receperit, et illum excessum in compoto suo tunc proximo futuro solvit in principio expensarum suarum antequam expensas faciat aut liberacionem. Et vocatur supplusagium tunc in proximo compoto, sic. In supplusagio extremi compoti, tantum et c.[1] (in Hockey 1975: 48)

And such possibility is provided for also by the mid-thirteenth century treatise on accounting in MS 7 (BM, Harleian MS. 1005, fos. 93^{r-v}, in Oschinsky 1971: 459) when it ends the *ordo compoti* in part ii with the sentence: 'Finito compotus tantum debet unus vel alter alteri.'[2]

Although the Beaulieu Abbey rules may suggest that the *excessus* is indeed no more than the excess of the amount spent over the amount received, nei-

---

[1] 'The *excessus* arises when someone spends more than he receives, and he satisfies that *excessus* in his next account as the first item of his expenses before he deals with the expenses or the liveries. And it is called *supplusagium* in the next account, i.e. *supplusagium* from the previous account, so much etc.'
However, the word 'solvit' in this rule may be ambiguous. *Solvere* may mean to pay or to free oneself from debt (and is often used as such at the foot of manorial accounts, as in, for example, 'solvit post compotum et quietus est.') If this rule were translated as 'he pays that *excessus* in his next account' that might be consistent with the findings of Postles (1981), and practice on the Crowland Abbey estates, referred to in the text. Although *Freund's Latin Dictionary* shows *expendere* and *solvere* as synonyms, the use of the two words in this rule could therefore well be significant.

[2] 'At the end of the account, so much is owed by one or the other to the other.'

ther those rules, nor MS 7, give any guidance as to how the accountant managed to spend more than he received (if, indeed, he did). The Beaulieu Abbey accounts too are simply illustrative of rule 4, that for Soberton, for example, beginning the *expensa necessaria* with 'in supplusagio extremi compoti x.li.xv.s.vj.d' and ending the account with the simple statement 'et excedit xxj.li.xv.s.iij.d.q.' (Hockey 1975: 115–16)

Postles, however, provides an answer in part to his questions in his study of the accounts of the glebe demesnes of Oseney Abbey, where he shows that the *excessus* there represented items in the discharge which had not actually been paid, i.e. it represented the indebtedness of the reeve to certain creditors. He illustrates this (p. 106) with evidence from the Chastleton account of 1338–9 and the Waterperry accounts of 1339 and 1340, e.g.:

. . . et sic excedit iiij.li. ob. qu. Nomina debiti videlicet vicario loci xxiij.s.x.d. . . . Item pro stipendiis famulorum per totum annum xj.s.viij.d. . . .[3]

Some support for Postles's contention may be found in the accounts of the manors of Crowland Abbey which provide further examples of the *excessus* balance dating from rather earlier than the examples from Oseney Abbey. However, these accounts also suggest other factors affecting the closing balance which may explain the apparent ability of the accountant to spend more than he received.

THE *EXCESSUS* BALANCE AT CROWLAND ABBEY

The account roll of all the Crowland manors for the year 1258–9 contains eleven examples of an *excessus* balance.[4] In each case the money accounts end with variants of the paragraph:

Omnibus ergo computatis subtractis et allocatis dominus debet preposito viij.s x.d.q. Et idem prepositus debet omnia in rotulo compoti contenta adquietare et in stipendiis seruientum prout in rotulo continento scilicet usque ad hanc diem compoti.[5] (Wellingborough, 1258/9)

suggesting that on these manors, as in the Oseney Abbey accounts, it was common to account in both the charge and the discharge on the accrual basis

---

[3] 'And so there is an *excessus* of £4 0s. 0¾d. The names of the creditors, that is to say the vicar of the place 23s. 10d. . . . the wages of the farm labourers for the whole year 11s. 8d. . . .'

[4] Oakington, Dowdike, Whaplode, Aswick Grange, Wellingborough, Addington, Elmington, Morborne, Langtoft, Bowthorpe, and Bucknall.

[5] 'Therefore all things being added, subtracted and allowed for the lord owes the reeve 8s. 10¾d. And the said reeve must settle everything contained in this roll, and the wages of the servants as contained in this roll, up to the day of this account.'

rather than when payment was received or made. It should, however, be noted that similar wording appears also in the accounts of those manors showing the more familiar *arreragia* balance, suggesting that even in those cases the amount shown as owing to the lord was not necessarily a measure of the cash in the hands of the reeve; he may well have been holding money pending payment to creditors. Few of the Crowland accounts give more detail of the composition of the closing balances, though the account roll for the reeves of Wellingborough in 1304–5 is—like the Oseney account rolls—more specific when it notes:

Summa totius expensarum et liberationum xx.li ij.d. ob. q. et sic expense excedunt Receptas in iiij. li. v.sol. j.d. q. quorum lvj. sol. debentur pro stipendiis famulorum.[6]

Thus far the Crowland accounts seem merely to reinforce the findings of Postles. Evidence may also be found elsewhere to support the suggestion that the *excessus* balance includes amounts owing to third parties. For example, in the action of Bogo de Clare against Walter de Reygni in the Exchequer of Pleas in 1286—albeit this was a case involving the keeper of his wardrobe rather than a manorial reeve—an *excessus* of £375 3s. 0d. was found owing to Walter; in evidence, Walter stated that the amount was 'owed to diverse creditors and a certain part to himself' (*Select Cases in the Exchequer of Pleas*, 116). However, the particular interest of the Crowland accounts lies in the way that the *excessus* balance was very common in these accounts for much of the latter part of the thirteenth century, but—on the basis of the admittedly very restricted evidence available—seems to have become less common shortly after the turn of the century. As well as in the 1258–9 rolls referred to above, in the Wellingborough account rolls as edited by Page (1936) an *excessus* balance appears in 1267–8, and although it does not appear in 1271–2 or 1276–7 it otherwise appears twenty times in the reeve's accounts (and several times in the Collector's accounts) in the account rolls available for the period 1280–1313. It does not, however, appear in the rolls for 1314–15 or 1322–3. Of the fewer accounts available for the other manors, as edited by Page (1934), an *excessus* appears in the rolls of Oakington, Drayton, and Cottenham in 1267–8, Oakington 1292–93, and Cottenham 1314–15, but not in those of Drayton or Oakington 1314–15, nor for any of the three Cambridgeshire manors in 1322–3. Surprisingly, given this trend, the balance reappears on the Oakington reeve's account roll 1361–2 where a change in the terminology of the *excessus* is evident; in that account the phrase *Et sic*

---

[6] 'Total expenses and liveries £20 0s. 2¾d. and so the expenses exceed the receipts by £4 5s. 1¼d. of which 56s. is owed for the wages of the farm labourers.'

superexpense c.i.s.xj.d has replaced the more usual form and a separate heading *superexpense* has appeared in the account roll as the first item amongst the expenses: 'Idem computat in superexpensis ultimi compoti anni precedentis ix.li. vij.s.'[7] There is, however, no obvious significance in this change in terminology which may be found elsewhere, particularly in Scottish accounts such as that for the earl of Mar, Chamberlain of Scotland, as early as 1264 (*Exchequer Rolls of Scotland* 1878: 11).

THE *EXCESSUS* AND SALES AT THE AUDIT

What can explain the apparent change in the frequency with which the *excessus* balance occurs? It appears to coincide with the formal introduction into the accounts of 'sales at the audit', the '*venditio super compotum*'. As is well known, following Drew's description of accounting and audit at St Swithun's Priory, Winchester (Drew 1947), these often represented shortfalls in the corn and stock accounts, or other deficiencies, which the accountant was charged with by the auditors when the account was heard, and which were commuted into money and entered in the charge. In the Wellingborough accounts these seem first to appear on the roll for 1312–13, when amongst the receipts Ricardus Palere is charged with:

De iiij quarteriis iij.b. brasei ordei venditis super compotum xxj.sol. iiij.d.ob. Item de xix aucis venditis super compotum iij.sol. xj.d.ob. Item de iiij$\overset{xx}{}$ columbella venditis super compotum xx.d.[8]

On this particular account there was an *arreragia* balance, representing an excess of receipts over expenses of fifteen shillings six pence. It is obvious that the sales at the audit considerably exceed this sum and that had the reeve not been charged with them there would in fact have been an *excessus* balance, as in earlier years. The sums involved at Wellingborough the following year were considerably in excess of this; there was an excess of receipts over payments of 74 shillings but sales at the audit were more than twice this amount, so that again, but for the sales at the audit, there would have been an *excessus* balance.

The other manors of Oakington and Drayton in 1314–15 also include sales at the audit amongst the charge, albeit in those cases not of sufficient

---

[7] 'The same accounts for £9 7s. 0d. *superexpense* from the last account of the preceding year.'

[8] 'For 4 quarters 3 bushels of malt barley sold at the audit 21s. 4½d. For 9 geese sold at the audit 3s. 11½d. For 80 pigeons sold at the audit 20d.'

amount materially to affect the excess of receipts over payments. Interestingly, however, Cottenham's account roll for that year does not include any such sales and as noted earlier it is the only one of the three manors still to show an *excessus* balance. In the 1322–3 roll of Oakington, sales at the audit amount to £9 12s. 1d., compared with an *arreragia* balance, before allowances, of £8 17s. 3d.

The impact of accounting for 'sales at the audit' on reducing the *excessus* balance, often turning it into an *arreragia* balance, does not of course affect the actual nature of the *excessus* in cases where it existed. It does, however, suggest that one should be careful in drawing too definite a distinction between different types of balance or in imparting too great a significance to any particular type of balance. An *excessus* might still be represented by specific amounts owing to sundry creditors just as an *arreragia* balance might still be struck after providing for amounts payable but not yet paid. In some cases, however, we might at least surmise that the *excessus* did indeed represent a genuine excess of payments made over money received—a situation that was in part present in the Bogo de Clare case, noted above—for on the Crowland Abbey estates, although carry forward to the next account was often the method of treating an *excessus* balance, in at least two cases the excess seems to have been paid to the reeve at the time of the account. The Wellingborough account for 1280/1 notes:

Et sic excedunt expense receptas in xxix.sol.vj.d. quos recepit super compotum per manus fratris Thomas de Well[9]

while the Drayton account for 1267/8 concludes:

. . et sic excedunt expense receptum xxxj.s. viij.d. et idem prepositus debet omnia adquietare in hoc rotulo contenta usque ad diem compoti. Memorandum quod dominus soluit dicto preposito omnia arreragia in isto compoto et omnibus aliis precedentibus ita quod quietus est.[10]

Despite the usual injunction here to settle everything contained in the roll, it is at least conceivable that the reason for the *excessus* being paid to the reeve in these cases was that the reeve had in fact financed the manor from his own resources—or from the 'secret reserves' of the manor, not unlike the way in which Chaucer's reeve used to lend his lord the lord's money. And the 'sales

---

[9] 'And so the expenses exceed the receipts by 29s. 6d. which he receives at the account from the hand of brother Thomas de Well.'

[10] 'And so the expenses exceed the receipts by 31s. 8d. and the said reeve must settle everything contained in this account up to the date of the account. Note that the lord paid the reeve all the arrears in this account and in all the other earlier ones and is quit.'

at the audit'—or rather, the fewer such penalties in earlier accounts—might help explain how he did so.

As noted above, sales at the audit often reflected the monetary value of differences between the accountant's claims of yields from corn and livestock and the yields that the auditors expected, based upon standards laid down in treatises on estate management and accounting and, no doubt, their experience. Even after these checks and penalties were introduced as part of the audit, it is likely that the auditors were happy with charging the accountant with the standard yield. As the anonymous author of *Husbandry* recognized:

Now, if the land yields more than the accountant was charged by the method 'by the grain' the lord will lose, if it yields less the accountant will be out of pocket. But although this method of charging corn offers no certainty many people apply it. (c. 4, in Oschinsky 1971: 419)

And we may suspect that often the lord did lose. Drew, for example, points out that at St Swithun's from the 1320s onwards, every manor was showing in its accounts a yield of 60 piglets, 28 goslings, 60 chickens, and 300 eggs, and that since most of the manors could support more breeding stock than this 'a capable, enterprising man could make money in this direction' (Drew 1947: 28). This would be consistent with the 'explicit and illuminating instruction for "cooking accounts"' (Denholm-Young 1946: 100) in Robert Carpenter's treatise (in Oschinsky 1971: 461) when he suggests—amongst other things—that '*ad bene reddendum compotum*'[11] the reeve might, for example, understate the number of lambs born. In short, the enterprising reeve could pay more than he received by using money accumulated from apparently defrauding the lord.[12]

This raises the question why the auditors—presumably with the lord's blessing—appear often to have been content with the meeting of standard yields, given that it would naturally be in the lord's interest to maximize the yield of his demesnes and to minimize fraud. It may be that the tools of agency theory as a branch of positive accounting theory can help explain this.

AGENCY RELATIONSHIPS ON THE MANOR

Jensen and Meckling (1976: 308) have pointed out that an agency relationship is based on a contract, as part of which:

[11] 'For the better rendering of the account.'
[12] Denholm-Young (1946: 100) noted about Carpenter, 'there can be little doubt that [he] was an astute and dishonest fellow who did not scruple to cheat his master. No doubt many others were like him . . .'.

The principal can limit divergences from his interest by establishing appropriate incentives for the agent and by incurring monitoring costs designed to limit the aberrant activities of the agent. In addition in some situations it will pay the agent to expend resources (bonding costs) to guarantee that he will not take certain actions which would harm the principal or to ensure that the principal will be compensated if he does take such actions.

The relationship between the lord and the reeve on the manor may be classified as one of principal and agent. The reeve's day-to-day powers were considerable and, as Bennett (1937: 168) puts it, 'the claims of the reeve to be considered as the "pivot man" of the manorial administrative system are very great'. However, he did not have a totally free hand in decision-making, and in particular was restricted in the expenses he could incur on behalf of the lord; for example, if the treatises are to be taken at face value, he ought not to sell corn or stock without authority from the lord (*Seneschaucy* c. 41, in Oschinsky 1971: 279). From the reeve's point of view, these limitations on his decision-making power may be thought of as examples of the bonding costs cited by Jensen and Meckling (1976: 325), since they would appear to limit the scope for taking advantage of favourable opportunities as they arose. However, it is one thing to posit a principal:agent relationship; it is quite another to suggest that this was founded in any way on contract or agreement.

The reeve was a villein tenant and, according to Plucknett (1954: 7), in many cases his office became compulsory. Bennett (1937: 169) points out that the system for appointment of the reeve varied enormously from one estate to another. In some places it depended purely on autocratic selection by the lord, and in such cases the idea of a consensual relationship seems hard to accept. In other cases, however, selection of the reeve might be by preliminary selection by the peasants, with final selection by the lord, or by democratic election by the peasants. The idea of agreeing to act seems more credible in these circumstances, particularly once allowance is made for the possibility of paying a fine to avoid having to serve as reeve, a practice that became fairly common[13] (*Select Pleas in Manorial Courts* 1889: 23, 45, 168; Bennett 1937: 171, Drew 1947: 27). If one could avoid service by paying a fine, willingness to serve seems more consensual and may be regarded as compatible with the

---

[13] For example, in the pleas of the manor of the abbey of Bec in 1275 it is noted that 'William Ketelburn gives the lord 6s. 8d. that he may be removed from the office of reeve', and in 1296 'John Robin offered lord a mark of silver for leave to retire from the office of reeve' (*Select Pleas in Manorial Courts* 1889: 23, 45). In the cases noted by Drew (1947: 27) the fines appear to be rather larger, e.g. 40s. in Portland in 1311, 20s. in Michelmersh in 1325; this may be why, according to Drew, few villeins at St Swithuns chose to pay the fine.

requirement that a contract for service must be sufficiently attractive to prevent the agent offering his services elsewhere—or in this case not offering his service at all. Combined with the swearing in by the lord or his steward in the presence of the court (Bennett 1937: 172), during which the reeve no doubt took an oath to carry out his duties honestly and to account to the lord for his doings, the idea of at least a quasi-contractual relationship seems less absurd. Indeed, Chaucer—a perceptive observer of these matters—notes in his General Prologue that the reeve:

> . . . by his covenant yaf the rekenynge
> Syn that his lord was twenty yeer of age.

The term 'covenant' may be taken as corresponding to 'contract' nowadays. (It is worth observing that Chaucer's reeve appears to have served his lord for many years in a relationship that was presumably found satisfactory to both parties.)

In keeping with the assumptions of agency theory, there are clearly reasons to believe that the reeve would not always act in the best interests of his master. The treatises were well aware of the incentive to cheat. Quite apart from Robert Carpenter's text on creative accounting, Walter of Henley warns:

Suche as have other mens things in theire custodie ought by good reason to knowe theise fowre things: to love theire maister and to feare him; and in making of profite they ought to thynke that the thing is theire owne but in making expence they should thynke it an other mans. But fewe servauntes or reeves bee theare which have alle theise iiii things together. Yea, many theare bee which have loste the first three and doe reteyne the fourthe but yet have turned it out of his right course. And knowing that the thing is an other mans and not theire owne they take it with the right hand and the lefte as they may best extort it and theire unfaithfulnes not be perceaved. (c. III, 112 in Oschinsky 1971: 341)

And Walter gives a specific warning that:

it cometh often to passe that those which buy and selle doe in their accompt increase the things boughte and dyminishe the things solde. If you bee to selle or buy [by weight] bee well advised for theare is muche fraude to suche as cannot espie it. (c. 108, in Oschinsky 1971: 341)

Indeed, the scope for personal enrichment is well illustrated by the accusations levelled against Michael Reeve on the Elton (Hunts.) Manor of the Abbey of Ramsey in 1278 (*Select Pleas in Manorial Courts* 1889: 95), when he complained that his defamers had accused him of:

collecting his own hay by means of the labour services due to the Abbot, and with reaping his own crop in autumn by means of boon works done by the abbot's customers, and with ploughing his own land in Eversholmfield by means of ploughs booned from the vill and with releasing the customers from their labours and carrying service on condition of their letting and handing over their land to him at a cheap rate, and of taking gifts from the richer tenants as a consideration for not turning them into tenants at money rents and with obliging the poorer tenants to become payers of money rent.

He received damages from his defamers for their 'vile words'.

The management problem facing the lord, therefore, was deciding on what terms to deal with the reeve to ensure that the reeve acted in the interest of the lord. Agency theory suggests that the principal will try to devise an incentive scheme to get the agent to act in the principal's interest while the agent may incur bonding costs as evidence of his good faith.

INCENTIVES AND BONDING

As far as bonding costs go, the reeve might be said to have incurred such costs in a number of ways. First, he was personally liable for errors, omissions, and sins of commission and was therefore effectively pledging his all against his good behaviour and wise administration. Secondly, these pledges may often have extended beyond the possessions of the reeve himself, for *Husbandry* is specific that:

All those on the manor who hold in villenage of the lord ought to elect as reeve some one for whom they are willing to be responsible, because if the lord suffers any loss through the fault of the reeve and if the reeve has no property of his own to repay the loss, they will have to pay for anything which he cannot pay from his own pocket. (c. 55 in Oschinsky, 1971: 441)

Plucknett (1954: 7) further points out that in some places where the reeve was elected by the villeins 'villeins were ready to buy this privilege although it carried with it the corollary that they became liable to guarantee the reeve's account'. This could be taken as an example of 'explicit bonding against malfeasance on the part of the manager' (Jensen and Meckling 1976: 325) (though it is certainly different from the more obvious examples of 'bonding' by medieval guild masters and wardens, cited in Watts and Zimmerman 1983: 618, who by the fifteenth century at least were apparently often required to post bonds, the balance of which would be returned on their retirement). Although the residual claimant to the benefits of the manor was the lord, it would also seem to follow from this doctrine of strict liability that the residual loss—at least to the extent that it was thought to be within his control—was borne by the reeve, perhaps a rather unusual bearing of risk in a principal : agent relationship.[14] Indeed, it may be presumed that, on those manors where it was possible to pay a fine to avoid service as reeve, it was the risk-averse reeve who did so, to avoid just these sorts of risk. Those who chose to serve—and often to serve for more than one term—must presumably have thought the rewards sufficient to compensate for the risks assumed.

As far as rewarding the agent goes, in a situation where the principal can observe the effort expended by the agent, or can deduce the effort from *ex post* knowledge of the state of the world, agency theory suggests that an incentive contract would pay the agent a fixed sum if he takes proper action and impose a penalty if he shirks his responsibility. When the principal cannot observe the agent's efforts, it is likely to be optimal to have the agent share in the outcome of his efforts so as to provide the incentive (Watts and Zimmerman 1986: 185). The typical arrangement with the reeve may be considered in this light.

Naturally, the precise terms of service differed from one manor to another. Drew (1947: 38) has shown that on the typical manor of St Swithun's Priory the reeve received no direct wage as such. However, his rent was remitted, as were his customary works, and he usually received a lamb and a fleece and sometimes a piglet and cheese. Moreover he was entitled to feed at the lord's expense during the harvest period. Together these might have amounted to some 24s. per annum. Bennett (1937: 158, 176) has suggested that the reeve was often given a small money payment (five shillings at Berkhamsted in 1300), but that the bulk of his remuneration came from remission of rent, the temporary grant of special pieces of meadow or close, and the relaxation of many services. In the Crowland accounts the most common allowance appears to be allowance of rent; for example, the account roll for Oakington regularly contains an allowance, amongst the discharge, of four shillings for the reeve's rent remitted.

The formal remuneration of the reeve would thus appear to consist of a largely fixed package. Moreover, as part of this arrangement, even before sales at the audit were formally instituted, the auditors would impose occasional penalties on the reeve for underachievement (e.g. in prices obtained or quantities produced); this would be evidenced by striking items through on the face

---

[14] In the analysis of residual claims by Fama and Jensen (1983: 328) it is envisaged that 'the contract structures of organisations limit the risks undertaken by most agents by specifying either fixed payoffs or incentive payoffs tied to specific measures of performance. The residual risk is borne by those who contract for the rights to net cash flows.'

of the accounts and substituting larger amounts (Drew 1947: 17; Harvey 1976: 52). The arrangement would therefore seem to be compatible with the situation where the principal can observe or deduce effort by the agent. However, it is obvious from the size of some of the penalties imposed on him—as from the size of the more formal 'sales at the audit'—that the reeve could not possibly pay them from the meagre fixed remuneration he was given. For example, Drew (1947: 20) has shown that in 1267 the reeve of Stockton suffered penalties totalling £8 3s. 8d., while it was noted above that at Oakington in 1322–3 sales at the audit amounted to £9 12s. 1d. Hoskin and Macve (1986: 115) conclude from this that the auditors' control of the reeve was more apparent than real. But a different explanation, still compatible with an agency-theoretic approach, is possible. This is that, provided some predetermined yields were achieved, the lord was prepared to permit the reeve at least to share in—if not take the whole of—any excess, as his incentive for good performance. In other words, he was effectively adopting an outcome-related contract, or more specifically a budget-based contract which, at its most generous and most severe, would be of the form $Y_A = a + (X - b)$ where Y_A = the reeve's income, a = a fixed sum, X = outcome and b = a predetermined yield. Thus, the enterprising reeve was not so much defrauding his lord as benefiting from the results of his good administration, and contributing to an increase in the utility of both of them. This in turn—in answer to Postles' question posed earlier—would allow the successful reeve ample funds to spend more than he received.[15] What is more, this approach would appear to be consistent with the treatment of the Sheriffs in the Royal Exchequer, who—in the twelfth century at least—were charged with the fixed 'farm' part of their receipts without enquiry being made as to how much they had actually been able to raise from the royal manors (Poole 1912: 129). The difference would represent their incentive to collect the king's revenues.

However, it was noted above that on the Crowland Abbey estates the incidence of the *excessus* balance diminished as that of 'sales at the audit' increased and we may surmise from this that it coincided with a reduction in the overall financial package that the reeve was able to enjoy. This seems to have occurred also at St Swithun's, for Drew (1947: 21) notes that in the late thir-

---

[15] There are obvious problems in ascertaining the effort expended by an agent in an agricultural situation. For example, although it might be thought that *ex post* knowledge of the actual state of the world such as weather conditions would help in ascertaining effort and honesty yet, 'although many manorial accounts contain references to weather conditions, correlations between patterns of weather and crop yields are poor' (Pretty 1990: 12. See also Titow 1960.) An outcome-related contract would overcome many of these problems.

teenth century penalties in the accounts were comparatively rare and 'in the days to come, reeves and serjeants looked back on this 1270–1315 period as a sort of "golden age"'. That raises the question why auditors and lords tightened up during the early fourteenth century. It may simply have been that with greater experience, and the greater spread of treatises on estate management, knowledge of what could be achieved as 'standard' became more widespread and it became easier to ensure an increase in the lord's utility whilst still providing sufficient—if reduced—incentive for the reeve. This would then represent a further change in a single course of development stretching from the early thirteenth to the mid-fourteenth century whereby the lord's control of the reeve became less and less direct and correspondingly less expensive; first a hierarchy of supervisors had been replaced by a system of written accounts and audit, then the reeve was effectively made part-lessee by the requirement for predetermined returns.

MONITORING COSTS

Agency theory not only seeks to explain the design of incentive contracts; it suggests also that the principal or agent will incur monitoring costs to see that the contract is kept to. And it is therefore entirely consistent with the theory that the lord should incur monitoring costs by way of the annual audit of the reeve's account by the lord's auditors (and sometimes by the view of account during the course of the year). Examples of the costs of the audit—which largely took the form of subsistence rather than any direct payment (though payment would occasionally be made to the scribe for preparing the roll)—are often found on the accounts themselves. For example, the account of Wellingborough in 1322 includes the following amongst the discharge:

In aduentu magistri Johannis rectoris . . . et Ricardi de Glatton ad visum compoti faciendum die Lune in . . . Evangeliste et in moram eorum die martis sequente et die mercurie. In pane ij. sol.ij.d. In ceruisia xv.d.ob. In carne bouina viij.d. In carne porcula vij.d. In carne iuuenculia iiij.d. In alettis et pisce iiij.d. In alaudis ij.d.q. In ouis j.d.ob. In allea pipere croco et . . . j.d.ob. Item in expensis Roberti clerici a die Sabbatici in vigilia sancti Luce Ewangeliste usque diem Lune in aduentu Ricardi de Glatton per duos dies et in moram suam post recessum Ricardi de Glatton a die Jouis sequente usque diem martis per quinque dies pro compoto . . . In pane iiij.d. In ceruisia vij.d. In carne vj.d. In allecis et pisce iiij.d. In ouis j.d.ob. In ij libris candele iiij.d.[16]

---

[16] 'For the visit of master John the rector . . . and Richard of Glatton to make a view of the account on the Monday of . . . the Evangelist and for their lodging on the following Tuesday and Wednesday. For

The counter roll for Bosham in Sussex (cited in Denholm-Young 1937: 133) is more concise when it notes:

In expensis computatorum pro compoto audiendo per talliam xlj.s. i.d. et quad.[17]

On the reeve's part, too, it would be entirely consistent with the reasoning of agency theory that he should agree to render the annual *compotus*.

The tenets of agency theory are often used to illustrate the voluntary undertaking of accounting and audit even in the absence of any legal regulation; the place of the law is seen as enforcing the contract at the heart of the theory. While agency theory might be consistent with the accounting and monitoring activities of medieval manors, the question as to whether those activities can be explained solely by the theory is at least debatable. Certainly as far as the reeve is concerned the distinction between a 'legal' requirement to account and a voluntary one might be thought a very fine one, depending on how one interprets 'legal'. As a villein tenant the reeve 'had his problems settled for him summarily in his lord's domestic or manorial jurisdiction' (Plucknett 1954: 31) and a reeve who failed to render his account would no doubt soon find himself amerced by his lord. Whether such amercement should be regarded as the use of 'law' to enforce an agreement, or whether it might be thought to represent an implicit legal requirement to account, is debatable. However, in some cases the accounting official was not the reeve at all, but rather a freeman, usually a bailiff. And of him Denholm-Young (1947: 154) notes:

the bailiff was more elusive than the reeve. He took oaths of fealty, found pledges, and so forth, but apparently seignorial justice was insufficient to deal with him. The aid of the exchequer had to be invoked. To deal with malfeasing officials an action of account arose. . . .

AGENCY AND THE ACTION OF ACCOUNT

In looking at agency and medieval auditing, Mills (1990) discusses the action of account. Following Langdell (1889) she stresses however that:

---

bread 2s. 2d. For ale 15½d. For beef 8d. For pork 7d. For veal 3d. For herrings and fish 3d. For larks 2¼d. For eggs 1¼d. For mustard, pepper, saffron . . . 1¼d. For the expenses of Robert the clerk on the Saturday of the eve of St Luke the Evangelist until the Monday of Richard of Glatton's arrival, for two days and for his lodging after the departure of Richard of Glatton on the Thursday following until the Tuesday, for five days for the account. . . . For bread 4d. For ale 7d. For meat 6d. For herrings and fish 4d. For eggs 1¼d. For two pounds of candles 4d.'

[17] 'For the expenses of the accountants to audit the account 41s. 1¼d. by tally.' Denholm-Young points out, however, that this is a drastic compression of the detail in the view.

the obligation to render account was not based on contract. The requirement was non-contractual in nature and was considered to exist independently of any agreement between agent and principal. (p. 62)

This view is supported by Plucknett when he points out that, far from being based on contract, by the fourteenth century it had been made clear that one could not even contract to make oneself subject to the action of account (Plucknett 1956: 635). Either the relationship giving rise to the action existed or it did not. Mills concludes that if the purpose of historically based studies 'is to argue that audits would exist without any legal intervention beyond enforcement of contract, the pre-modern evidence is at present insufficient to substantiate this claim' (1990: 62).

However, in considering agency theory and an unregulated environment, it is necessary to try to look at the situation before the action of account was invented. Before then, even if the duty to account could be said to have existed, there appears to have been no way it could be enforced in the courts. And without a remedy there was no right (and hence no obligation). At most there may have been a moral obligation to account. Prior to the action of account, all that existed was the action of debt, which applied only to liquidated sums, or covenant, which was limited to actions on agreements which were evidenced by sealed writings (Belsheim 1932: 469). In such an essentially unregulated environment, it could be argued that the account—when rendered—was rendered voluntarily, as a result of the relationship entered into between the lord and the accountant.

The problem, however, is in trying to identify just when the action arose, and how this related to the prior existence of manorial accounting. According to Fifoot (1949: 268) the action appears first to have been recorded *circa* 1200 when:

the bailiff to the Archbishop of Canterbury was brought into the Curia Regis to explain why he had failed to render an account of chattels committed to his charge. . . . By 1232 the pleadings in such actions seem to have been crystallised although no writ of account appeared upon the Register until the middle of the century.

On the other hand, according to Hall (1903: p. xii), reference to a bailiff's *compotus* occurs as early as 1170, clearly predating the first recorded action. Moreover, there are reasons for believing that oral accounting and audit was a common occurrence on manorial estates long before the development of written accounts (Harvey 1976: 15, 31; Noke 1981: 138). If the appearance of the writ on the register is taken as formal recognition of the action, there would seem to be some fifty or so critical years during which written manorial accounting and audit developed outside the common law, and a rather longer period since oral accounting had developed.

However, Van Caenegem (1959: 345) has identified 'a solitary precursor of the writ' from *circa* 1163. This writ required Emelina de Ros to account for expenses and profits to the Abbot of St Augustines, Canterbury, 'as she and her ancestors in Henry I's time had done'. Van Caenegem notes about the writ that 'it seems that an executive measure, outside the courts, and to the benefit of individuals, is at the origin of what was later to become a distinct plea in the royal courts'. The question is whether such a writ, founded as it seems on custom in a particular case, might be thought to represent a general legal concept of accountability, or merely one peculiar to the facts. Certainly Stoljar (1964: 204) argues that the action of account proper 'did not begin as the expression of a general principle, such as a principle of accountability, of application to all manner of agents and fiduciaries. The action began rather as a specific remedy for an exceptional case' (the exceptional case being 'a special class of accountants: manorial bailiffs failing to account for money received and collected . . .').

The problem of trying to establish which came first—accounting or the obligation to account—is complicated by the thirteenth century (and earlier) system of justice. As Plucknett (1954: 23) notes, 'In the thirteenth century the bulk of the nation's litigation did not take place in the king's court but in the county courts . . . and so the absence or rarity of the action cannot be deduced from an examination of the plea rolls. Although rare in the king's court, actions of account may well have been frequent, by writs of *justicies*, in the county courts'.

However, whatever its relationship in time with manorial accounts, it may in any case be suggested that the action of account merely implies a prior obligation to *account*, not necessarily to submit to an *audit* (albeit the action itself involved the use of auditors appointed by the court). Since a voluntary accounting was a bar to an action of account (Baker 1990: 412), rendering an account that was not audited may well have sufficed. Milsom (1966: 544) notes that 'if a relationship of accountability existed between the parties it should be ended by an account; and this could be formal or private. A private accounting was as much a cause of action in debt as a formal account before auditors. . . . It was also as effective a plea if an action of account was brought on the original relationship.' All that was required to justify a plea of *plene computavit* as a defence to the action was for the 'defendant to show that he and the plaintiff had agreed upon all items of the account and had struck a balance' (Langdell 1889: 252). If an unaudited account was sufficient then it may be suggested that the monitoring of the accountant's actions that seems to have accompanied most manorial accounts was not itself a legal requirement but one that may be explained by agency theory.

In any case, it is important to note also that once the action of account had evolved, and brought with it an implied obligation to account, one of the defences to the action that a bailiff could plead was that it had been agreed that he would be free of the obligation to account, i.e. it was possible as part of the contract defining the relationship to contract out of the obligation. This is clear from the case of *Rivers* v. *Iseude* in 1311, where it was accepted as a defence to an action brought by Richard de Rivers against William Iseude that, by letters patent, Richard had 'granted for himself and his heirs that the said William should be quit of every kind of action of account' (Year Book 5, Edward II, 1311, p. 4). And the deed appointing William as Bailiff of West Mersea was accepted as evidence of this agreement.

THE ACTION OF ACCOUNT AND THE *EXCESSUS* BALANCE

As was noted above in relation to the Bogo de Clare case, the outcome of an action of account was sometimes the finding of an *excessus* balance in favour of the accountant. And it is clear from such actions that this balance must have represented payments made by the bailiff from his own money (whatever the source of that). However, those cases where the accountant was found in credit provide some interesting observations on the 'one way character of accounting relationships which treated payments as diminishing the obligations created by receipts but not as creating positive claims' (Milsom 1966: 540). Langdell (1889: 252) explains the problem:

The theory of these items of discharge was that they were paid by the defendant, not out of his own pocket, but out of the money in his hands belonging to the plaintiff; and hence they did not constitute independent claims in favor of the defendant and against the plaintiff, but were mere items in the account; and the only way in which the defendant could enforce them or avail himself of them was by procuring them to be allowed in his account. And this was so, even though as sometimes happened the defendant's payment exceeded his receipts. . . .

The accountant in credit therefore had to rely on the audit for his justice, and the audit, under the action of account, had to be conducted—in the words of Bereford CJ in 1311—according to 'reason and equity' (Plucknett 1954: 28). These words were reiterated in 1326 by Stonor J. in a case where an *excessus* balance arose, when he noted:

Account shall be conducted by equity and not by the rigour of the law, as by allowing things which ought to be allowed and by disallowing things which ought to be disallowed; wherefore, since it is found before the auditors that he had used his own money for the profit of the manor, and that allowance was given to him for this in the account, it seems that is enough to entitle him to be answered. (Quoted in Plucknett 1954: 29)

It would appear, however, that, in view of this one-way accountable relationship, an accountant who knew himself to be in credit was not able to bring an action of account against the lord, and if the lord refused to assign auditors to hear the account, or to hear it himself, presumably there was little the accountant could do.[18]

CONCLUDING COMMENTS

There are obvious problems in trying to compare historical relationships based on feudal institutions to the relationships posited by modern economic theory where free agents may contract as they wish. There may be problems, too, caused by chance survival of legal and accounting records. However, it does seem tenable that many of the financial relationships between a lord and the reeve may be explained by the tenets of agency theory and that manorial accounting and audit would have existed—and indeed did exist—independently of any general legal concept of accountability.

The *excessus* balance—as Postles noted—is an ambiguous phenomenon, reversing as it did the normal indebtedness between lord and reeve, and raising the question how the accountant paid more than he received. Both the existence of the balance, and its subsequent scarcity, may, however, be seen to be compatible with that aspect of agency theory which strives to ensure and explain maximization of the joint utility of principal and agent through the design of incentive schemes for remuneration.

---

[18] A further technical distinction in the nature of the relationship is shown by the different treatment accorded by the law to the lord in credit compared with the accountant in credit. If the auditors found a balance owing to the lord, they could commit the accountant to prison until he paid what was owing. If, however, the balance were in favour of the accountant, the auditors had no power to commit the lord, nor could they order payment of the amount due. In such circumstances the accountant had to bring an action of debt to enforce payment of the amount due to him. Even then the lord was able to wage his law; such wager was, however, denied to the accountant even when, as occurred later on, the auditors lost their power to commit so that the lord had to bring an action of debt to recover the amount due (Milsom 1981: 277).

References

Baker, J. H. (1990), *An Introduction to English Legal History* (London: Butterworths, 3rd edn.).

Belsheim, E. O. (1932), 'The Old Action of Account', *Harvard Law Review*, 45/3.

Bennett, H. S. (1937), *Life on the English Manor* (Cambridge: Cambridge University Press).

Davies, R. R. (1968), 'Baronial Accounts, Incomes, and Arrears in the Later Middle Ages', *Economic History Review*, 2nd series, 21/2.

Denholm-Young, N. (1937), *Seignorial Administration in England* (London: Frank Cass & Co.).

——(1946), 'Robert Carpenter and the Provisions of Westminster', *Collected Papers on Medieval Subjects* (Oxford: Basil Blackwell).

Drew, J. S. (1947), 'Manorial Accounts of St Swithuns Priory, Winchester', *English Historical Review*, 62.

The Exchequer Rolls of Scotland (1878), vol. i, ed. J. Stuart and G. Burnett (Edinburgh: HM General Register House).

Fama, E. F., and Jensen, M. C. (1983), 'Agency Problems and Residual Claims', *Journal of Law and Economics*, 26.

Fifoot, C. H. S. (1949), *History and Sources of the Common Law: Tort and Contract* (London: Steven and Son).

Hall, H. (1903), *Pipe Roll of the Bishopric of Winchester 1208–09* (London: London School of Economics).

Harvey, P. D. A. (1976), *Manorial Records of Cuxham, Oxfordshire, c. 1200–1359* (London: HMSO).

Hockey, S. F. (1975), *The Account Book of Beaulieu Abbey* (London: Royal Historical Society).

Hoskin, K. W., and Macve, R. H. (1986), 'Accounting and the Examination: A Genealogy of Disciplinary Power', *Accounting, Organizations and Society*, 11/2.

Jensen, M. C., and Meckling, W. H. (1976), 'Theory of the Firm: Managerial Behavior, Agency Costs and Ownership Structure', *Journal of Financial Economics*, 3.

Johnson, C. (ed.) (1950), *Dialogus de Scaccario* (London: Thomas Nelson and Son).

Langdell, C. C. (1889), 'A Brief Survey of Equity Jurisdiction', *Harvard Law Review*, 2/6.

Mills, P. A. (1990), 'Agency, Auditing and the Unregulated Environment: Some Further Historical Evidence,' *Accounting Auditing and Accountability Journal*, 3/1.

Milsom, S. F. C. (1966), 'Account Stated in the Action of Debt', *Law Quarterly Review*, 82.

——(1981), *The Historical Foundations of the Common Law* (London: Butterworths, 2nd edn.).

Noke, C. (1981), 'Accounting for Bailiffship in Thirteenth Century England', *Accounting and Business Research*, 42.

Oschinsky, D. (1971), *Walter of Henley and Other Treatises on Estate Management and Accounting* (Oxford: Oxford University Press).

Page, F. M. (1934), *The Estates of Crowland Abbey* (Cambridge: Cambridge University Press.

——(1936), *Wellingborough Manorial Accounts A.D. 1258–1323* (Kettering: Northamptonshire Record Society).

Plucknett, T. F. T. (1954), *The Mediaeval Bailiff* (London: University of London).

——(1956), *A Concise History of the Common Law* (London: Butterworth, 5th edn.).

Poole, R. L. (1912), *The Exchequer in the Twelfth Century* (Oxford: Clarendon Press).

Postles, D. (1981), 'The *Excessus* Balance in Manorial Accounts', *Bulletin of the Institute of Historical Research*, 54/129.

Pretty, J. N. (1990), 'Sustainable Agriculture in the Middle Ages: The English Manor', *Agricultural History Review*, 38.

Select Cases in the Exchequer of Pleas (1932), ed. H. Jenkinson and B. E. R. Formay, Selden Society, vol. 48 (London: Bernard Quaritch).

Select Pleas in Manorial and other Seignorial Courts (1889), vol. i, ed. F. W. Maitland, Selden Society, vol. 2 (London: Bernard Quaritch).

Stoljar, S. J. (1964), 'The Transformation of Account', *Law Quarterly Review*, 80.

Titow, J. (1960), 'Evidence of Weather in the Account Rolls of the Bishopric of Winchester 1209–1350', *Economic History Review*, 2nd series, 12/3.

Van Caenegem, R. C. (1959), *Royal Writs in England from the Conquest to Glanvill*, Selden Society, vol. 77 (London: Bernard Quaritch).

Watts, R. L., and Zimmerman, J. L. (1983), 'Agency Problems, Auditing and the Theory of the Firm: Some Evidence', *Journal of Law and Economics*, 26.

——(1986), *Positive Accounting Theory* (Englewood Cliffs, NJ: Prentice Hall International).

Year Book 5 Edward II 1311 (1947), ed. G. J. Turner, Selden Society, vol. 63 (London: Quaritch).

POSTSCRIPT

The *excessus* balance is a particular form of the balance of the manorial account that has proved puzzling. But even the composition and significance of the more usual *et sic debet* balance is not always clear. And once one looks at other examples of charge and discharge accounting as it developed in the fourteenth, fifteenth, and sixteenth centuries, rather than just at manorial accounts, other accounting entries may be identified which affect the closing balance. In particular 'respites' occur in several sets of accounts examined, for example in fourteenth-century city receivers' accounts and in sixteenth-century ironworks' accounts. Respites in charge and discharge accounts were illustrated by Myatt-Price (1966) in her description of the fifteenth-century building accounts of Tattershall Castle, and Ross (1968) referred to them in her description of the Talbot household accounts for 1417–18 and 1424–5 (describing the Tattershall examples as 'a more puzzling example of respites'). Although Myatt-Price does not specifically examine the impact of the respites on the balances carried forward and brought forward, examination of the Tattershall Castle accounts shows that they do indeed affect those balances. In view of the different types of respite that seem to occur, it would seem that further examination of the nature and impact of respites in charge and discharge accounting would be informative.

Traditional analyses of manorial accounting as it developed during the thirteenth century have seen as its purpose that of establishing the liability of the accountant to the lord. Although there is a great deal of evidence that profit calculations were performed on some estates (and the Gloucester Husbandry, for example, contains fourteenth-century rules for profit calculation) the charge and discharge form of account was not a profit and loss account nor does it seem readily to lend itself to calculation of profit and loss, and indeed the connection between the charge and discharge money account and the figures sometimes reported as *profectus* or *wainagio* is not always clear. An alternative view has been proposed by Bryer (1992). He suggests that the emergence of manorial charge and discharge accounting during the thirteenth century should be viewed in the context of Marx's analysis of the social relations of feudalism, in which the lords were concerned not with capitalist notions of profit but with the measurement and maximization of total labour rent.

Local history societies, and others, continue to publish transcriptions and/or translations of medieval accounts and these offer more material to accounting historians wishing to investigate the techniques of charge and discharge accounting.

References

Bryer, R. A. (1992), 'Manorial Accounting in the Age of High Farming: Primitive Capitalism or Sophisticated Feudalism?' Warwick Business School Research Papers no. 64, November.

Myatt-Price, E. M. (1966), 'Examples of Technique in Medieval Building Accounts', *Abacus*, 2/1.

Ross, B. (1968), 'The Accounts of the Stewards of the Talbot Household at Blakemere: An Example of Medieval Accounting Practice', *Abacus*, 4/1.

6 · THE OLDEST EUROPEAN ACCOUNT BOOK: A FLORENTINE BANK LEDGER OF 1211

G. A. Lee

INTRODUCTION

It is from thirteenth-century Tuscany, and especially from Florence and Siena, that modern accounting takes its rise. From this period and region come the earliest business accounts in debit and credit form, as distinct from manorial and public accounts in charge and discharge form, whose history goes back to classical Greece and Rome, and even, in some aspects, to ancient Mesopotamia, Egypt, Crete, and Mycenae. It was the Tuscans also who, by a series of insights and tentative improvements, evolved, probably by 1300, that scheme of double-entry bookkeeping which is now in use throughout the civilized world as the basis of every well-ordered accounting system, from the simple hand-written books of a shopkeeper to the most sophisticated electronic data processing complex of the largest American industrial corporation.

Sienese and Florentine account books have survived in considerable numbers from the latter half of the thirteenth century onwards. Previous to that the evidence for the development of accounting is very sparse, and the most primitive Italian business records have reached us only by fortunate accidents. The oldest memorial of all comes from Genoa. It consists of three small sheets of paper found between the pages of the cartulary, or book of contracts, of the notary Giovanni Scriba; this cartulary is the earliest known, and extends from 1155 to 1164. The papers were elucidated by Guido Astuti in 1933. They contain profit calculations, in 'single entry' form, for three voyages in the Mediterranean in 1156–8, by the Genoese merchant Ansaldo Baialordo for himself and his home-based partner Ingo da Volta, who contributed most of the capital and took the lion's share of the profits. These

First published in *Nottingham Medieval Studies* (1972), revised by the author.

were respectively £74, £245, and £282; Ansaldo received a total of £171, and Ingo, of £430.[1]

Even for substantial books of account the odds against survival were very heavy. Medieval Italian partnerships in trade and in banking—the only types of firm which normally needed any elaborate records—were short-lived. Merchants (such as Ansaldo and Ingo) formed joint ventures for single voyages; at the end of each one they withdrew their whole capital (hopefully with a profit) and wound up the venture. Banking partnerships tended to be more stable; but even these were usually entered into for no more than four or five years at a time, at the end of which the firm was liquidated—though it was often re-formed soon after, with at least some of the old partners. Once liquidation had taken place and the proprietors' capital had been agreed and repaid, no one was interested in preserving the books; and the dearness of parchment generally caused the leaves to be washed or scraped and used for other purposes, including book-binding.

It has been known for a long time that the flyleaves of the *Codex aedilis* 67, in the Biblioteca Medicea-Laurenziana of Florence, show traces of thirteenth-century accounts. Apropos of them, Bandini's catalogue of 1774–8 states: 'sub anno MCCXI, MCCXC notata sunt varia nomina debitoris alicuius qui mercaturam Florentiae exercebat'.[2] It was not until the 1880s, though, that any serious attempt was made to decipher the writing, which, *pace* Bandini, dates entirely from 1211 and does not extend to 1290. The task was performed by Pietro Santini, whose findings, with a transcription of the text, were published in the *Giornale storico della letteratura italiana*, 10 (1887), 161–77, under the title 'Frammenti di un libro di banchieri fiorentini scritto in volgare nel 1211'. The text only was reprinted by Ernesto Monaci in *Crestomazia italiana dei primi secoli* (Città di Castello, 1889) and, with more critical editing, by Alfredo Schiaffini in *Testi fiorentini del dugento e dei primi del trecento* (Florence, 1926). The translation below is based primarily on Santini, but takes cognizance of many of Schiaffini's readings; Monaci's edition has little independent value.

The editors were philologists, principally interested in the text as the earliest-known long fragment of pure Italian, and in particular Tuscan, prose. It has no pretensions to literary grace, and its vocabulary is severely restricted by its subject-matter; but it is invaluable as evidence of the proficiency which

---

[1] Florence Edler de Roover, 'Partnership Accounts in twelfth century Genoa', *Bulletin of the Business Historical Society*, 15 (Dec. 1941), 87–92; repr. in A. C. Littleton and B. S. Yamey, *Studies in the History of Accounting* (London, 1956).

[2] Santini, op. cit. in text.

quite ordinary Florentines had already attained in the writing of the vulgar tongue, and of its nearness, even at that period, to the language of Dante and Boccaccio. It is also remarkable as a specimen of the use of Italian in accounts having something of a public character, as being admissible as evidence in proceedings for the recovery of debts—at a time when all official and legal records in Florence were in Latin, as they continued to be for centuries. In fact, the 1211 accounts contain many stereotyped phrases and formulae which seem to have been literally translated; Santini[3] suggests that, in view of the determination of medieval legislators to preserve Latin forms in legal documents, accounts in Italian must have been in use for a long time among merchants and bankers, in order to break down the prejudice of lawyers against them. The relative sophistication, too, of the accounts indicates a historical development extending well back into the twelfth century; but beyond this all is conjecture.

The fragments are obviously of as much interest, or more, to the economic historian and the accountant. The most notable treatment of the text from the former point of view is, perhaps, that of Mario Chiaudano, in *Studi e documenti per la storia del Diritto Commerciale Italiano nel sec. XIII* (Turin, 1930). Among historians of accounting, it has been noticed briefly by Fabio Besta in *La ragioneria* (Milan, 1922), and more fully by Federigo Melis in his *Storia della ragioneria* (Bologna, 1950), as well as by the American Raymond de Roover.[4] The ensuing translation and exposition constitute, as far as the writer knows, the first full study of the document in English.

THE MANUSCRIPT

The text, in Italian with a few Latin formulae, is written cursively on both sides of two sheets of parchment (as thin as tissue-paper and very fragile), each measuring 43 × 28 cm. They now form the flyleaves of the *Codex aedilis* 67, a fourteenth-century MS of the *Digestum novum cum glossa*, a legal work in the Biblioteca Medicea-Laurenziana in Florence.[5] On the two rectos the writing is generally well preserved and legible, except for some damage at the foot of *carta* 1 *recto*, and some cropping of the right-hand margin of *c.* 2

---

[3] Santini, 177–8 (footnote).

[4] Raymond de Roover, 'The Development of Accounting prior to Luca Pacioli According to the Account-books of Mediaeval Merchants', in Littleton and Yamey, *Studies in the History of Accounting.*

[5] The author is most grateful to the Director and staff of the Laurenziana for the supply of excellent photocopies of the MS, which have been found very useful in interpreting the printed transcripts. At that time he had not been able to visit the library.

recto. On *c*. I *verso*, however (the inside of the front flyleaf), some three-fourths of the original text has been scraped off completely and overwritten with the table of contents of the *Digestum*, in three columns of book script which, owing to the depth of the erasure, show through on the *recto*. Only the bottom one-fourth of the 1211 text is legible, and even that is mutilated; while the page exhibits many legal notes and trials of the pen, by various hands. *C*. 2 *verso* is free from overwriting, but the surface has been scraped all over, and only a few words here and there are decipherable with the naked eye. Santini applied chemicals, line by line, to this page in order to bring out the writing, and was thus able to read practically all of it, at the price of further injury to the MS. Both leaves have a few holes in them, mostly small except for one in *c*. I, some 2.5 cm., and one in *c*. 2 about 3.5 cm., in diameter. These must have been flaws in the skin, for the text is written around them without any lacunae: perhaps, for cheapness, inferior parchment was used.

From the character of the contents it is plain that the fragments are those of the customers' ledger of an unidentified firm of bankers, operating in Florence, Bologna, and Pisa in the year 1211. All the entries, except for one or two cryptic ones to be noticed in due course, relate to loans made by the bank, and to repayments of the principal. Each page is ruled down the middle, and each of the two columns is divided by horizontal lines into six to eight blocks of varying depth, as represented schematically in Figures 6.1–6.4. Each block is allocated to one loan, the bookkeeper leaving what he deemed to be adequate space; sometimes it was not quite filled, sometimes it proved too little, and writing had to be crowded in. The entries are not in chronological order, even as regards the original advances, but must have been made as and when evidence of the loan was furnished to the bookkeeper—very quickly if the transaction took place locally, a few days later if it occurred at a distance.

Each block of entries may be likened to an account in a modern ledger. First comes a statement of the borrower's name, the amount advanced, and the date, followed in many cases by the due date of repayment, the rate of interest to be charged for late payment (almost always, 4 *denari* per *libra* per month, or 20 per cent per annum—not an unduly high rate for the thirteenth century), sometimes the names of two or more witnesses, and sometimes, again, the name of a guarantor of the loan, principal, and interest. Then follow repayments of the principal, generally by instalments; nothing is said about interest as a rule. The successive entries are written straight on in prose, separated only by an abbreviation of the word *item*; all sums of money, in *libre*,

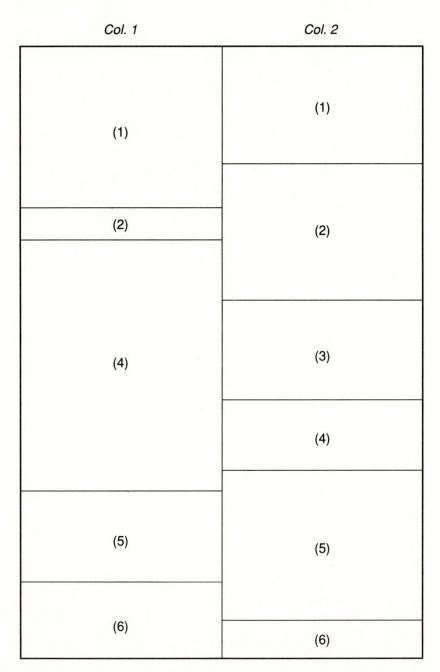

Fig. 6.I Carta I recto.

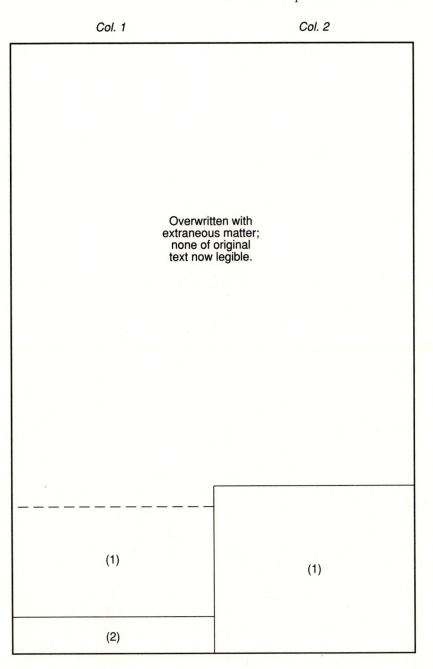

Col. 1

Col. 2

Overwritten with
extraneous matter;
none of original
text now legible.

(1)

(1)

(2)

Fig. 6.2 Carta I verso.

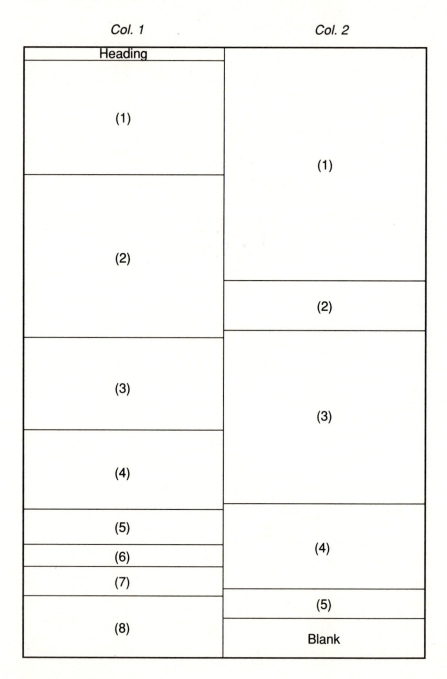

Fig. 6.3 Carta 2 recto.

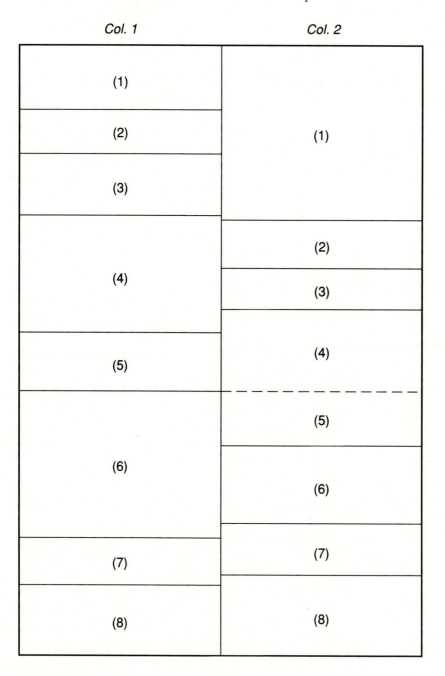

Fig. 6.4 Carta 2 verso.

soldi, and denari, are set out in roman numerals, with no attempt to order them in columns. There are no totals or balances; when repayments were equal to the advance, the account was closed by striking through it with slanting lines (as has been done in all cases). In other words, the first entry in each block was equivalent to a debit in a personal account for the borrower, and successive entries to credits; there was no balancing while the account was open, but cancellation of the paragraph was tantamount to totalling the two sides and proving them equal. The system appears even more modern if it is compared with electronic data processing, in which the computer is programmed to treat debits as positive sums and credits as negative ones (presented to it sequentially and regardless of any visual ordering), and to print out the balance, and/or write it on to a magnetic file, as an algebraic sum of otherwise unrecorded amounts. Indeed, this simulates the operations of the medieval clerk with his abacus, as he set up beads for the amount of the advance, and then took away beads representing the successive repayments, until he had none left; upon which he crossed out the entries.[6]

The two leaves of the MS are not consecutive; c. 2 seems to be the earlier, since it relates largely to loans made in Bologna for the fair of San Proculo (San Brocolo), which opened on 1 May, while most of the advances in c. 1 were made in June. The dates are all given according to the consuetudo bononiensis, by which the first fifteen days of the month were counted directly, while the last fifteen or sixteen were reckoned backwards from the Kalends (first) of the next month; e.g. 2 August is stated as due di intrante agosto, while tredici dì anzi kal. luglio means 19 June.[7] Since, however, it is clear that the main business was in Florence, it cannot be presumed that the ledger was kept at Bologna; perhaps the bookkeeper was a native of that city.

THE TRANSLATION

There appears in Figures 6.1 to 6.4 a schematic presentation of the entries on the four pages of the MS, on a scale of 1 : 2.5 as compared with the dimensions of the originals. The entries are numbered, on the diagrams and in the translation, purely for reference purposes, there being no such numbering in the text.

[6] The Liber abaci of Leonardo Fibonacci of Pisa had already appeared in 1202—from which date Melis judges the medieval era in accounting to begin: Storia della ragioneria, 381–4.

[7] Melis, ibid. 394 (footnote). He states that, relative to the second half of the month, the Bolognese system would give a date as so many days usciente, or exeunte, the month in question. In the 1211 accounts the reckoning is always from the kalends (1st) of the next month. This would suggest the Roman practice of counting in the kalends as the first day involved.

In the translation the original setting-out cannot, for typographical reasons, be preserved. The entries are given consecutively, column by column, with notes at the end of the section. The spelling of proper names has been modernized throughout; dates are given in their English equivalents; and sums of money are set down in arabic numerals in £.*s.d.*, representing *libre, solidi,* and *denari.*

Carta I recto, columna I

(1)

1211

Aldobrandino Pietro and Buoninsegna Falconi

are due to give us, each [for himself], in total £52. 0. 0*d.* for £18. 0. 0*d.* in Imperial *mezzani* at the rate of 35 less a third [*libre* in *mezzani* to 100 *libre* Florentine] which we gave them on 19 June, and they are to pay on 19 June; if [the moneys] are outstanding longer, [interest is] at 4*d.* in the £ per month, for as long as we may permit. Witnesses: Alberto Baldovini and Guittieri Alberti, of the Porta del Duomo.

Item Buoninsegna is due to give 12*s.* 0*d.* for one *massamutino.*

Buoninsegna Falconi has given us £40. 0. 0*d.*; Jacopo brought it at the due date. *Item* he is due to receive £4. 2. 0*d.*; we deducted from Buoninsegna's account what he was due to receive in respect of Ser Calcagno on 26 June. *Item* he gave £2. 19. 0*d.* on behalf of Tornaquinci, who paid him in cloths of his. *Item* Buonincontro da Poppio gave us £2. 0. 0*d.* personally on 29 June. *Item* Aldobrandino gave us £2. 19. 0*d.*; Giannozzo brought it.

(2)

To Messer Cancellieri we lent 2*s.* 0*d.* personally; we have added under his account what he was due to receive.

(3)

To Mainetto Passarimpetto we lent £1. 0. 0*d.* personally: [signed] Aldobran [dino]. *Item* he gave us £1. 0. 0*d.*; we deducted from his account what he is due to receive in respect of Buonaguida Forestani.

(4)

Jacopo, son of the Barone degli Acquarelli, and Simone his brother are due to give us, each [for himself], £52. 0. 0*d.* for £18. 0. 0*d.* in Imperial *mezzani* which we gave them on 19 June at [the rate of] 35 less a third; and they are due to pay us on 19 June. If [the moneys] are outstanding longer, [interest is] at 4*d.* in the £ per month, for as long as we may permit. Witnesses: Alberto Baldovini, Gaglietta de Pecora, Buontalento Macchetti, and Ruggieri, stepson of Buonfantino of Borgo San Lorenzo.

Item Buonincontro, son of the Barone degli Acquarelli, gave us £14. 11. 0*d.*; Cambio and Tornaquinci brought it on 28 July. *Item* Arrighetto Arrigoni gave us £5. 0. 0*d.*: [signed] Buonincontro; Tegghiaio brought it at the above date. *Item* Jacopo has given us £15. 0. 0*d.*, of which Ricovero, partner of Piero Rossi of San Firenze, received £6. 0. 0*d.*, Buonafede Varliani £5. 0. 0*d.*, and Testa di Codarimessa £4. 0. 0*d.*, on 2 August on our behalf. He also gave on our behalf to Cambio Morandi (?) £10. 3. 0*d.* on 20 September. *Item* Jacopo gave us £5. 6. 0*d.*; Jacopo brought it on 27 September. *Item* we were due to receive £2. 0. 0*d.* in respect of Dato Guidotti (?) on 8 October. *Item* Jacopo gave us £1. 10. 0*d.*; Aldobrandino brought it.

(5)

1211

Buonagiunta da Somaia is due to give £23. 18. 0*d.* for £23. 0. 0*d.* which we lent him on 30 June; we added what he is due to receive, and repay, on 1 August. If [the moneys] are outstanding longer, [interest is] at 4*d.* in the £ per month, for as long as we may permit; and if he does not pay, then Buonone, son of Farolfo of the Duomo [parish], promised to pay us interest and principal, as much as they shall amount to. Witnesses: Prestorso of Oltrarno, Lutieri, son of Galgano Balsimi, and Ugolino, son of Sassolino da Capiano. *Item* Buorricchetto del Grecio gave us £23. 18. 0*d.*; we added it.

(6)

[This account is illegible and mutilated.]

Carta I recto, columna 2

(1)

1211

Ristoro, son of Piero the pursemaker, and Jacopino, son of Sigolo, are due to give us, each [for himself], in total £8. 10. 8*d.* for £8. 0. 0*d.* which we gave them on 21 May at [a charge of] 1*s.* 4*d.* in the £, and are due to pay on 21 July; if [the moneys] are outstanding longer, [interest is] at 4*d.* in the £ per month, for as long as we may permit. Witnesses: Alberto Baldovini and

Consiglio dei Castagnacci.

Item he is due to pay in interest 19*s.* 4*d.*

Ristoro has given us personally £2. 0. 0*d.*; Tegghiaio brought it on 3 December. *Item* Tadellato del Buono gave on our behalf £7. 10. 0*d.* on 21 March [1211/12].

(2)

1211

Banzara del Garbo is due to give us £15. 0. 0*d.* in new Provins coin which we gave to Bartolo the apothecary (?) on 20 June, and which they are due to pay on 1 July; if [the moneys] are outstanding longer, [interest is] at 4*d.* in the £ per month, for as long as we may permit. If he does not pay, then Benvenuto, son of Romeo del Garbo, promised to pay us interest and principal, as much as they shall amount to. Witnesses: Alberto Baldovini and Buonaccorso, son of Villano of San Michele Berteldi. *Item* Banzara is due to give 2*s.* 4*d.* for his share of the interest. *Item* we refunded him 1*s.* 4*d.* *Item* Benvenuto is due to give 3*s.* 0*d.* for interest.

Banzara has given us £4. 13. 8*d.*; Tegghiaio brought the £4. 0. 0*d.* from Gerardo del Papa on 30 July. *Item* he gave on our behalf to Todino Allero £3. 0. 0*d.* on 29 July. *Item* Benvenuto, son of Romeo del Garbo, gave us £7. 16. 0*d.*; Jacopo brought it from Guidotto (?) Rusticucci for mid-September.

(3)

1211, 21 June.

Buonaccorso Manfreducci of San Martino del Vescovo is due to give us £40. 11. 0*d.* on behalf of Domenico of San Firenze; we have added what he is due to receive, and repay, on 1 September. If [the moneys] are outstanding longer, [interest is] at 4*d.* in the £ per month, for as long as we may permit. If he does not pay, then Dietaiuti del Banzara promised to pay us interest and principal, as much as they shall amount to. Witnesses: Alberto Baldovini, Varliano di Codarimessa, and Buonaffè his partner.

Buonaccorso has given us £40. 11. 0*d.*; we received it in Bolognese coin (?), and he has paid us the interest.

(4)

Gerardo, son of Buonaccorso Monteloro, is due to give [us] £1. 0. 10*d.* in respect of Buoglione, son of Traverso, which [sum] he was due to give Traverso in the old book.

[The rest of this account is erased, and a legal note in Latin written over it.]

(5)

Appollonio Tribaldi is due to give us 8s. 0d. which we lent him; he said that he was giving it to the apprentice of Aldobrandino the smith, for corn.

Item he is due to give £1. 15. 6d. on behalf of a pilgrim, to whom we gave it in coin of Tours; he said that he [the pilgrim] was giving him some linen cloth.

Item he is due to receive £1. 0. 11d. in respect of Servodeo, tenant of Mainetto del Medico. *Item* he is due to receive 5s. 0d. which he gave to Arnolfino . . . [illegible—MS damaged] . . . Attaviano (?) dell' Acerbo. *Item* Appollonio gave us 17s. 5d. personally.

[The rest of this account is illegible.]

(6)

[This account is illegible, mutilated, and overwritten with sundry legal notes and trials of the pen.]

Carta I verso, columna I

[The first three-fourths of the page have been erased and overwritten with the table of contents of the *Digestum Novum*, in three columns, with some notes and trials of the pen on part of the blank space remaining. The last fourth of column I reads:]

(1)

Item Mainetto Tornaquinci gave £12. 0. 0d., which we were keeping (?) for him on behalf of the mother of Sinibaldo Rinuccetti in the new register at the due date. *Item* Buonaguida della Gina gave us, on behalf of Mainetto Tornaquinci, £8. 0. 0d. which he owed him in respect of Benintendi Pizzichelli, on account of Buonaiuti Riccardini, on 12 July. *Item* Buonaguida of San Romedio gave us £2. 0. 0d. on behalf of Mainetto Tornaquinci; we deducted it from the account of Benintendi, son of Pizzichelli.

(2)

Bencivenni Marci of San Firenze is due to give us £3. 0. 0d. for £3. 3. 0d. in Bolognese coin [*a to* . . . (next word illegible)—meaning unknown] to Buonaccete, son of Gaiazzo, which we gave (?) on his behalf. *Item* he is due to give £9. 0. 0*d*.; we lent it on his behalf, through (?) Aldobrandino, personally. *Item* he is due to give 10*s*. . . . £4. 8. 0*d*. we deducted . . . [fragmentary]

[The rest is illegible, or torn away.]

Carta 1 verso, columna 2

[See headnote to column 1.]

(1)

. . . on 8 July. If [the moneys] are outstanding longer, [interest is] at 4*d*. in the £ per month, for as long as we may permit. Witnesses: Alberto Baldovini, Ristoro Cafferelli, and Compagnino, brother of the Tebalducci. Buonaguida Bencivenni has given us £2. 12. 4*d*.; we added what he is due to give further back. *Item* he is due to receive £1. 14. 0*d*. on behalf of Caccia, son of Arringhiero of Borgo Sant'Apostoli; we deducted it from his account at the due date.

Buonaguida Bencivenni has given us £37. 0. 0*d*. and *item* Chierico, son of Arrigo Malverni, gave us £5. 0. 0*d*.; he said that he was giving it to us on behalf of Buonaguida Bencivenni at the due date. *Item* Buonaguida Bencivenni [has given us ?] £14. 19. 8*d*.; the mother of Sinibaldo Rinuccetti received it on behalf of Sinibaldo; written yesterday in the new register. She said that she is having it paid into the bank of Fornaio, son of Rosso del Fornaio, whom Canollo and Ubaldino had engaged for her. *Item* Ispinello the cheesemonger gave us on behalf of Buonaguida, son of Bencivenni del Chierico, £11. 13. 0*d*.; Arrisalito, son of Turpino, has paid on our behalf into the . . . [cropping] on 9 July. *Item* he gave on our behalf . . . [cropping] Avvogadi (?) £8. 0. 0*d*. *Item* . . .

[The rest of this account is torn away.]

Carta 2 recto, columna 1

In nomine Domini, amen. San Proculo.

(1)

1211

Orlandino the leatherdresser, of Santa Trinità, is due to give us £26. 0. 0*d*. by mid-May for Bolognese coin which we gave him at Bologna for the fair of San Proculo. If [the moneys] are outstanding longer, [interest is] at 4*d*. in the

£ per month; and if he does not pay, then Angiolino Bolognini the leather-dresser promised to pay us. Witnesses: Compagno Avanelle and Bellacalza. *Item* he is due to receive £2. 3. 0*d*. in respect of Michele, son of Galletto; we deducted it from the account of Scilinguato Mainetti.

Orlandino has given us £7. 9. 0*d*.; Mainetto, son of Guido dell' Avvogado, received it on behalf of Aldobrandino Avveccari, Porcelle di Guittoncino, son of Gianni, and Griffo, with other moneys (?), on 20 May. *Item* Orlandino gave us £6. 4. 0*d*.; Jacopo brought it at the date aforesaid. *Item* Orlandino has given us £4. 16. 0*d*., which he gave to Arrigo, son of Ruggiero dello [I]ngem-mato; he was paying him on behalf of Guascone Tortolini on 22 May. *Item* he gave on our behalf to Buonaguida della Gattaia £2. 7. 0*d*. which we owed him on account of Rinieri Orlandini, on 23 May. *Item* he gave on our behalf to Uguccione, 23 son of Castellano, £2. 10. 0*d*., on 28 May. *Item* Orlandino gave us personally 11*s*. 0*d*.; he accounted for it to (?) Giannozzo.

(2)

Angiolino the leatherdresser is due to give us £40. 0. 0*d*. for Bolognese coin which we gave him at Bologna for the fair of San Proculo, and is due to pay by mid-May. If [the moneys] are outstanding longer, [interest is] at 4*d*. [in the £ per month]; and if he does not pay, then Orlandino the leatherdresser promised to pay us interest and principal, as much as they shall amount to. Witnesses: Mazzingo, Mainetto d'Albizzocco (?), and Bernardo Berti.

Angiolino has given us £11. 0. 0*d*. personally on 29 May. *Item* Benevieni the leatherdresser gave us on behalf of Angiolino £3. 10. 0.: Albizzo da Ferrara (?), leatherseller of Lungarno, brought it at the date aforesaid. *Item* Orlandino gave us £10. 0. 0*d*.; Cambio brought £3. 0. 0*d*. from Scotto the leatherseller, and £3. 17. 0*d*. from Jacopo del Campo, and Orlandino gave £3. 3. 0*d*. personally, at the date given above.

Item Angiolino [gave us] personally £5. 10. 0*d*. on 31 May and has paid the interest. *Item* Orlandino gave us £3. 16. 0*d*. on behalf of Jacopo on 31 May. *Item* Orlandino gave us £4. 3. 0*d*.; Cambio brought it from Bernardo the leatherseller on 3 June. *Item* Orlandino gave us personally £2. 0. 0*d*. on account of Arnolfino on 14 June. *Item* Orlandino gave [us] 3*s*. 0*d*., and has paid in settlement of his liability to Aldobrandino by mid-June.

(3)

Guglielmo, son of Gianni Guadagnuoli, is due to give us £16. 11. 0*d*. for Bolognese coin which we gave him at Bologna for the fair of San Proculo, and is due to pay on I June; if [the moneys] are outstanding longer, [interest is] at 4*d*. in the £ per month.

Jacopo Parisci has given us £13. 0. 0*d*.; we received £3. 9. 0*d*. of it from Gaglietta del Pecora; Albizzo brought it at the due date. *Item* Jaco[po] gave us personally £3. 11. 0*d*.; Rinaldo and Gianni brought it.

[A legal note in Latin has been written in the blank space at the end.]

(4)

Diede Bilicozzi is due to give us £9. 13. 4*d*. for Bolognese coin which we gave him at Bologna for the fair of San Proculo, and he is due to pay at mid-May; if [the moneys] are outstanding longer, [interest is] at 4*d*. [in the £ per month].

Mainetto Tornaquinci has given us £9. 13. 4*d*.; he paid it on our behalf to Vinedico Prestazzi, to whom we owed it on behalf of Dello, son of Mainetto dello Scilinguato, with other moneys, on account of Rinieri, son of Orlandino of Lungarno.

(5)

Ristoro Cafferelli is due to give us 10*s*. 0*d*., which we lent him for Ristoro's expenses (?), personally. *Item* to Ristoro personally £1. 0. 0*d*. of . . . [illegible]; it is added in the new register under his account.

(6)

To Aldobrandino Capi we lent 10*s*. 0*d*.; [also?] Aldobra[ndino] said that Ser Ni[ccolò] Capi (?) was giving it to him; added under Capi's account what he is due to receive.

(7)

Gerardo dell'Asino is due to give us 8*s*. 0*d*. in Bolognese coin which we lent him; added under his account, what Bentivegna is due to receive.

(8)

Albertino del Ripaio is due to give us £37. 17. 5*d*. in respect of the account further back, as Uguccione Brunetti says above that he settled (?) the £6. 10. 8*d*. of interest. We settled it for mid-November.

Carta 2 recto, columna 2

(1)

[The right-hand margin is cropped in the first part of this account, and the text slightly mutilated, but it is easily restored.]

1211

Donato, son of Ciaffero, and Guido della Spada are due to give us, each [for himself], in total £107. 7. 8*d.* for Bolognese coin which we gave them in Bologna for the fair of San Proculo, and are due to pay on 1 June; if [the moneys] are outstanding longer, [interest is] at 4*d.* in the £ per month.

[In the blank space following there has been written, in a later hand: *Mcccxvi mense martii die xvi*—presumably a trial of a new pen.]

Buonaccolto Salintorri has given us £17. 17. 10*d.*: Messer Aldobrandino, son of Rinieri Foresi, received £14. 0. 0*d.* of it on behalf of Simone Gianrolandi, and Albizzo brought the remainder on 13 June, when Rinieri, son of Martinello the binmaker (?), brought us the £14. 0. 0*d. Item* Rinieri (?) Rinucci gave us £17. 17. 11*d.*; we received £5. 10. 0*d.* of it from Corbizzo della Pressa; Jacopo brought it, and Giannozzo brought the remainder at the date aforesaid. *Item* he [Donato] gave on our behalf to Torsello Giugni £18. 0. 0*d.*; we paid it on behalf of Capo the dyer on 8 June. *Item* Donato gave us £9. 10. 0*d.*; Albizzo brought it at the date aforesaid. *Item* Ciaffero gave us personally £18. 12. 0*d.* on 11 June. *Item* he is due to receive £17. 17. 10*d.* which Arrigo dell'Erro gave us; we deducted from his account what he was due to receive at the due date. *Item* he is due to receive £2. 0. 0*d.* in respect of Caro the goldsmith; we deducted it from the account of Guarnelletto, son of Gregorio, on 5 July. *Item* he gave on our behalf to Accolto, son of Ughetto of San Firenze, £4. 0. 0*d.*; Donato, son of Ciaffero, paid it on 9 July. *Item* Donato gave us £1. 12. 0*d.* and his share of the interest he accounted for to (?) Tornaquinci on 9 July.

(2)

Ser Accorri, son of Panconsole, is due to give us £6. 0. 0*d.* in Bolognese coin which Arnolfino lent him at Bologna for San Proculo.

Item Ser Accorri gave us £5. 9. 0*d.* in Pisan coin; we made an allowance on (?) the Bolognese coin of 2*s.* 0*d.* in the £.

(3)

1211

Albertino Paganelli is due to give us £42. 8. 10*d.* for the account which was [opened] for San Proculo, which [sum] Arnolfino gave him at Bologna; and the remainder he is due to give to Mainetto, and is due to pay by St Peter's Day. We returned to Albertino Paganelli £5. 9. 8*d.*; we added what Guidalotto is due to receive.

Albertino Paganelli, in June, has given us £7. 2. 10*d.*; Tornaquinci brought it from Vezzoso dei Baroncelli on 1 September. *Item* he is due to receive 9*s.* 0*d.* in respect of Taone, to whom we accounted for money which Giucco del Compagno owned him, on 28 September.

Item he is due to receive £2. 2. 7*d.* in respect of Ispinello di Calimala on 28 June. *Item* Taone gave us £7. 15. 0*d.*; Albizzo brought it from Rinuccino, son of Alamanno Anselmini, on 8 July. (*Item* Dietisalvi, son of Rodolfo of the Porta San Pancrazio, gave us £3. 8. 11*d.*; Ugolino di Cosa received it from Abbraccia del Garbo (?) at the date aforesaid. *Item* he gave on our behalf to Bencivenni, son of Grispignano, £10. 0. 0*d.*; he was (?) paying it on behalf of Baldovino his brother on 30 July).

[The words in brackets have all been crossed out, line by line, and the following paragraph written in, mainly between the lines of the cancelled one:]

Item he is due to receive £12. 3. 9*d.* in respect of (?) Guidalotto; [we deducted] from his account what he is due to receive. Taone has given us 4*s.* 2*d.* and has paid the interest. *Item* Davidalo gave us £3. 11. 0*d.*; he said that Taone was paying us . . . [illegible]; we deducted from his account what he is due to receive. *Item* Taone gave us £4. 0. 0*d.*; Arnolfino brought it from Rinuccino Simoni on 9 August.

Item Mainetto Tornaquinci gave us £5. 5. 2*d.*; he paid it on our behalf to Buonaguida Bencivenni. He said that he was returning for the account what Albertino had overpaid him on 19 August.

Item Capitano gave us £5. 5. 1*d.*; Buonaguida Bencivenni received it on 22 August.

(4)

[This account is badly mutilated by cropping of the right-hand margin— hence the many lacunae.]

Mainetto is due to give us £7. 1. 1*d.* for the *storamento* of San Bran . . . colo. Mainetto has given us £2. 8. 2*d.*; we added that he is due to give £3 . . . *Item* he is due to receive £3. 15. 0*d.* in respect of the account which we had settled, which he has [. . .] us . . . had overpaid in the old book. *Item* he is due to receive £1. 2. 0*d*. less . . . *d*. . . . in respect of the account of the £150. 0. 0*d*. which we settled.

   (Mainetto Tornaquinci is due to give us £7. 1. 1*d*. for the account (?) of San Proculo, which . . .)

   (*Item* he is due to receive £7. 1. 1*d*. in respect of Ricovero, son of . . . to; we deducted from his account what he was due to receive . . . half-*denari*.)

   [The two paragraphs in parentheses have been crossed out, line by line.]

(5)

Ristoro dell'Arlotto is due to give us 18*s*. 2*d*. . . . [cropping] for the account of San Proculo; we have refunded to Mainetto 5*s*. 0*d*. of it. Ristoro has given us £1. 0. 0*d*. in Bolognese coin . . .

   [The rest of the account is erased.]

Carta 2 verso, columna I

[Owing to the condition of the parchment, only a few words here and there can be identified on the photocopy. Santini's transcript has thus to be taken largely on trust, but it appears very full.]

(1)

Guidalotto Rustichelli of Somaia is due to give us £13. 6. 0*d*. on behalf of Attaviano Becchi, who was giving it to us on behalf of Uguccione Godini.

   Donosdeo Begnoli has given us £5. 12. ?*d*. (?); Albizzo received it.

   Item Guidalotto is due to receive £13. 0. 0*d*.; we deducted from his account at the due date . . . [cropping] . . . mo Ughetti da Buonaccorri, nephew [or grandson] or Ughetto Giambuoni. We have added it. Riccardo brought £1. 14. 2*d*.

(2)

Brunetto Godini is due to give 14*s*. 0*d*. (?) for Baldovillano's share of the interest.

[The rest of this account is illegible.]

(3)

Cavalcante, son of Cavalcante, is due to give us £41. 13. 2*d*. for £46. 0. 0*d*. in Bolognese coin which Arnolfino gave on his behalf to Abbonizzo Maltempo for the . . . [illegible] at 2*s*. 1*d*. in the £.

Item Jacopo Simoni gave us £41. 13. 2*d.*; he paid it on our behalf to Mainetto Tornaquinci. We owed it him in the account for £150. 0. 0*d.* of dell'Orfo (?).

(4)

1211 *Item* he is due to give us interest £2. 9. 0*d.*

Lutieri Calcagni is due to give us £44. 11. 0*d.* for £41. 18. 6*d.* of new coin which he received in Pisa at [a charge of] 1*s.* 3*d.* in the £ on 11 June, and is due to pay it on 11 July; if [the moneys] are outstanding longer, [interest is] at 4*d.* in the £ [per month]. He said that it is between him and Cardinale. *Item* Cardinale is due to give £24. 2. 6*d.* in respect of the account of Rinuccino, son of Macigno (?), which we settled on 13 November [1210?].

Lutieri has given us personally £2. 10. 6*d.* on 13 July. *Item* Cardinale gave us £2. 15. 5*d.* (?); we added it.

Item £50. 0. 0*d.* of new coin which he gave on our behalf to Guarnieri, son of Gaiazzo of the Porta San Pietro, which [money] he caused to be given to Bernardo, the banker of Pisa, on 13 November. *Item* Lutieri and Cardinale gave us £15. 16. 6*d.*, nine parchments further on.

(5)

To Pacie (?), son of . . . evino we had lent £3. 17. 8*d.*, which Mainetto Tornaquinci gave him, which he was giving us on behalf of Abbraccia del Gatto (?). *Item* he is due to give 2*s.* 4*d.* which we gave him personally; he said that Allalbardo was paying him in cloths of his.

Pacie (?) has given us £4. 0. 0*d.*; we deducted from his account what he is due to receive in respect of Alberto Rosso.

(6)

In nomine Domini, amen.

Arnolfino is carrying with him to the Badia £103. 15. 0*d.* in Veronese coin which we took for him from Gualterotto. *Item* he is carrying £31. 0. 0*d.* in Veronese coin . . . [illegible] *di cambio* (?). *Item* he is carrying £1. 0. 0*d.* in Bolognese coin for expenses. The Veronese coin amounts to £78. 0. 0*d.* *Item* he is due to give £8. 17. 0*d.* which we gave on his behalf to Guascone, son of Rinieri Ubertini, for the exchange (?) of the Veronese coin. We added what he is due to receive: *item* from Paganello del Garbo, £90. 2. 1*d.*; *item* from Bene Prestasini, £47. 17. 3*d.*; *item* [from] Buoninsegna dell'Anguillaia, £45. 4.

1*d.* (?); *item* from Ser (?) Arrigo, [son of ?] Rinieri Medici (?), £94. 5. 6*d.*; *item* from Ruggiero, stepson of Buonfantino, £69. 13. 4*d.*; [*item*] from Arrigo, son of Rinieri Medici (?), £53. 2. 0*d.*, *item* he is due to give for the interest £14. 3. 0*d.*; *item* from Bencivenni, partner (?) of Guarniero, £2. 6. ?*d.* . . . . [illegible] It amounts in total to £504. 9. 2*d. Item* we recovered (?), including payments by those whose debts had been remitted (?), £504. 12. 0*d.*

(7)

Lutieri, son of Ruffolo, is due to give us £4. 0. 0*d.* on behalf of Benci di Borgo, who was giving it us for new coin. We added what he is due to receive. *Item* he gave on our behalf to Cambio Minerbetti £4. 0. 0*d.*

(8)

Alberto, son of Ubertino, is due to give us £1. 2. 4*d.* for two *massamutini*. Ubertino has given us £1. 2. 4*d.* We added under his account what he is due [to receive]; he had overpaid us (?) three parchments further on.

Carta 2 verso, columna 2

(1)

1211

B.) Ridolfo, son of Gualfredo dell'Anguillaia, is due to give us £37. 13. 6*d.* for £35. 0. 0*d.* of new coin which Aldobrandino gave him in Pisa at [a charge of] 1*s.* 6*d.* in the £; he gave it him on 23 May, and he is due to pay on 22 June. If [the moneys] are outstanding longer, [interest is] at 4*d.* in the £ [per month], for as long as we may permit; and if he does not pay, then Jacopo Riccardini of the Porta del Duomo promised to pay us interest and principal, as much as they shall amount to. [Witnesses: (?)] Chierico, son of Gerardo Tornaquinci, and Bartolo dell'Istorna. *Item* he is due to give 13*s.* 0*d.*, on account of our having overpaid Fierletto his brother.

Donato, son of Guido Fancelli, has given us £22. 10. 0*d.* on 30 June; we received it from Alberto Ubertini. We added it. *Item* Fornaio, son of Rosso del Fornaio, gave us £8. 1. 10*d.*; Cambio brought it at the date aforesaid. *Item* Gaglietta del Pecora gave us £7. 14. 0*d.*, from which we deducted 10*s.* 0*d.* which we owed him on behalf of Consiglio, partner of Dietiguardi of Borgo San Lorenzo; £6. 3. 0*d.* he gave on our behalf to Amizzo del Secca, and £1. 1. 0*d.* Redita (?) counted out on his behalf. *Item* Redita (?) gave 8*d.*

(2)

Compagno Soldi is due to give us £1. 19. 0*d.* on behalf of Uguccio[ne], son of Brunetto Godini, for the account which we settled in the old book on 1 July. *Item* he is due to give 2*s.* 6*d.* on behalf of Baldovillano di Sotto (?) *Item* he is due to give 6*s.* 0*d.* for interest.

Compagno has given us £2. 8. 0*d.*; we deducted from his account what he is due to receive by 1 March [1211/12].

(3)

Baldovillano di Sotto (?), of the household of Brunetto Godini, is due to give us £1. 5. 6*d.* on behalf of Uguccione, son of Brunetto Godini, for the account which we settled in the old book, which . . . [illegible] Compagno Soldi (?).

Baldovillano has given us £1. 3. 0*d.*; Aldobrandino brought it. *Item* Compagno Soldi gave us 2*s.* 6*d.*; we added what he is due to give, above.

(4)

1211. He is due to give 2*s.* 8*d.* for interest.

Jacopo, son of Guido Lunghi, is due to give us £12. 19. 0*d.* for £12. 0. 0*d.* of new coin which we gave him, at [a charge of] 1*s.* 7*d.* in the £, on 25 May. We added it. He is due to pay us on 24 June; if [the moneys] are outstanding longer, then he promised to give for a penalty 4*d.* in the £ [per month] for two months, and after the two months, 6*d.* in the £ [per month], for as long as we may permit; and if he does not pay, then Albizzo Ar . . . [hole in parchment] manni promised to pay us interest and principal, as much as they shall amount to. [Witnesses:?] Scilinguato Mainetti and Guarniero, son of Guido Guarnieri.

Bernardo, [son of?] Madonna Diana, has given us on behalf of Jacopo £13. 1. 8*d.*; Buonaguida Bencivenni received it on behalf of Guidotto Rusticucci.

(5)

Guglielmo, brother of Rinuccino Simoni, is due to give £3. 0. 0*d.* for Bolognese coin, and is due to pay us on 28 July; if [the moneys] are outstanding longer, [interest is] at 4*d.* in the £ [per month]. If he does not pay, then Rinuccino promised to pay us interest and principal.

Bandino has given us £2. 14. 0*d.* on behalf of Guglielmo. We added it. *Item* he has given us £1. 0. 0*d.* (?) for the interest.

(6)

Crispino Attiglianti is due to give us £5. 0. 0*d.* for the account in the old book, which [sum] we overpaid Attigliante.

Attigliante has given us £3. 1. 9*d*. which he is due to receive for sterling and other currency (?). *Item* Attigliante has given us £1. 8. 3*d*.; we deducted from his account what he was due to receive.

(7)

Bandino . . . [illegible] Attaviani is due to give £2. 14. 0*d*. on behalf of Guglielmo, brother of Rinuccino.

Bandino has given us £2. 14. 0*d*.; he brought it to Arnolfino.

(8)

Attaviano Becchi is due to give us £2. 10. 0*d*. for his share of the account, six parchments back, as Uguccione, son of Brunetto Godini, says above.

Attaviano has given us £1. 0. 0*d*. personally. *Item* Attaviano gave us £1. 10. 0*d*. personally, and the interest from (?) December [1210].

NOTES ON THE TRANSLATION

Carta I recto, columna I

Account (1)

The original text is set out below, as nearly as possible as it appears in the MS (except for writing out of obvious abbreviations, and omission of words deleted), as it gives examples of most of the standard phrases used in the ledger generally.

MCCXI
Aldobrandino petro e buonessegnia falkoni
      Nodino dare katuno in tuto lib. lii per liure
diciotto d'imperiali mezani arrascione ditrenta e cinque meno terza
kedemmo loro tredici dì anzi k. luglio e dino pagare tredici dì anzi kal.
      luglio.
se più stanno, a iiii d. lib. ilmese quantofusse nostra voluntade.
testi alberto baldovini e quitieri alberti diporte delduomo.
      Item die dare buonessegnia s. xii per umassamutino.
      Buonessegnia falkoni ciadato lib. xl: rekò
iakopo a termine. Item die auire lib. iiii e s. ii:
leuammo dirascione buonessegnie oue doues auire
per ser kalkagnio vi dì anzi k. luglio. Item diè lib. iii meno
d. xii per tornaquinci, keipagò nei panni suoi.

Item cidiè Buoninkontro dappopio s. xl dissuamano
tredì anzi kal. luglio. Item cidiè aldobrandino lib. iii meno d. xii:
rekò giannozo.

(no) die/dino dare: *die/dino avire:*
   'is/are due to give (us)';   and   'is/are due to receive'.

These phrases represent the earliest, and most natural, usage of the words *dare*
and *avere* in their accounting senses of 'debit' and 'credit'. In thirteenth-century bookkeeping, though, they are not yet thought of as direct opposites, for
with them are associated, respectively

(ci) diè/diede/ha(nno) dato: *(li) demmo/avemmo dato:*
   'gave (has/have given) (us)'; and   'we gave/have given him/them'.

Thus the early medieval ledger-keeper thought of two sets of fluxes and
refluxes—a loan to someone, and its repayment, on the one hand; and a loan
or deposit from someone, and its repayment, on the other (*mutatis mutandis* for
sales and purchases). He was also familiar with the idea that the same customer might deposit money with the bank *and* take a loan from it, and equally
with the practice whereby a customer used his deposit to pay a debt of his
own to another customer who had borrowed from the bank. In either case a
transfer between the deposit account and the loan account, in the banker's
books at the request of the depositor, would settle the borrower's liability in
whole or in part. Hence arose a third pair of opposed entries, of which many
examples occur in the 1211 ledger, viz.,

levammo ove die/dovea avere:
'we deducted what he is/was due to receive' (i.e. 'we debited his account
which has had a credit balance'); and

ponemmo che die/dovea avere:
'we added what he is/was due to receive' (i.e. 'we credited his (loan)
account with what stood to the credit of his (or another's) (deposit)
account').

It will be noted that the translator has scrupulously avoided rendering any of
these six expressions, or their variants, by phrases involving the words 'debit'
and 'credit'; it would have been quite anachronistic to do so.

e dene/dino pagare . . .:
'and is/are due to pay (on a certain date)'.

In the example above, this is the actual date of the advance! More usually, it is
one (occasionally two) months later. The significance of the date is clearer
from the phrase which normally follows, viz.—

se più stanno, a iiii d. lib. il mese:

'if [the moneys] are outstanding longer, [interest is] at 4*d*. in the £ per month'.

In other words, it appears that interest began to run, at the rate of 20 per cent per annum, from the due date, which, as in the first account, might be the date of the advance. In that case the borrower paid the full 20 per cent for as long as the loan was outstanding. Otherwise he had (say) one month free of interest (there was normally no intention that he should pay within that time), so that his actual rate was somewhat less than 20 per cent.

quanto fusse nostra voluntade: 'for as long as we may permit'.

This formula gave the bankers the right to call in the loan at any time after the due date. In fact, many of the loans run on considerably beyond it, and there is no evidence of a policy of punctually enforcing payment.

testi (abbreviated '*tt*') *A. B. e C. D.:* 'witnesses: A. B. and C. D.'.

The names of two or more witnesses appear in connection with eleven of the loans in the fragments. The amounts advanced range from £8. 10. 0*d*. to £52. 0. 0*d*., with one mutilated account whose repayments indicate a larger sum. On the other hand, advances as high as £107. 7. 8*d*. are made without specifying witnesses. There would be a notarial record in all cases, except where the sums were trivial, and the first 'witness' was probably the notary, as is suggested by the recurrence of names; that of Alberto Baldovini occurs six times. The witnesses' names were presumably omitted to save space, once it was realized that a legal record existed anyway.

di sua mano: 'personally' (literally, 'with his own hand').

rekò A. B.: 'A. B. brought it'.

This could refer to A. B. either as a messenger who brought money to the bank or as a partner who received it and accounted for it to the firm. The recurrence of the same Christian names suggests the latter, in the majority of cases. Eight names occur, in these and other contexts, between three and eight times each, and it would seem that they were those of the partners. They are, with the numbers of times their names appear:

Arnolfino (8); Jacopo (6); Albizzo, Aldobrandino, and Cambio (5); Giannozzo and Tornaquinci (4); and Tegghiaio (3).

The surnames are omitted, as being unnecessary for identification; in any case, fixed surnames were only gradually coming into use among the non-noble classes of Florence, as may be seen from the frequent identification of a customer by his father's Christian name, or by his trade.

a termine:

'at the due date' (already written).

Points peculiar to account (I) are:

buonessegnia falkoni:

According to Santini, Buoninsegna Falconi is mentioned by the eighteenth-century Tuscan antiquary Ildefonso di San Luigi as having been admitted to the *Arte della Seta*, or silk-mercers' guild, in 1225.

katuno:

'each [for himself]'; the loan was a joint one, since the repayments total only to £52. 0. 0*d.*, the amount of the one advance.

imperiali mezani:

'Mezzano' is defined by C. Battisti and G. Alessio, *Dizionario Etimologico Italiano* (Florence, 1950), as a coin having half the value of a standard coin. The identity of the currency is thus conjectural. The exchange is stated to be 'at the rate of thirty and five less a third', resulting in a liability of £52. 0. 0*d.* Florentine for £18. 0. 0*d.* in *mezzani*. If the rate is interpreted as £34. 13. 4*d.* in *mezzani* to £100. 0. 0*d.* Florentine, the sum works out very closely (£18. 0. 0*d.* × 100/34⅔ = £51. 18. 6*d.*).; hence this seems the most probable explanation.

porte del duomo:

The Porta del Duomo was the north gate in the Roman walls of Florence; it stood near the Baptistery. By 1211 the old walls must have been in decay, having been superseded by the much larger enceinte of 1174–76.[8]

massamutino:

This is defined by Battisti and Alessio[9] as a Hispano-Arabian gold coin of the twelfth century. Curiously, the repayments in the account allow nothing for the *massamutino*.

Buoninkontro dappopio:

The natural reading is 'Buonincontro da Poppio'. Melis,[10] however, emends it to '*da proprio*', meaning, presumably, 'for his own part'. In that case 'Buonincontro' may be a mistake for 'Buoninsegna'. It seems more reasonable to assume that Buonincontro was a debtor of Aldobrandino or Buoninsegna, who was directed to pay part of *their* debt to the bankers.

---

[8]   Yves Renouard, *Les Villes d'Italie de la fin du Xe siècle au debut du XIV siècle* (Paris, 1961–2).

[9]   *Op. cit. supra.*

[10]   *Storia della ragioneria*, 393.

Account (2)

Cancellieri, and Testa in account (4), are shown as witnesses to a boundary agreement between the Communes of Florence and Siena, dated 4 June 1203.[11]

This loan is settled by a transfer from Cancellieri's deposit account.

Account (4)

The total instalments come to £51. 10. 0*d*., if the £2. 0. 0*d*. due on 8 October was not in fact received; yet the account is struck through as settled.

Arrighetto Arrigoni is stated by Ildefonso to have made oath on the peace with Siena, on 29 May 1201.[12]

Account (5)

Here, for the first time, is mentioned a guarantor of the loan. The form is: *e s'ei no pagasse si no promise di pagare A. B. prode e kapitale quant'elli stessero.*

A charge seems to have been made for new coin, as in *c*. 2 verso, *col*. I, acc. (4).

Carta I recto, columna 2

Account (1)

It is unusual in these accounts to enter interest (as is often done in later Italian ledgers), nor is it clear just how the amounts are computed, or whether they represent the whole liability. Here it looks as though 4 *denari* were charged for each whole *libra* for each month or part-month after the due date, thus:

£8. 0. 0*d*. for 5 months at 4*d*. = 13*s*. 4*d*.
£6. 0. 0*d*. for 3 months at 4*d*. = 6*s*. 0*d*.
                                    ————
                                    19*s*. 4*d*.

This, however, may be fortuitous, as it does not seem to hold good in other cases.

Account (2)

Here no charge seems to have been made for the *provesini nuovi* (new coin of Provins, in Champagne—seat of two of the celebrated six annual fairs of that region). Also, the total 'debits' are £15. 6. 8*d*., and 'credits', £15. 9. 8*d*.

---

[11] Santini, 'Frammenti'.   [12] Ibid.

Account (4)

The 'old book' (*libro veckio*) probably refers to the ledger of a previous partnership, of which some, or all, of the partners have continued with the existing firm.

Account (5)

Coin of Tours was the royal money of France.

Repayments appear to be 2*d*. short, but the bad state of the MS makes it impossible to be sure.

Carta I verso, columna I

Account (1)

Here, and in the surviving account in the other column, are references to deposits made on behalf of 'Mamma Sinibaldi Rinuccietti' in a 'new register' (*quaderno nuovo*). This may have been the depositors' ledger of the bank. The Florentines of the thirteenth and fourteenth centuries (unlike the Venetians in the time of Luca Pacioli,[13] *c.*1494) do not appear to have used *quaderno* to mean 'ledger', but called the latter *libro dei debitori e dei creditori*.[14] Dante's sole reference, concerning the steps up to San Miniato which were made in the times

ch'era sicuro il *quaderno* e la doga,

has misled more than one commentator, and translator; it alludes, in fact, to a public *register* which was tampered with, not to a ledger.[15] All the same, one cannot be dogmatic about an isolated reference a century earlier.

Carta 2 recto, columna I

Account (1)

This is the first of several accounts relating to loans at Bologna for the fair of San Proculo (from I May)—a profitable time for the bank, as the pious headnote indicates. The amounts lent are all stated in Pisan *denari*, the common silver currency of Tuscany at that period; Florence did not begin to coin

---

[13] See e.g. R. G. Brown and K. S. Johnston, *Paciolo on Accounting* (New York, 1963).

[14] Melis, and R. de Roover, 'Accounting Prior to Luca Pacioli'.

[15] Dante, *Purgatorio* XII, 105; see N. Sapegno's edition of the *Commedia*, with his note on this passage.

fiorini grossi (= 12*d.*) until 1237.[16] Bologna had her own coinage already, and the *buolognini* are known, from other accounts in this ledger, to have been reckoned at 22*s.* 0*d.* to 20*s.* 0*d.* Florentine. Here, though, all amounts are stated in Tuscan currency.

Account (2)

Note that in this case the guarantor (whose own loan had been guaranteed by the debtor, just before) had to repay part of the loan himself. (Total payments were £40. 2. 0*d.*; the third item, £10. 0. 0*d.*, comprised the three following ones.)

Account (4)

Settlement seems to have involved six parties, including the bank!

Account (5)

It is not clear how this account was settled.

Account (8)

This account is squeezed in at the foot of the page, and 'we settled it for mid-November' (*sodammoli per mezzo novembre*) perhaps means that the balance was transferred to another page, where the 'credit' entries were set out.

Carta 2 recto, columna 2

Account (1)

This account has been underpaid by 1*d.*

'Martinello the *binmaker*' is a tentative rendering of *arciolaio*, a word otherwise unknown and (apparently) ignored by all lexicographers. Following a hint given by Parodi in his linguistic commentary on Santini's article, the present writer supposes it to mean a maker of *arcili*—*arcile* being a Lucchese word for 'flour-bin'.[17]

Account (2)

This makes it clear that Bolognese coin exchanged for Pisan in the ratio 22*s.* 0*s.* : 20*s.* 0*d.*—or, at any rate, that was what the bankers allowed. The calcula-

---

[16] Renouard, *Les Villes d'Italie.*

[17] *Giornale storico della letteratura italiana,* 10 (1887), 178–96. In this and other linguistic matters the writer is deeply indebted to Dr Barbara Reynolds, Reader in Italian Studies in the University of Nottingham, for her explanations and help in tracing references.

tion is quite accurate, the precise figures (to the nearest *denaro*) being £5. 9. 1*d*. Pisan for £6. 0. 0*d*. Bolognese.

Account (3)

This account has been overpaid by 1*d*.

The deleted words seem to have been entered here by mistake, and transferred to another page.

The Porta San Pancrazio (in the original, 'San Brancazzo') was the west gate in the Roman walls of Florence, at the end of the Via Strozzi.[18]

Account (4)

The meaning of *storamento* is impossible to decide from the context, because of the mutilated state of the text.

Carta 2 verso, columna I

Account (3)

There is little probability that Cavalcante, son of Cavalcante, was the Cavalcante dei Cavalcanti (father of the poet Guido) who figures in *Inferno* X, 52–72. Guido Cavalcanti was born during the 1250s, and it is unlikely that his father was born as early as *c*.1190 or before. Perhaps the person mentioned was Guido's grandfather.

In this account Bolognese coin is valued at 22*s*. 1*d*. to 20*s*. 0*d*. Tuscan, and the equivalent of £46. 0. 0*d*. Bolognese is worked out very accurately.

Account (4)

Here 20*s*. 0*d*. of new Pisan coin are valued at 21*s*. 3*d*. in ordinary Florentine coin—despite the nominal equality of the silver coinage of Pisa, Lucca, Florence, and Siena around 1211.[19]

In order to make sense of this account, the writer has emended Cardinale's payment of £51. 15. 5*d*., as given by Santini, to £2. 15. 5*d*. (reading *lib. ii* for *lib. li*—perhaps a misprint). Total advances of £68. 13. 6*d*. are then matched by payments totalling £71. 2. 7*d*.—without any addition for the £50. 0. 0*d*. of *new* coin. The excess is probably interest, included in the balance transferred from 'nine parchments further on'.

---

[18] Renouard, *Les Villes d'Italie.*

[19] Chiaudano, *Studie e documenti per la storia del Diritto Commerciale Italiana nel sec. XIII.*

The Porta San Pietro was the east gate in the Roman walls of Florence; it stood at the end of the Via del Corso.[20]

Account (6)

This is the most difficult section of the accounts to understand, and as to which the Italian authorities are least helpful; nor is interpretation aided by two lacunae—though, from minute examination of the photocopy, neither seems very long.

Arnolfino, a partner in the bank, carries to the 'Badia' two sums in Veronese coin, totalling £134. 15. 0*d.*, as well as £1. 0. 0*d.* in Bolognese coin for expenses. The illegibility of a few words makes the nature of the transaction uncertain; then it is stated that the Veronese coin amounts to £78. 0. 0*d.*—presumably, the sum in Florentine currency for which Arnolfino has exchanged it. (Evidently 20*s.* 0*d.* in Veronese was worth about 11*s.* 7*d.* Florentine.) What 'Badia' means here is hard to say; the only place of that name known to have existed in Florence is the Benedictine abbey. More probably, the passage refers to the meeting-place of the *Arte di Cambio*, the guild of moneychangers and bankers; the corresponding building in Milan was called *la badia de' mercanti cambiatori*.[21] Indeed, the words *di cambio* are doubtfully read by Santini after the lacuna, and retained in the translation.

There follows a statement that Arnolfino owes the bank £8. 17. 0*d.* for a payment made on his behalf for *storamento* of the Veronese coin; this seems to refer to the charge for changing the money.[22] It is then stated that the bank has 'added' what Arnolfino is owed *per* ('from') seven named persons, one of whom is said also to owe interest; the total due from these persons is £416. 13. 3*d.*, plus between 1*d.* and 11*d.* from the last named (Bencivenni)—Santini being unable to read the number of *denari*. After another tantalizing lacuna come the words: *Monta in tutto lib. Diiii e sol. viiii e d. ii* ('It amounts in total to £504. 9. 2*d.*'). The last entry is: *Item rauemmo trappagatori per quelli di laska lib. Diiii e sol. xii* ('Item we recovered (?), including payments from those whose debts had been remitted (?), £504. 12. 0*d.*'). This assumes *laska* to be a mistake for, or misreading of, *lascia* ('remission of payment')—which presumably accounts for the excess of 2*s.* 10*d.* over the previous figure.[23]

---

[20] Renouard, *Les Villes d'Italie.*

[21] P. Petrocchi, *Novo dizionario universale della lingua italiana* (Milan, 1908).

[22] Battisti and Alessio, *Dizionario*, give *contraccambiare* (exchange) as an old meaning of *ristorare*, and this appears to be the only interpretation which fits the context.

[23] Ibid. Is this a reference to the writing off of bad debts, which were later recovered? If so, it antedates by 66 years the next earliest reference, in Bene Bencivenni's debtors' ledger, of 1277: Arrigo Castellani, *Nuori testi fiorentini del dugento* (Florence, 1952).

The hypothesis now advanced is that all this is a record of cash introduced into the firm, and loan debtors assigned to it, by the partner Arnolfino as additional capital contributed, less expenses paid by the firm on his behalf. He appears to have brought in £78. 0. 0*d*. in cash and £504. 9. 2*d*. in debtors, and refunded expenses of £8. 17. 0*d*.—a net sum of £573. 12. 2*d*., on the assumption that the second gap in the text contained at least one futher debtor of the order of £88. 0. 0*d*., to make the total up to £504. 9. 2*d*. (The £1. 0. 0*d*. in Bolognese coin would be the firm's money, on this supposition.) Correspondingly, £78. 0. 0*d*. would appear as a receipt in the cash book, and eight loan accounts would be opened for a total of £504. 9. 2*d*., with a 'debit' account for Arnolfino in the sum of £8. 17. 0*d*. Subsequently, when a total of £504. 12. 0*d*. had been recovered from the debtors, some of whose balances appear to have been written down, this sum would be transferred to an account for Arnolfino, already credited with the £78. 0. 0*d*. of cash introduced.

The implications of the hypothesis for the study of early Italian accounting are discussed later.

Carta 2 verso, columna 2

Account (1)

There is an overcharge of £1. 0*s*. 0*d*. for the new coin. The £7. 14. 0*d*. repayment comprises the three amounts which follow.

Account (2)

Compagno appears to have overpaid 6*d*. Note that the second 'debit' of 2*s*. 6*d*. has its counterpart 'credit' in account (3) following—thus confirming the interpretation of the standard terminology of entries given in the note to *c*. I recto, *col*. I, acc. (I).

Account (4)

This is notable as the only account in which the interest is called a 'penalty' (*pena*). The rate is nil for one month, 20 per cent per annum for two, and 30 per cent thereafter; perhaps Jacopo's credit was less good than the average, or the bankers wished to discourage him from extending the loan unduly. The headnote, written in later, perhaps refers to interest unpaid on an earlier loan; if it does not, then it is difficult to see how it has been computed, or whether it represents the whole amount due.

Account (5)

It is not clear how this account was settled. Cf. note on Account (2) above, for the cross-referencing of this one to Account (7) below.

Account (6)

This account seems to have been paid 10s. 0d. short; possibly one of the amounts (in *soldi*) has been wrongly entered, or transcribed.

'For sterling' (*issterlino*) refers to an English silver penny of the period, bearing on its reverse a cross extending to the edge. Its value in France was fixed at a maximum of 4 *deniers tournois* by an ordinance of Louis IX (1265). In Italy, it was (after 1252) taken generally at 17s. 0d. in sterling to one gold florin (= £1. 9. 0d. in the local silver currency);[24] i.e. the rate of exchange was approximately 20s. 0d. English to 34s. 1d. Tuscan.

THE PLACE OF THE 1211 LEDGER IN THE HISTORY OF ACCOUNTING

As the only fragment of a commercial accounting system which antedates 1255, the bankers' ledger of 1211 is of inestimable value. To the economic historian it provides evidence of the early development of banking in Florence—albeit on a modest scale, as shown by the small sums dealt in—at a time when Siena was taking the lead in this respect, thanks to the employment of her bankers in collecting and managing the Papal revenues, and when the great days of the Bardi, the Peruzzi, and the Alberti had yet to come. The ramifications of the business in Bologna point to the activity of the Florentines in opening up to their cloth trade the rich markets of the North Italian plain and, beyond that, of France; using as a base the first important trans-Apennine city, with which a commercial treaty had been made in 1203.[25] More generally, the ledger reveals relatively complex modes of settling debts, by the setting-off of liabilities between customers of the bank and their own debtors—perhaps by the use of bills of exchange or promissory notes—and by transfers between accounts at the bank. All this argues considerable sophistication in the conduct of financial business, in a growing city of some 50,000 inhabitants, already autonomous, possessed of an extensive *contado*, pre-eminent in the manufacture and exportation of fine cloths, having

---

[24] Castellani, *Nuovi testi fiorentini (glossario)*.
[25] Santini, 'Frammenti'. A further treaty was made in 1216.

excellent communications with other Italian cities, and soon destined to take a leading part in resisting the attempts of Frederick II to assert his imperial authority in northern and central Italy.[26] The accounts, too, throw light upon the contemporary attitude to 'usury'—condemned by theologians as un-Christian and unnatural (was it not making money breed money?), but tolerated in practice, in the guise of a penalty for lateness in repaying a loan which there was no intention of liquidating by the due date—which could be the date of the advance itself.

Most of all, though, is the 1211 ledger a vital piece of evidence for the early development of advanced accounting techniques in medieval Italy. Charge and discharge accounting—i.e. periodical accounts of cash (and sometimes goods) receivable, and disbursed, with the two totals equalized by entry of the opening, and closing, balances due to the 'accountant's' masters—had been known to the Romans, and reappeared in thirteenth-century Italy, most notably in the six-monthly accounts rendered, from 1226, by the officers of the *Biccherna*, or revenue office, of Siena.[27] Such accounts were in Latin, and the technique may well have survived from classical times under the aegis of the Roman Church, which must have needed some such system to keep records of its revenues and expenditures, and to control the officials who handled them. In relation to accounting for landed estates, large households, and ecclesiastical and public bodies, the cash-flow and produce-flow aspects—particularly the former—were paramount, and the profit/loss aspect unimportant or irrelevant; hence the persistence in these areas of charge and discharge accounting, down to the nineteenth century.

For a merchant it was highly important to measure profit or loss from time to time. As long as trade was thought of as a series of separate ventures, though, it was sufficient to account for the cash flows on each venture, and to strike a balance of profit/loss, on a cash basis, when it was concluded. For this purpose simple cash accounting, supplemented by *ad hoc* calculations as for the Baialordo-da Volta partnership, was adequate to ensure correct division of capital and profits. It was only when credit began to be given and taken, extensively and for long periods, that there was much incentive to keep more elaborate accounts.

In contrast, a banker's business, by its very nature, necessitated the keeping of proper records of sums deposited by, and lent to, customers, as well as an account of cash received and paid. It is thus no accident that debit and credit, as opposed to charge and discharge, accounting should have developed in

[26] Renouard, *les Villes d'Italie*.   [27] Melis, *Storia della ragioneria*.

Italy as soon as banking businesses became organized on a scale larger than that of the single-handed moneylender or pawnbroker. A bank had to be conducted by several partners, and each had to commit his capital to the firm for several years at a time; hence it was necessary that the initial, and any subsequent, contributions of each partner should be recorded, if only in the cash book. Some method, too, was needed for recording each partner's drawings from the firm, either directly in cash or by having his private expenses paid out of the firm's funds; again, a sufficiently detailed cash record would have provided the information. Ascertainment of profit or loss need take place only when the partnership was wound up, after four or five years; it could be effected by 'single-entry' procedure—valuing the total assets (mostly cash and loan debtors), less liabilities (mostly depositors' balances), adding back the partners' total drawings, and deducting their contributed capital. Each partner then took his agreed share of the profit, less his total drawings (or refunded net overdrawings), plus his contributed capital; or, if he entered into a new partnership, carried forward his capital, including undrawn profits, to the new firm's books.

The books of an early Italian bank, then, could have been adequately kept by combining the charge and discharge principle, embodied in the cash book, with the debit and credit principle, exemplified by the personal ledger. That the cash book was derived from the charge and discharge account is probable, as witness the earliest extant specimens (of an unknown Sienese merchanting and banking firm of 1277–82, and of Ruggiero da Firenze, Pope Nicholas III's treasurer in the Marches, 1279–80), in which receipts are entered consecutively in the front half of the book, and payments in the rear half.[28] The paragraph form of personal account, illustrated in the 1211 ledger and in many later Tuscan specimens up to 1300 and beyond, may also have been derived from the charge and discharge account (the debtor being charged with his advance, and discharged of his repayments), but could equally well have evolved empirically, in response to the special need of a banker for such a record.

Fairly obviously, all entries relative to the principles of deposits and loans would appear in both the cash book and the ledger, or in two ledger accounts in the case of transfer entries, and each pair of entries could be cross-referenced, one to the other—as was not done in the 1211 ledger, but appears in others from the second half of the thirteenth century. Less obviously, it might be observed that an advance to a borrower created a debt from him to

---

[28] Melis, ibid. The text of the Nicholas III *libro d'introiti e d'esiti* is printed in Castellani, *Nuori testi fiorentini*; each receipt is prefixed *Domino Papa (Niccolò terzo) de avere*, and each payment *D.P. de dare*—showing some assimilation to the debit and credit system.

the bank (an asset), and at the same time lessened the cash balance (another asset), and conversely when the loan was repaid; while a deposit by a customer increased the cash balance (an asset), but also created a debt to the depositor (a liability), both asset and liability being reduced if the depositor withdrew money from the bank. The principle of double entry was thus latent, even in the most rudimentary Italian system; but in order to actualize it two more elements were requisite: capital accounts for the partners, and a profit and loss account (with or without supporting income and expenditure accounts). Only thus was it possible to account for the equity of the proprietors, as a sum of money initially equal to the excess of assets (positive) over liabilities (negative), but of opposite sign (i.e. negative, as representing the residual claim of the proprietors to the net assets); and, by means of the profit and loss account, to make periodical adjustments to the partners' equity, so as to maintain the said equality (with opposite sign) as the making of profits (or losses) caused net assets, and equity, to grow (or decline).

The bankers of 1211 had certainly not achieved double entry, for there is no reason to suppose that they kept a profit and loss account, or could have computed their profit at any time before liquidation of the firm. They probably did not even keep any record of interest received and paid, except in the cash book. On the other hand, it is the writer's hypothesis that they must have kept capital accounts, at least in embryo form, and this he deduces from his analysis and interpretation of *c*.2 verso, *col*. I, acc. (6).

This account, seemingly ignored by previous enquirers, he believes to record the introduction of fresh capital by the partner Arnolfino, partly in cash but mainly in the form of book debts—possibly taken over by him in the liquidation of another banking firm in which he was also a partner. Had all the capital consisted of cash introduced and undrawn profits, ascertained only on liquidation, there would have been no need of regular capital accounts, credited with each partner's share of the equity. With this introduction of capital in kind, though, it would be necessary to record the amount formally, as it might easily be missed if it appeared only in the middle of the borrowers' ledger. It is therefore possible that, in some other book now lost, there were capital accounts in paragraph form for all the partners, showing all amounts of capital introduced in cash or kind—or, at least, notes thereof, whether in proper account form or not. In short, accounting for equity may, on this evidence, be several decades older than authorities such as Melis[29] are disposed to allow.

[29] *Storia della ragioneria*, 425–523. Melis sees evidence of a capital account, *to which revenue was credited*, in the ledger of some unidentified Sienese merchants operating in Champagne in 1255–62. He can only surmise the existence of *any* kind of capital account at earlier dates.

Lastly, it should be noted that the paragraph form of account was histori-cally no bar to the gradual recognition in Tuscany of the essentially two-sided nature of all business transactions. As the notes on *c.* I recto, *col.* I, acc. (I) explain, a bookkeeper of 1211 seems to have thought of the operations of (*a*) making a loan, and obtaining repayment, (*b*) receiving a deposit, and repaying it, and (*c*) making a transfer between a deposit and a loan account as three distinct pairs of entries, denoted by six different forms of words. We do not know how many years elapsed before it was generally realized in accounting circles that the six categories could be effectively reduced to two—positive (debit) entries, denoted by *de dare*, and negative (credit) ones, denoted by *de avere*: perhaps it was the adoption of the modern type of bilat-eral account, by the Venetians and Genoese in the fourteenth century, which emphasized the dichotomy and enforced the standardization of entries in two forms only. What is certain is that by 1300 some Florentine firms at least, while still using the paragraph layout, had begun meticulously to cross-refer-ence all entries, positive to negative, and to fill out the system with 'nominal' accounts for income and expenditure, summarized in a profit and loss account—thus attaining to double entry, or something remarkably near it.[30] Use of the two-sided 'debit and credit' account (first seen in the celebrated double-entry accounts of the *massari* of Genoa in 1340) was probably retarded by the need to economize on expensive parchment or paper, espe-cially where an account had many debits and few credits, or vice versa, thus leaving one half largely blank.[31] All in all, then, the form of ledger exemplified by that of the anonymous Florentine bankers of 1211 proved extremely serviceable, and was the seed-bed of that mighty revolution in accounting techniques whose effects endure to this day.

[30] Castellani, *Nuovi testi fiorentini.* He identifies the first double-entry books of account as those of Rinieri Fini and his brothers, Florentine merchants trading to the fairs of Champagne, in 1296–1305, and of the Farolfi Company of Florence, for their branch at Salon, in Provence, in 1299–1300. These are still in paragraph form, though much neater than the 1211 accounts; the Fini ones have totals of the debit and credit items in each account, and the Farolfi ones have the figures set out in columns. (Raymond de Roover is more sceptical; see his 'Accounting Prior to Luca Pacioli'.)

[31] Melis, *Storia della ragioneria.*

7 · EARLY ACCOUNTING: THE TALLY AND THE CHECKER-BOARD

W. T. Baxter

TYPES OF TALLY

History shows us (or so historians claim) how mankind once coped with conditions that now seem impossibly adverse. Certainly this is true of accounting history. It shows how accounts could be kept when paper was still unknown or costly, coins were scarce and bad, and most men were illiterate.

In these straits, our ancestors made good use of two devices. To record numbers, they cut notches on tallies. To calculate, they used the abacus, notably in its form of the checkerboard.

Meanings of 'tally'

The word 'tally' suggests various things:

(1) A simple record of numbers, such as notches on a stick or chalk marks on a slate.
(2) An object divided into two interlocking bits, thus giving proof of identity, e.g. a split seal or die.
(3) A combination of (1) and (2), such as a stick that is first notched to show e.g. the number of £s lent by A to B, and then is split to give both A and B a record.

All three types have in the past helped business, but (3)—the split tally—probably has been by far the most useful.

First published in *Accounting Historians Journal* (Dec. 1989). I have received much help from M. T. Clanchy and A. Grandell. I am grateful also to: G. de Ste. Croix and D. Wormell (classical references); G. Tegner (Scandinavia); D. Forrester and M. Stevelinck (France); F. E. L. Carter and C. Coleman (England).

Wood's importance for records

Most of the tallies described below were bits of wood. ('Tally' comes from the Latin *talia*, a cutting, rod, or slip for planting.)

To us, wood must seem a clumsy material for records. But our ancestors were short of alternatives. The most obvious was parchment (sheep or calf skin); but this was costly. Such paper as was used in Europe came from the outside till the twelfth century, when its manufacture started in Italy or Spain; Britain had to rely on imports till the late sixteenth century.[1] And wood was in fact a surprisingly suitable means of recording. It could take ink and seals, and was for long regarded as the most important writing material after parchment. Even lengthy documents such as charters could be written on birch bark.[2]

A wooden tally had many virtues. It cost practically nothing. It was easy to score. It was intelligible at a glance to both the literate and illiterate. Its harder varieties withstood rats and decay better than paper and parchment; on many survivors, every notch is still as clean and true as it was six hundred years ago. And, as we shall see, it could serve as a flexible aid to sophisticated systems.

The many roles of the 'carved stick'

Marked sticks have been able to fill many roles in many lands—e.g. management records in Sweden,[3] and 'message sticks' (mnemonic aids for messengers) in ancient Greece and among Australian aborigines, etc.[4] The counting tally must be seen as only one part of a wide range of 'carved sticks'.

Scandinavia in particular has kept many specimens of the *karvstock*, chiefly for their value as a 'rich and subtle' form of folk art. A few date back to the Vikings, but some examples in museums at Stockholm and Helsinki were still in use in the mid-nineteenth century. They have been aptly described as 'neglected bearers of a cultural tradition' because of their importance for administration as well as counting.[5] For instance, some aided village headmen: the 'alderman' had a rod on which was recorded the mark—such as a

---

[1] D. C. Coleman, *British Paper Industry* (Oxford, 1958), 4. Alex Murray, *Reason and Society* (Oxford, 1978), 301 and 475.

[2] M. T. Clanchy, *From Memory to Written Record* (London, 1979), 95.

[3] Scandinavian examples (mentioned on this and later pages) are in museums in Stockholm and Helsinki; many are described in Axel Grandell, *Karvstocken* (Ekenas, 1982). *Tidskrift for Svensk Antikvarisk Forskning*, No. 2 (1986), *Daedalus*, Swedish Technical Museum, 1987, and *Historiska studier i folkliv*, Academic Press, Åbo 1989. (Swedish with English summaries.)

[4] Horniman Museum, London.

[5] Grandell, *Karvstocken*.

variant of the swastika—of each household; he had also a ceremonial staff of office (cf. the university's mace and the magic wand?). Some were used by tax-gatherers to note receipts in cash or kind. Some long and slender survivors were measuring rods (e.g. for checking labour on fencing). Some are carved roughly, others with loving care; thus one ell-stick has been pared into a basket-like frame enclosing loose balls of the wood.

The reckoning tally

Such measuring rods, etc., had more or less permanent markings and functions. But a stick used for recording numbers might from time to time get extra notches, e.g. to note additional payments; and it might have only a brief life.

The unsplit tally (function I of the list above) was a handy means for recording both physical quantities and money. Thus an English monastery used a tally to note milk yields.[6] Surviving specimens show e.g. numbers of seals caught (Sweden), reindeer herded (Siberia), and loaves baked (Albania).[7] The tally's role in cargo checking is recalled by our use of 'tally-man'.

Crude examples of the unsplit counting tally might be no more than a rough stick on which (an English survivor) a wood-cutter scratched a line for each bundle of faggots made, presumably because he was paid by piece-rate.[8] A slight improvement gave a short notch to each unit (e.g. bundles of hides handled at Bergen docks) and an extended notch to every nth unit. And some tallies took elaborate forms. A Finnish survivor, recording day labour (rent by tenant farmers) is a long stick ruled into two columns; the left column shows each man's mark; a small indentation was made on the right column, opposite his mark, after each day's work. Other examples of management records were multi-sided. Thus, where a Swedish flour mill was owned co-operatively, somewhat complex records were needed to keep track of each owner's days of use and his contributions of upkeep work; an octagonal tally met the need. And a sixteen-sided tally of 1863 served a Swedish mine foreman as output record (one side per worker).[9]

The transition from physical measure to money must have been easy. Notches proved a convenient way of showing wage and tax payments, also credit sales at inns and shops. The word 'tally' sometimes meant a credit

---

[6] Clanchy, *From Memory to Written Record*, 32.
[7] Horniman Museum, London.
[8] British Museum.
[9] Grandell, *Historiska studier i folkliv*, 49.

transaction: 'ye shall not have redy mony neyther, but a taly' (1545);[10] and it was further stretched to cover records on materials other than wood, e.g. a slate.

Antiquity of the tally

In the nature of things, tallies of prehistoric times were unlikely to survive till now. But (a historian of numbers tells us) 'we can deduce that the recording of numbers by notches carved on suitable objects is of great antiquity and was virtually a universal practice' (i.e. function I of the list above). A few such objects have been found, including a wolf bone from Moravia, some 30,000 years old; it has fifty-five notches, arranged in groups of five.[11]

Tallies of classical times were also unlikely to survive (though Roman remains dug up in Kent include a bone with scratched notches). But we get help from literary references. The Greeks used the word *symbolon* for 'tally' in the sense of two matching parts, usually of a coin or other hard object. Unfortunately the references do not always make clear whether such a tally filled function 2 (identification) only, or 3 (identification and number); but some early writers were clearly familiar with the use of split sticks in financial transactions.[12]

A moral tale of 500 BC is germane to business. It tells of Glaucus, a Spartan who has a reputation for justice above all other men. A traveller from Miletus therefore entrusts him with gold and silver, and adds 'take these tallies and be careful of them . . . give back the money to the person who brings you their fellows'. But later, when the Milesian's sons come to claim the money, Glaucus is tempted to deny remembrance of the matter. He asks the Delphic oracle whether he can safely swear that he never received it; rebuked, he hands it over, but—for even contemplating the perjury—he and his are 'utterly uprooted out of Sparta . . . there is at this day no descendant of Glaucus, nor any household that bears Glaucus' name'. It is tempting to argue that such *symbola* would not be much use unless they were marked with the *amount* of money—function 3.[13]

Plato gives the tally a role that far transcends accounting. He makes one of his characters suggest the *symbolon* as an explanation of sexual desires, as follows. Originally, humans were united in pairs as spheres. Each sphere had

---

[10] *Oxford English Dictionary.*

[11] Graham Flegg, *Numbers in History* (New York, 1983), 41.

[12] Society of Antiquaries, *Proceedings* (1899–1901), 78. S. West, 'Archilochus' Message-stick', *Classical Quarterly*, 38/1 (1988), 42.

[13] Herodotus, *VI*, 86, a5, b1. S. West, 'Archilochus' Message-stick'.

two faces, four arms, four legs, etc. Some spheres were man–man, some woman–woman, some man–woman. They had surprising strength and vigour, and planned to assault the gods. So Zeus sliced every sphere into two. Each of us therefore is only 'the tally of a man', ever yearning to be grafted again to the tally that will fit him. All men who are sections of man–man delight to be clasped in men's embraces; all women who are sections of woman–woman 'have no great fancy for men'; men who are descended from the hermaphrodite spheres are women-courters and adulterers, and the women are man-courters and adulteresses.[14]

A Latin equivalent to the *symbolon* was the *tessera hospitalis*. This too consisted of two matching halves, normally of something durable such as a die. And it too confirmed identity, e.g. of a stranger bringing a letter of introduction.

THE MEDIEVAL SPLIT TALLY

Thanks in part to its central role at the English exchequer, we have abundant evidence of the medieval tally's use in England. And some references come from further afield. Describing his Chinese trip (1271), Marco Polo tells us that he saw illiterate persons recording their business dealings by notching and splitting sticks 'exactly as it is done with our tallies', i.e. in Venice. The 1407 statutes for university students at Paris include:

Whoever wishes to have wine beyond this portion, whether at table or away, should record it on his tally, and reckon it according to his conscience. Of which tally the one part remains with the servitor and the other with his master, and the receipt is to be tallied as soon as he gets his wine.[15]

Again, monasteries in medieval Italy accepted deposits of goods and money for safe-keeping, giving the depositor part of a split tally (of wood or parchment). This he presented at withdrawal.[16]

According to the late Sir H. Jenkinson (deputy-keeper at the Public Record Office), in medieval England the split tally was the ordinary accompaniment of government and private business. After studying hundreds of exchequer and private tallies, he concluded: 'the more we examine financial conditions . . . the more do we find that all development is conditioned at

---

[14] *Symposium.* 191d.

[15] W. Marsden, trans., *Travels of Marco Polo* (London, 1908), 251. Asterie L. Gabriel and Gray C. Boyce (eds.), *Acutorium Chartularii Universitatis Parisiensis* (Paris, 1964).

[16] Florence Edler, *Glossary of Medieval Terms of Business* (Cambridge, Mass., 1938), 21.

every turn . . . by that system of tally cutting that was already well established in the twelfth century'.[17]

Physical form

Tallies intended for splitting were usually made of well-seasoned hazel or willow (woods that split easily), and were square in cross-section. Originally they were slender, and their length often was the space between the tip of the index finger and the outstretched thumb, i.e. was less than six inches if we allow for our growth in physique over the centuries; but, as we shall see, they were later to become much bigger.

Even the exchequer tallies for large sums could be crude: some of the survivors have knots, follow the slight curve of the original branch, and still have bark along one side. A hole might be bored at one end, so that as many as fifty tallies could be strung on a thong or rod.

Stock and Foil

Typically the medieval tally was split into two bits of unequal length. The longer (the 'stock', with a stump or handle) was kept as a receipt by the person who handed over goods or money. The shorter (the 'foil' or 'leaf') was kept by the receiver. Figure 7.1 shows the two parts of a modern Kent tally with notches for physical units (hops gathered).

Fig. 7.1 Modern Kent hop-picker's tally. Horniman Museum, London.

The literate often wrote ink 'superscriptions' on both stock and foil, to show the nature of the payment. The writing of the exchequer officials was normally in Latin, but in Hebrew at the 'exchequer of the Jews'. The writing tended to be neat and compact on the short early tallies, but to sprawl across

---

[17] H. Jenkinson, 'Medieval Tallies, Public and Private,' *Archaeologia* (1923–4), 290.

the later ones. Some private tallies also bore words—occasionally scratched on, and then perhaps rewritten later in ink.[18]

Cutting the tally

An anonymous description (perhaps eighteenth century) of the exchequer's cutting method runs:

A thick stick was put into a vice and roughly squared. On one side was written in Latin the name of the accountant [e.g. a sheriff bringing cash to the exchequer] and for what service the money was paid; on the opposite side the same particulars were written. On the other two sides were written, in front, the test or day of the payment and the year of the reign of the king . . . and on these two sides the sum paid in was represented by notches of various sizes cut in the wood, each size denoting a certain amount. . . . Thus written upon and notched the stick was put into a strong block, and on one of the written sides, about three inches up, a short thick knife was placed diagonally and struck with a heavy mallet, cutting the wood halfway through; the stick was then turned and the knife inserted on one of the notched sides, at the diagonal cut, when two or three sharp blows split it down to the end into two parts, one part having exactly the same writing and notches as the other.[19]

Complex splitting

In Scandinavia, the splitting process was sometimes complex. Where three parties were concerned in a transaction (e.g. the consignor of goods, the carrier, and the consignee), a 'triple tally', split into three parallel pieces, could be used. But the high point in tally technology was the 'fork tally'. The two ends of a four-sided stick were cut apart in such a way that each consisted of a butt with two prongs; the four prongs interlocked neatly when joined. This device was used in eighteenth-century Sweden, and enabled illiterate smiths to record transactions in two currencies—the *daler* (silver) and *ore* (copper), coins whose relative values varied over time.[20] Members of the staff at the Stockholm Museum have recently made copies of the pronged tally, and have found this task easy once the trick is learned.

The tally as a receipt

Thanks to the diagonal cut (the projection seen in the illustrations), stock and foil could at any time be squeezed together again, so that extra cuts for

---

[18] Hubert Hall, *Antiquities and Curiosities of the Exchequer* (London, 1891), 119.
[19] *Notes and Queries* (1881), 493.
[20] See n. 3 above.

new transactions could be made across the split, or the genuineness of the record could be tested: 'when these two parts came afterwards to be joined, if they were genuine they fitted so exactly that they appeared evidently to be parts the one of the other.'[21]

The split tally thus gave a form of receipt that was simple yet almost fraud-proof—'an intricate but robust form of record, not replaceable readily till carbon copying'.[22]

At settlement, the creditor would often hand over his stock to the payer. The latter could then break both stock and foil, or keep them spliced together as a permanent record. Any balance could be put on a new tally.

The Dialogus

Our knowledge of medieval tallies comes in part from two remarkable books by exchequer officials. About AD 1179, Richard Fitznigel, head of the permanent staff at the exchequer and later bishop of London, wrote his *Dialogus de Scaccario*. It is cast as a textbook for fledgling civil servants, and takes the lively form of question and answer. In 1711, another official (Thomas Madox) again described the exchequer's procedure ('if I do not err in my observation'), confirming that it had hardly changed during the intervening five centuries. An accounting textbook of 1793 still defined a tally, in its dictionary of 'the abstruse words and terms that occur in merchandise', as

a cleft piece of wood, to score up an account upon by notches. They are used by the officers of the exchequer, who keep one of the clefts in the office, and give the other to persons who pay in the money.[23]

Notch language

A simple form of tally had parallel notches of much the same width, each representing a single unit, as in Figure 7.1. But this form was clumsy where numbers were big. Then some of the numbers might be shown by other types of cut. In Scandinavia, the angle was varied; / stood for 5, × for 10, and ✕ for 20.[24] In England, notches of different breadth and depth have been used for different numerical units. Thus I was denoted by a mere scratch, but 12

---

[21] Thomas Madox, *History and Antiquities of the Exchequer* (1711), 709.

[22] M. T. Clanchy, *From Memory to Written Record*, 27.

[23] Charles Johnson (trans.), *Dialogus de Scaccario* (London, 1950). T. Madox. *History and Antiquities of the Exchequer.* John Mair, *Book-keeping Modernized* (1793).

[24] See n. 3. above.

by a slightly bigger cut, and 240 by a still bigger cut. A tally marked with a I-notch and 12-notch could be a receipt for one plus a dozen units of goods, or for a penny and a shilling. We must remember that the pound and shilling were for long merely convenient units of account, i.e. coins worth a pound or shilling did not yet exist; the only English coin was the silver penny (240 of which were in theory equal to one pound weight of silver).[25]

At the exchequer, a strict ritual governed the breadth of the notches (and private persons may well have used the same dimensions). The *Dialogus* states that the cut for £1,000 had the thickness of the palm of the hand; £100, of the thumb; £20, the little finger; £1, of a swollen barley corn; a penny, a mere scratch. Later, inches were used as measures. The exchequer then allotted 1½ inches to £1,000, and 1 inch to £100; such big notches tended to be U-shaped. Half-an-inch as a V-shaped notch denoted £20, and ⅜ inch denoted £10; as a v-shaped notch, it meant £1 in late years. ⁄₁₆ inch meant a shilling; a hair's breadth, 1*d.*; and a small hole 'prickt only by a bodkin', a halfpenny.[26]

If there were many notches of different sizes, they might be grouped on both the upper and lower sides of the tally:

If you hold a tally in your hand with the thick part and hole to the left, and with the note recording the name of the person to whom the business relates and the cause of the payment towards you, then you will find the cuts for the largest denomination—whether thousands, hundreds, scores of pounds or smaller amounts—on the lower edge near the right-hand extremity, and no other denominations will be cut on that edge. The lower denominations are all cut on the upper edge with pennies nearest the right-hand end.[27]

Figure 7.2 shows a stock of 1293, issued as a receipt by the exchequer to the sheriff of Surrey.[28] It has two deep triangular notches, and is thus for 2 × £20 = £40. Figure 7.3 is a diagrammatic view of one end of an exchequer tally acknowledging the receipt of £236 4*s.* 3½*d.* on 25 October 1739, as a loan to the king on 3 per cent annuities repayable out of the Sinking Fund.[29]

Thanks to notches of different sizes, it was easy for even an illiterate stall-holder to cut and to recognize elaborate money numbers. But perhaps we are wrong to dismiss him as completely illiterate, since his notches surely can be looked on as a form of writing. (It has indeed been suggested that the tally's

---

[25] John Lubbock (Lord Avebury), *A Short History of Coins and Currency* (London, 1902).
[26] H. Jenkinson, *Proceedings of Society of Antiquaries* (1913), 33. J. E. D. Binney, *British Public Finance and Administration, 1774–92* (Oxford, 1958), 222.
[27] R. L. Poole, *The Exchequer in the Twelfth Century* (Oxford, 1912), 88.
[28] PRO. E 402.
[29] *Parliamentary Papers*, 1868–9, XXXV, ii. 339.

Fig. 7.2 Exchequer stock of 1293. Public Record Office, E402.

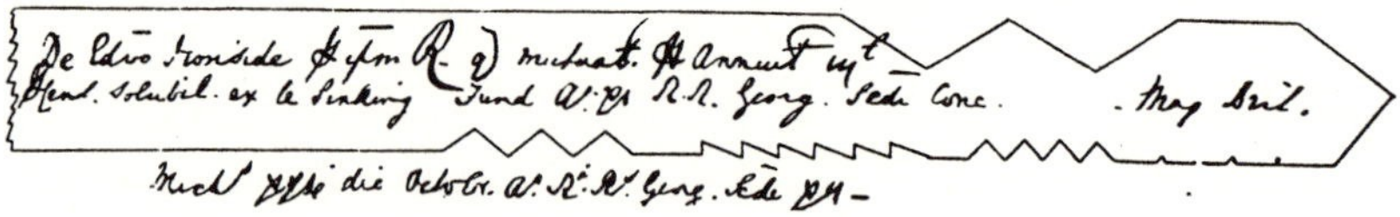

Fig. 7.3 Exchequer tally, 1739, for £236 4s. 3½d.
Source: Parliamentary Papers (1868–9), XXXV, ii. 339.

vertical and diagonal notches may be the ancestors of some ancient alphabets—runic in Scandinavia, and ogham among the Celts—and conceivably of Roman numerals.)[30]

The tally grows bigger

The tally's dimensions could readily be varied to suit the breadth and number of the notches.

Accordingly, as prices rose over the centuries, the tally's length tended to grow. (Maybe its growth could yield a rough index of general prices.) The collection at the Public Record Office (PRO) includes specimens dating from medieval times to the early nineteenth century. Its fourteenth-century stocks are slim and short (say, 5 inches), and thus in outline look rather like a toothbrush. By the eighteenth century, prices had risen perhaps fifteen-fold, and the length of some PRO tallies had stretched to between two and five feet. The famous specimen at the Bank of England is eight feet long. The

---

[30] Grandell, *Historiska studier i Folkliv*, 9, tells of a Viking tally with cuts for both numerals and Ogham words.

sides grew to about an inch, and the weight to a quarter of a pound or more.

THE MEDIEVAL EXCHEQUER TALLY

From earlier pages, one might well suppose the tallies at the exchequer to have mainly been its own receipts—issued for instance to a lender of cash, and brought back by him for cancellation at repayment date. But in fact some tallies came to concern more than those parties, and took on roles far more ambitious than those of straightforward receipts.

The tally as an order on the exchequer

In one of its extra roles, tallies became rather like a modern bill of exchange or bearer cheque drawn on the exchequer. Various officials other than those of the exchequer (e.g. of the 'King's wardrobe') issued their own tallies in return for goods that the king needed urgently but could not pay: for 'supplies could not wait upon arithmetic'. For instance, when the king and his vast household travelled, he had the right of purveyance, for which large numbers of tallies were issued to suppliers. Other officials might live far afield. A surviving account of the bishop of Carlisle tells how he bought nails on credit for work on the king's behalf at Carlisle castle; he gave stocks to the suppliers, and rendered his account (rolls) to the exchequer with the foils attached by thread as vouchers. Again, kings increasingly decentralized supply work by off-loading it onto sheriffs (e.g. these might be told to send 500 lambs to Westminster); the sheriffs issued their own tallies to sellers, as claims to be paid presently.[31]

The holder of these stocks was presumably paid later by the sheriff, etc. Or he might approach the exchequer for allowance; whether he then got satisfaction was, as we shall see, quite another question.

Orders on distant debtors

In financial matters, the medieval king faced two difficulties. First, he at times needed more ready cash (e.g. for a campaign) than lay in his London

---

[31] H. Jenkinson, *Proceedings of the Society of Antiquaries* (1913), 33; *Archaeologia* (1923–4), 306. Anthony Steel, *Receipt of the Exchequer, 1377–1485* (Cambridge, 1954), p. xxxv. W. A. Morris, *Medieval English Sheriff* (Manchester, 1925), 267.

exchequer. Second, much of his revenue was gathered and held by officials who were scattered across the realm; this cash could not readily be sent to London. He contrived to lessen both these difficulties by promoting the tally to yet another role.

The king's far-off debtors included the sheriffs and various other tax collectors, such as the port officials who levied customs dues on e.g. wool exports (the 'customers', of whom Chaucer was for some years the head). In an age without banks and safe roads, these men had great trouble in remitting money to London. For instance, on one occasion when the Boston customers brought coins, the exchequer had to command sheriffs *en route* to provide armed guards and accommodation, to be paid for out of the customers' treasure.[32]

To circumvent this difficulty, the exchequer had by about 1320 invented an ingenious use of the tally that enabled the king to settle accounts with his remote agents, and moreover to do much of his business without cash. The tally turned into an instrument for many-sided transfers.

To paraphrase Jenkinson: 'If X owes B, but is owed by A, let him—X—make out a receipt to A and give it to B, and let B not part with it till he receives the money'. In other words, if the exchequer—X—was short of funds, it would cajole creditor B into taking not cash but a tally addressed to some tax collector A. The tally purported to be a receipt by the exchequer for such-and-such a sum, paid in by the collector A out of such-and-such type of revenue: in fact, it recorded not A's payment but what he was someday likely to owe. Armed with this tally of assignment, creditor B presented himself to the collector, and—if all went smoothly—exchanged it for cash. The tally would afterwards serve the collector as his acquittance at the exchequer.[33]

On occasion, the tally followed a more roundabout path. The first holder B used it to pay C (at a discount?); C in turn might pass it to D; and so on. It thus circulated like a negotiable bill of exchange before reaching A. It became a kind of wooden money, useful to eke out the poor coinage.[34] Here then was a great innovation, but with the old primitive form preserved.

Assignment and anticipation

These assignment tallies came to play a big part in royal finance. They enabled the king to anticipate revenue: 'a pernicious process by which the

---

[32] Hubert Hall, *History of the Customs Revenue* (London, 1892), i. 10, 193; ii. 27.

[33] H. Jenkinson, *Archaeologia* (1911), 369; *Proceedings* (1913), 34. T. F. Tout, *Chapters in the Administrative History of Medieval England 11* (London, 1920).

[34] Philip Norman, *Archaeological Proceedings* (1902), 288.

crown sought to stave off present disaster by imposing severe penalties on the future'.[35] Such tallies also let exchequer officials shift the trouble of debt collection onto other shoulders. This was a mixed evil. If creditor B and collector A both worked in London, the system might do them little harm. If they worked in the same remote area, the system was positively beneficial to both, in that it cut out the costs, fatigues, and dangers of taking money to London and back; thus a royal employee B could conveniently get his salary from nearby collector A. But if B worked in London, and a high-handed exchequer gave him a tally on a remote A, the system was grossly unfair. B might be forced to go on a long journey, with no assurance of a favourable reception at the end.[36]

Delays and default at the exchequer

If a creditor's tally was drawn on the exchequer, he could face many troubles. His tally might take the form of an order on the Treasurer, payable at sight out of either revenue at large ('so much of the treasure remaining in your hands'), or some specified source of revenue.[37] But, if the exchequer's funds were running low, such orders could not guarantee payment.

Kings were not systematic in their spending, and the exchequer sometimes faced claims for two whole years of arrears. It therefore had to rank claims in some order of preference. Its chosen system affronts today's ideas of fairness. A creditor was most likely to get paid if he was (I) a member of the king's family or household; (2) a current supplier who threatened to withdraw; and (3) someone who could trade services, e.g. make a fresh loan, or (members of parliament) grant a tax.[38]

If he was not on this privileged list, the tally-holder could follow various courses. He could employ an attorney with inside knowledge to solicit on his behalf. He might pay a fee (perhaps a bribe) to officials who could 'spy out an assignment'. He might try to 'catch the king's ear'—especially by offering to cut down the size of the debt, sometimes by half. The king was apt to drive a hard bargain. If he finally favoured the claim, he gave the creditor a warrant on the exchequer. But even this might not be enough to secure attention there. Some creditors would in the end despair of being paid, and look on their claim as gifts to the king.

[35] T. F. Tout, *English Historical Review*, 39 (1924), 411.

[36] Steel *Receipt of the Exchequer*, p. xxxi.

[37] Hall, *History of the Customs Revenue*, 188.

[38] G. L. Harriss, 'Preference at the Medieval Exchequer', *Bulletin of the Institute of Historical Research* (1957), 17, *et seq.*

Even where the creditor was lucky, he would probably receive not cash but ('with somewhat tempered satisfaction') a tally of assignment. In most years, the exchequer paid more by tally than by cash; in 1381, the assignments rose to £47,000 while cash payments were only £7,000.[39]

Troubles with assignment tallies

The winning of an assignment tally could herald fresh tribulations. If it were drawn on (say) a customer in Cornwall, the holder faced an arduous journey (a prospect that might prompt him to discount the tally in London, with a merchant or perhaps an enterprising official at the exchequer itself). Arrived in Cornwall, he might be met by a harassed customer who was already overdrawn, or who faced a proliferation of preferences. Delay and insolence were common. The customer's difficulties might be genuine, e.g. where he had been ordered (assignments notwithstanding) to send all his money to the exchequer. But he sometimes used his position as discretionary paymaster to line his own pockets.

A system of preferences here again affected the tally-holder's prospects. His chances were good if he was a local baron; they might be good too if he was a local merchant, especially one whose tally was levied on customs arising from his own goods; he might even contrive to be appointed collector, and pay himself. A peremptory writ from the king reinforced a claim. A less-favoured holder might try to discount the tally with the collector, or perhaps hint at a bribe; but he would still be in competition with other claimants. An insignificant pensioner was likely to get only a 'saucy answer'.

If the holder's importuning finally came to naught, as was often the case, he had to take his dishonoured tally back to the exchequer. There the clerks cancelled his original entry in their accounts; and he wearily joined the queue for a fresh tally, probably on a different revenue. Another journey followed. Years might pass before he got his money. Yet all these (and other) imperfections in the system 'do not seem to have disturbed the equanimity of the exchequer'.[40]

The exchequer's accounting for tallies

The exchequer kept its accounts as lists of receipts and payments on separate sheepskin rolls ('pells'). This simple method worked efficiently until the tally of assignment came into use.

[39] J. F. Willard, 'The Crown and its Creditors', *Eng. Hist. Rev.* (1927), 12. Steel, *Receipt of the Exchequer*, 345.

[40] Ibid. 364. H. Hall, *History of the Customs Revenue*, i. 11, 190. G. L. Harriss, 'Preference', 25.

Not surprisingly, the exchequer could not readily fit entries for these new tallies into its cash accounts, which became endlessly confused. On striking an assignment tally, the clerks entered not only the notional receipt but (as cash was not in fact received) also a notional payment. More trouble came when the tally was finally returned by the customer, etc. for his acquittal. The clerks sometimes took refuge in explanatory glosses and fictitious loans.[41]

Discounting

We may guess that, as tallies circulated so freely, many private firms engaged in discounting; and that the big risks and delays made for stiff rates. But we know little about the details and rates of discounting, presumably in part because canonical rules against usury made explicit mention indiscreet. We do know that the customers' discount charges on tallies (bribes rather than time discount?) were looked on as an abuse of power, and were denounced in popular petitions.[42]

We likewise know little about rates of loan interest. Despite the ban on usury, the king was able to raise loans; and the rich lenders grew richer. Interest must have been allowed in some guise or other. Possibly the exchequer issued loans at a deep discount; in one instance, the lender of £2,703 seems to have paid in only £2,000, the £703 shortfall being described as war expenses. Or a lender might get a seemingly unconnected reward such as a post as tax 'farmer'.[43]

Royal control of sheriffs *via* the tally

In the early Middle Ages, the English kings (notably Henry I, 1100–35) were bent on wresting administrative power from feudal barons, and giving it to royal servants. These included the sheriffs of the counties. Besides their many other duties, sheriffs collected revenues that included certain taxes, receipts from the royal estates, and the 'rich spoils of law' (i.e. fines).

Sometimes the office of sheriff was filled by a powerful baron and became hereditary; but, whenever possible, the king put his own men into these key posts. He used the exchequer as a means of clamping tight controls on them. And the exchequer relied heavily on the tally. (Curiously, the king does not seem to have used this tally system in his southern French domains.[44])

[41] H. Jenkinson, 'Medieval Tallies', 306. C. D. Chandaman, *The English Public Revenue, 1660–88* (Oxford, 1975), 288.

[42] H. Hall, *History of the Customs Revenue*, i. 10.

[43] Steel, *Receipt of the Exchequer*, p. xxxvii, 319; *Cambridge Economic History*.

[44] See n. 47 below.

Twice a year, the sheriff had to present himself at the exchequer to defend his stewardship, i.e. act as 'accountant' for all details of the revenues and expenses of his shire. (The civil servant at the head of a British government department is still its 'accounting officer'.) He then paid in sums that he owed, and was given tallies as receipts; in early days, he might be given separate tallies for individual items of revenue (e.g. on one occasion, the Yorkshire sheriff got 972 at once), but later on he received a collective *dividenda* tally for all petty items. He produced tallies as vouchers for some of his expenses.[45]

Tax and tallies

Throughout Europe, taxes and other dues were levied with the tally's aid. Scandinavia in particular gives proofs that tallies were used when taxes and tithes were gathered. Thus a Finnish court record of 1522 tells how Thomas had to pay a heavy fine for breaking the collector's tally 'with which it is the custom to collect tax'.[46] Again, a French document of 1578 orders villagers near Dijon to stop using tax tallies.[47]

Two interesting questions follow. First, as some taxes had names that resemble 'tally', were these names derived from the tally? Examples are:

> *Tallage*, imposts levied by English kings and feudal superiors. Serfs protested 'they would rather go down to hell than be beaten in this matter of tallage'.[48]
>
> *Tallia*, a Swedish tax.
>
> *La taille*, the vexatious French tax originally levied on ignoble persons to raise funds for e.g. their lord's crusade, and later levied by the king (till the Revolution).

Voltaire tells us that the name *la taille* did indeed come from the 'odious collectors'' practice of marking each payment on a tally;[49] and some later writers find this plausible. But the balance of expert opinion traces the name to an allied stem, *taliare*, to cut (cf. 'tailor'); thus the French king cut (apportioned) the tax total between provinces according to reports on their crops, etc., and

---

[45] Helen M. Cam, *The Hundred and the Hundred Rolls* (London, 1930), I, *et seq.* Judith A. Green, *Government of England under Henry I* (Cambridge, 1986), 195. *Parliamentary Papers* (1868–9), xxxv. ii. 339. H. Jenkinson, *Archaeologia*, 368; 'Medieval Tallies', 300. Sheriff = shire-reeve. Reeve = steward.

[46] Grandell, *Historiska studies i folkliv*, 12.

[47] J.-J. Hemardinquer, 'La Taille: impat marqué sur un baton', *Bulletin philologique et historique* (1972), 508–11.

[48] H. S. Bennett, *Life on the English Manor* (Cambridge, 1937), 139.

[49] *Larousse*, 'la Taille'; Voltaire, *Oeuvres* (Paris, 1819), xiii. 80; xiv. 371.

so on down to parishes, and then (by 'friendship, party, animosity, and private resentment') to persons.[50]

Second, did the collection process rely on the split form of tally? Probably not. The unsplit tally was better in two ways: it displayed the apportionment of taxes between households, and it served the collector as voucher when he accounted to his superior for all sums due.[51]

Records of as late as 1784 show the procedure still extant in remote villages of the Landes and Pyrenees. The 'coarse and ignorant' inhabitants met in general assembly, and assessed themselves (in kind) according to their means; the collectors, also illiterate, notched the tax roll on a 'baton'.[52] Sweden has hundreds of unsplit tax tallies. A rather fine one, from 1627, looks somewhat like a broadsword. It has a line down the middle of each side. One of the resulting strips lists the payers' marks: alongside each mark, in the other strip, are notches recording the payers' dues. Finland has a planchette of as late as 1820, for day labour on roads, etc., by twenty families. Thanks to such tallies, the villagers could see the fairness (or otherwise) of the sharing between households, the payers were given a receipt before witnesses, and the collector had a complete record.[53]

THE PRIVATE TALLY

The more remote the tally was from a government office, the less likely it was to survive. The PRO has preserved several hundred private tallies (vouchers to accounts); otherwise few remain. However there can be little doubt about the 'extreme popularity' of the private tally. Estates and monasteries found it convenient; some surviving stocks, notched by a reeve when he collected rents from monastery tenants, served to acquit tenants in the eyes of the abbot. Wyclif denounced 'lords who take goods of the poor and pay for them with white sticks'. There is evidence of the tally's common use among traders by the thirteenth century (and presumably it had come into use earlier). Chaucer's characters mention it twice ('so be I faille [to pay] . . . write it upon my taille'). Many tallies, anticipating bills of exchange, were passing from hand to hand at a discount. 'English medieval finance was built on the tally.'[54]

---

[50] *Oxford English Dictionary.* Adam Smith, *Wealth of Nations* (Dublin, 1776), iii. 307.

[51] Grandell, *Historiska studier i folkliv*, 12.

[52] J.-J. Hemardinquer, 'La Taille'.

[53] Grandell, *Historiska studier i folkliv*, 12.

[54] Jenkinson, 'Medieval Tallies', 293; *Archaeologia*, 379. Steel, *Receipt of the Exchequer*, p. xxxv. Clanchy, *From Memory to Written Record*, 72, 95. Chaucer, Prologue, *Canterbury Tales*, l. 570.

At a time when coins were both scarce and bad, the tally helped to foster the process by which a credit economy flourished even though debt settlements depended ultimately on barter. A barter system could hardly function well if it consisted only of discrete transactions—if (say) tailor and peasant had to swap a coat for a pig. The tailor might not want a pig that day; and the coat might be worth more than a pig. Dealings became feasible if the tailor sold the coat on credit, and at later dates bought such items of farm produce as he needed, crediting the peasant; tallies enabled the necessary accounting to be done. They likewise enabled merchants to trade with one another on a two-way basis, with the balance swinging from side to side (as in Colonial America, where however ledger accounts kept track of the deals).[55]

Private persons used much the same notch language as the exchequer, but their writing—if any—tended to be terse and less likely to stick to the full and rigid formulas of officialdom.[56] Notches thus might perhaps stand for money or pigs or corn. The users relied on memory and witnesses for the full story.

The tally's everyday use is attested in several ways. It is for instance taken for granted in the matter-of-fact evidence at an 'inquisition' into the wounding of Walter, an estate servant: Walter was lifting a table, and Hugh was cutting tallies ready for use, when Walter tumbled and fell on Hugh's upturned knife.[57] Consider, too, comments by judges, and the tally's contributions to our speech.

Judges and tallies

Tallies featured in legal cases, for instance where a creditor demanded payment for goods or repayment of loan. His stock would then at least support his claim; but it might be accepted, not merely as evidence, but as itself generating liability. Its validity was increased if it bore the debtor's seal (important with illiterates).

In 1294, a judge went out of his way to help a merchant who produced an inadequate tally:

He who demands this debt is a merchant, and therefore if he can give slight proof to support his tally, we will incline to that side . . . Every merchant cannot always have a clerk with him.

[55] W. T. Baxter, *The House of Hancock: Business in Boston, 1724–75* (Cambridge, Mass., 1945).
[56] Jenkinson, 'Medieval Tallies', 319.
[57] Ibid., 312.

Again, a creditor in 1310 proffered two sealed tallies to witness a debt due by a parson. When the latter tried to evade liability, he provoked the following argument:

'To that you cannot get: for we have produced tallies sealed with your hand. 'We are not put to confess or deny this tally.'

At which Chief Justice Bereford thundered:

'Are not the tallies sealed with your seal? About what would you tender to make law? For shame!'

But Bereford in a later case disparaged the tally (somewhat inconsistently?), pointing out its defects:

'The tally is a dumb thing and cannot speak . . . The notches too; we cannot tell whether they refer to bullocks or to cows or to what else, and you may score as many notches as you like; and so we hold this to be no deed which a man must answer.'[58]

The tally's imprint on our speech

The wide use of tally is suggested by its many contributions to our everyday speech, e.g.:

To tally, i.e. to match or agree.

Stock. The tally's use as receipt led to 'government stock', 'stock exchange', etc. (But 'stock-in-trade' stems from the other use of 'stock' as 'wealth'.)

Counterfoil, 'counter' probably meaning a control or check.

Score has led to e.g. 'pay off old scores' and 'refused on the score of —'. Its meaning of 'twenty' is said to have come from the herd's habit of counting his beasts by scoring a stick (using the Scandinavian /, $+\!\!+\!\!+\!\!+$, ×, and ✕ for 1, 5, 10, and 20). The meanings in sport come from recording cricket runs, etc., with notches; eighteenth-century pictures of cricket matches often show two scorers notching the runs on short sticks.

In the nick of time suggests last moment victory.

Hop-scotch is related.

Indenture, a paper cut zig-zag—an alternative to the wooden tally.

Less common now are 'tallyman' (a trader selling goods on credit, and collecting the price by instalments); 'on tally' (on tick) and 'to live on tally' (outside wedlock).[59]

[58] C. H. S. Fifoot, *History and Sources of the Common Law* (London, 1949), 224–46.
[59] *Oxford English Dictionary*; but see K. Thomas, 'Numeracy in Early Modern England', *Trans. Royal Historical Society* (1987), 119.

The decline of the private tally

Jenkinson argued that tallies reached their peak of popularity in the fourteenth century, and that their private use declined thereafter (though the exchequer clung to them, ostensibly because they were necessary for the safety of the king's revenue, but also because the staff had a vested interest in the old ritual). He dated private tallies by their use of Latin or English; he saw many with Latin inscriptions (i.e. early date), only two with English (later date). He ascribed the decline to increased literacy and the coming of paper.[60]

But we may well suppose that the decline was slow, and stretched over centuries. Paper may perhaps have appeared in urban England by the thirteenth century, but it remained an expensive import. In Tudor times, a quire of writing paper (twenty-four sheets) cost a labourer's day wages; and probably the fringes of Scotland and Ireland had not yet heard of it. The invention of printing must have strained supplies of both paper and parchment; one parchment copy of the Gutenberg Bible needed the skins of three hundred sheep.[61]

The tally in many ways compared badly with paper. It was less easy to use and store. And it could hardly be adapted to the needs of the new breed of literate men who were learning to use Arabic numerals, the alphabetical index, cross-references, and then the ledger.[62] Paper's convenience came to outweigh cost, in the eyes at least of substantial merchants. The Yamey volume of accounting pictures shows Renaissance counting-houses in rich detail, but not a single tally.[63]

Yet some lesser folk must have stayed loyal to the tally. Shakespeare would hardly have mentioned it in a poem of personal feeling if it had not been in fairly common use ('nor need I tallies thy dear love to score'). Another of his lines perhaps suggests that, though still familiar, the tally was coming to be looked on as out-worn ('whereas, before, our forefathers had no other books but the score and tally').[64]

Can we regard the tally as being, in any direct sense, the ancestor of double-entry accounts? Clearly not. But the tally did foster credit transactions and multi-sided transfers; and so it must have made merchants familiar with notions that later won better expression as debits and credits.

---

[60] Jenkinson, 'Medieval Tallies', 313.

[61] Coleman, *British Paper Industry*, 4.

[62] K. W. Hoskin and R. H. Macve, 'Accounting and Examination', *Accounting, Organization, and Society* (1986), 105.

[63] B. S. Yamey, *Arte e Contabilita* (Bologna, 1986).

[64] Sonnet 122. *2 Henry VI* IV. vii. 39.

THE CHECKER-BOARD

Despite its merits as a record, the tally was hardly an efficient means of calculating. It became more helpful when it was used alongside the abacus.

The latter has taken several forms, some of which were already familiar in antiquity. It might be no more than a board sprinkled with dust on which lines were scratched ('abacus' possibly comes from Hebrew 'abaq', dust); and pebbles might serve as counters (Latin *calculus* means 'pebble'). By late Norman times, however, it had developed into the superior form (imported from Moorish Spain) of the checker-board (*scaccarium*, a chess-board). This

Fig. 7.4 Checker-board and counters (Hans Schäufelein, parable of the unjust steward, early sixteenth century)

Source: Courtesy of B. S. Yamey, *Arte e Contabilità*, 107.

might literally be a board, or a table-top, or a 'worked reckoning cloth' to be put on a table. It was criss-crossed with suitable lines; calculation was done by moving counters onto and off the resulting spaces. The counters usually were bits of metal like coins.[65]

Rulings

There were several forms of ruling (geared to the Roman numerals). One of 1691 appears in Figure 7.5. The circles represent counters, here for 1,000, 50, and 1, i.e. a total of 1,051. As can be seen, counters were put either on the lines, or (to represent intermediate numbers such as V and L) half-way between lines.[66]

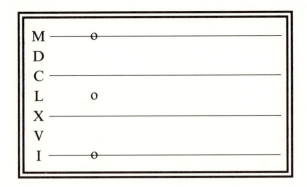

Fig. 7.5

For money arithmetic, some slightly more complex form was useful. Two such forms are shown in Figures 7.6 and 7.7. The first ('the merchants' use') had a horizontal row for each denomination of money:

> *Pence*—lowest row (nearest operator). A counter on the line stood for 1*d*.; above the line, for half a shilling, i.e. 6*d*.
> *Shilling*—next row. A counter on the line and to the right stood for 1*s*., to the left for 5*s*.; above for half a £, i.e. 10*s*.

and so on for the £ and for scores of £s. The abacus might accordingly appear as in Figure 7.6.

[65] F. P. Barnard, *The Casting-Counter and the Counting Board* (Castle Cary, 1981), 29.
[66] Ibid. 235.

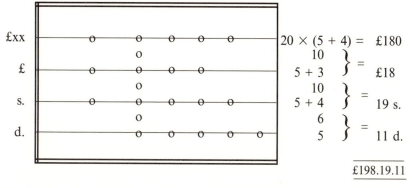

Fig. 7.6

The second form ('the auditor's use', employed at the exchequer) had vertical columns for the denominations; the operator used as many horizontal rows as he found helpful (e.g. for distinguishing revenues from expenses):

> *Pence*—right-hand column; counters stood for 1*d*. if placed low, and for 6*d*. if high.
> *Shillings*—next column; low counters stood for 1*s*.; high counters for 5*s*. (at right) and 10*s*. (at left)

and so on for £s, etc. The exchequer used seven columns (£10,000, £1,000, £100, £20, £1, 1*s*., 1*d*.),[67] and thus reflected the various sizes of notches on tallies, as in Figure 7.7.

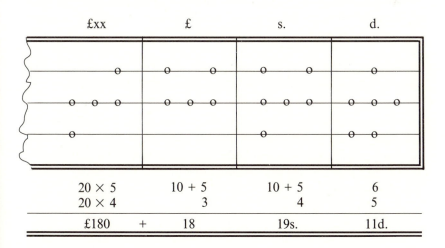

Fig. 7.7

[67] *Dialogus*, 31.

Calculation technique

To see how addition sums were done on the abacus, we can turn to the description of a tax audit at a German city (adapting it by substituting English money units). A gentleman of standing (the 'reckoner' or 'calculator') had the cloth before him, and a bowl with silver counters. The burgomaster read out the various sums due; for each sum, the calculator placed counters on the appropriate spaces. As soon as there were counters for 12*d*. in the penny space, he took them off and put one counter in the shilling space. As soon as there were counters for 20*s*. on the shilling space, in like manner he took them off and put a counter in the space for £s. A second gentleman examined the vouchers. A prelate read out a duplicate copy of the accounts (to ensure that the church got its share?). When the reckoning was finished, the calculator stated the amount shown on the cloth; the burgomaster was responsible for the accuracy of the result.

Subtraction could be done by removing counters. Even multiplication and division were possible, but only by a skilled abacist.[68]

The counters

Coins could serve as counters. But, soon after AD 1200, the French court took to using special 'casting counters' (*jettons*), and this fashion spread. Persons of refinement might have their own silver pieces, stamped with fanciful designs that illustrated proverbs, verbal conceits, etc. The less affluent used crude pieces made of base metal. Sometimes counters served too as small change.

Though few 'boards' have survived, there are still counters in plenty. One collector tells us that he owned 7,000 and had examined 35,000 others.

From the standpoints of numbers and interest to later collectors, French counters reached a peak under Louis XIV. They were employed until the Revolution (and acquired extra uses as medals and as largesse to be thrown to the poor). But the Revolution brought its simpler decimal units of money, weight, etc.; moreover the old system savoured of royalism. Many counters went to the melting pot.[69]

---

[68] Barnard, *Casting-Counter*, 233; Charles Singer (ed.), *History of Technology*, ii (Oxford, 1957), 766.
[69] Barnard, *Casting-Counter*, 22; J. M. Pullan, *History of the Abacus* (London, 1968), 45; David E. Smith, *History of Mathematics*, ii (New York, 1958).

Decline of the abacus

In Britain, the counting board probably dropped out of use somewhat earlier. Shakespeare still had references to it: Iago speaks scornfully of 'this counter-caster', and an ignoramus 'cannot do it [arithmetic] without compters'.[70]

Two things lessened the need for the abacus. One was cheap paper. The other was the use of Arabic numerals. Europe was slow to accept these. The author of the *Dialogus* knew of them (thanks to the writings of Moorish scholars), but preferred the Roman system. 'Ciphering' was long regarded as a bizarre and mysterious art. Arabic figures had, however, percolated into common use by the seventeenth century, and 'made the elementary rules of arithmetic accessible to every child'. An arithmetic book of 1668 explains manual accounting, but omits this section in its 1699 edition.[71] The Scots exchequer abandoned its board perhaps about 1660.[72] Only in the East has the abacus (in its form of beads on wires) remained popular.

THE MEDIEVAL AUDIT

Manor accounts

A feudal lord could own many manors. His whole estate was often supervised by a steward, and each manor by a reeve. The latter was either appointed from above or elected by his fellow serfs.

The reeve as accountant

One of the reeve's most troublesome tasks was to draft the yearly accounts for his manor. For this work, he relied on his memory, tallies, and perhaps notches on barn-posts. (We are told that some nineteenth-century farmers still kept complicated accounts on tallies, cutting the amounts with a billhook 'as fast as you could write them with a pen'.) The reeve's figures were put into writing by trained scribes, who made a round of manors each Michaelmas for this purpose; or the priest might do the writing.

---

[70] *Othello*, I. i. 31; *Winter's Tale* IV. iii. 38.
[71] *Dialogus*, p. xxxvii; Singer, *History of Technology*, 767; Thomas, 'Numeracy', 122.
[72] A. L. Murray, 'Procedure of the Scottish Exchequer', *Scot. Hist. Rev.* 40 (1961), 95.

In form, the reeve's accounts seem the obvious ancestor of the 'account charge and discharge', still used by Scottish solicitors for trust funds, etc. The reeve was charged to deliver, e.g.:

Rents
Sales
Fines receivable

The discharge allowed him such items as:

Tithes
Repairs to castle
The fines of tenants too poor to pay

Then came the balance payable by the reeve for this year, plus any balance due from earlier years. (Sometimes the latter balance prefaced the charge; but that arrangement blurred the current year's results.) A physical inventory of livestock might be appended on the back of the account. Tallies might be attached to the foot of the account, to record payments by the reeve to his lord.

Hearing the accounts

The feast of St Michael (29 September) was the 'season for hearing the accounts'. The reeve at that time faced a whole team of auditors: it might include the steward and (if the manor belonged to a monastery) the cellarer. These men were well informed, and would 'take inquest of the doings which are doubtful'. To help their probings, they brought with them the rolls of the manor, and so could—with seemingly uncanny knowledge—check the current figures with earlier ones. In many surviving accounts, some entries in the scribe's writing are struck out and replaced by entries in an auditor's hand. The reeve used tallies to vouch his outlays, and received a tally when he handed over his balance. If we may judge from the well-known procedures at the exchequer, the manor auditors did the needed sums with the help of a reckoning cloth.

A reeve might be put in the stocks because of his arrears. But sometimes the auditors would forgive a debt because of the reeve's 'weakness and poverty'.[73]

---

[73] Bennet, *Life on the English Manor*; John Hacker, *Rural Economy and Society in the Duchy of Cornwall* (Cambridge, 1970). *Proceedings of the Society of Antiquaries* (1893–5), 309. P. D. A. Harvey, *Manorial Records*, British Records Association, Archives and the User, No. 5 (1984).

The exchequer audit

Just as many a pub is called 'The Chequers', the principal treasury of England took its name from the checker-board, which was central to its working. An earlier name was 'The Tallies'.

The exchequer was first mentioned in 1110.[74] It was organized in two divisions:

Upper. This was a court of the 'Kings Baron's and Great Men', e.g. the Justiciar (first subject of the realm, entrusted 'with the king's very heart'), Chancellor, Constable, and Treasurer. They made sure that the royal revenue was properly collected, largely by the sheriffs. The Treasurer was the main-stay of the whole exchequer. Fitznigel had himself obtained the post (by purchase); his *Dialogus* lingers affectionately over the procedures, particularly the sheriff's audit. The upper division became also a court of law, popular because it gave prompt judgement over disputed dues, and enabled citizens to appeal against harsh collectors.

Lower. This had the humbler roll of cash office. It was staffed by lesser officials, differing in their duties (Fitznigel tells) 'but alike in their zeal for the king's advantage when justice permits it'. They deputized in their masters' names; thus, when in time the Chancellor stopped attending the meetings, his clerk took his place, eventually coming to be called the Chancellor of the Exchequer and then superseding the Treasurer as chief official; there were likewise two understudy Chamberlains and a Constable. Other officers included four tellers to count the cash, a silver-smith and melter (to assay coins paid in), a tally-cutter, and an usher who went to the royal forests to fetch wood for tallies. Some of these functionaries assisted their masters in the Upper Court when it was in session.[75]

The sheriff's 'farm'

Because trustworthy officials were not always available, medieval kings tended to privatize tax gathering, i.e. to use tax farmers. A sheriff paid a fixed rent—his 'farm' or 'ferm'—for the right to collect certain of his county's taxes, rents of royal manors, etc. (but he also had to collect and hand over some other items). A surplus on his farm was his wages; a deficit had to be made good out of his own pocket. He thus had strong reason to act as 'the hammer of the poor'.[76]

---

[74] Green, *Government of England under Henry I*, 41.

[75] *Dialogus*, p. xxxv et seq.; *Dictionary of the Middle Ages* (New York, 1984), 532.

[76] *Cambridge Economic History*, iii (Cambridge, 1963), 437. It is not clear how much the sheriffs could

The king summoned a sheriff ('see, as you love yourself and all that you have, that you be at the exchequer there and then') at Easter and at Michaelmas. The Easter visit was provisional, i.e. the sheriff then paid in about half of his dues on account—the 'sheriff's profer', for which he received a memorandum tally. His accounts were not audited till his Michaelmas visit, when he came back for another profer and then his audit, final payment, and acquittance.[77]

Analogies with chess and criminal courts

On taking his place in the court, the sheriff found himself facing a formidable team that was arrayed on three sides of a table (see Figure 7.8). The table was rather small (10 feet by 5 feet), with a rim to stop the checkers from rolling off. On it was spread a dark cloth 'figured with squares like a chessboard' with lines 1 foot apart. The row of barons overlapped the top of the table. The sheriff sat opposite them; beside him were his assistants

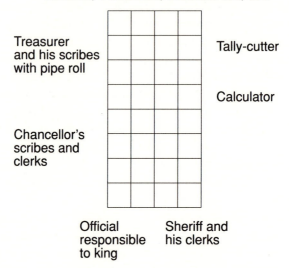

Fig. 7.8

involved outlays, yet were prized. An honest sheriff was at least entitled to various small fees and some hospitality. A dishonest sheriff could exact other fees ('the sheriff's welcome'); he could cheat the exchequer; he could commandeer horses and carts; and he could be ambidextrous as a judge, i.e. take bribes from both sides—Morris, *Medieval English Sheriff*, 279.

[77]   *Dialogus*, 79; Hall, *History of the Customs Revenue*; Poole, *Exchequer in the Twelfth Century*.

(bailiffs, and clerks with stocks and vouchers). His opponent, the Treasurer, sat on the left side, also with supporters.[78]

Fitznigel relishes the confrontation between Treasurer and sheriff, and the analogy with a chess game: just as 'on a chessboard, battle is joined between two kings . . . here too struggle is joined between two persons, to wit, the Treasurer and the Sheriff who sits at his account, while the rest sit by as judges to see and decide'.

Fitznigel carries the analogy further by describing the minor officials as pawns. There were many of these, and there was much duplication of work. Not only was each item in the sheriff's account checked carefully and entered in several rolls, but many of the officials were watched over by colleagues; as Fitznigel puts it, 'a three-fold cord is not easily broken'. Such excessive checking prompts one to wonder whether the officers perhaps were too ill-educated for accuracy, or were intent on making jobs for hangers-on, or were prone to corruption. Fitznigel must have permitted himself the same doubts; when, as 'master' in his dialogue, he has described the officer who acted as watchdog over the Treasurer, he makes his 'scholar' interject: 'Well then, saving the Treasurer's reverence, this appointment seems to detract from his dignity, since his honour is not absolutely trusted.' At which, the master replies:

God forbid! Say rather that his labour is spared and his security assured. For it is not because either he or anyone else is not trusted that so many sit at the Exchequer; but because it is fitting that such great matters and the public affairs under so great a prince should be entrusted to many great personages, not merely for the King's profit, but to honour his excellence and royal state.[79]

Audit by ear

Medieval audit procedure had to suit men who were illiterate, i.e. to whom the ear was more important than the eye; even nobles and monks 'wrote' by dictating to a scribe, and could 'read' with most understanding by listening to someone with reading skill. 'Inspecting a document' meant hearing it read. Auditors accordingly listened as the details of an account were related. (This presumably explains our rather odd use today of 'auditor'—rather than, say, 'scrutineer'—and of 'to hear from' those who write to us.)[80]

At the sheriff's audit, therefore, most of the court's exalted members sat

---

[78] Madox, *History and Antiquities of the Exchequer*, 105 *et seq.*

[79] *Dialogus*, 29. The rolls were not exact duplicates of one another, e.g. fines levied by different courts were classed differently in the various rolls. Modern attempts to reconcile the rolls may baffle researchers. M. H. Mills, *Eng. Hist. Rev.* (1921), 349.

[80] Clanchy, *From Memory to Written Record*, 97, *et seq.*

back and listened to a dialogue between the (attacking) Treasurer and the (defending) sheriff.

The audit ceremony

This can be visualized as follows. The Treasurer has made meticulous preparation; he has brought tallies awaiting matching and each shire's sheepskin records (pipe-rolls, so called because of their shape). Known revenues (e.g. fixed rents) and payments are already entered in the rolls, and blanks are left for the unknown. The Treasurer is supported by his 'lynx-eyed' scribe; next sits the Chancellor's scribe (copying what the other writes), and the Chancellor's clerk to watch that no mistakes are made. Yet another official is directly responsible to the king for another roll; he sits on the sheriff's left. At the table's right is the calculator; he sits at the middle of his side (in front of the £ column) so that his hand can move freely and everyone can see him. Beside him is the tally-cutter. Others present include suppliers, etc., holding tallies from the sheriff; alerted by public notices, they could attend the audit to check that their claims were allowed.[81]

The Treasurer starts by calling the name of the accountant, i.e. the sheriff, who is put under oath, and is charged—almost like a criminal—with having money of the king. The accounting (like that of the manor) follows the system of charge and discharge. The Treasurer carefully dictates from his roll the known amounts of the charge—the farm, arrears from former years, etc.; also the sheriff has to confess his variable revenues (including fines, the chattels of fugitives from justice, of those mutilated for their crimes, and of deceased usurers). His discharge covers fixed payments such as tithes, alms, and the wages of royal servants (e.g. pipers and wolf-takers). It covers also his variable payments. As authority for making these, he may plead custom (e.g. the expenses of trial by ordeal), or he may hand in the royal writs sent to him (e.g. orders to fortify castles, and to give 'honours and succour' to royal guests). Even where the court knows well that such-and-such outlays have been made, it may hotly contest the sheriff's claim if he does not submit writs as authority and vouchers proving payment.[82]

Meantime the calculator—who can perhaps be likened to a slick modern *croupier*—listens to the proceedings, and says the amounts as he flips his counters on and off—a 'confusing and laborious process . . .'

---

[81] *Dialogus*, 18, *et seq.*; *Dictionary of the Middle Ages*; iv. 530; *Parliamentary Papers*, 341; Morris, *Medieval English Sheriff*, 252.

[82] *Dialogus*, 24, *et seq.*; Hall, *History of the Customs Revenue*, 196.

> Tongue, eyes, hand and restless brain
> Work with all their might and main.

He puts out the charge items as heaps of counters, and then the discharge items as heaps on a lower line. In simple cases (no 'blanching'—see below), the lower line is next subtracted from the upper; the sheriff is responsible for the remainder. His stocks for earlier payments are duly matched with foils held by the exchequer.

The above description is oversimplified in various ways. For instance, the sheriff's dealings may be split between his main farm and various minor sections, each of the latter being treated as a separate account charge and discharge. Again, some of the items may be entered by tale (the stated number of pence being accepted without deduction for clipping, forgery, and other faults), or may instead be subject to blanching (deduction for the faults). For the blanching process, the melter takes from the sheriff's cash a random sample of 240 silver pence, melts them over a 'cleansing fire', skims off the impurities, and ends with a silver ingot. This is brought back to the court and weighed. If (say) it is 12*d*. (= 5 per cent) short of a pound weight, and the sheriff's payment is £100 of coin, the heap of counters at his credit is cut down to only £95. Then, in order that the Treasurer can account for the actual number of coins, two tallies are struck—one for the £95 (given to the sheriff), and a shorter 'combustion tally' for £5.[83]

Moreover, doubtful questions continually come up during the audit. Do the rents accord with ancient custom? Has the sheriff acted properly? The Justiciar and other barons resolve these points and declare the law: 'the highest skill at the exchequer does not lie in calculations but in judgements'.[84]

After two days of grilling, the sheriff's ordeal ends. He publicly takes his affidavit that he has made his account to the best of his knowledge and belief. If the balance is adverse, he pays it in; the two halves of his tally are put together, and the payment is recorded in fresh cuts across the splits; if he cannot pay, he is liable to go to the Tower. If a balance is due to him, it is carried forward or set off against any sums due by him on other accounts.[85] Finally 'he is quit' is written in the rolls,[86] and he is 'cast out of court'. His account cannot in future be called in question; like a person discharged by a criminal court, he cannot be tried twice on the same charge.[87]

---

[83] *Dialogus*, 38, 125.

[84] Ibid. 15–30.

[85] Ibid. 21, 126; Hall, *History of the Customs Revenue*, 186.

[86] 'Quietus est'; this gives point to Hamlet's 'he himself might his quietus make with a bare bodkin'.

[87] J. E. D. Binney, *British Public Finance and Administration 1774–92* (Oxford, 1958), 216, 238.

After Fitznigel's time, some details of the procedure changed. Thus the duration of a typical audit rose to seven days; perhaps as a result, the date fixed for an audit might be many months after the fiscal year.[88]

Audit of lesser officials

Much the same procedure was continued further down the official scale, e.g. between a sheriff and minor accountants (such as bailiffs from whom the sheriff exacted a farm for the right to collect part of the revenue).[89] The sheriff had his own 'exchequer', often in the castle of his county town, with an elaborate machinery of records and private tallies.[90]

THE EXCHEQUER TALLY'S SPECTACULAR END

The private tally disappears

After the fourteenth century, as we have seen, substantial merchants used the tally less and less, though petty traders still found it helpful till the eighteenth century or even later. Hogarth's picture of the milk-woman shows her brandishing a tally at her poet-debtor. (Sly milk-women could sometimes, without detection, 'cut dead men'—i.e. two notches for one on the split tally.[91]) A historian, recalling his stay in Paris during the 1830s, tells us:

The baker's man in the morning brought with his basket a bundle of tallies on a ring. The maid produced her counter-tally, and the number of rolls or loaves was marked with a file on tally and counter-tally laid together, just as described in the *Dialogus*.

Such a baker might keep tallies not only for his debtors, but also for his creditors; these supplied wheat, and were later paid by barter (a loaf in return for a kilo of flour).[92]

One comes across stray references to the split tally even in the early twentieth century. It has served as a record of output (e.g. bins filled by Kent hoppickers), and of timber deliveries to the University of Åbo (Turku). Its use was often associated with dirty materials (e.g. charcoal deliveries in Sweden), presumably because these would soil paper records.

[88] M. H. Mills, *Eng. Hist. Rev.* (1921), 484.
[89] Morris, *Medieval English Sheriff*, 250.
[90] Ibid. 283. Jenkinson, *Archaeologia*, 368; 'Medieval Tallies', 301.
[91] Dorothy Davis, *A History of Shopping* (London, 1966), 217; Thomas, 'Numeracy', 119.
[92] J. H. Ramsey, *Revenues of the Kings of England* (Oxford, 1925), 13; M. Stevelinck in correspondence. The tally was still used in some Kentish hop farms in 1938. The stocks were kept by the tallyman (strung on a cord at his belt) and the foils by the pickers. A notch was scored with a file across both bits for every five bushels—notes by Museum of Kent Rural Life, Maidstone.

The exchequer's late ritual

Far from disappearing, the exchequer tally kept and even increased its importance for some centuries.

The exchequer has given historians much scope for colourful prose. It was 'elephantine in its movements but elephantine in its memory . . . its lethargic ritual concealed a curiously sluggish vitality'. Its ancient custom was 'already a fetish' in the thirteenth century. Nevertheless it ran 'the most efficient system of public finance in Europe'; at it, the English 'showed their systematising genius'.[93]

The exchequer's cutting and notching method persisted with little change for six centuries. A thirteenth-century clerk could have interpreted an eighteenth-century tally (though, as we shall see, he would have been startled by its extended functions). Roman numerals and Latin were used till the end.

However, time brought a shift to new taxes that the sheriff did not collect, and so his half-yearly visits grew less important; nevertheless the antique manner of *viva voce* audit survived (till 1834), with a kind of dress-rehearsal the day before.[94] For other transactions (e.g. day-to-day dealings with tax-collectors and lenders), the tally ritual had by the sixteenth century become as follows. The sum of money received was entered in an account book and then on a strip of parchment—the 'teller's bill'. To prevent fraudulent alteration by the payer, the bill was thrown down a pipe into the tally court, i.e. a room below. Here entries were made in two more books; a tally was struck by two deputy-chamberlains, and a tally-writer put on the narration; then entries and tally were checked and rechecked. The payer could collect his stock on application, usually on a later day. If his payment was a loan, he would at its maturity present his stock; another elaborate ritual followed as the officials sought out the foil, joined it to the stock, and made suitable entries in the rolls.[95]

Given such strict procedures, how are we to explain the stocks that were not returned to the exchequer, and are now prized by antiquarians? Part of the answer may be that, while lenders had good reason to return their tallies at maturity date, other men might have less reason, e.g. a payer of certain kinds of tax, of a fine, or of a fee for a baronetcy. In theory, some of these payers later took their stocks back to the exchequer to have their accounts acquitted; the officials then kept the stock and spliced it with the foil. But a

---

[93] *Dictionary of the Middle Ages*, iv. 531; Jenkinson, *Archaeologia*, 368; Henry Roseveare, *The Treasury* (London, 1969), 21.

[94] Binney, *British Public Finance*, 213.

[95] *Parliamentary Papers* (1835), xxxvii, p. 342.

payer might not bother with this sterile drill; and so stocks remained in private muniments.[96]

Tallies of *sol* and *pro*

At one time or another, the exchequer used perhaps a dozen different kinds of tallies (including e.g. memorandum and combustion—described above). But, for our purposes, the later tallies can still be classed under the two familiar heads:

1. *Tally of receipt*. This was the straightforward acknowledgement of actual in-payment. The first word of the entry in the pell was *solutum* (= paid); hence *sol* tally.

2. *Tally of assignment*. This was the instrument for securing payment from a third party. It usually was still a *sol* tally; the payee was not named, so that transfer was possible. But it might be a *pro* tally; here the inscription stated that it was struck *pro* (= for the benefit of) a named person, on a specified revenue. Such revenue was alienated, i.e. the right to money was transferred to the favoured creditor, who could in his own name sue the revenue receiver. A *pro* tally was clearly less flexible than a *sol* tally, and perhaps less useful to the king as a means of anticipating revenue.[97]

To woo cautious investors and lessen the king's dependence on goldsmiths, yet another kind of assignment tally was devised by exchequer officials early in the reign of Charles II. This was the 'tally of loan', which can perhaps be regarded as the first government stock. It was backed up by a repayment order that carried 6 per cent interest and was negotiable by endorsement. Such tallies were to be cashed in regular sequence from taxes granted by Parliament; but officials at once extended the system to other kinds of revenue that the original Act had not contemplated. The tallies passed from hand to hand, e.g. goldsmiths (whose banking activity was expanding fast in this period) cashed them at a discount.[98]

Climax under Charles II

Charles II inherited an impossible financial position, and needed a growing revenue; yet a hostile Parliament was niggardly in voting him taxes. The

---

[96] Jenkinson, 'Medieval Tallies', 293.

[97] Binney, *British Public Finance*, 224; Chandaman, *English Public Revenue, 1660–88*, 288.

[98] John Clapham, *The Bank of England* (Cambridge, 1944), 11; W. A. Shaw, 'The Treasury Order Book', *Economic Journal* (1906), 37.

exchequer was thus hard-pressed. One of its troubles now seems odd. The revenues of a financial year came in only after some delay, whereas expenditures began immediately. Modern states have learned how to smooth over this temporary shortfall; 'the process seems so easy to the modern mind that we are almost reluctant to acknowledge the difficulty of the problem that beset Charles'.[99]

The tally, particularly the new tally of loan, gave the king an unseen and unsuspected way of creating credit almost at will. He exploited it to the full.

We are lucky in having first-hand accounts of the issues from a high civil servant. Pepys, as secretary to the navy, had to rely on tallies to meet the fleet's needs. The exchequer gave him new tallies which he then tried to turn into cash. His diary has more than eighty references to them, e.g. 'To the exchequer, and there got my tallys for £17,000, the first payment I ever got out of the exchequer . . . and away home with my tallys in a coach, fearful every step of having one fall out or snatched from me' (19 May 1665). His fears were not groundless. On 26 November 1668, a subordinate lost a £1,000 tally. However when Pepys came to his office two days later, he heard to his 'great content' that a porter had found the tally in Holborn, and had brought it in; for which honest act the man was rewarded with twenty shillings.

Charles II at first managed the issues with prudence. But soon, hard-pressed by the demands of war and love, he grew reckless. The issue of tallies rose to a *crescendo*. In consequence, they became hard to cash. Pepys tells how he went to the 'Excise Office where I find that our tallys will not be money in less than sixteen months; which is a sad thing, for the king to pay interest for every penny he spends—and which is strange, the goldsmiths with whom I spoke do declare that they will not be moved to part with their money upon the increase of the consideration by 10 per cent' (21 Jan. 1665). The tally office became overworked, and its ancient form of accounts grew bewilderingly complex; Pepys denounces its clerks as 'lazy rogues . . . Lord, to see what a dull heavy sort of people they are there, would make a man mad' (16 May 1665).

By the 1670s, the royal finances were in great disorder. The debt rose to £1 million, a whole year's revenues. Bankers were 'ground between their angry creditors and an empty exchequer'. The legal limit on interest rates was 6 per cent, but Charles had to pay 20 or even 30 per cent. In 1672, he was forced to suspend all payments of interest for twelve months—the 'stop of the

---

[99] Shaw, 'Treasury Order Book', 35.

exchequer' by which 'the common faith of a nation was violated', and some goldsmiths were incapacitated.[100]

Tallies and the founding of the Bank of England

Despite this disaster, the exchequer in following decades was still able to issue tallies and notes. But the 'stop' meant that no one would accept these unless they were backed by high interest. Moreover they circulated at a discount. The rate reflected the status of the taxes on which the tallies were secured. It reflected too the king's fortunes: those of William III did not inspire confidence, and so (according to a somewhat jaundiced pamphlet) great numbers of his tallies lay bundled up like faggots in the hands of brokers and stock-jobbers, who 'devoured the King and the army . . . scarce 50% of the money granted by Parliament has come into the hands of the exchequer, and that too late for service, and by driblets'.[101]

Trade was expanding greatly in these years. Traders and Crown both needed a solid establishment that could advance money at a reasonable rate. So there was a strong case for the 'daring idea' of a Bank of England. It was duly founded in 1694.

Tallies were important in its financing. The government wanted to get the flood of tallies off the market; and, after hard bargaining, the Bank agreed to help, on very advantageous terms. Subscribers to its capital ('engrafted stock') could pay four-fifths in tallies, taken at par; the government then paid the Bank 8 per cent interest on the tallies' nominal value. It also instructed the Bank (1696) to buy up other tallies (said by then to be selling on average at a 40 per cent discount), and on these too it paid the Bank 8 per cent interest.[102]

Even after the Bank was founded, tallies played some part in finance. Coins were still scarce, and so 'all great dealings were transacted in tallies, bank bills, and goldsmiths' notes'.[103]

By the eighteenth century, the Crown relied increasingly for its short-term needs on exchequer bills rather than tallies. But it still issued tallies to investors in the national debt. And it experimented with a new form, the annuity tally: lenders got the right to an assignable annuity, for life or a fixed term such as ninety-nine years.[104]

---

[100] John Clapham, *Bank of England*, 12; E. Lipson, *Economic History of England* (London, 1956), iii. 236.
[101] J. Francis, *History of the Bank of England* (London, 1847), 58.
[102] Clapham, *Bank of England*, 47.
[103] A. Andreades, *History of the Bank of England* (London, 1924), 23.
[104] Philip Norman, 'Exchequer Annuity Tallies', *Proc. Archeological Soc.* (1902), 300; Binney, *British Public Finance*, 127.

The end of the exchequer tally

It was obvious by the eighteenth century that the routines of the exchequer, once admirable, had become a confused farce. But they lingered on, even though they had to be buttressed with a parallel system more suited to the times. Clerks from the Bank of England came daily to take charge of the cash transactions and make the effective accounting entries; and payers got a written quittance as well as a stock.

The exchequer could not reform itself even if it had wanted to do so. It was hamstrung by its own rules, which had grown into non-statute law. The tally was the only form of quittance allowed to it. And its officials, now sinecurists who delegated their work, had the strongest reasons to fight change. They were paid fees on all receipts; as the national revenue grew, so did their pickings. A teller was rumoured to earn what was, for the times, the immense income of £30,000 a year.[105]

But, as part of the popular campaign for political reforms, change came at last. An Act of 1782 abolished the sinecures at the exchequer—though still with a reprieve; an indulgent Parliament provided that the Act should not take effect till the death or retiral of the two Chamberlains. These were young patricians (one was still at Eton), and they clung to their offices for another forty-four years, i.e. till 1826. Then methods were reformed also; paper replaced wood as the material for receipts (but still with the old Latin formula). The obsolete accounting routines were abolished soon after—the sheriffs' in 1833, and the exchequer's in 1834.[106]

A fair number of the late tallies are in the PRO. They, and their accompanying accounts, show some odd quirks in state finance. An unknown American in 1805 sent conscience money. The account of an official at Gibraltar includes money spent for the release of captives in Morocco, and (1752, the year of calendar reform) shows deductions from salaries for 'the eleven days in September annihilated by Act of Parliament'. Some tallies suggest extreme dilatoriness in settling accounts; thus an 1825 tally is for transactions in the 1808–14 Spanish campaign; and the executors of a contractor got his 'stipend', for work in Florida during 1767 and 1781, only in 1826.[107]

---

[105] Binney, *British Public Finance*, 224; *Illustrated London News* (1858), i. 446.

[106] R. L. Poole, *Exchequer in the Twelfth Century*, 91; M. T. Clanchy, 'Burning the Tally Sticks in 1834', *Literacy and Law in Medieval England* (London, forthcoming 1995); Dickens was satirical about the exchequer's reluctance to replace sticks with paper: 'all the red tape in the country grew redder at the bare mention of this bold and original conception', *Speeches and Letters*, ed. K. J. Fielding (Oxford 1964), 204.

[107] PRO F 402/301; British Museum, OA 9443–8.

Parliament blazes

But the tally's story has a postscript of high drama. The exchequer had from time to time used old tallies as firewood. (Clearly it viewed records of wood with disdain; paper and parchment were preserved at some cost.) Between 1826 and 1834, however, more than twice the usual quantity had accumulated in the tally room at the exchequer. Then space was needed for a bankruptcy court, and so in 1834 the Lords of the Treasury ordered most of the tallies ('which my Lords understand to be entirely useless') to be destroyed.

The site chosen for the bonfire was a yard that then lay between Parliament and the Thames; the men in charge were cautioned to be careful as the Parliament building was only wood and plaster. But the Clerk of Works—keen on the up-to-date technology—decided that the new iron stoves under the House of Lords would instead be a safe and proper place for the burning. On the evening of 15 October, two workmen employed by contractors moved the tallies (enough to fill two carts) to the cellars. At 6.30 next morning, they began to stoke the stoves, putting in only some ten tallies at a time, and damping them occasionally with water. But by afternoon they had grown impatient, and were pushing in the tallies as fast as they could. At 5.00 p.m. one witness saw an 'astonishing blaze'; a member of a guided tour in the House of Lords felt the heat through his boots. An hour later, the fabric burst into flames.[108]

The Times reported that

people living nearby were thrown into the utmost confusion and alarm by the sudden breaking out of one of the most terrific conflagrations that has been witnessed for many years past . . . countless numbers swarmed upon the bridges, the wharfs, and even upon the housetops; for the spectacle was one of surpassing though terrific splendour . . . Not even the most zealous exertions could save the edifice from absolute destruction.[109]

The tally did not die tamely.[110]

---

[108] *Parliamentary Papers* (1835), xxxvii, p. 329.   .

[109] *Times*, 17 Oct. 1834.

[110] Earlier articles are: R. Roberts, 'A Short History of Tallies', *Accounting Research* (July 1952); W. E. Stone, 'The Tally', *Abacus* (June 1975); R. H. Parker, 'Accounting Basics', in G. Macdonald and B. Rutherford (eds.), *Accounts, Accounting and Accountability* (London, 1989).

Fig. 7.9

DOUBLE ENTRY

8 · THE GALLERANI ACCOUNT BOOK OF 1305–8

C. W. Nobes

This chapter discusses the *Libro dell'entrata e dell'escita* of the London branch of the Gallerani company between the years 1305 and 1308. It appears that it has not been considered in detail before by an accountant. The question of whether it represents double entry is examined. The Farolfi ledger, which may be the earliest extant example of double entry, is only six years older (Lee 1977). This research should be of interest to those who are not accounting historians because it deals with the period when bookkeeping was developing into the Italian fifteenth-century double-entry system which is still the basis of accounting throughout most of the world. Further, because it is not immediately clear whether this account book uses double entry, it raises interesting questions about the exact nature of the characteristics of double entry.

HISTORY OF THE *LIBRO*

This surviving book of 'entry and exit', which is written in medieval Tuscan Italian, is akin to a journal. It is at present in Belgium where it arrived with Tommaso Fini, who was a member of the Gallerani company and also a Flanders agent of Robert of Béthune. It is not clear exactly when and why the Gallerani left London, but it *is* clear that foreign merchants and bankers were in danger from the king, Edward II. De Roover (1956: 126) refers to the records of the flight of the Frescobaldi partners from England to escape arrest in 1311–12. But difficulties were not confined to England, and Fini had to leave 'Belgium' hurriedly in 1309, whereupon the documents were

First published in *Accounting Review*, 57/2 (Apr. 1982). I am very grateful to R. H. Parker for prompting the work leading to this paper; to him, G. A. Lee, B. S. Yamey, and anonymous reviewers for their many helpful comments on earlier drafts; and to R. Bruni for help with translation.

confiscated by the Count of Flanders and thereby preserved. They may now be found in the State Archives at Ghent.[1] There they were noticed in passing by P. de Decker[2] in 1844 and subsequently transcribed by Georges Bigwood, whose work was carried on after his death in 1930 by Armand Grunzweig. The latter completed the study and published a two-volume work (Bigwood 1961 and 1962).

The Bigwood books contain much history of the Gallerani company and its international operations, and also deal with other early fourteenth-century records which relate to their Paris branch. Bigwood's transcription work is obviously of great value. However, his readers should note that it is possible to detect some errors. There are a number of simple transcription errors where the Italian date in the entry is different from that in the margin.[3] In addition, it should be mentioned that the marginal dates are sometimes the dates of the entry and, at other times, the dates of the transaction. In the present writer's opinion, there is also misinterpretation of some entries.[4]

Bigwood (1962: 257) suggests that the *Libro* represents *'comptabilité en partie double'*. Martinelli (1974: 480) quotes Bigwood in translation and does not disagree with him. However, Bigwood was not an accountant, and there is no specific backing for the claim. He was relying on a discussion with and reading of Melis (1950: 474), who refers to the Gallerani papers as *'partita doppia senese in piena maturita'*.[5] However, de Roover (1956: 123), who was consistently more sceptical about such claims, comments[6] that 'a cursory examination led Professor Melis to the conclusion that the Gallerani unquestionably kept their books in double entry. This is possible, but by no means established without more careful study'. It appears that no accountant has given the question 'more careful study' in published form since the publication of the transcription. It is intended to do this here, after a brief digression on the London branch of the Gallerani.

---

[1] When Melis (1950: 475) wrote, the *Libro* was in Brussels. However, it has now returned to the Rijksarchief at Ghent, where I worked on it in May 1981.

[2] Cited in Bigwood (1962) as de Decker (1844).

[3] For example, entries 318–23, 377, 378, 394, and 395.

[4] See entry 402 quoted in text (*Dr.* fol. 128 in *GI*; *Cr.* fo. 57 in *LDC*). Bigwood thinks fo. 57 in the *LDC* is a clothes account. However, why should this be *credited?* There must have been a credit to either 'cash' or 'Frescobaldi'. I believe fo. 57 contained the Frescobaldi account.

[5] 'Fully developed Sienese double entry'.

[6] De Roover's writing was published five years *before* the publication of the Bigwood transcription.

THE GALLERANI IN EARLY FOURTEENTH-CENTURY LONDON

The Gallerani, we are told (Bigwood 1962: 5), was a Sienese merchant company of medium size. Its London branch was closely linked with that in Paris.[7] It borrowed and lent money; bought and sold horses, lead, gems, and other merchandise; and settled and collected debts relating to other branches. Most of the bookkeeping was carried out by a London partner called Biagio Aldobrandini, as the *Libro* records. It is not clear exactly where they did business, but they paid for premises at what they called 'Valbrocco' (Walbrook, in the City of London) (Bigwood 1962: 120).

At the beginning of the period of the *Libro*, England was ruled by Edward I (reigned 1272–1307). The Prince of Wales was the future Edward II (reigned 1307–27) of considerable notoriety and unusually unpleasant demise, as historians and playwrights have recorded (e.g. Keen 1973, Marlowe 1598). Biagio went to the coronation of Edward II, as entry 402[8] records:

402. (*escita*)   £7. 8. 0*d.* to expenses, to be given to the Frescobaldi for gold cloth and robes they bought for us for the King's coronation.

It is clear that the Gallerani dealt with the mighty: there are many entries concerning lords, knights, and cardinals. One of the characters who looms large in the history and drama relating to this period is Piers Gaveston, the favourite of Edward II. In the Gallerani records, there are two interesting entries dealing with 'Piero di Ghavestona'. Entry 400 notes that on 4 August 1306, Biagio spent 28 shillings and 6 pence sterling[9] on merchandise, including some for the said Piers Gaveston. More fascinating is entry 190:

190. (*entrata*)   £8. 13. 4*d.* charged to the Treasurer of the Prince (*LDC* fo. 37) for a horse ('*sardo leardo*') received by Piers Gaveston [see 179 and 351 below].

---

[7] For more details on the activities of the company and its organization, see Melis 1950: 472–76 and Bigwood 1962.

[8] Entry numbers are those allocated by Bigwood (1961). Narratives are the author's abbreviated translations.

[9] All of the entries are in sterling, and in the pounds (£), shillings (*s.*), and pence (*d.*) system adopted from the Romans, and only abandoned in England in 1971. In this case, there are 12 pence to one shilling, and 20 shillings to one pound.

THE NATURE OF THE 'LIBRO'

The *Libro dell'entrata e dell'escita* (*LDE*) is a form of journal organized in two parts, as was Sienese custom (de Roover 1956: 122, 123, 127). Each page has five or six entries which consist of narratives, amounts of money in sterling, and references to other books. Although the *Libro* is clearly related to a cash book and probably evolved from it, it would be misleading to call it by such a name, for many entries have no direct cash involvement. Folios 1–26 (including the *verso* in each case up to folio 25) contain entries concerning sterling receipts or the creation of sterling debits in some other way. At the end of each piece of narrative there is a folio reference to another book of account, the *Grande libro* (*GL*). This book is missing, as are all others apart from the *LDE* itself. However, in all cases, the reference for the credit is to this *Grande Libro*. Where cash is received there is no reference to an account to be debited (clearly this implies a debit to cash); where another account is to be debited because cash has not been received, there is a folio reference to a third type of book, the *Libro dei conti* (*LDC*).

Then there are blank pages from 26^v to 36^v. The second part of the *LDE* runs between folios 37 and 54. It contains sterling payments or the creation of other sterling credits. In each case there is a narrative, a reference to an account to be debited in the *Grande libro*, and, where the transaction is other than a cash payment, a reference to an account in the *Libro dei conti* to be credited.

The first half of the *Libro* (*entrata*, inflow) contains entries involving either *da* (i.e. received from) or *che dieno* (or *debeno*) *avere* (i.e. who should have or should be credited). The second half (*escita* or *uscita*, outflow) contains entries involving either *a* (i.e. payment to) or *che dieno dare* (i.e. who should give or should be debited).[10] In the case of non-cash entries, it is often unclear why the debit, rather than the credit, goes to the *Grande libro*, that is, why the transaction is an *escita* rather than an *entrata*. Most accounts seem to have existed in both the *Grande libro* and the *Libro dei conti*.

Possibly, an attempt was made to put frequent transactions through the latter in order not to clutter the former. Alternatively, perhaps stricter security and secrecy were attached to the former.

The dates of the entries are a slight problem because, as mentioned above, some are the dates of transactions, and others are the dates of recording.

---

[10] Similar expressions were noted by Lee (1973: 141) in a Florentine bank ledger of 1211.

Many dates are missing. The *LDE* does not follow strict chronological order, which is not unusual for 'early' accounting. However, within any folio the order is mostly chronological, and the two halves of the *LDE* generally move forwards, starting from May 1305 and ending in October 1308, but with several exceptions.

As has been mentioned, the *Grande libro* and the *Libro dei conti* are missing. However, the accounts that they contained can be inferred from the many references to them in the *LDE*. Bigwood (1962: 246–54) lists the accounts that must have been on the various folios in these two books. However, he omits a cash account which, judging by closing entries in the *LDE*, would have been on folio 30 of the *Grande libro* (entry 427, see below). The accounts in the *Libro dei conti* are transferred to the *Grande libro* at the end of the period (entry 423, see below).

The first two entries in the *LDE* (Figure 8.1) are balances brought forward at 1 May 1305 from the previous period. Entry 1 is the cash balance of £15. 0s. 10d.; entry 2 is the excess of all other debit balances over all credit balances remaining in the previous period's *Libro dei conti*, £109. 4s. 11d. (detailed as the entries necessary to close the previous *Libro dei conti*).

		Dr.	Cr.
1. (*entrata*) 1 May 1305	£15. 0. 10d. cash left on 30 April 1305.	(Cash)	From previous *LDC* via the *GL*.
2. (*entrata*) 1 May 1305	£109. 4. 11d. balance of the *Libro de' conti* i.e. 224. 17. 6d. to be collected and 115. 12. 7d. to be given to others. [Thus, some entries would be the opposite of those shown on the right.]	Various accounts in *LDC*	From previous *LDC* via the *GL*.

Fig. 8.1

Judging by the procedure of October 1308 (discussed below), the entries to close the previous *Libro dei conti* had their counterparts in the *Grande libro*. The entries are here reversed to open up the new *Libro dei conti*. The *Grande libro* had not been closed down. Its balance could have been used to determine profit and to draw up a balance sheet. Sadly, any evidence of either of these activities has not come to light.

Turning to the end of the period on 31 October 1308 and the end of the *LDE* (*escita* half), we have a closing cash balance of £34. 1s. 8d. as entry 427, and a closing list of debit balances (mostly personal debtors) of £153. 7s. 1d. as entry 423 (Figure 8.2).

		Dr. in GL	Cr. in LDC
423 (*escita*) 31 October 1308	£153 7. 1d., which amount remained in *LDC* on the last day of October 1308; written to the debit of accounts in the *GL* fos. 26 to 29.	fos. 26–9	Various accounts in *LDC*.
427 (*escita*) 31 October 1308	£34 1. 8d. The closing cash balance held by Nicoluccio.	fo. 30, Cash	Nicoluccio fo. 59 in *LDC*.

Fig. 8.2

Entry 423 is supported by a detailed schedule of 26 constituent balances which are to be transferred to accounts in the *Grande libro*, which remains open.

Thus it might be hoped that, if the *Grande libro* is to balance, then the total of the *entrata* half of the *LDE* (which creates credits in the *Grande libro*) would be equal to the *escita* half (which creates debits). This is also exactly the case, as will now be shown.

There is a memorandum at the end of the *LDE* written to Nicoluccio di Cante, a Paris partner, which gives totals: *Avere* (credits) £9481 8s. 9d., *Resta* ('the other' or 'the rest'?) £9477 16s. 1d. Bigwood has noted some errors in the folio totals which help to account for the small difference above. The present writer, taking these and another I have found[11] into account, has totalled all the *entrata* entries (£9484 12s. 8d.) and all the *escita* entries (£9482 19s. 1d.). A degree of error of this size seems more than acceptable over a three-and-a-half-year period, particularly as many of the entries were in cumbersome Roman numerals.

---

[11] There seems to be a mistake in entry 281 to 8 Oct. 1305: '£0. 18. 0d. to equipment; given to Bindo di Pari of Florence; and £0. 2. 0d. more for other small things.' The 2s. was missed when the folio was totalled, and not noticed by Bigwood.

SOME SPECIAL CASES

There are a few exceptions to the otherwise consistent use of the rules for the use of the *LDE* explained above. There are some non-cash *entrata* entries which create only a credit, but these are matched by *escita* entries of the same date which create only a debit.[12] This practice is especially common for the purchase of horses (a purchase: 179 and 351; the subsequent sale: 190) (Figure 8.3).

		Dr.	Cr.
179. (*entrata*) 5 June 1306	£7. 0. 6*d.* to be credited to Paris branch for 94 16. 3*d. tournois* paid for a horse ('*sardo leardo*') bought by Biagio in Paris. Written to the horse account.		fo. 102 in GL, Paris branch
351. (*escita*)	£7. 0. 6*d.* debit a horse ('*sardo leardo*'), for 94 16. 3*d. tournois* which Paris paid and Biagio bought from a Genoese. Credit to Paris.	fo. 24 in GL, Horse account.	
190. (*entrata*)	(see p. 239 above)	fo. 37 in LDC	fo. 24 in *GL*.

Fig. 8.3

Further, for the period I June 1306 to I November 1308, a joint venture for the trading of horses was run with the Frescobaldi company. The joint venture is set up by entry 377 and closed by entry 216 (Figure 8.4).

The difference between purchase and sale prices is noted as profit.[13] It is fairly clear that the bookkeeper was initially uncertain about how to deal with the joint venture. There is a cancelled entry on I June 1306 which mistakenly credited the Frescobaldi account in the *Grande libro* with their contribution to the capital of the joint venture. Also, the opening entry credits an account in the *Libro dei conti* rather than the capital account in the *Libro dei cavalli*. This seems to have been altered by the date of the closing entry, 216.

[12] Entries 20 and 249, for example.

[13] Profits of about 23 per cent for the single horse, and 18 per cent for the joint venture.

		Dr.	Cr.
377. (*escita*)	£133. 6. 8*d*. debited to the Horse Joint Venture with the Frescobaldi.	fo. 25 in *GL*, Horse J-V.	J-V account, fo. 39 in *LDC*.
216. (*entrata*) 1 Nov. 1308	£156. 14. 10*d*. to our capital in the Horse Joint Venture, including £23. 8. 2*d*. of profit.	Capital account in *Libro dei cavalli*, i.e. fo. 2	fo. 25 in *GL*, Horse J-V.

Fig. 8.4

Lastly, the penultimate and pre-penultimate entries of the *escita* half of the *LDE* are to debit the expense account in the *Grande libro* for two petty cash accounts which have been running throughout the three-and-a-half-year period. These are the *dentro* (inside the office) and *fuore* (outside) petty cash accounts. These entries are necessary because transfers from cash to petty cash are not recorded in the *LDE* as they occur (as *Dr* Petty Cash; *Cr* Cash). Thus, at the end of the period, the closing entries are not (*Dr* Expenses; *Cr* Petty Cash) but (*Dr* Expenses; *Cr* Cash).

THE ESSENTIALS OF DOUBLE ENTRY

Before asking whether the London branch of the Gallerani was using double-entry bookkeeping in 1305, it is necessary to recognize some criteria for double entry against which to judge the Gallerani system as evidenced by the *LDE*. Here we are assisted by useful precedents set by Lee, de Roover, and Martinelli. Lee (1973: 154) notes that double entry requires that 'there is (supposed to be) a debit for every credit, with full cross-references'. In a later work, Lee (1977: 85 and 90) suggests more detailed criteria, including the presence of concepts of accounting entity and proprietor's equity, the use of accounting periods and a single monetary unit, the calculation of profit and loss, and the periodic collection of balances to prove equality of debits and credits.

How well does the Gallerani accounting system measure up to these criteria? It is very clear that the Gallerani company was accounted for as an entity and that there was even a strict separation of the branches within the company.[14] For instance, there are many entries of debit or credit to the account

[14] Melis (1950: 475) says: 'Hence, such branches had an autonomous bookkeeping system, which must have included some accounts linking up with the central office bookkeeping'.

of the Paris branch.[15] Lee's criterion of monetary homogeneity is also strictly respected. Although the narratives for many entries *refer* to other currencies, the actual entries are always recorded in sterling: for example, entry 116 (see Figure 8.5).

		Dr.	Cr.
116. (*entrata*)	£0. 19. 0*d.* to the credit of the Paris branch for 12. 7. 6*d. livres tournois* received by Nicoluccio and charged to his account in *LDC*.	Nicoluccio's account, fo. 6 in *LDC*.	fo. 100 in *GL*, Paris Branch.

Fig. 8.5

It is apparent from the entries in the *LDE* that the London partners, including Aldobrandini, had capital accounts. Sadly, it is not possible to tell what they contained or how the profits were split up. Nevertheless, there were accounts for profits, interest, and other expenses: for example, entries 87 and 166 (Figure 8.6).

		Dr.	Cr.
87. (*entrata*) 9 Nov. 1305	£3. 18. 6*d* to the 'bay horse' account. The amount has been written to the lead expenses in the *LDC* (fo. 8) because the horse has become lame.[16] It has been given to God [charity ?].	Expenses of lead account, fo. 8 in *LDC*.	fo. 10 in *GL*, horse account.
166. (*entrata*) 29 Aug. 1306	£0. 12. 0*d*, to profit, gained on the purchase and sale of gold doubloons.	(Cash)	fo. 120, profit.

Fig. 8.6

There also appears to be a regard for accounting periods: the *LDE* runs for exactly three-and-a-half years. It could be argued that this period was merely the term set for the partnership or the stint of the bookkeeper. However, even if periodicity cannot be read into this one account book, the importance of periodicity as a prerequisite for double entry might well be questioned. Surely it is more telling that, at a point in time, there are closing entries,

---

[15] Entries 116 and 179, for example.

[16] Presumably, the lead expense account is debited because the horse became lame as a result of carrying too much of this heavy metal.

and the balances are collected together to prove equality of debits and credits.

De Roover (1956: 125) would require each transaction to be recorded twice, and the existence of accounts for expenses and operating results. It has been shown that the *LDE* creates two entries for each transaction: one for the *Grande libro* and usually one for the *Libro dei conti*. For cash amounts, it is presumably the physical existence of the cash which acts as the record of the other entry. An actual counterpart entry is created at the end of periods when the cash is counted to establish a closing entry to the *Grande libro*. At the same time, the *Libro dei conti* is closed down and a total balance in the *Grande libro* is achieved at the end of the period. It is possible that there was a separate cash book, but this seems unlikely as the *LDE* itself looks so much like a cash book which has just been adapted to include non-cash entries. As for de Roover's other point, it has been shown that there were accounts for expenses and profit.

Martinelli (1977: 11) would look for 'the presence of two complete sets of antithetical accounts,[17] constant reference for each entry to its cross-entry, and constant application of the same monetary unit'. These requirements seem to be satisfied, except for the criterion about cross-references (also mentioned by Lee, above). It is not possible to be sure on this point because of the absence of the *Grande libro* and the *Libro dei conti*. However, there are full references in the *LDE*.

CONCLUSION

The *Libro dell'entrata e dell'escita* of the London branch of the Gallerani from 1305 to 1308 was written in Italian, using typically Tuscan expressions and with a characteristically Sienese format. Because of the clear evidence for the creation of double entries, and because the two halves of the *LDE* are in almost exact balance, it seems that this bookkeeping contained, at the least, substantial elements of double entry. Incidentally, if this view is accepted, then these records represent the earliest extant accounting records using a form of double entry in the British Isles. However, as the Gallerani in London was a (short-lived) branch of a foreign firm, there is no suggestion that indigenous English records were kept in this advanced way either during or following its presence.

[17] It is supposed that Martinelli means 'two complete sets of antithetical entries'.

References

Bigwood, G. (ed. A. Grunzweig) (1961), *Les Livres des Comptes des Gallerani, Book I* (the transcription) (Brussels: Commission Royale d'Histoire).

——(ed. A. Grunzweig) (1962), *Les Livres des Comptes des Gallerani, Book II* (the commentary) (Brussels: Commission Royale d'Histoire).

de Decker, P. (1844), *Études historiques et critiques sur les Monts de Piété* (Brussels: The Author).

de Roover, R. (1956), 'The Development of Accounting Prior to Luca Pacioli According to the Account-books of Medieval Merchants', in A. C. Littleton and B. S. Yamey (eds.), *Studies in the History of Accounting* (Irwin; reprinted in 1978, New York: Arno Press), 114–74.

Keen, M. H. (1973), *England in the Later Middle Ages* (London: Methuen).

Lee, G. A. (1973), 'The Development of Italian Bookkeeping, 1211–1300', *Abacus* (Dec.): 137–55.

——(1977), 'The Coming of Age of Double Entry: The Giovanni Farolfi Ledger of 1299–1300', *Accounting Historians Journal* (Autumn): 79–95.

Marlowe, C. (1598), *The Troublesome Raigne and Lamentable Death of Edward the Second* (London).

Martinelli, A. (1974), 'The Origination and Evolution of Double Entry Bookkeeping to 1440' (unpublished doctoral thesis. University Microfilms, Ann Arbor, Mich.).

——(1977), 'Notes on the Origin of Double Entry Bookkeeping', *Abacus* (June): 3–27.

Melis, F. (1950), *Storia della ragioneria* (Bologna: Zuffi).

9 · BALANCING AND CLOSING THE LEDGER: ITALIAN PRACTICE, 1300–1600

B. S. Yamey

I

Ledger-closing procedures occur chronologically at the end of the bookkeeping cycle; and early writers on bookkeeping and accounts almost invariably treated these procedures at or towards the end of their expository texts. Lodovico Flori was an important exception. In his treatise of 1636 he places the *bilancio* (balance account)—the end-product of the balancing and closing procedures—in the forefront of his exposition of double-entry bookkeeping (after having dealt with such preliminary matters as how to make entries in the journal and the ledger).

Flori writes that it may seem as if discussion of the *bilancio* should come at the end of his text, only after the nature and purpose of all other ledger accounts have been explained. He decided, however, that it was better to begin with a short explanation of the *bilancio*. That account, he writes, is the purpose and goal (target) of all the other accounts. It is a brief summary or abstract of all the accounts with balances that are left open at the balancing date, these balances being reduced to equality. The *bilancio* compresses the open accounts into a small space. It represents the state of affairs of an administrative entity (*amministratione*) with such clarity and distinction that anyone at a glance can gain a good understanding of the entity's situation.[1]

For Flori, the balancing and closing procedures were designed to produce a succinct statement of the entity's affairs which the financial administrator could submit, together with the profit and loss and capital accounts, as a compact record of his stewardship. The procedures also served to establish the arithmetical accuracy of the ledger; and they facilitated the closing of one ledger and the

---

[1] Flori 1636: 44; see also 99.

opening of the next. Nevertheless, Flori placed the main stress on the *bilancio* as an informative condensed statement of affairs, a desirable end-product in its own right. Flori, following the pioneering treatise of 1586 by Angelo Pietra, a Benedictine, advised that new account books be opened every year.

It may be significant that Flori, a Jesuit priest, set out in his treatise to explain the keeping of double-entry accounts for a monastery or ecclesiastical college, that is for an entity in which there was a collectivity of 'owners' and, in modern parlance, a divorce between ownership and management. Pietra's treatise also deals with the accounts of a monastery.

In this chapter I review ledger-closing practices and procedures of business firms in Italy, and of firms of Italian origin in business in other European countries. The period covered is broadly from 1300 to 1600. Because of the limited number and limitations of available studies, the review is somewhat impressionistic. It nevertheless throws light on the extent to which the practice of double-entry bookkeeping by natives of the country of its birth measured up to Flori's standards.[2] It also illustrates the variety of practices employed.

II

There were several different methods for effecting the closure of a ledger and the opening of its successor (or for closing the accounts in a ledger and reopening them in the same partly used book).

The simplest method was to close the nominal accounts through the profit and loss account into the capital account. The remaining accounts (for assets, liabilities, and capital) were then closed, and new accounts were opened in the new ledger. This method is described in two versions in Luca Pacioli's *Summa de arithmetica . . .* (1494).[3] In one version there is no intermediating compilation of account balances. In the other, a trial balance (called *bilancio el libro* by Pacioli) is drawn up on a sheet of paper outside the ledger, and used to generate the closing entries in the old ledger and the opening entries in the new ledger. This method was used in the famous ledger of 1340 of the stewards (*massari*) of the commune of Genoa, though it is not clear which of the two versions was used.[4] It was also used in the early sixteenth-century ledger of

---

[2] I have included references to the accounts of a few non-Italians who, however, had strong connections with Venice and who were greatly influenced by Italian practice.

[3] Pacioli 1494, chs. 34 and 36.

[4] Martinelli 1983: 110.

the Venetian Alvise Pisani dal Banco, where, according to Pilla, account balances were transferred directly from the old ledger to the new.[5]

Another method, common in practice, was to have a balance account in the old ledger into which were posted the balances of all the remaining open accounts after the elimination of the nominal accounts. The opening entries in the new ledger were made from the items in the balance account in the old ledger.

A third method was a refinement of the second. The balance account in the old ledger was repeated as the first account in the new ledger, but with debit balances entered as credit balances, and vice versa. Flori used this method, and in his model set of accounts illustrated the use of the closing balance account and the corresponding reversed opening balance account. Balance accounts of this type seem to have been in frequent use. An early example is the early fifteenth-century ledger of Andrea Barbarigo, Frederic Lane's 'merchant of Venice'.[6]

A fourth method was to dispense with the balance account. Instead, the balances of open ledger accounts were transferred to the capital account. This probably unusual method was used in the ledger (1318–24) of the Del Bene in Florence.[7] It appears to have been used also in the even earlier ledger of the Florentine Giovanni Farolfi partnership that operated with its head office in Nîmes in France.[8]

III

Pacioli tells his readers that *el bilancio del libro* is made when a new ledger is needed to replace one that is full.[9] The evidence suggests that Pacioli was reflecting Venetian practice. According to Lane, the 'only kind of balancing of the ledger which can be shown to be common at Venice was connected with closing one ledger when all its pages had been used up and opening a new ledger'.[10] Francesco Vrins, a Flemish merchant established in Venice, had ten successive ledgers, and corresponding journals, between May 1586 and October 1603. Eight of the ledgers had closing balance accounts. The period covered was not the same for any two ledgers, and varied from nine to thirty-six months.[11]

---

[5] Pilla 1974: 271.   [6] Lane 1944: 172 n. 4.   [7] Melis 1950: 517–18.

[8] Lee 1977: 91.   [9] Pacioli 1494, ch. 32.

[10] Lane 1944: 171–2. Andrea Barbarigo carried out only one general balancing before his ledger (1431–49) ran out of space. He did this in 1435, shortly before his marriage: Lane 1944: 173, 174.

[11] Brulez 1965: i. 644–56.

According to Paola Massa, practice in sixteenth-century Genoa was similar. Thus Vicenzo Usodimare di Rovereto, active in the silk business, closed his ledger when it was full five years after it had been opened.[12] Two Genoese merchants of the preceding century who kept their own accounts opened balance accounts only on the termination of their surviving ledgers: Giovanni Piccamiglio's ledger 1456–9, and Battista de Luco's, 1472–6.[13]

Some merchants closed their ledgers, at irregular intervals, even when they were not full. This appears to have been the practice in the fourteenth century of the important Florentine partnerships of the Peruzzi and of Alberti del Giudice.[14] Maarten de Hane, a Fleming who settled in Venice, compiled balance accounts on nine occasions, at irregular intervals, between 1541 and 1555. Jan della Faille, a Fleming who acquired his knowledge of commercial matters from de Hane in Venice and later acted as his factor in Antwerp, had six irregularly spaced balances between 1576 and 1578. His son, Maarten, on the other hand attempted only one balance in the period 1589 to 1594.[15]

By the fifteenth century the large Florentine partnership businesses had annual balance accounts. The Medici bank had annual balancings both for the head office in Florence and for the subsidiary partnerships elsewhere in Italy and in major commercial centres outside Italy.[16] In nearby Prato, Francesco Datini, Iris Origo's 'merchant of Prato', had introduced annual balancings already towards the end of the fourteenth century.[17] The practice was not confined to partnerships. Giovanni Borromeo, a Florentine trading in Milan in the 1420s, appears to have had a new ledger every year, with balance accounts at each year end.[18] On the other hand, the only surviving ledger of the Borromeo partnership's establishment in London was balanced only when it was full in 1439, after more than three years of activity.[19]

How widespread in the sixteenth century was the practice of annual closure of the ledger in Italy, and elsewhere? In an important article Flavio Pilla proposed tentatively that annual closure may have been a reasonably widely spread practice by the sixteenth century. He noted that there had been little study of surviving sixteenth-century account books, and therefore he based his conjec-

---

[12] Massa 1974: 269.

[13] Heers (1959) and Balletto (1979) reproduce the respective ledgers. The closing balance account in Piccamiglio's ledger has the title *Exitus presentis cartularii*, and that in De Luco's *Exitu prezente cartularo*. Neither was completed. These two Genoese ledgers perhaps do not qualify as double-entry ledgers, as their editors note. But it seems that both merchants attempted to use the system, and nearly succeeded in doing so.

[14] Pilla 1974: 258.   [15] Brulez 1959: 440.   [16] De Roover 1963: 84.

[17] Melis 1962: 146, 150, 412.   [18] Zerbi 1952, ch. 9.

[19] According to G. Biscaro, it was not until 1460 that firms in Milan required their branches abroad to render an annual balance (*bilanzo del libro*): Kats 1926: 95, referring to Biscaro's study of the Borromeo partnership accounts.

ture on other evidence. Simon Stevin, the celebrated Dutch mathematician, scientist, and man of affairs, around 1600 wrote his *Coopmans Bouckhouding op de
Italiaensche Wyse*, included in his *Vorstelicke bouckhouding . . .*, which was published in
1607. Stevin, according to Pilla, advised that every firm should have an annual
balance. On the basis that writers of treatises were apt to reflect practice rather
than to lead it, Pilla proposed his conjecture that annual balancings must have
been common.[20] He observed, however, that Raymond de Roover regarded
Stevin as an innovator, and believed that his ideas would have been received
with reserve by his business contemporaries.[21] In fact, Stevin's treatise on *commercial* bookkeeping had little influence even on the literature of the subject, his
main follower being the Englishman Richard Dafforne.

In any case, the particular discussion is misconceived, because Stevin did
not recommend, advise, or desire that firms should close their ledgers annually. What he wrote was as follows (the French version reflecting accurately
the Dutch version): 'Il est en usage pres de plusieurs Marchands, d'examiner
annuellement comment gaing & perte est succedé sur icelle année . . .'. In a
later chapter he observed that when a journal and ledger are fully used ('rem-
pli d'escriture') so that new ones are needed, the closing of the ledger is necessary, with the balances of the old ledger being brought into the new. He
added that the closing of the ledger is required also when the merchant
ceased trading because he had retired or died.[22]

Thus, as Pieter de Waal wrote in 1927 in his exemplary monograph on
sixteenth-century bookkeeping in the Netherlands, Stevin did not prescribe
the drawing up of an annual balance; he was merely referring to a practice he
had observed among many merchants.[23] Pacioli had written something similar about a century before. He remarked that large-scale merchants (*gran mer-
catanti*) in well-known centres (*luochi famosi*) changed ledgers at the beginning
of each new year, and so had an annual *bilancio*.[24] Jan Coutereels, Stevin's con-

---

[20] Pilla 1974: 277. He refers, also, to a 1625 contract of a Venetian five-year partnership for the manufacture and sale of silk cloth that stipulated the 'making of a *bilancio* of all the business each year at the
end of December'.

[21] De Roover 1937: 288.   [22] Stevin 1607, chs. 9 and 10.

[23] De Waal 1927: 273. The erroneous reading of Stevin's text goes back at least several decades. De
Roover 1937: 288, refers to his supposed recommendation of an annual closure ('il recommande la clôture
annuelle . . .'), though he refers generally to De Waal's correct discussion. Max Weber 1923: 238, wrote
that Stevin was the first to require the compilation of a balance account ('Bilanz')—which his English
translator rendered as follows: 'The device of the balance was first insisted upon by the Dutch theorist
Simon Stevin in the year 1698 [error for 1608]': Weber 1961: 207. Eugen Schmalenbach wrote that
Stevin was the first to emphasize the necessity to make the balance account ('Bilanzziehung') annually:
Schmalenbach 1931: 59. Werner Sombart wrote that Stevin (1607) was the first to require that the books
should be closed annually, in addition to closures on the death of the merchant or shutting-down of his
business: Sombart 1928; ii/1. 115.

[24] Pacioli 1494, ch. 32.

temporary and fellow-countryman, did, on the other hand, recommend annual balancings in his treatise of 1603: 'If one wants to close one's books, and make a balance of all one's business, which ought to be done once a year . . .'.[25] Again, Pacioli had made a similar point: 'It is always good to close [*saldare*] the ledger each year, notably if one is in a partnership; for frequent accounting makes for long friendship.'[26]

IV

The Venetian author Giovanni Antonio Moschetti noted that if the sums of the debit and credit balances in a *bilancio* were discordant, even if to the extent of only a *piccolo* in a total of a hundred thousand *ducati*, this meant that there was an error in the ledger. The ledger had to be checked again so that the error could be discovered and the ledger rectified. The satisfaction of discovering the error, Moschetti continued, dispelled the fatigue and boredom of the search. He referred to Hercules and the cleansing of the Augean stables.[27] The checking routine was described in detail by Pacioli, and other early treatises usually gave some space to the subject.

In practice, merchants and bankers, or their bookkeepers, were often unwilling to follow Moschetti's advice to the letter. There is ample evidence of ledgers and *bilanci* out of balance and left unbalanced, or, though perhaps less frequently, of ledgers forced into equilibrium by a one-sided balancing entry. Partnerships as well as one-man businesses provide examples:

> Francesco Datini (Barcelona branch 1411); Giovanni Borromeo (1427 and 1428); Medici bank (Florence head office 1433; branches: Rome 1427, Venice 1427, Basle 1442, Milan 1460, Lyons 1467, London 1477, Pisa 1486, Rome 1495); Andrea Barbarigo (1435); Borromeo & Company (London branch 1436, Bruges branch 1438); Antonio della Casa & Simone Guadagni (1454); Nicolò Barbarigo 1483; Piero Saliti & Company (1527); and Affaitadi & Company (Antwerp 1562, Rome branch 1568, Seville branch 1569).[28]

---

[25] Coutereels 1603, section headed 'Van de Balance'. The relevant words in Coutereels are: 't'welck eens int iaer behoort te gheschieden' ('which ought to take place once a year').

[26] Pacioli 1494, ch. 29.

[27] Moschetti 1610: 17.

[28] Melis 1962: 410 (Datini); Zerbi 1952: 342, 344 (Borromeo); De Roover 1963: 207, 215, 231, 246, 278, 292, 336, and Sapori 1973: 205 (Medici Bank); Lane 1944: 173 (Andrea Barbarigo); Zerbi 1952: 420, 439 (Borromeo partnership); Cassandro 1976: 672 (Della Casa/Guadagni); Lane 1944: 173 (Nicolò Barbarigo); Spallanzani 1978: 613 (Saliti); Denucé 1934: 133, 171 (Affaitadi).

Nicolò was one of the sons of Andrea Barbarigo. The Florentine Della Casa/Guadagni partnership

This listing of examples, which together amount to a substantial proportion of *bilanci* published or described in the literature, is not intended as retrospective criticism of the merchants or bookkeepers who failed to balance
their books. They must have had good reasons for not going through, perhaps for a second or third time, the laborious checking procedures. Perhaps
they were pressed for time and had better things to do with it. It is true, also,
that in most of the above instances the *bilancio* was out of balance by only
absolutely and relatively small amounts. However, the merchants and bookkeepers must have known that a small imbalance could be the end-result of
several partially offsetting individual errors, some possibly large—though this
obvious point was not usually made in the bookkeeping manuals.

The transgressing merchants and bookkeepers could have drawn comfort
from the words written by the Jesuit friar Lodovico Flori in 1636. He noted
that 'Quandoque bonus dormitat Homerus'. The poor bookkeeper also
makes mistakes, fatigued as he is by his concern now with numbers, now with
weights, now with measures, now with accounts of various kinds, and now
with a diversity of currencies. If the ledger has been checked, rechecked, and
checked again, any remaining imbalance in the *bilancio*, provided it was a small
amount, could be offset by a single entry in the capital account.[29] But few
writers were as comforting as Flori.

The frequency of errors in the ledger is interesting in suggesting that the
merchants and bankers of Tuscany—most of the examples are Tuscan—were
perhaps not so precise and careful in their reckonings as is often supposed.[30]
The phenomenon also has some bearing on the reasons for the adoption
(possibly even the origination) of double-entry bookkeeping.

Alvaro Martinelli has explained the rapid spread of the use of the system
in terms of, *inter alia*, 'the mathematical controls which the system provides'.[31]
Edward Peragallo expressed a similar view, though he noted that in practice
the controls were not made use of extensively.[32] Indeed, the frequency with
which merchants and bookkeepers evaded the arithmetical discipline of the
double-entry system does suggest that its special feature was not highly
prized.

operated in Geneva. Piero Saliti and his partners traded in Nuremberg. The Affaitadi were Cremonese who
had settled in Antwerp. The Borromeo and the Della Casa/Guadagni balance accounts were forced into balance by the introduction of a single entry in an account other than the balance account. It is not known
whether other early balance accounts that balance were similarly brought into balance by such single entries.

[29] Flori 1636: 80, 109.

[30] For the conventional view, see for example Burke 1987: 199, and Bernard 1972: 329.

[31] Martinelli 1983: 117.

[32] Peragallo 1971: 529.

James Aho has recently suggested a radically different approach.[33] For him, double-entry bookkeeping was an 'outgrowth' of the 'art of rhetorical discourse'. It was designed to justify business activities that were viewed with suspicion or hostility in medieval Christian Europe. Double-entry bookkeeping 'provided the apology for the rational pursuit of wealth *par excellence*'.

Aho bases his argument largely on the duality of entries and the balance account in the double-entry system. He stresses the 'conclusion implicit in an error-free ledger' that for 'every credit there is an equal and corresponding debit'. He interprets this equality between debit and credit to mean 'in ordinary language' that: 'I own a particular amount because I have given an equivalent amount at some other time, and I owe a particular amount because I have received its equivalent at some other time.' After further elaboration, Aho proceeds to the following inference:

The conclusion of the balance sheet, then, is not simply that such and such is the net worth of our business, but rather that such profit is morally legitimate. And it is so, because it arises from a fundamentally equitable and balanced transaction. 'We owe no more than what we have received and we have no more than what we have already given'.

It will be noted, in passing, that Aho failed to recognize that an unrequited gift or the accidental finding of a sum of money is as readily accommodated in a double-entry ledger as any ordinary business transaction involving an exchange, and that it does not disturb the equilibrium of the balance sheet; or that a thief who keeps his books by double entry would have no difficult in recording the proceeds of his enterprise, and that his balance sheet would balance if his ledger was error-free. The double-entry system (like any other system of recording) is indifferent as to whether what is to be recorded is or is not an 'equitable' or 'balanced' transaction. The system cannot sanitize a transaction or event that, at the particular time and place, is regarded as illicit, inequitable, or morally reprehensible.

What is relevant here, however, is that the frequency of early balance accounts that do not balance is highly inconvenient for Aho's conjecture. If an error-free ledger and a balanced balance account carried so heavy a weight of significance and implication, it would be surprising that the surviving evidence of practice is so perverse as to show the frequency of early ledgers that were not error free.

Another major question raised by Aho's conjecture can be dealt with briefly by way of digression. To whom was the rhetoric of double-entry

---

[33] Aho 1985, *passim*.

bookkeeping addressed? Who had to be convinced that business activities and their conduct by the business man in question were just and legitimate? Aho's answer is that the rhetoric was addressed at the community, 'but more importantly, [at the business man] himself'. As for the latter, it is surely bizarre to suppose that any medieval merchant or banker who entertained serious doubts about his business rectitude or the legitimacy of his activities would have had them set at rest by his use of double-entry bookkeeping. Does a modern taxpayer feel he is not cheating, when engaged in tax evasion, because his ledger is kept in impeccable double entry? As for the community, I am not aware that the judgement of the Church, courts of law, tax authorities, or guild (or similar) organizations as to the propriety of a particular enterprise or type of transaction was affected by whether the firm or business man in question kept his books according to the tenets of double-entry bookkeeping rather than in some other way.[34] Men of affairs would have known that the balance account in an error-free ledger will balance even if the ledger is that of a thief, an embezzler or blackmailer, or of a money-lender taking advantage of the ignorance of the proverbial widows and orphans.

V

When we think of a balance sheet today, we have in mind a concise financial statement containing a small number of entries, the items helpfully grouped and ordered. It was different in fifteenth- and sixteenth-century Italy. 'Medieval statements were not systematically arranged as are modern balance sheets; they listed separately debit and credit balances in the order in which the accounts appeared in the ledger, without any further attempt at classification.'[35] The balance account of the Peruzzi family business in 1336 covers ten pages of the ledger.[36] The June 1427 balance account of the Rome branch of the Medici bank has over 500 entries.[37] The balance accounts attached to the tax returns of the Medici Bank in Florence are small booklets. The balance account of the Antwerp company of the Affaitadi in 1567 extends over twelve pages, with 81

---

[34] I am not aware of any specific evidence that courts of law or other judicial authorities gave greater probative weight to a merchant's account books when they were kept by double entry rather than in any other way. It is interesting, however, that Flori declared, in 1636, that a double-entry ledger, if well kept (*ben tenuto*), acquired credit (*fede*) among almost everyone, a fact confirmed by the attitude of the public authorities in almost all nations (Flori 1636: 3). But Flori left it at that. It is evident, though, that Flori was referring here to the credibility of the merchant's accounting records, and not to his ethical behaviour or the theological legitimacy of his business operations—the latter hardly a major matter of concern to business men in the seventeenth century.

[35] De Roover 1963: 100.   [36] Peragallo 1938: 20.   [37] De Roover 1963: 206–7.

debit and 96 credit entries. The only subtotals are those at the foot of each page.[38] The balance accounts of smaller businesses were naturally less voluminous, though compiled in the same way.

As de Roover has shown, copies of the detailed annual *bilanci* of each of the Medici branch establishments were sent to the head office in Florence. There the individual entries were scrutinized, usually in the presence of the branch manager concerned, to assess the recoverability of the debts and to ascertain the reasons for high levels of merchandise inventory.[39] Presumably the balance accounts of the various Datini overseas partnerships were similarly examined in Prato.

The typical profit and loss account was not an account taking up a single opening of the ledger or a number of successive openings. The profit and loss account was more likely spread over several (non-successive) ledger openings. When the space allotted to the account was used up, the balance was carried over to a later opening. In the Borromeo ledger for 1427 the profit and loss account is to be found in five different places.[40] In ledger B of the Della Casa/Guadagni partnership, covering some sixteen months in 1453 and 1454, the profit and loss account appears on four openings, and in total has almost 200 individual entries.[41] Unlike in a *bilancio*, the entries in a profit and loss account were not all made at the same time, i.e. when the ledger was being balanced; most entries were made at other times as and when particular events occurred.

Balance accounts and profit and loss accounts of the kind described above were not statements whose main messages the reader could take in at a glance or even after several glances. Clearly, they were not prepared for such a purpose. The interesting question is whether and how frequently, say, the Medici or Datini had analytical summaries or abstracts compiled from the entries in those compendious 'final' accounts. There appears to be no clear information on this point in the Medici bank records, and no such summary documents are referred to by de Roover in his well-known monograph. For Datini, on the other hand, a few summary *bilanci* have survived. Melis described the *bilancio sintetico* as a rarity (*rarissimo*); and he reproduced only one, namely that of the Avignon business at the beginning of the year 1410 (= 1411), described by Melis as the oldest surviving example of its kind.[42] Its composition was as follows (amounts omitted):

[38] Denucé 1934: 198–215.   [39] De Roover 1963: 100.

[40] Zerbi 1952: 327. The ledger folios are numbers 83, 165, 218, 261, and 269.

[41] Cassandro 1976: the ledger folios are numbers 34, 64, 106, and 162.

[42] Melis 1962: 162; also Melis 1972: 459. Peragallo 1938: 29 reproduces another, even earlier, Datini summary statement of assets and liabilities.

Debtors, goods and cash

Goods in house and warehouse (one total)
Cash
Furniture and implements in house and warehouse (one total)
Victuals and provisions (one total)
41 Debtors (one total)

Total

Creditors

Profit for year ended December 1410
11 Creditors (including profits of earlier years) (one total)

Total

The evident inclusion of the partners' capital account balances with the outside creditors may seem a weakness. Perhaps the compiler regarded them as amounts owed by the partnership to the individual partners.

Melis gives the details also of a Datini summary profit and loss account. This document, likewise on a loose sheet, is of the Pisa partnership for a period of less than a year, ended in October 1399. There are only seven entries in all: debit entries for household expenses for the period, a *riserbo* (see below) and the shares of each of the two partners; and credit entries for (trading) profits for the period, profits on exchange for the period, and profits from commissions (*provigioni*) and accommodation (*ostellagi*).[43]

VI

The early Italian treatises largely ignored questions concerning the valuation of assets for ledger-closing purposes, and have virtually nothing to say about the pro-rating of outlays and receipts that straddle adjacent accounting periods. Here they do not differ from the accounting literature in other languages. Surviving Italian account books for the period covered in this essay display a variety of practices, in this respect also showing few substantial differences from material for other parts of Europe. The rest of this section illustrates the diversity of practices.

[43] Melis 1962: 185. The profit and loss account in Flori's model ledger (*Spese generale* and *Entrata generale*) is also a summary account. There are separate nominal accounts for the various categories of expenses and revenues, the totals of each of which are entered in the profit and loss account at the end of the year: Flori 1636, ledger fo. 49.

The practice of eliminating truly bad debts from the ledger, by clearing them through the profit and loss account, was widespread; but no doubt there were large differences in the rigour with which such debtors' accounts were identified and removed. In the Datini ledgers the accounts of irrecoverable debts were eliminated, but for the record were entered into a separate account book, the *libro dei ma' debitori*, kept outside the main accounting framework.[44] Another procedure was to transfer *doubtful* debts to a separate account in the ledger, without cancelling them by transfers to the profit and loss account. Piccamiglio's fifteenth-century ledger has such an account, the *racio malorum debitorum*, whose balance appears among the debits in the closing balance account; di Rovereto's sixteenth-century ledger has a similarly titled account.[45] Several of the Medici Bank balance accounts include debts labelled as bad (*debitori cattivi*) or as long overdue and doubtful (*debitori lunghi e dubbiosi*).[46] The sixteenth-century Affaitadi balance accounts include individual debts identified as bad as well as collective accounts with titles like debtors of little hope (*debitori di poco speranza*), debtors who are bankrupt, old, and irrecoverable (*debitori . . . che tutti sono falliti e vechij non sine ricavara nulla*), and debtors lost and without hope (*debitori persi . . . di nessuna speranza*).[47]

Stocks of unsold merchandise were valued on a variety of bases. In the early fourteenth-century ledger of the del Bene partnership the stock of merchandise on hand was valued at current wholesale prices. Thus when the same lot of goods was present at two successive annual stock-takings, its value could be calculated at different prices; and Armando Sapori lists a number of examples in his study of the accounts.[48]

According to Melis, in the Datini ledgers unsold stocks of merchandise were valued at cost or current price, whichever the lower. Apparently it was unusual for the current price to be lower than the cost price—perhaps this means that current price was taken to be the current realizable price, not the current replacement cost. Packing materials were stated at an estimated price.[49]

The treatment of merchandise accounts in Giovanni Borromeo's ledgers is unusual. Goods that were traded in an effectively continuous market were valued at the current wholesale price, subject to a prudential reduction of some 10 per cent; but the average actual cost of acquisition was used when this was below the modified current cost of acquisition. There were, however, items such as jewellery and expensive fabrics that did not have active markets.

[44] Melis 1962: 379, 416; Melis 1972: 69.
[45] Heers 1959: 96; Massa 1974: 30.
[46] De Roover 1963: 246, 264, 278, 292.
[47] Denucé 1934: 116, 141–2, 144, 149, 167.
[48] Sapori 1932: 235.
[49] Melis 1962: 412–13, 413 n. 1, 418.

Here, until the entire lot had been sold, the remaining unsold stock was 'valued' at the figure that balanced the debits and credit sides of the relevant goods account: there was no adjustment for the profit or loss on the sales that had been made up to that point. It was possible, therefore, for the asset account to have a negative (i.e. credit) balance, i.e. when the proceeds of sales to date exceeded the costs of acquisition of the entire lot. Zerbi explains that there were such instances.[50] When the entire stock had been sold, the profit or loss on the goods was ascertained, and carried to the profit and loss account. The creation, in the meantime, of a reserve, by way of an asset with negative value, is difficult to explain, since the merchant must have been well aware of what his bookkeeper was doing.[51]

In the Della Casa/Guadagni ledger, the merchandise (*merchatantie*) account was balanced on two occasions. On the first, the unsold balance was inserted at a value whose basis is not indicated. The second balancing, a few months later, was achieved simply by insertion of the balancing figure.[52]

In the fifteenth-century ledger of the London branch of the Borromeo partnership, some of the remaining merchandise at the end of the period was valued at amounts higher than their cost, thus anticipating future profits. It seems, however, that the practice of overstating current profits may have been a temporary expedient (later ledgers have not survived). The London branch was a subsidiary of the Bruges branch which at the time was doing badly. The London profits were therefore boosted, it seems. Similarly, debts considered uncollectable were not written off, and depreciation was not recorded in respect of *masserizie* (see below).[53]

The question of inventory valuation was largely avoided by merchants who drew up balance accounts only when the ledger was full. The published analyses of Venetian ledgers do not describe how unsold goods, whether in the warehouse or in the hands of agents abroad, were valued when the ledger was eventually closed.

Fixed assets such as land and buildings are rare in surviving early Italian account books. The personal property of Francesco Datini was recorded in his headquarter's ledgers in a single collective account, the *conto possessioni*, the details being kept in a separate *libro di possessioni*. It appears that most of the assets were kept on the books at their cost of acquisition.[54]

---

[50] Zerbi 1952: 332–4.

[51] Zerbi noted other examples of Borromeo's (or his bookkeeper's) 'conservatism' in under-stating profits: Zerbi 1952: 335–6. According to Massa 1974: 271 n. 3, the closing merchandise inventory in di Rovereto's ledger was almost certainly understated as against market values.

[52] Cassandro 1976: 614 and 654.

[53] Sapori 1932: 235 n. 19.

The only fixed asset accounts that are frequently encountered are those for 'furniture, utensils and implements', which is probably the most useful translation of the word *masserizie*. Federigo Melis explained that expenditure on *masserizie* was usually capitalized in the ledgers of merchants in Tuscany and of merchants of Tuscan origin. The asset account was credited periodically for loss of value through use or age, the debits being entered in the profit and loss account. Examples of this treatment are to be found in the ledgers, among others, of the Farolfi, the Del Bene, the Lippi and Del Bene partnership, Datini, the Medici Bank, and the Della Casa and Guadagni partnership.[55]

Melis contrasted this Tuscan treatment of the asset *masserizie* with practice elsewhere in Italy. He showed that non-Tuscan merchants usually did not capitalize expenditures on *masserizie*, but debited them to the profit and loss account in the period in which they were made. He gave the example, *inter alia*, of Giacomo Badoer's ledger. He noted that Andrea Barbarigo, also a Venetian, did capitalize the expenditures, but did not make adjustments for the depreciation of the assets.[56]

Melis observed, in 1972, that various early Genoese, Milanese, and Venetian ledgers, long regarded in the historical literature as perfect examples of double entry, were, in his judgement, imperfect. The double entry in them was incomplete or unfinished (*incompiuta*). The treatment of *masserizie* in these ledgers meant that the series of asset accounts in them was incomplete; and the profit and loss account in those years in which *masserizie* were bought were burdened excessively with outlays that should properly have been capitalized and amortized.[57] In drawing attention to the relative sophistication of Tuscan practices, Melis was unduly critical of non-Tuscan accounting. In particular, he failed to address the question whether non-Tuscan enterprises and establishments were at any practical disadvantage because their ledgers did not measure up to the Melis standard. It is difficult to see how they could have been disadvantaged in any way. There is no merit in Melis's attempt to add his 'depreciation' criterion in the definition of the double-entry system.

Accounting for the depreciation of a fixed asset is an example of the pro-rating or apportionment among accounting periods of an expenditure whose

---

[54] Melis 1962: 378.

[55] Melis 1972: 384 (Farolfi); Sapori 1932: 238–9, 356 (Del Bene); Zerbi 1952: 231 (Lippi and Del Bene); Melis 1962: 414–15 (Datini); De Roover 1963: 266, 298 (Medici Bank); Cassandro 1976: 250 (Della Casa and Guadagni). The credit entry in the Del Bene *masserizie* account reads: '. . . perduti di queste masserizie che sono loghore e vecchie, e che sono ragionate meno . . .' (. . . lost on that *masserizie* which is worn out and old, and which is estimated at less . . .); in the Della Casa/ Guadagni account it reads: '. . . ragoniamo di perdita nelle chontrascritta masserizie . . .' (. . . we estimate the loss on the *masserizie* on the debit side. . .).

[56] Melis 1962: 414 n. 3, and Melis 1972: 58, 58 n. 2.   [57] Melis 1972: 57–8.

flow of services straddles several periods. Other examples in several early Italian ledgers include the apportionment of rent payments, payments for supplies of food and salary payments.[58] An interesting example is the pro-rating of a payment made by Datini's Barcelona branch for a trading licence or concession (*guidaggio*) to the King of Aragon.[59] Apportionment of expenditures seems to have been largely a Tuscan practice.

The creation of reserves was another form of adjustment connected with the closing of the ledger, the few examples available all being in the records of Tuscan enterprises. Some reserves were established for specific purposes, such as reserves for doubtful debtors in various Medici Bank balance accounts.[60] The more interesting reserves were general reserves, created so as to avoid overstatement of the profits of a completed accounting period. The earliest example appears to be an adjustment of this kind in the Peruzzi ledger of 1308.[61] General reserves of this kind were common in Datini ledgers. Thus in the first ledger of the Pisa branch a reserve (*riserbo*) of 200 *fiorini d'oro* was set up. It was to cover unpaid expenses and possible losses on bankrupt debtors, as well as errors pertaining to the profit and loss account (*erori si trovasono a detto conto*): the latter item presumably related to inadvertent overstatement of revenues or understatement of expenses.[62] A general reserve is also to be found in the earlier of Giovanni Borromeo's two ledgers.[63]

VII

In the preceding section I have indicated certain features that, according to the available evidence, were wholly or largely confined to business firms established in Florence and other centres in Tuscany, or established elsewhere and run by business men from Tuscany. The features all relate to practices affecting the calculation of profit in the profit and loss account, and hence also the net asset figure derivable from the balance account.

The greater sophistication of accounting in Tuscany than in other parts of Italy, especially in the fifteenth century, calls for explanation. The conjecture offered here is one that draws on Flavio Pilla's article (1974) in which he

---

[58] Lee 1977: 90 (Farolfi); Zerbi 1952: 420 (Borromeo partnership); Melis 1962: 417 (Datini); De Roover 1963: 206, 207, 215, 227 (Medici Bank).
[59] Melis 1962: 415.
[60] De Roover 1963: 227, 247.
[61] Melis 1962: 402 n. 3.
[62] Melis 1962: 419.
[63] Zerbi 1952: 336.

compared Venetian and Florentine balance accounts. The explanation turns on the prominence of the partnership form of organization in Tuscany, and its absence or unimportance in Venice.

Partnerships in fifteenth-century Tuscany were for specified short periods, typically for periods of from three to five years. It was usual for a terminating partnership to be replaced by a new partnership—there would be the old partnership and the succeeding new partnership. There usually was a large measure of continuity in the composition of the two successive partnerships, though there could be some change. A partner might drop out; a new partner might be admitted; or, if the partners remained unchanged, capital and profit shares could be altered. The assets and liabilities of the old partnership were transferred to the new (though sometimes the new partnership acted in effect as collecting agent on behalf of the old partners as regards debts due to the old partnership). Third parties might well have been ignorant of the changes that had taken place in the partnership's composition and structure.

It is not surprising that assets would be calculated carefully on the actual dissolution of any partnership business, regardless of the nature of the accounting system being used. This calculation would be necessary for the distribution to the partners of any undistributed profits and the remaining assets and liabilities. When a new partnership was to take over the old partnership business as a going concern, it would be necessary to value the depreciating assets on an acceptable basis and also to allow for prepaid and accrued expenses. Moreover, precautionary or prudential 'reserves' might also be allowed for to protect the interests of the members of the successor partnership.

What is more difficult to explain is why depreciation of *masserizie*, adjustments for prepayments and accruals and the creation of reserves were included in the profit and loss account and reflected in the balance account in the intermediate years in which a partnership did not come to an end as a separate entity. These adjustments did not affect the interests of the various partners in a partnership that was continuing unchanged in composition and in profit and capital shares. Perhaps the explanation is that the practice of dealing with such matters at the end of a partnership's life was carried over to ledger closings performed during the life of the partnership as well. Careful accounting for profits and asset values may have become entrenched as custom and practice in partnership businesses in fifteenth-century Tuscany.

What can be said with confidence is that by the fifteenth century some partnerships in Tuscany had adopted accounting devices affecting the calculation of profits and net assets for continuing enterprises that have a modern ring. These sophisticated devices were not discussed in Pacioli's elementary exposition, nor indeed in other early treatises. As there have been few studies of Italian double-entry account books of the sixteenth, seventeenth, and eighteenth centuries, it is not known whether the practices in question continued to be commonly used in Tuscany, and whether they came to be used to any extent elsewhere in Italy in these centuries.

References

Aho, J. (1985), 'Rhetoric and the Invention of Double Entry Bookkeeping', *Rhetorica*, 3.

Balletto, L. (1979), *Battista de Luco mercante genovese del secolo XV e il suo cartulario* (Genoa).

Bernard, J. (1972), 'Trade and finance in the Middle Ages', in C. Cipolla (ed.), *The Fontana Economic History of Europe*, vol. i (London).

Brulez, W. (1959), *De firma della Faille en de internationale handel van Vlaamse firma's in de 16e eeuw* (Brussels).

——(1965), *Marchands flamands à Venise (1568–1605)* (Brussels and Rome).

Burke, P. (1987), *The Historical Anthropology of Early Modern Italy* (Cambridge).

Cassandro, M. (1976), *Il libro giallo di Ginevra della compagnia fiorentina di Antonio della Casa e Simone Guadagni 1453–1454* (Prato).

Coutereels, J. (1603), *Den stijl van boeck-houden* (Middelburg).

Denucé, J. (1934), *Inventaire des Affaitadi banquiers italiens à Anvers de l'année 1568* (Antwerp).

De Roover, R. (1937), 'Aux origines d'une technique intellectuelle: la formation et l'expansion de la comptabilité à partie double', *Annales d'histoire economique et sociale*, 9.

——(1963), *The Rise and Decline of the Medici Bank 1397–1494* (Cambridge, Mass.).

De Waal, P. G. A. (1927), *De leer van het boekhouden in de Nederlanden tijdens de zestiende eeuw* (Roermond).

Flori, L. (1636), *Trattato del modo di tenere il libro doppio . . .* (Palermo).

Heers, J. (1959), *Le livre de comptes de Giovanni Piccamiglio homme d'affaires Génois, 1456–1459* (Paris).

Kats, P. (1926), 'Double-Entry Book-keeping in England before Hugh Oldcastle', *Accountant*, 74.

Lane, F. C. (1944), *Andrea Barbarigo, Merchant of Venice 1418–1449* (Baltimore).

Lee, G. A. (1977), 'The Coming of Age of Double Entry: The Giovanni Farolfi Ledger of 1299–1300', *Accounting Historians Journal* (Autumn).

Martinelli, A. (1983), 'The Ledger of Cristianus Lomellinus and Dominicus De Garibaldo, Stewards of the City of Genoa (1340–41)', *Abacus*, 19.

Massa, P. (1974), *Un'impresa serica genovese della prima metà del Cinquecento* (Milan).

Melis, F. (1950), *Storia della ragioneria* (Bologna).

——(1962), *Aspetti della vita economica medievale* (Siena).

——(1972), *Documenti per la storia economica dei secoli XIII–XVI* (Florence).

Moschetti, G. A. (1610), *Dell'universal trattato di libri doppii* (Venice).

Pacioli, L. (1494), *Summa de arithmetica . . .* (Venice).

Peragallo, E. (1938), *Origin and Evolution of Double Entry Bookkeeping* (New York).

——(1971), 'A Commentary on Viganó's Historical Development of Ledger Balancing Procedures . . .', *Accounting Review*, 45.

Pilla, F. (1974), 'Il bilancio di esercizio nelle aziende private veneziane', *Studi Veneziani*, 16.

Sapori, A. (1932), *Una compagnia di Calimala ai primi del Trecento* (Florence).

——(1973), 'Il "bilancio" della filiale di Roma del Banco Medici del 1495', *Archivio storico italiano*, 131.

Schmalenbach, E. (1931), *Dynamische Bilanz* (5th edn., Leipzig).

Sombart, W. (1928), *Der moderne Kapitalismus* (6th edn., Munich and Leipzig).

Spallanzani, M. (1978), 'Le compagnie Saliti a Norimberga nella prima metà del Cinquecento', in J. Schneider (ed.), *Wirtschaftskräfte und Wirtschaftswege*, vol. i (Bamberg).

Stevin, S. (1607), *Vorstelicke bouckhouding op de Italiaenische wyse* (Leiden).

Weber, M. (1923), *Wirtschaftsgeschichte* (Munich and Leipzig).

——(1961), *General Economic History* (New York).

Zerbi, T. (1952), *Le origini della partita doppia* (Milan).

10 · THE SCOTTISH ENLIGHTEN-MENT AND THE DEVELOPMENT OF ACCOUNTING

M. J. Mepham

THE SCOTTISH ENLIGHTENMENT

The 'Scottish Enlightenment' is the name given in recent years to the remarkable epoch which Dugald Stewart described as a 'sudden burst of genius' (1854: 551). Although it is difficult to give firm dates, it is commonly considered that the Enlightenment extended from the Act of Union (1707) to the death of Sir Walter Scott (1832) with the peak of its achievements occurring in the second half of the eighteenth century.

The period is sometimes characterized by describing the major developments in areas such as economics, philosophy, and law, associated with the names of Adam Smith, David Hume, and Lord Kames, but the Enlightenment was not restricted to a small group working in a narrow range of subjects. Many other important advances occurred in a wide range of disciplines such as medicine, mathematics, agriculture, chemistry, geology, sociology, anthropology, and psychology. The roll call of luminaries would include such people as William Hunter, Andrew Duncan, William Cullen, Colin Maclaurin, James Hutton, Joseph Black, William Robertson, Adam Ferguson, and John Millar. The Enlightenment also saw a flowering of the arts, so that there were great architects (such as Robert Adam) and a notable literary revival (Sir Walter Scott, Tobias Smollett, and the poetry of Robert Burns).

The eighteenth century was also a period in which a number of important accounting texts emanated from Scotland and this chapter considers the connection between these texts and the Enlightenment.

First published in the *Accounting Historians Journal*, 15/2 (Autumn 1988).

ACCOUNTING IN EIGHTEENTH-CENTURY SCOTLAND

In 1700 there were few professional accountants in Scotland and the 'Italian Method of Book-keeping' was not widely used, but by 1800 there were professional accountants operating in the major Scottish towns and a knowledge of accounting was common in the business community. This improvement in the general level of accounting knowledge was aided by the important series of texts which appeared during the century. J. Crawford wrote that:

The first Scottish book on accounting was published in 1683. That book heralded a century during which Scotland established its reputation as a land of accountants: a steady stream of textbooks, including some which ran to so many editions that they could be called classics, appeared from Scottish presses (Pryce-Jones and Parker 1974: p. v).

The most notable of the accounting authors wrote clear expositions of the 'Italian Method of Book-keeping'. Moreover they wrote in a way which showed their enthusiasm for the merits of the new technique that they were explaining. They were committed advocates of the art and the impact of their writing was not merely parochial since it exercised a considerable influence beyond the borders of Scotland to the rest of the British Isles and to America. The importance of the Scottish texts has been noted by other commentators and the period when they were written has been described as one of 'Scottish Ascendancy' (Yamey, Edey, and Thomson 1963: 170–3).

Any study of the Scottish Ascendancy invites the question as to why the phenomenon should have occurred in Scotland, which was a relatively backward country, when the conditions would seem to have been much more propitious in England. The increase in the demand for accounting texts in Scotland can readily be explained by the country's improving trade but economic factors do not explain why this demand could not have been satisfied by imported books.

This chapter attempts to answer this question. It seeks to show that the ascendancy may be regarded as part of the more general flowering of the sciences and arts in eighteenth-century Scotland which has become known as the Scottish Enlightenment.

It is appropriate to note, at this juncture, that the question considered by this essay may be regarded as part of the larger question of 'Why the Scottish Enlightenment?' Devine comments on 'the central paradox of the phenomenon, namely the emergence of an age of cultural distinction within a society apparently deprived in both economic and social terms' (1982: 26).

It will be appropriate to identify some factors which may have encouraged both the Enlightenment and the Ascendancy in accounting texts but first the backgrounds and achievements of the four most important of the Scottish accounting authors will be described. These writers are:

Alexander Malcolm	1685–1763
John Mair	1702 (or 1703)–1769
William Gordon	1720 (or 1721)–1793
Robert Hamilton	1743–1829

'PHILO DOGMATICUS'—ALEXANDER MALCOLM[1]

Alexander Malcolm was born in Edinburgh in 1685. His father was minister of the Greyfriars Kirk in Edinburgh but the family moved to England when he was deprived of his post on the re-establishment of Presbyterianism in Scotland in 1689 (Scott 1915). Alexander, nevertheless, seems to have been educated at the University of Edinburgh and to have graduated Master of Arts (Bywater and Yamey 1982: 157) although his name cannot be traced in the university's records, which are incomplete for this period.

He became a teacher of mathematics and bookkeeping in the city and in 1718 he published *A New Treatise of Arithmetick and Book-keeping.*[2] His approach to these topics was scholarly, imaginative, and innovative, with a recognition of the importance of stressing the need for an understanding of principles rather than encouraging rote learning. Whereas the majority of his contemporaries emphasized accounting practice by providing page upon page of illustrative material, but little in the way of supporting text, Malcolm gives a full explanation of principles and he emphasizes accounting's role in the maintenance of justice. This Malcolm considered to be important, as justice was a necessary condition for the development of commerce (pp. 113–14). Colinson had adopted a similar viewpoint in the dedication of *Idea rationaria*, the first Scottish book on accounting (1683).

Malcolm's abilities were considerable and three years later he published a major book on the theory of music (*The Treatise of Musick*), which was the first important book on the subject published in Scotland. The music historian Sir John Hawkins (1719–89) claimed that this was 'one of the most valuable

---

[1] This is the title of a contemporary sketch of Malcolm (drawn by his friend Alexander Hamilton) which is contained in *The Tuesday Club Record Book*, preserved by the Maryland Historical Society of Baltimore.

[2] The text shows the influence of North's book *The Gentleman Accomptant* (1714) but in no sense is it a copy of this.

treatises on the subject of theoretical and practical music to be found in any of the modern languages'.

Soon after the appearance of his music text Malcolm moved to a teaching post in Aberdeen and in 1730 and 1731 he published separate books on mathematics and bookkeeping. These are based on, but not direct copies of, material from his 1718 book which had covered both subjects. In *A New System of Arithmetic, Theoretical and Practical* his aim is to combine practice and theory. De Morgan described this book as 'One of the most extensive and erudite books of the last (i.e. the eighteenth) century' (1847: 66). *A Treatise of Book-keeping* has an approach which is consistent with that of his earlier work but there is specific recognition of the use of accounting for planning purposes and its role as a tool of justice is no longer emphasized.

Immediately after the appearance of his *Treatise of Book-keeping* Malcolm migrated to America where he became a teacher in New York (Sadie 1980). The reason for his emigration is unclear but it is possible that it may have followed the death of Mary, his wife (Lloyd 1928). It is clear, however, that he became very unhappy with his situation there. He writes in a letter to a friend, Charles Macky (who was later to become the first Professor of History at the University of Edinburgh) that he feels 'Damned alas to the Slavery of Teaching Latin and Greek to the Cubs of a Stupid ungrateful purse proud race of Dutchmen. I shall say no more on this Subject But that Learning is the Very worst Cargo can be brought to America.'[3]

Malcolm remained in this post until 1740 when he became rector of St Michael's Church at Marblehead, Boston. This was both a change of vocation and a change of religious allegiance. At Marblehead he became friendly with Dr Alexander Hamilton (1712–56), a fellow Scot who emigrated from Edinburgh to Annapolis in 1738–9. Dr Hamilton, a physician and social historian,[4] was an uncle of Robert Hamilton (who is considered later in this article). Alexander Hamilton was also a vestryman at St Anne's, Annapolis, and this probably had a part to play in Malcolm's move to the rectorship of that parish in 1749. It is likely that Malcolm also taught at King William's School in Annapolis (Fletcher 1986: 211). In 1753 he was made Chaplain in Ordinary to the Assembly of Maryland. In 1754 he became rector of St Paul's in Queen Anne's County and from 1755 he was also master of the county Free School. He died in 1763 (Maurer 1952).

---

[3] Letter to Charles Macky, dated 3 July 1738 in the Manuscript Collection of the University of Edinburgh (La. II. 91).

[4] Alexander Hamilton (1712–56) was the author of *Itinerarium*, which was written in 1744 when he made a tour through the northern colonies; this was published privately in 1907, and more recently by the University of North Carolina Press in 1948.

Although Malcolm had emigrated well before the peak of the Enlightenment, his books on mathematics, music, and accounting were scholarly, analytical works which deserve recognition as part of the achievements of that movement. His letters in the archives of the University of Edinburgh convey his sense of loss at being separated from the intellectual stimulation of his Edinburgh friends.

'THE ELABORATE MAIR'—JOHN MAIR[5]

John Mair, the most successful accounting author of the eighteenth century, was born in 1702 or 1703, in Strathmiglo, Fife. His father 'was a portioner or small proprietor in that parish, and also carried on business as a manufacturer, to a considerable extent' (A. Mair 1830: p. iv). John and a younger brother, Alexander, both entered the University of Saint Andrews in 1722 and they both graduated with MA degrees in 1726. John then enrolled as a divinity student but in 1727 he applied for the position of 'doctor' (assistant master) in the Grammar School at Ayr which, incidentally, is still in existence.

John's application for this post was unsuccessful and, instead, he took up an appointment as 'Governor to Mr. Charles Cathcart, son to the Honourable Collonell Chas. Cathcart'.[6] A few months later, however, the Ayr post was again vacant and Mair was appointed at a salary of 200 merks (McClelland 1953).

For the next nineteen years Mair was actively initiating and implementing important curriculum developments in addition to carrying out his regular teaching duties and engaging in an extensive writing programme which included the most popular bookkeeping text of the century. This book, *Bookkeeping Methodiz'd*, exerted a major influence in North America as well as Britain. Sheldahl's inspection of some 160 eighteenth-century library, retail, and auction book listings enables him to state that 'Contemporary sales listings and library catalogs imply that *Mair's book-keeping* was easily the most popular accounting text in the major American cities during the latter half of the eighteenth century' (1985: 7). In 1775 this text was published in a Norwegian translation by Jasper Vande Velde de Fine and through this translation it became both the first English language book on the subject to

---

[5] A description used by J. Morrison, *The Elements of Book Keeping by Single and Double Entry* (London: Longman, Hurst, Rees, Orme, and Brown, 1813), 2.

[6] From a letter to Ayr Town Council, November 1727.

be translated into another language and the first Norwegian book on book-keeping. Various editions of the book were republished in Ireland and several other books were based on sections of it.

Mair's writing was characterized by the emphasis that he paid to detail and his attempts, as each new edition was issued, to make his book even more complete and relevant to business needs. The second edition (1741) included an additional section on 'Monies and Exchanges'; accounting for the tobacco trade with the colonies was added in the third edition (1749) and the fifth edition had two new sections on accounting for the sugar trade (based on Weston's book which had been published three years earlier) and shopkeep-ers' accounts. These additions meant that the 251 pages of the first edition (1736) had swollen to 416 pages by the 5th Edinburgh edition (1757).

In 1746 Mair became Rector of the school and First Master and teacher of Arithmetic, Book-keeping, and other Sciences. Immediately he began to introduce radical changes. The Ayr Council supported the creation of a new kind of school aimed at 'the training up of youth in the knowledge of litera-ture and preparing them for business in the most expeditious way possible' (Boyd 1961: 76–7). The remodelled school, based on plans drawn up by Mair, was, in his words, designed to be a 'sort of Academy where almost every sort of the more useful kinds of Literature will be taught, and the want of College Education will in great measure be supplied to boys whose parents cannot well afford to maintain them at Universities' (Taylor 1966: 62).

Mair remained at Ayr until 1761 when he accepted an invitation to become Rector at a newly founded Academy at Perth. This was to become a model for several other such academies which were built later in the century at Dundee, Inverness, Elgin, Fortrose, Ayr, and Dumfries (Magnusson 1974; 24–5).

Mair died in February 1769 at 66 years of age. His *Book-keeping Moderniz'd* (based on *Methodiz'd* but 50 per cent larger with 620 pages) was published posthumously and nine editions appeared over the next thirty-five years, the last appearing in 1807. *Methodiz'd* and *Moderniz'd* were thus standard texts in Britain and America for one hundred years and they fully earn the description of the first 'book-keeping series' (Mepham and Stone 1977). A total of thirty-two different printings of these texts have been identified in the period from 1736 to 1807 and *Methodiz'd* subsequently continued as the basis for Langford's *Merchants' Accounts*, which had nine editions between 1808 and 1853.

During his life Mair was also a prolific author on other subjects, with suc-cessful textbooks on history, geography, mathematics, and Latin to his credit (see Appendix). These writings and his educational vision and the innovations that he introduced at Ayr and Perth qualify him for recognition in educational history as a pioneer in Scottish science, mathematics, and business education (Sutherland 1952: 422). Although his books were less erudite than those of Malcolm, they were more successful and influential in spreading a knowledge of the subjects on which he wrote. If the motto of the Enlightenment was 'improvement', then Mair was part of the Enlightenment.

'THE INGENIOUS GORDON'—WILLIAM GORDON[7]

William Gordon is reputed to have been the son of the Third Duke of Gordon, by an early marriage to a French lady in Tours. The legend is that the marriage was not recognized in Scotland, the mother died young of a 'broken heart' and William did not succeed to the dukedom (Bulloch 1905: 145; Aberdeen Journal, *Notes and Queries* (1908), 107; Murray 1930: 34). Although the story must be false, since the Third Duke was born at about the same time as William, it seems likely that there is an underlying element of truth in the claimed connection to the ducal line since William received considerable help from the dukes of Gordon and dedicated several of his books to the Fourth Duke, referring to him as 'illustrious patron and Generous benefactor'.

William Gordon studied at Marischal College (one of the two universities in Aberdeen) from 1732 to 1736 and graduated, Master of Arts, in 1736 (Anderson 1898: 309). About 1750 he became schoolmaster at Fochabers which is adjacent to Gordon Castle. This appointment may indicate the exercise of some influence by the duke. He left this post in 1753, just after the death of the Third Duke, to take up a post as writing and mathematical master at the High School, Stirling.

In Stirling, he married Elizabeth Christie, daughter of the Town Provost, but other things did not go well. In 1755 he was suspended from his church preceptorship because of some domestic scandal and, in the following year, there was a complaint that he was not taking proper care of the boys under his charge. Shortly after this, in the same year, he resigned from the post.

William next moved to Glasgow where, in the same year, he founded and ran a Mercantile Academy with James Scruton and Robert Dodson (and later Alexander Jack). In 1767 he received a loan of £300 from the Fourth Duke

---

[7] A description used by Morrison, *Elements of Book Keeping by Single and Double Entry*, 2.

of Gordon to purchase the part of the premises that he occupied. While at Stirling, William had written his first book, *Every Young Man's Companion*, but his period in Glasgow saw the appearance of his major works, *The Universal Accountant and Complete Merchant* and *The General Counting-House and Man of Business*. While these were not so influential as Mair's bookkeeping texts they were important and well regarded with their worth recognized in America, where Chauncey Lee used them in preparing the bookkeeping section of his book *The American Accomptant* (1797).

The Academy continued until 1783 but latterly it does not seem to have been successful. Gordon's partner, James Scruton, was ill and Gordon himself was in perpetual financial difficulties because of a propensity for ill-advised business ventures. In September 1782 he was imprisoned in Glasgow's Tolbooth for non-payment of outstanding debts but in December 1782 he obtained a *cessio bonorum* (a form of bankruptcy) and was released from gaol.[8]

In 1783 Gordon moved to Edinburgh to become 'Master of the Mercantile Academy' there. He established his new Academy in the Scale Stairs at the head of Blackfriars' Wynd (*Caledonian Mercury*, 30 September 1786), where he continued his writing, including a major revision of *The Universal Accountant* in which he makes a case for the establishment of Chairs in Accounting at all universities. He says:

it would tend much to the prosperity of trade, that not only such as are intended for the commercial line, but that all youth of distinction also, should be early introduced to the knowledge of figures and accounts . . . For this purpose, it is to be regretted, that a proper Professor is not appointed in every University in Britain . . . (5th edition (1787), ii. 14–15)

In 1793 he is recorded as being in partnership with George Paton at the Commercial Academy, South Bridge, Edinburgh (Williamson 1794) but he died on 12 December later that year. His will shows the total value of his estate to be only £76 3s. 3¾d. and there was still the matter of the duke's outstanding £300 loan.

'THE JUDICIOUS HAMILTON'—ROBERT HAMILTON[9]

Robert Hamilton, in retrospect the most important of this group of writers, was born in Edinburgh into an influential family with strong kirk and

---

[8] Document in the Scottish Record Office, Edinburgh, CS 25/7 Dec. 1782.

[9] A description used by Morrison, *Elements of Book Keeping by Single and Double Entry*, 2.

university connections and important business interests. Robert's father, Gavin Hamilton, was a prominent Edinburgh publisher, bookseller, paper maker, and bailie of the burgh who, two years after Robert's birth, distinguished himself by his brave loyalty to the British crown when, during the 1745 Rebellion, Bonnie Prince Charlie's father was proclaimed King James VIII of Scotland in Edinburgh.

Robert was educated at the University of Edinburgh (where in 1732 his grandfather had been Principal and where two uncles were currently professors). Following this he was employed in the banking-office of Hogg and Son, but in 1766, at the age of 22, he applied for the Chair of Mathematics at Marischal College. He was unsuccessful but the decision was close.

After the failure to secure the Aberdeen professorship Robert became involved in managing the family's paper mill but, on his father's death, he took the opportunity to divest himself of these irksome obligations. In 1769 the rectorship of Perth Academy became vacant on the death of John Mair and Hamilton applied for and was appointed to this post. At Perth, Hamilton wrote his main accounting work, *An Introduction to Merchandize* (1777–9). This book is much in advance of its time, with an emphasis on the managerial uses of accounting information which is absent from the other eighteenth-century books. Although it is exceptional in many other respects, its chief claim to fame is the remarkable description of a costing system that it contains (Mepham 1988).

In 1775, Hamilton obtained an LL.D. from the University of Edinburgh and in 1779 he was appointed to the Chair of Natural Philosophy at Marischal College, Aberdeen. Hamilton's preference, however, was for an appointment in mathematics and he soon came to an amicable agreement with the professor of that subject to exchange classes. Thus, although he remained professor of natural philosophy, he in fact taught the mathematics classes until 1817 when he officially transferred to the Chair of Mathematics.

At Aberdeen, Hamilton continued his writing but his next important work was not published until he was seventy. This was a book on *The National Debt* (1813), in which he sought to demonstrate the fallacy of attempts to redeem that debt painlessly by means of a sinking fund. This work has always been regarded as his main claim to fame. Hamilton died in 1829. Throughout his life he was active in humanitarian, religious, civic, and philanthropic activities and he wrote several essays on social problems which were published posthumously.

Robert Hamilton's work on the national debt qualifies him for recognition as part of the Scottish Enlightenment but it will be claimed here that his

Merchandize also deserves recognition as a pioneering work which emphasized the use of accounting as a decision-making aid to manufacturers and traders. In the past the merits of this book have been seriously underestimated (Mepham 1983).

THE ECONOMIC BACKGROUND

There is evidence that some Scottish businessmen, at the start of the eighteenth century, were developing accounting systems which helped them to improve their efficiency (Marshall 1980) and throughout the century there was a growing demand for books which explained sound accounting procedures. It is relevant to outline some of the economic developments which created this demand.

At the end of the seventeenth century Scotland had been hit by successive failures of the harvest. There was the aftermath of the Darien[10] disaster and the effect of war. Trade between Scotland and England was minimal and Scotland was poor in comparison with its southern neighbour. There were, however, encouraging signs of developing economic activity. In 1683 Colinson, in the first Scottish book on bookkeeping, expressed his view that the number of new Scottish trading ventures was increasing and that there was optimism that trade would grow and flourish (p. 1).

Early in the century the Treaty of Union (1707) created an Anglo-Scottish Common Market. Previous trade patterns were modified and expansion encouraged. There was not an instantaneous growth of trade with England but there was a steady improvement. Internal, coastal, and overseas trade were also expanding. In 1700 Scotland's trading partners were the countries of northern Europe, with the trade with the Netherlands being particularly important. At the Scottish end of this trade the east coast had an advantage. This led to the development of trading activity in the east of Scotland and Edinburgh, whereas Glasgow and the west were at a distinct disadvantage.

During the first half of the century, however, the balance shifted. The 1707 Treaty gave Scottish traders entry to England's jealously guarded colonial markets without payment of customs duties, and Scottish-owned ships obtained the protection and privileges afforded by the Navigation Acts.

---

[10] In 1698 the Company of Scotland Trading to Africa and the Indies (the Darien Company) had attempted to establish a Scottish colony (New Caledonia) on the narrow Isthmus of Darien linking North and South America. The adventure was a complete failure; 2,000 died, and the money cost of £300,000 was a considerable drain on the nation's cash resources.

Seventy years after the Treaty of Union, John Gibson, an eighteenth-century Glasgow accountant, describes Glasgow's subsequent commercial development as follows:

The Union with England opened a field of trade, for which the situation of Glasgow was greatly to her advantage; the commerce of the east coast, since that period, has declined: that of the west has increased to an amazing degree. (1777: 205–6)

In the same year James Scruton, Gordon's partner in the Academy in Glasgow, asked the rhetorical question, 'what was Scotland before its union with England? or, to come nearer home, what was Glasgow . . . ?' (1777: 2). In writing this, he had in mind Glasgow's flourishing trade with the West Indies and North America—a trade which was only possible after the Treaty of 1707. Mair had introduced a chapter on the tobacco trade into the 3rd edition of *Book-keeping Methodiz'd* (1749). Although this trade collapsed with the American War of Independence, Scotland consolidated its industrial success in the second half of the century and started a period of economic expansion which lasted until the 1870s. The sugar trade with the West Indies, which had been in existence since the beginning of the century, developed rapidly, partially filling the gap caused by the demise of tobacco. Mair had included a chapter on the sugar trade since the 5th edition (1757).

The linen industry, which was Scotland's major manufacturing industry in the middle of the eighteenth century, also received benefits from the Union with England in the form of export bounties and tariff protection from the competition of Dutch and German manufacturers. The industry experienced an era of rapid growth in the period from 1740 to 1780. Hamilton hints that his description of a costing system for a linen manufacturer is based on a real system, and Perth, where he wrote his book, was an important centre for the trade. At the end of the century the profits earned from the linen trade became an important additional source of capital for the developing manufacture of cotton yarn and cloth. This new branch of the textile industry, which was centred on Glasgow and Paisley, was soon making use of spinning machines driven by water power.

The partnership form of business organization became increasingly important as the century passed and it was recognized that sound bookkeeping practices were essential to foster the mutual trust that was required among partners. Colinson had claimed that the 'honourable and profitable Science of Book-keeping is the only help, that encourages many to join their small stocks together . . .' (1683: 1). Although the textbooks concentrated on the accounts of the sole trader they all considered partnership accounts in some detail. The Bubble Act of 1720 ostensibly banned partnerships with freely transferable shares and limited liability but the accounting texts continued to describe a form of organization, 'the fixt company', which had similarities to the modern limited liability company (Malcolm, *A Treatise of Book-keeping* (1731), 65). Methods of accounting for transferable shares in such companies were developed and even the question of shares issued at a premium was discussed.

As a group the eighteenth-century writers provided a body of literature which moved bookkeeping towards accounting. This development should be viewed along with the increasing adoption of the system by merchants and manufacturers, as the century passed, and the birth of the Scottish accountancy profession. At the beginning of the eighteenth century there were one or two 'professional' accountants in Edinburgh; in the last decade of the century the number was over thirty. All three developments assisted the expanding Scottish economy.

THE SCOTTISH EDUCATIONAL SYSTEM

The 'Scottish Enlightenment' and the 'Scottish Ascendancy' in accounting texts were, in part at least, due to the calibre of the Scottish educational system in the eighteenth century. The four accounting authors were all educationalists and all were products of the Scottish university system. Higher education facilities were good in Scotland, where there were five universities (compared with two in England) and it has been claimed that 'In the eighteenth century there was a greater proportion of the population possessed of a university education in Scotland than in any other country in Europe' (Feuer 1963: 216).

The century was one of general educational advance and commercial education facilities also improved considerably. In the seventeenth century commercial education had been catered for by the apprenticeship system. Towards the end of the century, however, it was increasingly the case that aspiring young merchants with ability and the necessary financial backing, were attending special schools abroad, often in Holland. The formal teaching of the subject in Scottish schools was also improving at the beginning of the eighteenth century. In the first decade of that century both Glasgow and Edinburgh Councils established the official post of teacher of bookkeeping and there were other developments.

In the first half of the century a grammar school education was almost entirely devoted to Latin and the classics, but by 1750 changes in the curriculum were taking place and mathematics, science, and bookkeeping were finding a place.

George Watson, Scotland's first professional accountant (Brown 1905: 183), who had received his own commercial education in Holland, demonstrated his conviction that bookkeeping should have a place in the school curriculum when, in leaving instructions in his will for the establishment of a school, he provided that the scholars should be taught accounting and bookkeeping. This was his only stipulation on curriculum matters. Watson died in 1723; his school, George Watson's Hospital (now George Watson's College) opened in Edinburgh in 1741.

The four accounting authors contributed to the educational developments. The achievements of Mair and Hamilton at Ayr Grammar School and Perth Academy have been mentioned. The new academies, which built on their pioneering work, typically included mercantile studies as an important part of the syllabus. Alongside this development there was also a rapid growth in the number of private educational establishments run by writing masters and bookkeeping teachers such as Malcolm and Gordon.

SCOTTISH PUBLISHING

A trade which prospered in step with the progress of the Enlightenment was publishing and printing. In Edinburgh (and Glasgow), as the century passed, printing flourished. Arnot (1779: 438) states that in 1739 there were only four printers in Edinburgh but forty years later the number had risen to twenty-nine. From the 1730s the Edinburgh firms produced cheaper texts than the London printers (Jones 1985: 92) and, towards the end of the century, it even seemed possible that Edinburgh might supplant London as the main centre of publishing in Britain.

In part the large number of printing firms was sustained by reprinting English books. Before 1710 Scottish printers had been free to reprint such works without restraint but, in that year, a Copyright Act imposed restrictions. Considerable litigation followed this Act but this did not put a brake on the Scottish progress (McDougal 1988). The strength of printing in Edinburgh also encouraged Scottish writing and, since the book trade was profitable, publishers were able to offer substantial advances to authors (Chitnis 1976: 38). When Stevenson, Professor of Logic at Edinburgh University, assisted in the defence of Scottish printers in one of the copyright actions, he claimed that the Scottish printing activities were designed 'to encourage learning in Scotland, and to give an opportunity to good Scottish writers who might otherwise never appear in print at all' (McDougal 1988: 8). If this point is tendentious it is, nevertheless, true that the strength of printing and publishing in Edinburgh, the availability of credit for prospective writers and the climate of the Enlightenment all encouraged Scottish writing. The Enlightenment fostered a belief in the printed word as an instrument in the advancement of society and gave encouragement to the publication of 'academic' texts of all kinds, including books on bookkeeping.

The majority of the bookkeeping texts by Scottish authors were published in Edinburgh. Authors frequently published their own works but there were also important publishing houses and Hamilton had family connections with the major publishing firm of Hamilton, Balfour, and Neill. This firm alone published 400 titles between 1750 and 1762 (McDougall 1974).

THE ACCOUNTING TEXTS CONSIDERED AS PART OF THE ENLIGHTENMENT

The effect of the Enlightenment on the intellectual life of Scotland was dramatic and the four accounting writers display the versatility which was common in the period. It has already been noted that Malcolm wrote a major work on music; Mair was a pioneer of science education in the school curriculum; and Gordon campaigned for the inclusion of accounting in university studies. The importance of Hamilton's treatise on the redemption of the national debt and his social writings is generally acknowledged and both he and his father are listed by Camic among 375 Scottish eighteenth-century 'intellectual achievers' (1983: 243–56). An appendix details the writings of the group.

David Hume emphasized the catalytic effect of the 'spirit of the age':

The same age which produces great philosophers and politicians, renowned generals and poets, usually abounds with skilful weavers, and ship-carpenters. We cannot reasonably expect, that a piece of woollen cloth will be wrought to perfection in a nation which is ignorant of astronomy, or where ethics are neglected. The spirit of the age affects all the arts; and the minds of men, being once roused from their lethargy, and put into a fermentation, turn themselves on all sides, and carry improvements into every art and science. (1963: 301)[11]

---

[11] In contrast, Adam Smith relates improvements in the arts and sciences to a prior improvement in trade and material prosperity (Smith 1776: III. iv. paragraph 10).

In their activities and in their accounting writings it is reasonable to suggest that the Scottish accounting writers were encouraged and influenced by the intellectual 'ferment' of the period and the 'spirit of the age'. This does not, however, mean that the Scottish Ascendancy in accounting texts should necessarily be counted among the achievements of the Enlightenment since some would argue that bookkeeping texts (however good) are too lowly for consideration alongside the other achievements of the age.

Young, however, makes the point that

the Scots thinkers of the Enlightenment not merely refused to recognize any distinction between the pure and applied sciences, but were prepared to treat the practical applicability of their speculations as a yardstick of their merits. (1967: 11)

With this criterion of 'practical applicability', the bookkeeping texts, and particularly those of Mair and Gordon, must surely rank as achievements of the Enlightenment in that they were important contributions to the development of systematic business systems which were of considerable practical use and extremely influential. These texts played a major role in spreading a knowledge of sound accounting methods to the rest of Britain and to America and Norway (through the translation of Mair's book).

Accounting did not feature in university studies but it has been noted that Gordon considered that the 'science' had advanced to the point where it should be taught in all universities. If this were to be done, he claimed 'we should not only have more intelligent merchants, but the members of both Houses of Parliament, would thereby become better judges of political economy' (vol. ii (1787), 14–15). This reference to political economy is particularly interesting because it has been claimed that Adam Smith's 'political economy was a new discipline produced by the Scottish Enlightenment' (Chitnis 1976: 9).

Smith's *Wealth of Nations* (1776) is rightly regarded as a major contribution of the Enlightenment. On his death, in 1790, his obituary in the Caledonian Mercury claimed that he had converted his Chair at Glasgow University to one of trade and finance. It should be recognized, however, that the *Wealth of Nations* was not designed to give practical advice to the business man. The accounting texts, however, did have this aim and Hamilton's *Merchandize* is particularly relevant in this respect.

The first volume of the first edition of Hamilton's book appeared one year after the *Wealth of Nations*. Although Smith discussed opportunity cost, he did not consider how the businessman could make use of the concept. In contrast Hamilton appreciates its uses in business decision-making and sets out to develop practical tools. Writing after Smith had suggested that society was improved by the 'invisible hand' of competition, he outlines a cost accounting system which is designed to improve the manufacturer's efficiency. He does this by advocating an opportunity cost approach in discussing transfer prices for his comprehensive costing system and as the basis behind a residual income method of appraising performance. In this way Smith's analysis was converted, perhaps coincidentally, to a management decision-making end and Hamilton produces a work whose worth remains unchallenged in the field for the next century. Nothing of any note was published (in English) on this subject for over 100 years after Hamilton's book until the appearance (in the 1880s) of three books on cost accounting (Metcalfe 1885; Garcke and Fells 1887; Norton 1889).[12]

CONCLUSION

If the Scottish Enlightenment has a focus it was probably a focus on the improvement of society through a study of 'the science of man' (Hume 1975: 273) and the search for the laws underlying human behaviour. Malcolm argues that 'Societies are supported by Commerce' and he claims that a sound system of bookkeeping is a prerequisite for ensuring the justice which is required for the promotion of commerce and hence the advancement of society (*A New Treatise on Arithmetick* (1718), 113–14). The eighteenth-century Scottish accounting authors considered their texts as more than sound, utilitarian manuals which explained a useful, but optional, technique. The Italian Method had 'practical applicability' but the authors thought of it as a major advance which would lead to major improvements in trade and commerce and their writings convey their excitement and enthusiasm for its outstanding virtues. Gordon, for example, considers that 'Regular books frequently examined, will contribute more to prosperity in trade, than great address and abilities without them' (*The Universal Accountant* (1765), ii. 12). The writers were outstandingly successful in spreading a knowledge of this important system and the benefits arising must have been considerable.

Economic advances and the growth of capitalism created a demand for accounting texts in Scotland, England, Ireland, and America. To a considerable extent this demand was met by Scottish textbooks which, in the case of America, were exported from Glasgow or through London (McDougall

---

[12] Garner 1976, ch. 2, notes some earlier discussions of industrial accounting, but these do not seem sufficiently important to falsify this statement.

1988: 14–20). This chapter has argued that the Scottish Enlightenment provided the conditions which encouraged a group of able academics to supply the needed books. The texts were practical, technical works but they were also, it is posited, a part of the general intellectual ferment of the 'Enlightenment' and there is a basis for considering them an important part of this movement and complementary to more renowned works in economics and law. If the accounting writings lacked the glamour of some of the other publications of the period, and some of the other works of their authors, they had an influence throughout the English speaking world which is arguably as profound.

References

Aberdeen Journal (1908), 'The Author of the *Universal Accountant*', *Notes and Queries*, I: 107.

Anderson, P. J. (ed.) (1889/1898), *Fasti Academiae Mariscallanae, Aberdonensis 1593–1860: Selections from the Records of Marischal College and University* (Aberdeen: New Spalding Club), vols. i, ii.

Arnot, H. (1779), *The History of Edinburgh* (Edinburgh: W. Creech, London: J. Murray).

Boyd, W. (1961), *Education in Ayrshire through Seven Centuries* (London: University of London Press).

Brown, R. (1905), *History of Accounting and Accountants* (Edinburgh: T. C. and E. C. Jack).

Bulloch, J. M. (1905), 'The Romance of a Duke', *Scottish Notes and Queries*, Second Series, 6 (Apr.): 145–7.

Bywater, M. F., and Yamey, B. S. (1982), *Historic Accounting Literature: A Companion Guide* (London: Scolar Press).

Camic, C. (1983), *Experience and Enlightenment, Socialization for Cultural Change in Eighteenth Century Scotland* (Edinburgh: University Press).

Chitnis, A. C. (1976), *The Scottish Enlightenment: A Social History* (London: Croom Helm).

Colinson, R. (1683), *Idea rationaria* (Edinburgh: David Lindsay, James Kniblo, Josua van Solingen and John Colmar).

De Morgan, A. (1847), *Arithmetical Books from the Invention of Printing to the Present Time* (London: Taylor and Walton; repr. London: H. K. Elliott, 1967).

Devine, T. M. (1982), 'The Scottish Merchant Community, 1680–1740', in R. H. Campbell and A. S. Skinner, *The Origins and Nature of the Scottish Enlightenment* (Edinburgh: John Donald), 26–41.

Fletcher, C. (1986), 'King William's School Survives the Revolution', *Maryland Historical Magazine* (Autumn): 210–21.

Feuer, L. S. (1963), *The Scientific Intellectual* (New York: Basic Books).

Garcke, E., and Fells, J. M. (1887), *Factory Accounts* (London: Crosby Lockwood and Co.).

Garner, S. P. (1976), *Evolution of Cost Accounting to 1925* (University, Ala.).

Gibson, J. (1777), *The History of Glasgow from the earliest accounts to the present time; with an Account of the Rise, Progress, and Present State of the Different Branches of Commerce and Manufactures now Carried on in the City of Glasgow* (Glasgow: for the Author).

Hume, D. (1963), 'Of Refinement in the Arts', in *Essays Moral, Political and Literary* (1st edition 1741; repr. Oxford: University Press).

——(1975), *A Treatise of Human Nature* (1st edn. 1739; repr. Oxford: Clarendon Press).

Jones, P. (1985), 'The Scottish Professoriate and the Polite Academy, 1740–6', in I. Hont and M. Ignatieff (eds.), *Wealth and Virtue* (Cambridge: University Press).

Lee, C. (1797), *The American Accomptant* (Lansinburgh: W. W. Wands).

Lloyd, M. (1928), 'Alexander Malcolm, Writer in Mathematics and Music', *Scottish Notes and Queries* (Dec.): 234–6.

McClelland, J. (1953), 'Schools', ch. 14 of A. O. Dunlop, *The Royal Burgh of Ayr: 750 Years of History* (Edinburgh: Oliver and Boyd).

McDougall, W. (1974), 'Gavin Hamilton, John Balfour and Patrick Neill: A Study of Publishing in Edinburgh in the Eighteenth Century', Ph.D. thesis, University of Edinburgh, 1974.

——(1988) 'Copyright Litigation in the Court of Session, 1738–1749, and the Rise of the Scottish Book Trade', in *Edinburgh Bibliographical Society Transactions*, 5/5: 2–31.

Magnusson, M. (1974), *The Clacken and the Slate* (London: Collins).

Mair, A. (1830), *A Brief Explication of the Assembly's Shorter Catechism* (New Edition, Montrose: Smith and Co.).

Marshall, G. (1980), *Presbyteries and Profits* (Oxford: Clarendon Press).

Maurer, M. (1952), 'Alexander Malcolm in America', *Music and Letters* (July): 226–31.

Mepham, M. J., and Stone, W. (1977), 'John Mair, M.A.: Author of the First Classic Book-keeping Series', *Accounting and Business Research* (Spring): 128–34.

——(1983), 'Robert Hamilton's Contribution to Accounting', *Accounting Review* (Jan.): 43–57.

——(1988), 'The Eighteenth-Century Origins of Cost Accounting', *Abacus* (Mar.): 55–74.

Metcalfe, C. H. (1885), *Cost of Manufactures and the Administration of Workshops, Public and Private* (New York: Wiley and Sons).

Murray, D. (1930), *Chapters in the History of Bookkeeping, Accountancy and Commercial Arithmetic* (Glasgow: Jackson, Wylie and Co.).

North, R. (1714), *The Gentleman Accomptant* (London: E. Curll).

Norton, G. P. (1889), *Textile Manufacturers' Bookkeeping for the Counting House, Mill and Warehouse* (Huddersfield: Alfred Jubb).

Pryce-Jones, J., and Parker, R. H. (1974), *Accounting in Scotland* (Institute of Chartered Accountants of Scotland, Edinburgh).

Sadie, S. (ed.) (1980), *The New Grove Dictionary of Music and Musicians*, vol. ii (London: Macmillan Ltd.).

Scott, H. (1915), *Fasti Ecclesiae Scoticanae* (Edinburgh: Oliver and Boyd, New Edition), vol. i.

Scruton, J. (1777), *The Practical Counting House* (Glasgow: James Duncan).

Sheldahl, T. K. (1985), 'America's Earliest Recorded Text in Accounting: Sarjeant's 1789 Book', *Accounting Historians Journal*, 12/2 (Autumn): 1–42.

Smith, A. (1776), *The Wealth of Nations* (London: W. Strahan and T. Cadell).

Stewart, D. (1854), *Dissertation: Exhibiting the Progress of Metaphysical, Ethical and Political Philosophy*, vol. i of the *Collected Works*, ed. W. Hamilton (Edinburgh: Thomas Constable and Co., 2nd edition).

Sutherland, D. J. S. (1952), 'John Mair, The Pioneer of Science Teaching in Scotland', *Scottish Educational Journal* (4 July): 422.

Taylor, A. L. (1966), 'The Grammar School of Ayr 1746–96', *Collections of the Ayrshire Archaeological and Natural History Society*, 7: 58–89.

Weston, W. (1754), *The Complete Merchant's Clerk: or, British and American Compting-House* (London: R. Griffiths).

Williamson, P. (1794), *Williamson's Edinburgh Directory 1794–1796* (Edinburgh: Williamson).

Yamey, B. S., Edey, H. C., and Thomson, H. W. (1963), *Accounting in England and Scotland: 1543–1800* (London: Sweet and Maxwell).

Young, D. (1967), *Edinburgh in the Age of Reason* (Edinburgh: University Press).

APPENDIX

Books written by Alexander Malcolm (1685–1763)

A New Treatise of Arithmetick and Book-keeping Edinburgh: printed by John Mosman and William Brown for John Paton	1718
A New System of Arithmetick, Theoretical and Practical. Wherein the Science of Numbers is Demonstrated . . . London: J. Osborn and T. Longman, F. Fayram and E. Symon	1730
A Treatise of Book-keeping, or Merchants Accounts; in the Italian Method of Debtor and Creditor 1st edition, London: printed for J. Osborn and T. Longman	1731
(facsimile reprint as vol. xi of *Historic Accounting Literature*, London: Scolar Press, 1979; facsimile reprint, New York: Garland Publishing, 1986) 2nd edition, London: printed by Dan. Browne for D. Browne	1743
A Treatise of Musick, Speculative, Practical and Historical 1st edition, Edinburgh: printed for the Author	1721

2nd edition, London: J. Osborn and T. Longman	1730
London: J. Osborn	1731
Malcolm's Treatise of Music . . . Corrected and Abridged by an Eminent Musician	
London: printed for J. French	1776
2nd edition, London: printed for J. French	1778
2nd edition, London: printed for J. Murray	1779

Books and articles written (or edited) by John Mair (1702/3–1769)

BOOKS

Book-keeping Methodiz'd 1st edition, Edinburgh: T. and W. Ruddimans for the	
Author	1736
(facsimile reprint as vol. 12 of *Historic Accounting Literature*, London: Scolar	
Press, 1979)	
1st edition, Edinburgh: W. Sands, Brymer *et al.*	1736
2nd edition, with Additions and Improvements, Dublin: printed by Mary	
Fuller	1737
2nd edition, Edinburgh: printed by W. Sands, Brymer *et al.*	1741
2nd edition, Edinburgh: printed for, and sold by W. Sands . . . and by Mess.	
Midwinter, Innys *et al.*, London	1741
2nd edition, Dublin: printed by Isaac Jackson	1742
2nd edition, Dublin: printed by Isaac Jackson	1748
3rd edition, with Additions and Improvements, Edinburgh: printed by	
W. Sands, A Murray, and J. Cochran	1749
the Last Edition, with Additions and Improvements, Dublin: printed and sold by Isaac	
Jackson	1750
4th edition, Edinburgh: printed by Sands, Murray *et al.*	1752
3rd edition, Dublin	1754
4th edition, Dublin	1754
5th edition, with Additions and Improvements, Dublin: printed and sold by	
I. Jackson	1754
5th edition, Edinburgh: printed by Sands, Donaldson *et al.*	1757
6th edition, Edinburgh: printed by Sands, Donaldson *et al.*	1760
Norwegian translation by Jasper Vande Velde de Fine, Norway	1775
7th edition, Edinburgh: printed by Sands, Murray *et al.*	1763
7th edition, Dublin: printed by H. Saunders	1763
From the last edition printed at Edinburgh and revised, Dublin: printed and	
sold by I. Jackson	1764
8th edition, Edinburgh: W. Sands, A. Murray *et al.*	1765
8th edition, Dublin: printed by H. Saunders	1767

9th edition, Dublin: printed by H. Saunders	1772
From the last edition printed at Edinburgh . . . with many additions and improvements, Dublin: R. Jackson	1773
Book-keeping Moderniz'd 1st edition, Edinburgh: A Kincaid, W. Creech, and J. Bell	1773
2nd edition, Edinburgh: John Bell and William Creech	1778
3rd edition, Edinburgh: J. Bell *et al.*	1784
4th edition, Edinburgh: John Bell and William Creech	1786
5th edition, Edinburgh: Bell & Bradfute and Wm. Creech	1789
6th edition, Edinburgh: Bell & Bradfute and Wm. Creech	1793
7th edition, Edinburgh: Bell & Bradfute and Wm. Creech	1797
8th edition, Edinburgh: Bell & Bradfute	1800
9th edition, Edinburgh: Bell & Bradfute	1807
Arithmetic, Rational and Practical 1st edition, Edinburgh: A. Kincaid and J. Bell	1766
2nd edition, Edinburgh: A. Kincaid and Wm. Creech	1772
3rd edition, Edinburgh: John Bell and Wm. Creech	1777
4th edition, Edinburgh: John Bell and Wm. Creech	1786
5th edition, Edinburgh: Bell & Bradfute and Wm. Creech	1794
6th edition, Edinburgh: Bell & Bradfute and Wm. Creech	1799
Ancient History Epitomized Edinburgh: T and W Ruddimans	1750
Also published as part of *An Introduction to Latin Syntax* (next item)	

An Introduction to Latin Syntax . . . to which is subjoined, An Epitome of Ancient History . . .
1st edition, Edinburgh, 1750; 2nd edition, Edinburgh, 1755; 3rd edition, Edinburgh, 1760; 4th edition; 5th edition; 6th edition, Edinburgh, 1770; 7th edition; 8th edition, Edinburgh, 1777; 8th edition, 1779; 9th edition, 1786; another edition, Dublin, 1790; another edition, Glasgow, 1790; 11th edition, Kilmarnock, 1790; 10th edition, Glasgow, 1797; another edition, Edinburgh, 1797; 1st American edition, Philadelphia, 1799; 11th edition, Dublin, 1800; 12th edition, Edinburgh, 1793; another edition, New York, 1804; 12th edition, Edinburgh, 1805; 13th edition; another edition, New York, 1807; another edition, Baltimore, 1811; another edition, New York, 1811; 15th edition, Edinburgh, 1811; another edition, New York, 1813; 17th edition, Edinburgh, 1815; 18th edition, Edinburgh, 1816; another edition, New York, 1817; stereotype edition, Edinburgh, 1818; another edition, Baltimore, 1820; stereotype edition, Edinburgh, 1821; another edition, New York, 1821; stereotype edition, Edinburgh, 1823; another edition, Baltimore, 1824; stereotype edition, Edinburgh, 1826; another edition, Edinburgh, 1827; another edition, New York, 1830; another edition, Edinburgh, 1831; another edition, New York, 1833; another edition, New York, 1836; another edition, New York, 1838; another edition, New York, 1839; another edition, New York, 1843; another edition, New York 1846; another edition, New York, 1848; another edition, New York,

1853; another edition, Philadelphia, 1857; revised by A. R. Carson, Edinburgh, 1860; another edition, Philadelphia, 1861

The Tyro's Dictionary, Latin and English 1st edition, Edinburgh, 1760; 2nd edition, Edinburgh, 1763; 3rd edition, Edinburgh, 1778; 4th edition, Edinburgh, 1785; 5th edition, Edinburgh, 1793; 6th edition, Edinburgh, 1801; 7th edition; another edition, New York, 1809; 8th edition, Edinburgh, 1812; 9th edition, Edinburgh, 1817; 10th edition, Edinburgh, 1822; revised by G. Ferguson, Edinburgh, 1846

A Radical Vocabulary, Latin and English 1st edition; 2nd edition; 3rd edition, Edinburgh, 1772; 4th edition; 5th edition, Edinburgh, 1779; 6th edition, Edinburgh, 1785; 7th edition, Edinburgh, 1791; 8th edition, Edinburgh, 1799; 9th edition, Edinburgh, 1803; American edition, New York, 1809

The First Four Books of C. Julius Caesar's Commentaries of his Wars in Gaul, with an English Translation 1st edition; 2nd edition, Edinburgh, 1757; another printing, Edinburgh, 1769; 3rd edition, Edinburgh, 1770; 4th edition, Edinburgh, 1770; 5th edition; 6th edition, Edinburgh, 1792; another printing, Edinburgh, 1793; 7th edition, Edinburgh, 1808

Sallust's History of Catiline's Conspiracy, and the War with Jugurtha 1st edition, 1741; 2nd edition; 3rd edition, Edinburgh, 1770; 4th edition, Edinburgh, 1774; 5th edition; 6th edition, Edinburgh, 1793; another printing, 1822; another printing, 1831; another printing, 1847

A Brief Survey of the Terraqueous Globe Edinburgh and Perth, 1762; republished 'with great additions, amendments and improvements', Edinburgh, 1775; another printing, Edinburgh, 1789; another printing, London, 1795; 2nd edition, London, 1802

A Select Century of M. Cordery's Colloquies Glasgow, 1775; another printing, 1786; another printing, 1788; 7th edition, Dundee, 1792; another printing, 1797

ARTICLES

'Arithmetick', section in *Encyclopaedia Britannica* 1st edition, Edinburgh: Bell & Macfarquhar, pp. 365–423   1771

'Bookkeeping', section in *Encyclopaedia Britannica* 1st edition, Edinburgh: Bell & Macfarquhar, pp. 582–620   1771

Books edited and/or revised by Mair

Cocker's Arithmetic, revised by Mair

Edinburgh: Sands, Murray and Cochran	1751
51st edition	1756
Edinburgh	1760

A new edition, Edinburgh: Alexander Donaldson	1762
A new edition, Edinburgh: A. McCaslan	1765
another edition, Glasgow: James Brown	1771
another edition, Edinburgh	1771
another edition, Edinburgh	1780
another edition, Glasgow	1787

Wilson's Introduction to Arithmetic, edited and revised by Mair, 2nd edition,
Edinburgh: W. Sands *et al.*   1752
(First edition, which was not edited by Mair, was 1741)

Adaptations of Mair's works

*Essays on Book-keeping wherein the Art is fully explained, To which is added a Large Appendix
containing a Variety of Specimens in Company Accounts . . . by a Teacher of
Book-keeping.* Glasgow: printed for John Orr   1758
(The major part of the contents of this book comes from Mair's *Book-keeping
Methodiz'd*, the remainder is Webster's *An Essay on Bookkeeping*)

An Essay to Make A Compleat Accomptant . . . by Richard Roose, London: for
Hannah Roose   1760
    (contains 'The Six Questions in Company Accompts' from Mair's
    Book-keeping Methodiz'd)

Book-keeping epitomized or a compendium of Mair's methodical treatise of merchants-accompts
by the Rev. John Shaw, Leeds: J. Binns and London: J. Johnson, Ogilvy
and Speare, and Vernor and Hood   1794

Merchants' Accounts; or Book-keeping according to the Italian Method of Double Entry
London: Published by R. Langford   1808
    (preface describes the book as *Mair's Book-keeping Methodized, with some corrections
    and additions*)

another edition	1822
another edition	1824
another edition	1826
another edition	1828
another edition	1830
another edition	1835
another edition	1843
another edition	1853

Clavis Mairiana, or a Key to Mair's Introduction to Latin Syntax by *a young gentleman*
1st edition, New York: J. Seymour, 1809; 2nd edition, revised by
Muirhead, Edinburgh: Wallace & Co., 1814; Another edition by John
Black, Edinburgh: University Press, 1818; Another printing, Edinburgh,
1822

Books written by William Gordon (1702/1–1793)

Every Young Man's Companion 1st edition; 2nd edition, London: J. Hodges,
  1757; 3rd edition; 4th edition, London: J. Rivington, H. Woodfall *et al.*,
  1765; 5th edition, London: H. Woodfall, 1769; 6th edition, London
  and Salisbury: H. Woodfall, J. Rivington *et al.*, 1777

The Universal Accountant and Complete Merchant (2 vols.) 1st edition, Edinburgh:
  printed for the author and A. Donaldson   1763/65
(facsimile reprint of vol. ii, New York: Garland Publishing, 1986)
  2nd edition, Edinburgh: printed for Alexander Donaldson   1765
3rd edition, corrected, and revised by the Author, Edinburgh: printed for
  Alexander Donaldson   1770
4th edition, Edinburgh: A. Donaldson   1777
5th edition (New Modelled) (2 vols.) Edinburgh: printed for A. &
  J. Donaldson & C. Elliott   1787
6th edition, Dublin: printed by T. Henshall   1796
The General Counting-House and Man of Business 1st edition, Edinburgh: printed
  for A. Donaldson   1766
2nd edition, Edinburgh: A Donaldson & S. Crowder   1770
Glasgow   1770
The Elements, Analysis and Practice of Arithmetic 1st edition (written with Robert
  Dobson), vol. i of 3 according to title-page, Glasgow: printed by R. Urie
  for the Authors   1771
2nd edition (NOT with Robert Dobson), Glasgow   1775
Institutes of Arithmetic, elementary and practical Edinburgh: W. Creech   1779
Edinburgh: W. Creech   1789
Revision of Hayes translation of Livy (8 vols.) Edinburgh   1761
Titus Livius Roman History, translated into English Edinburgh: W. Smith 1783;
  Edinburgh, 1809; Edinburgh: Bell & Bradfute, 1813
Cornelius Nepos, Vitae Excellentium Imperatorum . . . with an English translation
  Edinburgh   1790
A New Geographical Grammar and Complete Gazetteer Edinburgh: Alexander Guthrie   1789
Another Issue, Edinburgh: Martin, McDowall, and Company   1789
(This book seems to have been initially issued in parts)

Books and articles written by Robert Hamilton (1743–1829)

BOOKS

An Introduction to Merchandize 1st edition (2 vols.) printed for the Author;
    sold by T. Cadell, London and John Balfour, Edinburgh   1777/79
2nd edition, Corrected and Revised, Edinburgh and London: Charles Elliot   1788
(facsimile reprint as vol. xv of 'Historic Accounting Literature', London: Scolar
    Press, 1979)
    3rd edition, Edinburgh, Glasgow, Aberdeen, Perth and Leith: J. Hunter;
    Bell & Bradfute *et al.*   1797
4th edition, Corrected and Revised, Edinburgh, London, Glasgow, Aberdeen,
    Perth and Leith: J. Hunter, G. G. and J. Robinson *et al.*   1799
5th edition, Edinburgh   1802
New-modelled edition revised by Elias Johnston, Edinburgh, Aberdeen and
    London: Archibald Constable and Co. and Fairbairn & Anderson *et al.*   1820
A Short System of Arithmetic and Bookkeeping 1st edition, London and Edinburgh:
    C. Elliott & T. Kay   1788
2nd edition   1796
3rd edition, Edinburgh, Glasgow, Perth and Leith: J. Hunter, Bell & Bradfute
    et al.   1798
4th edition
5th edition, Edinburgh   1802
6th edition
7th edition, Edinburgh   1810
8th edition, Edinburgh   1815
Another edition *Enlarged and Improved* by James Welsh, Aberdeen and
    Edinburgh: A Constable and Co. *et al.*   1826
An Essay on Peace and War . . . published anonymously, London: G. G. J.
    and J. Robinson   1790
Heads of a Course of Lectures on Mathematics Aberdeen: A. Brown and Edinburgh:
    W. Creech   1800
An Inquiry Concerning the Rise and Progress, The Redemption and Present State, and the
    Management of the National Debt of Great Britain 1st edition   1813
2nd edition, Enlarged, Edinburgh: Oliphant, Waugh and Innes   1814
American Edition, 'From the 2d London ed', Philadelphia: M. Carey   1816
French Translation by J. Henri La Salle, *Recherches sur l'origine, les progres, le rechat,*
    l'etat actuel et la regie de la dette nationale de la Grande-Bretagne Paris: Gide fils   1817
3rd edition, Enlarged (title extended by the addition of the words *and*
    Ireland), Edinburgh: Oliphant, Waugh, and Innes   1818
Part reprinted in J. R. McCulloch (editor), *A Select Collection of Scarce and Valuable*
    Tracts and Other Publications on the National Debt and Sinking Fund, London   1857
(reprinted New York: Augustus M. Kelley, 1966)

An Address to the Inhabitants of Aberdeen on the Management of the Poor Aberdeen   1822

Observations upon the causes of distress in the country, and proposals of a plan for ameliorating the condition of the poor . . . Glasgow: printed by J. Curll   1822

The Progress of Society London: John Murray, Albemarle Street   1830
(reprinted New York: Augustus M. Kelley, 1969)

Essays Aberdeen: printed by D. Chalmers and Co.   1831

Mathematical Tables: continuing logarithms of numbers . . . *also, Tables of Compound interest, probabilities of life, and annuities for years and lives* 1st edition, Edinburgh: printed for William Creech   1790

2nd edition with several additional tables, Aberdeen: printed by Chalmers for William Creech, Edinburgh   1807

2nd edition, Edinburgh: J. Fairbairn   1816

A book entitled *Remarks on the necessity and the Means of Extinguishing a large portion of the National Debt* (1818) has been attributed both to Hamilton and Thomas Bunn (S. Halkett and J. Laing, *Dictionary of Anonymous and Pseudonymous English Literature* (Edinburgh: Oliver and Boyd 1929), v. 75).

ARTICLES

'Book-keeping', section of *Encyclopaedia Britannica* 2nd edition, vol. ii, Edinburgh: J. Balfour *et al.*   1778

3rd edition, vol. iii, Edinburgh: Bell and Macfarquhar   1797

4th edition, Edinburgh: A. Bell   1801

5th edition, Edinburgh   1810

6th edition, vol. iv, Edinburgh: Constable & Co. (an additional section is appended on a *New Method of Book-keeping*   1823

7th edition, Edinburgh: Black (includes a reference to Cronhelm, F. W., *Double Entry by Single*, 1818)   1842

CORPORATE ACCOUNTING

II · EARLY CANAL COMPANY ACCOUNTS: FINANCIAL AND ACCOUNTING ASPECTS OF THE FORTH AND CLYDE NAVIGATION, 1768–1816

D. A. R. Forrester

Economic and accounting historians have tended to study railway developments, and companies incorporated under the British 1856 and 1862 Acts, rather than the earlier experience of parliamentary or statutory companies out of which general, consolidating legislation, and limited liability for companies evolved.

The Forth and Clyde Canal or Navigation is of interest in so far as private finance was subscribed in Scotland and London in 1768, adequate according to first estimates, and postponing the need for Exchequer support. As work progressed, retrospective and prospective statements of sources and applications of funds were required, anticipating more general charge–discharge annual statements sent from Glasgow to London from 1791 to 1856. Transactions on credit were curtailed; receipts were lodged in and payments made from the Royal Bank of Scotland. New corporate and cash accounting systems thus emerged at precisely the time of Exchequer reforms of the Imprest system. Periodic income was quickly ascertained, tabulated, classified, and graphed as early as 1815. A final significant innovation in printing and circulating reports and accounts to proprietors took place after Glasgow interests outvoted the London and landed shareholders.

Account books as such have not survived, but minute books and a series of reports and accounts sent from Glasgow to London from 1787 are available in the Scottish Record Office. These records have been used by Lindsay to describe the Canal's general history, but do not permit replication of J. R.

First published in *Accounting and Business Research* (1980).

Ward's socio-economic analyses of the finance of English canals;[1] but they offer contemporary vignettes which can be supplemented in local archives. The stature of individual entrepreneurs becomes clear as the freedoms advocated in Adam Smith's *Wealth of Nations* were increasingly realized. Administrative and accounting skills learnt in the mercantile field were applied effectively to this Canal, which was not completed to the Firth of Clyde until 1790, and paid no dividend till 1800, thereafter liberally rewarding the patient investors.

We therefore find here examples of intersectoral migration of skills, of relationships between Exchequer, legislature, and a private company, and also of a co-ordination of private interests and common weal. The infrastructural development described was of importance not merely in facilitating and cheapening the transport of passengers and freight (almost 3 million tons were to be carried in 1866) but also by its direct tendency to make different districts and different places feel that each had need of the other, as Buckle wrote in his *History of Civilisation in England*.[2]

INTRODUCTORY

A canal through the narrow central belt of Scotland had seemed attractive since the 1660s: both naval and commercial traffic would be facilitated. A century later, Edinburgh's interests with the Continent and Glasgow's booming trade with the Americas promoted rival plans, until that for a Great Canal for sea-going ships received effective support.

Glasgow's promotion of a shallower canal could be replaced by a 7-feet deep navigable cut[3] only if support was obtained from public funds, it was thought. But negotiations proved fruitless. Tired of delays, aristocrats, and merchants and bankers, chiefly in Edinburgh and London, opened a subscription list to raise the £150,000 required according to John Smeaton's, the great civil engineer's, plans and estimate. Meetings were held in both cities, and a Private Bill was presented to Parliament for incorporation. This received royal assent as 8 Geo. III cap. 63 in 1768.

Twelve more times up to 1820, the company had to obtain Private Acts amending its constitution, altering its fund-raising powers, or for acquiring land on modified routes. There was thus advantage in having members and

---

[1] Works referred to are listed by author in the References. FCN1/- indicates Scottish Record Office files.
[2] Buckle 1867: iii. 181.
[3] Progressive deepenings to 10 feet took place up to 1814.

influence in the Houses of Commons and Lords. Parliamentary companies may well have seemed 'little republics',[4] growing up in the shadow of Westminster till they reached the independence which Robert Lowe aspired for them in 1856. The experience then gained by the legislature enabled incorporation by simple registration.

But with poor communications and parochialism, tension and problems inevitably arose, especially as the cut proceeded westward from Grangemouth on the Forth and reached the vicinity of Glasgow in 1776. Thither the management was moved and Edinburgh found itself increasingly ignored in negotiations between London and Glasgow. London's control was tightened after funds had run out in 1773 with the sea-to-sea canal scarcely half complete. The position was made specially difficult by the collapse of Douglas Heron & Co.'s Ayr Bank.

Economies were insisted on, and more formalized subcontracting. Faith in the contract method was later voiced by Superintendent Colquhoun who found it the least expensive mode of conducting the business, and proposed that his estimates of maintenance and operating costs under twelve heads be the basis for putting these operations out to contract: 'in spite of every kind of vigilance on the part of those entrusted with management, like all public undertakings there is a propensity to waste . . . which if not checked by the most vigilant eye of an auditor, will accumulate and increase year after year'.[5]

ACCOUNTING

In addition to the Chief Engineer, Smeaton, a site engineer, MacKell, and a surveyor or estimator, a key appointment at the start was that of Oversman or Clerk to the Cheque for the whole works. Nine candidates applied for the post in June, 1768, including a factor, a former Carron Iron company clerk, and an army lieutenant. Several had powerful patrons. The successful applicant, a former merchant in Edinburgh called Alexander Stephen, was awarded a salary of £70. His duties at first were to pay wages and to keep accounts, with a journal of work done, reporting to the Law Agent in Edinburgh weekly. Some months later he was instructed to make a full and distinct account of monies received and disbursed. Invoices for more than £20 were required to be checked against current and agreed prices, and to be signed by

---

[4] The phrase is Robert Lowe's, used in the debate on the 1856 Companies Act. (*Hansard*, 3rd Series, cxl, col. 134.)

[5] FCN1/37, p. 186.

the Engineer before submission to the Committee for approval. Stephen was also instructed to draft a State of Accounts owing, and to prepare an Account of Utensils and Materials. This was later described as a Ledger of Ware, distinctly accounting for the diverse applications of wood, etc. In 1771, Speirs sent over from Glasgow an assistant to keep this record at a salary of £30. The task was not facilitated by MacKell who attested receipts and uses of wood without informing Stephen. From 1769, a General Account of materials on hand was to be laid before Quarterly Meetings. No such stocks appear in the 1792 or 1815 Balance Sheets, even though in January 1797 it was prescribed that an annual inventory of materials and utensils should be taken, and the value fixed 'by some disinterested person'.

The Edinburgh Agent had early opened a Minute Book, a Letter Book, a Book to register precepts or cheques drawn on the Bank, a share or Stock journal and Ledger for transactions. (The Book for bank precepts has been reduced today to cheque counter-foils; but in the eighteenth century Treasury at Westminster, such a system had replaced cumbersome instructions to the lower Exchequer by means of tallied foils and counterfoils.) The agent had been ordered to prepare a plan of share transfer books in the manner of the great companies in England, but instead adopted the 'plan' of the Royal Bank of Scotland. All these books, together with Stephen's Accounts, were ready for examination in November 1768, when a full Committee was adjourned so as not to interrupt the Lord Provost and Mr Speirs in the examination subcommitted to them.

But the auditing of ever increasing expenses proved onerous for Committee members. Relations with the Royal Bank were so close that, in 1770, its Secretary was made part-time Comptroller and Auditor of Accounts to the company. After he had taken the oath of faithful administration, and provided sureties or guarantees of £1,000, Archibald Hope's salary was to be £60 per annum. He was to audit the accounts of the London and Edinburgh Agents, and of Stephen, while his account would be audited by a committee member. Full committee approval of expense might be necessary in special circumstances. The title of Hope's function was borrowed directly from the Exchequer. But the days of combining many offices which could be delegated to assistants were numbered, after the 'one man, one job' reforms in the Treasury from 1776 to 1782 spread out.[6]

London of course required an overview of sources and applications as work proceeded. Those in Parliament required from Hope an abstract of

---

[6] Cf. Roseveare 1973: 85, 181/2.

bank accounts, and a clear statement of proposed works and expenses before they left town in March 1771. Later that year, the Committee approved the books audited by Hope as 'giving full satisfaction to all concerned, especially the distant proprietors, who have no opportunity of seeing the works and inspecting the respective Accounts'. Next spring, London requested estimates of sources and applications for the coming season, and to the completion of works, along with accounts of work to date including information on average costs per yard dug and of masonry built, which had to be obtained from those on site. (The best estimates or forecasts, we will see, were prepared by Colquhoun for the last stages of canal construction.)

As work moved west and finance became increasingly hard to find, responsibilities were transferred to Glasgow in 1775. London resolved that Stephen should be Agent in Scotland and cover all meetings, while Hart in Edinburgh should be demoted to company solicitor, after he had transferred the books to Hope. An Edinburgh General Meeting however continued Hart as chief clerk, agent, accountant, and bookkeeper at a salary of £200, to include all his assistants and office expenses.

In May 1775, the Committee in Glasgow invited a member, Jackson by name, to examine the books and vouchers of the company from the very start. He replied that it would be too time consuming and distracting from his own business; he was doubtful of the propriety of interfering with accounts contracted under the former Committee, and refused to take custody of the books.

By March, 1776, it was resolved in London that there was no occasion for an agent, clerk, auditor, or comptroller in Edinburgh. Hope was downgraded to company cashier at a salary of £30; and even this appointment was terminated subsequently.

Many responsibilities thus rested with Stephen: he was ordered to receive toll receipts each week, and to lodge accounts and vouchers monthly with the member of Committee responsible for 'contingent affairs' between meetings. By 1779 London was complaining of his slowness in transmitting committee minutes. From the start of 1781, Accounts of Revenue and Expenditure were demanded quarterly.

Edinburgh felt even less well served. A General Meeting there in 1782 appointed a committee to investigate problems in the Falkirk area, and were told from London that this was contrary to regulations. Edinburgh complained of this reaction to 'a very innocent recommendation': but the value of meeting subsequently was not clear to members, only two of whom attended that September. Early in 1883 Stephen was ordered to transmit Committee of Management minutes to Edinburgh. Yet in 1784, Glasgow and London had got a Bill through first and second readings in the Commons before news of it reached Edinburgh. The Bill was designed to put the whole canal under control of a new Glasgow Customs House, and to reduce proxy powers at London meetings. Edinburgh was goaded to self-defence, and to demand that the agent in Glasgow forward a full report monthly, and copies of accounts which a committee of five were to audit. Unless the system of management was entirely changed, wrote John Knox in Edinburgh,[7] there was risk of a total loss of capital. The Glasgow Committee also asked for a clarification of the roles of general meetings and committees.

By 1786 many influential Glasgow merchants had added to their interests in West Indian trade or in cotton importing and processing some shares in the Forth and Clyde Navigation. Such names occur in the list of proprietors at that date as Henry Glassford and his collaborator Patrick Colquhoun, who as Provost of Glasgow had chaired Committee meetings for two years prior to 1784. Other members were the Speirs, who had intermarried with the family of Sir Thomas, later Lord, Dundas of Kerse on whose lands stood Grangemouth. Dundas was established as a rich government contractor in London. Together then, the London and Glasgow interests secured the out-numbering of the Edinburgh vote, and the passing of an Act confining General Meetings to London. The Secretary of the company there was required to keep a true and perfect account of all Acts, Proceedings, and Transactions of the new Governor, Council and General Meetings. Sir Thomas was elected Governor, and re-elected in each of the next twenty-six years.

Meanwhile, perhaps before demitting office as Provost in 1784, Patrick Colquhoun had instigated proposals for a new ledger, which were approved by London. In August 1785, Richard Smellie, accountant and bookkeeper, was appointed because of:

the absolute necessity of employing an able accountant to post up the books of account in a methodised and accurate manner and upon the principles of double-entry, showing the stock of the company and specifying such heads of expenditure as shall be thought necessary to give the proprietors a clear and distinct view of the application of the money.

Three terms in this suggest the varied derivation of the accounting to be applied. *Methodized* was familiar from the title of John Mair's *Book-keeping* in its first eight editions. *Heads* was a typical Exchequer accounting term. *Application* suggests fund or trust accounting, where misapplication had to be guarded

---

[7] His pamphlet is quoted by Pratt (1922).

against. The supremacy of the traders' forms is indicated by the instruction to Smellie to buy a waste-book, journal and ledger. Stephen was to supply evidence, and the accounts of the proprietors were to come from Edinburgh.

The new books were to cover transactions since 1775. Tersely, Smellie was told to record receipts only from clear and distinct vouchers. Soon it became clear that there were more than trivial errors in Stephen's accounting. In April 1786, he acknowledged blunders and inaccuracies, the largest of which was a failure to record £825 received from the Carron company. His account showed total debits of £25,287 and credits of £23,683. After some eighteen adjustments his debt to the company (cumulated over the years) was agreed at £1,223 14s. 8½d. This sum the Committee had to recover by the sale of his house, and from his sister and James Dennistoun, who were his guarantors. Stephen had been ill and was put on half-pay, before he was brusquely replaced by Patrick Colquhoun.

Stephen suffered like many another of the period not so much through dishonesty as from imperfections in accounting. He had had to cope with the first commitment of proprietors' funds to unprecedentedly large engineering works, with changes in administrative centre and responsibilities, and with financing problems now to be examined. These imperfections could not be remedied by bookkeepers or officials trained to this type of operation, for there were none. The problems arose within the tradition of stewardship or factor's accounts, where interim audit and even discharge of accountability for one period were less important than the final reckoning. In Exchequer and similar accounting, only on death or retiral was the final settlement demanded.[8] Security was obtained not from foolproof, ongoing accounting and audit systems, but from a continuing personal responsibility of office-holders, guaranteed by the sureties which they had to provide on appointment. But novel in many respects as the systems introduced to the Forth and Clyde after Stephen's retiral might be, the traditional ideas and form of charge and discharge account continued to coexist alongside them till 1856.

FINANCING

The financial history of the Forth and Clyde Navigation may conveniently be studied with reference to calls on subscribed capital, bank lending, bonds and annuities, and government aid. (Later we will describe a dispute on

---

[8] Cf. Forrester 1978, *passim*.

whether improvements should be financed from retained profits or from borrowing.)

Accountants in Britain have been neither knowledgeable nor sensitive on how their techniques have evolved and may evolve to meet changing circumstances and to exploit changing technical media. Accordingly the system of progressive calls on subscribed capital, which was developed by statutory companies in the eighteenth and nineteenth centuries to finance extended infrastructure developments was still covered in bookkeeping texts until very recent years, even though such companies and such developments had long been absorbed into the public sector of the economy. The history of the system has to be sought in such books as O. C. Williams's *Historical Development of the Private Bill Procedure and Standing Orders in the House of Commons.* F. Clifford's earlier *History of Private Bill Legislation* is there referred to, showing how Parliament's accumulated experience of local initiatives proved invaluable, and was eventually applied in the general enabling legislation for companies in 1844, 1856, and 1862, complemented in the case of infrastructure companies by increasing bureaucratic interventions prior to nationalization.

Canal legislation has not received the same attention as that for railways. But the first problem of competition from alternative navigations had been faced in 1761/2 for the Duke of Bridgewater's Canal Bill. With the Forth and Clyde Bill, Glasgow's alternative Bill and the proposal of Bo'ness that a cut be made east to serve that town were each withdrawn on the offer being made to repay their legal expenses.

The problem faced by the legislature was to ensure the seriousness of each proposal, and that finance was adequate. Estimates by respected engineers were therefore sought, together with sufficient subscriptions by persons of worth to carry through the works which often yielded little income till complete. With experience the problem of subscribers being unable to honour all calls was encountered and partially overcome by the transferability of part-paid shares. In the case of the Forth and Clyde, the financing problem was accentuated not only by Smeaton's initial underestimating of construction costs (which may appear typical of most projects), but also by the eight years before toll income became considerable, the twenty-two years before sea-to-sea navigation was completed, and the thirty-two years before dividends were paid and the shares ceased to be a speculation. More particularly, in the year after the canal was incorporated, Douglas, Heron, and Co. formed the so-called Ayr Bank, with the duke of Queensberry in its chair also, and with the duke of Buccleuch involved. The management operated with a mixture of 'aggressiveness, euphoria and self-deception' which was extended also to the proprietors, a nation-wide speculative frenzy giving way to the Bank's collapse along with thirteen Edinburgh private banks in 1772.[9] Such events lay ahead as the Forth and Clyde began.

Of the £128,700 nominal value of shares subscribed for, 10 per cent was due before incorporation. The first call of £5 was payable to the Royal Bank of Scotland by 1 December 1767, and the second two months later, till which date new subscribers were admitted. These calls of course would be absorbed in initial legal expenses and compensation monies. The incorporating Act permitted calls to be made each of not more than £10 per share, nor less than three months apart. Subsequent calls, payable to the Royal Bank or at Drummond's Bank in London, may be traced from the Minute Books in part but were not always approved by General Meetings.[10]

By 1773 the tenth to twelfth calls were advertised for funds to cover the work which had proceeded briskly but expensively towards the west. Many contributed promptly, but for others it appears to have been a semi-voluntary matter. The company's powers to forfeit shares or charge interest on unpaid calls were extended by private Act in 1771, and appear to have been more readily enforceable in Scotland. Counsel's opinion was there obtained that October; and in May, 1773, a Court of Session summons was to be executed. In November 1780, the Carron Iron company had to be forced to pay interest due by Court of Session decree. Complicated relations could, however, arise with individual proprietors. In 1787, new powers were obtained from Parliament for partial forfeiture after crediting actual payments to a proportion of shares now treated as fully paid; and this was done for George Chalmers, a lawyer who had been active in initial flotation and was then allowed his expenses, but denied a similar claim in 1788 for charges possibly incurred in representing Edinburgh's interests against London and Glasgow.

In England the enforcement of calls was always a matter of imperfectly documented difficulty.[11] A Forth and Clyde meeting in 1769 felt that 'arrears from noble-men and gentlemen require only a reminder'. In February 1774, slow payers were to be reminded prior to Drummond, the bankers, calling on each, bearing a receipt. In November 1779, the Lord Chancellor advised that a Bill in Equity was not to be recommended, but that declarations should be filed in the Court of the King's Bench. If a subscriber died, his executors might be forced to pay £1,000 overdue, plus the cost of King's Bench process, as for Luke Scrafton's shares in 1781. In February of that year, £14,300 was still recorded as outstanding; two members in total arrears

---

[9] Checkland 1975: 124–34.   [10] Cf. *Issues in Accountability*, 3/12.   [11] Ward 1974: 118.

were struck off; and a polite reminder was sent to Lord Elphinstone! In May 1783 law charges in one case alone totalled £100; ten months later it was decided to debit such charges to the subscriber. In March 1785 as subscribers' capital in relation to the Exchequer participation had to be confirmed, interest on arrears was demanded because thereafter 'interest on interest' (i.e. compounded) would be payable. Yet legal process against Henry Isaac's executors in March 1787 was dismissed with costs.

In 1789, Colquhoun calculated the situation as follows: the statutory capital was 1,500 shares; 213 shares not initially subscribed had been entrusted to Sir Lawrence Dundas, and 136 had subsequently been sold. Thus 77 shares had not been issued; 85 had been forfeited under the 1771 Act, and 41 more under 27 Geo. III cap. 55 leaving 1,297 shares in the hands of 136 proprietors. Under this latter Act, capital which had received no reward for up to seventeen years had interest allowed at 5 per cent per annum from the date of each individual contribution. Each share issued at £100 was thus revalued at £167 3s. 6d., with total paid-up capital showing as £216,125 19s. 6d.[12] This of course represented an 'opportunity cost' to the proprietors rather than actual capital paid in. Extra cash was then, as earlier, needed.

On several occasions, additional finance was offered. Glasgow pressed to finance from its own resources a connecting canal in 1771. In March 1773 additions to subscriptions of £16,700 were proposed, Glasgow expressing a willingness to subscribe if other proprietors were also willing.[13] In March 1781 a new subscription of £30,000 was also discussed. In 1789 the Glasgow Committee urged that the 203 remaining shares should be issued above par, increasing the private capital to ⅚ of the whole, with the Exchequer's share reduced to ⅙. But London vetoed the idea of a prospectus for circulation to shareholders.

More effectively and frequently the Royal Bank of Scotland helped with finance. It had agreed to charge only 4 per cent interest on its loans to such a 'national concern' in 1768, on condition that all payments should be made in its bank notes.[14] But the Bank was unwilling to lend to a company without personal security. In 1770, the Praeces or Chairman in Edinburgh was to accept bills of exchange presented by the company's agent, and discount them at the Royal, thus raising immediate funds which were to be repaid out of the receipts from the sixth call on the shareholders. In this and other ways, £11,500 was owed to the Bank in June 1770: and the debt increased to £19,600 by 1772.[15] On subsequent occasions we learn of the company seek-

---

[12] FCN1/35.
[13] Marwick 1876–1917: vii. 399.
[14] *Three Banks Review*, Dec. 1964.
[15] Checkland 1975: 233.

ing to relieve the Dundases and others of their liability on its behalf to the Bank. In 1794 Bonds of Relief are mentioned as issued by the company under its seal to the Governor and proprietors who had signed personal bonds to the Bank.

A new source of finance was clearly required by March 1773. A London Minute recorded Smeaton's estimate five months earlier that the cost of works from the Logie Water to the 'West Sea' would amount to £70,000, and in addition a further 243 acres of land would have to be purchased at £30 per acre. Salaries were estimated to add £4,500 before completion, and £19,610 was due to the Royal on bonds given by Sir Lawrence and Thomas Dundas. Funds still required were estimated at over £102,000, but arrears on calls, and the 15 per cent of subscribed capital still to be called were estimated to bring in £39,000. Allowing for £6,500 contingencies, some means of raising £70,000 was sought.

This was to take the form of an issue of bonds resembling in many ways those by which Queensberry and Buccleuch were seeking to pay off the debts of the Ayr Bank. They had raised £450,000 by placing 'annuity bonds' on the London capital market, despite the opposition of the East India Company.[16] Precedent for the new means of raising finance also came from the toll-roads. By Act of 13 Geo. III cap. 104, the company was permitted to print bonds for £70,000, granting or assigning the navigation and its future tolls as security. Books recording these assignments 'by way of life annuities or otherwise' were to be open at all times to proprietors and creditors. In March 1774, the London Meeting minuted its confidence in this form of finance; further bonds should be issued to complete the canal.

But whether owing to the interruption to trade resulting from the American War of Independence or for other reasons, no further work was undertaken for several years after the canal had reached Hamiltonhill one mile from Glasgow. Bond interest must have remained a heavy, prior charge on the revenues of the incomplete canal. In 1787 Colquhoun noted that bonds bore interest at 5 per cent as compared with bank interest of 4 per cent. In preparation for the final stage, in 1787 he calculated the sums held or owing to the company or likely to be received in each of the three following years. A surplus over requirements of £30,000 was disclosed until 1790; and this surplus he suggested might be used to repurchase the bonds for £26,000 held by Messrs Forbes and Cumming. In March 1788, bonds for £20,000 were redeemed and delivered to the proprietors who had signed them. In the

---

[16] Checkland 1975: 132–3.

1792 Balance Sheet two bonds totalling £25,000 are shown as due to the Royal Bank. Typically for the period, Colquhoun proposed that a surplus of £5,000 could form a sinking fund, but with the purpose of repaying cash-credits and overdrafts. Recourse to bonds, of £100 up to £1,000 each nominal, was adopted again in 1799, for the purpose of repaying the Exchequer participation.

The flexibility and other advantages of Scotland's unique Bank 'cash-credit' system[17] gain further evidence after the transfer of management to the West, where the Royal had no branch at first. In 1783 Stephen was ordered to lodge receipts punctually with the Glasgow Arms Bank. In that year, David Dale and Scott Moncrieff started operations on behalf of the Royal, and by 1786 were entitled to receive a copy of Committee of Management Minutes.

A new importance for cash accounting and for Bank records can be discerned, displacing aperiodic, personal and imprest accounts. From 1 January 1781, a quarterly Account of Receipts and Expenditure was required for London. In that month, a copy of the Account from 1786 was provided by the Royal, £5 being charged for this 'work of much labour'. By 1786 the Royal Bank Account was being copied monthly and transmitted to London, where it took up about 100 pages of the Reports which were bound together each year. With the monthly and annual classified summaries, this account obviously played a central role as a day-book for a company which sought to avoid imprests or debtor accounts.

A very similar transfer to cash accounting, year by year, was being instigated in the Treasury by the Commissioners for Examining appointed by Parliament to reform outmoded procedures.[18] One of these Commissioners was George Drummond, possibly related to John and Adam Drummond who were proprietors of the Forth and Clyde Navigation. It is not necessary to attribute to individuals a natural extension of state accounting developments which would be known to every parliamentarian.

In the north the balance sheet of 1792 shows that £2,761 was still imprest with the company servants or contractors, and was due to become part of the cost of the canal when accounts were settled. In January 1794, it was specified that all accounts and outlays formerly paid by the surveyors and others from advances made to them, should be paid monthly and quarterly at the company's offices by drafts on the Bank. All revenue and expenditure were to pass through the company's account at the Bank, and be directly debited or credited to respective nominal accounts for receipts and disbursements. The

---

[17] Checkland 1975: 267.   [18] Cf. Binney 1968, *passim*.

account was to be examined, compared with vouchers and initialled monthly by a member for the Committee.

In 1791, the offer of a leading proprietor, Hopkirk, to lend £12,000 for 5–7 years at 4¾ per cent was rejected because of the flexibility of the Bank's overdraft system. In 1795, it was decided to pay off all small sums which bore interest so that the company would pay interest to the Bank only.

From July 1775 toll-collectors had been urged to avoid giving credit, and to pay in takings weekly to the agent, and by him to the Bank. Even Henry Glassford was pressed to settle accounts for lime moved from his quarries each month; this was modified however, since, provided these dues were brought to account within the year, it was felt of little consequence in which month.[19] In general, means were sought to facilitate punctual analysis of monthly revenues and speedy year-end accounts.

GOVERNMENT PARTICIPATION

Government systems were not always copied or welcomed. The story of Exchequer aid must now be told, marking as it does an early rejection by nobles and merchants of the merchantilist ideas which had informed the applications for state support for the canal in the 1760s and again in 1776. In 1780, the Board of Trustees for Fisheries and Manufactures was approached once more without success. Further efforts were made, however, and in 1783, the Dukes of Argyll, Buccleuch, and Queensberry, and the Lord Advocate, with Sir Thomas Dundas waited on the Earl of Shelburne at the Treasury. Only in February 1784, after a similar deputation to Pitt and the Treasury Lords, was agreement reached for an intricate manœuvre. This related to the estates of former Jacobites, which after the '1715' had been sold but which after the 'Forty-five' had been retained in a major effort to civilize the Highlands.[20] Forty years later those disinherited had shown their loyalty to the Hanoverian kings so clearly that resale of lands to them could be considered. The Forth and Clyde Navigation appeared first among the petitioners for the funds to be realized from the sale, and indeed bore £200 of the cost of the Disannexing Act. The company was to receive £50,000: and this sum was to rank equally for dividends with subscribed capital as increased by interest up to Martinmas 1784. The Act 24 Geo. III cap. 57 prescribed that dividends were to be declared from the free annual produce of

[19] FCNI/14–9/vi/1801.   [20] Cf. Smith 1974, *passim.*

the canal, once the company's debt had been paid off, and a sufficient fund retained for contingent expenses and repairs. The Exchequer's dividends were earmarked for road and bridge building.

The Act required the company to deliver to the Court of the Exchequer annually an abstract from their books, showing the state of their funds and debts as well as the gross revenues and deductions therefrom. (Significantly the basis of state accounting in specific funds was altered through their consolidation in 1787—since which time the plural form 'funds' has lived on in state and company accounting from which specific, earmarked revenues and funds have progressively disappeared.)

Between London and Glasgow, detailed debate took place as to what precise accountability was required. Colquhoun in Glasgow advocated a 31 December year-end, rather than accounts to Martinmas (11 November). He also supported a General Account Current, clarifying charges and discharges rather than a Cash Account. By 20 May 1789, the Scots Exchequer demanded accounts for the previous five years.[21]

London transmitted accounts which were to be sent on from Glasgow. James Loch for the Exchequer then wrote that the accounts submitted did not sufficiently convey the information intended by Parliament. He proposed that the King's Remembrancer should travel to Glasgow and obtain a more particular state, to give the Court a complete view of the situation in 1784 and of alterations since, 'adjusting with the managers a plan of the Accounts for the future'.[22]

Glasgow was at this time instructed to co-operate, while later negotiations were reserved to London. But resistance to the Exchequer was hardening: in December 1788, it was ordered that an account showing the Exchequer as proprietor of 2,999 shares should be replaced by one showing the £50,000 as 'Money granted by Parliament . . . from the Act it could not be inferred that the government were either partners or proprietors, with any voice or control in direction or management'.

In March 1797, Glasgow defended itself against further Exchequer criticisms. In 1798, the company felt able to offer repayment of the initial sum with interest. Two accounts of the Cost of the Navigation, with and without interest, went to the Chancellor. But when the time came, confusion arose as to whether repayment should be to London or Edinburgh.[23]

---

[21] SRO–E.310/2, p. 326.

[22] FCNI/38–8/viii/89.

[23] In Edinburgh, public records show only a request from the South that payment be accepted. SRO-E307/10, p. 329.

TOLLS

The toll-charging of the canal also reveals influences from the mercantilist period, and in particular from Customs and Excise. On incorporation, rates were fixed at 2 pence per ton-mile, except for ballast or ironstone which was to be charged at one penny. This was by agreement with the Carron Iron Company, which in March 1773 suggested that if the produce of lands in the neighbourhood of the canal was to be exempt, all their materials, which were listed *extenso* might be similarly treated. Such requests were typical of the pressures from particular interests, in resisting which Smeaton was asked for the experience of the River Calder Navigation in Yorkshire. Its Schedule and Book of Rates was obtained from a Mr Simpson of Halifax.

Adam Smith in *The Wealth of Nations* ignored the effects of speed and wash in suggesting that charges based on weight were the most equitable for such works.[24] But the problem of calculating the weight of mixed cargoes was speedily reported by the Stockingfield collector, and was resolved by equating a barrel to 5 cubic feet or ⅛ ton, as in the Customs service. By 24 Geo. III, cap. 57 the company was authorized to calculate tonnage on this basis, and was relieved of the obligation to apply equal rates throughout, provided due notice was given and maximum charges were not exceeded. Endless committee hours were spent in discussing rates for specific commodities, with few underlying principles of pricing or rate-moderation emerging. Yet in 1787, a further Act reduced rates for cargoes of lime, ironstone, and manure only at times of ample water supply over the locks. It was thus sought to secure marginal traffic and income without need for further reservoirs.

In the 1790s frequent requests for lower tolls were received to favour specific cargoes or persons, but were forwarded to the Governor. From 1794 to stimulate export of coals dug beside the Monkland Canal, such coals were charged at ½*d*. per ton-mile provided that water was ample. Two years later, resistance to a proposal by Pitt to tax canal traffic was successfully organized with the English canals. But in 1806, wartime inflation prompted a Bill authorizing full freedom in setting tolls up to 4*d*. per ton-mile.

As in the Customs service, receipts were analysed by commodity carried, and neatly tabulated for months and years. Indeed they formed the subject of a lithographic chart which presented these statistics up to 1814, in mode pioneered for economic data by William Playfair. Playfair's brother John was

---

[24] ii. 216.

Professor of Natural Philosophy at Edinburgh, and suggested that whatever can be expressed in numbers may also be represented by lines. William's drawing skills learnt for engineering with Meikle, Boulton, and Watt were applied to statistical presentation in his *Commercial and Political Atlas* (1786) and *A Statistical Breviary*. The method soon found imitation in France.[25] Evidence of earlier application than this to company statistics in Britain has still to be found.

But Customs procedures and dues had a detrimental effect on the growth of canal traffic, especially via the Firth of Forth to Leith; dues payable equalled the complete cost of land carriage from Edinburgh to Glasgow. Sea-to-sea passage was secured just before the French wars made the English Channel dangerous and greatly increased traffic. But Customs problems were typical of those prompting campaigns for *laisser-passer* and free trade which were finally successful only years after the Napoleonic wars were over.

NEW CONTROL SYSTEMS

We may now return to our study of the company's administration. The engineer MacKell had died in November 1779. His successor with the title of Surveyor was Nicol Baird, who had been a toll collector. In 1785 Robert Whitworth, who had worked with Brindley, became engineer with the task of completing the works from Stockingfield to Bowling on the Clyde estuary.

With Stephen's dismissal a new strong administrator was also required. The Glasgow Committee proposed that Patrick Colquhoun be appointed Inspector and Superintendent from April 1786. Ten years before, at the age of 31, he had returned prosperous from Virginia and became closely involved with the Glassford interests. In 1778 he helped raise money for a regiment to fight against the American rebels. As Provost of Glasgow he founded the first Chamber of Commerce in Britain (preceded by one in New York), and from 1782–3 chaired canal committee meetings. The *Dictionary of National Biography* records his later effective advocacy of poor relief, and of a London Metropolitan Police force, as well as his authorship of *The Wealth, Powers and Resources of the British Empire*, which C. R. Fay described as 'the statistical bible of the early English socialists'. These activities are said to have been based in London from 1789 till his death in 1820. Other less known activities include the arrangement of trading outlets on the Continent during the Napoleonic

---

[25] See Funkhouser and Walker 1935.

Wars. In 1806, he became London agent for the Senate of Hamburg, and established thereafter a Chamber of Commerce on Heligoland where Scots exporters had their agents.[26]

All this, however, lay in the future for Colquhoun, whose energies and abilities are documented in volume after volume of the Forth and Clyde Navigation's records. On his appointment no salary was mentioned, but in 1787 a sum of £300 was approved supplemented later by a gratuity of £100 plus £50 for his clerks. His chief task was to support Whitworth in the completion of the canal. We have already seen how he estimated and scheduled future expenditure balanced against funds as they became available. Probably when he took over the chief account for the company was a 'General Account Current' to which all expenditure was debited, but where also operating expenses and income were reflected leaving a balance at any time called 'Cost of Navigation to date'. The duke of Bridgewater's canal was similarly accounted for, deficit balances being inflated each year with interest at 5 per cent.[27] For the Exchequer's purposes Colquhoun preferred an alternative calculation which showed the proprietors' contributions together with interest thereon, as accepted in the Disannexing Act, plus the grant from Parliament, all increased by simple interest since 1784 at 5 per cent. The total of £371,000 was then increased by outstanding debts of £39,000, less sundry disposable properties and debtors to give 'a total and exact cost of the Canal in its finished state' of £394,545. This he preferred to the £294,473 18s. 3d. shown in the ledger 'General Account Current' which included no interest since 1784, and had been reduced by £104,000 of toll dues.[28]

Colquhoun's final account on demitting office may now be examined. It was accompanied by a meticulous report on the whole venture to date. The balance sheet is described as a 'General Aggregate of the Affairs of the Company'. Property is itemized on the left side starting with debts receivable. The seven realizable forms of 'property' are aggregated with forfeited and unappropriated shares to give a total at the bottom of 'Property which can be turned into cash'. Items 8–13 appear to be capable of producing rents or other income in several cases. The canal itself is shown in terms of net costs of old and new lines, with sums still outstanding on the latter, 'impressed' and not yet accounted for. We may note that the forfeited shares were valued including interest, while the unissued capital was shown at par. These two items appear identically in the Capital Section on the other side of the balance sheet, emphasizing the sense of a fixed stock, authorized and modifiable

[26] Crouzet 1958: 190.   [27] Ward 1974: 27.   [28] FCN1/37 Appx. 2.

only by statute. Of the debts due by the company, the largest is the bonds of £25,000.

This balance sheet shows a final account of the period, but interim reporting systems had been developed and formalized immediately on Colquhoun's taking over. From 1787 it was necessary to account to London only. On sheets all of the same size were transmitted Committee Minutes monthly, a General Report and Abstract of Tolls quarterly, a copy of the Ledger and Journal annually, copies of all stock transfers, and 'an authenticated General Abstract of the State of the company's Affairs as they stood at balancing'. Annual Reports were to reach London ten days before the Annual General Meeting on the first Wednesday of February.[29] The year's reports were then all bound together. That this system was arranged jointly between London and Glasgow is suggested by the fact that a copy of the Standing Orders of the House of Commons relating to Canal and Navigation Bills was sent north in 1786 to assist deliberation on a new constitution for the company, which would require parliamentary approval. The reporting procedures just described were adopted as company 'standing orders' by a General Meeting in August 1791. Thus terms in use in 'the Mother of Parliaments' were adopted naturally by the companies to which she gave birth.

Difficulty was encountered in meeting the tight deadlines for reporting. The 1788 accounts were delayed; and in March 1791, London enjoined obedience to Standing Orders. In 1794 a timeous submission was urged so that 'every proprietor in England may, when he requires it, have all the necessary information relative to the company's affairs'.

But Colquhoun's effectiveness is evident in every line of his reports. On resigning in March 1792 he proposed a mode of arranging and estimating the annual expenditure under heads of repairs to locks and bridges, banks, tow-paths, reservoirs and houses; for wages and salaries of artificers, lock- and bridge-keepers, and officers. After Repairs, the sixth head was for Adventitious Damages and Accidents; and a tenth head was for Contingent Expenses. While many expenditures could be forecast, and indeed, as we saw above, made matter of subcontracting, reserves would presumably be built up to cover these sixth and tenth classes. In his estimate of annual expense at £1,961 4s. 0d., however, Colquhoun modified his classification, and based his calculation on numbers of locks, bridges, miles, and persons employed.

An additional report was prepared to explain to the Governor how the debts of the company had increased during 1791. The books, Colquhoun wrote, were

[29] FCNI/27–25/iv/1789.

kept upon the Principles of Double Entry, and every transaction is detailed according to the most accurate and approved Rules of Accomptanship . . . but as this mode admits of being shaped into any Form that may be most familiar to the mind, and as the idea of a Factor or Steward's Account has been suggested as a kind of model I shall adopt this system . . .

He proceeded to consider himself responsible to the company of proprietors for all the debts, property, and effects at year-start, charging himself with revenue received and new debts contracted, and to show what became of this property, or 'in other words the exact Application, not departing at all from the statements in the Books'. His illustration showed a *Charge* for debts, from arrears, etc., plus properties, adding increases in debt during the year and the revenues. His *Discharge* showed closing debts to the company and properties, an increase in sums imprest out for new works, expenses, interest, and salaries, balancing to a ½d. He added a two-sided illustration showing only increments or changes during the year. Such a report from one trained in trader's double entry to a Governor accustomed to stewardship accounts, must represent an antecedent of our present day Sources and Applications Statements.[30] Accounts of 'Charge and Discharge—both on Account and in Cash' continued till 1856 to be transmitted from Glasgow and tabled at meetings of the Forth and Clyde Navigation.

The London Minutes of 1792 evidence doubts about Scots accounting: Mr Black, a local accountant, was to be employed to inspect the Journal and Ledger 'for any mode more eligible for keeping the same and to have proper allowance for his trouble'. His account for £46 15s. 0d. was submitted in 1794, but consideration of his report was postponed, apparently indefinitely.

Audits, as we have seen, were usually a matter for Committee members. In 1796 the Glasgow Provost compared Journal and balanced Ledger with every statement in the State Book, before copies were sent south. In 1821 when Mr Wallace of the Committee was unable to examine the books and accounts on his own, Robert Grahame and Professor Millar were appointed a Committee of proprietors to assist. But at all times, and especially at General Meetings, the Books or copies of them were available for inspection by proprietors.

---

[30] As suggested by Yamey 1962: 43. Origins of this statement may thus be traced 65 years before those suggested by Park (1966) or by Rosen and DeCoster (1969).

SHARE TRANSFERS

A few facts may be added to what is known of stock markets at this period.[31] One of the essentials of a joint-stock and continuing company was an ability for membership to change: indeed this was secured by the Forth and Clyde's incorporating Act, which laid down a form of share-transfer certificate. We have already noted that the company preferred to copy the Transfer Books of the Royal Bank to 'the Plan of the great companies in England'. Transfer responsibilities were moved to Glasgow, at least by 1787. In June 1792, it was instructed that transfers were to be booked only on original instructions, an extract of sale, by heredity or probate of will. A memorial on the subject was prepared by an advocate, Archibald Campbell, in 1800. One year later, transfer fees paid to the Superintendent were fixed at 1 guinea for five shares, and 2 guineas for more than ten, payable by buyer or seller and excluding stamp duty and postage. Two guineas including stamp duty was reported as the fee in all general companies in England. By 1779, 192 transfers were recorded; and by 1848, a total of 1715.[32]

The prices at which transfers took place are not evident in the early years. In 1794, the Secretary in London enquired of Glasgow as to what the Superintendent considered a justified price. From this time, the latter charged himself with the price received from the buyer, and in his discharge showed his payment to the seller. Thus the market appeared to be made by and through the company. Once dividends were declared, prices were more readily calculable. Sometime before 1831 transfers were normally completed through brokers. From that year dates the first list of stock prices printed by James Watson, a Glasgow accountant and stock-broker, who quoted the price of the company's shares of £400 16s. 0d. nominal with dividend of £28 at £560–2.

DIVIDENDS

The opening of the canal from sea to sea was followed by war with France, which made the English Channel dangerous and the use of the canal more attractive. Toll revenues increased, and exceeded £20,000 from 1796. At first the income was absorbed by new works and improvements as by the repay-

---

[31] Michie 1978, *passim*.   [32] Copy transfers are found in Vols. FCNI/48–90.

ment of debt. But in 1800, the long-patient stockholders received a first dividend of £10 per share. Such payments continued till 1814, with the company paying the new Income Tax equal to 11*s*. 4*d*. per share. In 1814 the dividend was raised to £15, and next year to £17 10*s*. 0*d*. In 1817, it was raised again; and officers, surveyors, and master carpenters, who had been refused an increase in wages, were assured they would benefit with shareholders later. Five years later, proportionate changes in dividends and wages and salaries were considered 'in order to identify as much as possible the two interests'.

GLASGOW TAKE-OVER

Glasgow's trade and manufactures had on the whole flourished during the Napoleonic Wars. This is documented in the ledger of James Finlay and Co. for 1800 (stored at Glasgow University). Therein are accounts for agents in St Petersburg, Berlin and other German cities, Alsace, and Italy. (Friedrich Engels' father was their agent in the Rhineland.) In all, Kirkman Finlay claimed, they had 700 correspondents on the Continent prior to 1803.

In the history of James Finlay and Co. published in 1951, only very brief reference is made to Kirkman's chairmanship of the Forth and Clyde Navigation from 1816 till his death in 1842. He most ably represented brash, new Glasgow energies which had over the years come into increasing conflict with Lord Dundas whose estates lay at Grangemouth, who had family ties with the Speirs and contacts in the House of Lords. The conflict was fought out over long-standing personal resentments, partially in legal forms, and climaxed in an important accounting innovation.

Dundas adopted a proprietorial attitude, and had forgotten about his long-standing debt of £3,000 to the company. The expense of the first ever steamboat experiment was also held against him. Also recalled was confusion about the purchase of gravel beds at Bantaskine to provide ballast for ships without cargo. In 1803, he informed the Royal Bank that the land had been acquired by the company.[33] But in that year of 'uncommon pecuniary distress', neither the company nor Dundas nor Speirs had available the necessary funds. A Glasgow Committee member had then stepped in and bought the land in his own name—to the profit, he claimed, not only of himself but also of the company since ships had access to ballast at cheap prices. Personal enterprise thus complemented corporate efforts, but did not receive credit for so doing!

---

[33] *Three Banks Review*, Dec. 1964.

More serious were the doubts raised from London about the competence
of Scots law-courts to intervene in the affairs of a company whose meetings
could only be held in Westminster, since 1787. This the Scots held was a
matter of internal regulation, since the property, profits, and cash of the company were in Scotland: there share-transfers were registered; and there creditors of individual shareholders could 'arrest' their shares. In 1786, 1,213
shares of the company were held by natives of Scotland, and only 130 by
English people.[34] Now, in 1815, out of 127 shareholders only 40 owning
365 shares had fixed residences in the south. The lawyers had to consider
whether the real estate of the company could be considered real estate 'in the
person of a partner'. If shares were personal property, then personal rights
had no *situs* or fixed location. Such matters had not been resolved in the decision *Syme* v. *Balfour* of 1804, and formed part of the controversy in 1815.[35]

The immediate cause of the open rift was financial. Glasgow shareholders
led by James Hill and Robert Grahame of Whitehill objected to the application of surplus revenues not to dividends but to the extension of the docks
and other works at Grangemouth, which they suggested would chiefly benefit
Dundas as landowner. The Governor replied in print that projections of revenue under four new 'heads' might total £8,849 10s. 0d. per annum and thus
equal a return of 6 per cent on the project's cost, the investment appraisal
being undertaken by Rennie the engineer. But no such justification had been
given to the 'packed' meeting which Dundas had got to approve the application to Parliament for the private Bill necessary: the objectors replied that a
less warrantable estimate had never been palmed off upon any company! The
Londoners had meanwhile attempted to transfer the surplus of £23,000 from
a Scots to an English bank, only to have an interdict successfully raised in
Scotland. No mention was made in the controversy of the drop in canal revenues nor to the need for more employment which would result from the end
of the Napoleonic Wars.

Thus at the same time as the House of Commons was rebelling against an
extension of wartime income tax, the shareholders in the Forth and Clyde
were revolting against restrictions on their dividends in order to finance new
works—which if necessary at all they felt should be financed from new borrowings. The war of pamphlets brought alternatives into focus. Did the Scots
believe, asked the Governor, that the extraordinary (or capital) expenditures
of £76,000 in the previous twenty-two years should not have been taken
from revenues? Where full profits were distributed without abiding by a fixed

---

[34] Lindsay 1968: 29/30.
[35] The pamphlets printed during the controversy are stored in the Mitchell Library, Glasgow.

annual dividend and without reserving against eventualities, 'the stock would bear no fixed or determined value in the market': speculators might examine minutely the company's books and see the precise state of its affairs; but no person unacquainted with business would think of buying its shares: 'The immediate injury to the stock and to the credit of the company by any diminution of dividend is much greater than any advantage arising from any temporary increase.' Referring to an Irish Canal scandal, the Governor suggested that only stock jobbers would want a temporary increase in dividends and share prices, before selling out and leaving the company to shift for itself. He observed:

As English capitalists could not derive any consequential benefit from the canal except by making it productive as a navigation, they might be supposed to be altogether unbiassed as to their views of management.

He quoted the opinion of legal Counsel in Edinburgh:

Every corporation has a discretionary power to fix upon a sum as neat profits, leaving surpluses . . . as undivided profits which may be applied by the company to any expense whatever that occurs in the management of its affairs, subject to the claims of creditors till distributed.

Finlay and his supporters first submitted calculations that an increased dividend was reasonable: dividends should be related not to the nominal value of capital, nor to the value of £325 per share enacted in 1799, nor to the value of £420 calculated by the Governor by adding the shortfall of dividends not equal to legal interest rates. Instead they applied compound interest to capital contributed since 1768, and deducted dividends when paid, and thus calculated a value per share of £643, using what would now be called 'opportunity costs'. The Governor, they said, would adopt simple rather than compound interest when it suited his purpose. Current dividends were still not equal to 4 per cent of share values as calculated in Glasgow.

At one stage Hill and Grahame suggested that each proprietor should lend the company for its new works his share of the surplus revenue, and receive therefor a transferable document. But the chief Glasgow case was that all shareholders should be kept informed and allowed to decide. In 1804, an abstract of accounts had been printed; but the motion at the meeting held in April 1814 that a printed abstract should be furnished to each proprietor at the same time as his dividend was paid, had been negatived. 'To make such information public and general', one of the pamphlets suggested, 'would tend more than any other thing to prevent jobbing in shares of stock, either in buying or selling.'

The Governor wrote in justification:

It is a thing which is never done in any copartnery. It never was heard of that a chartered bank or any company . . . printed and published to the world annual states. . . . It is sufficient for every proprietor that he has access at London and Glasgow to examine the books at all times—as they have twice a year to call for their dividends, they can easily make this examination.

The cost of posting statements to proprietors was avoidable. Any proprietor who was in Parliament could and did take advantage of free mail services for all purposes. It was suggested that James Finlay and Co. saved about £1,000 each year in postage while Kirkman was an MP.[36]

The outcome may be briefly recorded. At a General Meeting held in the British Coffee House in the Liberty of Westminster on 20 March 1816, there was a large turnout of nobility, six redoubtable Glasgow spinsters, and Glasgow merchants including Robert Owen as executor of David Dale.

Tabled at the meeting was a weight of books and documents: the Journal and Ledger; an Abstract of Accounts with the Royal and the Bank of Scotland; accounts of tolls and commodities for the year and previous decade; accounts of charge and discharge for the company as a whole, for toll collectors and two others. There were also abstract or summary Receipt and Expenditure accounts for passage-boats, a General Account Current, and a Balance Account. Such were the forms of corporate reporting to this company in session—supplemented by copies of the Interdict case, and Counsel's opinion on the attempted transfer of funds south of the Border.

The battle was quickly over. Dundas and his relatives and supporters were voted out of office and Finlay was elected Governor. The capital expenditure at Grangemouth was rescinded as was the transfer of funds from Scotland to England. Indispensable works were to be financed from borrowing.

A dividend of £25 per share thus became possible and was approved. (Share prices rose promptly to £500.)[37] It was also ordered unanimously that the Governor and Council prepare and print States of the Company's affairs, as at present, and furnish each proprietor with a copy, and in the future prepare states of affairs and of their Revenues and Expenditure by 10 March yearly. Longer notice was to be given of any bills proposed for parliament.[38]

Thus more participation at meetings was sought by proprietors—as also by providing a Memorandum Book for their suggestions at the Glasgow

---

[36] Cf. Binney 1968: 46–7 and the *History of Jas Finlay* (1951), 28.

[37] Michie 1978: 161.

[38] The accounts are reproduced in full in *Issues in Accountability*, 3.

office from 1824. And from 1831, they also were to receive a printed Chairman's statement. Whether attendance and participation, or the opposite, were thereby promoted is open to discussion. But the Forth and Clyde initiative is clear, and was not promptly imitated.

The next stage in publishing company accounts may have come in 1837 when the London Joint Stock Bank found its results good enough to be used as an advertisement. Other joint stock banks followed suit, chiefly in the London area; although Sir Robert Peel in 1844 replied to suggestions:

I do not wish to pry into the affairs of each bank. . . . It has frequently been proposed to require from each bank a periodic publication of its liabilities, its assets and the state of its transactions generally. But I have seen no form of account which would be satisfactory.[39]

In 1847, Peninsular and Orient Company shareholders were informed that:

it was not considered for their interest that such a course should be pursued . . . Proprietors at a distance forming their opinion of the future position of the company from published accounts of past transactions could scarcely avoid arriving at erroneous conclusions.[40]

The 1855/6 Companies Acts in an optional schedule made it easy for a company to adopt Articles of Association requiring printing and circulation of accounts, a week before the meeting. Thus far in advance was the Forth and Clyde in 1816.

CONCLUSION

History is composed of both fact-finding and generalization or theory-building. Here we have been chiefly engaged in the former, providing footnotes for a survey of company accounting which cannot start in 1856, since so much had by then been decided, and which need not spend too long on the earlier incorporations and monopolies of a pre-industrial age. Our footnotes relate to a company not of adventurers, but of proprietors of a thin strip of land through the narrow waist of Scotland on which was dug a waterway with a capacity for ships large for that time. In that company were landowners, bankers, and merchants, led by the provosts of Glasgow and Edinburgh and by noblemen in London. It was necessary that they contribute more than

---

[39] W. F. C. Crick and J. E. Wadsworth, *A Hundred Years of Joint Stock Banking* (London, 1936), 20, 30, 284.

[40] Quoted Naylor 1960: 12.

capital, since rights had to be obtained or modified by legislation, engineers had to be appointed, and supervision exercised over the progress of work and the details of expenditures unprecedented in the north.[41] Audit was an early and continuing responsibility.

Since shareholders included some proprietors of the ground through which the canal was to pass, a system of shareholders' accounts had to be created to which sundry debits and credits could be posted. The initial impression is of shareholder democracy working through regular meetings and agreement rather than through voting and a delegation of responsibilities to directors. Throughout, books of accounts and other records were open to inspection as a result of the repeated copyings necessary where there were three centres. Only gradually formal reporting procedures from Glasgow to London were established derived from a new set of accounts.

In these accounts, as is appropriate to a transport undertaking, 'cash' transactions were the prime entries, with regular payments into the bank of revenues, month by month and year by year, while expenses were also paid from the bank account instead of by officers from imprests. The bank which had helped in the early years and provided a Comptroller and Auditor for the Company was unable to provide the large sums necessary to complete the cut to Glasgow and later towards the sea. In the mid-1770s bonds had to be issued, yet we find the Bank holding these. In the 1780s state participation was accepted in return for investment of monies realized by Highland land sales. The Scots Exchequer required a very precise accountability. Once the canal was complete and profitable the private shareholders hastened to repay the state investment before declaring a dividend.

In such negotiations some may see precedent for a co-operation of public and private interests two centuries later, although others will sense the death-throes of mercantilism. But in the controversy which climaxed in 1816, more is to be found than Scots resistance to manipulations from London. (This Glasgow had earlier condoned when it was Edinburgh interests which were threatened.) A system of proxies had been built up at the start to enable those sufficiently interested to be represented in both centres. Proxies could not act effectively however, unless their principals were informed. Glasgow accordingly pressed for fair notice of proposed Parliamentary bills, and for precirculation of abstracts of accounts. The focus of attention of accounting historians has thus moved from the Great Book or Ledger where Roger North sought 'a perpetual and limpid state of all accounts',[42] to the Balances

---

[41] Military road-works in Scotland cost only £300,000 from 1730–1800. See Haldane 1962: 11.

[42] Yamey, Edey, and Thomson 1963: 36.

and printed abstracts derived from it since 1816. A one-way stream of information is now accepted, very different perhaps from the improvements intended by the innovators of 1816.

References

Binney, J. D. (1968), *British Public Finance, 1774–92* (Cambridge: Cambridge University Press).

Buckle, J. T. (1867), *The History of Civilisation in England* (London: Longmans).

Checkland, S. G. (1975), *Scottish Banking* (London: Collins).

Crouzet, F. (1958), *L'Économie britannique et le blocus continental, 1806–1813* (Paris: Presses Universitaires).

Finlay, James & Co. (1951), *A History of the Firm, 1750–1950* (Glasgow).

Forrester, D. A. R. (1978), 'Whether Malcolm's is Best or Old Charge & Discharge', *Accounting Historians Journal*, 5/2 (Autumn).

Funkhauser, H. S., and Walker, H. M. (1935), 'Playfair and his Charts', *Economic History* (Feb.)

Haldane, A. R. B. (1962), *New Ways through the Glens* (London: Nelson).

Issues in Accountability 3 (1978), *The Great Canal which linked Edinburgh, Glasgow & London* (Strathclyde Convergencies).

Lindsay, Jean (1968), *The Canals of Scotland* (Newton Abbot: David & Charles).

Marwick, J. (1876–1917), *The Records of the Burgh of Glasgow* (Glasgow: Scottish Burgh Records Society).

Michie, R. C. (1978), 'The Transfer of Shares in Scotland 1700–1820', *Business History* (July).

Naylor, G. (1960), *Company Law for Shareholders* (London: Institute of Economic Affairs).

Park, C. (1966), 'Funds Flow Statements', in M. Backer (ed.), *Modern Accounting Theory* (Englewood Cliffs, NJ: Prentice-Hall).

Pratt, E. A. (1922), *Scottish Canals and Waterways* (Selwyn & Blount).

Rosen, L. S., and De Coster, D. T. (1969), 'The Funds Statement, a Historical Perspective', *Accounting Review* (Jan.)

Roseveare, H. (1973), *The Treasury, 1660–1870* (London: Allen & Unwin).

Smith, A. M. (1974), 'The Forfeited Estates, 1752–84', in Barrow (ed.), *The Scottish Tradition* (Edinburgh: Scottish Academic Press).

Three Banks Review (1969), 'The End of an Enterprise—The Forth & Clyde Canal' (Dec.)

Ward, J. R. (1974), *The Finance of Canal Building in 18th Century England* (Cambridge: Cambridge University Press).

Williams, O. C. (1948), *The Historical Development of Private Bill Procedures and Standing Orders in the House of Commons* (London: HMSO).

Yamey, B. (1962), 'Accounting in England, 1500–1900', in W. T. Baxter and S. Davidson (eds.), *Studies in Accounting Theory* (London: Sweet & Maxwell).

Yamey, B., Edey, H. C., and Thomson, H. W. (1963), *Accounting in England and Scotland, 1543–1900* (London: Sweet & Maxwell).

POSTSCRIPT

Some time ago,[1] Peter Bird requested information on the 'total blank' in the recorded history of the accountability of joint-stock companies for almost three hundred years to 1844. Important information on that history was therefore sought in the origins of printed accounting information. Wider company and capital market developments could thus be investigated, focusing on communications in particular with distant shareholders. The first and subsequent reliance on print deserves study now, because of increasing use of alternative communication technologies in markets and firms today.

One contested proposal to print annual statements was researched for 'The Great Canal that linked Edinburgh, Glasgow and London', *Issues in Accountability*, 3 (1978/80). The excerpts now reproduced were published in *Accounting and Business Research*, Special Accounting History Issue (1980). Further and collaborative investigations were focused on the 4th International Congress of Accounting Historians, Pisa, August 1984. My wide-ranging review[2] noted that eighteenth-century charities published appeals and reports; and State Accounts and statistics were commonly printed, while shareholders might be fined for non-attendance at company meetings! There listed were the dates of company legislation in different countries, often with the requirement that a copy of the Accounts had to be accessible at Registries or published in Gazettes rather than circulated by post.

Multinational collaboration was received for an Exhibition at Pisa; and the research continues. States or Balances of Accounts were required in the English East India Company from 1621; but the printed State of 1782 seems to have been exceptional.[3] Presentations of course can change. An early chart has been reproduced: but US companies have used pictures in reporting typically from 1947 only.[4]

---

[1] See *Accounting History*, 1/1 (Feb. 1976), 8.

[2] 'The Medium not the Message . . .', *Congress Proceedings* (1984), 217–29.

[3] V. Baladouni, *Accounting Historians Journal* (Spring 1986 and June 1990).

[4] Flesher and Jordan, *Accounting Historians; Notebook* (Spring 1990), 41. Recently maintained is that 'accounting numbers merely add the gloss': C. Cooper, Pheby, Pheby and Puxty to BAA and EAA Congresses, Spring 1992.

it might have been enough, in order to be derived from the UNION CANAL, merely to mention, that its object to be derived from the UNION CANAL, merely to mention, that its object up the fine countries of Linlithgowshire, abundant in Lime, and Stirlingshire, abounding in Coal, and to connect the populous and flourishing Cities of Edinburgh and Glasgow, and their respective sea-port towns, by a cheap and safe conveyance for their inhabitants, for the Produce of the country, and the respective Manufactures and Commerce of these cities and towns. It is certainly from these sources, and these alone, that a great Revenue must naturally flow, whatever may be the opinions of persons, as to the particulars, and extent of each article of Revenue.

I beg leave to present with this, a Chart of the Revenue of the Forth and Clyde Canal, which shews the rapid increase it is making.

I am,

GENTLEMEN,

greatest respect,

obedient humble Servant,

H. BAIRD.

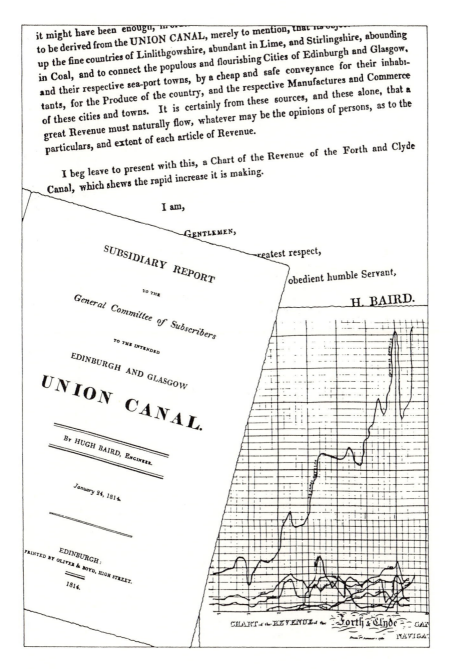

SUBSIDIARY REPORT

TO THE

General Committee of Subscribers

TO THE INTENDED

EDINBURGH AND GLASGOW

UNION CANAL.

By HUGH BAIRD, ENGINEER.

January 24, 1814.

EDINBURGH:
PRINTED BY OLIVER & BOYD, HIGH STREET.

1814.

CHART of the REVENUE of the Forth & Clyde CANAL NAVIGATION

Fig. II.I

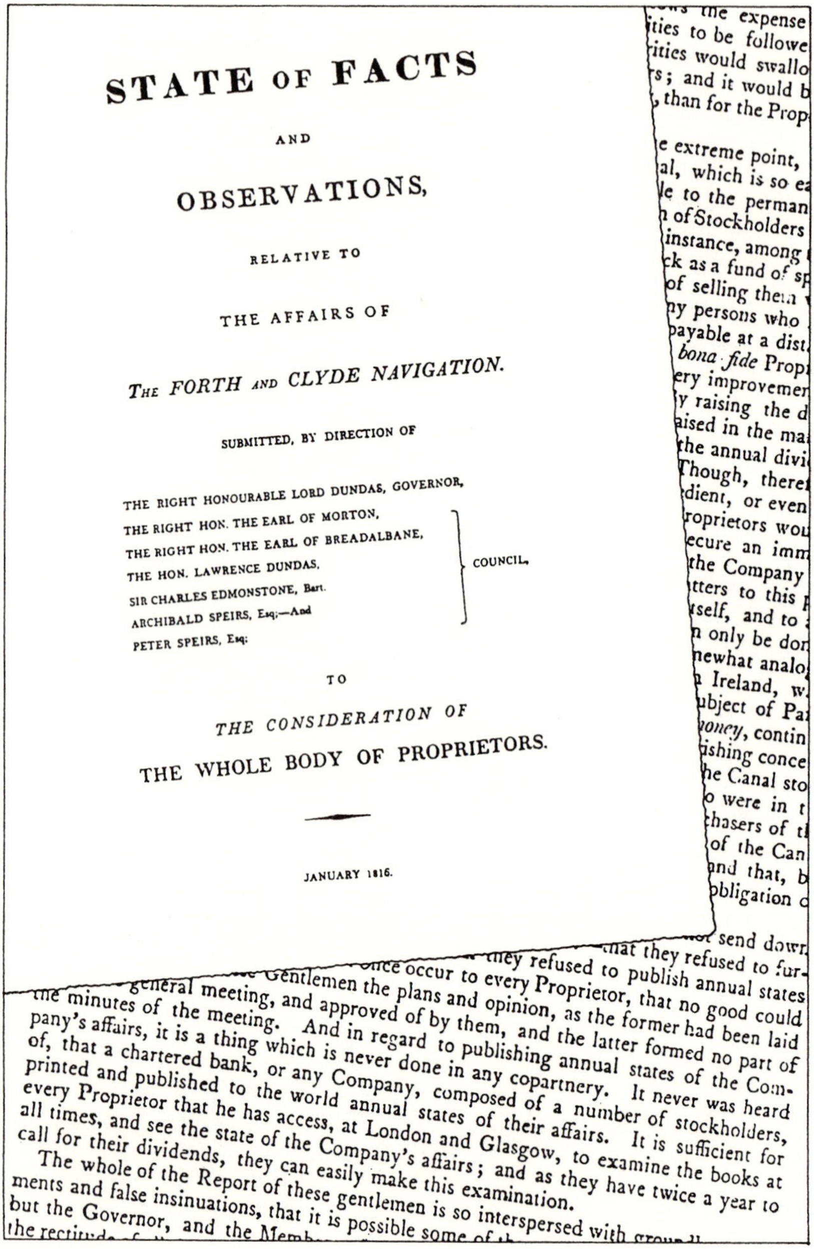

STATE of FACTS

AND

OBSERVATIONS,

RELATIVE TO

THE AFFAIRS OF

The FORTH and CLYDE NAVIGATION.

SUBMITTED, BY DIRECTION OF

THE RIGHT HONOURABLE LORD DUNDAS, GOVERNOR,
THE RIGHT HON. THE EARL OF MORTON,
THE RIGHT HON. THE EARL OF BREADALBANE,
THE HON. LAWRENCE DUNDAS,   } COUNCIL.
SIR CHARLES EDMONSTONE, Bart.
ARCHIBALD SPEIRS, Esq;—And
PETER SPEIRS, Esq:

TO

THE CONSIDERATION OF
THE WHOLE BODY OF PROPRIETORS.

JANUARY 1816.

the expense
ities to be followe
ities would swallo
s; and it would b
than for the Prop

e extreme point,
al, which is so ea
e to the perman
n of Stockholders
instance, among
k as a fund of sp
of selling them
ny persons who
payable at a dist.
bona fide Prop
ery improvemer
y raising the d
aised in the ma
the annual divi
Though, there
dient, or even
roprietors wou
ecure an imm
the Company
tters to this
self, and to
n only be dor
newhat analo
n Ireland, w
abject of Pa
money, contin
ishing conce
he Canal sto
o were in t
chasers of t
of the Can
and that, b
obligation c

send dowr
that they refused to fur
once occur to every Proprietor, that no good could
general meeting, and approved of by them, and the latter formed no part of
the minutes of the meeting. And in regard to publishing annual states of the Company's affairs, it is a thing which is never done in any copartnery. It never was heard
of, that a chartered bank, or any Company, composed of a number of stockholders,
printed and published to the world annual states of their affairs. It is sufficient for
every Proprietor that he has access, at London and Glasgow, to examine the books at
all times, and see the state of the Company's affairs; and as they have twice a year to
call for their dividends, they can easily make this examination.
The whole of the Report of these gentlemen is so interspersed with grou
ments and false insinuations, that it is possible some of
but the Governor, and the Memb
the rectitude

Fig. II.2

12 · THE DEVELOPMENT OF BRITISH RAILWAY ACCOUNTING: 1800–1911

J. J. Glynn

INTRODUCTION[1]

While the intention of this essay is to concentrate on accounting aspects arising from the development of the railways, it is also necessary to have an appreciation of the economic and political climate of the time. Railways in the nineteenth century had a major influence in reshaping some of the legislative procedures in Parliament, the development of the capital market, and the economy at large. The first government regulations for the control of railways as a whole came in 1840, when the Board of Trade Railway Department was set up. This was the forerunner of the present Ministry of Transport, which was established in 1919. Some twenty-eight years later, in 1868, the Regulation of Railways Act made it obligatory for all railways to render accounts half-yearly according to the forms prescribed in the first schedule of that Act. Many historians regarded the early and middle decades of the nineteenth century as being the heyday of *laissez-faire* for companies. Why then were steps taken to regulate the railways?

From 1800, many railways were built by private agreement with landowners, often as feeders to canals. Occasionally, canal owners would allow the public to pay a toll and use these lines. The first public railway, in its own right, was the Surrey Iron Railway; authorized by Act of Parliament in 1801, and opened in 1803. The first engine was developed in 1804 by Richard Trevithick and ran on the Pennydarren tramroad near Merthyr Tydfil. This

This is an abbreviated version of a paper presented by the author at the Association of University Teachers of Accounting Conference, Dundee, April 1981, first published in *Accounting Historians Journal*, 11/1 (Spring 1984). I am very grateful for the comments received on earlier drafts of this paper; especially those from Professors J. Kitchen and R. H. Parker.

[1] For a general history of British Railways see Francis (1968), Ellis (1960), and Perkins (1970).

was a time of rapid technological advance in the design of engines, rolling stock, and track. The Stockton and Darlington Railway, opened in 1825, became the first commercial steam driven railway, but with steam for mineral merchandise traffic only. Railways, at this stage, aroused little public interest outside their immediate locality. The *Yorkshire Gazette* thought the opening of the Stockton and Darlington Railway was only worth eight lines. Also at this time financial backing was localized, coming mainly from the new, sturdy liberal class of the industrial cities of the North and Midlands.

The end of this second decade saw the first large-scale awareness of the public of the age of the railway. On 15 September 1830 thousands gathered in Oldfield Lane, Manchester, to see the Duke of Wellington and to witness the opening of the first steam passenger service operated by the Liverpool and Manchester Railway. This company issued a first prospectus on 29 October 1824. Only after a stormy debate did the Liverpool and Manchester Act become law in 1826. Three subsequent Acts also became law, allowing for the raising of a loan, as funds were running short, and for certain route deviations and extensions. The cost of these four Acts was estimated at £27,000. By the end of 1830, the line had carried 70,000 passengers. In the first eighteen months of operation, nearly ten times that number were carried. Net receipts from all traffic, by 1835, were about £80,000 per year; £20,000 more than estimated. Total costs of building and equipping the line had, however, exceeded the estimate of £800,000; the actual expenditure coming to about £1,200,000. The half-yearly dividend rose from £4. 10s. per cent for the first half of 1831 to £5 for the first half of 1845 and the price of shares soon rose to £200, after they had been issued at £100.

PROMOTION OF A RAILWAY COMPANY AND THE BEGINNINGS OF REGULATION

Each railway was formed by its own separate Act of Parliament so that from the start a joint-stock company was created with limited liability. This was necessary due to the very size of each project. The average canal in 1825 had a capital of £165,000, and employed a few score of lock-keepers and maintenance men. The average cost of constructing twenty-seven railways opened between 1830 and 1853 was nearly £2 million, and the average labour force in 1851, excluding construction workers, was upwards of 2,500 (Pollins 1952: 407).

Private Acts for the creation of railway companies were often criticized on several counts.[2] Then, as now, the most important stage was the committee stage. Nowadays the committee is a judicial body noted for its impartiality. Then, the committee on a private Bill was composed of all locally interested members, and the knowledge of local circumstances was the hallmark of a committee man. Committees were large, attendance was not compulsory, and often members only attended to vote without having heard the evidence. Members were often canvassed by interested parties and were, in many instances, interested parties on their own account (either as proponent or opponent of a particular Bill). On one occasion, a Member's vote was disallowed on the grounds that he was a subscriber to the company whose Bill was under discussion. The Speaker took the line that it was wrong to victimize one, when so many offended in the same manner. Another pointed out that Members' names were often excluded from the published list of subscribers, as his own had been (Parris 1965: 20).

It was not until 1844 that radical changes to this system were made, brought about by the activities of railway promoters but effective on all future Bills whatever their concern. As O. C. Williams has stated:

it was the expansion of the railways that for the first time brought more clearly than ever before the consciousness of Parliament that in private legislation there was an aspect of public, as well as one of private interest, to which no government could be indifferent; and that the function of Parliament was, not merely to act justly as between parties, but also to consider and promote the interests of the public as a whole. (Williams 1948: 67)

The main features of the new procedure, introduced experimentally in 1844 and made permanent in the following year, were:

1. large, locally interested committees were replaced by small, less partial bodies;
2. Bills were grouped so that comparable schemes were referred to the same committee;
3. attendance was made compulsory.

All through the 1830s there had been lively debates in both Houses of Parliament concerning the control of railways. As early as 1836 James Morrison introduced a motion for railway legislation (Hansard, xxxiii. 977). He was concerned with the monopoly situation of railways which he believed had led to excessive charging as a result of collusion between rival companies.

The reason that years of indecision occurred concerning railway regulation

---

[2] For a fuller account of the passage of these Acts see Parris (1965).

was the conflict between the capitalistic economic philosophy of the time and the fact that governments of the day were concerned that the vast amounts of capital that were invested (by the public) should be wisely invested. Many companies were large with paid-up capital of as much as £30–40 million. Such contradictions can often be discerned from the reading of parliamentary debates, editorials, and letters of the time. Poulet Thomas, a minister at the Board of Trade, summarized this view when he said at one point, 'It is by the Government not meddling with capital that this country has been able to obtain a superiority over every other country' (Hansard, xxxvi. 1161–2). Yet he had previously told the house that 'he was not unfriendly to the great works to which these Bills related, but at the same time, he felt bound from the situation which he held in government, to take care that the capital of the country was not improvidently or unwisely applied' (Hansard, xxxi. 684–5).

In 1840 Lord Seymour's Railway Regulation Act was passed, and from thence forward all new railways had to be inspected and approved by the 'Lords of the Committee of Her Majesty's Privy Council appointed for Trade and Plantations', or, as it later became known, the Board of Trade. This Act, though much resented at the time by the railway companies, gave the government limited powers of investigation into the safe operating of various lines. Further important Acts came into being in 1844 and 1845 but these again concentrated mainly upon the regulation of railways with respect to maintenance and operation.

RAILWAYS: THEIR EFFECT ON THE CAPITAL MARKET

One historian has said, 'the buying and selling of shares, unimportant before the coming of the railways, was an essential part of the Victorian commercial structure' (Porter 1912: 552). Railways were instrumental in enlarging the investment market by attracting large numbers of hitherto untapped investors. Such expansion was not always to the good. Some of the more unfortunate side-effects were:

1. speculation in shares which, at times, amounted to 'feverish gambling, on a scale big enough to entail a financial panic and a national slump';
2. a widening gap between the ownership of companies and their management;
3. following from (2), the opportunity for directors to mismanage shareholders' funds.

'Being first in the field, the railway companies were open to all the tempta-
tions of unregulated competition in avarice and speculation: but they were
also the whipping boys of public indignation and the guinea-pigs for the first
experiments in parliamentary control and the development of modern company law' (Perkin 1970: 179–80).

There were three railway investment booms: 1824–5, 1836–7, and (by far
the largest) 1845–7 (Perkin 1970: 180). In 1824–5 schemes amounting to a
total expenditure of nearly £22 million were put forward but, while these
could be termed 'main lines', few were proceeded with. In 1836 thirty-five
railway Acts were passed, twenty-nine of them for new lines covering 994
miles at an estimated cost of approximately £17.6 million. The third boom
period is often referred to as the 'railway mania' of 1845–7. In November
1845, when the whole capital investment in existing railways amounted to
£71 million, *The Times* estimated that the cost of 620 new railway schemes
(not including 643 other companies which had not yet registered their
prospectuses) came to £563 million, equivalent to over two-thirds of the
National Debt.

This 'mania' was brought to a close in 1846, when the Bank of England
raised the bank rate in an effort to stop the drain on gold and credit. As a
result of this intervention the price of shares tumbled and thousands of shareholders found themselves holding paper script worth less than they had paid
or promised for it, often with money they did not have. Gullible investors
had been at the mercy of unscrupulous company promoters. Many instances
occurred of fraud on a grand scale. Leopold Redpath, registrar of the Great
Northern Railway, was transported for life in 1857. A more notorious character was George Hudson,[3] a former draper from the city of York, who
became known as the 'railway king' of the 1840s. Having succeeded to the
chairmanship of several railway companies he was eventually unmasked as
one who had 'doctored the books' to improve balance sheets, had paid dividends out of capital, had bought and sold Great North of England shares on
behalf of other companies in which he had interests and pocketed the difference, and had made contracts in his private capacity with these companies to
his own personal profit. His alleged frauds added up to a total of £598,785.
In 1855 he was forced to move abroad to avoid lawsuits from his old companies.

Up until 1830 the London Capital Market was mainly involved with the
dealing of government stocks. In that year only four railway companies, out

---

[3] A full account of Hudson's life is given by Lambert (1968).

of a total of 205 companies, had stock exchange quotations. By 1844, the number had increased to sixty-six railways out of the 705 companies quoted. These companies had the largest single block of paid-up capital, £47 million, compared with the £26 million of the joint-stock banks. By the end of the railway 'mania' in 1847 the railways' capital had risen to over £200 million (Reed 1969: 162–83). Also at about this time stock exchanges began to operate in the provinces; notably in Manchester, Liverpool, Birmingham, Leeds, Glasgow, and Edinburgh. An early Liverpool share price list, dated 9 August 1836, named seventy-one companies whose shares were dealt in; thirty-eight were railways, and banks, the next largest class, provided fifteen companies. The remaining eighteen were miscellaneous insurance, ferry, and utility companies. Significantly, no canals were named, suggesting that business was mainly confined to 'new' companies (*The Liverpool Stock Exchange Centenary Books* 1900: 22). The development of these provincial centres re-emphasizes the point mentioned earlier that much of the speculative capital did in fact come from areas outside London.

THE NEED FOR ACCOUNTING LEGISLATION[4]

Prior to 1868 no precise form of accounts was prescribed for railway companies, although certain requirements with reference to accounts were placed on such companies as came within the scope of the Railway Regulation Act, 1844, and the Railway Clauses Consolidation Act, 1845.

The keeping of accounts was, however, obligatory on all railway companies (in common with other companies carrying on undertakings of a public nature) under the provisions of the Companies Clauses Consolidation Act, 1845. Section 115 provided that:

The directors shall cause full and true accounts to be kept of all sums of money received or expended on account of the company by the directors and all persons employed by or under them, and of all matters and things for which such sums of money shall have been received or disbursed and paid.

While 'full and true accounts' were required, the form in which such information had to be prepared was left very much to the discretion of individual companies. This led to a diversity of practices which not only rendered such accounts incapable of comparison but in many instances led to charges of deliberate deception.

[4] All relevant Acts can be found in Edwards (1980).

Many nineteenth-century writers argued that railway accounts were not merely badly drawn up, incomplete, and incomprehensible but that directors, either individually or in collusion, deliberately sought to distort presentation to investors and other interested parties. Writing in 1867, Joseph Lee Thomas said:

My own impression is that an impartial and complete investigation of Railway Accounts, would show that dividends have been paid which could not have been, had all the items strictly chargeable against revenue been so debited; the average working expenses of Railways would not, I fear, . . . [be] found to be much less than sixty per cent of the receipts. (Thomas 1867: 14)

Up to this time, accounting provisions had been contained within the individual private Acts which formed each company. Such provisions were extremely varied. The Act incorporating the Stockton and Darlington Railway in 1821 consisted of 104 sections. One section only (s. 56) vaguely required the company to keep 'proper Books of Account'. The company was also empowered to pay dividends (s. 38). Fourteen years later, in 1835, the Great Western Railway was established. Its Act contained 251 separate sections. It was provided that accounts be made up half-yearly and that they be laid before a half-yearly general meeting of the company. If shareholders at the meeting considered the accounts to be unsatisfactory, they could appoint a committee to examine them and make a report. Dividends could be made from 'clear profits' of the company, provided that 'no dividends shall be made exceeding the net amount of clear profit at the time being in the hands of the said company, nor whereby the capital of the said company shall in any degree be reduced or impaired' (s. 146).

It could be said that, with the progression of time, additional clauses began to appear in subsequent Acts. However, there was little guidance provided by the terminology used. What, for example, did the term 'profit' mean? What were 'proper books of account'? It would be useful today if we knew the thoughts of the draftsmen of such Bills and Acts. The term 'gross income' was partially regulated since each Act laid down maximum charges that could be made, and interest on loans was declared a prior charge. Sometimes part of the gross profit had to be reserved as a contingencies fund. An analysis of the Acts relating to twenty-six railway companies, contained in Appendix 31 to the Second Report, Select Committee on Railways, PP 1839, x. 449–541, shows the extent of the variations in the enactments.

Much of the legislation was a direct result of abuse of one form or another. In 1844 the Railway Regulation Act (s. 19) stated:

And whereas many railway companies have borrowed money in a manner unautho-
rised by their acts of incorporation or other acts . . . upon the security of loan notes
or other instruments purporting to give a security for the repayment of the . . . sums
. . . and whereas such loan notes . . . have no legal validity . . . but such loan notes . . .
issued . . . and received in good faith . . . in ignorance of their legal invalidity, it is
expedient to confirm such as have already been issued.

Prior to 1844, railway companies had often borrowed without any legal
authority on the basis of loan notes, the holders of which had no legal remedy
whatever for the recovery of their money, against either the company or the
directors. Railway borrowing powers were included in the relevant Private
Acts, and companies were most frequently empowered to borrow on a mort-
gage or by issuing bonds. A further common restriction was that borrowing
powers were normally for use if the share capital proved insufficient. This latter condition had previously been ignored by most companies. In practice,
there developed a heavy reliance on loan capital during the years of construction as it enabled cash receipts to be matched more exactly to construction
costs. Authorizing Acts invariably placed limits on the size and frequency of
share capital and required notice to shareholders. Such practice also meant that,
as revenue was not yet earned, interest payments had to be met from capital.

Bank credit was a common form of finance at this time, though it is difficult to judge from surveying company reports its exact accounting presentation. Was the finance merely in the form of short-term overdrafts on current
account or was it perhaps longer term and an indication of financial weakness? Accounts of the Birmingham and Gloucester Railway in the 1840s
show how there was in fact a reliance on bank loans once authorized borrowing powers had been exhausted.[5] Under sections 115–19 of the Companies
Clauses Consolidation Act of 1845 a bookkeeper was to be appointed to
'enter up the accounts . . . in the books', and the accounts were to be kept and
books were to be balanced at prescribed periods.

On the books being so balanced an exact balance sheet shall be made up, which shall
exhibit a true statement of the capital stock, credits, and property of every description belonging to the company at the date of making such balance sheet, and a distinct view of the profit or loss which shall have arisen on the transactions of the
company in the course of the preceding half-year.

The balance sheet had to be examined by at least three directors and
signed by the chairman or his deputy. This balance sheet, together with

---

[5] BTHR. BGR I/I accounts for years ending 31 Dec. 1841 to 31 Dec. 1844. Referred to in Pollins
(1952).

related balanced supporting books, was to be available for inspection by the shareholders at the company's office at least fourteen days before a meeting. The balance sheet was also to be produced at this meeting. Auditors, holding at least one share in the company but without an executive appointment, were to be appointed. They, too, were to receive the accounts, for examination, at least fourteen days before the shareholders' meeting. By sections 101–8, a report or confirmation of the accounts had to be made by the auditors. While it was not a requirement that auditors should sign such a report, in practice they often did. This Act was however not retrospective, although many companies who had not previously appointed auditors did so as a result of public concern arising after the crises and scandal of the late 1840s.

There were other Acts of Parliament which affected railway accounts. For example, the Railway Passenger Duty Act, 1842, required railway companies to keep books giving details of passenger receipts. Copies had to be sent monthly to the Commissioners of Stamps and Taxes. This was for the purpose of assessing liability for passenger duty. Matters were slow to improve and public concern led the House of Lords in 1849 to appoint the Select Committee on the Audit of Railways in order to 'consider the possibility of providing a more effectual audit of accounts'.

THE SELECT COMMITTEE OF 1849

As stated above, it was not until 1845 that there was any general legislation compelling the preparation of accounts. Writing in 1850, Dionysius Lardner said:

It is well known that on the presentation of each half-year's report, auditors are appointed by the meeting of shareholders to examine and check the balance-sheet. The witnesses produced before the House of Lords [in 1849], consisting of public accountants, eminent railway directors, and others, distinguished by special knowledge on such subjects, were unanimous in declaring this system of audit destitute of all efficiency. (Lardner 1850: 510)

This report is interesting as it provides an insight into Victorian attitudes regarding the need for a uniform format of accounts; the need for an impartial audit and the division of expenditure between capital and revenue. The examination of three witnesses is briefly reviewed.

On 12 March 1849 Charles Russell, the chairman of the Great Western Railway (GWR), was called as a witness. At the time the GWR Bill had come before Parliament he had been chairman of the select committee. He subsequently resigned his seat and became, first, a director and, two years later, chairman of GWR. In response to questioning, Russell stated that he would never contract business with another railway company on the basis of published financial statements alone. He was also wary of third parties (such as the select committee) devoting attention to his industry and claimed that railway accounts presented greater information than analogous modes of investment such as the Bank of England, the East India Company, and various canal stocks.

Another witness, W. Andoe, a government auditor, was called before the committee two days later. He had been requested to examine several sets of accounts and found that there was little sign of uniformity between them. At this time government departments probably had the most efficient audits and Andoe was strongly of the opinion that independent public accountants should be employed to fulfil a similar function for railway companies.

A pioneer of the late Victorian generation of public accountants, William Quilter, was likewise called to attend. He was a partner in the firm of Quilter, Ball & Co. (later merged with what became Deloitte Haskins & Sells). He had been involved in examining the affairs of three failed railways: the Eastern Counties Railway, the South Eastern Railway, and the East Union Railway. He later became, in 1870, the first president of the old Institute of Accountants (London Institute of Accountants).[6] As with Andoe, Quilter was strongly in favour of a uniform presentation of accounts and the appointment of independent public accountants as auditors. In his words, 'I should be unfit to enter upon the duties without I felt myself to be an independent man, not intending to show favour or affection to either parts [party].'[7]

These three witnesses reflect the views of many of those called before the committee. There were those who argued for the status quo and the maintenance of *laissez-faire*, perhaps more for their own individual interests. Others, indeed the majority, argued for uniformity and greater disclosure because they considered an injustice arose to the greater mass of investors. Despite the forceful arguments presented, it was not until eighteen years later that a statutory form of accounts became obligatory.

---

[6] Refer to biographical reference in Parker (1980).
[7] In reply to Q2221 of the Select Committee on the Audit of the Railways.

THE INTRODUCTION OF STATUTORY REGULATION

The Regulation of Railways Act, 1868, made it obligatory for all railway companies to render their accounts half-yearly in line with the forms prescribed in the first schedule of that Act. Judged by present standards, the financial and statistical information contained in the proforma accounts of the Act were extremely meagre. No machinery existed in order to decide the items to be included under the various headings. Companies still had the ability to enter results to suit their individual purposes. In the years that followed the 1868 Act many railway companies diversified their interests into the allied areas of hotels, docks, and steamships. Although section 3 of the 1868 Act provided that 'the Board of Trade, with the consent of a company, may alter the said forms as regards such company for the purpose of adapting them to the circumstances of such company, or of better carrying into effect the objectives of this section', the power does not appear to have been exercised.

The 1868 Act was also the first statutory recognition of the 'double-account system'. The principal distinction between the double- and single-account systems is the method of setting out receipts and expenditure on capital account. In the double-account system separate statements are prepared for capital and revenue expenditure and receipts. The capital account is a cash basis statement, showing, on one side, all moneys subscribed by share and debenture-holders, and, on the other, how such sums were expended in the purchase of fixed assets. The balance of receipts over expenditure, or vice versa, is carried to the balance sheet. There was, therefore, no pretence that asset figures represented market value; simply a statement of the disbursement of capital receipts on capital expenditure. It was very much a stewardship-orientated system; and according to Dicksee (1911: 141–5) a system very much favoured by the Chancery Division.

With the double-account system, the assets charged to capital are not written down by reason of diminished value due to wear and tear or obsolescence, but, where necessary, a depreciation fund is created by charging the revenue account with an annual sum and crediting the fund with a like amount. The original designers of the double-account system appear to have decided that a provision for depreciation would not be necessary, and that the periodic renewal of assets out of revenue would be sufficient to maintain the value of the capital assets. Under the form of accounts set out in the 1868 Act, no specific provision was made for depreciation funds.

In later years the necessity for instituting proper depreciation funds became more apparent and the companies provided the funds for the replacement of track, rolling stock, etc. Such charges tended not only to equalize annual charges to revenue, but also to cover the expired life of assets falling due for complete renewal at a subsequent date.

In the late 1840s, and particularly following the intervention (in 1846) of the Bank of England in raising the bank rate, many companies found that they had to call a halt to their capital expenditure programmes. Several limited the amount of their capital expenditure to the unexpended balance on their capital accounts. Once these accounts were balanced off, further capital was simply passed through the revenue account. Sometimes a suspense account would be opened and expenditure charged over several accounting periods. Owing to the large amounts required for expanding or maintaining the railways such a process meant that investors could suffer fluctuating dividends.[8] A leading text of the time had the following quotation, which summarizes the application of depreciation of which the authors much disapproved.

In the case of most railways, for instance, the deterioration of the plant is taken to be adequately and fairly provided for by the current expenditure upon repairs and renewals which is debited to revenue account. This practice is defended on the ground that by the very nature of railway property the repairs and renewals must be at least equivalent to depreciation, and that an effectual check against any starving in maintenance is furnished by the certificates which heads of the spending departments periodically give as to conditions of the permanent way, plant, tools, buildings and rolling stocks. (Fells and Garcke 1887: 95–6)

A further Regulation of Railways Act was passed in 1871, under section 9 of which railway companies were required to render anually to the Board of Trade returns of their capital, traffic, and working expenditure in the form contained in Schedule I to that Act. Subsequently, under section 32 of the Railway and Canal Freight Act, 1888, the powers of the Board of Trade were further extended to enable them to call for additional statements and to amend the returns rendered under section 9 of the 1871 Act, in such manner as they deemed expedient. As with section 3 of the 1868 Act, section 32 appears not to have been brought to bear. Despite legislation it very often was the case that items suddenly appeared in, and just as suddenly disappeared from, the accounts; separate figures were given for items one year, and

---

[8]   See e.g. the case of the London and North Western Railway referred to in Reed (1969: 154).

composite figures the next. Each company adopted its own method of ascertaining the results for embodiment in the statutory pro formas.

FURTHER DEVELOPMENTS IN FINANCIAL REPORTING

The unsatisfactory condition of railway accounting, as governed mainly by the 1868 Act, led the Railway Companies Association to attempt to remedy these anomalies when, in 1903, they appointed a committee to devise a formula to secure some uniformity of practice. This committee was composed of accountants employed within the industry and had no outside (impartial) input. It held over fifty meetings and issued its final report in 1905. The report contained many decisions concerning the allocation of receipts and expenses but, as there was a lack of unanimity among various companies, these deliberations served little purpose.

The Board of Trade set up a Departmental Committee in June 1906 with the following terms of reference: 'To consider and report what changes, if any, are desirable in the form and scope of the Accounts and Statistical Returns (capital, traffic, receipts and expenditure) rendered by railway companies under the Railway Regulation Acts' (Newton 1930: 4). Sixty-seven meetings were held and the work of the 1903 working party was acknowledged. Their report was issued in 1909 and the recommendations contained therein were subsequently given effect in the Railway Companies (Accounts and Returns) Act, 1911.

THE RAILWAY COMPANIES (ACCOUNTS AND RETURNS) ACT, 1911

The 1911 Act prescribed that, as from 1 January 1913, every railway company must prepare annually accounts and returns in accordance with the form set out in the First Schedule and submit them to their auditors in that form. The accounts were to be made up to the uniform date 31 December in each year; but power was given to the Board of Trade to fix some other date, if necessary, in the case of any company, or class of companies, to meet special circumstances of that company or class of company.

The obligation imposed on railway companies under section 3 of the 1868 Act to compile accounts half-yearly was repealed, and companies were specifically exempted from the necessity of compiling accounts or balance sheets, or holding ordinary general meetings, more than once a year. It was provided, however, that this should not relieve a railway company of any obligation in connection with a guarantee of dividend under any statutory provision.

Authority was also given to the directors of incorporated railway companies to declare and pay interim dividends, if they so desired, for the first half-year with no need for the accounts to be audited or submitted to the shareholders.

Section 3 of the Act empowered the Board of Trade to add to or alter the accounts contained in the First Schedule. Such intention was to be advertised in the London, Edinburgh, and Dublin *Gazettes* and provision did exist for appeal. The rights conferred upon the Board of Trade by section 9 of the Regulation of Railways Act, 1871 (as amended by section 32 of the Railway and Canal Traffic Act, 1888) were preserved under section 5 of the 1911 Act, but provided that such returns would be called for on request.

The accounts and returns prescribed in the Act are framed on definite lines: Part I consisting of 'Financial Accounts' (capital, revenue receipts and expenditure, and balance sheet), and part II 'Statistical Returns'. Part II was arranged to illustrate statistically the operations dealt with financially in Part I. Provision was made, for the first time, for showing separately those operations which were subsidiary to the railway operations. As with the 1868 Act, this Act adopted the double-account system but special provision was made in the balance sheet for dealing with depreciation funds.

GOVERNMENT CONTROL OF RAILWAYS

The accounts of railway companies for the year ended 31 December 1913 were published in accordance with the provisions of the 1911 Act. In the following year, at midnight on 4 August, owing to the outbreak of the Great War, the government exercised its power under section 16 of the Regulation of the Forces Act, 1871, and took control of the railways. Broadly speaking the terms of compensation were such that each company was guaranteed, for each year of control, the net receipts of the year 1913, covered by the first seven items in account No. 8 of the First Schedule of the 1911 Act, this being the main Revenue Account. There were a few minor adjustments to this rule of thumb approach, for example, the introduction of works brought into use 31 December 1912. There was also a discontinuance of settlements between one company and another. The Board of Trade (and, from 1919, the Ministry of Transport) authorized, for the year 1914 and onwards, that the accounts be published in abridged form. This period was from 1914 to 1921 inclusive.

The railways never again existed in their former state. In 1919 control of the railways passed to the newly created Ministry of Transport. Two years later the Railways Act (1921) provided for the reconstitution of the railways (with a few exceptions) into four great groups styled:

1. The Southern Group (Southern Railway);
2. The Western Group (Great Western Railway);
3. The North Western, Midland and West Scottish Group (London, Midland and Scottish Railway);
4. The North Eastern, Eastern and East Scottish Group (London and North Eastern Railway).

It had taken over eighty years (since the first commercial railway was established in 1830) to produce a standard presentation of accounts and financial reporting but by then railways were moving into another era devoid of the capitalistic ideals upon which they had been founded.

References

Bagwell, P. S. (1968), *The Railway Clearing House in the British Economy, 1842–1922* (London: Geo. Allen & Unwin Ltd.).

Broadbridge, S. (1970), *Studies in Railway Expansion and the Capital Market in England, 1825–1873* (London: Frank Cass & Co. Ltd.).

Campbell, C. D. (1932), *British Railways in Boom and Depression: An Essay on Travel Fluctuations and their Effects, 1878–1930* (London: P. S. King & Son Ltd.).

Dicksee, L. R. (1911), *Advanced Accounting*, 4th edn (London: Gee & Co.).

Edwards, J. R. (1980), ed., *British Company Legislation and Company Accounts, 1844–1976*, vols. i and ii (New York: Arno Press).

Ellis, H. (1960), *British Railway History: An Outline from the Accession of William I to the Nationalisation of Railways, 1830–1947*, vols. i and ii (London: Geo. Allen & Unwin Ltd., 3rd impression).

Fells, J. M. and Garcke, E. (1887), *Factory Accounts* (London: Crosby Lockwood & Son).

Francis, J. (1968), *A History of the English Railway: Its Social Relations and Revaluation, 1820–1845*. 1st pub. 1851. Reprints of Economic Classics (New York: Augustus Kelley Publishers).

Gourvish, T. R. (1972), *Mark Huish and the London and North Western Railway: A Study in Management* (Leicester: Leicester University Press).

Kitchen, J., and Parker, R. H. (1980), *Accounting Thought and Education: Six English Pioneers* (London: Institute of Chartered Accountants in England and Wales).

Lambert, R. S. (1968), *The Railway King, 1800–1871* (Newton Abbot: David & Charles).

Lardner, D. (1850), *Railway Economy: A Treatise on the New Art of Transport* (London: Taylor, Walton & Maberley).

Newhook, A. E. (1914), *Railway Accounts and Finance* (London: Sir Isaac Pitman & Sons Ltd.).

Newton, C. H. (1930), *Railway Accounts* (London: Pitman's Transport Library).

Parker, R. H. (1980), ed., *British Accountants: A Biographical Sourcebook* (New York: Arno Press).

Parris, H. (1965), *Government and the Railways in the Nineteenth Century in Britain* (London: Routledge & Kegan Paul).

Perkin, H. (1970), *The Age of the Railway* (Newton Abbot: David & Charles).

Pollins, H. (1952), 'A Note on Railway Construction Costs, 1825–1850', *Economica*, 19: 395–507.

Porter, G. R. (1912), *The Progress of the Nation* (London: Methuen).

Reed, M. C. (ed.) (1969), *Railways in the Victorian Economy: Studies in Finance and Growth* (Newton Abbot: David & Charles).

Thomas, J. L. (1867), A Letter on the Present Position of Railways (retained in the library of the London School of Economics).

Williams, O. C. (1948), *The Historical Development of Private Bill Procedures and Standing Orders in the House of Commons* (London: HMSO).

Worthington, B. (1978), *Professional Accountants* (New York: Arno Press).

13 · FIXED ASSET ACCOUNTING IN THE SHIPPING INDUSTRY: P. & O. 1840–1914

C. J. Napier

INTRODUCTION

Although accounting historians have long recognized the significance of fixed asset accounting for the development of financial reporting, much of the existing literature is very general, being based on secondary sources such as professional accountancy journals and legal cases. For example, the pioneering contribution of Brief (1966) is of this nature. More recently historians have seen a need to investigate primary sources so as to ascertain the accounting policies actually adopted by companies, in order to provide an empirical basis for the generalizations of earlier researchers and, perhaps, to challenge conclusions drawn from inadequate evidence. Such primary investigations are inevitably dependent on the survival of original accounting records, whether published financial reports or the underlying books of account, and the vicissitudes of history have reduced substantially the amount of primary material available to the researcher. Useful studies have been made of a few businesses and industries (for example, the investigations reprinted in Edwards 1986), but additional evidence is still necessary, particularly in industries not yet studied in detail.

One such industry is merchant shipping. In the nineteenth and early twentieth centuries Britain's merchant fleet dominated the world shipping market

First published in *Accounting, Business and Financial History*, I/I (1990). The P. & O. archives are deposited at the National Maritime Museum, Greenwich, and my thanks are due to P. & O. and to the Museum staff for their help in the preparation of this chapter. I should also like to thank Freda Harcourt, late of Queen Mary College, University of London, for introducing me to the P. & O. archives and for sharing with me her researches into P. & O.

An earlier version of this chapter was presented at the conference 'Accounting and Decision Making in Companies 1844–1938', held at the Cardiff Business School in September 1989, and I should like to acknowledge the useful comments of the participants at that conference.

(Mathias 1983: 286), and British shipping companies represented a significant (and rapidly growing) sector of the London capital market (Essex-Crosby 1938: tables I–III). One of the largest and most influential of these companies was the Peninsular & Oriental Steam Navigation Company (P. & O.), which by 1914 owned a fleet of about half a million tons (representing about 5 per cent of the world's total merchant shipping tonnage) and had a stock market capitalization of over £7 million—second only to the £8 million of its close contemporary the Royal Mail Steam Packet Company. The survival of a remarkable series of published accounts, business records, ledgers, and other accounting documents, covering the whole of P. & O.'s history from its incorporation in 1840, allows us to study the evolution of one company's accounting for its fixed assets during a period of time roughly coextensive with the development and formalization of the historical cost convention.

The P. & O. archives reveal clearly the interaction between depreciation, reserve accounting, and dividend determination during the nineteenth and early twentieth centuries. Edwards has observed:

Although profitability was sensitive to changing economic conditions, managers believed that their shareholders required a steady dividend. This led some of them to employ valuation procedures designed principally to produce a pattern of reported profit sufficient to cover the planned level of dividend. The aim was profit smoothing on a large scale. (Edwards 1989: 116–17)

P. & O.'s depreciation practices bear this out: for long periods dividends would be maintained at a steady rate, and reported profits would be adjusted, through overt transfers to reported reserves, disclosed additional depreciation, and the use of secret reserves, to a level approximately equal to the dividend that the Directors of P. & O. decided to pay. P. & O.'s early practices lend less support, however, to the criticisms of early nineteenth-century accounting offered by Brief (1965: 14): P. & O.'s accounts (except perhaps for the first three or four years) exhibit neither 'the failure to systematically distinguish between capital and revenue expenditures' nor 'the failure to periodically allocate the original cost of fixed assets to expense'.

The main purpose of this chapter is to provide an exposition of P. & O.'s changing approach to fixed asset accounting. The evolution of P. & O.'s accounting becomes easier to understand in the light of the company's commercial development, and the first section of the chapter provides a historical outline for P. & O.[1] This reveals that significant changes in P. & O.'s

---

[1]   This is largely based on the three corporate histories of P. & O.: Cable 1937; Divine 1960; Howarth and Howarth 1986.

accounting may be identified with both important external developments in P. & O.'s business and changes in senior management. The main section of the chapter examines how P. & O. accounted for its fleet between 1840 and 1914, while the third section appraises P. & O.'s practices and attempts to identify their rationale.

THE COMMERCIAL DEVELOPMENT OF P. & O.

P. & O. was one of several British companies formed at the end of the 1830s to exploit the technology of steam propulsion of ships. P. & O. was incorporated by Royal Charter on 31 December 1840 (the simple incorporation by registration introduced by the Joint Stock Companies Act, 1844 was not yet available). P. & O. could, however, trace its roots to earlier steamship ventures to the Iberian peninsula, sponsored by the ship-broking partnership of Willcox and Anderson. This firm, founded by Brodie McGhie Willcox in 1815 (he was joined by Arthur Anderson, previously his clerk, in 1822), had carried on an irregular service from Falmouth in south-west England to ports in Spain and Portugal. In 1835 Willcox and Anderson were joined in business by Richard Bourne, an ex-naval captain whose family held the government contract to distribute the mails in Ireland, and who also ran a steamship line, the Dublin and London Steam Packet Company. It is probably through the efforts of Bourne that the fledgeling Peninsular Steam Navigation Company gained a contract from the British government to carry the mails from England to Spain and Portugal. This contract was signed on 22 August 1837, regarded by P. & O. as the date of its foundation.

Early steamships were inefficient vessels in comparison with sailing ships of similar size. The steam engines were extravagant in their demand for coal and were prone to breakdown. Unreliable engines meant that a full set of sails had to be carried to provide a back-up, while the need to carry large volumes of coal restricted the space available for freight and passengers. Thus early steamships were viable only if some form of regular and high-value income could be guaranteed. This came in the form of mail contracts. The independence from the winds provided by steam power made it possible for steamship companies to promise a regular service, something attractive to users of the mail. The availability of mail contracts provided a boost to steam navigation on the part of British companies, and thus indirectly favoured British commerce.

During the three years from 1837, the British government considered a mail service to India and China, using the 'Overland Route' through Egypt. The contract was given to the by now renamed P. & O., which started with a service covering the route England–Gibraltar–Malta–Alexandria. The East India Company already carried the mails from Suez to Bombay, and P. & O. adopted the route Suez–Aden–Ceylon–Madras–Calcutta, until the East India Company's route was eventually taken over in 1852. In 1845 a mail service was initiated from Ceylon to Hong Kong. Later P. & O. was to run a service to Australia, while the Hong Kong service was to be extended to Shanghai and ultimately to Japan.

For the first twenty years of P. & O.'s life profits were high. Dividends on P. & O.'s shares climbed from 7 per cent in 1841 to 10 per cent in 1851, and averaged over 10 per cent throughout the 1850s. This level of profit was achieved despite the economic handicaps faced by steamships, because P. & O. specialized in high-value business. The restricted amount of space available for freight (after allowing for coal and for the mails) made it necessary for P. & O. to concentrate on cargoes whose owners were prepared to trade off high freight charges against speed and regularity of service. Thus P. & O. built up a large business in precious metals and specie, silks, indigo, and (although P. & O. scarcely boasted about it) opium (Harcourt 1982). P. & O. steadily improved its fleet, with most new ships after 1845 being built of iron and most after 1850 relying on screw propulsion rather than paddle wheels. Ships gradually became larger, but P. & O. rarely experimented with new and untried technologies.

The good years of the 1850s were not to last, however. As P. & O.'s founders grew older, they became complacent, and less ready to respond to challenges. The most significant of these was the Suez Canal. P. & O.'s service to the East required two distinct fleets. One of these carried passengers from England (and from other Mediterranean ports such as Marseilles and Brindisi) to Alexandria, while the other ran from Suez to India, China, and Australia. Ships were designed for particular services and, once a ship was 'placed on station' in the East, it tended to stay there for the rest of its life. P. & O. thus had to maintain a full repair facility for its eastern fleet as well as one for its Mediterranean fleet. In addition to this, the 'transit through Egypt' required a wide range of facilities (steam launches to take passengers up the Nile, camels and horses to cross the desert to Suez, hotels, farms, water condensers) which P. & O. had to provide. Unfortunately, even though plans for a canal had been under discussion throughout the period from P. & O.'s incorporation, with construction beginning in 1859, P. & O. did not take the Suez Canal seriously.

Ships built during the 1860s were not designed for service in both the Mediterranean and the Indian Ocean, and the draught of several of the newest ships was too great for them to be able to pass through the canal when it opened in 1869. Moreover, in the 1860s P. & O. had to face the challenge of competition from the French Messageries Impériales company and others: P. & O. argued that this competition was unfair, as the French company was being subsidized by the French government at a rate some five times greater than the mail subsidy received from the British government by P. & O. Messageries Impériales entered the specie trade, and by 1863 was carrying bullion to Egypt at rates so low that it was impossible for P. & O. to compete (P. & O. Annual Report 1863, P. & O./6/1).[2] The French company even threatened to compete in the lucrative opium trade (Harcourt 1982: 18). P. & O.'s business was further hit by the financial crisis of 1866, which badly affected the Indian trade in general. To make matters worse, several of P. & O.'s ships needed major refits, including new boilers: repair costs which had run at about £90,000 a year during the early 1850s shot up to over £350,000 a year in the early 1860s, reaching as much as £439,400 in 1866. The crisis year for P. & O. was 1867, when for the first time a loss was recorded, amounting to £181,129, reflecting the virtual disappearance of the specie business, combined with a rise in the cost of coal. In 1867, for the first time (and, until 1932, the last), P. & O. passed its dividend.

P. & O. was saved at this time by two factors in particular. First, the mail contracts came up for renewal. Under the new contract, the Post Office guaranteed P. & O. an income sufficient to pay a dividend of 6 per cent, after charging 5 per cent on the value of its fleet for insurance and a similar amount for depreciation. Against this, if P. & O.'s profits were large enough to allow it to pay a dividend in excess of 8 per cent, the Post Office was entitled to share in the excess profits. In 1868 and 1869 it was necessary for P. & O. to call on the Post Office to subsidize the dividend. The other factor that helped P. & O. was the extraordinary receipt of some £215,000 from the British government during 1868 and 1869 for the charter of P. & O.'s ships to carry troops on an expedition to Abyssinia. This charter income was earned with little adverse effect on P. & O.'s other receipts and payments. As a result of what were in effect subsidies, P. & O. was able to recover from its 1867 loss. Moreover, the mail contract was quickly renegotiated to increase

---

[2] References of the style P. & O./X/X are to documents in the National Maritime Museum, Greenwich. P. & O. made its accounts up to 30 September each year: references to the Accounts or Annual Report for a particular year relate to those for the twelve months ended 30 September in that year.

the flat rate payment to P. & O. (from £450,000 to £500,000 a year) while dropping both the dividend subsidy and the right of the government to participate in 'excess' profits: just as P. & O.'s rate of dividend started to rise towards 8 per cent.

The crisis of 1867 was well documented in P. & O.'s annual and half-yearly reports to its shareholders. By the early 1870s, however, shareholders might have thought that all was now well. The Suez Canal was opened in November 1869, but P. & O. (making a virtue of necessity, perhaps) adopted a 'wait and see' policy towards running through the canal. Whereas, up to the opening of the canal, P. & O. had a near monopoly of the India service, after the canal was opened it faced substantial competition from both other British and foreign shippers. Freight rates fell rapidly, but P. & O. had still to bear the costs of transshipment of passengers and goods across Egypt, while competitors' ships sailed straight through. It was only in 1874 that the majority of P. & O. vessels went through the canal. While during the five years 1866 to 1870 P. & O. had spent £1,264,000 on fifteen new ships, the five years 1871 to 1875 saw expenditure of £1,939,000 on nineteen new ships, now designed to run through the canal and suitable for service in both northern and tropical seas. P. & O. was able to finance the later asset additions without substantial recourse to new capital, but liquid funds were run down by nearly £400,000, and by 1874, and even more so 1875, a new crisis seemed to be looming.

It was P. & O.'s great fortune at this time that the general management of the company came into the hands of Thomas Sutherland, who was to dominate P. & O. for over forty years. Sutherland had joined P. & O.'s London office in 1852 at the age of 18, but two years later he was sent out to the Far East. He made his reputation there over the next twelve years, and was recalled to London in 1866, being appointed Assistant Manager two years later. He clearly impressed the Board greatly, as he became one of the three Managing Directors in 1872, and Chairman in 1880, which offices he held until 1914. In 1911 Sutherland was to look back on those earlier days:

[I] remember the very first occasion on which I had the honour to address a meeting of the Shareholders of the Company. . . . The circumstances were indeed peculiar and mortifying. At that time our exotic overland trade had been annihilated by the opening of the Suez Canal. We had 120,000 tons of really noble ships, but all of them unfitted for this new Suez Canal trade, and standing in our books at a cost of £3,000,000 sterling, for we had no reserve fund in those days as we have at the present moment. Our dividends were lowered until they had become invisible or almost so, and in fact there would have been no dividend if we had charged in our accounts a proper amount for depreciation. We were, therefore, as you can easily imagine, in a very impecunious position. (Proceedings of Annual Meeting, 12 Dec. 1911, P. & O./6/21)

In the crisis year of 1875 serious investigations took place with a view to retrenchment, and these investigations revealed inadequacies in P. & O.'s internal accounting system. Sutherland himself was to prepare a memorandum recommending improvements in internal accounting, designed to show P. & O.'s performance on a more detailed basis than hitherto.[3] Improved management, cost savings, a slashing of the dividend to 3½ per cent in 1875 (it was increased gradually to 7 per cent by 1881), and the impact of more efficient ships all served to carry P. & O. into the 1880s. For the next thirty-five years P. & O. was to face competition and suffer fluctuating revenues in line with the business cycle, but it was able to grow steadily, until by the eve of the First World War it was one of the largest, most substantial, and soundest of British shipping companies.

The years around 1900 were ones that saw widespread moves towards merger and consolidation in many industries (Hannah 1983), and shipping did not escape this trend. P. & O. was relatively late in joining the merger movement, as it was not until 1903 that its Royal Charter was amended to allow it to take controlling interests in other companies. The first take-over was in 1910, when the 'Blue Anchor' Line, which specialized in carrying emigrants from Britain to Australia via the Cape of Good Hope, was bought. During the next few years P. & O.'s name was associated in the press with several other shipping companies, but the next acquisition was a highly significant one: P. & O. took over the British India Steam Navigation Company in May 1914. British India owned 131 ships representing nearly 600,000 tons, and its fleet was therefore larger than P. & O.'s. The two companies were complementary in that British India tended to provide local services that fed or were fed by P. & O.'s lines. Moreover, British India gave P. & O. something that it lacked: management succession. While Sutherland's period of domination of P. & O. was in many respects a good one for the company, he failed to develop possible successors within the P. & O. management. British India, however, was under the direction of James Lyle Mackay, Lord Inchcape, who was not only a younger man than Sutherland but was also able to bring a fresher and more entrepreneurial spirit to the company. After the acquisition, the day-to-day management of the two companies continued as before, with P. & O. managed from London and British India from Calcutta

---

[3] This memorandum was discussed briefly in 1956 by the then General Manager of P. & O. in an article in *The Accountant* (Aston 1956).

by Inchcape's firm Mackinnon Mackenzie & Co. Sutherland soon retired from the chairmanship of P. & O., however, to be succeeded by Inchcape. In some ways, therefore, the P. & O./British India merger might be regarded as an early example of a 'reverse take-over'. The year 1914 provides a convenient place at which to close this brief history of P. & O. Not only was there a change in management and to some extent in philosophy, but the outbreak of the First World War was to change the British shipping industry, leading ultimately to its loss of dominance in world trade.

ACCOUNTING FOR THE FLEET

Introduction

The most important assets of any shipping company are, naturally, its fleet of ships. During the period 1840 to 1914 P. & O.'s fleet lists show 230 steamships (Cable 1937: 243–8), in addition to numerous tugs, launches, and lighters. These range from the *Royal Tar*, a 308-ton wooden paddle steamer, built in 1832 and acquired from the predecessor Peninsular Company, to the 12,358-ton *Medina* of 1911, which cost some £330,000, and was brought into service after being used as the Royal Yacht during King George V's visit to India for the Delhi Durbar. (By comparison, P. & O.'s current flagship, the *Canberra*, is nearly four times as large, being of 45,000 gross tons.) P. & O.'s fleet tended to consist of between forty and fifty ships at any one time, and some statistics for the period under review are given in Table 13.1.

When P. & O. was incorporated, its initial fleet was taken over from various owners in exchange for shares with a nominal value of £304,600. Subsequent additions to the fleet were nearly always commissioned by P. & O. rather than bought second-hand. Few ships were retained for more than twenty years; they would be sold either for breaking up or for use as tramp steamers. P. & O. ships were often sold to Indian or, later, Japanese purchasers, and steps were taken to ensure that subsequent owners did not use the ships to compete with P. & O. This finite life for ships came about partly because the ships (and in particular the engines) would wear out and partly because the rapid technological developments affecting steamships made it essential to replace ships with new and more efficient vessels. An important factor in the timing of replacements and improvements was the requirements of the mail contracts. When these were renewed they often specified that the

Table 13.1. *P. & O. fleet: comparative statistics*

Years	Number of ships in fleet	Average age (years)	Total tonnage	Average per ship	Total cost (£)	Average cost		Net book value (£)	Average NBV		Average years' dep'n
						per ship (£)	per ton (£)		per ship (£)	per ton (£)	
1845	14	7.00	14,333	1,024	625,301	44,664	43.63	529,301	37,807	36.93	3.07
1850	22	6.95	24,713	1,123	1,058,978	48,135	42.85	825,034	37,502	33.38	4.42
1855	37	7.00	44,685	1.208	1,841,911	49,781	41.22	1,554,174	42,005	34.78	3.12
1860	52	7.63	71,345	1,372	2,923,032	56,212	40.97	2,153,600	41,415	30.19	5.26
1865	44	8.77	69,442	1,578	3,087,291	70,166	44.46	2,274,900	51,702	32.76	5.26
1870	43	10.12	80,247	1,866	3,561,272	82,820	44.38	2,727,250	63,424	33.99	4.68
1875	47	8.81	117,473	2,499	4,490,184	95,536	38.22	3,496,000	74,383	29.76	4.43
1880	46	10.17	127,060	2,762	4,480,222	97,396	35.26	2,212,634	48,101	17.41	10.12
1885	50	10.00	172,694	3,454	5,345,496	106,910	30.95	2,517,604	50,352	14.58	10.58
1890	49	10.47	192,658	3,932	5,404,909	110,304	28.05	2,476,732	50,546	12.86	10.83
1895	49	10.39	223,837	4,568	5,646,572	115,236	25.23	2,417,173	49,330	10.80	11.44
1900	54	9.72	278,564	5,159	6,460,376	119,637	23.19	2,747,018	50,871	9.86	11.50
1905	52	9.62	317,460	6,105	7,537,141	144,945	23.74	2,960,149	56,926	9.32	12.15
1910	59	9.66	407,894	6,913	9,242,334	156,650	22.66	3,655,561	61,959	8.96	12.09
1914	57	11.10	442,719	7,767	10,096,948	177,139	22.81	3,299,546	57,887	7.45	13.47

Note: Based on P. & O.'s 'Cost of Ships' books (P. & O./5/610–13), with ships' ages and tonnages verified in Rabson and O'Donoghue (1988).

mail service should be accelerated: in 1880, for example, P. & O.'s Australian mail contract required a saving of two and a half days on the previous thirty-five days between Brindisi (the mails being carried there from England by train) and Adelaide, while between 1873 and 1887 'the Bombay mail time was reduced from 23 to 16½ days, Shanghai from 45½ to 37½ days, Melbourne from 48 to 35 days' (Cable 1937: 183). When a ship was replaced P. & O. would almost always order a larger, faster, and more powerful replacement. Cost per ship also rose, although P. & O. was able to achieve some economies of scale by having several ships built to virtually the same design.

During the period 1840 to 1914 P. & O.'s approach to the publication of its annual accounts developed, and this development may be broken down into three periods: 1840 to 1853, 1854 to 1875, and 1876 to 1914. As the form and content of P. & O.'s published accounts changed, so did its approach to accounting for its fleet. During the first of these periods P. & O. tabled various financial statements at Annual General Meetings. These developed from statements that were little more than trial balances in the early years, to 'Statements of Debts, Credits and Effects' (balance sheets) and 'Capital Accounts' (summarized balance sheets) by the end of the period (P. & O./6/52). In the published Annual Reports P. & O. started by disclosing only isolated numbers, but steadily increased the amount of information until by 1854 the Capital Account was presented, together with statements showing the movements on reserves. During this period, the statements showed the cost of the fleet, while a reserve was described as the 'Depreciation Fund'. The years 1854 and 1855 were transitional: P. & O. now disclosed the Capital Account, but continued to show the gross cost of ships; movements on the Depreciation Fund were also disclosed. From 1856 to 1875 P. & O.'s published accounts consisted of the Capital Account, in which the fleet (referred to in the accounts as 'Stock in Ships') was shown net of depreciation, together with a summarized Revenue Account and a Proprietors' Underwriting Account. From 1876, a more detailed format was adopted, with an extensive 'General Working Account' for P. & O.'s revenues and expenses (on average, the General Working Account classified revenues under five headings and expenses under as many as twenty), a 'General Balance Sheet', and statements of the various reserve accounts. During this period, the balance sheet showed a 'Stock in Ships' figure, which was reconciled to the previous year's figure by adding the cost of new ships and deducting depreciation and the disposal proceeds of ships sold; depreciation was based on 5 per cent straight line.

We are able to trace the evolution of P. & O.'s accounting for its fleet not only through the information made available to shareholders at Annual General Meetings and in published accounts but also because of the survival of a series of 'Cost of Ships' books (P. & O./5/610–13), covering the period from 1840 until well into the twentieth century. While the form of these books changed over time, together they allow us to identify precisely the accounting treatment of the fleet each year, and highlight various unusual practices that might be adopted in some years but not others.

1840–1853

From the beginning P. & O. saw depreciation as only one element in achieving the overall aim of maintaining the value of the P. & O. fleet: the other elements were repairs and insurance. At the first half-yearly meeting on 27 May 1841 the following statement was made:

It will be borne in mind by the Proprietors that the Ships and Floating Property of the Company are insured for £200,000, which principle will not be departed from without their concurrence, and on due notice being given. This provision against loss or accident, together with the determination of the Directors to continue applying annually, out of profits, a portion thereof to meet deterioration, until a fund be credited to the extent of £50,000 for this purpose, will be the best guarantee to the

Proprietory that *the value of the Company's property will be maintained.* (P. & O./6/1; emphasis in original)

Over the next few years several funds were built up out of appropriations of profit and amounts charged as expenses, until by 1848 a total of about £360,000 had been accumulated in three funds: the Repairing, Insurance, and Depreciation Funds. The existence and size of these funds were explained at length in the 1848 Annual Report (P. & O./6/1). The size of the Repairing Fund was based on an estimate that the annual average cost of repairs for an ocean-going steamship was about 10 per cent of the ship's book value net of depreciation. However, as P. & O.'s fleet was relatively new, actual repair costs represented less than the 10 per cent estimate, so a balance had been built up to provide in advance for subsequent higher repair costs. The Depreciation Fund was needed because:

It is well known that ships and machinery, although kept up in efficient repair will, in time, gradually deteriorate in value. This gradual depreciation has been estimated at about 5 per cent per annum on the value of the ships and machinery. It became therefore necessary, in order to keep up the property of the Company at its original value, to set aside, out of earnings, a Fund to meet this deterioration. This has been done at the rate above mentioned, and the amount £173,902 6s. 8d. so reserved out of earnings has been applied from time to time to the construction of new Vessels and Machinery. (P. & O./6/1)

The Insurance Fund was accumulated in order for P. & O. to act as a 'self-insurer' of its fleet, rather than underwriting the risks of loss to its ships externally. Between 1845 and 1848 the Insurance Fund was accumulated out of transfers from the Profit and Loss Account. During this period P. & O. paid a steady dividend of 8 per cent, so the profits set aside in the Insurance Fund could potentially have been used to pay higher dividends. At the same time, the proportion of the fleet insured externally dropped steadily, until from 1849 P. & O. had no significant external insurance cover. In P. & O.'s accounts from 1849 a transfer would be made annually from the Profit and Loss Account to the 'Proprietors' Underwriting Account'. The transfer was based on the book value net of depreciation of the fleet, and was notionally at the rate of 5 per cent, although in practice the amounts transferred represented a marginally lower percentage.

Was the notional 5 per cent a realistic premium? When P. & O. commenced operations, it paid premiums to external underwriters at 6 per cent, later falling to 5¼ per cent. It is unlikely that P. & O. would have persisted in using a 5 per cent rate if this had become excessive compared with the external insurance market. However, the large shipping companies tended to self-insure, so market rates might not have been appropriate measures of the likely cost that P. & O. would have had to pay. P. & O.'s actual experience of losses was a highly favourable one. Between 1849 and 1875 the total charge for insurance was £2,522,000, while the total written off for losses was £970,463. Most of the balance was paid to shareholders as bonus dividends, while the Insurance Fund was on occasion 'raided' to write off losses on ships sold (for example in 1867 and 1871) and for extraordinary repairs.

From 1845 depreciation was credited to the Depreciation Fund, being calculated in principle at 5 per cent of the value of the fleet. In practice, the depreciation charged in the Profit and Loss Account was normally a round number, for example £40,000 in 1848 and £45,000 in 1851. The amount charged for depreciation was normally equal to (or slightly greater than) the amount charged for insurance and credited to the Insurance Fund (or later the Proprietors' Underwriting Account). The level of charge for repairs was normally about twice that of depreciation, up to 1855, when the use of a repair fund for smoothing out the cost of repairs was dropped.

In setting up the various reserve funds, the Directors of P. & O. were conscious of the significance of capital maintenance:

Without making such provision previously to the division of any profits, no steamship navigation enterprize [sic] can be said to be placed in a sound financial position, and . . . to do otherwise would be tantamount to paying a Dividend out of Capital. (Annual Report 1848, P. & O./6/1)

It is interesting that P. & O.'s Directors should have made such a statement in 1848: this was a year when many large railway companies were accused of paying dividends out of capital (Bryer 1991, Edwards 1985), and the Directors may have wished to forestall criticisms.

P. & O. attempted to maintain its capital in physical as much as in financial terms in the early years. The 'Original Stock in Ships'—the initial fleet taken over on incorporation in 1840—was regarded as a special entity. In the annual balance sheets the cost attributed to these ships was reported as one amount, when subsequently purchased ships were listed separately. Similarly, the original share capital of £304,600 was shown as a separate component of share capital. Moreover, when some of the original ships were lost at sea, and were replaced, the new ships were recorded in the accounts at the same cost as those they replaced, even though their actual cost was greater. For example, one of the initial fleet, the *Great Liverpool*, which had been valued at £80,000, was lost in 1846. P. & O. replaced this ship with the *Ripon*, at a cost of

£96,250. The excess cost of £16,250 was immediately written off to the Depreciation Fund, and the cost of the *Ripon* was subsequently reported in the accounts as £80,000. Thus the financial value of the Original Stock was maintained, but it is noteworthy that the *Ripon* was not an exact physical replacement for the *Great Liverpool*, as it was about 15 per cent larger and had engines twice as powerful.

During this initial period P. & O.'s fleet expansion was financed partly from the reinvestment of reserves (including the Depreciation Fund), but more significantly from increases in share capital. In the next period, the regular depreciation provisions were to become more important as a source of funds.

1854–1875

In 1854 the depreciation charge of £62,500 was exceptionally large, in comparison with previous annual charges of £45,000. P. & O. was thus able to show all its ships at a net book value figure accurately based on 5 per cent reducing balance depreciation. For the next few years P. & O.'s practice was to round the cost of a new ship down to a multiple of £100 in the year of acquisition and thereafter to provide 5 per cent reducing balance depreciation. In addition to this, extra depreciation might be provided in respect of ships that were very old or had gone for a long time without an overhaul, while the net book value of other ships might actually be increased (normally when the ship in question had undergone major repairs). Exceptionally, in 1857, P. & O. provided 7½ per cent depreciation of £138,750, as well as making a special transfer from the Profit and Loss Account of £40,000 and utilizing a suspense account of £100,000 set up in 1855 as extra depreciation. Thus P. & O. allocated a substantial proportion of its abnormally high profits during the Crimean War to depreciation. The effect of this was that in 1860 (when the second Cost of Ships book—P. & O./5/611—commenced) P. & O.'s fleet of fifty-two ships had a total cost of £2,923,032 and a net book value of £2,153,600.

The second Cost of Ships book reveals clearly that the publicly stated amount for depreciation was not necessarily the total actually written off the value of the fleet. Over the five years 1861 to 1865, for example, the stated depreciation was £115,000 each year, but this was augmented by different amounts each year and applied in various ways to normal depreciation, writing off losses on disposal, additional depreciation, and upward revaluations of particular ships. The sources of amounts used to augment depreciation (a practice which continued until 1876) were quite varied and included miscellaneous charger receipts, revaluations of other assets (such as workshops in Bombay and Hong Kong), and, in 1863 to 1866, the balance of undistributed profit for the previous year. In 1862, for example, the augmentations to the reported depreciation of £115,000 totalled £47,950. Normal 5 per cent depreciation totalled £107,650, write-downs of twenty-two ships totalled £114,700, and upward revaluations of five ships totalled £59,400.

During the period 1855 to 1859 P. & O. had spent about £200,000 a year on repairs, although included in this total were various substantial items that represented improvements: ships such as the *Malta*, *Candia*, and *Colombo* were lengthened, and several new engines were provided. Repair expenditure accelerated in the early 1860s to between £300,000 and £360,000 a year. During this time, P. & O.'s practice was to debit the cost of the improvement to the Repair Account (and thus to the Profit and Loss Account) and make an adjustment (not necessarily equal to the amount of the improvement) to the net book value of the ship concerned. In 1866, however, the repair cost was so large that P. & O. decided not to provide any depreciation that year. In the Annual Report for 1866, the following explanation appears:

The repairs and renewals of [nine ships] come into the accounts for the financial year, and the consequence is that the amount expended in this way has exceeded the total of that spent in repairs and renewals, together with the sum set apart for depreciation in former years, when the repairs had been of the average character. In the accounts submitted prior to the Annual Meeting of December, 1865, the cost of

repairs for the year stood at	£294,457	7	10
And the amount set apart for depreciation was	115,000	0	0
Together	£409,459	7	10

In the accounts for the present year the amount expended
in repairs and renewals alone reaches the unusual sum of   £439,399   16   7

but, as the vessels repaired and renewed during this and the preceding year have been rendered in many respects as good as new, the Directors have not considered it necessary to charge any reserve for depreciation against the revenue of the last financial year. (P. & O./6/7)

By omitting the depreciation charge in 1866, P. & O. was able to show sufficient profits to cover a 6½ per cent dividend. In the following year, 1867, a loss would have been made whether or not depreciation was provided, and a full 5 per cent charge of £125,000 was made. Repair expenses fell steadily, until by 1871 the annual repair expense was £220,000.

It has already been observed that the first half of the 1870s was a difficult period for P. & O. In 1870 four ships with a total book value of £170,700 were sold for £61,661. The loss of £109,039 came out of the depreciation charge, leaving only £55,268 for writing down the other ships: only the older ships had any depreciation provided that year. In 1871 a further seven ships were sold, one at a small surplus over book value, the other six at a substantial loss. Most of this loss (£69,800) was written off against the balance on the General Reserve Fund (the name given to the Insurance Fund from 1863), and net depreciation provided on the remaining ships was approximately equal to the theoretical 5 per cent. The accounts for 1871 also saw the opening of a Renewal Fund of £20,000 to cover expected abnormal repairs in future years. Next year, the Renewal Fund was augmented by £23,039, the balance on the Proprietors' Underwriting Account, but expenditure began to be debited against the total. The practice of transferring the balance on the Underwriting Account to the Renewal Fund continued, but expenditure increased rapidly, with £128,198 in 1874 (ordinary repairs charged in the Profit and Loss Account were £198,459) and £270,573 in 1875. In the latter year, £80,000 of the total initially allocated to extraordinary repairs was transferred out of the Renewal Fund and added to the ordinary repairs cost in the Profit and Loss Account. This was explained in the Annual Report for 1875:

The amount to the debit of [the Renewal] account for the present year is very large, viz. £278,773 [including a debit balance brought forward from 1874 of £8,200], but of this a very considerable portion appertains to ships which were still under repair at the end of the financial year. The Directors have therefore no hesitation in carrying forward a portion of this debit.

The General Repairs Account is for the past year £175,310 against £198,459 for the previous year. But as the supply of new machinery, combined with extensive alterations, involves a general overhaul, which every ship must receive at stated intervals, and which is properly chargeable as ordinary repairs, the Directors have considered it necessary to charge this Account with a proportion of the expenditure standing in the first instance to the debit of Renewal Account. They have accordingly charged the sum of £80,000 to the General Repairs Account.

Crediting this amount together with the balance of the Underwriting Account, £86,227, there remains the sum of £112,545 to be carried forward to the Renewal Account in respect of ships not completed, or not at work during the past year.

In giving this reason for carrying forward so considerable an amount, the Directors would state that in the accounts presented for this year they have actually charged the sum of £473,338 for repairs, renewals and depreciation [ordinary repairs £175,310, extraordinary repairs £270,573, and depreciation £140,000, less debit balance on renewal account carried forward £112,545], and are therefore doing ample justice to the maintenance of the Fleet.

The Directors have before them the precedent of 1866 for employing the depreciation of the year to cover any extraordinary expenditure for repairs, and by acting in the same way it would be unnecessary to carry forward any balance of the Renewal Account. They do not, however, consider it advisable to adopt this precedent at the present time. In some cases, the large additions made to the tonnage, and the radical alteration effected in several of the ships, might have justified some portion of the outlay being placed to Capital Account, but in no instance has this been done, although the sum so expended during the last four years has been very heavy. (P. & O./6/9)

Even with a 'full' depreciation charge in 1875, it had to be recognized that the depreciation provided on the P. & O. fleet had become seriously out of line with the notional 5 per cent reducing balance being provided. On a fleet costing £4,490,184 at 30 September 1875, depreciation of only £994,184 had been provided, giving a net book value of £3,496,000. On a 5 per cent reducing balance basis (even allowing for no depreciation except rounding down in the year of acquisition) the net book value of the fleet should have been just over £3 million, while on a 5 per cent straight line basis the net book value would have been £2,740,000. As part of the accounting reforms adopted in 1875, a 5 per cent straight line basis was adopted: this was more realistic, given that ships tended to be disposed of after about twenty years for very small residual amounts. But on the new basis, the P. & O. fleet was overvalued by £750,000.

1876–1914

The 1876 Annual Report is significant not only for the introduction of a new form of published financial statements but also for the very detailed discussion of accounting matters. The General Reserve Fund, which had stood at £432,124 for the last five years, was converted into a Reserve Account, and a combined amount for the year for insurance and depreciation of £300,000 credited to the account. Shareholders were warned that the practice of paying a 'bonus' dividend out of surpluses on the Underwriting Account in years when insurance losses were significantly less than the amount transferred from the Profit and Loss Account to the Underwriting Account would cease, and insurance would be dealt with inside the Reserve Account. The Annual Report for 1876 explained:

Though the fact of the Company insuring their own vessels instead of effecting insurances outside was a very distinct gain, the advantage thus obtained ought to contribute, not to a special, but to a general profit on the working of the Company, after making such reserves, for the purposes of depreciation, renewals of the fleet, or reserve fund, as may be considered legitimate or necessary.

The Directors act on this principle in dealing with the charge of £300,000 for insurance and depreciation made on the General Working Account for the present year. The amount thus charged is £30,000 more than last year, but the advisability of increasing the reserve for the purpose of depreciation as opportunity offers, will explain this. (P. & O./6/9)

In fact, out of the £300,000 credited to the Reserve Account, some £40,600 was allocated to insurance charges and £200,000 written off the value of the fleet. The amount provided for depreciation was only £4,803 short of the correct charge on a 5 per cent straight line basis.

The practice that had been adopted a few years earlier of a Renewal Account for extraordinary repairs was continued, and transfers were made from the Reserve Account and the General Working Account so that, after the year's expenditure, only a small debit balance remained. From 1878 the purpose of the Renewal Account was changed so that it included *all* repair expenditure. Between 1878 and 1887 the renamed Repair and Renewal Account acted as an equalization account, with £250,000 a year being transferred from the General Working Account and the actual expenditure (which during this period ranged from £195,000 to £275,000) charged to the account. In the Annual Report for 1878 this change was justified on the basis that the distinction between ordinary and extraordinary repairs was in practice an arbitrary one 'as the work carried on under both heads is more or less inseparably connected' (P. & O./6/9). From 1888, by which time the credit balance on the Repair and Renewal Account was about £250,000, the amount transferred from the General Working Account each year was equal to the repair expenses charged to the Repair and Renewal Account (except in 1892, when the total costs were £255,049, but the transfer from General Working Account was restricted to £250,000). This rather artificial accounting practice continued until 1899, when the balance on the Repair and Renewal Account was credited to the Reserve Account; in subsequent years, repair expenses were debited directly in the General Working Account.

From 1876 the approach to depreciation was also modified, and this was reflected in a new Cost of Ships book (P. & O./5/612), which covered the period 1876 to 1879. In this book two double pages were allocated to each year. The ships in the fleet were listed at cost on the left-hand side of the pages, while the aggregate depreciation provision was shown on the right-hand side; there was no longer a specific calculation for each ship's depreciation. The pages for the year also included a calculation of the year's total depreciation charge, and this was now based on 5 per cent straight line. In the General Working Account, a round sum amount for insurance and deprecia-tion was debited (during the period to 1889): this was £300,000 a year for 1876 to 1879 and £315,000 for 1880 to 1889. This amount was credited to the Reserve Account. In addition, between 1877 and 1884 a total of £485,000 was transferred from the General Working Account to the Reserve Account as 'extra depreciation'. The Reserve Account was debited with vari-ous 'insurance charges', including outside insurance premiums paid in respect of ships in port, various claims for collisions, general average, groundings, and so on, and the book value of ships lost at sea. The Reserve Account was further debited with depreciation. It was not until 1879 that the depreciation settled down to an accurate 5 per cent straight line charge (to which *ad hoc* extra provisions might be added). In 1876, as we have already seen, a round £200,000 was provided, in 1877 the normal depreciation provided was £293,626, together with £200,000 extra depreciation, and in 1878 the nor-mal depreciation was £259,000: in both these latter years a 5 per cent charge would have been only £207,596. In 1877 and 1878 the 'excess' normal depreciation came about because P. & O. transferred all of its total charge of £300,000 for depreciation and insurance to depreciation, less only some triv-ial insurance charges (and, in 1878, a 1 per cent bonus dividend of £29,000). In 1879, as well as the normal 5 per cent charge of £205,184, the balance to the credit of the Reserve Account at 30 September 1876 of £436,531 was also deducted as depreciation. At this point the shortfall of depreciation inherited in 1875 had been completely recouped.

In these three years, there were extensive explanations in the Annual Report of what P. & O. was doing. These explanations are detailed and sophisticated, but they are somewhat disingenuous. The substantial shortfall in depreciation was correctly identified with the use of the reducing balance rather than the straight line method to calculate depreciation and the failure to make a provision in 1866. However, it was then asserted that the Reserve Account could be regarded as an additional depreciation fund. Such an asser-tion is absent from earlier Annual Reports: indeed, an analysis of the origins of the amounts making up the balance on the Reserve Account at 30 September 1876 shows that it consisted almost entirely of surpluses arising over nearly thirty years transferred from the Underwriting Account.

In 1878, an extra amount of £100,000, debited to the General Working Account for insurance and depreciation, was left in the Reserve Account, increasing the balance to £536,531. In 1879 a revaluation of P. & O.'s coal and naval stores and its London head office provided a total surplus of

£242,000. As a result of these credits, the Reserve Account was considered by P. & O.'s Directors to be greater than the level of business required, and, as noted above, the 1876 balance of £436,531 was applied as additional depreciation and written off the 'Stock in Ships' account. The notion that the Reserve Account could be looked on as a form of supplementary depreciation fund was to recur in the years after 1900.

From 1880 normal depreciation of 5 per cent was provided, and for the five years up to 1884 small amounts of extra depreciation were also charged. These extra charges appear to have been made in order to appropriate profits in excess of the amount thought necessary to allocate to paying a dividend in those years. Where these extra charges were justified at all in the Annual Reports, the reason given was that it was necessary to supplement the normal depreciation to allow for the increased cost being incurred at the time that ships were replaced, in order to incorporate improvements required by mail contracts and the need to compete with other shipping lines. By 1884 the total extra depreciation deducted from the cost of the fleet was some £290,000, representing about 5½ per cent of cost (or an extra year's depreciation over the normal amount). It was to stay at or about this level for another ten years.

It has already been pointed out that the balance sheet each year showed a reconciliation of the Stock in Ships account by taking the net book value for the previous year, adding the cost of new ships and deducting the depreciation and the proceeds of ships sold (or the net book value of ships lost) to arrive at the net book value for the current year. This reconciliation could itself conceal various abnormal practices to do with the determination of cost of new ships. When a ship was being built an account would be opened in the general ledger, and this would be debited with the various payments made to the shipbuilder, together with the cost of fitting the ship out. The latter cost was open to manipulation to some extent, however, as items such as the initial set of ship's stores and equipment (including such things as china and glass and passenger bedding) might be debited to the cost of the ship or alternatively debited to the ships' stores account and ultimately written off to profit and loss account. Similarly, costs might be debited to repairs rather than cost of ships. In 1884, for example, the three new ships in that year each had their costs as reported in the published accounts understated by £10,000, and an annotation in the Cost of Ships book states that this represented 'outfits not included in above figures'. Similarly, in 1890, a total of £51,784 was omitted from the cost figure in respect of six new ships, represented by 'stores, outfits, and preliminary charges'.

Another point where flexibility was possible was the exact date on which the depreciation of a ship commenced. From 1880 the policy was to include a new ship in the Stock in Ships account only when it was fully paid for but to commence depreciation from the month in which P. & O. took the ship over from the builders and it first sailed. The effect of this was that a few ships might have more than twelve months' depreciation in their first year in the Stock in Ships account (if they were taken over from the builder before the previous year end but payment was not complete—perhaps because of fitting out charges—until the current year). This policy continued until 1908, when two changes were made. First, depreciation commenced *twelve months* after the date the ship first sailed; second, only nineteen years' depreciation was provided, so that after a total of twenty years a ship would be written down to a residual value of 5 per cent of cost. No publicity was given to this change of accounting policy, even though the effect in the year of change was to reduce the depreciation charge from £420,216 on the old basis to £379,779 on the new basis.[4] The various adjustments to cost of ships were noted against each affected ship from year to year in the Cost of Ships books. Maybe the sensitivity of this information, together with the build-up of extra depreciation (the total of which was also noted from year to year), explains why the Cost of Ships books were provided with locks and apparently written up only by P. & O.'s chief accountant.

The other adjustment in arriving at the Stock in Ships account balance each year related to ships sold or lost at sea. The latter (with two minor exceptions) were written off at cost less depreciation at 5 per cent on the straight line basis either to the Reserve Account (up to 1889) or to the General Working Account, as part of the total 'Insurance Charges'. Under normal circumstances, P. & O. would expect to sell two or three ships a year, as they came to the end of their lives. Most of the ships involved were sold for more than their written-down value at the time of sale (in many cases the ships had been fully depreciated). Indeed, over the period 1876 to 1914 P. & O.'s total profits less losses on the sale of ships amounted to £271,448. By crediting the proceeds to Stock in Ships, rather than just the written-down value, P. & O. 'captured' these profits as extra depreciation. It may be that the recurring profits of disposal stimulated the change in accounting policy in 1908, as up to then there had been a net loss on ship sales in only one of the previous fifteen years. The occasional earlier practice (for example, in

---

[4] In the 1908 pages of the Cost of Ships book (P. & O./5/613), there is a slip of paper showing the calculation on the old basis and an annotation 'Depreciation not to commence until 1 year has expired, as per Chairman's instruction.'

1867) of writing off losses on sale of ships against reserves is not found after 1876.

From 1899 the practice of providing extra depreciation in addition to the normal 5 per cent straight line charge was recommenced. The early years of the twentieth century were good ones for P. & O. It benefited from troop-carrying contracts during the Boer War (1899–1902), and during the Russo-Japanese War in 1905 was also in a favourable position to benefit from increased trade in the Far East and somewhat reduced competition. Over the period to 1912 P. & O. was able to provide a total of £1,213,000 of extra depreciation out of operating profits. By 1914, on a fleet with a book value of £10 million, normal depreciation of £5 million had been provided, but the extra depreciation had accumulated to £1.7 million. The impact of the extra depreciation may be seen in Table 13.1, by comparing the average age of the fleet with the average years' depreciation[5] provided. It will be observed that the under-depreciation of the 1870s had been remedied by 1880. By 1895, the extra depreciation represented about one year's normal depreciation. In 1900, the impact of the extra depreciation is more significant, and this trend continues, until by 1914 a fleet on average eleven years old (less than ten years old if age is weighted by cost) had been written down by thirteen and a half years on average. During the 1910s Sutherland was to comment regularly at Annual General Meetings about the low amount to which the fleet was written down. He would normally quote the net book value of the fleet per ton, and then deduct from total book value the various reserves shown on the balance sheet to argue that the fleet stood at virtually nothing. In 1913, for example, Sutherland said:

If we turn to our Balance Sheet . . . the book value of the fleet . . . works out at £7 13s. per ton, but if we allow for those cash reserves to which I have had to call your attention very often, the actual value of the fleet is only £3 7s. 3d. a ton. As the fleet up to that point cost in round figures ten millions, or to be perfectly and absolutely exact, £9,994,524, it will be seen at once that the Company's financial policy has been worked for many years on sound lines. (Report of Proceedings, Annual General Meeting 10 Dec. 1913, P. & O./6/21)

The following year, in his final Chairman's Report, Sutherland was to be even more specific, claiming that 'the fleet of our Company, as a going concern, instead of being worth [its book value of] £7 9s. per ton, is worth at least £14 per ton'.

---

[5] This is calculated by the formula:

$$\text{Average Years' Depreciation} = 20 \times (1 - \text{Net Book Value}/\text{Total Cost}).$$

P. & O.'S ACCOUNTING PRACTICES APPRAISED

P. & O.'s accounting for its fleet, and the interrelated use of reserves, was influenced by a number of factors, some of which were recognized explicitly in statements made by the Directors to the P. & O. shareholders, while others need to be deduced from the evidence of P. & O.'s actual practice. We have already noted the early recognition of the significance of *capital maintenance*, and P. & O. emphasized on many occasions the importance of maintaining its fleet intact through adequate repairs, insurance to protect against outright loss of ships, and depreciation to allow for the orderly replacement of ships. The notion of capital maintenance adopted by P. & O. cannot, however, be easily labelled as a physical capital maintenance or a financial capital maintenance one. In this context, we may note a highly suggestive comment at the 1846 Annual Meeting, that the number of ships, and consequently the capital required and the revenue necessary for maintaining the company's trading, had not yet been fully ascertained. The implication is that P. & O. regarded its physical capital as a fleet of ships of sufficient number, size, and quality to service the business it had undertaken. As that business grew, so the fleet would have to expand, until some sort of steady state was reached. From this point, it would not be considered legitimate for P. & O. to finance asset replacement out of new issues of capital.[6] In fact, by about 1875 the steamship routes that P. & O. would serve had been determined, and these were maintained with virtually no change (except for a gradual speeding up of the service) until 1914: P. & O. made no issue of share capital (indeed, it actually reduced its capital) from 1875 to 1912. P. & O. did not regard it as sufficient simply to maintain a particular level of operating capacity: when ships were replaced, P. & O. would almost always acquire a larger, faster, and more powerful vessel.

Depreciation was, from P. & O.'s viewpoint, seen almost entirely as a matter of providing resources for *asset replacement*. There were some early comments relating to the role of depreciation as a measure of the cost of wearing out of assets (see the Annual Report for 1848 quoted above), but the ambivalence regarding the function of depreciation—was it a charge against profits for the cost of wearing out or an appropriation of profits to provide resources for replacement?—which has been identified by many writers (for

---

[6] We might see an analogy with the desire of canal and railway companies to close their Capital Accounts once the work of constructing the route and equipping the service was complete (Edwards 1985).

example Brief 1965; Edwards 1989; Yamey 1960) is present in the Annual Reports of P. & O. Certainly, P. & O. regarded it as important to provide annually for depreciation: only in 1866 was a depreciation charge omitted altogether, while the amounts provided each year for normal depreciation were, at any rate by the criteria publicly adopted by P. & O. from time to time, adequate sums (even though they might have been regarded as inadequate with the benefit of hindsight). The switch from reducing balance to straight line depreciation in 1875, though possibly a decade too late in terms of the evolution of P. & O.'s fleet, was a reasonable one in that it achieved the aim of writing off the cost of ships over their normal working lives. The less material change in the computation of depreciation in 1908 could also be regarded as reasonable, as ships tended when sold at the end of their lives to have a residual value, while the larger ships that P. & O. was by now having built required several months after P. & O. took delivery to work up to service: delaying the commencement of depreciation for twelve months could be regarded as reflecting this.

From 1875, even with the move to straight line depreciation, the replacement aspects of depreciation tended to dominate. In the Cost of Ships book, depreciation was treated as an aggregate amount, and allocations to individual ships were made only when they were sold or lost at sea. Substantial additional amounts were provided out of profits, as the cost of replacing ships rose. The form in which movements on the Stock in Ships account were presented each year suggested that the proceeds from the sale of ships and the amounts written off for depreciation were to be regarded as funding the new ships acquired in the year. It is significant that in 1914 the book value of P. & O.'s fleet was disclosed at an amount some £200,000 *less* than in 1875, even though the tonnage of the fleet was four times as great and the cost well over double the 1875 amounts: the aim of financing replacements out of depreciation had been achieved.

Depreciation, and reserve transfers, played another role, that of *dividend smoothing*. Throughout the period under review P. & O. did not build up substantial balances of undistributed profits within the Profit and Loss Account: even as late as 1914, the balance carried forward was only £68,703. In determining the level of dividend to be paid P. & O.'s Directors worked within various constraints. First, there appears to have been an expectation on the part of shareholders that all of the available profits would be divided, as seems to have been the general practice at the time in most companies. Thus the onus was on the Directors to justify profit retentions. Direct transfers to Reserve Account were infrequent, while reserves were much more likely to be built up through some form of indirect route (for example, the Repair and Renewal Account, which had become a *de facto* reserve in the 1880s but was only merged with the Reserve Account in 1889). An abnormal jump of £40,000 in the undistributed balance on the General Working Account in 1908 was also specifically justified: as a precautionary move to equalize future dividends. The second constraint that the P. & O. Directors considered to bind them was a wish to maintain a consistent level of dividend. In the early years, this was achieved despite some fluctuation by labelling some dividends as 'bonus' dividends, signalling that they were to be regarded not as regular but rather as irregular elements of the total. Thus, during the period 1855 to 1865, the total dividend ranged from 8½ to 15 per cent, but in every year (except 1860) the accounts broke this down into a normal 7 per cent dividend and variously described bonuses. After P. & O. reduced its share capital in 1890 and split it into Preferred and Deferred Stock, in every year until 1914 P. & O. paid on its Deferred Stock an interim dividend of 3½ per cent and a final dividend of 6½ per cent, and in most years this was supplemented by bonus dividends: between 1902 and 1911 the dividend was maintained at an overall 13 per cent, while from 1912 it rose to 15 per cent.

Fluctuations in reported profits could be smoothed out by providing extra depreciation or making transfers to reserves. These adjustments were clearly disclosed and explained by P. & O. However, profits could also be smoothed by the use of 'secret' or 'inner' reserves: balances representing the understatement of assets or overstatement of liabilities, the existence of which was not publicly disclosed. By the beginning of the twentieth century the use of secret reserves was widespread (Yamey 1960) and P. & O. had such a reserve, the 'Special Outlays Account'. This account was apparently opened in 1878, although details of its movements survive only from 1892 (P. & O./5/638). The Special Outlays Account had been accumulated largely out of surpluses arising on P. & O.'s coal and stores accounts,[7] but also out of abnormal receipts from the British government for troop-carrying charters. Up to 1892 £360,800 had been credited to the Special Outlays Account, of which £245,653 had been spent on ships' improvements (for example, installation of electric lighting, refrigerated holds, and refitting one ship to provide a luxury cruising service) and on improvements to P. & O.'s head office. Thus in

---

[7] Coal (which was P. & O.'s largest single cost) was charged in the General Working Account at an average cost per ton for the year, and this average seems to have been set at a higher level than the amounts actually paid by P. & O., less discounts and rebates, would imply. Surpluses could arise on stores accounts (which covered the food and drink supplied to passengers and crew and the various consumable supplies used on board ship) in a similar way. In addition, P. & O. gained revenues from the sale of wines and spirits on its ships, which were not disclosed in the General Working Account.

1892 P. & O.'s secret reserve amounted to £115,147. The balance grew rapidly over the next twenty years, to £464,699 in 1900 and £772,060 in 1905 (the main contributions coming from troop-carrying charters during the Boer War), and reached a maximum of £1,038,713 in 1911, before declining to £861,862 in 1914. On P. & O.'s balance sheets, the Special Outlays Account was included in a total described as 'Sundry Balances; and Accounts not closed': indeed, it represented about 90 per cent of the total.

The effect of the extra depreciation and transfers to open and secret reserves during the period 1893 to 1914 is shown in Table 13.2. Annual profits (after providing the regular 5 per cent depreciation) fluctuated between £160,000 and £615,000, but the transfers to the secret reserve

Table 13.2. *P. & O.: appropriation of profits 1893–1914*

Year	Actual profit net of normal depreciation	Transfer from/(to) special outlays account	Profit disclosed in general working account	Appropriations of disclosed profit			
				Extra depreciation	Net transfer to reserves	Dividends paid	Retained in general working account
	(£)	(£)	(£)	(£)	(£)	(£)	(£)
1893	224,940	(54,531)	170,409	—	—	174,000	(3,591)
1894	242,942	(66,060)	176,882	—	—	174,000	2,882
1895	171,258	—	171,258	—	—	174,000	(2,742)
1896	232,353	(56,868)	175,485	—	—	174,000	1,485
1897	413,127	46,500	459,627	—	250,000	208,800	827
1898	175,503	(2,678)	172,825	—	—	174,000	(1,175)
1899	437,977	(215,915)	222,062	21,250	523	197,200	3,089
1900	554,516	—	554,516	182,200	162,791	208,800	725
1901	159,441	14,159	173,600	—	—	174,000	(400)
1902	494,692	(21,270)	473,422	263,576	—	208,800	1,046
1903	457,431	1,505	458,936	—	250,000	208,800	136
1904	614,287	(282,853)	331,434	123,296	—	208,800	(662)
1905	398,113	(18,902)	379,211	170,000	—	208,800	411
1906	382,783	(94,877)	287,906	79,000	—	208,800	106
1907	330,146	(34,269)	295,877	80,000	—	208,800	7,077
1908	241,700	7,396	249,096	—	—	208,800	40,296
1909	268,131	(51,272)	216,859	—	—	208,800	8,059
1910	247,818	45,675	293,493	84,000	—	208,800	693
1911	483,041	(139,306)	343,735	134,500	—	208,800	435
1912	245,699	68,824	314,523	75,000	—	239,375	148
1913	445,717	46,027	491,744	—	200,275	291,000	469
1914	229,469	62,000	291,469	—	—	291,000	469
Total	7,451,084	(746,715)	6,704,369	1,212,822	863,589	4,568,175	59,783

helped to reduce the variations. In abnormal years fluctuations could be attributed to unusual events that might well be known to shareholders from other sources: thus in 1900 the high reported profit could be attributed to Boer War troop-carrying charters, while the low profit in 1901 could be explained as the effect of the loss of one of P. & O.'s newest ships, the *Sobraon*. Thus transfers to reserves in apparently 'good' years could be defended, allowing dividends to be maintained at a steady level. Out of the total profits for the period 1893–1914 of nearly £7½ million, some £4½ million went in dividends, leaving £3 million to be reinvested in the business. This was more than enough to provide the P. & O. Directors with all the flexibility they could possibly need: indeed, in 1914 P. & O.'s balance sheet revealed a portfolio of marketable investments worth over £2½ million, so most of the undistributed surplus represented free resources. (This could be argued to indicate a lack of entrepreneurship on the part of the P. & O. Directors towards the end of Sutherland's chairmanship.)

How did P. & O.'s depreciation policies compare with those of other companies during the period under review? As was to be the case for most companies subsequently, however incorporated, P. & O.'s Royal Charter contained a stipulation about dividends:

It shall not be lawful for the said Corporation to distribute any portion of the Capital of the said Undertaking by way of dividend in respect of profits other than and except any portion of the profits of the said undertaking which may have been reserved out of the profits thereof and afterwards agreed to be divided. (P. & O./30/21)

This constraint continued to apply until P. & O.'s Ninth Supplementary Charter of 8 September 1903, when the emphasis of the relevant clause was changed slightly from a 'no dividends out of capital' stipulation to a 'no dividends except out of profits' one: the change in wording does not appear to have led to any change in dividend or accounting practice on the part of the Directors of P. & O. Given that P. & O. was incorporated in 1840, it could have decided to adopt the double-account system, as such systems were at that time widely found in the context of railways and other large businesses. The use of the double-account system would have largely avoided the issue of depreciation, but, unlike the railways, where a substantial part of capital was sunk in the permanent way and associated engineering works, which might reasonably be assumed *ex ante* to have a non-finite life, P. & O.'s principal assets all too clearly had finite lives. The problem of asset replacement would have to be faced sooner or later, and would loom much larger for a shipping company owning forty or so ships whose replacement would not take place on a smooth pattern than for a railway, with several hundred engines and several thousand carriages that could be replaced gradually.

Another possible model would have been that of the 'single-ship' company. Such companies were relatively common in the latter part of the nineteenth century. A firm of shipping managers would incorporate a separate company for each ship that it managed. The net cash inflow from the ship, after paying a commission to the managers, would be divided among the shareholders in the company. When the ship was finally sold or broken up, the residual proceeds would also be divided. No provision would be made for depreciation. In his textbook *Advanced Accounting* Dicksee was to use the example of the single-ship company to introduce the distinction between capital and revenue expenditure, and to point out that, in such companies, 'the Revenue Account, omitting as it does to provide for Depreciation, *does not show the profit earned*' (Dicksee 1903: 4, emphasis in original). In a single-ship company shareholders were well aware that their money was invested in a business with a finite life, and that part of their cash return should strictly be regarded as a return of capital. The founders of P. & O., however, had every intention of forming a company that would continue indefinitely, and they very quickly came to view P. & O. as a 'semi-national institution'. Thus an accounting policy predicated on the termination of the business would have been considered irrelevant.

P. & O.'s actual accounting practice during the period under review stands favourable comparison with those practices observed in the generality of companies. In his study of iron and steel companies Edwards has noted the extent to which depreciation tended to fluctuate in line with the general level of profits: this is clear not only in the case of the Shelton Iron, Steel & Coal Co. during the period 1889 to 1929, discussed in detail by Edwards (1980), but seems to apply generally in the case of companies in that industry (Edwards 1981: 21–5). Practices in the shipping industry appear to have varied greatly, but P. & O.'s treatment of depreciation after 1875 is comparable with that adopted by companies such as Cunard (Hyde 1975: 149–50), albeit the amounts provided by P. & O. were, given the larger size of its fleet, substantially greater. Unlike many companies, however, P. & O.'s depreciation was never (except in 1866) to be reduced below its stated rate in order to smooth out short-term profit fluctuations. Every year from 1877 to 1914 P. & O. provided 5 per cent straight line depreciation on its fleet: in nearly half of those years, it provided more.

CONCLUSION

The extent to which the adoption of particular accounting policies enhances or otherwise the performance of a business is one that is perhaps incapable of resolution. It is possible that 'sound' accounting policies are as much an effect of good management as a cause. P. & O. was possibly the most successful shipping company of its time. Of course, the dice were loaded in its favour: during the early years it had no substantial competition while being heavily subsidized by the British government through the mail contracts. It was able to recover from crisis (again often helped by government subsidy or by the propensity of British imperialism to require troopships every few years), and by the 1880s had certainly achieved the ambition of becoming a semi-national institution. Its securities were the bluest of blue-chips, and its credit was, by the end of the nineteenth century, better than that of many governments.

In achieving this reputation of financial strength P. & O.'s ability to pay a dividend in all years but one up to 1914 must have made a significant contribution. Although dividends in the earliest years might have been inflated somewhat at the expense of depreciation, after 1876 this position started to reverse itself, so that by the end of the nineteenth century P. & O. was able to pay a high dividend while still retaining resources through overt reserve transfers, additional depreciation, and transfers to a secret reserve. P. & O.'s fixed asset accounting epitomizes the development of the concept of depreciation during the nineteenth century, from an almost optional reserve for asset replacement to a regular (and unavoidable) measure of the cost of using fixed assets. However, P. & O.'s public attitude to depreciation during this period also reflects the ambiguity in the nature of depreciation which has perhaps still not been settled: is depreciation a cost or a retention of funds for asset replacement? As late as 1914 the latter purpose was uppermost in the minds of P. & O.'s Directors.

P. & O.'s accounting policies thus reflected the company's rise to being a pillar of the establishment. Early practices were advanced by the standards of the time, while later practices were sophisticated (though, like P. & O.'s approach to ship technology, seldom innovative). After 1914 the quality of published accounts was to decline, and it appears that P. & O. adopted some of the potentially problematical practices common elsewhere in the shipping industry. There is evidence (Jones 1989) that P. & O. continued to use secret reserves during the 1920s, suggesting that Lord Inchcape supported P. & O.'s dividends before 1932 with accounting devices similar to those for which Lord Kylsant of the Royal Mail group faced prosecution. In 1914, however, such problems were far from the minds of the P. & O. Directors and share-holders, who could look back with Sir Thomas Sutherland[8] to a company that had started in 1840 with £300,000 worth of ships and was now, after the British India merger, in a position to 'command the employment of a cap-ital of fifteen millions sterling . . . [and] a tonnage of a million and a quarter tons, and this tonnage and this capital will be worked with a common aim and purpose for the prosperity of a great national enterprise'.

References

Aston, Chas. W. (1956), 'There is No New Thing . . .: An Early Treatise on Accounting for Management', *Accountant* (17 Nov.): 512–13.

Brief, Richard P. (1965), 'Nineteenth Century Accounting Error', *Journal of Accounting Research* (Spring): 12–33.

——(1966), 'The Origin and Evolution of Nineteenth-Century Asset Accounting', *Business History Review* (Spring): 1–23.

Bryer, R. A. (1991), 'Accounting for the "Railway Mania" of 1845: A Great Railway Swindle?', *Accounting, Organizations and Society*, 16/5–6: 439–86.

Cable, Boyd (1937), *A Hundred Year History of the P. & O.* (London: Ivor Nicholson & Watson).

Dicksee, Lawrence R. (1903), *Advanced Accounting* (London: Gee & Co. Repr. New York: Arno Press, 1976).

Divine, David (1960), *These Splendid Ships: The Story of the Peninsular and Oriental Line* (London: Frederick Muller).

Edwards, John Richard (1980), 'British Capital Accounting Practices and Business Finance 1852–1919: An Exemplification', *Accounting and Business Research* (Spring): 241–58.

——(1981), *Company Legislation and Changing Patterns of Disclosure in British Company Accounts 1900–1940* (London: ICAEW).

——(1985), 'The Origins and Evolution of the Double Account System: An Example of Accounting Evolution', *Abacus* (Mar.): 19–43.

——(1986) (ed.), *Reporting Fixed Assets in Nineteenth-Century Company Accounts* (New York: Garland Publishing).

——(1989), *A History of Financial Accounting* (London: Routledge).

Essex-Crosby, Alan (1938), 'Joint Stock Companies in Great Britain 1890–1930', M.Comm. thesis, University of London.

---

[8] At the Extraordinary General Meeting in June 1914 to approve the take-over of the British India Steam Navigation Company (P. & O./6/21).

Hannah, Leslie (1983), *The Rise of the Corporate Economy* (London: Methuen).

Harcourt, Freda (1982), 'The P. & O. Company: Flagships of Imperialism', in Sarah Palmer and Glyndwr Williams (eds.), *Charted and Uncharted Waters: Proceedings of a Conference on the Study of British Maritime History* (London: National Maritime Museum).

Howarth, David and Stephen (1986), *The Story of P. & O.: The Peninsular and Oriental Steam Navigation Company* (London: Weidenfeld & Nicolson).

Hyde, Francis E. (1975), *Cunard and the North Atlantic 1840–1973* (London: Macmillan).

Jones, Stephanie (1989), *Trade and Shipping: Lord Inchcape 1852–1932* (Manchester: Manchester University Press).

Mathias, Peter (1983), *The First Industrial Nation* (London: Methuen).

Rabson, Stephen, and O'Donoghue, Kevin (1988), *P. & O: A Fleet History* (Kendal: World Ship Society).

Yamey, B. S. (1960), 'The Development of Company Accounting Conventions', *Three Banks Review* (Sept.): 3–18.

POSTSCRIPT

Although the main purpose of this chapter was to describe and analyse a major company's changing approach to accounting for its fixed assets over an extended period of time, it also touched on the use of secret reserves. In British accounting history, the classic example of the use of secret reserves was the Royal Mail Steam Packet Company, which was in many ways comparable with P. & O. Thus it was not surprising that evidence of secret reserves turned up in the P. & O. archives. A companion paper (Napier 1991) examines in detail how P. & O.'s Chairman Lord Inchcape deliberately manipulated reported profits over the period 1914–31, by the use of a wide range of transfers to and from secret reserves. This permitted P. & O. to maintain its dividend during the 1920s, a very difficult time for the British shipping industry, while still depreciating its fleet of ships.

Recent research (Arnold 1991; Ashton 1986) has begun to criticize the interpretation of the accounting practices of the Royal Mail company as involving 'abuses' of secret reserves. They suggest that to a large extent what was involved was undisclosed *provisions* for unascertained liabilities and losses, rather than free *reserves*. This new interpretation has some validity in the case of P. & O., whose Directors certainly never regarded the company as having substantial undisclosed free reserves. However, P. & O. was able during the 1920s and 1930s to draw upon the profits and reserves of its subsidiaries in order to maintain its own reported profits, and the contribution from its allied companies was crucial in allowing P. & O. to overcome the financial and economic crises which brought down Royal Mail. One subsidiary in particular contributed nearly £10 million to P. & O., with virtually no disclosure. This was P. & O.'s New Zealand subsidiary the Union Steam Ship Company, and recent archive work in both Britain and New Zealand has provided unambiguous evidence of the existence of clear free reserves in the accounts of at least one major company (Napier 1992).

The secret reserves of the Union Steam Ship Company pose a problem to traditional analyses of the use of such reserves by Directors aiming to smooth profits and thus dividends in the interests of shareholders. Given that Union was a 100 per cent subsidiary of P. & O. from 1917, and P. & O. was advised in general terms of Union's 'true' financial position, from whom were the secrets being kept? Documents in the Union archives suggest that the company concealed its financial strength from potential competitors but more significantly from the New Zealand government, who might have been quick to impose price and other regulations on the company. Is this an early example of the selection of profit-reducing accounting policies to minimize 'political costs'?

References

Arnold, A. J. (1991), 'Secret Reserves or Special Credits? A Reappraisal of the Reserve and Provision Accounting Policies of the Royal Mail Steam Packet Company, *Accounting and Business Research* (Summer): 203–14.
Ashton, R. K. (1986), 'The Royal Mail Case: A Legal Analysis', *Abacus* (Mar.): 3–19.
Napier, C. J. (1991), 'Secret Accounting: The P. & O. Group in the Inter-war Years', *Accounting, Business & Financial History* (Sept.): 303–33.
——(1992), 'Secret Accounting in New Zealand: P. & O. and the Union Steam Ship Company, 1917–1936', in Atsuo Tsuji (ed.), *Collected Papers of the Sixth World Congress of Accounting Historians*, vol. iii: 1333–58 (Osaka: Accounting History Association).

LOCAL GOVERNMENT ACCOUNTING

14 · ACCOUNTING IN ENGLISH LOCAL GOVERNMENT FROM THE MIDDLE AGES TO *c.*1835

R. H. Jones

The historical accounting literature significantly underemphasizes the persistence and pervasiveness of non-commercial non-double-entry bookkeeping in England. Attention has typically been focused on the Exchequer pipe rolls and manorial accounting in the Middle Ages, whereas, in fact, non-commercial non-double-entry bookkeeping persisted for over 700 years. In addition, it pervaded the economy throughout this time: it was not only adopted in the pipe rolls from 1130 until 1832 but also by the organs of government in the localities,[1] namely the counties, boroughs, and parishes. These covered the whole country and at the end of the eighteenth century they were represented by over 15,000 separate organizations. To varying extents they collected money, paid money over, borrowed and repaid money, spent money, made rates, produced accounts and had them audited; their use of double entry was not common until the nineteenth century.

The overall purpose of this chapter is to provide a synthesis of this aspect of the history of accounting, concentrating on accounting in the government of localities. In addition, there are three more specific objectives. First, to clarify what is meant by 'charge–discharge' accounting: there is confusion in the literature about terminology and doubt about what the method involves. Second, to understand, for its own sake, what 'local government' accounting meant before government regulation and professionalization in the nineteenth century. And, third, to make a contribution to an earlier discussion about

First published in *Accounting and Business Research* (Summer 1985), The author acknowledges the advice given by Professor K. V. Peasnell on an earlier draft.

[1] This may seem an unnecessarily contrived way of saying 'local government'. However, as the Webbs pointed out (1922: 355), they did not find that term in use before the middle of the 19th century. The phrase 'local government' implies a 'system' of government which in their opinion did not prevail before the 1830s.

which characteristics of double entry led to its dominance over charge/discharge.

We begin by attempting to clarify what was involved in charge–discharge accounting. We then discuss in turn accounting in the parishes, accounting in the boroughs, and accounting by county treasurers. Finally we offer a synthesis of accounting in the government of the localities throughout this period, drawing conclusions about its relationship with what government itself meant and suggesting why double entry eventually held sway.

CHARGE–DISCHARGE ACCOUNTING

Baxter (1980) offers a clear and concise summary of what in fact is generally implied by economic and local historians when they talk of charge–discharge accounting. He associates it with both manorial and pipe roll accounting in the medieval period. For him, it is a 'system of stewardship' where 'the steward was charged with the sums for which he was responsible (opening balance, plus receipts), and discharged of his legitimate payments; the end balance showed what he must hand over to his lord or keep in his charge for the next period' (p. 69).

There are, however, at least two writers in the accounting literature who have taken a different view. Chatfield (1977: 25) states that it was 'developed in fifteenth century Scotland by government accountants'. Since he previously discusses the English Exchequer pipe rolls, he clearly does not categorize them as charge–discharge. Boyd (1905: 58) adopts the same pattern: having discussed the pipe rolls he subsequently states that the 'earliest examples of this form of account (charge and discharge) which we find . . . are those of the Lord High Treasurer of Scotland', the oldest extant copy of which dates from 1473/4. Even more explicitly, Boyd also states that accounts of a priory dating from 1354, which include opening balance, arrears brought forward, receipts, payments, arrears carried forward, and balance, 'can hardly be said to be stated in that form [of charge–discharge]' (p. 58).

It is not easy to resolve the terminological question. It is true that the English Exchequer pipe rolls do not use the words nor Latin words which could be translatable as charge–discharge. An early publication of the Pipe Roll Society (1884) does discuss them in terms of 'Charge and Allowance' though this does not appear to be a translation and the same author recasts one of the accounts as a 'Balance Sheet' (p. 51), which tends to suggest terminological looseness. Two of the most substantial theses available on manorial accounting do not use the phrase charge–discharge accounting (Oschinsky 1971 and Harvey 1976). Booth (1981) does and in fact segregates his specimen accounts using these words, though it is not clear that they are translations. In the text he says that 'the first task at the audit of each account was to calculate the "charge" (onus)' (p. 18). This is interesting because in the accounts which we discuss later the first use of these words occurs in 1547/8, when the opening section of the account of a parish is headed 'Onus' and the first entry says that the wardens 'chargythe themselvys' (Savage n.d.). In 1589, for the same parish, the words 'chardge' and 'dischardge' appear throughout the account (pp. 81–2). No doubt a more extensive hunt for these terms would yield similar results. Perhaps it is simply one more of many examples of phrases in accounting whose etymology is not clear and which are used in different senses by different writers.

It seems to the present writer that the most generally accepted meaning of charge–discharge in fact represents a family of accounting statements drawn up on the basis of single entry. The other unifying theme is that they represent the account of a steward being held responsible for financial transactions of a period to a higher authority. The steward is a debtor to the extent of the charge; in many cases the charge includes recurring amounts from previous years although it is often supplemented by 'extraordinary' amounts. The emphasis is on the amounts being due unless there is good reason for a shortfall, the discharge. In the context of the pipe rolls, this is graphically brought out in the *Dialogus de Scaccario* (Johnson 1950). However, the accounts themselves are only a 'family' because some are, as Baxter suggests, statements of opening cash in hand, receipts and payments, and closing cash in hand. However, many are statements of cash and debtors in hand, income and payments, and cash and debtors carried forward (Oschinsky 1971: 218; Booth 1981: 24; Harvey 1976: 68; Johnson 1950: 84). We know of many examples where the charge–discharge account is one of physical inventory such as corn and animals (Harvey 1976 provides a detailed discussion). In the accounts we discuss later there are a few examples of physical inventory being included within the monetary charge–discharge account, and even of inventory being valued. Creditors are not commonly assumed to have been included, although as a matter of technique they could have been handled in the same way as debtors. And, as Baxter (1980) explains, the charge–discharge account was used in trust accounts to distinguish between capital and revenue. Thus we can say that charge–discharge was able to handle the necessary adjustments to produce accrued income from cash entries; in practice, the most common adjustment in government accounts related to debtors.

The pipe rolls were charge–discharge accounts which included debtors, though their treatment of these was not as sophisticated as other examples. In contemporary terms we would tend to think of the pipe rolls as the accounts of central government; they were in fact the written accounts of the monies due to the Crown by the sheriffs in the counties. They were, in the Middle Ages, the accounts of the government of the county on behalf of the Crown. However, in one county, Cheshire, the charge–discharge accounts were considerably more sophisticated. We know this because of the substantial thesis of Booth (1981), which is concerned with the financial administration of Cheshire between 1272 and 1377. In 1301 the revenues of the county 'passed forever off the pipe rolls on to the annual accounts rendered by the Chamberlain of Chester at the local exchequer' (Stewart-Brown 1938: p. x). By 1365, perhaps earlier, the form of these accounts was as sophisticated a form of charge–discharge as is known to us from this period (see Fig. 14.1).

Amounts owed by the Chamberlain (the Steward) to the county do not confuse the year's charge–discharge. Payments by the Chamberlain are divided between payments for this year and payment of arrears. Any of this year's charges which the auditors accept as not collectable are deducted from the foot of the account, the implication being that this does not necessarily mean they will be uncollectable next year. But even after allowances there may be charges which have not been collected by the Chamberlain (i.e. his personal debtors) but which the county still insists the Chamberlain should collect; these appear within the final balance of arrears presumably in addition to any shortfall in cash paid by the Chamberlain.

The Exchequer pipe rolls were in effect made up only of sections 1, 2, and

1.	*Charge*	
	Monies due for this year	X
2.	*Discharge*	
	Payments	X
3.	*Balance of Charge–Discharge* (1 minus 2)	X
4.	*Joint Sum of Indebtedness*	
	Balance of Charge/Discharge (3 above)	X
	Arrears from previous year's account	X
5.	*Foot of Account*	
	Payment of cash	
	Of arrears	X
	Of balance of Charge–Discharge	X
	Allowances for monies due but not collectible etc.	X
6.	*Arrears* carried forward (4 minus 5)	X
	(including debtors)	

Note: Adapted from Booth 1981: 33, 23.

Fig. 14.1

3. This meant that where items of charge were not cash but represented debtors of the steward, then the accounts themselves had to be marked to this effect and the mark 'cancelled' when payment was made. The Cheshire method clearly segregates the arrears figures, enabling control to be maintained periodically without referring back to previous pipe rolls.

There has been debate amongst historians about whether the system of administration of Cheshire in this period was *sui generis* (Booth 1981: ch. 1); it seems that its accounting method was not adopted by other governments of the localities.

ACCOUNTING FOR PARISHES

The counties in the Middle Ages, in the person of the sheriffs, were organs of government of the localities on behalf of the Crown. Of equal, if not greater, antiquity were the organs of government of the localities on behalf of the Church: the parishes. The Webbs' seminal volumes on the history of English local government began with the parish. The reason given was that of the other local authorities the parish was by far the most numerous (at the turn of the eighteenth century there were over 15,000) and it was the only unit of local government which covered the whole of the country (Webbs 1963: 3–7).

From the financial point of view they were also important. The statutory power to levy a rate is often dated from the Poor Law Act of 1601 (43 Eliz. I, c. 2); this Act conferred the power on the parishes (as well as boroughs and counties). In fact, as Cannan (1912) reminds us, there had been statutory rates as early as 1427. More important, there had been non-statutory rates from time out of mind (Cannan 1912: chs. 1, 2). In the parishes the rates had been primarily for the upkeep of the church[2] but down the years they were supplemented by poor rates, highway rates, police rates, and others.

The parish, then, began as an ecclesiastical unit centred on a church. The main duty of parishioners was upkeep of the church. Particularly from the sixteenth century onwards, and not unrelated to the dissolution of the monasteries by Henry VIII, it increasingly took on civil duties.

Overall responsibility for the management of the parish in some cases was vested in the parishioners as a whole. The room in the church where meetings were held ('the vestry') came to be used for the parishioners' meetings. These

---

[2] Compulsory church rates persisted until 1868 (Tate 1969: 28).

came to be known as the open vestries. Some vestries were close vestries, where a local oligarchy was preserved with the power of re-electing itself. The increasing number of close vestries, with increasing allegations of impropriety, eventually resulted in the reform of the parochial unit as an administrative arm of local government.[3]

Responsibility within each parish for the specific functions was given to (often forced on) the officers of the parish. The four most common offices were those of the churchwarden, the constable, the highwaywarden, and the overseer of the poor. Each statutorily kept accounts and was required to submit them to the justices of the peace annually. For example, the 1601 Act states that the churchwardens and overseers:

shall within four days after the end of their year . . . make and yield up to two such justices of peace . . . a true and perfect account of all sums of money by them received, or rated and sessed and not received, and also of such stock as shall be in their hands, or in the hands of any of the poor to work. (section II (2))

Though each officer produced accounts, those of the churchwarden are the most important and have most frequently been published. Cox (1913) provides a catalogue of the extant accounts and this has been updated by Blair (1939). The publications are random and numerous. Most are only partial transcriptions because their main purpose is to illuminate the content of the accounts rather than the accounts themselves. We have chosen to discuss the full transcriptions/translations which provide good coverage of the time from the late Middle Ages to the early nineteenth century.

The most sumptuous[4] publication is that of the accounts of St Martin-in-the-Fields, 1525–1603 (Kitto 1901). A full reproduction in actual size, this book is as close as one could come to reading the originals. Four other valuable examples are:

    Ashburton, Devon, 1479–1580 (Hanham 1970);
    St Nicholas, Warwick, 1547–1621 (Savage n.d.);
    Bodicote, Oxfordshire, 1700–1822 (Fearon 1975);
    Hooton Pagnell, Yorkshire, 1767–1820 (Whiting 1938).

All the accounts are accounts of an officer or officers. When there was more than one churchwarden, as there often was, there was usually only one account. Generally, the accounts were written records of an approximately annual 'audit' where the churchwardens offered the detailed items of account for approval by the vestry (parishioners as a whole or representatives), then

---

[3] The reforms began in 1834 with the first of a series of Poor Law (Amendment) Acts.

[4] Webbs' adjective (1963: 7), but it seems even more apposite today.

physically handed over any money still held (or claimed reimbursement of money due) and any inventory of goods, animals etc. These accounts typically include an amount of money paid to a clerk for writing up the account.

All the accounts contain the following five elements, in one form or another:

1. A heading, giving the names of the churchwardens, the period of account, and the name of the parish.
2. The balance brought forward from the foot of the previous period's account.
3. Receipts (or revenues) of the period.
4. Payments of the period.
5. The balance of the account carried forward.

The headings appear invariably and in some cases are so elaborate they are works of art (e.g. Kitto 1901: 224, 287). The order in which the next three items appear varies from parish to parish but is usually consistent from period to period. Most often the first item recorded is the balance brought forward from the previous year's account though there are examples of this being brought into the final reckoning at the end. In most cases, receipts appear before payments. However, in the Hooton Pagnell accounts payments consistently appear first.

The balance of the account is usually described as being offered up by the existing churchwardens (assuming there was a surplus). It may be described as being offered to the (named) churchwardens elect. There may also be signatures or marks. In the Hooton Pagnell accounts these are sometimes accompanied by phrases such as 'Allowed by us', 'Examined and allowed by us . . .'.

With the exceptions of Hooton Pagnell and Bodicote, the accounts adopt roman numerals. These two do relate to later periods, but because there is no explicit comment about the treatment of numbers in the transcription (cf. Hanham 1970: p. xx) we cannot assume that the originals were in Arabic. The entries in each set of accounts can be grouped into three different forms: paragraph form, separate lines but figures not in columns, and separate lines with figures in columns. Ashburton and Hooton Pagnell are in paragraph form. St Nicholas are an example of the second form. Bodicote and St Martin-in-the-Fields are written in separate lines with figures in columns; however, Bodicote are strictly columnar (pounds, shillings, and pence strictly segregated) whereas St Martin's are only left-adjusted.

In two sets of accounts (Bodicote and Hooton Pagnell) the receipts are put in one group, the entries being chronological with a sum total at the end.

This applies also to payments. However, the other three adopt different categorizations within the groups of receipts and payments. St Martin-in-the-Fields are grouped in quarters (Lady Day, Midsummer, Michaelmas, Christmas). In Ashburton, for the account 1510/11, there are the following groups:

> Arrearages (i.e. balance b/f)
> Rent
> Ale
> Wax-silver
> Gifts
> Cross & burial
> Other receipts
>   Sum total of receipts
> Rent resolute
> Expenses etc.
> Repair of various tenements
>   Sum total of payments

The receipts classification remained almost uniform throughout the period; the payments were sometimes placed in one group only. St Nicholas also adopts a detailed breakdown of receipts and payments.

As to the content of these accounts, we can say that, almost without exception, they used the cash basis. Most entries included the words 'received' or 'paid'. There was a small number of occasions when the balance at the foot of the account explicitly included reference to monies still owed to the church-warden. For example at the foot of the Ashburton account for 1505/6 appears the following: 'And so they have clear—£8. 10s. 11d. with 40s in the hands of the ale wardens . . . and 2s. rent of Richard Hogge and Thomas Peche and five shillings in wax which they delivered (Hanham 1970: 34).

The 2s. rent appears under 'Gifts, rent, etc' and is added in to the 'Sum of all receipts'. Therefore, the amount of £8 10s. 11d. *includes* this 2s. rent (actually 12d. from each man). Since the explanation is that this amount is still owed the original entries can hardly have been cash receipts.

In the 1506/7 account the two amounts of 12d. are recorded as rent from Hogge and Peche. At the foot of the account the wording has (unfortunately) changed to the amount clear 'with 6s. 8d in pledges' (p. 35). This could include 4s. rent unpaid from our two heroes but it is unlikely. The 1507/8 account similarly shows 12d. rent from each of them but the account has no totals: no receipts totals, payments totals, or net total of the account.

This is very rare in the accounts we are examining. There is a footnote given by the transcriber to the effect that the 1507/8 account is in a 'new hand' (p. 35) but this hand does not change again until 1509/10, and the 1508/9 account does include totals. It is difficult to accept the explanation, therefore, that the lack of totals was because of the particular clerk writing the account. The 'arrearages' at the beginning of the 1508/9 account are £13—an unusually round number which in fact does not agree with the individual items. Hogge and Peche do not appear in the accounts from 1508/9 onwards.

We have expended some effort in recounting this incident because it is unusual to find mention of amounts unpaid in churchwardens' accounts and also because the attempt to include debts in what had been a receipts and payments account produced the kind of difficulties one might expect particularly if the debts were never paid. Had they been paid, there would have been no problem—the balance on the account would revert to being cash rather than cash plus debtors. But when the arrears were not paid, what was to be done? The 1507/8 wardens could not equitably have been charged with the bad debts since they originated with the 1505/6 wardens. They could simply have been forgotten, by excluding them from the foot of the account, but then the account would not balance. Perhaps there were other reasons why the 1507/8 account was so different from its predecessors and successors—the accounts themselves give a 'cold' view of historical events. Nevertheless, we can say that this attempt to introduce debtors was a failure.

The accounts of Bodicote, Hooton Pagnell, and St Nicholas are wholly cash accounts and there is no inclusion of physical inventories of goods held by the churchwardens. St Martin-in-the-Fields, however, do occasionally include inventories. From the beginning of the series of Ashburton's accounts, physical items of stock are included in the main body of the account. In the 1479/80 account, the first entry under Arrearages (which is the balance b/f) is:

First they answer for £4. 7s. 9½d. Item they answer for a ring of silver.
    Sum thereof: £4. 7s. 9½d. and a ring. (Hanham 1970: 1)

There is no further mention of this ring in the account. The 1482/3 account (which is the next one printed) has only money in the arrearages but the foot of the account reads:

And so remains clear—£7. 3s. 10½d. which we delivered William Erle, Henry Hoper, Thomas Wylke and John Coche, wardens elect for the year following. And there remains likewise in lead—49 lbs. And in tin—17½ lbs. And in ocre—8 lbs. And there remains 3s. 4d. in the hands of Thomas Dorset for the grave of Cecila Dolbear lately wife of William Dolbear. And there remains in the hands of the said wardens 1 silver spoon, 1 plater and 1 cover. (Hanham 1970: 3)

The 1483/4 account includes a 'silver spoon' with the money amounts of receipts; and the foot of the account includes only 'a silver spoon, a plate and a cover' (p. 4).

This is very typical of the entries for physical inventories. The movement of inventories is not traceable through the accounts and the opening and closing items are not reconcilable. Indeed, from 1485/6 the inventory is not included in the feet of the accounts, only in the arrearages of the new accounts.

The 1509/10 account put 'valuations' on the inventory: 'Arrearages £8. 18s. 8d, 2½oz. of silver worth 7s. 11d. and 14s. in wax.' Physical inventories were regular entries until 1557/8, when the accounts reverted to being entirely cash-based.

Churchwardens' accounts present a picture of the warden or wardens being held accountable for receipts and payments and also by implication being responsible for the actual collection and payments out of money. In the Ashburton accounts, however, there is revealed a network of other officers who themselves collected and paid out money, who sometimes paid money over to the wardens, and whose balances were accounted for in the wardens' accounts. The 1517/18 accounts are a particularly elaborate example.

There remains little else to say about these sets of accounts which will add to the general description provided above. There is, however, one incident which is worth recounting.

In 1816, in Bodicote, one of the churchwardens, called Hadland (at this time each warden submitted separate accounts), dabbled with double-entry bookkeeping. Instead of the entries running down the consecutive pages, as in the past, the payments appeared on the left-hand folio and the receipts on the right-hand. The left-hand side was headed, 'Dr. Chas. Hadlands Acct 1816' and the right-hand side, 'Churchwarden (pr Contra) Credit' (Fearon 1975: 116). It is an editor's note which tells us that these appear opposite one another in the original (p. 116). Most of the payments entries are prefaced by 'To' and two of the receipts are prefaced by 'By'. This practice had actually crept into the 1809/10 accounts (of a different warden), though not to the same extent.

Other than this change of form, the account is much as it was previously. The two sides were totalled thus:

$$\begin{array}{cc} \underline{20.\ 4.\ 2} & \underline{20.\ 5.\ 9\frac{1}{2}} \\ & \underline{20.\ 4.\ 2} \\ \text{In Hand} & 1.5\frac{1}{2}\ [sic] \end{array}$$

Hadland was warden until 1822 but did not repeat his foray into double entry, although he sporadically began his payments entries with the word 'To'.

One has an uneasy feeling that his debits and credits are the wrong way round; if the account is a cash account then of course they are. Did he really know he was putting together an income and expenditure account? If he did, this would support the view that the charge–discharge account was a modified income and expenditure account. Whether he knew what he was doing or not, presumably the experiment was abandoned because without the corresponding entries the change was purely cosmetic.

ACCOUNTING FOR THE BOROUGHS

The county and the parish may be older but it is the borough which has the romance. 'Borough' means 'walled town'. The 'burgesses' controlled the boroughs. The word 'bourgeoisie' comes from the same root. In terms of succeeding centuries, we might see the boroughs as pockets of resistance against feudalism and eventual victors over it. We might also see them as the manifestation of monopoly rights over local manufacture and trade. It is clear that they *were* the urban revolution in England, the revolution which has so transformed our lives.[5] The most significant development in their history was the granting of royal charters of incorporation. These represented hard-won and initially costly freedom from financial and judicial interference by the feudal lords. The earliest ones date from the middle of the fourteenth century (Weinbaum 1937: 47) but what is known as the classic age of incorporation came a century later. The essence of these corporations was then summarized in five characteristics: 'perpetual succession, power of suing and being sued as a whole and by the specific name of the corporation (e.g. mayor, aldermen and burgesses of this or that town), power to hold lands, a common seal and authority to issue by-laws' (Weinbaum 1937: 18). The chartered boroughs, the 'free' boroughs, had total control over the trading which took place within the city walls (and lack of it in the immediate environs). They had

---

[5] See e.g. Mumford (1966), particularly pp. 302–20.

their own courts and fines collected from offenders accrued to them, not to the Crown. They owned much of the land and buildings, extracted rents therefrom, and levied tolls on traders. They were run on behalf of the burgesses and a major objective was to control the town's manufacture and trade. Many were extremely wealthy. The poorer boroughs had been accustomed to levying rates on the burgesses. Cannan (1912: 18–20) cites the case of Ipswich in the second half of the fifteenth century where regular rates were made, accounts were drawn up of monies received, and burgesses who refused to pay were threatened with disenfranchisement. However, it was not in fact until the 1835 Municipal Corporations Act that general statutory authority was given for incorporated boroughs to levy rates, and even then the emphasis was on boroughs levying rates only if their other income was insufficient.

Within the free boroughs the Crown still had overall power. But the law of the land was administered by the boroughs themselves. The Church remained important: parishes were as ubiquitous within the walls as they were outside. Economic life was determined by the burgesses.

Over many years, these local monopolies became, some would say inevitably, inefficient, extravagant and corrupt—certainly in the eyes of the nineteenth-century reformers. The 1835 Act forced the management of these boroughs to be directly accountable to ratepayers (not until the twentieth century were they directly accountable to the inhabitants) but, at the same time, crucially, maintained and indeed reinforced their 'freedoms'. In important respects, and this applies directly to the accounting function, they remained separate from the rest of what came to be known as 'local government' (until 1972 that is). It is no exaggeration to say that the local government accounting profession came from boroughs.

In one small but significant sense the importance of boroughs has been recognized in accounting history: namely, the work of Miss D. M. Livock (1965 and 1966) on the city of Bristol. On the other hand, economic and local historians have been less concerned with borough accounts, so there are few good examples available of transcribed or translated accounts: the best two are for the boroughs of Hull (Horrox 1983) and Leicester (Chinnery 1967).

The financial affairs of boroughs were typically vested in the officer known as the chamberlain and it is the chamberlain's accounts which have most often survived. The office was usually held for a year or small number of years and, because the town was often in debt to the chamberlain, it was held by a wealthy burgess. The chamberlains' accounts of Hull (there were two chamberlains in each year) have been published for the years 1321/4 (one account) and 1464/5. These are interesting because of their antiquity, the former coinciding with the period discussed earlier in the context of Cheshire. In fact there is nothing otherwise exceptional about them. They are in the form of charge–discharge. They are the accounts of named individuals which record, below the head, receipts, payments, and a summary. They are in paragraph form and were originally written in Latin. Separate paragraphs were used for each category of receipt and payment and each was totalled. A total of all receipts was recorded. In the summary paragraph a total for payments was written and then the balance shown. As it happens, both accounts recorded amounts of money owing by the town to the chamberlains. The former account also details that the amount owed should be paid off at the rate of 20 marks per annum (which Horrox 1983: 24 calculates would have taken about eight years). Between the two accounts Hull was granted its charter of incorporation (1440) and whereas the former account had receipts mainly from taxes the latter records the rentals and lease payments from the newly acquired holdings. This changed the form of the chamberlains' account in one respect. One amount is shown for the 'rents and farms' as a receipt. But this was not in fact a cash receipt; it was the amount supposed to be collectable (Horrox 1983: 173 n. 47). Against this amount had to be set discharges because of 'decayed' payments. These were summarized in a paragraph at the end of the payments section and added into the total sum of 'payments, decays and diminutions' which was then deducted from total receipts to produce the balance of the account.

The Chamberlains' Accounts of the Borough of Leicester (Chinnery 1967) is an astonishing publication. It covers the period from 1689 to 1835. It reproduces in full the accounts for eight of those years (at approximately twenty-year intervals). It also produces summaries of the missing years, analysed over the paragraphs of account. We are told in the Introduction that these *were* the accounts of Leicester until 1835, when double-entry bookkeeping, among the other reforms, was introduced.

The accounts are in columnar form with pounds, shillings, and pence strictly segregated. After the head of the account, receipts are recorded and grouped into common items, then come payments similarly grouped. The curious thing about all the accounts is that there are no subtotals (either of groupings or of pages) and in fact the accounts for 1688/9 and 1708/9 are not summarized at all. The latter do record another group of items at the end called 'Supers', which we are told represent the decayed rents and lease payments. The 1729/30 account also lists 'Supers' and these are included in an overall summary which produces a balance due to the Corporation. In fact the summary records many adjustments to the basic entries. These suggest that the annual audit, which was held every year between March and May and consisted of the chamberlain accounting to a group of something like twenty-four Aldermen and Councilmen, did have an effect on the accounts (p. viii). One adjustment relates to an additional amount of £2 16s. 2d. being charged to the account because in the payments section was included an amount paid to 'Mr. Hart' overstated by that amount. There was also an adjustment for a single receipt which had been charged in two separate places.

These accounts are indeed astonishingly comprehensive. Their publication is justified in terms of their value to economic and local historians rather than to accounting historians. What they do clearly demonstrate however is the continuity of chamberlains' accounts over, in this case, 150 years.

Bristol Corporation is the only example known to the present author of the accounts of a borough having been examined in depth by an accounting historian *qua* accounting history.[6] D. M. Livock's researches in the early 1960s resulted in a paper in the *Journal of Accounting Research* called 'The Accounts of the Corporation of Bristol: 1532 to 1835' (1965) and a transcription of the accounts for 1557 and 1628 which was published by the Bristol Record Society (1966).

Perhaps the most important point to note about her work is that, as far as the accounting records were concerned, the period from 1532 to 1835 is better seen as two distinct periods; the years 1785/6 mark the change. Before 1785 the 'accounts' were primarily made up of the annual audits with which we are now familiar (they are referred to as 'Mayor's Audit'). Written up after the year end, the chamberlain's account was the written record of the chamberlain's incomings and outgoings as offered up to the common chamber. In 1786, though the change had been presaged as early as 1615, the 'accounts' became what Livock describes as 'a full double-entry form of accounts' (1965: 96) with cash books, journals, and a ledger. On the introduction of these accounts the annual audit was no longer written up, at least in the previous form. Instead, summaries were given in the journal and the ledger and it was these which were signed by the auditors.

The transcriptions of the chamberlains' accounts for 1557 and 1628 are examples of the written record of the annual audit and, in fact, are a combination of many elements that we have already seen in churchwardens' and others' accounts. Both sets have a written heading (the 1557 heading is in

---

[6] *Pace* Wren (1948 and 1949); valuable though these papers are (they incidentally confirm that the City of London used charge–discharge accounting in the 17th century) they are primarily concerned with economic history.

Latin) which identifies what follows as the account of a named officer of the city of Bristol for the year ended at the feast of St Michael. However, there is more than one 'account' for the year. Separate accounts, with separate headings and separate feet, are produced for the 'town lands' and for (three) other groups of lands.

The first section is the charge, the main group of which is made up of rentals of town lands. These are further divided into the (named) streets, bridges or areas where the properties are. Then comes the discharge. These are in chronological order classified into the four quarters with each divided into weeks. At the end of all the individual accounts is a summary. The balance between charge and discharge is recorded with the four signatures of the auditors. These accounts are not simply receipts and payments. In the first place, the entry for each rental is the amount that would be due assuming each property to be occupied. For some pages, where the property is empty the abbreviation 'vac' is written to the left of the entry. There are three subtotals for each page:

> Sum of all amounts;
> Sum of the ones not occupied (may or may not be marked 'vac');
> Balance (marked 'Rest clere').

In other words, the individual items are the charges, while the subtotal for the page in effect discharges the chamberlain of the rents not due because of voids. It is the balances (marked 'Rest clere') which are carried forward to the overall summary.

This form also suggests that the balances called 'Rest clere' are not subtotals of receipts: some of the rents due from occupied houses must have remained in arrears on some occasions, in which case the balances would include accrued rents. Livock (1965: 90) confirms this. She tells us that it was only when an individual chamberlain went from office that the arrears of rent were explicitly identified. In other years rents included arrears of rent, as did the balance of the account as a whole. That there were arrears was the chamberlain's problem, not the city's. But this would be inequitable for a new chamberlain (in Bristol, chamberlains held office for more than one year). Consequently, a calculation of the total arrears was made to divide the balance from the foot of the outgoing chamberlain's account into cash and arrears. The new chamberlain thus became responsible for the old one's uncollected rent although presumably the fact that it had been identified as having originally resulted from previous office-holders' actions was equitable enough.

There is no obvious suggestion that these accounts otherwise included any accruals of either receipts or payments. As late as 1780 Livock (1965: 95) is able to say that 'if the total arrears of rent are deducted from the amount said to be due from the chamberlain the result is the balance as shown by the cash book'.

If the foregoing suffices as a summary of the formal accounts of the chamberlain up to 1786, it does not describe the accounts of the city which were kept. It is not surprising to find, particularly in view of the number of entries which were recorded in the Mayor's Audit, that there were subsidiary records. We know from Livock that these included rent books, day books, books of loan transactions and cash books.

Details of why a double-entry bookkeeping system was instituted in 1785 and whose expertise was used are not available. What is particularly interesting about the accounts is the form of the final accounts. First, a balance sheet was not produced although with one exception it could easily have been: the exception relates to the personal accounts, which were not balanced annually. The movement on the capital account over the year was explained in terms of 'Receipts' and 'Expenditure'. Second, an amount was brought into this capital account representing the capitalized value of rentals and lease payments of properties owned by the city. This practice lasted until 1817, when the surveyors recommended these valuations be written out because they were 'merely visionary' (Livock 1965: 99). The effect of the write-out was to reduce the capital stock from £174544 3s. 6¾d. to £11738 13s. 8¼d.[7]

The reform of Bristol in 1835 saw some changes reflected in the accounts, though they were relatively minor. In common with many other boroughs the office of chamberlain was replaced by that of the 'Treasurer'.[8] However, the new treasurer was the same man as the old chamberlain (Ralph n.d.: 30). Another change was that the audit certificate appeared now in the Cash Book. The folio for August 1836 had a certificate relating to the period 1 March to 31 August 1836 which states that the two 'Auditors of the Borough' and the 'auditor appointed by the Mayor' have audited the account of the sums of money received and paid by Thomas Garrard, Esq. (the Treasurer), 'and we find them to be correct'.

---

[7] Additional details not provided by Livock were gleaned from the archives by the present author.

[8] This was because the 1835 Municipal Corporations Act used the word 'Treasurer' rather than 'Chamberlain'. It is not clear if there was political significance in this. The Chamberlain of the City of London, which office was the model for Bristol, still exists; the city of Plymouth also still has a 'City Treasurer and Chamberlain'.

THE ACCOUNTS OF COUNTY TREASURERS

There are two obvious lacunae in our discussion of the early development of 'local government' accounting. The first relates to the *ad hoc* local authority, what the Webbs (1922) call 'Statutory Authorities for Special Purposes', which played such an important role in the eighteenth century. In addition to being guardians of the poor, they were concerned with turnpikes, paving, lighting, cleaning, and watching the streets. Perhaps not surprisingly, the accounts of these many authorities[9] have not been published, if they are still available. The turnpike trusts, for example, were originally subject to detailed control by the justices of the peace but from the middle of the eighteenth century 'no new provisions were inserted (in their originating Acts) requiring the Trustees to account for their receipts and expenditure to any public authority' (Webbs 1922: 165).

The second gap in our discussion relates to the county level after the Middle Ages, when the justices of the peace took over from the sheriffs as the judicial representatives of the Crown. The important development as far as they are concerned was the gradual imposition of civil duties in addition to their judicial ones. Henry VIII gave them overall responsibility for the financial affairs of bridge building and maintenance in 1530 (22 Hen VIII, c. 5) and Elizabeth I added some responsibilities for poor relief in 1572 (14 Eliz. I, c. 5) and, more significantly, in 1601 with the Poor Law. This included the provision that the justices should elect treasurers who would collect money for the relief of the prisoners in the King's Bench and Marshalsea Prisons.

Whereas the 1601 Act significantly increased the civil duties of the justices and introduced the notion of a County Treasurer, it was a 1739 Act (12 Geo. II, c. 29) which created the office of County Treasurer uniformly throughout the country. The Act also brought together all the separate county rates which had developed over the years into one rate levied by the justices. Section VII required that:

the said respective treasurer or treasurers shall and are hereby required to keep books of entries of the several sums respectively received and paid by him or them in pursuance of this Act; and is also hereby required to deliver in true and exact accounts upon oath if required . . . of all and every sum and sums of money respectively received and paid by him or them, distinguishing the particular uses to which such

---

[9] The Webbs say that there were something like 1,800 of them collecting in total £3m. gross by 1835 (1922: 2).

sum or sums of money have been applied . . . and shall lay before the justices at such sessions the proper vouchers for the same.

This requirement for audit had particular force, at least in theory, because section X also required that no new rates could be made 'until it shall appear to the said justices . . . by the accounts of their respective treasurer or treasurers or otherwise, that three fourths of the money collected by virtue of the preceding rate have been expended for the uses and purposes aforesaid'. It is perhaps difficult to imagine how one would 'otherwise' know that three-quarters of the rates had been spent but it was not an unwise precaution for the drafter of the Act to take in view of subsequent problems in obtaining accounts at all from some of these treasurers.[10] The 1739 Act remained in force until 1888, when county government lost its judicial function, in effect becoming the branch of local government we recognize today.

The accounts of the County Treasurers have not been published but there are some useful articles which have been written about the office and which include consideration of archival material.[11] What these do suggest is that charge–discharge accounting was employed, although at the end of the eighteenth and the beginning of the nineteenth century there are suggestions of double-entry bookkeeping being introduced in some areas. What is also interesting is that three of these papers point to financial difficulties which led to treasurers being relieved of office and/or new systems of accounting being introduced, all during the decade of the 1780s. In Middlesex in 1782 the Bench concluded that 'the present method of auditing . . . is not such as affords that satisfaction which is required in matters of account' (Staff of the Middlesex County Record Office 1952: 277) and the treasurer was instructed 'to keep his accounts by double-entry, classed under distinct heads showing debits and credits' (p. 278). During Michaelmas 1780, in Warwickshire, 'the financial storm broke' and the treasurer was discharged from office because of 'neglect of duty' (Hughes 1955: 95). And in Glamorgan, at the Easter Session of 1786, the treasurer was 'discharged from that office he having neglected to settle his accounts' (Elsas 1957: 260). Nor was this confined to the counties. In July 1789 Liverpool suspended and later dismissed their treasurer for improper conduct. The books were then 'required to be balanced monthly and laid before the Council at each meeting' (Chandler 1954: 155). Recall also that it was 1785 when Bristol first intro-

---

[10] See for one example Staff of the Middlesex County Record Office (1952).

[11] Cornwall (1955–9) is the best example. See also France (1952), Staff of the Middlesex County Record Office (1952), Walne (1954), Hughes (1955), Steer (1955), and Elsas (1957).

duced double-entry bookkeeping, including balance sheet valuations of capital assets.

Though the connection has not, to this writer's knowledge, been made before, these events seem to be a natural part of the movement for 'Economical Reform' which was born in the 1780s but which was more directly concerned with central government. As Roseveare (1969) puts it:

the winter of 1779/80 saw the beginning of a movement which was . . . to introduce into public life a new morality, into finance a new probity and into government as a whole new standards of efficiency and economy. (p. 118)

At the centre the most obvious manifestation of this movement was the establishment of a Commission for Examining, Taking and Stating the Public Accounts which reported first in November 1780 and issued its last report in December 1786. Binney (1958) discusses this period in considerable detail but there is no suggestion that it had any direct effect on government in the localities. Neither does there seem to have been a significant role for double-entry bookkeeping. Binney tells us that it had already been in use by the Treasury (but not the pipe rolls or the spending departments) since the revolution in 1688 and it was not until the nineteenth century that it was adopted universally in central government (Roseveare 1969: 138).

The decades around the end of the eighteenth century also saw increasing demands for accounts of local government to be published, which can again be seen as part of the 'Economical Reform' programme. Indeed, one of its acknowledged founders, Lord Shelburne, said:

It has been found by experience that this is the grand principle of economy and the only method of preventing abuses; far better than oaths or any other checks which have been devised. Instead, therefore, of oaths there should be an obligation to *print* at the end of the year every expenditure and every contract, except in the cases of Secret Service, which may be subject to checks of another nature. (quoted in Binney 1958: 268)

The statutory requirement of published accounts for local authorities came with the County Rates Act 1815. The first published abstract of accounts for the County of Buckinghamshire for 1816/17, for example, was a one-page account, receipts on the left-hand side, payments on the right, with a statement by the auditors that the accounts themselves 'were verified upon the oath' of the treasurer and were 'examined and allowed by us'. In common with many other examples, the 1815 Act did not introduce abstracts of accounts nor even their publication but it did introduce a uniform requirement to publish. Halcrow (1953) tells us that it was at this time that pressure was brought to bear on the borough of Newcastle to publish their accounts, and Chandler (1954: 155) says that Liverpool's accounts were published in 1815 after years of agitation, when the Mayor arranged for the accounts from 1797 to 1816 to be published. Thus, although there was undoubtedly concerted effort throughout the country at the turn of the eighteenth century for the accounts of boroughs and counties to be published, the statutory result was applied first of all to the counties.[12] It was not until the 1835 Municipal Corporations Act, after years of inquiry into the finances of boroughs, that the same requirement was forced on incorporated boroughs.

SYNTHESIS

The foregoing, while it does not purport to be a comprehensive history, does suggest that what we are dealing with is a homogeneous set of accounts. Each authority's accounts are remarkably consistent and, more importantly, are, at least in terms of fundamentals, remarkably comparable. The author has examined many other fragments of published accounts and there is nothing in them of importance which contradicts the following synthesis.

All the authorities used charge and discharge accounting (although some, including the pipe rolls themselves, do not adopt this terminology). They are all accounts of people, not of organizations. Even in the incorporated boroughs, the accounts are those of the chamberlain, not of the legal fiction. They are the accounts of a steward addressed to a higher authority. 'Accounting' by the steward and 'auditing' by the higher authority took place simultaneously and were bound up with each other. The auditors would typically assume that the recurrent income would be a part of the steward's account. The steward would 'account' for any differences and any non-recurrent items. A clerk would record the results of these exchanges, for a fee. It is the clerk's record of the proceedings which is available and which we have primarily been discussing.

In the Exchequer, the account was heard twice a year (primarily so that cash could be collected on account—the 'profer'); in the local authorities,

---

[12] Is it purely coincidental that the surveyors in Bristol recommended in 1817 that valuations of rental and lease agreements of corporate land be written out of the accounts, as being merely visionary? The County Rates Act did not in fact apply to the incorporated boroughs, even though Bristol was a county as well as a borough. It would be surprising however if Bristol were immune from the non-statutory pressure that was applied to Newcastle and Liverpool, major ports all. The selling off of corporate lands to members of the councils was undoubtedly an issue at this time—so much so that the only central government control introduced by the 1835 Act was the requirement that any alienation of real estate was to be approved by the Treasury, under s. 94.

generally once a year. Obviously, 'accounting' was not a continuous or even a frequent provision of financial information. The event required that the steward turn up. For the Exchequer, it was a matter of law: he was summonsed. In the small parishes there was presumably little difficulty in obtaining the churchwarden in the normal run of events. In the counties in the eighteenth century it was common for the steward to give surety on taking up the post which provided some incentive to turn up at the court (though it was obviously not too successful in some counties during the 1780s). The proceedings were, particularly at the Exchequer, highly formal, combative, ritualistic and even mystical. They were equivalent to, if not the same as, courts of law.[13] It seems unlikely that the same ritual, to the same extent, took place at the local level. It was very common for the audit to take place in a public house and the accounts themselves often include items for ale and wine at the audit. For the parishes and the counties the hearing of accounts by the justices was by definition a legal event.

As for the form and content of the accounts themselves, the emphasis is on the charge rather than the discharge. The former is almost invariably recorded first, takes up more of the account and is classified more consistently and in more detail. There are many examples of the desire for the account to separate the cash position out from the debtors position. The 'Cheshire method', which dates from the middle of the fourteenth century, could handle this, at least where the number of entries was manageable, but it was not adopted in later accounts. Individual stewards down the years confronted the problem of debtors in an *ad hoc* way, usually as a memorandum and without much success.

The charge–discharge accounts were nowhere concerned with separating out the revenue position from capital. They were also generally concerned with cash and debtors. Some dabbled with inventories but in effect only as memoranda and, on the face of it, without much conviction.

The subclassification of the charge and discharge had always been a matter to which some attention had been given. Once it had been agreed upon it remained consistent for many years. In some cases this did reflect management considerations. The recurrent receipts were usually dealt with in a stereotyped way, as one might expect rentals and lease payments from property to be. Management which took as its starting-point 'what happened last year?' is reflected in these accounts. A significant and non-trivial explanation for why the accounts of a given year are the way they are is because they were that way the previous year.

---

[13] One reason why the ancient course of the exchequer survived into the 19th century was that it was hidebound in law.

The whole thrust of the charge–discharge account was that even before the account was heard the steward was in debt to the higher authority. The burden of proof that the actual position was otherwise fell on the steward. This was undoubtedly true at the Exchequer: as the *Dialogus de Scaccario* (Johnson 1950: 78–9) puts it, '[a]ll the Sheriffs and Bailiffs, then, to whom the Sommonses are addressed, are bound by the same legal compulsion (that is by the authority of the King's order), to wit that they must assemble on the day named, at the place appointed, and answer for their debts'. It has been suggested that what double-entry bookkeeping was to capitalism so charge–discharge accounting was to feudalism (Bailey 1984: 28). It did develop in England in the context of feudalism and the burden was on the steward. However, one must be careful not to emphasize this one-sidedness too much.[14] The sheriff typically held a fee farm and it was often the fixed payments due under this that were accounted for at the Exchequer. For the Crown, the benefit of this system was that a fixed return could be relied on from Crown lands. This left the risk but also the flexibility (to collect more than was strictly due) to the sheriff. The crucial part of the deal, from the Crown's point of view, is no risk. In that context, any suggestion that this fixed income was not forthcoming was likely to be treated with some scorn. Feudal the context may have been but the one-sidedness of the account had some justification.

From the Webbs' point of view (1922: 355–65), government of the localities before 1835 could be characterized by the principle of the 'obligation to serve'. The obligations in a particular kind of authority arose in different ways but however they arose the Webbs tell us 'they included, not merely a duty to obey, but also a direct *charge* on the will to act. They involved not only personal responsibility to a superior, but also such power over other persons as was incidental to the due performance of the public service. Thus, however men might differ in faculties and desires, or in status and fortune, they were all under obligations to serve in one way or another' (p. 355–6, emphasis added). The account charge and discharge admirably suited the purpose of discharging the steward's obligations. It seems important, particularly in the context of close corporations,[15] to emphasize, as the Webbs did in general terms, that the obligation of the chamberlain to serve was onerous. It is difficult to see that it was as onerous a relationship as that of a parish churchwarden towards the vestry and the justices. Nevertheless, however

---

[14] Binney (1958: 244) suggests an analogy between this and single-entry bookkeeping's 'one-sidedness'—and contrasts it with double entry's two sides.

[15] Both Leicester and Bristol were examples: Webbs (1908: 443–81).

wealthy the chamberlain was, there still was an obligation to serve seen in the accounts.[16]

Our conclusions would be then that charge–discharge accounting was determined by its originally feudal context but that it persisted down the years and pervaded the economy as a written manifestation of the 'obligation to serve' imposed by governments of the locality on inhabitants.

An expert, professional bureaucracy was a nineteenth-century development, but it would be too glib to say that the abandonment of the 'obligation to serve' caused the adoption of double entry. The question of why double entry superseded other methods is addressed in the commercial context by Yamey (1956). He identifies three main advantages. The first two are uncontroversial: namely, that it is a 'more comprehensive and orderly' approach and its 'duality' provides a check on accuracy and completeness (p. 7). As local authorities' financial transactions grew these must have been significant advantages: charge–discharge emphasizes the final account at the expense of the individual transactions which make it up; double entry emphasizes each individual transaction. This is nowhere more clearly seen than in Bristol (in the eighteenth century second in importance only to London), where the charge–discharge account increasingly demanded subsidiary books of account to the point where these needed to be linked in a structured way. The third main advantage Yamey identifies is that under double entry the ledger 'contains the material for developing, as part of the system, statements of profit-and-loss and of capital, assets and liabilities' (p. 7). In the commercial context, Yamey's concern is with whether these statements were a by-product of double entry's first two advantages; or whether they were central in the context of the Sombartian thesis linking double entry with capitalism. In the context of the foregoing, we would want to lend support to Yamey's preference for the former view. As Baxter (1980) explains, income and capital could be calculated within the charge–discharge account. In our discussion what is missing from charge–discharge is not the impersonal accounts but the real accounts and more importantly the personal accounts. The 'Cheshire method' dating from the fourteenth century could handle the summary of personal accounts to give the total debtors figure but it did not provide the records required for a day-to-day control of debtors (or for that matter of cash, although the physical contents of the chest obviated the need for this).

When Bristol introduced double entry in 1785 we know that it was accompanied by the introduction of capital valuations of rental and lease

---

[16] Horrox (1983: 22) says that in Hull 'as elsewhere' holding the office of chamberlain was treated as a prerequisite to higher office in order to provide encouragement to take the job.

agreements and a statement showing the movement of funds over the year. Bristol was one of the wealthy boroughs and without difficulty could be classified as a capitalist body. Whether economic measures of income and wealth motivated the reform is only a matter for speculation; it is certain that these valuations were relatively quickly dispensed with.

In 1867, when parishes were for the first time uniformly required to adopt a double-entry system, an accompanying letter from the Poor Law Board explained that ratepayers had not received full information about their finances by publishing only a 'receipts and expenditure' statement (which meant receipts and payments). The problem was as the Board saw it that 'they had no information as to the amount of outstanding liabilities' (Poor Law Board 1866–7: 125).

Of course, the stewardship role of double-entry is much more easy to accept in local authorities (outside the wealthy boroughs) than it is in companies. Nevertheless, there is nothing in this review of accounting in the government of localities which suggests anything other than that double entry was a better stewardship model than charge–discharge when organizations carried out a substantial number of financial transactions involving debtors and creditors. As Baxter (1950: 32) once observed, 'the first and most fundamental reason for keeping accounts is to aid in remembering what we have trusted to our debtors'. Charge–discharge accounting did precisely that, since the steward was a debtor to the higher authority; but it was of limited use to the stewards themselves as their own credit transactions grew. Double entry solved that problem and was able to provide the necessary final accounts to render the charge–discharge account redundant. If its benefits exceeded the costs of acquiring the additional bookkeeping skills, how could it lose? Given time, it could not.

References

Bailey, Derek T. (1984), 'Towards a Marxian Theory of Accounting', *British Accounting Review* (Autumn): 21–41.

Baxter, W. T. (1950), 'Credit, Bills and Bookkeeping in a Simple Economy', in W. T. Baxter (ed.), *Studies in Accounting* (London: Sweet & Maxwell), 31–48.

——(1980), 'The Account Charge and Discharge', *Accounting Historians Journal* (Spring): 69–71.

Binney, J. E. D. (1958), *British Public Finance and Administration 1774–92* (Oxford: Clarendon Press).

Blair, J. (1939), *A List of Churchwardens' Accounts* (Ann Arbor, Mich.).

Booth, P. H. W. (1981), *The Financial Administration of the Lordship and County of Chester 1272–1377* (Manchester: Manchester University Press for the Chetham Society).

Boyd, Edward (1905), 'Early Forms of Account', in Richard Brown (ed.), *A History of Accounting and Accountants* (Edinburgh: Jack).

Cannan, Edwin (1912), *The History of Local Rates in England*. 2nd edn. (London: P. S. King & Son).

Chandler, George (1954), 'Mr. Treasurer—Liverpool', *Local Government Finance* (July): 153–6.

Chatfield, Michael (1977), *A History of Accounting Thought*, rev. edn. (New York: Robert Krieger).

Chinnery, G. A. (1967) (ed.), *The Chamberlains' Accounts 1688–1835*, vi: *Records of the Borough of Leicester* (Leicester: Leicester University Press).

Cornwall, Julian C. K. (1955–9), 'The Archives of the Treasurers of Buckinghamshire before 1889', *Journal of the Society of Archivists*, I: 70–4.

Cox, J. Charles (1913), *Churchwardens' Accounts: from the Fourteenth Century to the Close of the Seventeenth Century* (London: Methuen).

Elsas, M. (1957), 'Mr. Treasurer, Glamorgan—before 1889', *Local Government Finance* (Nov.): 260–4.

Fearon, J. H. (1975), *Parish Accounts for the 'Town' of Bodicote, Oxfordshire 1700–1822* (Banbury: Banbury Historical Society 12).

France, R. Sharpe (1952), 'Mr. Treasurer—Lancashire before 1889', *Local Government Finance* (July): 153–6.

Halcrow, Elizabeth (1953), 'Mr. Treasurer—Newcastle upon Tyne before 1835', *Local Government Finance* (July): 151–3; (Sept.): 200–2.

Hanham, Alison (1970), *Churchwardens' Accounts of Ashburton, 1479–1580* (Devon and Cornwall Record Society, NS 15).

Harvey, P. D. A. (1976) (ed.), *Manorial Records of Cuxham, Oxfordshire, circa 1200–1359* (London: HMSO for Historical Manuscripts Commission).

Horrox, Rosemary (1983) (ed.), *Selected Rentals and Accounts of Medieval Hull, 1293–1528*, Yorkshire Archaeological Society, Record Series, CXLI, 1981.

Hughes, C. J. (1955), 'Mr. Treasurer—Warwickshire before 1889', *Local Government Finance* (Feb.): 38–40; (Apr.): 95–8.

Johnson, Charles (1950) (ed.), *Dialogus de Scaccario* (The Course of the Exchequer) (London: Nelson).

Kitto, J. V. (1901), *St. Martin-in-the-Fields: The Accounts of the Churchwardens, 1525–1603* (London: Simpkin, Marshall, Kent, Hamilton, & Co.)

Littleton, A. C., and Yamey, B. S. (1956) (eds.), *Studies in the History of Accounting* (London: Sweet & Maxwell).

Livock, D. M. (1965), 'The Accounts of the Corporation of Bristol 1532–1835', *Journal of Accounting Research* (Spring): 86–102.

——(1966) (ed.), *City Chamberlains' Accounts in the Sixteenth and Seventeenth Centuries* (Bristol: Bristol Record Society's Publications XXIV).

Mumford, Lewis (1966), *The City in History* (Harmondsworth: Pelican).

Oschinsky, Dorothea (1971), *Walter of Henley: And Other Treaties on Estate Management and Accounting* (Oxford: Clarendon Press).

Pipe Roll Society (1884), *Introduction to the Study of the Pipe Rolls* (London: Pipe Roll Society III).

Poor Law Board (1866–7), Appendix to *19th Annual Report 1866–67*.

Ralph, Elizabeth (n.d.), *Government of Bristol 1373–1973* (Bristol: Corporation of Bristol).

Roseveare, Henry (1969), *The Treasury: The Evolution of a British Institution* (London: Penguin Press).

Savage, Richard (transcriber) (n.d.), *The Churchwardens' Accounts of the Parish of St. Nicholas, Warwick 1547–1621* (Warwick: Henry Cooke & Son).

Staff of the Middlesex County Record Office (1952), 'Mr. Treasurer—Middlesex—before 1889', *Local Government Finance* (Dec.): 276–82.

Steer, Francis W. (1955), 'Mr. Treasurer—Sussex', *Local Government Finance* (Nov.): 267–71.

Stewart-Brown, R. (1938), *Cheshire in the Pipe Rolls 1158–1301*, Record Society of Lancashire and Cheshire 92.

Tate, William Edward (1969), *The Parish Chest: A Study of the Records of Parochial Administration in England*, 3rd edn. (Cambridge: Cambridge University Press).

Walne, Peter (1954), 'Mr. Treasurer—Berkshire', *Local Government Finance* (Apr.): 88–91.

Webb, Sidney and Beatrice (1908), *English Local Government: The Manor and the Borough*, parts I and II (London: Longmans, Green & Co.).

——(1922), *English Local Government: Statutory Authorities for Special Purposes* (London: Longman, Green & Co.).

——(1963), *English Local Government: The Parish and the County* (London: Cass & Co.).

Weinbaum, Martin (1937), *The Incorporation of the Boroughs* (Manchester: Manchester University Press).

Whiting, C. E. (1938) (ed.), *The Accounts of the Churchwardens, Constables, Overseers of the Poor and Overseers of the Highways of the Parish of Hooton Pagnell, 1767–1820*, Yorkshire Archaeological Society, Record Series XCVII.

Wren, Melvin C. (1948), 'The Chamber of London in 1633', *Economic History Review*, 2nd ser. I: 46–53.

——(1949) 'The Chamber of the City of London', *Accounting Review*, 24: 191–8.

Yamey, B. S. (1956), 'Introduction', in Littleton and Yamey (1956).

POSTSCRIPT

This chapter was originally written as part of my Ph.D. thesis, submitted to the University of Lancaster and published as *The History of the Financial Control Function of Local Government Accounting in the UK* (New York: Garland Press, 1992). The primary purpose of the thesis was, however, to understand the accounting model adopted by local authorities at the time I was writing. My knowledge to that date had suggested that the answers to many of the important questions lay in the distant past: hence the emphasis on accounting history. Also, I was (and for that matter remain) keen that public sector accounting should not become compartmentalized: it was important to me to understand how this subset of accounting fits into accounting as a whole.

Although I was writing a thesis, from the beginning I had an open-ended commitment to write the necessary history. Had this needed too much time, given the constraints of doctoral work, I would simply have narrowed the focus. But it was strikingly true of the approximately 500-year period covered by this chapter that, whereas I began its research with a seemingly endless stream of opportunities, diminishing returns rapidly set in. There seemed remarkable consistency in the accounting, over time and between different authorities: I had wanted to call this 'clerical consistency' (with the additional attraction of the pun in the context of parishes) and now I cannot remember why I did not. Although I accept that it may have been a failure of imagination on my part, the effect of this clerical consistency was, over the period before the nineteenth-century reforms, that I only had this one chapter to write.

COST AND MANAGEMENT
ACCOUNTING

15 · THE DEVELOPMENT OF INDUSTRIAL COST AND MANAGEMENT ACCOUNTING BEFORE 1850

J. R. Edwards and E. Newell

The application of accounting techniques in business management continues to be a largely unexplored area of business history.[1] This is not to suggest that there is any lack of comment on the subject in the literature, but rather that many inferences and conclusions drawn so far have been based on limited evidence. For instance, it is generally held that cost accounting—the principal device of management accounting—was adopted relatively late by British industries. It is argued that little interest was shown in the analysis of costs for the purpose of making decisions about levels and methods of production, or for the pricing of products, until the arrival of 'scientific management' at the end of the nineteenth century. There was certainly an absence of technical cost accounting literature until then; the first practical handbook in English on the subject was not published until 1887, for instance.[2] But it is by no means clear that this reflects a corresponding lack of interest in costing on the part of businessmen. Given the nature of the changes which took place in British industries in the eighteenth and nineteenth centuries, the notion that industrial costing procedures developed on a significant scale only from the end of the nineteenth century is surprising and seems inconsistent with the persuasive 'demand/response' theory of accounting development, which sees accounting as a 'social technology' continually responding to changes in business requirements. Yet this view of stagnation until the late nineteenth century persists in the literature.[3]

First published in *Business History* (1991).

[1] The authors wish to thank Charles Feinstein and an anonymous referee for their comments on earlier versions of this chapter. For further discussion of certain aspects covered here see J. R. Edwards, 'Industrial Cost Accounting Developments in Britain to 1830: A Review Article', *Accounting and Business Research*, 19 (1989).

[2] E. Garcke and J. M. Fells, *Factory Accounts: Their Principles and Practice* (London, 1887).

[3] Most recently, E. Jones, *Accountancy and the British Economy, 1840–1980: The Evolution of Ernst and Whinney* (London, 1981), 111–16; R. S. Kaplan, 'The Evolution of Management Accounting', *Accounting Review*, 59 (1984).

The purpose of this essay is to demonstrate that a growing body of evidence, produced mainly by specialist accounting historians, sheds new light on the development of cost and management accounting before 1850. The results of these studies are of importance to business historians concerned with the development of management practices. In particular, it is now possible to reassess a number of issues raised in Pollard's pioneering work *The Genesis of Modern Management*, which remains the only general study in this field written specifically for economic historians.[4] Recent findings reinforce Pollard's view of the relative sophistication of 'partial costing' and *ex ante* cost estimation to the extent that it can now be shown that cost and management accounting techniques previously supposed to date from the late nineteenth or early twentieth century were used in metal and other industries up to three hundred years earlier. It is suggested, however, that in the light of new evidence Pollard's conclusion that 'The practice of using accounts as direct aids to management was not one of the achievements of the industrial revolution . . . it does not even belong to the later nineteenth century, but to the twentieth'[5] is unduly pessimistic. It is shown that a number of firms operated advanced 'total' cost accounting systems much earlier than he supposed, and it is argued that greater use was made of *ad hoc* costings and estimates in guiding management decisions before 1850 than he suggests.

This essay is in three sections. In part I the established views of the development of cost and management accounting are examined; in part II the techniques of cost and management accounting are described; and in parts III to VI the results of recent research are assessed in relation to the established views.

I

Solomons undertook the first thorough examination of the development of cost accounting, and identified the year 1875 as being of particular importance.[6] From the early fourteenth century until 1875, he argues, major cost accounting developments dealt with the bringing of records of industrial activity within the double-entry framework of bookkeeping and the devising of means of tracking internal transfers of goods from one process of manu-

---

[4] S. Pollard, *The Genesis of Modern Management: A Study of the Industrial Revolution in Great Britain* (London, 1965).

[5] Ibid. 248.

[6] D. Solomons, 'The Historical Development of Costing', in D. Solomons (ed.), *Studies in Cost Analysis* (2nd edn., London, 1968).

facture to another. After 1875, the broader issue of using accounting to provide information for managerial decision-making is given greater stress, and in this respect Solomons refers to the 1880s and 1890s as witnessing a 'costing renaissance'. His explanation for the lack of progress in cost accounting before then is that, in the absence of keen competition, prices could be set at levels which produced generous profit margins, and therefore the need for detailed costing data was not strongly felt by industrialists.

An alternative explanation has been put forward by Garner, who argues that the initial impetus for the development of cost accounting was the replacement of domestic production by more capital intensive factory-based methods. In Garner's view, it was the growth in the scale of centralized production which promoted cost-consciousness. Large production units generated high costs which were not easy to measure. Under such conditions the potential for inefficient use of resources and loss-making was increased, and this provided a strong incentive for managers to introduce accounting systems which gave them greater information about, and control over, costs.[7] Plausible as it is, this explanation only makes the delay in the use of cost accounting even more puzzling: it implies that industry had to attain some critical level of centralization before cost accounting became necessary, and that this was not reached until the end of the nineteenth century.

The conclusions reached in both works suffer from the fact that at the time of writing there was a dearth of published material available describing cost accounting practices before the late nineteenth century. Pollard subsequently drew upon a large volume of archival material which demonstrates a high degree of cost-consciousness on the part of entrepreneurs from the eighteenth century. Nevertheless, he too is drawn to the conclusion that 'accountancy in its wider sense was used only minimally to guide businessmen in their business decisions, and where it was so used the guidance was often unreliable'.[8]

Important contributions to this field have since been made, and of the new evidence, studies by Stone and Johnson have demonstrated that fully integrated cost and financial accounting systems were in operation at the Charlton cotton mills (Manchester) and Lyman mills (Boston, Massachusetts) in 1810 and 1854 respectively.[9] In surveying these findings, Johnson has echoed Garner in arguing that it was the change in the

---

[7] S. P. Garner, *Evolution of Cost Accounting*, (University, Ala., 1954), ch. 2.

[8] Pollard, *Genesis of Modern Management*, 245.

[9] W. E. Stone, 'An Early English Cost Accounting System: Charlton Mills, 1810–1889', *Accounting and Business Research*, 4 (1973); H. T. Johnson, 'Early Cost Accounting for Internal Management Control: Lyman Mills in the 1850s', *Business History Review*, 46 (1972).

organizational structure of business activity from the domestic system to factory production which provided the principal stimulus for the development of cost accounting, though he places the crucial period of change in the eighteenth century.[10]

Prior to 1780, Johnson argues, much industrial activity took place within the domestic system, and comprised a fairly simple series of market transactions. The businessmen purchased materials which were then 'put out' to a variety of artisans for each to perform a particular processing function paid for on a piece rate basis. At each stage of manufacture the businessman needed very little by way of accounting information to decide which course of action was preferable, such as whether to process further or to sell a good: he could readily calculate the costs of production from material input costs together with the piece rates paid to labour, and he knew the market prices of the good he produced and so could easily estimate the relative profitability of various options. Furthermore, under the piece rate system, productivity was linked directly to costs: if labour productivity changed, output changed, and so did the wage bill, all in proportion to each other. By switching to factory production and wage labour this direction relationship between labour costs and production broke down: wages were no longer determined by output, and it was now necessary for the employer to manage labour productivity in order to control costs. It was to achieve this, Johnson claims, that industrial cost accounting evolved, and it was made possible, he argues, because of the relative simplicity of industrial organization. Since firms tended to produce single products rather than a range of goods, basic cost accounting techniques were easily implemented while complicated accounting systems to apportion costs to different goods were not required. It is, therefore, within what Johnson describes as the 'single activity organization' which flourished between 1780 and 1900, that the internalization of employment and manufacturing processes gave rise to the need for the development of cost and profit finding techniques as the basis for both performance assessment and resource allocation decisions.[11]

Johnson's findings suffer from the general problem that hitherto much of the attention devoted to the impact of industrialization on accounting developments has focused on the textile industries. Indeed, Mepham has stated that there are grounds 'for believing that the origins of industrial accounting'

---

[10] H. T. Johnson, 'Towards a New Understanding of Nineteenth-Century Cost Accounting', *Accounting Review*, 56 (1981), 510–18.

[11] H. T. Johnson, *The Role of Accounting History in the Education of Prospective Accountants* (Glasgow, 1984), 5–7. See also H. T. Johnson and R. S. Kaplan, *Relevance Lost: The Rise and Fall of Management Accounting* (Boston, Mass., 1987), ch. 2.

are to be found here.[12] Prominence is given to the textile industries probably because important technological changes in the second half of the eighteenth century facilitated a dramatic conversion from the domestic system to factory-based production, making these industries obvious candidates for finding evidence of cost accounting. However, the seeds of industrial change were sown much earlier, and recent work has emphasized that it was the cotton industry *together with* the metal industries which achieved high levels of real output growth in Britain in the eighteenth and early nineteenth centuries.[13] Furthermore, centralized production in metal industries pre-dates the industrial revolution by a considerable margin. And although recent gradualist studies have stressed the persistence of domestic production into the nineteenth century,[14] this is not to suppose that there were not strong incentives to introduce cost accounting in other work-places: Roll demonstrated sixty years ago how an advanced costing system was used in Boulton & Watt's Soho works in the late eighteenth century,[15] and McKendrick has described how Josiah Wedgwood used cost accounting in his pottery works in the 1770s.[16]

It is unlikely that these firms were exceptional, but the scarcity of well-documented examples has, perhaps, conveyed this impression. The lack of attention given to primary material is partly attributable to the fact that many business records have not survived. There is a strong possibility that costing records have been discarded because they were kept separate from the other account books, and were often written up as loose-leaf memoranda. They were kept in this way primarily because the analytical aspects of cost accounting were not undertaken by 'financial' bookkeepers (who recorded their messages in robust ledgers), but were the work of owners or managers. A bookkeeper, who was normally preoccupied with keeping track of a firm's obligations in the form of cash, debtors and creditors, rarely possessed the necessary commercial expertise or knowledge of production methods to undertake cost accounting. The owner or manager was much better placed to make such calculations, and was also keen to maintain a high degree of

---

[12] M. J. Mepham, 'The Eighteenth-Century Origins of Cost Accounting', *Abacus*, 25 (1988), 57.

[13] For instance, C. K. Harley, 'British Industrialization before 1841: Evidence of Slower Growth during the Industrial Revolution', *Journal of Economic History*, 42 (1982), 268–9; N. F. R. Crafts, *British Economic Growth during the Industrial Revolution* (Oxford, 1985), 23.

[14] For instance, A. E. Musson, 'The British Industrial Revolution', *History*, 67 (1982), 252–3; M. Berg, *The Age of Manufactures: Industry, Innovation and Work in Britain, 1700–1820* (London, 1985), 42.

[15] E. Roll, *An Early Experiment in Industrial Organisation: Being a History of the Firm of Boulton and Watt, 1775–1805* (London, 1930), 244–52.

[16] N. McKendrick, 'Josiah Wedgwood and Cost Accounting in the Industrial Revolution', *Economic History Review*, 2nd series, 23 (1970).

secrecy in order to avoid the possibility of important information being transmitted to competitors. For instance, costing calculations undertaken by the copper smelter H. H. Vivian in the 1840s, which will be considered later, were kept under lock and key in a private business diary.[17]

The historical analysis of accounting practice therefore requires the careful interpretation of limited evidence and, moreover, a treatment which considers in practical terms how contemporary industrialists made decisions about production using cost criteria. Such an approach is adopted by Jones in a recent study of accounting practice in the management of landed estates and of iron and copper smelting works in Wales.[18] Significantly, he finds evidence in the metal industries of a high degree of cost consciousness dating from the sixteenth century. Had Jones looked beyond Wales, he would have found further evidence of the early use of cost analysis in the metal industries. Hammersley's recent transcription of the notebook of the younger Daniel Hechstetter includes detailed costings for the production of copper and silver at the Mines Royal metal works near Keswick in the late sixteenth and early seventeenth centuries.[19] However, before proceeding with an analysis of these and other studies, it is first necessary to define the principles and objectives of cost and management accounting.

II

Management accounting is the term developed since the Second World War to describe the provision, for management, of statistical information for the purposes of *planning, decision-making*, and *control*. The term 'cost accounting' has older origins and is concerned specifically with the identification and accumulation of costs and, as such, provides much of the basic information required by management accountants.[20] The distinction between the two elements of internal reporting has become increasingly blurred, and many accounting texts now treat them as synonymous. Both forms of accounting may be distinguished from financial accounting, the primary aim of which is to provide external users of accounting information, such as shareholders, employees,

---

[17] National Library of Wales (hereafter NLW), Vivian Papers, E18, Hafod Smelting Charges.

[18] H. Jones, *Accounting, Costing and Cost Estimation: Welsh Industry, 1700–1830* (Cardiff, 1984).

[19] G. Hammersley (ed.), *Daniel Hechstetter the Younger: Memorabilia and Letters, 1600–1639* (Stuttgart, 1988). The use of cost accounting at Keswick is noted in M. B. Donald, *Elizabethan Copper: The History of the Company of Mines Royal* (London, 1955), 221–30.

[20] See, for instance, C. Drury, *Management and Cost Accounting* (2nd edn., London, 1985), 19–20.

and the government, with a historical overview of the trading position of a firm.

Planning involves the identification of corporate objectives and, at this stage, cost accounting techniques may be used to identify the incremental costs and revenues associated with alternative courses of action so as to enable them to be ranked in terms of their expected financial merit. The kinds of decisions to be taken range from long-term strategic decisions (such as whether to relocate plant, supply a new product, or switch to more capital intensive methods of production), to short-term tactical decisions (such as whether to increase production to satisfy an unforeseen upturn in demand or to accept an overseas order at a price lower than is ruling in the home market). Making and implementing a decision is, therefore, a job for management which may be made on the basis of financial data, but bearing in mind possible constraints such as unfavourable effects on the environment or local employment.

Modern cost accounting systems are designed to measure on a routine basis actual costs incurred in two ways: the total cost of each of the various activities of a business, and the cost per unit of a firm's output or outputs. These costings are achieved by dividing a firm into 'cost centres' of distinguishable locations, operations, processes, and so on, and by dividing the firm's outputs of goods or services into 'cost units' of cost per unit of the goods or services produced. Within cost centres and cost units, costs are further broken down into the separate 'elements' of material costs, labour costs, and expenses. These elements may be identified with particular cost centres or cost units (direct costs), or they may be identified with several (indirect costs), in which case accountants have to apportion them between cost centres or cost units accordingly.

When a firm produces a single good on a continuous basis, the relatively simple technique of 'process costing' is used. This divides total process costs, identified in the manner described above, by an appropriate measure of output to give an average cost per unit, such as cost per ton. In workshop and building trades it is more common for firms to produce differentiated goods for sale. These require different and sometimes more complicated accounting procedures known as 'job costing' to apportion actual costs, as compared with average costs, to particular units of output or jobs.[21]

An element of total costs which deserves special consideration in this context is the accounting treatment of fixed assets; this is because the amounts

---

[21] Ibid. 30–1.

involved are substantial in capital intensive industries and because their accounting treatment is both subjective and arbitrary. Although there are more sophisticated approaches, the total costs involved in operating a fixed asset may be said to comprise depreciation, maintenance costs, and interest on capital. Today, maintenance charges will invariably be charged against profit and depreciation is also deducted, although a choice may be made from a range of different depreciation methods depending upon the pattern of benefit derived from using the asset. In practice, assets are usually written off in equal instalments over their expected useful life, although an 'activity-based' charge (the amount written off during an accounting period as a function of the level of usage) is sometimes used for internal reporting purposes. The accuracy of the charge suffers from the difficulty of obtaining reliable estimates of the useful life of and residual value of assets.[22]

Using the various techniques described, cost accountants are able to identify costs incurred and measure performance. To help management make a sensible appraisal, comparisons may be made with independent yardsticks such as the results achieved by the same business in a previous year or another business during the same accounting period. The degree of control may be further improved if management employs the practice of evaluating actual performance by reference to predetermined 'standard costs' and 'budgets'. Standard costs are estimated costs, calculated in advance of production for the various elements of cost incurred for each product supplied. They are designed to represent the anticipated minimum costs that would be incurred assuming the most efficient production methods are used (ideal standards), or assuming a high but realistic level of efficiency (attainable standards). Budgets are set for an entire operation or activity using standard cost data to provide overall financial targets which can be achieved by efficient production.[23]

The determination of standard costs and the setting of budgets require production methods to be monitored carefully, or experiments in production methods to be made, in order to ascertain acceptable levels of costs. Once such benchmarks are determined, actual costs can be compared with corresponding standard costs at the end of accounting periods, and any variance between the two can be analysed into its component parts, using statistical methods, to determine whether or not the variance is acceptable. For instance, if an excess of actual costs over standard costs proves to be significant, it should then be possible for the cost accountant to locate the cost centres or

---

[22] The accuracy of the calculation also suffers, in common with most other accounting calculations, from the use of historical costs rather than current costs.

[23] For a detailed description see Drury, *Management and Cost Accounting*, ch. 17.

cost units where this occurs and to identify the high cost elements. With this information managers can then decide what action should be taken to reduce actual costs incurred in the future.

To achieve maximum control, it is necessary to use an accounting system which can trace the internal movement of goods through various stages of production so that costs can be allocated to their sources accurately. To facilitate this high degree of control, it is now standard practice for firms to integrate cost accounts with financial accounts in a single accounting system in such a way that accounting information can be readily extracted for use by financial and cost accountants. The process of integrating the two types of accounts requires devising a financial accounting system which identifies costs and apportions them to appropriate cost centres and cost units. By doing so, such a system can provide managers with cost data on a regular basis—typically weekly, fortnightly, or monthly—which is readily comparable with data for other periods.

III

The use of costings in industry is by no means a product of the eighteenth or nineteenth centuries. In his history of the early development of iron-making in Wealden, Straker, for example, cites a number of costings from business records covering the period 1330 to 1773. Some are extremely rudimentary, but of particular interest is an estimate of the cost of producing one ton of bar iron at Ashdown Forest, Newbridge, in 1539, and an annual cost estimate for the Heathfield furnace for 1746.[24] Although correctly described as estimates, it is likely that these were measures of actual costs incurred rather than measures of costs likely to be incurred if a particular project was undertaken. At the same time, the calculations provided information on which a decision could be taken, such as whether or not to continue operations.

Another early example of cost finding is contained in a document issued in 1620 by the London members of the Worshipful Co. of Bakers, which includes a careful build-up of the weekly costs of production. This document was produced in response to price controls. Under the English Bread Assize of 1266, bread prices were fixed but the baker was allowed to vary the *weight* of loaves in response to changes in the price of grain, according to a set scale of weights and grain prices. This system was designed to ensure that the price

---

[24] E. Straker, *Wealdon Iron* (Newton Abbot, 1969), 196 and 199.

was high enough to cover the baker's profit, set at two loaves plus bran sales per quarter of wheat, and estimated cost of production. The purpose of the document was to support a claim for an increase in the allowance made for production costs.[25]

These examples show two distinct approaches to costing: the use of cost estimates and the compilation of detailed cost statistics. The records examined by Jones display a keener interest in cost estimates than in monitoring the actual costs incurred in undertaking a particular activity. This probably reflects the general absence of detailed record-keeping and, more important, the lack of any conviction that the benefit obtained from such information would justify the work involved in its preparation in circumstances where the owner and/or manager remained in close contact with all aspects of day-to-day activity.

Nevertheless, exercises in cost estimation were not simple, and the careful thought devoted to the preparation of estimates is particularly noticeable in some of the earliest examples. Hechstetter's remarkably detailed estimate of the relative cost of producing 'rough copper' near Keswick in 1615 indicates that comprehensive accounts of all aspects of production were kept. Here, weekly costs for labour, carriage, horses, allowances, and various materials are listed. They are multiplied by 52 and added to the cost of copper ore, charcoal, and other smelting materials along with miscellaneous items including rent and interest to give a total annual cost. This is compared with the sales price of the copper produced to show an annual profit of £225. The costing is also compared with one undertaken in 1600 to assess the changes in production costs over this period.[26]

Similarly, the records of the Landore copper works for the 1730s contains a sophisticated assessment of the cost of making one ton of copper. The calculation sets out the various direct costs of smelting and refining—materials, labour, and expenses—for the various stages of production: calcining, melting, roasting, and refining. Carriage inwards is included, as are allowances for candles, smithwork, and repairs to furnaces at each stage. Added to the total direct costs of production are certain indirect costs, such as the salary of an agent, rent of premises, sales commission charges, and freight costs in transporting copper from Neath to London.[27] A similar exercise was undertaken at the Pontypool Forges in 1704 by John Hanbury, who prepared a theoreti-

[25] D. A. R. Forrester, 'The Records of an Incorporated Baker's Guild, with Reference to Prices, Costs and Audits', *Accounting History*, 3 (1978), 10–11; Garner, *Cost Accounting*, 31–3.

[26] Hammersley (ed.), *Daniel Hechstetter*, 82–5.

[27] Jones, *Accounting, Costing and Cost Estimation*, 22–3.

cal calculation of the total cost of making 300 tons of bar iron over twelve months. The result was divided by 300 to give a cost per ton of £13 2s., which compared favourably with the estimated selling price of £15.[28]

In contrast to the construction of cost estimates, Daniel Peck, proprietor of lead works in Flint, prepared a calculation in 1707 which set out the *actual* direct cost of the weekly output (distinguishing between smelting, refining, and conversion costs), the values of the products and by-products produced, and a comparison of the two totals, to produce a balance called 'weekly profit'. This was multiplied to produce an annual figure from which certain overhead costs were deducted, leaving a residual annual profit figure.[29]

Burley's investigation of the records of Thomas Grigg, an Essex textile manufacturer, for the period 1742 to 1760, identifies an early accounting system where interest was shown in the flow of goods into and out of individual processes, and the identification of actual costs incurred.[30] In the production of cloth, five main processes were employed: wool sorting, cleaning, combing, spinning, and weaving. The first three stages, which appear to have involved relatively little in the way of labour and capital requirements, were performed on the premises, whilst the remaining work was undertaken by approximately 500 outworkers. Surviving records focus on the activities of the latter, presumably because records were not required to provide information about transactions under the owner's direct supervision. The records have been likened by Burley to those maintained by the Medici family in Florence almost 200 years earlier,[31] but Grigg's records seem significantly less advanced: they are not on the double-entry basis, they do not contain overheads, and the financial data is fairly patchy compared with the reasonably comprehensive costings contained in the Medici records. Perhaps of more interest are the forty or so *ad hoc* direct costing calculations made for various fabrics between 1749 and 1759, a time when demand was low and direct costs were high. As was the case with Wedgwood in 1772, poor results and unfavourable market conditions seem to have stimulated cost-consciousness.[32]

These examples demonstrate how accounting data were used to estimate and calculate actual costs incurred and to indicate overall profitability. However, there is no indication as to what use was made of such information. With the exception of Hechstetter's calculation, they do not provide the comparative

[28] Ibid. 13–14.

[29] Ibid. 15 and 18.

[30] K. H. Burley, 'Some Accounting Records of an Eighteenth-Century Clothier', *Accounting Research*, 9 (1958).

[31] Cf. R. de Roover, 'A Florentine Firm of Cloth Manufacturers', *Speculum*, 16 (1941).

[32] McKendrick, 'Josiah Wedgwood', 48.

information required for the appraisal of production efficiency, neither do they refer to choices about the allocation of resources. They do, however, imply a strong interest in planning and a desire to monitor general profitability.

Nevertheless, a number of examples have been found where businessmen made decisions about future resource allocation which utilized accounting techniques. These industrialists were acting far in advance of the more celebrated proponents of the use of costing for forward planning of the early twentieth century.[33] This evidence not only reinforces the Pollard view of the sophistication of partial cost accounting,[34] but demonstrates both the earlier use of certain methods and an even greater variety of accounting techniques employed. For instance, in the late sixteenth century, Hechstetter calculated the effect on profit of selling copper in a different geographical area and also the effects on cost of changing the level of production.[35] An analysis undertaken by the Mine Adventurers of England in 1710 compares the cost of smelting and refining copper ore at Neath with undertaking the same processes in Garreg.[36] Similarly, an investigation was undertaken at the Melincryddan works in about 1740 to determine the relative costs of manufacturing copper at various levels of production at Neath and Redbrook, Gloucestershire, in order to determine which was the better location for smelting.[37] This cost–benefit analysis is also of importance in that it demonstrates the recognition of a clear distinction between fixed and variable costs, something not made explicit in economic literature until Charles Babbage did so in 1832.[38] Furthermore, this distinction of costs is given a precise practical application. Calculations were made of the relative costs of producing and selling five, six, seven, and eight tons of copper per week at both locations. Some costs, such as the cost of copper ore purchased in Cornwall, were the same at both locations, other costs differed, such as freight costs, which were greater for St Ives to Redbrook than for St Ives to Neath. Of the sixteen elements of total cost, ten were treated as directly variable with production, three as semi-variable, and three as entirely fixed. The total costings were then compared with estimated sales revenue to show an advantage for Neath at each planned level of production.

Other early examples of the recognition of the differential behaviour of costs have also been found. In a letter to the mining engineer John Taylor, dated 11 May 1824, Richard Cort, son of Henry Cort, states that 'the increased scale of [copper] Smelting, lessens also the [impact of] fixed

[33] R. H. Parker, *Management Accounting: An Historical Perspective* (London, 1969), 22–6.

[34] Pollard, *Genesis of Modern Management*, 219–20.   [35] Hammersley (ed.), *Daniel Hechstetter*, 117–18.

[36] Jones, *Accounting, Costing and Cost Estimation*, 222.   [37] Ibid. 30.

[38] C. Babbage, *On the Economy of Machinery and Manufactures* (London, 1832), 174. See Parker, *Management Accounting*, 59–60.

expenses which . . . are as much on 1,000 as on 6,000 tons'. Such costs are also contrasted with 'all other items [which move more or] less in proportion to the quantity of ores smelted'.[39] In a similar vein, Josiah Wedgwood observed in 1772 that some expenses 'move like clockwork & are much the same whether the quantity of goods [produced] be large or small'.[40]

The Tredegar manuscripts record consideration being given by the lessors in 1746 to the renewal of a lease yielding £150 per annum, or whether instead to take over and operate the iron works located on the land.[41] The lessors estimated that £7,600 would have to be invested to cover the cost of fixed assets and operating expenses over the first twelve months. The conclusion reached was that a minimum of £530 would have to be generated to cover interest at 5 per cent on £7,600, i.e. £380, plus the rental forgone of £150. This is a creditable early attempt to apply the opportunity cost concept to industrial decision-making.

Clear recognition of the impact of changing levels of output on the selling price and profit is contained in a calculation made by John Vivian in 1785, as deputy governor of the Cornish Metal Co., a marketing enterprise which handled a large proportion of the British output of copper at the time. With the company facing financial difficulties over accumulation of stocks, Vivian argued that the sale of three-quarters of available copper would enable a higher price to be charged to produce a greater profit than by selling the entire amount, so that 'it will be in [the mine owners'] interest to keep the overplus in reserve, in the hope of an increased demand or a decreased produce'.[42]

During the 1820s, the management of the Mona Mine Co. investigated on several occasions whether it should continue to smelt copper at Amlwch in Anglesey and market the finished product through Liverpool, or sell more copper ore through Swansea. This was provoked by R. J. Nevill, of the Llanelli Copper Co., who in 1820 approached the Mona Mine Co., having conducted his own cost analysis, in the hope of persuading the company to send ores to Swansea, where his company would be able to purchase them. This suggestion was not taken up, but between 1820 and 1824 data were collected and an analysis undertaken which favoured the continuation of smelting at Amlwch.[43] A similar analysis was made in 1828, and a comparison of the expected outcomes this time favoured the shipment of ore to Swansea.[44] This was then subjected to a 'sensitivity analysis'[45] by the

---

[39] Jones, *Accounting, Costing and Cost Estimation*, 105.   [40] McKendrick, 'Josiah Wedgwood', 55.

[41] Jones, *Accounting, Costing and Cost Estimation*, 187–9.   [42] Ibid. 190.

[43] University College of North Wales, Bangor (hereafter UCNW), Mona Mine MSS, 1599.

[44] Jones, *Accounting, Costing and Cost Estimation*, 231–6.

[45] Sensitivity analysis revises the data in a costing calculation to discover whether possible changes in any of the variables would have a marked effect on the expected outcome.

company accountant Thomas Beer, with the financial effects of a series of assumptions more favourable to Liverpool incorporated into the calculation. The Swansea option retained its advantage, and the Anglesey works were closed in 1833.

An important feature of these analyses was the use made of total rather than marginal costing. In some industries total costings were no doubt used to help management arrive at individual tenders. But in most industries, where competition existed and prices were fixed by market, producers were price-takers, and businessmen presumably required total costings to decide whether to supply goods at given market prices.[46] Often, market conditions were somewhere between the two extremes of monopoly and perfect competition. The copper smelting industry was oligopolistic, and market behaviour fluctuated from collusion to price warfare. Though less concentrated, the iron industry faced similar market conditions. Both industries had the potential to generate excessive costs through the inefficient use of resources—particularly fuel—and companies were acutely aware of the necessity to cover all their costs in the long run. This provided a constant incentive to control costs, an incentive that was increased when market conditions squeezed profit levels, such as during periods of price warfare. With straightforward production methods, and little by way of by-product manufacture until the latter part of the nineteenth century, these metal industries were ideally suited to the use of simple process costing to produce figures for total costs. Normally, total costs were expressed as averages, in cost units of 'cost per ton of metal produced'. Such units could be compared over time to provide indicators of changes in production costs and compared with the market price of metals to indicate whether sales of metal or purchases of ore would lead to a profit or loss. Edwards and Baber have shown that the Dowlais Iron Co. produced up-to-date figures for costs per ton of finished product from the first half of the nineteenth century using a relatively sophisticated accounting system,[47] and Newell has identified the use of such 'output costing' amongst south Wales copper smelters in the same period.[48]

An interesting application of costing information by copper smelters was its imputation into calculations to make decisions about the purchase of ore, either by private contract with mining companies or through the public sales

---

[46] Whether this comparison is sensible, for *short-run* decisions, would of course be questioned by advocates of marginal costing who claim that goods should be supplied provided avoidable costs are covered.

[47] J. R. Edwards and C. Baber, 'Dowlais Iron Company: Accounting Policies and Procedures for Profit Measurement and Reporting Purposes', *Accounting and Business Research*, 9 (1979), 147.

[48] E. Newell, 'Interpreting the Cornish Copper Standard', *Journal of the Trevithick Society*, 13 (1986), 41–2.

of ore, known as 'ticketings', which were held regularly in Cornwall and Swansea for much of the eighteenth and nineteenth centuries. The following calculation was made in 1824 by Thomas Beer, the accountant of the Mona Mine Co., to decide whether or not to adopt a course of action which, on the face of it, appeared very unlikely to prove worthwhile; namely the payment of £126 by private contract for sufficient copper ore (12.5 tons) to produce a ton of copper when the market price of copper was £112 per ton.

Under trade conventions, the payment of £126 to the mine owner was nominal. The actual payment made by the smelter was net of 'returning charges', an amount set to cover transport and processing costs. In practice, the returning charge was the cost unit measured by copper smelters, i.e. the cost of transporting, smelting, and refining one ton of ore. With returning charges set at 55s. per ton of ore, the net payment was £126 − (55s. × 12.5), or £91. 12s. 6d. As was common throughout the industry, the returning charge overstated the true costs incurred. It is clear that a more accurate costing of production had taken place, since Beer adds £21. 17s. 6d. to the net price, as the true production cost (which is equivalent to a returning charge of 35s. per ton), to give a figure of £113. 10s. As it was the normal practice to measure copper ore in a 21 cwt. ton rather than the conventional 20 cwt. ton, an adjustment was made to reduce the cost by the sales value of one cwt. of copper, i.e. £5. 12s., to give a net cost of £107. 18s. The cost of rolling the copper, £5 per ton, was then added to produce a final figure of £112 18s., which was recognized as not taking account of commission to the selling agent, interest on capital, and so on, to give an 'apparent loss' of just 18s.[49]

Correspondence between the proprietors of Pascoe Grenfell & Son and Alfred Jenkin, the firm's Cornish agent responsible for bidding for ore at the ticketings, show how the unit cost of smelting copper ore was used to regulate bids at the ticketings.[50] It was well known that the unit cost, or returning charge, changed according to the 'produce', or copper content, of the ore. Costings made by John Vivian for the Mona Mine Co. in 1811 demonstrate the point clearly, when he calculated that, *ceteris paribus*, higher produce ore yields a higher profit than lower produce ore.[51] Pascoe Grenfell & Son undoubtedly conducted similar analyses, and, like smelters such as Vivian & Sons,[52] produced a set of tables which cross-tabulated returning charges (or unit costs) with the percentage of copper in the ore over a range of prices for

[49] Jones, *Accounting, Costing and Cost Estimation*, 205.
[50] Royal Institution of Cornwall, Truro, Hamilton Jenkin Papers, HJ/2.10, *passim.*
[51] Jones, *Accounting, Costing and Cost Estimation*, 204.
[52] NLW, Vivian Papers, E18, p. 141.

one ton of copper, to give the maximum price which could be paid for ore to allow it to be smelted at profit given the prevailing price for copper. At the ticketings, Jenkin was given a maximum price for copper at which he could bid, and it was his responsibility to set bids accordingly by recourse to his 'variation tables'.

In 1831, the Mona Mine Co. decided to adopt the same system. The manager, John Sanderson, reported: 'I applied to Mr. [J. H.] Vivian for the loan of their tables of calculations, who refused, saying that their tables were in terms that they would not divulge. When Mr. Keates [of the Ravenhead copper works, St. Helens] was here I asked him whether he would inform any one of their method of purchasing C[opper] ore, and he gave me the same answer I rcd. before'.[53] Undaunted, Sanderson went on to construct his own set of tables.

It is clear from these examples that unit costs were used on a regular basis in the copper industry for the purpose of *control*. Whilst the underlying calculations to determine unit costs may have been made on an irregular basis, it is nevertheless evident that they were applied to purchasing copper ore on a weekly or fortnightly basis, given the organization of the ticketing system of marketing ore. This is a particularly interesting application of cost accounting for control purposes, since it links production costs directly with input prices as well as to calculations regarding profitability.

Further evidence of ingenuity in the use of costings in the copper industry can be found in the business notebook of H. H. Vivian, son of J. H. Vivian and grandson of John Vivian. Here, Vivian recorded annual breakdowns of historical costs in the various parts of the business covering the period 1822 to 1866, indicating that elsewhere detailed cost accounts based on individual cost centres had been kept.[54] Unfortunately, these have not survived. Vivian also records *ad hoc* costings relating to the manufacture of copper sheathing for ships, Yellow Metal (a brass alloy), copper rollers, as well as the smelting of copper, for which he provides a detailed example of determining its unit cost.[55]

Most of the costings considered so far have been *ad hoc* exercises. These would have been undertaken either *ex ante* or *ex post*, although it is not always possible to categorize cost calculations as such with certainty. Calculations made before the event would have been used for planning and resource allocation purposes, whereas calculations made after the event enabled actual results to be appraised and may have led to a reallocation of resources. The

[53] UCNW, Mona Mine MSS, 1,026.
[54] NLW, Vivian Papers, E 18, *passim*.
[55] Ibid. 162, 173, 245, and 255.

potential usefulness of these calculations is increased where both types are available at the same time: the *ex ante* figure represents a standard which should be aimed for, against which *ex post* results may be judged.

The use of standards goes back a very long way. In agriculture, it is known that standard yields were established for crops and livestock in the thirteenth century;[56] what were called 'trial smeltings' of copper ore were undertaken at Keswick at the beginning of the seventeenth century to provide standards of smelting costs, whilst standards, based on 'time and motion' measurements for different types of cost, were established at the Carron Co. in the eighteenth century to enable results to be monitored and a target profit to be achieved.[57] The accounting system today called standard costing developed out of these beginnings as a means of analysing standards and actual costs. The existing literature suggests that standard costing was developed for the use of engineers in the United States in the 1890s,[58] but the following example shows clearly that the basic principles were used to ascertain the efficiency of coal consumption at Vivian & Sons' Hafod works in 1848.

Coal was the major variable cost element in the copper smelting industry, and coal consumption could also vary greatly through inefficient use. Wary of this, Vivian recorded: 'To ascertain the quantity of coal used in each operation trials were made: the results multiplied by the total number of operations during the year, of which a record had been kept, should give the actual quantity used, which will be seen was not borne out in practice owing to bad work'. The results showed that 59,286 tons of coal were required, whereas 69,525 tons of coal had been used, indicating that fuel costs were over 17 per cent higher than necessary.[59] Results of similar coal trials held in 1836 are included in the notebook of William Jones, manager of the Hafod works, although the purpose of the exercise is not recorded.[60]

IV

Pollard acknowledges that *ad hoc* calculations of the type described above were in widespread use by the eighteenth century. However, he does not explore

[56] *Anonymous Husbandry*, in E. Lamond, *Walter of Henley's Husbandry* (1890), 71 ff.
[57] R. K. Fleischman and L. D. Parker, 'Managerial Accounting Early in the British Industrial Revolution: The Carron Company, a Case Study', *Accounting and Business Research*, 20 (1990), 218.
[58] M. J. Epstein, *The Effect of Scientific Management on the Development of the Standard Cost System* (New York, 1978), 51–6; M. L. Inman, 'The Relevance of the Historical Background to Standard Costing', *Association of Certified Accountants, Students' Newsletter* (Aug. 1989), 32–4.
[59] NLW, Vivian Papers, E18, p. 208.   [60] NLW, BLW MSS. 15113B., pp. 25 ff.

their range of possible applications and refrains from categorizing them as cost accounting proper, implying that such 'partial' cost accounts were inferior to fully integrated cost and financial accounting systems.[61] Indeed, he states that businessmen 'did not develop to any significant extent the use of accounts in guiding management decisions'.[62] The growing body of evidence shows that *ad hoc* costing data was much more widely used as the basis for management decisions than has previously been believed the case. Nevertheless, the integration of cost and financial accounts was an important advance in accounting practice which potentially gave managers improved control over operations and facilitated the regular appraisal of performance in factories where large numbers of workers were employed. This development is now examined.

Where a system of financial accounting is in place, independent *ad hoc* costing calculations may also be made, with both types of accounting drawing on a common source of information. Where *ex post* costings are prepared alongside financial accounts, cost-conscious businessmen will be aware that a natural development of their accounting procedure would be to modify and expand the system of financial accounting to incorporate costing calculations. This change would increase the arithmetic accuracy of the data—there being less chance of omitting costs within the more secure double-entry accounting framework—and would make it possible to produce a range of accounting reports on a regular basis. Nevertheless, businessmen would have also to consider the additional cost of operating such a system and assess whether or not it was advantageous to produce cost accounts on a systematic basis. A recent criticism of integrated accounts is that they tend to result in the production of routine reports which grow increasingly unrelated to the kinds of decisions managers need to take in a changing business environment. It is also the case that the arbitrary apportionment of overheads to cost centres—to ensure that all costs are 'accounted for'—produces total cost figures which are not always considered the most appropriate for business decisions. They are generally judged to provide a reasonably adequate basis for performance assessment and long-term pricing decisions, but not for short-term pricing and production decisions which are more rationally based on marginal costs and revenues associated with a particular option.[63] Thus, integrated accounts should not necessarily be regarded as the most useful or appropriate system for cost accounting.

---

[61] Pollard, *Genesis of Modern Management*, 220–1.   [62] Ibid. 248.

[63] The development of intricate systems for the apportionment of overhead costs, which became increasingly complex but no less arbitrary, was a major preoccupation of engineers and accountants in the late nineteenth and early twentieth centuries. It might be argued that this had a harmful impact on the development of cost accounting since it diverted attention from the future to the past and gave further emphasis to total (absorption) costing.

It should also be recognized that there is a possible intermediary stage between the use of *ad hoc* costings and integrated accounts, namely the preparation of routine costings independently of the financial accounting system. This happened at the Carron Co. between 1765 and 1784, where a costing system was developed to monitor the performance of individual departments. The principal features of this system (which are also common to a system of full integration) were the apportionment of overhead costs to individual departments, and the establishment of standards for the purpose of recharging major material costs, such as ironstone, to producing departments. This enabled the profitability of different departments to be measured on a monthly basis, and comparisons to be made with other companies to discover areas of relative advantage. It also enabled the performance of departmental heads to be monitored so that those producing poor results could be called to account. This is an early example of 'responsibility accounting'.[64]

By the end of the nineteenth century a number of large industrial concerns had established independent costing departments. Furthermore, the burgeoning cost accounting literature of that period continually emphasized the need for integration of cost and financial accounts. Understandably, the inference was drawn that the practice of integrating accounts began to develop only at this stage. Whilst acknowledging that the diffusion of integrated financial and cost accounting was slow in Britain,[65] Johnson was one of the first writers to challenge this 'late development' view by citing the example of the Charlton mills accounts of 1810, suggesting that it was in textile factories in the early nineteenth century where the principles of double-entry bookkeeping for the maintenance of cost accounts was first applied.[66] It is now known that even this does not identify the integration process with its first origins. Fleischman and Parker imply that the Carron Co. operated integrated cost and financial accounting following changes made in 1786[67]—though Campbell seems to fix the date at 1784.[68] Clearer evidence of early integration is provided by Jones, who shows that the Cyfarthfa Iron Co. used, from at least 1791, a system of double-entry bookkeeping to charge individual cost centres with the direct and indirect cost involved in the conversion of raw materials into finished goods.[69] Operations were divided between twelve distinct production centres; direct expenses were allocated to each of these, and

[64] Fleischman and Parker, 'Managerial Accounting', 215.
[65] Johnson and Kaplan, *Relevance Lost*, 141–4.
[66] Johnson, 'Nineteenth-Century Cost Accounting', 511.
[67] Fleischman and Parker, 'Managerial Accounting', 214.
[68] R. H. Campbell, *Carron Company* (Edinburgh, 1961), 136–8.
[69] Jones, *Accounting, Costing and Cost Estimation*, 132.

production overheads, such as blacksmith work and the cost of operating the furnace, were apportioned between them. A 'manufacturing' account was periodically prepared for each production centre, containing quantities and values for opening and closing stock. The balances were transferred to the general profit and loss account, where non-allocated overhead costs, such as interest, common charges, and so on, were also accumulated.

In a number of cases, the output of one production centre was transferred to another. For instance, the output of pig iron produced at the Cyfarthfa furnace was allocated between the pig iron account, the castings account, and scrap. Transfers to pig iron production and castings were priced internally at 90s. per ton, and to scrap iron (which was recycled to castings at the same price) at 60s. per ton. For 1820, by which time the size of the concern had quadrupled, there is information available regarding the methods used to apportion overheads between production centres. For example, charges on the 'furnaces overhead account' were apportioned to individual furnaces on a time basis.[70]

The ledgers of the Mona Mine Co., commencing in 1817, are a further early illustration of integrated cost and financial records. There is much evidence of care being taken to ensure a proper allocation of expenses between the mine and the smelting works, and, beyond that, between different production centres. There, in 1830, and at the Cambrian Smelting Co. in 1822,[71] overheads were recharged to departments and products using the 'prime cost' method and 'direct labour hour' method respectively.[72] Clearly these methods were not improved upon for some time, since the accountant Thomas Battersby states that the percentage on prime cost was the most widely used overhead recovery method in Britain in 1878, and even in 1898.[73]

V

Whilst many studies in this area have focused on the chronological development of costing techniques, recent research also shed new light on the development of

[70] Jones, *Accounting, Costing and Cost Estimation*, 136 n.

[71] Ibid. 104.

[72] Ibid. 106. The purpose of recharging overheads is to produce total cost figures for goods produced. The direct labour method expresses overheads as a percentage of the labour costs that can be clearly identified with a specific department and/or product; the prime cost method uses direct materials and direct expenses, as well as direct labour, in the apportionment process.

[73] Solomons, 'Historical Development of Costing', 22–3.

other aspects of management accounting. The use of rates of return for the purpose of performance assessment and decision-making, and the inclusion of charges for interest and depreciation in costing calculations are examined in this section.

Johnson links the need for calculations of the percentage return on capital invested (ROI) with the twentieth-century development of vertically integrated and multidivisional organizations.[74] He explains the growing popularity of ROI on the grounds that it provided a more effective means of allocating resources than the capital market. While this may have been the case, it should not be assumed that the development of ROI awaited the emergence of such conglomerates. Moreover, although Hamilton may have been the only early writer in the English language to discuss the relationship between profit and capital employed,[75] Pollard's assertion that businessmen never used this measure is certainly wrong.[76] Again, early examples may be found in the metal industries.

Robert Morris, partner in the copper smelting firm of Lockwood, Morris and Co., estimated that 'Profit from May 1727 when Partnership was formed to Michaelmas 1728 was about £2,900, which upon a capital of £10,000 was 23 per cent per annum granting the time to be one year and a quarter'.[77] One hundred years later, Richard Cort commented that the British Iron Co.'s reported profit of £11,000 in 1826 was 'about 4 per cent on £267,616 total amount of real capital employed', and this contrasted unfavourably with the company's prospectus which forecast a return of 20 per cent.[78]

The use of interest as a business cost has also been examined. Garner's assertion that the inclusion of interest as a cost of production began to receive attention in the literature only in the last quarter of the nineteenth century[79] overlooks Hamilton, writing one hundred years earlier, who suggested that 'a period's profit should be charged for the use of funds employed in earning it'.[80] According to Pollard, 'Interest was treated as a cost, universally in computing the advisability of planned ventures, but frequently also in accounts of the past'.[81] While use of the terms 'universally' and, even, 'frequently' are possibly too strong, Pollard's conclusions receive a measure of support from Jones's findings and from elsewhere in recent literature.

Many of the financial calculations previously considered, prepared for Welsh and other companies to enable management to assess performance and choose between alternatives, incorporate an allowance for interest, usually of

[74] Johnson, *Role of Accounting History*, 11.
[75] Mepham, 'Origins of Cost Accounting', 63.
[76] Pollard, *Genesis of Modern Management*, 235.
[77] Jones, *Accounting, Costing and Cost Estimation*, 20.
[78] Ibid. 216.
[79] Garner, *Evolution of Cost Accounting*, 143.
[80] Mepham, 'Origins of Cost Accounting', 63.
[81] S. Pollard, 'Capital Accounting in the Industrial Revolution', *Yorkshire Bulletin of Economic and Social Research*, 15 (1963), 80.

5 per cent. The inclusion of an interest charge in the routine *post fact* accounts was, however, usually confined to partnerships, where the deduction was designed principally to ensure that individuals were properly remunerated for different capital contributions, rather than to produce a more accurate costing of business operations as, for example, in the Crawshay ledger for 1791–8.[82] Elsewhere, Mepham shows that the accounts of the British Linen Co. for 1748 includes an interest charge as part of the agreed profit sharing scheme between the partners.[83] At the Charlton mills, the calculated cost of business operations clearly includes interest imputed at 5 per cent on the owners' capital investment from 1810 onwards.[84] One further example of an interest charge in *post fact* accounts is contained in a calculation prepared for the Mona Mine Co. covering the seven years to 31 March 1800. The actual profit earned is compared with an interest charge of 10 per cent on 'average capital employed' to produce a shortfall designated 'loss by the mine, £29,789 15s 10d'.[85]

It is interesting to note that the evidence suggests that the use of interest charges on capital investment in industry is pre-dated by its use in agriculture, where the earliest example is found in 1617.[86] It is possible that, as with other industrial accounting developments, the use of interest may well have its origins in landed estate accountancy.[87]

The accounting treatment of depreciation is another topic which has attracted some interest. Mason gives a number of instances where it was discussed in the literature during the sixteenth and seventeenth centuries,[88] but it was slow to appear in business records. The first hint of systematic depreciation cited by Jones is found in the records of the Stanley Smelting Co. for 1788/9, though insufficient information is available, even there, to establish the precise significance of the following journal entry: 'To Stanley buildings for 10 per cent on first cost . . . £500'.[89] Other early examples of the use of depreciation in this way have been identified at the Carron Co. ironworks in 1769, where 8 per cent was charged on buildings, and Boulton & Watt's

---

[82] Jones, *Accounting, Costing and Cost Estimation*, 169.

[83] Mepham, 'Origins of Cost Accounting', 67.

[84] Stone, 'An Early English Cost Accounting System', 77.

[85] Jones, *Accounting, Costing and Cost Estimation*, 171.

[86] R. H. Parker, 'History of Accounting for Decisions', in J. Arnold, B. Carsberg, and R. Scapens (eds.), *Topics in Management Accounting* (Oxford, 1980), 262.

[87] Jones, *Accounting, Costing and Cost Estimation*, ch. 2.

[88] P. Mason, 'Illustrations of the Early Treatment of Depreciation', *Accounting Review*, 8 (1933), 210.

[89] Jones, *Accounting, Costing and Cost Estimation*, 159.

Soho Foundry in the 1790s, where 5 per cent was charged on buildings and 8 per cent on steam engines.[90]

After 1800 the use of depreciation in industrial accounting seems to have become more common. The practice was taken up in the textile industries,[91] while between 1830 and 1850 significant developments in the treatment of depreciation occurred in the railway industry. Initially, railway companies imputed depreciation in their accounts to cover the deterioration of rolling stock, but by the end of this period they began to establish depreciation funds for the eventual replacement of large sections of track.[92] A sophisticated scheme of this sort is outlined by Captain Mark Huish and others in a private report to the directors of the London & North Western Railway in 1853:

the amount [to be] laid aside was arrived at by first calculating the probable cost per mile of the operation of relaying [the track]—by estimating the number of years which, according to the experience of the day, would represent the 'life' of the road—and by then calculating the annual reserve which, at either 4 or 4½ per cent. compound interest, would be necessary in order to reproduce, at the end of the period, the total amount required to restore the line to its original condition.[93]

This calculation contains some of the basic features of a modern discounted cash flow investment appraisal, namely uncertainty and making allowance for the time value of money.

A less sophisticated method of capital project appraisal, but one popular with businessmen today, was used by the civil engineer Charles Vignoles in 1833 to explore the possibility of laying down a railway for horse-drawn waggons from the Parys and Mona mines to the port at Amlwch. A calculation of annual cost saving from adopting the proposed scheme is shown to pay back the initial investment of £5,354 within about three years.[94]

VI

Much of what has been written on the historical development of management and cost accounting has focused on what might be described as 'single

[90] Pollard, *Genesis of Modern Management*, 244.

[91] J. R. Edwards, *A History of Financial Accounting* (1989), 84–5.

[92] J. R. Edwards, 'Depreciation and Fixed Asset Valuation in British Railway Company Accounts to 1911', *Accounting and Business Research*, 16 (1986–7), 251–5.

[93] M. Huish, H. Woodhouse, and E. Watkin, '(Private) Report to the Permanent Way Committee of the London and North Western Railway on the Renewal Fund, 1853', in J. R. Edwards (ed.), *Reporting Fixed Assets in Nineteenth Century Company Accounts* (1986), 273.

[94] Jones, *Accounting, Costing and Cost Estimation*, 237–41.

variable solutions': the level of industrialization, the relative impact of fixed and variable costs, and the organizational structure of business activity have each been identified as principal causal factors.[95] In the light of recent research it does not seem that any simple explanation for the development of management and cost accounting will stand up to close scrutiny. Accounting has developed to serve management in an increasingly complex and constantly changing social and economic environment. The variety of the costing procedures employed by managers in Wales and elsewhere, their *ad hoc* nature, and the widely different circumstances in which innovations occurred, demonstrates the contingent nature of the contemporary accounting framework. Under these conditions managers first decided what they wanted to do—plan, choose, or control—and then structured the information accordingly. As the problem changed, so did the information required and generated. With the diffusion of ideas and techniques hampered by secrecy, unstandardized accounting methods were developed to meet the specific requirements of individual firms.

The findings surveyed in this essay show that it is now necessary to reappraise generalizations which have been made concerning the development of costing procedures within the factory and workshop. In summary, it can now be stated that the use of standards goes back to medieval times; the preparation of cost estimates dates at least from the early sixteenth century; the use of *ad hoc* procedures to identify incremental costs for planning and decision-making purposes dates from the late sixteenth century; the integration of cost and financial records to provide routine data for the purpose of transfer pricing, performance assessment, and control in large companies dates from the 1790s, and perhaps earlier; whilst the roots of standard costing can be perceived in the accounting practices employed during the second half of the eighteenth and the early nineteenth centuries.

Many of the tools of modern management accounting were, therefore, in use by 1850 and, since some of these procedures have very early origins, it is difficult to resist the conclusion that they must have been fairly firmly established in at least certain sectors of the economy. It is impossible to gauge the extent to which the techniques described above were utilized, and it seems likely that the more sophisticated advances occurred within the larger concerns undertaking a more complex range of activities, such as the Carron Co., which has been

---

[95] Hudson's identification of a range of possible variables affecting accounting developments in the West Riding textile industry is an important exception to this approach. P. Hudson, 'Some Aspects of 19th Century Accounting Development in the West Riding Textile Industry', *Accounting History*, 2 (1977).

described as 'an atypically large Scottish industrial undertaking'.[96] Nevertheless, the results of recent studies by Jones and others may be contrasted with the bleak observations made by Pollard and others concerning the nature and usefulness of accounting systems during this period. Future research into primary business records can only add weight to the conclusion that significant use was made of cost accounting data for planning, decision-making, and control before and during the industrial revolution.

POSTSCRIPT

Since the above chapter was written, in 1989, interest in the development of cost and management accounting has continued to grow. An important reason has been the publication in 1987 of Johnson and Kaplan's *Relevance Lost* which has been described as 'one of the most significant monographs on the history of accounting published to date'[1] and is attributed with having 'placed accounting history centre-stage not only in the research agenda, but also for practical business management'.[2] Moreover, it has given a particular impetus to management accounting history research because the major issue addressed is the process by which cost accounting and management control systems have developed to a state where top managers believe they can run their firms 'by the numbers'.[3]

We believe that an effective reappraisal of the present role of management accounting requires a solid understanding of the circumstances in which cost and management accounting procedures were first developed. While Johnson and Kaplan see US management accounting as a product of the second half of the nineteenth century, the research surveyed in the preceding article suggests to us a different timescale for development in Great Britain, and this view has been reinforced by further recent work.

Lee believes he has found 'rare precursors of modern industrial accounting'[4] among the colliery records of the Willoughbys of Wollaton, Nottinghamshire, covering the second half of the sixteenth century, and

[96] Fleischman and Parker, 'Managerial Accounting', 213.

[1] M. Ezzamel, K. Hoskin, and R. Macve, 'Managing it all by Numbers: A Review of Johnson & Kaplan's "Relevance Lost"', *Accounting and Business Research* (Spring, 1990), 153.

[2] Ibid. 164.

[3] Johnson and Kaplan, *Relevance Lost*, 15.

[4] G. A. Lee, 'Colliery Accounting in Sixteenth-Century England: The Willoughbys of Wollaton, Nottinghamshire', in O. F. Graves (ed.), *The Costing Heritage: Studies in Honor of S. Paul Garner* (Harrisonburg, Va.: Academy of Accounting Historians), 51.

demonstrates how charge and discharge based records were ordered to pro-vide a rudimentary basis for short-term decision-making.[5] Amongst the note-books of Daniel Hechstetter, the manager of the Keswick Works from 1597 to 1633, we find evidence of a wider range of calculations, possibly imported from Germany, used for the purpose of planning, decision-making, and con-trol.[6] From the late seventeenth century has survived a fully integrated system of cost and financial accounts, conforming entirely with the principles of double-entry bookkeeping, used to facilitate the administration of charcoal iron-making in the Sheffield region.[7]

The growing conviction that economic development and technological change is a gradual, ongoing process, rather than one that can be neatly ascribed to particular time periods receives further support from work on records surviving from the British industrial revolution. Fleischman and Parker present evidence of 'purposeful costing activities undertaken by own-ers and managers'[8] in a paper which also tentatively explores some of the environmental factors responsible for the observed levels of sophistication. These researchers extended their analysis to encompass also the textile indus-try in a survey of twenty-five firms which is judged to have revealed 'particu-lar emphasis on cost control (72%) and standards utilisation (80%)'.[9]

The above studies are principally concerned with identifying the existence and use of cost and management techniques, from which it is inferred that management must have regarded them as providing a relevant and rational basis for decision-making. Fleischman, Parker, and Vamplew have invited economic and accounting historians to address more directly the question of assessing the impact of observed techniques on decision-making and eco-nomic growth.[10] This will not be an easy task as there are strongly held views that cost accounting systems are adopted for reasons other than the search for increased efficiency. Hopper and Armstrong, for example, argue that the development of accounting controls were 'rooted in struggles as firms attempted to control labour processes in various epochs of capitalistic devel-

---

[5] Ibid. 71.

[6] J. R. Edwards, G. Hammersley, and E. Newell, 'Cost Accounting at Keswick, England, *c*.1598–1615: The German Connection', *Accounting Historians Journal* (June 1990), 61–80.

[7] J. R. Edwards and T. Boyns, 'Industrial Organization and Accounting Innovation: Charcoal Ironmaking in England 1690–1783', *Management Accounting Research*, 3 (1992), 151–69.

[8] R. K. Fleischman and L. D. Parker, 'The Cost Accounting Environment in the British Industrial Revolution Iron Industry', *Accounting, Business and Financial History* (Summer, 1992), 157.

[9] R. K. Fleischman and L. D. Parker, 'British Entrepreneurs and Pre-industrial Revolution Evidence of Cost Management', *Accounting Review* (Apr. 1991), 371.

[10] R. K. Fleischman, L. D. Parker, and W. Vamplew, 'New Cost Accounting Perspectives on Technological Change in the British Industrial Revolution', in Graves, *Costing Heritage*, 22.

opment'.[11] Others seriously doubt whether earlier identified technical innovations amount to a genuine system of management accounting, with the latter instead believed to date, in Britain as in the USA, from the late nineteenth century.[12]

Accounting history research is at an exciting stage, marked by a 'pluralization of methodologies and the attendant posing of new questions to the past of accounting [which] extends beyond accounting history'.[13] Undoubtedly industrial accounting is a particularly fruitful focus for further investigation.

[11] T. Hopper and P. Armstrong, 'Cost Accounting, Controlling Labour and the Rise of Conglomerates', *Accounting, Organizations and Society*, 16, No. 5/6 (1991), 405.

[12] Ezzamel *et al.*, 'Managing it all By Numbers'; K. Hoskin and R. Macve, 'The Genesis of Modern Cost Management: A Reappraisal of the Significance of European Initiatives', paper presented at the Fifteenth Annual European Accounting Association Congress, Madrid, April 1992.

[13] P. Miller, T. Hopper, and R. Laughlin, 'The New Accounting History: An Introduction', *Accounting, Organizations and Society*, 16, No. 5/6 (1991), 395. See also C. J. Napier, 'Research Directions in Accounting History', *British Accounting Review* (Sept. 1989), 237–54; M. Neimark, 'The King is Dead. Long Live the King', *Critical Perspectives on Accounting*, I (1990), 103–14; R. K. Fleischman, L. P. Kalbers, and L. D. Parker, 'Archival Research and the "New Accounting History": The Industrial Revolution Case', in Atsuo Tsuji (ed.), *Collected Papers of the Sixth World Congress of Accounting Historians*, iii (Japan: Accounting History Association, 1992), 675–715.

16 · SOME ASPECTS OF NINETEENTH-CENTURY ACCOUNTING DEVELOPMENT IN THE WEST RIDING TEXTILE INDUSTRY

P. Hudson

The fundamental requirement in studying business accounting techniques historically is to see developments as the response to particular and individual needs of industries as they themselves develop over time. These needs are the product of such things as technical and organizational change, the size of business units, the nature of products and markets. This basic structural determinant can be regarded as being tempered by two further factors. First, it may be tempered by 'external' influences, for example, the need to respond in particular ways to legal requirements, taxation demands, or outside pressure generally from shareholders and other interested parties.[1] Secondly, developments are modified by the extent to which requirements are met by the stage of evolution of accounting theory and practice, the background, education, and abilities of entrepreneurs in an industry, and the legacy of traditional methods handed down from earlier stages of economic development.

The advantage of a historian's approach to accounting evolution is the ability to relate specific developments to the changing nature and historical background of particular industries and thus to place accounting more squarely in the context of the emergence of industrial capitalism.[2] This chap-

---

First published in *Accounting History* (1977).

[1] For an exposition of the importance of these influences see R. P. Brief, 'The Origin and Evolution of Nineteenth Century Asset Accounting', *Business History Review*, 40 (1966), 1–23.

[2] For debate on this subject see Werner Sombart, *Der moderne Kapitalismus*, 6th edn. (Munich, 1924) ii/1. 118–25; F. L. Nussbaum, *A History of Economic Institutions* (New York, 1933), 159–61; B. S. Yamey, 'Scientific Bookkeeping and the Rise of Capitalism', *Economic History Review*, 2nd ser. 1 (1949), 99–113; and 'Accounting and the Rise of Capitalism: Further Notes on a Theme by Sombart', *Journal of Accounting Research*, 2 (1964), 117–36.

ter aims to use the example of the contrasting branches of the Yorkshire textile industry in the nineteenth century to highlight the determinants of methods used in various aspects of business accounting. First, an outline of the
Yorkshire textile trades in the period will be given to illustrate the contrasts
between different branches. Features of development which one would expect
to influence the nature of accounting will be isolated to form a theoretical
model. This will then be applied in studying aspects of accounting methods
used by a representative sample of Yorkshire textile concerns.[3]

In tracing the history of the West Riding textile industry one must first
make a clear distinction between the two major branches of the industry,
woollens and worsteds. Milled woollen cloth was the traditional product of
the county, carried on until well into the nineteenth century by a large number of small independent clothiers who employed their families and perhaps
one or two journeymen, owned their own tools, equipment, and materials-in-
process, and sold their finished pieces at the local cloth hall.[4] Worsted production, by contrast, only expanded significantly in the West Riding from
the second half of the eighteenth century and was organized from its inception on a merchant-capitalist basis, with a merchant clothier of fairly substantial means distributing work to an army of wage-dependent domestic
workers. The merchant capitalist owned the materials in the hands of his
workers and usually their tools and equipment also. He was responsible for
wool purchase in bulk and for the disposal of finished goods. He was thus
generally in charge of a fairly large organization with the attendant problems
of control over production, distribution and collection, pilfering, wage payments, etc.[5]

This contrast in the traditional means of organization in woollen and
worsted production not only had implications for the demands placed on
bookkeeping in the domestic system of the eighteenth and early nineteenth
centuries and hence the legacy of methods passed on, but also affected the
nature of transition to workshop and factory production and the accounting

[3] This sample is composed of those concerns whose surviving records have been catalogued in
P. Hudson, *The West Riding Wool Textile Industry: A Catalogue of Business Records* (Edington, 1974). The sample
includes firms of all sizes and varies from those concentrating primarily on merchanting to those specializ-
ing in one manufacturing process, vertically integrated firms, and firms producing a wide variety of yarns,
cloths, and clothing. References to archive collections in the book will henceforth be by name of firm and
relevant item number. The location of archives can be derived from the catalogue itself.

[4] The structure and organization of the West Riding domestic system of woollen production is well
described in H. Heaton, *The Yorkshire Woollen and Worsted Industries from Earliest Times up to the Industrial Revolution*
(Oxford, 1920); and in W. B. Crump and G. Ghorbal, *History of the Huddersfield Woollen Industry*
(Huddersfield, 1935).

[5] See Heaton, *Yorkshire Woollen and Worsted Industries*.

needs there. In general, as one might expect, the worsted industry was transferred to larger mill units as the merchant capitalists were often in a good
position to demand credit and capital facilities required to establish large
concerns. In the woollen industry concentration took more varied forms.
Domestic clothiers often grouped themselves together to form a company
mill, an early type of joint-stock concern set up under a trust deed and often
with a considerable number of shareholders. These concerns were fairly common from the 1780s, when some of the preparatory processes in the woollen
industry were mechanized and hence most economically carried out in centralized establishments alongside fulling.[6] In some cases the larger woollen
domestic clothiers managed to become factory producers in a small way aided
by loans, the hire purchase of machinery, multiple tenancy of industrial buildings, and the renting of room and power which saved on fixed capital outlay.[7]
These two means of concentration ensured that the average woollen business
was considerably smaller than the typical worsted factory concern (see Table
16.1). There was a minority of large woollen mills where cloth or wool merchants undertook centralized production of all stages in the industry, usurp-
ing the position of the traditional small manufacturers.[8] These latter
exceptions aside, woollen mills were generally smaller and this organizational
tendency was endorsed by the differential rate of technological change in the
two sectors. Worsted fibre is much more adaptable to mechanization, so that
the transition to mill production of the major branches of spinning and
weaving proceeded some two decades earlier in the worsted sector than in
woollens. Worsted spinning was mechanized in the first two decades of the
century and weaving from the mid-1830s. Combing, a process peculiar to
worsteds, was not mechanized until after mid-century. Some worsted firms
turned over each process to machinery as developments occurred but the general pattern in worsted factory production was towards vertical disintegration
and concentration on just one process, which enabled greater use to be made
of the economies of large-scale production. By the third decade of the nine-

---

[6] Fulling or milling—peculiar to woollen production—had been a centralized powered process since
the 13th century. In the late 18th century scribbling and carding processes were adapted to water power.
Company mills were most common in the heavy-woollen district Dewsbury/Batley area, e.g. Healey Mill,
Ossett Mill, Spring End Mill at Horbury, Whiteley Mill at Thornhill, all dating from late 18th century.
There were company mills also in the Leeds area but generally from a later date, e.g. Gill Royd Mill Co.,
Kellett Brown & Co. (both established 1834).

[7] For examples see Hudson, *West Riding Wool Textile Industry*, *passim*.

[8] A classic example is Benjamin Gott of Leeds, who by 1800 had the biggest textile factory in
Britain—Park Mill, Leeds. This was most common in the Huddersfield/Colne Valley fancy woollen area,
the incentive being a closer control over quality production and expensive imported wool. See Crump and
Ghorbal, *History*, 89–100.

TABLE 16.1 *Number of men employed in manufacturing establishments for which 'masters' sent in returns to 1851 Census: Yorkshire*

No. of men employed	Woollen cloth manufacture (%)[a]	Worsted manufacture (%)[b]
1–9	52.3	28.3
10–49	38.6	37.7
50–199	6.9	21.7
200+	2.2[c]	12.3[d]

[a] 581 employers.
[b] 106 employers.
[c] Includes 3 employers of 350, 420, 421 men and 2 employers of 500 each.
[d] Includes 9 employers with 350–550 men, 1 employer with 1,000 men, 1 employer with 3,000 men.

Source: 1851 Census Division IX: Employers: Yorkshire.

teenth century the capital threshold of entry into mill production of worsteds was high.[9] The woollen industry, by contrast, generally maintained its vertically integrated structure and was carried on in mills involving a much smaller capital outlay.[10] The slower and more piecemeal adoption of machine processing and steam power gave a lower capital intensity in this branch of the industry—many of the early factories incorporated the hand processes alongside machine production or 'sent out' work, particularly weaving, to domestic employees until well into the second half of the nineteenth century.

These basic distinctions between the woollen and worsted industries characterized their development through the entire nineteenth century. The smaller woollen concerns were slower in becoming public companies although the majority of firms in both branches typically maintained their private status as family concerns and small partnerships until after the First World War. The basic woollen/worsted contrast affected such aspects of accounting as the size and complexity of the system, the need to incorporate fixed capital costs and depreciation, departmental divisions of accounts, the separation or confusion of mercantile, estate, farming, and manufacturing accounts, and the need for formal account disclosures.

Superimposed on the major woollen/worsted contrast were other influences which determined the differentiation of firms and hence their accounting requirements. An important factor was the type of product produced and

[9] For a succinct account of the development of worsted factory production in the 19th century, see E. M. Sigsworth, *Black Dyke Mills: A History* (Liverpool, 1958), 1–135.
[10] Fixed capital values derived from insurance data indicate that worsted mills averaged about three to four times the investment of woollen concerns by 1835 (excluding the very large woollen concerns to avoid distortion): see D. T. Jenkins, *The West Riding Wool Textile Industry 1770–1835: A Study of Fixed Capital Formation* (Edington, 1975), 302–15.

the nature of the market for that product. Many of the products of the industry were manufactured for a market which was virtually perfectly competitive, e.g. worsted yarns, combings, and many of the plainer utility cloths such as certain coatings and blankets. In complete contrast was the fancy-cloth, fashion-determined side of the market for Yorkshire produce which became increasingly predominant, particularly after the introduction of cotton warps into worsted weaving from the 1830s followed by the use of silk, mohair, and alpaca fibres. These developments, together with increasing use of high-grade Spanish and Saxony wools in the woollen branch from the 1830s, resulted in the production of an immense variety of cloths with equally varied markets and merchanting methods. Fairly accurate costing and pricing was needed for fashion goods and for cloths made for specific contracts in order to allow a reasonable profit margin. A further influence on accounting requirements was the extent to which firms participated in their own purchasing and merchanting or other business ventures, or concentrated solely on textile manufacture. Given this brief outline of the main variables which would tend to influence accounting development, it is possible to express these more clearly as a general model in tabular form (see Table 16.2).

Before proceeding with a closer examination of the evidence regarding the way these determinants worked themselves out in practice in the textile sector in the nineteenth century, it is necessary to consider the available 'tools' of accounting which modified developments. These include the legacy of earlier bookkeeping methods in the industry, the industrial and educational background of entrepreneurs, the availability of trained office personnel, and the state of development of accounting theory and practice.

First, one must be aware of the strong influence of mercantile methods of accounting.[11] The majority of worsted and large woollen manufacturers were men from merchant backgrounds and the small amount of fixed capital involved in domestic production enabled *ad hoc* putting-out systems of accounts to be evolved in the eighteenth century in worsted production, which persisted but were found increasingly wanting, as manufacturing become more centralized and mercantile transactions a lesser activity. The putting-out systems, which were similar to mercantile practice but almost always single entry, and therefore lacking profit and capital accounts, did fulfil requirements of control and supervision of operations in the period when

---

[11] This was particularly strong where a merchant firm extended into manufacturing, e.g. William Lupton & Co. Ltd., Henry and Andrew Peterson.

TABLE 16.2 *Simplified model of variables affecting accounting development*

The demands placed on an accounting system are a function of:	Aspects of accounting affected
A. *Type of firm*	
Nature of the product (homogeneous, varied, fashion)	} Costing as an aid to pricing and decision-making
Nature of the market (perfect competition, monopoly, contract selling)	
Level of vertical or horizontal integration	Separation of departmental accounts
Extent of merchanting allied to manufacture	Separation or confusion of merchanting and manufacturing account
Private partnership organisation	Treatment of capital as an auxiliary to entrepreneurship—retardation of double-entry systems and calculations of periodic profit on capital of entire concern
Company mill	Responsibility of accounts to larger body of shareholders
Public company	Demand for formal account disclosures
B. *Development over time*	
Nature of the 'domestic system'	Need for control of complex operation (worsted) or primitive small farmer/manufacturer bookkeeping (woollen industry). Influence of mercantile accounting
Speed and nature of transition to factory production	Need to integrate fixed capital into costings (overheads), inventories, profit calculations
Size of factory unit and fixed capital; pace of mechanization & technological obsolescence	Requirement of a policy for depreciation
Experience of changes in economic conditions over time	The necessity to adapt accounting systems to changing conditions, e.g. policy regarding drawings and dividends, need for costings in changing market situations

fixed capital was small and technological change slow.[12] There was then no problem of large capital outlays on equipment or of costs varying with output and few innovations to be tested by their relative profitability. These conditions were however changing rapidly by the early decades of the nineteenth century.

The legacy of mercantile methods and theories of accounting also resulted in the separation of ventures, lack of continuity, and the absence of regular assessments of the profitability of an entire concern over time.[13] These

---

[12] e.g. John Foster & Sons 1–3, R. V. Marriner Ltd. 1–4, Box 68.

[13] See Grace & Jepson 1, 2 (1807–50). These features are true also of the accounts of William Lupton & Co. in the 19th century but in the 18th century the firm's predecessors had a double-entry system with regular yearly assessments of profit and loss. Clearly other influences were at work—possibly in this case the ability and foresight of one of the partners. Some firms only got round to assessing the balance of books at the time of a partnership change, e.g. Grace & Jepson.

tendencies were endorsed by the fact that both textbooks and teachers of bookkeeping concentrated on merchanting accounts with a much smaller emphasis on estate, factorage, and retailing—almost ignoring manufacturing accounts until the late nineteenth century.

Estate accounting methods were also transferred to some of the early factory industrial ventures. This resulted again in the virtual absence of capital accounts—purchases of fixed equipment being generally treated as costs to revenue for that year or accounting period. This led to gross distortions when profitability came to be examined, which were further enhanced by the lack of logical grouping of incomes with their appropriate expenditures. It was thus difficult to isolate and assess returns on investments.[14] Common in the small woollen manufacturing concerns where production into the nineteenth century was closely allied to farming, but also found in larger enterprises, was a general lack of any idea of firmly separating the textile business accounts from other business interests such as estate management, agriculture, quarrying, mining, or from strictly private affairs such as philanthropic donations, medical bills, fine art, victual, and other purchases.[15]

Relating these legacies to what is known of the evolution of factory production in the woollen and worsted industries one would expect to find the most adequate tools of accounting to be transferred to worsted factory production given the merchant-capitalist background of the majority of entrepreneurs. They tended to have more experience of accounting for manufacture and large-scale operations, whereas the smaller firms in woollen production often had only the domestic clothiers' methods to fall back on, which were generally a confusion of diary entries with business and personal memoranda inextricably mixed.[16]

Both branches worked in an environment in the nineteenth century where there were very few trained bookkeepers or personnel with numerate skills. Furthermore the prevalence of small private family partnerships with the concomitant and often extreme desire for complete secrecy of affairs meant that most businessmen preferred to do their own accounting. The sheer burden which this involved militated against the adoption of the more tedious but more thorough double-entry method, although some firms contrived to cir-

[14] e.g. John Foster & Sons 9 (1859–79), T & M Bairstow 1, 2 (1801–64), J. & J. Holroyd 1 (1783–1825), Joseph Lee (1796–1825).
[15] See n. 14 above; also Jonathon Akroyd 2 (1776–80), Robert Jowitt & Sons Ltd. 27–41 (1803–98), Joseph Rogerson (1808–14).
[16] See P. Hudson, *The Genesis of Industrial Capital: A Study of the West Riding Textile Industry, c.1750–1850* (Cambridge, 1986), 25–52.
[17] See John Foster & Sons 291 (1841).

cumvent the problem by multiplication of office staff so that no individual clerk had access to all the books. In general, however, there were very few office staff, even in firms employing several hundred workers, until the last quarter of the nineteenth century, when a small but specific group of clerks began to appear on the payrolls of some firms.[18]

All firms were also working at a period when the accountancy profession was undeveloped and where there were few theoretical examples available in published form. However, there is evidence of a fairly widespread interest in accounting texts at least amongst the larger Yorkshire manufacturers, particularly in the worsted industry. *Jones's English System of Book-Keeping*[19] seems to have been fairly widely read and commented upon.[20] Several prominent West Riding textile manufacturers appear among the testimonials in the front of editions of the book between the 1830s and 1860s.[21] John Foster & Sons, worsted manufacturers of Queensbury, were personal friends of Edward Jones's grandson Theodore Brook Jones, who became their professional accountant in 1858.[22]

Another accounting theorist with some influence in the West Riding in the first half of the nineteenth century was F. W. Cronhelm, who wrote his much celebrated book in 1818.[23] He was resident in Halifax, being employed by John Edwards & Son, worsted merchants and manufacturers.[24] Some of the examples in his book are West Riding concerns, including the important section on manufacturers' accounts in which the complete separation of ownership from the business and the method of recording property and changes in property rather than debt relationships is clearly laid out.[25] Little evidence has however survived to illustrate the extent of his influence in

---

[18] See T. & M. Bairstow Ltd. 170–2, Thomas Boyd (Leeds) Ltd. 18. More evidence is available of office staff employed in the first two decades of the 20th century: E. Fox & Sons Ltd. 6 (1901–6), James France & Co. Ltd. 7 (1911), J. D. Johnstone 41–7 (from 1912).

[19] E. T. Jones, *Jones's English System of Book-Keeping* (1796). There were more than twenty subsequent editions up to 1860. See B. S. Yamey, 'Edward Jones and the Reform of Book-Keeping, 1795–1810', in A. C. Littleton and B. S. Yamey (eds.), *Studies in the History of Accounting* (London, 1956), 313–24.

[20] e.g. Isaac Holden & Sons, Box V 7, 11, and 13.

[21] Ten of the nineteen 'Northern' firms testifying in 1832/3 were West Riding textile concerns. Six of the twenty-seven signatories of the 15th edition (1867) were West Riding woollen or worsted businessmen.

[22] For correspondence between Foster and his accountant concerning accounts see John Foster & Sons 166, 179, 182, 187. The 'English System' was not being used despite the testimonial in 1867.

[23] F. W. Cronhelm, *Double-Entry by Single* . . . (London, 1818).

[24] It was probably his influence which resulted in fairly elaborate *ex ante* costing being used by the firm in the 1860s. These included charges for overheads, a 10% addition for interest, and a profit margin allowance of around 15%. Rawson Papers, item 354. (In private hands, enquiries: Leeds City Archives.)

[25] Cronhelm, *Double-Entry*, 125–300. The example used is that of John Henderson, a Leeds woollen manufacturer.

the West Riding. The appeal of single-entry theories such as those of Jones and Cronhelm had a certain logic in the West Riding in this period when the majority of businessmen did their own books and were not under public pressure to disclose financial information.

Later in the century a further significant advance in the theoretical writings on manufacturers' accounts was again connected with the West Riding: this was G. P. Norton's *Textile Manufacturers' Book-Keeping*, published in Huddersfield in 1889.[26] This system was designed to allocate costs to departments and processes in such a way that the cost could be compared with the prices charged by outside specialists. The prevalent use of outworking concerns for some of the processes in vertically integrated concerns would endorse the logic of the standard costing notion, albeit in a primitive form.[27] There is little evidence of this form of costing being widespread in the West Riding before the twentieth century, but further research is required.

Little is known of the precise influence of theoretical works as compared with *ad hoc* modifications of accounting systems arising through trial and error. The slow but accelerating spread of the use of professional accountants in the last third of the century may have encouraged more uniformity in theory and practice.[28]

Having considered the distinctive features of the branches of wool textile production, suggested some possible determinants of the nature of certain accounting techniques, and qualified this by recognition of the tools available by virtue of the methods used in the domestic system, the background of entrepreneurs, and the extent of theoretical knowledge, it is now necessary to study certain aspects of accounting as they occurred in particular types of firm. In this way the model in Table 16.2 can be related to the empirical evidence. Examination of this evidence will, for convenience, be structured around three major areas:

1. The use of accountancy in costing and aiding management decisions.
2. Adaptation of accounting to large-scale manufacture. Integration of fixed capital purchases and overheads. The treatment of depreciation.
3. The adoption of regular accounting periods and returns, balance sheets, and attempts to estimate the profitability of an entire concern.

---

[26] Norton was a partner in a firm of woollen manufacturers' accountants: Armitage, Clough & Norton of Huddersfield, London, and Dewsbury. Unfortunately their records do not appear to have survived.

[27] It was only in his later work that Norton fully developed the use of proper standard costs; see G. P. Norton, *Cost Accounting and Cost Control* (London, 1931).

[28] The pressure of recommendations in the Companies Acts of 1856 and 1862 probably aided this also.

COSTING AND AIDING MANAGEMENT DECISIONS

There is little evidence that accountancy was systematically used in aiding management decisions via *ex ante* assessments of costs and projected profitability of various courses of action before the twentieth century.[29] Such costings as survive are mainly done to aid pricing and include prime costs but only unsystematic allowances, wild guesses, or complete omissions of such costs as overheads and marketing.[30] In vertically integrated firms there was a tendency towards the separation of departmental accounts (corresponding to successive processes).[31] Some attempts were made to assess the profitability of departments via *ex post* costings but overheads were always a problem and no principles seem to have emerged for treating joint products.[32]

It seems certain that the development of production costing in both branches of the industry was primarily determined by the type of commodity produced. Prices of the relatively homogeneous products of the various stages of worsted production—particularly combings and yarn—would, in an environment of horizontally integrated concerns, tend to be more market-determined than products in the successive stages of woollen manufacture. It was therefore only necessary to keep costs below prices and not to use costings to determine prices. In both branches an everyday utility cloth would be subject to an almost perfect market and profits would simply be a question of keeping costs down. Those cloths made for the fashion trade, with demand dependent on changes in taste and usually made in advance for each new fashion season, presented a different problem. The uniqueness of a successful fashion product would ensure some monopoly of supply at first and profits would then depend on the addition of a suitable margin after costing the product. Many examples may be found of *ex ante* costings first developed to serve this side of the trade. Few date from before 1850 and most include

---

[29] It may seem surprising that technological modifications and machinery improvements were not given any form of cost/profit analysis before being adopted. This may be partly because inventions were either obviously superior or because large profit margins in periods of good trade allowed old machinery to be utilized unquestioned.

[30] e.g. William Ackroyd Ltd. 1 (1844–52),T. & M. Bairstow Ltd. 302–9 (1854–1913), F. W. Bannister & Company Ltd. 18 (1891–1909), John Foster & Sons 62 (1845–6), 68 (1847), 116–20, 123–6 (1840–3), George Crowther & Co. 9 (1882–3), John Taylor & Sons Ltd. 16–22 (1870–1890s), William Rhodes Ltd. 2 (1896), G. & J. Stubley 11 (1858–1936), J. C. Waddington & Sons Ltd. 1 (1816–27), Messrs Walker 3 (1890s). The lack of formality in recording costings and their separation from the books of account may help to explain the survival of so few calculations.

[31] e.g. Kellett Brown & Co. Ltd. 6–48 (1835–1920s), T. & M. Bairstow Ltd. 14 (1889–1913).

[32] e.g. Hudson, Sykes & Bousefield 21 (1873–86).

only prime costs with no allowance for overheads. The fashion trade in worsted mixtures put particular pressure on the need for costing.[33]

Another section of the trade where *ex ante* production costing developed early was in the supply of army cloths. It is unclear whether the underlying factor was that prices had to be produced for a tender or that a definite order meant a guaranteed market. In either case it is the absence of market competition which is important.[34]

Company mills also commonly costed their work for various processes. They often had a local monopoly of services but, as they were established primarily to serve shareholders and to process their materials, pricing was usually just a question of making sure that costs were covered.[35]

Another costing example which was necessitated partly by the absence of competition is that done for the combing process by Isaac Holden & Sons, a Yorkshire firm who held machine patents and had a monopoly of combing in France. The surviving calculations date from the 1850s and 1860s and are *ex post* costings to enable profits to be calculated from sales. They include a 10 per cent per year charge to machinery and rents.[36]

In years of expanding trade large profit margins disguised inefficient pricing and planning and omission of overheads. Only when profit margins were depressed were firms stimulated to calculate their costs more seriously. There appears to be an increase in the number of costing attempts surviving from the onset of general trade uncertainties in the mid-1870s—particularly in the fancy worsted cloth trade.[37] No examples have been found of costing being used to value inventories. Most of the large firms were in the habit during most of the nineteenth century of doing a new inventory each year using current estimated values.[38]

---

[33] For examples see n. 30 above, particularly John Foster & Sons 116–26 (1840–73). John Edwards & Sons were more systematic in overhead allowances when calculating cloth prices and profits for the South American trade; see n. 24 above.

[34] e.g. T. & M. Bairstow Ltd. 302 (1855), Henry Booth & Sons Ltd. (1859–67).

[35] e.g. Ossett Mill Co. I (1785–92), Kellet Brown & Co. II *passim* (1835–1922), John Hartley & Sons Ltd. (formerly Gillroyd Mills), Morley, 3 (1835–61).

[36] It is not clear here whether machinery purchase is just being written off gradually to revenue or whether the 10% represents some attempt at allowing for machine overheads. The rent allowance is more obviously concerned with plant overhead but neither machinery nor rent allowances are included for all months. See Isaac Holden & Sons Ltd., Box VII, 7, 8.

[37] For problems in the trade during these years, see E. M. Sigsworth and J. Blackman, 'The Woollen & Worsted Industries, 1815–1914' in D. H. Aldcroft (ed.), *The Development of British Industry and Foreign Competition 1875–1914* (London, 1968), 128–57. For examples of costings from this period see George Crowther & Company (B) 9 (1882–3). Lister Bros. & Co. Ltd. XI, I (1873–85). John Taylor & Sons Ltd. IV (1870–1890s).

[38] See Hudson, *West Riding Wool Textile Industry, passim.*

ADAPTATION TO LARGE-SCALE MANUFACTURE

From the 1820s, with the widespread mechanization of worsted spinning, the size of mills in the Riding was increasing rapidly, as is evidenced by the fixed capital figures in Table 16.3. It was in the 1830s–1840s that some concerns, particularly in worsted production, adopted double-entry systems of account-ing and started to employ one or two regular office staff. This was really a function of the increase in sheer size of a firm's operations. Manufacturing accounts, particularly costings, remained quite separate from the double-entry systems.[39] The most notable feature encountered with the growth of fixed capital assets was the tendency to ignore it in the accounts except for annual interest. Additions and improvement were normally entered as costs to rev-enue, a practice which became more problematic by the mid-nineteenth cen-tury as the proportion of fixed to circulating capital increased. The absence of depreciation charges continued until the 1860s and 1870s in the West Riding and even after these decades few firms had a consistent policy. The earliest depreciation allowances found among West Riding textile concerns date from 1829–41, when a flat rate of 7½ per cent per year was allowed on the machinery of John Marshall, a Leeds flax spinner, but he was well ahead of his contemporaries in the scope and nature of his accounts.[40] The Property and Income Tax Act of 1842 and subsequent taxation changes probably stimulated the introduction among unincorporated businesses of more widespread depreciation allowances on fixed equipment in the hope of gaining maximum tax concessions. The need to allow for replacement, repair,

TABLE 16.3 *Average fixed capital per mill in the West Riding wool textile industry*

Date	No. of mills with insurance figures	Average fixed capital (£)
1810	64	1,443
1820	36	4,100
1835	67	5,527

Note: The fixed capital figures are derived from Sun and Royal Exchange Insurance policies and include buildings, machinery, and fittings in most cases. Several mills had fixed capitals of over £20,000 by 1835. The average is biased on the low side because of the large number of very small concerns, particularly in the woollen industry.

Source: D. T. Jenkins, *West Riding Wool Textile Industry*, 302–15.

[39] See e.g. John Foster & Sons Ltd. from 1841, R. V. Marriner Ltd., Box 22 (1838 onwards).
[40] S. Pollard, *The Genesis of Modern Management* (London, 1968), 288.

and maintenance without upsetting the balance of any one accounting period or permitting an overdistribution of dividends was a further pressure of the need to make allowances for depreciation.[41] Physical deterioration was often confused with the need to build up reserves against technological obsolescence and for betterment—a problem particularly acute in some branches of wool textiles, e.g. spinning in the first half of the nineteenth century.[42]

There was no consistent policy towards depreciation allowances among the textile concerns.[43] Some allowed it on the basis of historic cost (e.g. 10 per cent of the purchase price per year),[44] others on the basis of a percentage of the previous year's value.[45] Ad hoc methods were most common, such as rounding down to a 'tidy' sum for arithmetical convenience and varying irregular allowances possibly related to the desirability of a reduction in values on disclosed balance sheets, particularly in years of 'bad' trade.[46]

Sometimes a figure was allowed for all machinery and another for buildings; generally between 5 and 20 per cent on machinery and around 2½ per cent—if anything at all—on buildings.[47] There is no evidence of how the varying sums were arrived at except for reference to depreciation being equal to the sum spent on repairs, or on new machinery in some firms and in some years.[48] There are some examples from the 1870s and 1880s of concerns calculating depreciation on each individual machine or type of machine, the proportion allowed generally increasing with the age of the item.[49] This may well be indicative of wider practice of more exact depreciation allowances but insufficient evidence has survived.

ADOPTION OF REGULAR ACCOUNTING PERIODS

The prevalence of small partnerships throughout the West Riding in the nineteenth century encouraged a distinction to be drawn between the interest on

[41] Several firms first began to allow depreciation from the time of the Income Tax Legislation and the Companies Acts of 1856 and 1862. The latter acts stressed particularly the problem regarding dividends.

[42] Norton highlights the confusion prevailing in the West Riding in his book but is quite clear himself that depreciation has four separate causes, namely supersession by improvements, reduction of the cost of labour and materials, decline in profits, and wear and tear. Norton, Cost Accounting, 233–6.

[43] I am here indebted to Dr D. T. Jenkins, who has been making an investigation of depreciation allowances in the industry.

[44] e.g. Wormalds & Walker Ltd. 3 (1851–70).

[45] e.g. John Foster & Sons Ltd. 4 (1841–9).

[46] e.g. J. T. Clay & Sons Ltd. 301 (1882–92), Marshall, Kaye & Marshall 30–3 (1800–1900).

[47] These figures are derived from studying all firms whose records yield evidence of depreciation. Both woollen and worsted concerns are included c.1840s–1914. See Hudson, West Riding Wool Textile Industry.

[48] e.g. John Foster & Son 4, pp. 62, 120, 505–8 (1841–9), J. T. Clay & Sons Ltd. 12, 301 (1880s).

[49] T. & M. Bairstow Ltd. 362 (1880s), W. & E. Crowther 6 (1872–98), J. T. Clay & Sons Ltd. 12 (1875–87).

capital and the profits of the partners. The resultant treatment of capital in the accounts as an auxiliary to entrepreneurship instead of the central motive force behind a firm is pointed out by Pollard as being a fault common in the nineteenth century.[50] Profits were generally understood to be the surplus after interest was charged.[51] There was no shortage of capital in the West Riding in the nineteenth century and until 1832 the interest rate was fixed by the Usury Laws at 5 per cent. The businessman was seen as using capital as a tool for which he paid the going rate. Thus the 'accountants' pattern of thought was not consistent with a market ordained distribution of capital according to its marginal return, or any bidding for it based on promised earnings'.[52] This attitude was very important because whilst it persisted there would be no attempts made to calculate the profit rate on capital. 'The notion of capital as a continuous let alone autonomous factor is virtually eliminated.'[53]

The most common form of partnership determination of profits in the West Riding took the form of periodic inventories—a particular feature of single-entry systems. All claims except for the original partners' capital were deducted from total assets and the difference was capital plus profits.[54] This, compared with the previous year's total, showed the 'profitability', although few firms made the comparison. 'Periodic calculations of a firm's profits and statements of the value of its assets are of little interest to the businessman who is closely and continuously concerned with his own business operations.'[55] Entrepreneurs were more concerned with their cash situation and the inventory figures which represented their future earnings.

Wild fluctuations of the 'capital' of a company occurred from year to year in these statements of affairs depending on such things as the valuation of assets, treatment of depreciation, provision for bad debts, and varied policies towards drawings by partners. Some firms only allowed drawings when the account would bear it (often not for several years after the foundation of a concern).[56] Some firms divided partners' funds into two sections only one of which was withdrawable.[57]

[50] Pollard, *Genesis*, 271–6.

[51] See John Broadbent & Sons 35, J. T. Clay & Sons Ltd. 294, 298, 302, J. T. Holroyd 1, E. Posselt & Co. Ltd. 2, William Lupton & Co. Ltd. 9, R. V. Marriner Ltd. 48, Boxes 22, 68, John Foster & Sons 4–7, Wormalds & Walker Ltd. 2, 3.

[52] Pollard, *Genesis*, 274.

[53] Ibid. 275.

[54] e.g. John Barran & Sons Ltd. 1 (1845–69), T. & M. Bairstow Ltd. 3, 6, 78, 237, 241 (1839–82), John Broadbent & Sons 1–5 (1826–73), J. T. Clay & Sons Ltd. (B) 1 (1812, 1814), (Ha) 10 (1814).

[55] B. S. Yamey, 'Some Topics in the History of Financial Accounting in England 1500–1900', in W. T. Baxter and S. Davidson *Studies in Accounting Theory* (London, 1962), 38.

[56] See e.g. Sigsworth, *Black Dyke Mills*, 226; Wormalds & Walker Ltd. 2, 3 (1811–76).

[57] e.g. Benjamin Gott & Partners. Pollard, *Genesis*, 281.

There was little external pressure to involve a firm in more 'accurate' regular demonstrations of its profit or loss, however calculated, until after the limited liability joint-stock legislation of 1844, 1856, and 1862, after which a minority of firms became incorporated and disclosed their accounts regularly in accordance with statutory recommendations.[58] Divorce of ownership from management in some firms towards the end of the century had a similar effect. The company mills of the woollen industry were however under pressure as early as the 1790s to be more regular and formal in their accounting, to make regular statements, and to provide for shareholders to examine the accounts if they wished.[59]

In general the idea of capital as an auxiliary to entrepreneurship, the close control which the small partnership form of organization gave to the majority of textile concerns, and the lack of external pressures through most of the century discouraged the regular assessment of total profits in a consistent manner. This also explains the persistence of single-entry systems late into the period of industrial capitalism and contests Sombart's identity of double entry with capitalism. Despite the lack of a profit and loss account and a capital account 'the greater comprehensiveness and orderliness of the double-entry system are likely to be relatively unimportant for effective business management when the proprietor is in close touch with much of the detail of his firm'.[60] This was certainly the case in the West Riding.

Two important aspects of cost accounting remained very confused among West Riding textile concerns at the end of the nineteenth century. These were the relationship between cost records and commercial bookkeeping by double entry, and the policy in charging for overhead expenses. Further work is required on the evidence available to see for example whether Norton's ideas were typical of practices in the West Riding.[61] It seems that manufacturing accounts were kept separate from the double-entry systems but some were tied in resulting in the same net profit figure as that shown by the

---

[58] The mandatory provisions of the 1844 Act were subsequently dropped but the 1856 and 1862 Acts recommended fairly sophisticated disclosures with a regular audit, double entry, and allowances for depreciation. See H. C. Edey and Prot. Panitpakdi, 'British Company Accounting and the Law 1844–1900', in Littleton and Yamey (eds.), *Studies*, 356–79. For West Riding examples of the influence of legislation see J. Hepworth & Sons 1–8 (1895–1957), Lister & Co. Ltd. (1889–1952), M. P. Stonehouse 12 (1880–1915), Holly Park Mill Co. (L) 1 (1867–1918).

[59] e.g. Ossett Mill Co. 1, 2 (1786–1892), John Hartley & Sons Ltd. (formerly Gill Royd Mills), Marley, 1 (1835–61), Kellet Brown & Co. Ltd. 69 (1845–75).

[60] Yamey 'Accounting and the Rise of Capitalism', 134–5.

[61] G. P. Norton *Textile Manufacturers' Book-Keeping* (Huddersfield, 1889). For details of Norton's ideas see A. C. Littleton, *Accounting Evolution to 1900* (New York, 1966), 340–52.

trading account.[62] Littleton has summed up the problematic of accounting concepts at the close of the nineteenth century:

So long as exchange was its purpose and its environment, book-keeping expressed many expenditures for services as temporarily withheld deductions from capital—that is—practically as losses. With the advent of manufacturing however such expenditures as labour and services acquired must be regarded (with concrete materials) as property elements awaiting conversion; they represent investments of capital. This was a new view of bookkeeping.[63]

This view, however, is not consistently apparent in surviving West Riding textile records until well into the twentieth century.

In conclusion, it is first and foremost necessary to point out the need for further work to be done on this collection of business records, which is unique both in the number of firms represented and in the variety of surviving material. Some of the more obvious features of accounting development have been set against the historical and economic background of the industry concerned, but an in-depth study, by a trained accountant, could yield some interesting results. Why was there such a lack of uniformity in the accounts of different concerns? Can the woollen/worsted contrast be extended in the analysis? To what extent did the accounting techniques used fulfil the purpose required of them in this industry in the period? Where they fell short (e.g. in accounting for fixed capital, defining profit, and in making regular returns), why was this the case? Were carefully calculated depreciation allowances desirable and how important was accounting profit as a concept, compared with cash flow and inventories, to the businessman of the period? How does the West Riding compare with other areas and industries in its accounting development, its association with theoretical works, and its use of professional accountants? Some approaches which could help to answer these questions have been indicated here, together with strong advocacy of the need to place the study of accounting in the context of a detailed and specific knowledge of the history of the industry and its branches. Hopefully this may eradicate the problem of inferring purpose from the form and content of accounts and of analysing nineteenth-century books with the hindsight produced by twentieth-century concepts and requirements. The rest is up to the accountants.

---

[62] For examples see Hudson, *West Riding Wool Textile Industry*, 552: 'Accounts: Trading'. Further work is necessary on this aspect of accounting in the West Riding particularly in the first quarter of the 20th century.

[63] Littleton, *Accounting Evolution*, 350. This change of *concept* is incidentally perhaps more relevant to the needs of industrial capitalism than the change to double entry, which is a tool and not a concept. This 'new view of book-keeping' distinguishes 'valorisation from exchange' in the Marxist sense.

17 · THE MINISTRY OF MUNITIONS 1915–19 AND GOVERNMENT ACCOUNTING PROCEDURES

S. Marriner

INTRODUCTION

'An extraordinary improvisation beyond precedent without parallel in any country in the world took place in our industrial system. Thousands of persons who knew nothing at all about public business or public departments, thousands of firms which had never been used for warlike manufacture were amalgamated together'[1]—this was a description of operations by the Ministry of Munitions in April 1918 by its minister, Mr Winston Churchill. At the same time the Financial Secretary, Sir Worthington Evans, claimed that the Ministry itself was 'the biggest buying, importing, selling, manufacturing and distributing business in the world' dwarfing its nearest rival the United States Steel Trust.[2] He produced comparative statistics.[3]

The Ministry had indeed become a mammoth business. In 1913 total government expenditure for all purposes was £184 million[4]—by the year ending 31 March 1918 the Ministry of Munitions' turnover was £2,000 million and its net cost to the taxpayer £620 million.[5] In addition to Royal Ordnance Factories it owned over 200 manufacturing, transport, mining, and commercial enterprises and extensive housing estates. It acted as a large finance and

First published in *Accounting and Business Research* (1980). This chapter is based primarily on material in the Public Record Office. Although a great many of the Ministry of Munitions' records have been destroyed, a collection of files relating to accounting procedures has survived, mostly in MUN5. I should like to thank the staff of the PRO for their generous advice and assistance, especially Mr. E. W. Denham, who originally drew my attention to these records, Mr. M. Roper, and Dr. C. J. Kitching. For advice on the accounting aspects I am deeply indebted to Professors R. C. Morris and A. M. Bourn of the University of Liverpool. I am also grateful for a grant from the University of Liverpool's Research Fund which helped to finance the work.

[1] *The Parliamentary Debates, Official Report, House of Commons* (hereafter *Parl. Deb. H. of C.*), 25 Apr. 1918, p. 1157.
[2] Ibid. 1182.   [3] Ibid. 1187. See Table 17.1.
[4] B. R. Mitchell and Phyllis Deane, *Abstract of British Historical Statistics* (London, 1962), 398.
[5] Sir Worthington Evans, *Parl. Deb. H. of C.*, 25 Apr. 1918, pp. 1884–5.

TABLE 17.1 *Worthington Evans's statistics on the Ministry of Munitions*

	US Steel Trust	Ministry of Munitions
No. of employees	252,000	385,000
Payroll (£m.)	52	71
Net floating capital (£m.)	100	350
Annual sales to customers (£m.)	170	1,500
Annual inter-company sales (£m.)	60	500
Stocks in hand (£m.)	36	277

banking house and was sole importer of all vital raw materials, the sole market for the output of some industries and a major market for most others. In the words of Mr Webster Jenkinson, Controller of Factory Audit and Costs in October 1918, 'The Ministry of Munitions may be regarded as the driving wheel which supplies the motive power for almost every industry in the country and its accountants may reasonably claim to be one of the spokes which adds to its strength and enables it to bear the strain.'[6]

Unfortunately the Ministry's accounting system had *not* borne the strain. Familiar market mechanisms were extensively disrupted at a time of unprecedented wartime expansion in government trading and manufacturing. The Ministry's accountants had not only to account to Parliament for taxpayers' money but also to undertake unfamiliar tasks such as fixing prices and profits by simulating market forces (or by other means), and devising measures of efficiency and incentives for the production of essential goods. The accounting system was strained to breaking-point by 1917.

The Ministry's accountants had a dismal history of failure until 1918: many millions of pounds of taxpayers' money could never be accounted for and had to be written off. Inquiries by the Comptroller and Auditor General and by parliamentary committees sparked off public scandals: in 1918, the Chairman of the Public Accounts Committee described one report by the Comptroller and Auditor General as a 'nightmare'[7] and *The Economist* referred to some of his criticisms as 'horrifying as to the state of accountancy they reveal'.[8] The abuse continued post-war: in 1921 *The Accountant* accused the Ministry of 'wasteful and unbusinesslike methods'[9] and there were frequently

---

[6] Copy of lecture delivered at the London School of Economics on 'Costing at National Factories' by M. Webster Jenkinson, 9 Oct. 1918, p. 28, PRO, MUN5/107/450/9.

[7] F. D. Ackland, Chairman, *Report from the Committee of Public Accounts with Minutes of Evidence* (hereafter *PAC Report*), 4 Dec. 1919, Q. 2708.

[8] *The Economist* (20 Apr. 1918), 631.

[9] *Accountant* (4 June 1921), 712.

comments in Parliament such as 'the books of the Ministry are in an almost impossible condition'.[10]

In a short article it is difficult to do justice to the complexities of such a large organization[11] but the intention is to examine some of the major defects in accounting procedures, the attempted remedies, and the long-term implications.

GOVERNMENT ACCOUNTING PROCEDURES TO 1915

During the nineteenth and early twentieth centuries government accounting procedures had been designed simply to show that money allocated by Parliament had been properly spent. Accounting procedures were governed by the Exchequer and Audit Departments Act of 1866 (29 & 30 Vict., c. 39) and the Army and Navy Audit Act of 1889 (52 & 53 Vict., c. 31). The first empowered the Treasury to prescribe the records all departments kept to account for their disbursement of taxpayers' money. Each department had an Accounting Officer: a civil servant, usually appointed by the Treasury.[12] By 1914 the Accounting Officer was responsible for the correctness and regularity of accounts, for general financial administration, and for representing the department before the Committee of Public Accounts. He was responsible in the event of irregularities in payments.

The government accounting system so established was on a cash basis and consequently entries were only made when cash transactions occurred. Moreover bookkeeping was on a single-entry system. The Comptroller and Auditor General could require any department to produce a balance sheet but it appears that he rarely did so. When capital expenditure occurred it was usually charged to an Appropriation Account and immediately written off except for stores recorded in stock valuation accounts. The Royal Ordnance Factories were, however, exceptions, for they kept capital accounts and, unusually for government organizations at this time, even allowed for depreciation.[13] The Army and Navy Audit Act of 1889 was designed for govern-

---

[10] *Parl. Deb. H. of C.*, vol. 138, p. 870. Further revelations of the Ministry's inefficiency can be found in 'Report of the Ministry of Munitions Investigation Committee', 9 Nov. 1920, House of Lords Record Office, Bonar Law Papers, Box 103, Folder 10, and *Report of the Tribunal to Inquire and Report upon the Alleged Instructions by an Officer of the Ministry of Munitions as to the Destruction or Concealment of Documents* (Cmd. 1340, 1921).

[11] A twelve-volume official history was printed after the war but not published. Copies can be found in the Public Record Office, in a few libraries, and on microfiche (Harvester Press Ltd.).

[12] For an account of the historical development of the post of Accounting Officer see *Government Accounting: A Guide on Accounting and Financial Procedures for the Use of Government Departments* (London, 1974), Introduction to Section C.

[13] See *Capital Accounts of the Ordnance Factories, 1888–9 to 1900–1*, PRO SUPP 2/1.

ment shipbuilding and manufacturing establishments, especially for the Royal Ordnance Factories and naval dockyards. Their accounts had to be presented annually in a Treasury-approved form and audited by the Comptroller and Auditor General but, in addition, to accounting for their disbursement of money, they had to produce separate accounts showing expenditure on labour and raw materials by each establishment.

These accounts did not statutorily have to include capital expenditure and they were only produced six months after the end of each financial year—too late to be used for any form of cost-plus pricing of munitions or ships sold to customers.[14] It appears that when the War Office had sold its produce or services before the war customers had been charged an average cost calculated basically on prime costs in former years,[15] no allowance being made for capital costs. When the War Office had bought armaments from private firms it had usually asked for tenders from a small ring of large producers with whom it enjoyed long-standing special relationships.[16] A serious omission from this system was the lack of statutory provisions for what have, since 1921, been called 'trading' accounts for government departments.[17]

THE CREATION OF THE MINISTRY OF MUNITIONS

There had been some criticisms of this system but no substantial changes in principle by June 1915, when the Ministry of Munitions was created to take over from the War Office control of the production of anything required for war purposes (5 & 6 Geo. V, c. 51). In November 1915 the Ministry also took over the Royal Ordnance Factories.

The first Minister of Munitions, Mr David Lloyd George, regarded rapid production of war materials and produce as his first priority with financial considerations occupying a poor second place. From the outset staffing was a major headache. Civil servants came from the War Office, the Offices of the Crown Agents and High Commissioners; the first Director of Munitions Accounts, Oscar Barrow, had been India's Comptroller and Auditor General.[18] Some staff were recruited from railways—a notable recruit being Mr Eric Geddes;[19] the Explosives

[14] 'Use of Cost Accounts', Paper by Sir Charles Harris, 10 May 1917, *PAC Report*, 31 July 1917, app. 9.
[15] Ibid.
[16] For a discussion of the War Office's 'special relationships' with contractors see R. C. Trebilcock, 'A "Special Relationship": Government, Rearmament, and the Cordite Firms', *Economic History Review*, 2nd ser. 19/2 (Aug. 1966).
[17] See below: 'Post-war application of the Ministry's experiences'.
[18] PRO, MUN5 102/400/2.
[19] D. Lloyd George, *War Memoirs*, vol. i (London, 1933), 249. For a general discussion of the recruitment of staff see ibid. 245–55.

Department gained the services of Lord Fletcher Moulton, a judge with considerable experience in interpreting company law and company accounts;[20] Mr William Beveridge assisted with labour problems and Mr Seebohm Rowntree with housing. The greatest need, however, was for businessmen and accountants. Traditionally trained civil servants lacked the range of expertise for such large-scale operations and, even more seriously, few had any experience either of manufacturing and merchanting or of commercial accounting.

Mr Lloyd George decided that the Ministry must be 'from first to last a business-man organisation'.[21] By July 1915 he claimed that he had secured the services of '90 first class business-men'.[22] The acquisition of accountants proved more difficult. There was a serious shortage of trained accountants at all levels. Some firms such as Price, Waterhouse & Co. gave generously of their services. One of their partners, Mr (later Sir) Gilbert Garnsey, became extensively involved in advising and supervising and from 1917 he held a series of official posts.[23] Many other accountants volunteered full- or part-time service[24] and the Ministry regularly employed local firms of accountants to audit the accounts of government factories in their localities.

Throughout the war, however, the supply of qualified accountants in both industry and the government sector fell far short of demand and there were also grave shortages of bookkeeping staff. The net effect (as will be shown below) was that many industrial firms as well as government departments found that their basic cost-control systems were inadequate. From the Ministry of Munitions' point of view perhaps the greatest need of all was for cost accountants equipped with the necessary combination of accounting knowledge and a detailed understanding of all the technical, engineering, and manufacturing problems involved in costing explosives, iron ore and coal mining, shell, gun and aircraft production, etc.

The key appointment was that of Mr (later Lord) Samuel Hardman Lever as Accounting Officer. Mr Lever was not a civil servant. He was a practising accountant with extensive experience of cost accounting but Mr Lloyd George insisted that 'in the present case the interests of economy and the safety of public funds will best be served by Mr. Lever's appointment in this capacity. He alone of the persons who may be regarded as available and suit-

[20] See e.g. his judgment *In re Spanish Prospecting Company Limited*, 1911, I Ch. 92–108.

[21] Lloyd George, *War Memoirs*, 245.

[22] Ibid. 254.

[23] *PAC Report*, 8 Aug. 1916, Qs. 3103–14. Also ibid., 4 Dec. 1919, pp. 360–1. He also worked for the Air Ministry from its creation in 1918. For an account of his career generally see Jack Kitchen, 'The Accounts of British Holding Company Groups: Development and Attitudes to Disclosures in the Early Years', *Accounting and Business Research* (Spring 1972), 114–15.

[24] *PAC Report*, 31 July 1917, Qs. 2189, 2197–8.

able will have an intimate knowledge of the financial aspects of the enormous contracts which have to be made.'[25]

THE MINISTRY'S ACCOUNTING SYSTEM: PRINCIPLES

Though the new ministry broke with tradition in its appointments it could not so easily shake off the long tradition of government accounting procedures and statutory limitations. This Ministry's operations were so different from most traditional government business that difficulties immediately arose in combining the system of fund accounting required by statute for reporting purposes with an effective internal cost-control system. The Ministry's accountants were forced by circumstances to modify their practices but until 1917 they did not do so systematically. The inevitable result was confusion. At times it is difficult from the surviving evidence to tell what system was being used and it is clear from subsequent statements by accountants and civil servants to the Committee of Public Accounts that many officials did not themselves know exactly what principles were being or should be followed.[26]

Basically, however, it seems that some of the problems stemmed from an unimaginative reliance on the traditional principles of government accounting; some from the total lack of policies for certain classes of transactions; and others from the lack of any built-in checks on accuracy and completeness of recording.[27]

The most troublesome principle was the use of cash rather than accrual accounting. The problems arising from this were aggravated by the failure to keep personal accounts for contractors: instead there was one account per contract (and some firms had hundreds of contracts with the Ministry). The Ministry's bookkeepers, however, failed to keep the contract accounts accurately. Overall this meant that the Ministry's credit transactions—which were

[25] H. Llewellyn Smith quoting Mr David Lloyd George to the Secretary of HM Treasury, 24 Nov. 1915, PRO, MUN5/102/400/6. Mr Lever's appointment was also whole-heartedly supported by Dr Christopher Addison, Mr Lloyd George's right-hand man at the Ministry: C. Addison, *Politics from Within*, vol. i (London, 1924), 99. It was later suggested that the fact that Mr Lever had been allocated far more responsibility than any one man could possibly cope with was a contributory factor in the collapse of the Ministry's accounting system: *History of the Ministry of Munitions* (unpublished) vol. iii, part i, pp. 26–7.

[26] See e.g. Minutes of Evidence on the Ministry of Munitions Appropriation Accounts for 1916–17 before the Committee of Public Accounts, Evidence of Mr S. Dannreuther, 30 May 1918, Qs. 1892–8.

[27] The account given in the rest of this article has been built up from surviving Ministry of Munitions files in PRO, MUN5, supplemented by the Ministry's own annotated copies of reports from the Committee of Public Accounts (MUN5/106/400/12) and of the Ministry's Appropriation Accounts (MUN5/102/400/6). In order to avoid too many footnotes specific references to these sources are only given where examples are quoted or explanation is needed.

extremely numerous—either never entered the general accounts or were only entered after a long time-lag. In these circumstances, the reliance on cash accounting was conducive to omissions and errors.

IMPLEMENTATION

(a) Materials, components, stores

Some of the effects of this system can be illustrated from the Ministry's distribution of raw materials. Both imports and the home production of all important raw materials were controlled by the Ministry. Allocations to contractors engaged in war production were frequently made free of charge to reduce their need for working capital. Similarly manufacturers of components and semi-manufactured goods were frequently instructed (often by telephone) to send consignments directly to munitions producers, charging them to the Ministry. The cost of such consignments of materials and components should eventually have been deducted from the munitions producers' charges to the Ministry for their finished produce.

In practice, as no cash changed hands, such issues did not enter the Ministry's general accounts at the time. They should have been recorded in the account for the relevant contract. Each consignment was issued against a warrant which should have carried the contract number. There was, however, no provision for ensuring that the officials issuing the consignments had a record of the relevant contract numbers. Frequently they only had the name of the contractor (for whom there was no personal account) and so they had nowhere to record such issues. In fact, in 98 per cent of cases checked in 1917, warrants did not bear a contract number.[28] Because of the very long time-lag in settling bills with contractors—often two or three years—the chances of rectifying omissions at a later date were slender.

Furthermore, there was no effective check as late as mid-1917 that manufacturers used all these materials for war production. Accounting control systems of any sophistication were only beginning to be developed before 1914[29] and it is hardly surprising that progress was slow. Conversion rates

---

[28] 'Report on the Conditions and Difficulties of the Ministry [sic] Accounts Department' to Sir A. McDuckham, signed by Mr Dannreuther, Mr Barrow, and Mr Guy, 5 Mar. 1917, PRO, MUN5/108/450/16.

[29] For a historical account of the development of control systems see R. H. Parker, *Management Accounting: An Historical Perspective* (London, 1969), and D. Solomons (ed.), *Studies in Cost Analysis* (London, 1968).

were devised for some standardized products, e.g. so many shell cases per ton of metal, but for many products there were no accurate estimates of the number of units that should be produced from a given amount of material.

Partly because of these procedures, the accounting system also failed to make adequate provision for recording the Ministry's stores of materials and other produce. At the outbreak of war, Woolwich Arsenal was the government's main store and movements of goods in and out were carefully recorded: as the scale of operations increased new stores were opened all over the country but there was no systematic policy for ensuring that accurate records were kept for each store.[30] There was no provision either for regular stock-taking. Further complications arose from the failure to devise adequate policies for imported materials. Many consignments disappeared as ships were torpedoed; overseas agents could not, because of war conditions, specify in shipping documents the ports to which particular consignments were heading; when produce arrived it was frequently sent directly to contractors (free of charge) to save time and pressure on the railways. Consequently the Ministry's system failed to show how much was due to arrive, how much actually arrived in this country, to which ports it came, and where it was sent on arrival.

(b) Financial assistance to contractors

The accounting system was also defective in keeping track of the Ministry's advances of money to contractors. There was a grave shortage of financial capital: public issues were discouraged to keep the market free for government borrowing, banks were not eager to lock up their money in long-term loans and working capital was scarce. The Ministry had, therefore, to ensure that firms had sufficient financial resources to enable them to undertake war production. In addition to free issues of materials, direct grants were made to finance firms building or extending factories and housing estates, and for the purchase of plant and machinery on condition that the buildings and equipment were used to supply war materials.[31] Large advances of working capital were made in the form of money loans or overdrafts or by advance payments for goods yet to be delivered. Repayment terms should have been recorded but in many cases they were not. It was not until 1918 that full records were kept of advances of

---

[30] In the early days there was such a shortage of weighing machines that no check could in any event be kept on the quantities of materials entering and leaving stores.

[31] In many cases there was no formal arrangement at the time for interest charges or for deciding the ownership of the resultant assets. Subsequently the Ministry claimed many of them.

materials and money. A summary of receipts and expenditure[32] for the years 1915–19 contains no entry at all for advances to contractors until 1917–18 and yet by 31 March 1917 (according to one estimate) contractors probably owed well over £65 million for materials and cash and in addition there was 'a large quantity of material chargeable against contractors for which no basic information is at present obtainable'.[33] On 12 July 1917 it was estimated that something approaching £150 million was outstanding in loans and advances of materials for which no final accounts were available.[34]

(c) The Ministry's capital expenditure and fixed assets

The Ministry's accountants also failed to devise satisfactory ways of recording capital expenditure in its own factories. The pre-war practice of writing off most capital expenditure as it occurred was arguably satisfactory for the many government assets that had little or no commercial value. Pre-war the Royal Ordnance Factories, the War Office's main manufacturing assets, were, as we have seen, an exception to this practice. By the financial year 1913–14 their accumulated capital expenditure (less depreciation) was £2,287,895 with the cost of stores in hand at the end of the period £860,904.[35]

During the war large amounts of additional physical capital of commercial value were created by the Ministry of Munitions in the form of buildings, machinery and equipment, houses, and transport facilities. It was obviously highly desirable that plant registers should be kept so that government property could subsequently be identified and then sold at the end of the war. It was not until late in 1917 that systematic efforts were made to record the Ministry's assets. To this time (apart from the ROFs) the few surviving records of fixed assets show accumulated capital expenditure without depreciation; it was, however, more usual for capital expenditure to be indiscriminately mixed up with production costs. Subsequently such items frequently could not be retrieved to determine even the historic cost of surviving fixed assets because many accounting records had 'simply disappeared' and 'no-one knows why'.[36] Furthermore, even where records of capital items had survived there were no clear directives to 1917 about their allocation for pricing purposes.

[32] Ministry of Munitions *Appropriation Accounts* for 1918–19.
[33] T. L. Judd to J. H. Guy, 2 Apr. 1917, PRO, MUN5/108/450/16. It was not until 1918 that full accounts of these advances were kept.
[34] Report by Mr Guy and Mr Garnsey on the 'Weaknesses of the Accounts Departments', 12 July 1917, PRO, MUN5/108/450/16.
[35] *PAC Report*, 1 Aug. 1918, p. xxiii.
[36] *Appropriation Accounts* 1916–17, 1 Aug. 1918, Q. 2019.

CONTROL OF THE MINISTRY'S EXPENDITURE AND ACCOUNTS

The accuracy of all government accounting before the war had depended heavily on the Treasury and Comptroller and Auditor General. The Treasury had closely scrutinized estimates, checked expenditure, covered legitimate deficits, and recouped surpluses but, with the outbreak of war, Treasury control of the Admiralty's and War Office's expenditure was relaxed to avoid delaying war production; when the Ministry of Munitions was created it enjoyed the same freedom.[37] To 1917 the Treasury was merely informed in very general terms about estimated capital expenditure and no effective alternative method of estimating or controlling expenditure was devised in the early years. Estimates of future capital expenditure invariably proved disastrously off-target. As the *Builder* said after the war: 'it would seem that national estimating is a sort of pastime, and is performed in a manner which would bring a business firm into liquidation.'[38]

The only pre-war control that survived, in theory at any rate, was subsequent investigation by the Comptroller and Auditor General. This should have revealed errors and omissions but it usually occurred one or two years after the event, too late to compensate for omissions in recording. Furthermore the Comptroller and Auditor General was so short of qualified accounting staff himself that he only checked between 1 and 5 per cent of the Ministry's accounts.[39]

The system could have incorporated the use of methods to alert the Ministry's own accountants to errors and omissions but it failed on this score too. At the time many defects were blamed on single-entry bookkeeping, which meant that there was no automatic check on errors or omissions; in fact 'even the loss of a ledger would not be revealed'.[40] It is hardly surprising with the shortage of staff and abnormal pressure of work that errors, omissions, and inaccuracies abounded.[41]

---

[37] Expenditure by the Admiralty and War Office was freed from control in Treasury Minutes of 8 Dec. 1914 and 29 Mar. 1915 which were subsequently extended to the Ministry of Munitions, PRO, MUN5/107/420/1.

[38] *Builder*, 10 Dec. 1920, p. 653.

[39] Evidence of Mr Garnsey, *Approp. Accounts* 1916–17, 1 Aug. 1918, Q. 1878.

[40] Report by Mr Guy and Mr Garnsey on the Form of Public Accounts based on experience at the Ministry of Munitions, 16 Jan. 1918, p. 4, PRO, MUN5/107/450/5.

[41] The defects are too numerous to list in detail but they included the use of incorrect prices and obsolete specifications in contracts; extensive omissions; arithmetic errors; the loss of papers; and double payments to contractors.

CONTRACT COSTING

(a) Principles

The defects in the general accounting system spilled over to some extent into costing. The problem of calculating the prices to be charged to Allied governments for munitions did not unduly exercise the Ministry's accountants. Most attention was directed towards fixing the prices that the Ministry should pay to contractors from whom it bought munitions. For most 'warlike' products market mechanisms gave little or no guidance in the matter of fixing prices and profits. The pre-war system of competitive tenders from large firms (still regarded as the best procedure) could only be used in a minority of cases.[42] Frequently there was no competition: just one contractor doing business with one buyer—the Ministry of Munitions. In this bilateral bargaining position new methods had to be devised for fixing prices and this was one area in which the Ministry's accountants claimed some measure of success.

The objectives were to ensure that contractors earned a 'fair' but not 'excessive' profit, that they had an incentive to produce in sufficient quantities the goods most needed for the war effort and that they should do this in the most efficient way. Prices were either based on actual costs of production determined after the event or on estimates of cost made in advance of production. Whenever possible prices were fixed at the time the contract was signed by estimating costs and adding a margin for profit because this gave manufacturers an incentive to economize in order to increase their profits. This was however impracticable in the case of new products for which neither the manufacturer nor the Ministry had any previous experience. In such cases prices had to be based on the costs actually incurred plus a margin for profit. This type of contract was not favoured because contractors lacked any incentive to economize—in fact it encouraged extravagance because the higher the costs, the larger the actual profit earned. 'Cost-plus' contracts were only signed, therefore, when there was no alternative.

(b) Methods

The effectiveness of these procedures for determining the prices to be paid to contractors depended on the Ministry having adequate knowledge of produc-

[42] Notes by Mr Gibb on the work of the Contract Department under Sir John Mann, 31 Jan. 1919, PRO, MUN5/111/500/38.

tion costs. Various devices were therefore adopted to estimate and check costs. The chief ones were first the determination of unit costs in government factories and their application to the prices paid to private industry for the same products; secondly the costs of one or more firms were investigated, the results then determining prices to be paid to the rest of the industry; thirdly, special contracts with variable price provisions were devised for new products.

I. *Costing in national factories.* The first method, operated through the Royal Ordnance and National Factories, worked fairly well for routine processes such as shell-making. Some two hundred National Factories were established to supplement production in the Ordnance Factories and the private sector: they were managed by local firms and businessmen; some plant and buildings were borrowed and the Ministry met the remaining capital expenditure. In all the National Factories there was 'a very minute and exhaustive system of verifying costs—they are brought up month by month, tabulated and circulated amongst all factories interested'.[43] Printed booklets gave details of costing and tables were constructed to show the number of units of a commodity that should be obtained from given quantities of materials.[44] Conferences were organized so that accountants from National Factories could exchange views on costing generally. The Office of Works gave guidance on regional variations in wage rates. Costs were compared between factories to ensure efficiency and the results were then used as a yardstick against which to measure the efficiency of private manufacturers of similar products. The prices the Ministry paid to some armament manufacturers were reduced by 25 to 30 per cent as a result.[45]

This system was not, of course, foolproof. Clearly there is no such thing as a single 'true' cost for a unit of a commodity. It was openly admitted that in all costing there was a 'margin of error';[46] then too costs differed when firms used different types of machinery or production methods. The items included in 'cost' also caused difficulties because of a slavish adherence to the principles of fund accounting which were quite unsuited to the task in hand, namely to accumulate costs (both current and capital) in relation to each contract. Thus although some 'oncosts' were charged to production, they only

---

[43] Evidence of Sir John Mann, *PAC Report*, 31 July 1917, Q. 2524. See also 'Memorandum Explaining the System of Cost Accounts at National Shell and National Projectile Factories', Nov. 1915, PRO, MUN5/107/450/1.

[44] Printed weekly *Reports on Finance of the Ministry of Munitions of War* were also circulated to accounting staff. Those for 20 Nov. 1915 to 29 Dec. 1917 have survived in PRO, MUN2/23.

[45] *PAC Report*, 8 Aug. 1916, Q. 2819.

[46] Ibid.

included current factory and general establishment charges, the cost of power, and general repairs and renewals. The initial cost of tools, repairs to plant and buildings, and depreciation were not generally included until 1918 and neither were interest, sinking fund charges, or rent for buildings and land. The National Factories' costs were not therefore comparable with those in private industry and prices based on them had to include a margin to cover these additional costs.

2. *Investigations of manufacturers' costs.* The second main method adopted for pricing was for the Ministry's officials directly to investigate private manufacturers' books to establish their costs. The Ministry had powers to control all manufacturers engaged in war production under the Defence of the Realm Act and the Munitions of War Acts. The Munitions of War (Amendment) Act of 1916 (5 & 6 Geo. V, c. 99) specifically endowed the Ministry with powers to require firms to give information about costs. Naturally there was some resistance from manufacturers and many firms' records were in any event useless because of their deplorable state. The methods used even by many large firms 'were absolutely antiquated' and there were no standardized procedures for bookkeeping, for financial accounting, or for production methods.[47]

Gradually, however, manufacturers came to accept the Ministry's cost investigations as officials maintained complete confidentiality if firms co-operated and blacklisted those who did not[48]; many firms even came to regard the Ministry's methods as useful tools for improving their own business organization: 'In many cases the contractors' cost records were badly kept, unsound in principle or non-existent and the Ministry's investigation has often been beneficial in showing the contractor his real costs and in stimulating better methods of costing.'[49] Some firms were even glad to employ accounting staff trained by the Ministry because of the shortage of qualified people. To July 1917 it was estimated that the Ministry's accountants, assisted by advice on technical matters from engineers, had undertaken some 700 investigations.[50]

3. *Special contracts.* The aim of these investigations of private contractors' costs and of the costing system of the National Factories was to establish what they called 'standard costs' for traditional and mass-produced

---

[47] Evidence of Sir John Mann, *PAC Report*, 31 July 1917, Q. 2523. On the history of uniform costing see D. Solomons, 'Uniform Cost Accounting: A Survey. Part I', *Economica* (Aug. 1950). This does not, however, consider the effects of the war on procedures.

[48] 'Replies by the Finance Department of the Ministry of Munitions to a questionnaire from the Reconstruction Department', 4 July 1917, PRO, MUN5/102/400/6, hereafter cited 'Replies to Questionnaire'; also *Approp. Accounts* 1916–17.

[49] 'Notes on Profit' by Sir John Mann, 12 Nov. 1917, PRO, MUN5/111/500/66.

[50] 'Replies to Questionnaire'.

products.[51] These were then used as a basis for pricing with the addition of an allowance (a percentage or lump sum) for profit. Such contracts were not, however, the answer for many complex new war products: research and development were often necessary and costs could not be estimated in advance. In addition many firms were reluctant to experiment: they needed positive encouragement to switch to new types of production.

The Ministry tried out various types of contract to allay their fears: there was, for example, the 'co-operative contract', which contained a high 'standard price' but if costs fell below this the contractor and Ministry shared the savings. Some contracts guaranteed firms against losses. Some contained a 'safety-valve clause', i.e. they contained a maximum and minimum price. If the contractor could prove that the minimum price did not yield an agreed rate of profit it could be supplemented up to the maximum.

The question of the rate of profit contractors should earn was a thorny one: 'In theory, and very generally stated, the maximum profit aimed at is 10% of the cost of Wages, Materials and Expenses' plus 2.5 per cent for supervising subcontractors.[52] In practice, these rates were not rigidly maintained. In some cases higher rates (25–30 per cent) were allowed to encourage manufacturers to enter new lines of production.[53] If a contract involved no risk, a very quick turnover, or the production of large quantities of a standardized product, the contract price might be fixed to yield a profit rate as low as 5 per cent.[54] The actual return to the manufacturer was further complicated by the Excess Profits legislation. In some cases the Excess Profits tax was waived in lieu of a subsidy for capital expenditure (much to the annoyance of Treasury officials, who regarded this as improper procedure).

There were long debates about the success of the Ministry's costing systems. Its officials claimed considerable success in reducing prices charged by contractors, in concentrating dealings on 'efficient firms', increasing the efficiency of others and ensuring the efficiency of the National and Royal Ordnance Factories. It was claimed that large areas of British industry were introduced to best-practice cost accounting formerly restricted to small numbers of firms. The costing system did, however, suffer from some of the defects in the general accounting system, especially in the allocation of capital costs for pricing.

[51] The Ministry's officials frequently refer to 'standard' costs and 'standard' prices. Because of the term's special meaning to modern accountants I use it in inverted commas. The word 'target' would probably be more appropriate but that too has acquired a special meaning in 'target-cost contracts'.

[52] 'Notes on Profit' by Sir John Mann. See also memo by Sir John Mann, 12 Nov. 1917, in the same file.

[53] Ibid.

[54] Ibid.

REVISION OF THE ACCOUNTING SYSTEM FROM 1917

When the Ministry was created in 1915 it had been anticipated that the war would not last for long. In 1917 the end was still not in sight and costs were escalating to a hitherto unanticipated level. Attempts to discover the extent of taxpayers' expenditure and checks by the Comptroller and Auditor General exposed very serious defects in the Ministry's general accounting system and sparked off intensive efforts to devise a more satisfactory one. Despite the inadequacies in accounting in the private sector, government accountants were urged to adopt 'commercial' accounting practices to replace fund accounting. At the time great importance was attached to the rewriting of accounts in double entry from 1915 and to the use of double entry for all new transactions. This, it was predicted, would reduce future errors and omissions.

Complete records were now kept for each contract and control over stores was tightened. New recording systems for stores started in January 1917; by the summer a central stores organization was in operation to ensure adequate records of receipts and issues of both home-produced and imported materials and produce. Inventories were taken more frequently.

Renewed efforts were directed towards devising a more effective cost-control system. By 1917 there was a Joint Cost Committee of the War Office, Admiralty, and Ministry of Munitions to share data and keep a register of cost investigations to avoid wastage by departments competing for scarce resources and paying different prices for the same products.[55] Following the re-establishment of detailed Treasury control in October 1917, the Treasury set up a standing Inter-Departmental Committee on Contracts in February 1918. This became known as the Colwyn Committee from June 1918 when Lord Colwyn took over the chairmanship from Lord Inchcape. The committee's brief was to examine all matters relating to profits, forms of contract, and subcontractors for the Ministry of Munitions, Admiralty, and War Office.[56]

---

[55] There were many rivalries between the Ministry and other departments. The War Office in particular claimed priority in devising costing procedures. See especially 'Use of Cost Accounts in the War Office' by Sir Charles Harris, 10 May 1917, a paper reproduced in *PAC Report*, 31 July 1917, app. 9. In giving evidence to the Committee of Public Accounts, however, Sir Charles admitted that the Woolwich Arsenal had no real costing system under the War Office, *PAC Report*, 8 Aug. 1916, Q. 2984. It is also clear that the War Office's accounts generally were unreliable—see e.g. *PAC Report*, 14 June 1921, Q. 4656, and the *History of the Ministry of Munitions*, vol. iii pt. I, p. 92.

[56] The Committee did not have time to influence procedure before the war ended. Its first report (Cd. 9179) on building construction contracts was only published in Aug. 1918. A more important one (not

The Ministry's costing system also benefited from improvements in accounting for capital assets which made it easier to charge for the use of fixed assets when determining cost-plus prices. It now became normal practice to allow depreciation and in some accounts this was back-dated to 1915. One report by the Ministry's Financial Secretary instructed National Factories to include depreciation in manufacturing costs for pricing from February 1918 at the following rates:[57]

Permanent buildings (%)	10–17½	Machinery, tools (%)	25
Temporary buildings (%)	20–30	Furniture (%)	15
Plant (%)	20–25	Canteens (%)	20

From April 1917 a new Internal Audits section began to check all accounts. Attempts were also made to institute effective controls over new capital expenditure: early in 1917 a Munitions Works Board was set up to exercise general supervision over all new construction and in October detailed Treasury control of future expenditure was restored.

Intensive efforts were also made to reconstruct accounts from 1915 in order to compile a register of all the Ministry's assets. Contractors were asked for statements of all materials, components, and loans made to them since 1915 and a special unit, known as the 'breakdown gang', tried to reconcile contractors' records with the Ministry's. Unfortunately, in the words of Sir Gilbert Garnsey, many contractors' books 'were in as bad a state as ours'.[58] When there were no records of issues of materials to particular contractors some checks were possible through the railway companies' accounts of movements of goods to and from contractors.

In October 1917 instructions went out that inventories should be drawn up of all the Ministry's property, plant, machinery, etc. and in December a Special Committee for Land and Buildings was charged with the job of listing all the Ministry's property wherever it might be, including all capital assets in the National Factories, plant and machinery in the hands of contractors (paid for by the Ministry), and other property such as railway sidings built by the Ministry, cars, lorries, etc.

---

published but dated 31 Oct. 1918) suggested costing principles for all types of government contracts. According to F. R. M. de Paula this was used in negotiations with contractors during the inter-war years until superseded during the Second World War: *Developments in Accounting* (London, 1948), 246.

[57] PRO, MUN5/450/4. The reasons for choosing these rates are not disclosed and it is not clear how they were to be applied (i.e. straight line or reducing balance) or how they were to be allocated when more than one commodity was produced.

[58] *PAC Report*, 4 Dec. 1919, Qs. 2816–17.

FIRST PROVISIONAL BALANCE SHEET

In the spring of 1918 in an attempt to bring all this information together the first provisional balance sheet was drawn up for the Ministry of Munitions.[59] This included the Royal Ordnance Factories, some 200 National Factories, housing schemes and sundry other enterprises such as railway sidings and filling stations. The Ministry's 'fixed assets' appear at 24 April 1918 as £88,472,410 4s. 0d. and 'stocks and stores on hand' as £279,477,854 10s. 5d.[60] These totals were made up from various sources. The Central Stores organization now had records for stores all over the country. The process of trying to establish contractors' debts for loans and free issues was, however, still incomplete; in fact Messrs Guy and Garnsey warned the Minister that 'the first Balance Sheet will show upwards of £200,000,000 of money advanced but unaccounted for' and a further 'very large figure, probably well over £50,000,000 which is represented by unsettled items such as procrastination in fixing prices and disputes with Contractors'.[61]

Valuations of buildings, plant, and machinery were based on historic cost (if this was available) less depreciation and, failing this, on valuations. It is not clear whether these were attempts to reconstruct historic cost or to calculate the current value. The National Factories accounted for nearly £62 million of the fixed assets but the only National Factory for which the PRO has separate accounts is the Shell Factory at Rochdale: unfortunately these are not very helpful for in its balance sheet for 31 March 1918 there are no entries against 'Buildings' or 'Land'—these are left blank. 'Fixed assets' (£19,630 10s. 10d.) include only alterations to buildings, roads, plant, machinery, tools, furniture, canteen equipment, and 'miscellaneous construction charges' (£195 6s. 9d.).[62] As late as May 1920 the Comptroller and Auditor General reported that 'owing to the accounting conditions in the period preceding the revised system of book-keeping the [Ministry's] assets in the majority of cases do not represent firm valuations'.[63]

Although the Ministry's accountants attached a good deal of importance to this exercise, in retrospect, its main usefulness seems to have been in highlighting the defects in the recording system.

[59]   This aimed to show the position as at 24 Apr. 1918, PRO, MUN5/450/31 and 34.
[60]   Ibid.
[61]   J. H. Guy and G. F. Garnsey to the Minister of Munitions, 10 Jan. 1918, PRO, MUN5/105/400/34.
[62]   Nominal Ledger, Dec. 1915 to Sept. 1919, fo. 244, PRO, MUN3/16. Its buildings had probably been loaned to the Ministry.
[63]   'Report of the Comptroller and Auditor General', 12 May 1920, *Approp. Accounts 1918–19*, p. 18.

POST-WAR APPLICATIONS OF THE MINISTRY'S EXPERIENCES

(a) Reform of government accounting

The new accounting system was fully operational by 1 April 1918 but the rewriting of accounts from 1915 was far from complete when the war ended in November 1918. As late as June 1919 some 58,000 contractors' accounts still awaited confirmation and settlement. The end of the war brought immense new problems: manufacturing had to be closed down; a Disposals Board was created to sell buildings, plant, machinery, and the Ministry's vast stores of raw materials, semi-manufactured, and manufactured produce. Lack of space prevents any detailed consideration of the many post-war problems but it is relevant to ask whether this first traumatic experience of large-scale government enterprise from 1919 had any immediate post-war influence on government accounting practice and on costing in British industry.

The publicity and scandals referred to above sparked off demands for inquiries into how all government accounts should be kept. The report of a committee set up in October 1920 to 'consider the provisions of the Exchequer and Audit Departments Act 1866 and to report on any amendment needed therein'[64] led to an Act to Amend the Exchequer and Audit Departments Act (11 & 12 Geo. V, c. 52). For the first time departments were statutorily obliged to produce 'trading' accounts 'showing the income and expenditure of any shipbuilding, manufacturing, trading or commercial services conducted by Departments, together with such balance sheets, statements of profit and loss, and particulars of costs as the Treasury may require'. These were to be audited by the Comptroller and Auditor General.

There was also considerable pressure at this time for non-trading departments to adopt accrual accounting but the main experiments along these lines with the Army's accounts were abandoned in 1925.[65] In the longer term it was accepted that cash accounting was most relevant for government requirements provided it was properly operated and supplemented where necessary by a costing system.[66]

---

[64] The report was published on 23 June 1921, Cmd. 1382.

[65] *Third PAC Report*, 1922, paras. 56–7; *Second PAC Report*, 1925, paras. 50, 64; *Final Report of the Committee on the Form of Government Accounts* (Cmd. 7969, June 1950), app. C.

[66] *Report of the Committee on the Form of Government Accounts* (Cmd. 7969), 'Summary of Main Conclusions', 57.

(b) Effects on costing in the private sector

With regard to the effects of wartime experience on costing in the private sector, how valid were claims by the Ministry's accountants that they had introduced British industry to best-practice cost accounting? In 1926 F. R. M. de Paula commented, 'Speaking generally, costing in this country . . . is not satisfactory and considerable development is necessary in order to place it upon a satisfactory footing.'[67] This was borne out by investigations of the efficiency of British industry and trade by the Balfour Committee between 1924 and 1929; great difficulty was experienced in obtaining satisfactory data in a comparable form about production and distribution 'on account of the lack of consistent and scientific practice among many firms in respect of costing accounts'.[68] Throughout its investigations the Committee concentrated on coal, iron and steel, engineering and shipbuilding, electrical manufacturing, chemical, cotton, woollen, worsted, and clothing production, all industries very much affected by the Ministry of Munitions' control of raw materials and consumption of their output, but there is no reference to wartime experiences of costing.[69] The Committee found a serious lack of uniformity within and between industries and commented further that a 'striking feature of the reports of the committees under the Profiteering Acts was the frequency of reference to the unsatisfactory organisation of businesses in respect of their costing systems'.[70] It would appear that, if the Ministry of Munitions had any major and widespread influence on private industry's costing systems, this had long since been dissipated.

COMPARISON WITH EXPERIENCES SINCE THE SECOND WORLD WAR

(a) Recurrence of general problems

If the experiences of the Ministry of Munitions accountants are looked at in the context of more recent events it can be seen that they were battling with problems that have kept recurring even after many more decades of trial and error. Since the Second World War there have been charges against govern-

---

[67] F. R. M. de Paula, *Developments in Accounting* (London, 1948), 141.
[68] *Final Report of the Committee on Industry and Trade* (Cmd. 3282, Mar. 1929), 225.
[69] Ibid. 2, 225–6. See also Solomons, 'Uniform Cost Accounting'.
[70] *Report*, 225.

ment departments of inaccurate storekeeping,[71] failure to ensure adequate recording of equipment in the hands of government contractors,[72] estimates of capital expenditure that bear no resemblance to final costs, and difficulties in allocating overheads in pricing the produce and services of government manufacturies;[73] devising a satisfactory accounting system for the Royal Ordnance Factories has proved a prolonged and uphill task.[74]

(b) Pricing defence products

The most publicized aspect of government accounting since the Second World War, however, has been the persistent problem of fixing prices for government purchases of defence products. As in the 1914–18 War the most satisfactory procedure is still that of competitive tenders but in a high proportion of government contracts (especially for new products) this is not practicable. The same challenging problems therefore recur as those facing the Ministry of Munitions: how to fix prices so as to ensure that a contractor earns a 'fair' but not 'excessive' profit that is sufficient to encourage him to venture into risky new fields of research and manufacture and at the same time to ensure that he has an incentive to efficiency.

It seems that whatever system is adopted to try to reconcile these (often conflicting) objectives it must involve highly arbitrary calculations and it must encounter difficulties in implementation. There have been *post-mortems* and accusations of waste of taxpayers' money such as the inquiries into Ferranti's 'excessive' profits on the guidance system for the Mark I Bloodhound and into Bristol Siddeley Engines' profits for servicing aero-engines. Reports of investigations published in 1964, 1965, and 1967 exposed defects in the price-fixing system.[75] The first of these reports showed that 'not only is the system of estimating costs and profits on certain kinds of Government Contracts wanting but that even the system as laid down has not been worked properly'.[76]

---

[71] e.g. *Third PAC Report*, 1955–6, paras. 50–7.

[72] e.g. ibid. 1962–3, paras. 60–3.

[73] e.g. ibid., paras. 142–4.

[74] As late as July 1971 *The Report of the Committee on Government Industrial Establishments* (Cmd. 4713), though accepting that the ROFs were well-managed and had gone a long way towards establishing a 'commercial accounting system', was critical of some accounting procedures followed (para. 9).

[75] On Ferranti see *First Report of the Inquiry into the Pricing of Ministry of Aviation Contracts* (Cmnd. 2428, 1964) and *Second Report* (Cmnd. 2581, 1965). Also J. F. Flower, 'The Case of the Profitable Bloodhound', *Journal of Accounting Research* (Spring 1966), 16-36. On Bristol Siddeley Engines see *Second Special Report from the Committee of Public Accounts*, 4 July 1967, Parl. Papers, 1966–7, Paper 571.

[76] *Accountant* (8 Aug. 1964), 50.

(c) Types of contracts

As in the First World War, government departments buying the services or produce of private contractors could sign fixed-price contracts, they could pay the manufacturer's full costs after the event plus a profit calculated according to a pre-arranged formula (cost-plus contracts), or they could fix prices at an intermediate stage. Fixed-price contracts give the greatest incentive for manufacturers to improve their efficiency. Cost-plus contracts are easier to cost but offer the contractor no incentive for efficiency. Fixing prices at an intermediate stage in the production process should ease the problem of costing but, in fact, this happened in the Ferranti case and yet there were serious errors in estimating direct costs; as these were the basis for calculating overheads at a very high rate (558 per cent) the initial errors were multiplied.

Because of such difficulties the Ministry of Munitions had tried out 'co-operative' contracts and 'safety-valve' contracts and to reassure nervous contractors some contracts had made provision to compensate them in the event of losses. Since the Second World War the favoured alternative has been the 'target-cost' contract. In this type of contract the government department and contractor agree on a target cost and profit percentage but as an incentive to efficiency the contractor receives an agreed share of the amount by which actual costs fall below the target: equally he must pay part of the amount by which actual costs exceed the target.[77]

(d) Profits

I. *Determination of rates.* All contracts involve a definition of what constitutes a 'fair profit' and estimates of costs made before, during or after production. As we have seen earlier, during the 1914–18 War 10 per cent of the cost of 'wages, materials and expenses' was considered a fair profit although this rate was not rigidly enforced. Since the Second World War profits have been based on capital employed with additional allowances (based on cost) for efficiency and risk. Such calculations inevitably raise further problems: in particular 'capital employed' plays an important role in profit formulas and yet it is a term used very loosely by accountants. Furthermore, arbitrary allocations have to be made between commodities of both overhead costs and capital employed when considering a single product produced for the government by a multi-product

---

[77]   For an account of procedures since World War II see C. Turpin, *Government Contracts* (Harmondsworth: Penguin, Law and Society Series, 1972). On target-cost contracts see pp. 192–3.

firm.[78] In practice it is also necessary to have a conversion factor between percentage profit on costs and percentage profit on capital employed: this involves agreement between the contractor and Ministry on the costs (actual and estimated) of the whole of the contractor's business during the year: the conversion factor is then the ratio of these costs to 'capital employed'.[79]

The acceptable profit rates have changed several times: to the 1960s the aim was 7.5 per cent on capital employed which could be raised by allowances on cost to the equivalent of a maximum of 10 per cent on capital employed if there was no risk and 15 per cent if there was risk.[80] By 1970 it was considered fairer to aim for an average profit over all government contracts of 14 per cent on capital employed: 10.7 per cent if there was no risk and 16.1 per cent for risk.[81] As two-thirds of the contracts involved risk the weighted average would be 14.3 per cent. In 1975 to attract more capital into the industries serving the government and to cover the increasing rate of inflation the average was raised to 18–19.8 per cent for risky contracts and 14.4 per cent for safe ones.[82]

2. *Implementation.* Ensuring that contractors actually earn these rates involves accurate costing: the reliability of costing has depended on firms' accounting systems, on the Ministries' technical cost officers who furnish estimates of the cost of direct labour and materials, and on accountants who determine overheads. Problems of implementation have arisen due to inadequacies in contractors' costing systems[83] and shortages of technical costs officers. These difficulties have been seriously aggravated by Ministries' lack of information (compared with firms) about the general interaction between the technical and commercial aspects of most industries and more specifically by lack of information about contractors' costs. They did not have the Ministry of Munitions' sweeping powers to examine firms' books. This problem was

---

[78] For a consideration of these problems seeC. L. Parker, 'Capital Employed', *Journal of Industrial Economics* (Apr. 1955), 134–43, and R. C. Morris, 'The Book-Yield as a Performance Evaluator', Paper at the Southern Area AUTA Conference, 25 Sept. 1971, p. 35.

[79] *Second Special Report from the PAC,* 1967, app. IV, p. 131.

[80] For the position in the early 1960s see K. Hartley, 'Costing of Government Defence Contracts', *Accountant* (30 May 1964), 684–8.

[81] The intention was to aim for a return equal *on average* to the overall return on capital employed by British industry during the years 1960–6. This was estimated at 14%: Mr John Diamond, Chief Secretary to the Treasury, 26 Feb. 1968, *Parl. Deb. H. of C.,* vol. 759, p. 948. See also Review Board for Government Contracts, *First Report on the General Review of the Profit Formula for Non-competitive Government Contracts* (1974), hereafter *First Report on Profit Formula.*

[82] *First Report on Profit Formula* and Mr Joel Barnett, Chief Secretary to the Treasury, 20 Mar. 1975, *Parl. Deb. H. of C.,* vol. 888, written answers, pp. 525–30.

[83] See e.g. the report of the development of the 'Blue Steel' weapon in *Third PAC Report,* 1961–2, paras. 60–1.

particularly exposed by the Bristol Siddeley Engine investigation and, in 1968, the government and the CBI formally agreed to accept the concept of 'equality of information' up to the time prices were fixed.[84] It was also agreed that a Review Board for Government Contracts should find out what profits were earned, act as a referee in doubtful cases and review fixed-price contracts if profits exceeded 27.5 per cent or if losses exceeded 15 per cent.[85]

It was recognized that once prices had been fixed on the basis of 'equal information' they should not be modified and yet, as taxpayers' money was involved, there should be some check on 'excessive' profits (during the First World War this exigency had been covered by the Excess Profits legislation). To compensate for 'unfair' downward revisions, there should be some recompense for heavy losses. This process, of course, works against the long-accepted principle that fixed-price contracts give an incentive to efficiency. Obviously incentive is restricted if, by raising profits above the 'fair' profit limit, the contractor attracts an inquiry and downward revision of prices.

In 1974, the Review Board for Government Contracts, reporting on its investigations into the operation of contracts since 1968, reached the conclusion that the profit formulas had broadly reached their desired objectives although it recommended raising the average to 20 per cent and the upper point of reference for investigating excessive profits to 37.5 per cent; the lower point for losses should be changed from 15 per cent to 5 per cent.[86]

CONCLUSION

Perhaps in view of the fact that any procedures adopted must inevitably involve highly arbitrary and controversial decisions, the Ministry of Munitions' accountants deserve sympathy rather than the bitter criticisms they suffered in their efforts to tackle such intransigent problems with little previous experience and working in the very difficult operating conditions during the First World War.

---

[84] Mr John Diamond, 26 Feb. 1968, *loc. cit.*, p. 947 and *First Report on Profit Formula*, paras. 2–3.
[85] Cf. the Colwyn Committee set up in 1918.
[86] *First Report on Profit Formula*, paras. 80, 106, 138.

J. Freear

INTRODUCTION AND SUMMARY

Robert Loder's Farm Accounts, 1610–1620,[1] are held at the Berkshire Records Office, Reading. In this chapter, a brief description of the background to the accounts will be followed by an examination of the accounts from a management accounting point of view, using the main elements of the decision-making process as headings under which to consider the accounts. I have also included a brief note on some of the criticisms to which the accounts, as records, have been subjected.

A great deal has already been written about Robert Loder and his accounts.[2] However, very little has been written about the management or

First published in *Abacus* (1970). This chapter is based on the results of the research which I undertook on Robert Loder's Farm Accounts while P. D. Leake Teaching Fellow at the University of Kent at Canterbury. I should like to acknowledge my indebtedness to Mr P. A. Bird, Senior Lecturer in Accounting at the University of Kent at Canterbury, both for drawing my attention to the accounts and for his comments during the preparation of this paper.

[1] The accounts were edited by G. E. Fussell for the Royal Historical Society: *Robert Loder's Farm Accounts, 1610–1620*, Camden Society 3rd Series, LIII (London, 1936). All page references to the accounts refer to Fussell's edition.

[2] *Thirteenth Report* of the Historical Manuscripts Commission (1891), app. IV; H. Hall, 'The Dawn of Modern Farming', *Quarterly Review*, 256 (1931); Fussell, *Robert Loder's Farm Accounts; Farming Technique from Prehistoric to Modern Times* (Oxford, 1966); R. H. Tawney, 'The Rise of the Gentry, 1558–1640', *Economic History Review*, 11 (1941); H. J. Habakkuk, 'Robert Loder's Farm Accounts, 1610–1620', book review in *Economic History Review*, 9 (1938); M. Campbell, *The English Yeoman* (New Haven, Conn., 1942; London, 1967); E. Kerridge, *The Agricultural Revolution* (London, 1967); J. Thirsk (ed.), *The Agrarian History of England and Wales*, iv: *1500–1600* (Cambridge, 1967); B. S. Yamey, 'Accounting in England 1500–1900', in W. T. Baxter and S. Davidson (eds.), *Studies in Accounting Theory* (London, 1962), also 1st edn. W. T. Baxter (ed.), *Studies in Accounting* (London, 1950), and 'Accounting and the Rise of Capitalism', *Journal of Accounting Research* (Autumn 1964); R. H. Parker, 'Early History of Cost Concepts for Decision-Making', *Accountancy* (Sept. 1968), and *Management Accounting: An Historical Perspective* (London, 1969); A. Fletcher, *Elizabethan Village* (London, 1967); C. H. Robinson, 'Robert Loder: Farmer', in *Harlequin*, leisure magazine of the United Kingdom Atomic Energy Research Establishment, Harwell (Christmas 1954).

decision aspect of the accounts other than a mention of Loder's 'businesslike approach' and the use of small fragments of the accounts to illustrate Loder's use of ideas such as opportunity cost.[3] I hope to demonstrate that Loder made use of decision-making concepts and an information system which did not become officially recognized (i.e. in the governmental agricultural advisory services) as best practice until the 1960s. In this sense his techniques are superior to those contained in much nineteenth and twentieth-century accounting literature.

ROBERT LODER AND PRINCE'S MANOR FARM

Robert Loder of Harwell, Berkshire, died in 1638 aged 49 years. His account book contains detailed accounts for ten years only, 1611 to 1620. If he kept accounts after that date, as seems probable, they have not yet come to light. Although it covers only a decade, the account book has proved to be a fertile source of information about, for example, the techniques of Jacobean farming, wage rates, crop yields, and prices. Though writers such as Fussell and Tawney have noted in general terms Loder's 'businesslike approach' to farming, it was left to Yamey and Parker to draw attention to Loder's 'keen understanding of economic calculation for business decision-making', and to contrast this with his use of that 'primitive accounting form', the narrative paragraph.

Robert Loder farmed 'Upper' or Prince's Manor in the parish of Harwell, Berkshire. The manor was granted by the Black Prince to the College of St Nicholas, Wallingford Castle. In 1557, the manor was purchased from the Crown (the College of St Nicholas having been abolished in 1549) by Richard Loder, Robert's great-great-grandfather. John Loder, Robert's father, succeeded to the manor on the death of his father in 1593. However, John himself died two years later, when Robert was 6 years old. Until 1610, when Robert 'was of the adge of xxj', his uncles managed Prince's Manor on his behalf—not particularly well to judge from his comments on the state of disrepair of the thatched roofs—although when he was 16 he had taken over the replanting and running of one of the orchards, Fardinges.

Prince's Manor Farm in Loder's time comprised approximately 100 acres of enclosed downland, four orchards, and 150 acres, organized on a strip basis, in the two open fields. Most of the land in the open fields was sowed with wheat or barley, which were the main cash crops. Some was retained for

[3] See esp. the works of Hall, Fussell (1936), Habakkuk, Tawney, Campbell, Yamey, Thirsk, and Parker cited in nn. 1 and 2 above.

internal use, but most was sold, the barley largely in the form of malt. The orchards and pigeon house were also minor sources of cash revenue. As well as cattle, sheep, pigs, and poultry, Loder maintained horses for ploughing and carriage, and employed regular labour such as the carter, the shepherds, and the maids, hiring casual labour, paid by the day or by the piece, or contracting work out, as necessary.

Prince's Manor Farm is still in existence today; the orchards have been ploughed, and some of the meadowland sold, but the main arable areas, considerably added to over the intervening years, remain part of the farm.

'BEFORE ALL THINGS A BUSINESSMAN'

G. E. Fussell[4] summed Loder up in these words and later went on to amplify the statement: 'Loder's object in farming was to make his living from his estate. . . . He wanted as large a financial return for his expenditure of capital, managerial work and manual work as he could get, and he did his utmost to obtain it' (p. xxiii). Evidence of this objective can clearly be seen in many of the decision memoranda interspersed throughout the accounts such as his continuing review of the wheat and barley enterprises, his main cash crops. He was able to demonstrate that wheat was likely to be more profitable than barley in the majority of circumstances, and therefore over the years expanded his wheat acreage and reduced his barley acreage until the two were approximately equal. Originally his idea was merely to grow more wheat and less barley, but in about 1615 he had modified this to half wheat, half barley, because he wished to be in a position to take advantage of the high prices which barley occasionally fetched.

Decision-making theories usually have four basic requirements:

I. the objectives of the decision-maker must be clear, and preferably quantifiable.

Loder had a clear objective—to maximize the return on his investment of time, money, and effort in Prince's Manor Farm. How did he seek to achieve it? To answer this we must look to the remaining three decision-making requirements:

2. a willingness to consider a wide range of alternative courses of action;
3. an information system capable of producing relevant data both for planning and for control purposes;

---

[4] Fussell, *Robert Loder's Farm Accounts*, p. x.

4. the ability to select and to use appropriate concepts with which to evaluate the likely results of alternative courses of action.

I shall now discuss each of the last three in turn.

RANGE OF ALTERNATIVE COURSES OF ACTION

Loder appreciated the concept of opportunity cost—the value of the next best alternative use of scarce resources forgone—and would no doubt have been in complete agreement with Joel Dean's statement 'that it is dangerous to confine cost knowledge to what the firm is doing. What the firm is not doing but could do is frequently the critical cost consideration, which it is perilous but easy to ignore'.[5] The barley/malting enterprise offers an excellent example of the range of alternatives which Loder was prepared to consider (the dates refer to when the alternative was considered):

(*a*) the letting out of the malting of his own barley (1612);

(*b*) the purchase of barley 'out of the hill country' for seed, rather than using his own barley for this purpose (1613);

(*c*) the selling of his barley as barley, rather than malting it before sale (1614, 1615, 1616);

(*d*) the letting out of his barley for malting (1612) with the added check that he bought barley and malted it himself (1619), keeping strict account of the results;

(*e*) the storage of barley and malt when the selling price was low, and releasing it for sale when the price improved (1614, 1616, 1620). In considering pursuing this policy with his wheat crop he concluded (p. 29) 'soe that reckoning the losse a man is at in shrinking of his wheat, and in the spoile by mice; it was best sould this yeare at the first; even presently after harvest'.

Being aware of the existence of a range of alternatives is not in itself conclusive evidence that the concept of opportunity cost is known to the decision-maker. Loder's account book offers other evidence of this knowledge, even though of course he did not use the term 'opportunity cost'.

1. The most frequently quoted example is that of the inclusion among the charges against profits of the item 'The use of money borrowed; and of my stocke which lay dead until I had my crope. Imprimis the use afor money

---

[5] Joel Dean, *Managerial Economics* (Englewood Cliffs, NJ 1951), 260.

which I borrowed came to iiij L xiiij s vj d. Item the use of my stocke which lay dead, from the time I made an end of sowing untill I had it in my barne (it being as by my Notes appeareth the summe of lxxxx L xvij s iiij d) I reckon comes to for halfe a year iiij L xiiij s vj d.'[6]

In other words, Loder calculated the opportunity cost at 10 per cent per annum of tying up his money in growing crops when there existed an alternative course of action, that of putting out the land on a 'share-cropping' basis or renting it—in Loder's words 'All this yf I had let my lande to halfes or at a Rent, I had saved' (p. 22).

2. Perhaps the best example is that of charging inter-enterprise transfers at weighted average market price, which represents the cost of the opportunity forgone by retaining for internal use produce which would otherwise have been sold. This policy he carried out regularly, delaying the closure of his accounts until all sale crops had been sold and the weighted average price calculated.

The charging of internal transfers at market price representing opportunity cost is superior to the method advocated by Orwin in 1914.[7] Orwin quotes from Professor G. F. Warren's *Farm Management*:[8] 'The usual theory seems to be that if corn and hay can be easily and cheaply grown, they should be fed to livestock. Perhaps the basis of this error is the absurd practice of some institutions of charging feed to animals at the cost of producing it rather than what it can be sold for, less the cost of marketing.' Orwin replies to this, using the figures used by Warren as an example: 'In one case hay costs £1 a ton to produce, in another it costs £5, and Professor Warren, assuming the market price of hay to be £3, suggests that for record-keeping the cost should be abandoned in both cases and the market price substituted. Clearly this sweeps away the *principle of cost, and information as to facts, as to what has happened*, is lost. A sum of £2 is added to the £1 which the hay actually cost one of the farmers, whilst a sum of £2 is deducted from the £5 which it actually cost the other, and with this misrepresentation of their financial experience their accounts are carried on' (my italics). Orwin's opinion is not shared by recent writers such as Jeffrey and Camamile and Theophilus,[9] nor is it shared by Loder.

---

[6] By way of illustration, the last mentioned sum is £4 14s. 6d.

[7] C. S. Orwin, *Farm Accounts* (Cambridge, 1914), 23–4.

[8] New York, 1913.

[9] A. G. Jeffrey, 'Records and Accounts for Farm Management', *Ministry of Agriculture, Fisheries and Food, Bulletin No. 176* (HMSO, 1963); G. H. Camamile and T. W. D. Theophilus, *Records for Profitable Farming* (London, 1964).

LODER'S INFORMATION SYSTEM

The accounts have been described by Hall[10] as 'a gathering of paper sheets, small folio size, of which our farmer's writing, in a rather cramped but not illiterate hand, covers seventy-eight pages with notes, calculations and statistics which are not in the conventional form of medieval or post-medieval accounts, but resemble the rough journals or ledger books of merchants and officials'. The accounts contain two main elements: a recording element containing operating details organized on an enterprise basis, and decision memoranda containing comment, alternative courses of action, and other material relevant to decision-making. The decision memoranda are interspersed throughout the ordinary accounting records, which are themselves in the form of narrative paragraphs. As a result, the account book has, superficially, an untidy and ill-organized appearance, especially when it is compared with, for example, the neatly recorded income and expenditure records of the Toke estates (1616–1704), which, however, contain no decision memoranda. The editor of the Toke accounts commented in the introduction:[11] 'It is only in the early days of his account-keeping that Nicholas [Toke] gives us the benefit of a detailed list of his stock, his crops and his profits. Evidently as long as his father lived this was necessary in order that he might give an account of his stewardship; and for the first few years after he entered into the property he retains the habit; but very soon he omits this valuable record, and merely jots down expenditure without attempting to add up or estimate his position.'

Although Loder's accounts have been criticized as being mathematically inaccurate, arbitrary in content, and primitive in accounting form (criticisms which I shall examine later), they have at least four points in their favour:

1. They are consistent both in layout and in detail. Table 18.1 gives the summary accounts for 1615; the layout is almost identical in all the years 1612 to 1620, indicating that Loder decided on a model layout for his accounts and kept to it.

2. They contain relevant detail for decision-making and control—acreage, sowing, yields, costs, and full details of disposal.

3. The accounts are organized on an enterprise basis, rather than compris-

[10] Hall, 'The Dawn of Modern Farming'.

[11] Eleanor C. Lodge, *The Account Book of a Kentish Estate, 1616–1704* (London, 1927), p. xxix. I am grateful to Mr R. H. Parker, Reader in Management Accounting at the Manchester Business School, for referring me to these accounts.

TABLE 18.1 *Summary accounts 1615*[a]

	£	s.	d.
'The value of my whole crop' (A)			
Wheat	43	6	8
Barley	198	1	3
Straw, chaff, and hulcks	31	15	6
Pulse	15	14	4
Total	288	17	9
'Layinges out' (B)			
Tillage	53	10	—
Seed	31	13	10
Use of money	13	8	6
Harvesting	8	9	—
Threshing, etc.	13	16	11
Total	121	1	6
'Whole value of the Crope' (A) − (B)	168	13	10
Haymaking			
Revenue (C1)	57	17	6
Charges (C2)	4	9	2
Net profit (C3)	53	8	4
Other revenues (D)			
Orchards	14	2	1
Pigeon house	5	6	6
House, quit rents, etc.	17	2	8
Total	36	11	3
Other charges (E)			
Tithes, etc.	10	19	2
'The fulle and whole value of my profittes in this yeare'			
(A) + (C1) + (D)	383	6	6
'The whole summe of cleare profittes made upon my farm'			
[(A) − (B)] + (C3) , + [(D) − (E)]	257	13	3

[a] In the original accounts, this calculation was set out in narrative paragraph form, with some tabulation. Roman numerals were used, following Loder's usual practice. The original accounts also contained more detail than is shown here. The figures contain examples of the arithmetic inaccuracy referred to later in the chapter.

ing merely lists of expenditure and income. Under each enterprise, information is given relating to costs, revenues, yields, etc., and Loder includes his own comments and calculations in the memoranda interspersed at appropriate points among the records. These features, combined with the overall consistency of the accounts to which I have already referred, served to provide Loder with full details for each important enterprise for each year.

The organization of the accounts on an enterprise basis also represents, from the management accounting point of view, a considerable improvement over accounts prepared mainly for taxation or reporting purposes. Accounts prepared in the latter way had then to be analysed for management purposes on an enterprise basis. This traditional 'account analysis', combined with partial budgeting, continues to be used, although the use of 'gross margin' techniques has been advocated by such writers as Camamile and Theophilus and actively encouraged by the Ministry of Agriculture for about the last ten years. These enabled planning (partial budgeting) and control (account analysis) to be conducted on the same basis, using the same techniques for each.

Gross margin techniques require the initial organization of the accounts on an enterprise basis, charging to each enterprise all direct or variable costs associated with the output, and allocating all revenues from the sale of the output to the particular enterprise. The difference between the two is referred to as the gross margin, which may be expressed in £ per acre or per unit of livestock. The gross margins for all enterprises are then totalled and applied to the reduction or elimination of all 'fixed' costs, the difference being the profit or loss for the farm as a whole. In order to achieve strict comparability among farms, rules were made to ensure that each type of income or expenditure is treated in an identical way, being included either in the gross margin enterprise accounts, or in the non-allocated 'fixed' cost accounts. It is this rigid demarcation between fixed and variable costs which distinguishes gross margin techniques from partial budgeting techniques; in other respects, as I shall demonstrate in the following section, they are very similar.

Loder's sophistication in this respect is clearly illustrated by the ease with which the current Ministry of Agriculture M.A.4. Gross Margin Analysis form can be completed using Loder's figures almost entirely without the need to adjust them.

4. Loder stated in the opening paragraph of the accounts that he would begin all his years 'at our Lady Day' but he did not say when he would close them. In fact he kept them open until he had sold the whole of the produce which was earmarked for sale rather than for internal use. This enabled him

to avoid making year-end valuations of stock and also to value at a weighted average market price all internal transfers of produce, although it did mean a delay of several months before he was able accurately to calculate his 'profittes'.

MAJOR CRITICISMS OF THE ACCOUNTS AS RECORDS

1. *Arithmetic inaccuracy.* 'His arithmetic is often defective. His calculations are directed towards the exact assessment of his financial position, but his final balance sheets for each year's produce will not always work out. This is sometimes due to the omission of items in the final computation, and sometimes to poor addition.'[12] Fussell's criticism (p. xxiv) has strong evidence to support it; there are many inaccuracies in the accounts, some due to poor addition, others to a lack of care in relisting the items. Fussell does however go on to say that Loder does 'arrive at the position fairly closely'. It is significant that Loder was, almost without exception, accurate in his addition of the pounds, and that his only mistakes occurred in the shillings and pence.

2. *Arbitrary inclusion of enterprises.* Habakkuk[13] stated that the accounting was 'rather arbitrary' in what it included, a criticism which was also made by Fussell. Table 18.2 indicates the frequency of inclusion and the amount of detail given. The first five enterprises listed in Table 18.2, about which, significantly, information was given in every year, accounted for about 95 per

TABLE 18.2 *Main enterprises: frequency of inclusion*

	1611	1612	1613	1614	1615	1616	1617	1618	1619	1620
Wheat	D	D	D	D	D	D	D	D	D	D
Barley	D	D	D	D	D	D	D	D	D	D
Orchards	d	d	d	d	d	d	d	d	d	d
Pigeons	d	d	d	d	d	d	d	d	d	d
Provender	d	d	d	d	d	d	d	d	d	d
Cattle	—	d	D	—	—	—	—	D	—	—
Sheep	d	D	D	—	—	—	—	—	—	—
Pigs	—	—	D	—	—	—	—	—	—	—

Note: D = detailed calculations; d = less detailed calculations; — = no calculations.

[12] Fussell, *Robert Loder's Farm Accounts.*   [13] Habakkuk, review of *Robert Loder's Farm Accounts.*

cent of both the total revenue and 'cleare profittes' of the farm. It is probable that cattle, sheep, and pigs were usually omitted from the accounts because they were not sufficiently important, or perhaps also because the nature of these enterprises did not give Loder much scope for experimentation, but did enable him to exercise a direct physical control over them. In that case, why are they ever included? Usually the answer can be traced to a specific problem or question arising in a particular year. For example, in 1613 and 1614 his flock of sheep suffered from rot, and he had therefore to consider how to deal with the situation and to prevent its recurrence. Fussell appears to believe that the difference of treatment between the major and minor enterprises is due to Loder's intentions not being matched by his performance. The foregoing discussion should demonstrate beyond doubt that the difference in treatment is due largely to the very fact that some enterprises are important and are therefore regularly included and that some are not, and are therefore rarely included. As to Loder's intentions, the only available evidence is contained in a brief statement in the opening paragraph of the accounts, and the actual accounts; therefore we must compare the records with the evidence of Loder's recording policy—the records themselves!

3. *Primitive accounting form.* Yamey[14] criticizes the accounting entries as being in 'the most elementary form . . . the narrative paragraph'. Certainly the narrative paragraph is cumbersome to modern eyes, especially if used in conjunction with Roman numerals. For example (p. 34), 'Imprimis my whole layinges out being as is aforsayd, ciiij L xvj s and my whole profittes (as is here abovesayd) being cclxxxx L vj s j d ob; the cleare profittes then (I say) comes to more then my layinges out by the summe of clxix L xvij s ix d ob.' Nevertheless Loder does manage to note down important information, and the narrative paragraph does at least permit him to write observations about a particular transaction, a feature of Loder's accounts which is of considerable importance. To have separated the observations from the records might well have weakened the link between the two, and an elaborate system of cross-references might have been made necessary. I find it difficult to believe that, if the accounts were not sufficient for Loder's purposes, he could not have improved them, especially in view of his sophistication in other respects. The fact that they followed essentially the same pattern over the whole period suggests that they suited Loder's needs.

---

[14] Yamey, both works cited in n. 2.

EVALUATION CONCEPTS

Having established a range of alternative plans, and having organized a suitable information system, such as that described earlier, the problem is then one of evaluation and ranking the alternatives according to the extent to which they satisfy the objectives of the decision-maker.

Loder's knowledge of opportunity cost provides the underlying basis of evaluation concepts, although, as an operational concept, opportunity cost has been criticized. Gould[15] has pointed out that to rank the plans, we must know the opportunity cost; if we define opportunity cost as the value of the next best alternative use of scarce resources forgone, then we must know the value of the next best alternative—in other words, to find the opportunity cost we must rank the plans. He therefore suggests that evaluation should be carried out in terms of differential (or incremental or additional) costs; this permits such costs which do not change as a result of pursuing an alternative plan, or which change equally under alternative plans, to be omitted from the calculations, allowing concentration on the calculation of the costs which do change. This really represents a short-cut alternative to the method of costing fully each alternative and then comparing the total costs and ranking accordingly. In this way differential costing represents a refinement of opportunity cost techniques rather than a departure from them.

The use of differential costing does however depend on a knowledge of which costs can be avoided and which are unavoidable if particular courses of action are undertaken. Generally speaking, in other than long-run situations or major policy changes, fixed costs are unavoidable and variable costs are avoidable. Hence, in this situation differential costs will include only variable costs.

The distinction between fixed and variable costs is crucial to the application of gross margin techniques, indeed to most planning techniques. Giles,[16] writing in 1962, stated that all such techniques, from a series of simple adjustments to output to produce maximum gross margins within the physical and financial constraints imposed by the farm, to sophisticated programming techniques, are based on the

principle of the selection of enterprises on the basis of gross margins, i.e. the difference between the gross output from each enterprise and the direct or variable

---

[15] J. R. Gould, 'The Economist's Cost Concept and Business Problems', in Baxter and Davidson (eds.), *Studies in Accounting Theory*, 218–35.

[16] A. K. Giles, 'Gross Margins and the Future of Account Analysis', *University of Reading Miscellaneous Studies*, 23 (1962). My italics.

costs . . . of obtaining that output. This recognition of variable costs—as distinct from fixed or overhead costs—is no new concept in agricultural economics. The significance of these two types of farm costs has been recognised from the beginnings of the subject. It was, for example, the basis of the system of analysis developed by J. S. King in his *Cost Accounting Applied to Agriculture as long ago as 1927.*

Below I give some examples illustrating that Loder appreciated the importance of the distinction between fixed and variable costs as applied to decision-making:

1. In 1617 Loder, as usual, compared the wheat to the barley enterprise and concluded that

it were my best course to sow halfe my lande with wheat for in this year if I had done so I iudge I had gotten . . . xviij L vj s viij d or ther aboutes; besides I iudge that for the carying of my wheat to Marquet I may reckon it to stand me in but little more than my manes labour that goeth with my horses and in selling it, because my charge in keping my horses is never the more or less (so long as I keep vj horses and a Teame) for they would be els idle in the stable. (pp. 137–8)

Thus in calculating his carriage costs he rightly ignored the costs of the horses first because they were an unavoidable cost—he had to keep them for other purposes whether or not he used them for this purpose—and secondly because the opportunity cost of using them to carry wheat to market was letting them lie 'idle in the stable'.

2. In 1618, in the calculation of the costs of maintaining his small herd of cattle Loder referred to his maids' labour in milking the cattle (p. 155): 'excepting my maides labour was worth, which was I iudge but a small thing so long as I must keep ij maides, for yf they did not that, they would yarne but little any otherwayes.'

3. Loder also attempted to calculate the effect of turning the apparently unavoidable cost of maintaining horses into an avoidable cost by keeping none at all. He calculated (p. 35) that he would have gained £23 12s. 3d.

yf I had put forth my lande [to tillage] . . . and kept no teame at all; which is the best course out of doubt yf I could have my lands well plowed; my corne brought in when it is ready; and caryed out when I would my hay caryed in at the best season, & assone as it is ready my lande kept in good hart (as they call it) my dounge caryed forth; my woode brought home, my straw carried to my shep; etc and such like caryages; then I need not be troubled with vnruly servantes; (but this is worthy to be thought of) nor troubled with many businesses.

4. The wheat and barley comparisons contained in the memoranda in each year are themselves basically differential costing exercises. In Table 18.3 I use

TABLE 18.3

	£	s.	d.
Profits			
23½ lands (strips) of wheat producing a gross revenue of	53	7	3½
90½ lands of barley 'which is iiij times soe much			
ground as I iudge' produced a gross revenue of	193	5	1
'which wants of iiij times soe much profit by some of'	20	4	1
Seeding			
'And for the seed, the barly is more chargeable . . . by'	5	3	4
This is calculated:			
Total seeding costs if all lands sowed with wheat	26	13	6
Total seeding costs if all lands sowed with barley	32	6	10
Barley is 'more chargeable' by	5	13	4[a]
Reaping			
Barley, divided by four to equal the wheat area	4	2	4
÷ 4			
Total	1	—	7
Wheat	2	17	4
'Wheat comes to more then any quarturne of barly by'	1	17	—
Straw			
Barley, divided by four to equal the wheat area	25	4	—
÷ 4			
Total	6	6	—
Wheat	7	8	9
'Wheat straw comes to more then a quarturne of barly straw by'	1	2	9

[a] Not £5 3s. 4d. as Loder calculated—one of his minor arithmetic inaccuracies to which I referred earlier.

1612 as an example.[17] Loder concluded on this occasion that 'it were good to sow more store of wheat and lesse barlye'.

CONTROL

Giles has argued that the 'real and lasting problems of farm management in practice are the implementation of a plan and its day-to-day

[17] The whole of the information contained in the 1612 memorandum was laid out in the accounts in one long paragraph. I have reorganized the data into columnar form and I have converted the roman numerals into arabic numerals so as to make the calculations easier to follow.

control'.[18] This control must be in terms of a fairly precise plan or budget of what is expected to happen, against which actual results can be compared. Loder's memoranda on wheat and barley are in effect both control and planning memoranda, based on the results of the previous plans; nor did Loder neglect day-to-day control of the various activities on the farm, as the following examples demonstrate:

I. The malting enterprise offers the best example of the control which Loder exercised over current operations and consequently over the results of past decisions. The malting of barley causes an increase in the total weight of the barley after malting, provided that the malting is carried out successfully. In 1613, Loder calculated that the malting process caused an 'increase' of 4qrs. 3bu. 2½p., valued at £5 10s. 6¾d., with malt dust at a further 10s. He then estimated that the direct or variable costs associated with the malting process were: 'haire' (on which the barley is dried) 9s., straw (at 7d. the quarter 'but it costs me more I doubt') £2 13s. 8d. The gross margin is therefore £2 17s. 10¾d., which 'remaines towardes my maides labour'. In 1617 Loder's calculation of the increase in fact showed a loss, which worried Loder greatly—'what should be the cause hereof I know not, but it was in that yeare when R. Pearce and Alce were my servantes & then in great love (as it appeared to well) whether he gave it my horses . . . or how it went away, God onely knoweth'. Perhaps after further thought, he reluctantly admitted another possibility: 'that I mistoke the setting downe of x quarters (or some) at one time or other; which I do not think because I never did, to my knowledge.'

In 1620 Loder produced a profit and loss account for his experiment in buying barlye:[19] 'what the clxv qutrs j b. ij p. of barlye cost, & what was the Increase thereof when it was maulted, how I sould the same & what I got by it more then I payd for it and more then the charge of making, caryage, etc., comes to & what I have towardes the use of my stocke' (see Table 18.4).

2. Loder's concern with opportunity costs and other related concepts did not cause him to neglect everyday out-of-pocket expenses. On pages 88 and 89, Loder lists well over fifty items of cash outlay totalling £38 12s. 6d., prefacing the list with 'Money layd out from the jth of January in anno supradicto untill the sayd day in Anno 1615, for and aboutes divers other thinges not set downe in any other Note . . . written for this end that *I might see my divers and manie expenses and so to prevent them as much as might be*' (my italics).

---

[18]   A. K. Giles, 'Budgetary Control as an Aid to Farm Management', *University of Reading Miscellaneous Studies* 33 (1964).

[19]   In the original accounts this calculation was set out in narrative paragraph form, using roman numerals.

TABLE 18.4

	£	s.	d.	£	s.	d.
Barley cost				90	6	6
Making (1s. per quarter)				8	5	2
Carriage (4d. per quarter)				3	1	4
Entertainment of workers and carters					15	—
Hair					6	6
Total				102	14	6
Sales	118	14	4			
Increase	13	12	4			
Malt dust		6	8			
Ashes		2	6	132	15	10
'which is more then my charge by'				30	1	4

3. In 1615, he divided the total housekeeping sum by eight:

vij of us, which was my ordinarie household.

j as good as vj monethes and ij days in workmen as going to plow, thaching, hedging, carpenters etc.

j as good as v monethes ij weeks . . . in harvesting.

In other words he converted the short stays of taskers and other casual boarded labour into 'man-years' as a basis for past and future comparisons and to enable him to calculate the costs of boarding workmen.

CONCLUSIONS

Did Loder's decision-making procedures work? The most important decision related to the acreage of land to be put to wheat rather than to barley. His policy was, on the basis of his frequent and detailed evaluation of the question, that he should grow more wheat and less barley. Later, in 1615, this was modified to half wheat, half barley. In 1618, 1619, and 1620, the acreage of wheat equalled or was only a little less than the acreage of barley. Previously the wheat acreage had been about one quarter, or less, of the barley acreage. The figures given in Table 18.5 illustrate the success of this policy.

What general conclusions may be drawn about Robert Loder and his accounts? I suggest that, on the evidence in the accounts, he is best described as a 'pioneer practitioner' in management accounting, on the following grounds:

TABLE 18.5

	Average of the years 1612–17		1618		1619		1620	
	£	£	£	£	£	£	£	£
Gross revenue		252		280		322		378
Seed	33		31		30		24	
Harvesting etc.	30		34		31		19	
Carriage etc.	I	64	9	74	12	63	8	51
Gross margin		188		206		249		227

1. that his objective was clear—to obtain the maximum return from his farm;
2. that he had a sound knowledge of the concept of opportunity cost, and that he put this knowledge to use;
3. that he developed an information system which provided him with data for decision-making and control, although it has been criticized on various counts,
4. that he was aware of, and used in his calculations, the distinction between avoidable and unavoidable costs which is the basis of modern decision-making techniques,
5. that in all these respects he was not merely ahead of his time, but used techniques superior to those which were advocated and used at least three centuries later.

POSTSCRIPT

Over two decades ago, I concluded that Robert Loder was best described as a 'pioneer practitioner' in management accounting. I believe that my conclusion still holds, though with two modifications.

Robert Loder was a practitioner, not a writer of textbooks. How much of a pioneer he was remains an intriguing question. Conceivably, his uniqueness may lie as much in the survival of his records as in his analytical abilities, considerable though they were. There is evidence of systematic management accounting in earlier manorial, governmental, and other enterprises (see, for example, Sybil M. Jack, 'An Historical Defence of Single Entry Book-Keeping, *Abacus*, 2/2 (Dec. 1966), 137–58) and in later industrial firms (see, for example, R. K. Fleischman and L. D. Parker, 'British Entrepreneurs and Pre-Industrial Revolution Evidence of Cost Management', *Accounting Review*, 66/2 (Apr. 1991), 361–75). It is reasonable to assume that, like Loder, the firms and manors used management accounting techniques because they found them useful. Further, at least in the case of the firms, it is probable that each had discovered the techniques independently, given the secrecy that surrounded management accounting then, and indeed for the next hundred years. The records of manors and of firms during the industrial revolution were more likely to survive than were the records of an individual owner-manager.

Most of what had been written about Loder's accounts prior to my article had contained criticism of his 'untidy' accounting, notably, his use of the narrative form, roman numerals, his arithmetic errors, and his unwillingness to bind himself to the annual ritual of closing the books. If I were writing the article today, I should set those criticisms even more firmly in the context of the reasons for which Loder kept accounts—to assist him in making business decisions, to control their consequences, and to learn from his mistakes. He did not prepare the accounts for submission to outside agencies. He prepared them for his own purposes only. He had a clear economic objective, and he used effectively opportunity cost and related concepts towards that objective. He tailored to his needs an information system that he kept in place throughout the period. For example, in the article I noted that the 'decision memoranda are interspersed throughout the ordinary accounting records'. Now, I see the decision memoranda in an even more positive light, as integral to, and inseparable from, his entire system and structure of business information gathering and evaluation.

Robert Loder's accounts are personal documents. Unaided, he created an accounting model for his own use. Statements of generally accepted accounting principles did not exist, and so he devised his own. No management accounting 'guru' influenced him. As a result, his accounts are relevant today as a refreshing example of individual thought and practice, and of the importance of relating effects to causes, and measurement practices to objectives.

ACCOUNTING THEORY

19 · THE EARLY DEBATE ON FINANCIAL AND PHYSICAL CAPITAL

T. A. Lee

The concept of capital is central to the determination of periodic income, irrespective of whether the latter is based on the principles of economics or accounting. Without adequate and consistent definitions and computations of capital at succeeding points of time, there can be no credible income data. This has been well evidenced in the recent professional prescriptions of current cost accounting for external financial reporting purposes.[1] These pronouncements have focused attention on the need to understand the concept of capital which underlies each specific income proposal. In particular, they have identified the existence in practice of two alternative capital maintenance approaches—that is, maintenance based on capital defined in terms either of a specific monetary attribute such as the money unit or the purchasing power unit (hereafter termed *financial* capital); or a specific attribute of the reporting entity's physical asset structure such as its physical units or operating capacity (hereafter termed *physical* capital).

The distinction between the two concepts of capital (and their related maintenance functions) is not a new one. Sweeney (1933a), for example, presented one of the best analyses in this area, and his work should be required reading for interested students of capital definition and measurement. However, despite its antecedents, the distinction provoked a debate in the late 1970s and early 1980s concerning the utility and relevance of the financial and physical approaches for purposes of external financial reporting. Indeed, an international symposium was held on the subject.[2] Contributions

This chapter has benefited considerably from the comments of its reviewers. First published in *Accounting Historians Journal*, 10/1 (Spring 1983).

[1] e.g. Accounting Standards Committee 1980a; Australian Society of Accountants and the Institute of Chartered Accountants in Australia 1976, 1978; Financial Accounting Standards Board 1979.

[2] Lemke and Sterling 1982.

to this meeting discussed the relative merits of financial capital and physical capital and, in so doing, identified significant problem areas for the producer of current cost accounting information which utilizes a physical capital main-tenance approach—for example, the needs of external report users, the accounting treatment of holding gains, coping with changing asset structures and technologies, accounting for price decreases as well as increases, the feasi-bility of using current values in financial reports, and alternatives to current cost accounting.

It should not be surprising to find these matters debated in the 1980s. After all, if current cost accounting contains these problems, it is only right and proper to discuss them with a view to the establishment of current cost accounting as a credible system of financial reporting. However, it is of some concern to find the discussion taking place *ex post* the prescription of current cost accounting. What is even more disturbing is the discovery that the same issues were identified and debated in the early 1900s. Indeed, in 1930[3] a symposium on asset value appreciation covered much of the ground dealt with in the aforementioned one in 1981. And resolution of the issues identi-fied at that time is no further forward despite the passage of 50 years of thought and experience.

Not only was the debate about financial capital and physical capital raised in the early 1900s, it was also fully documented in the relevant accountancy literature, and contributed to by some of the leading academics and practi-tioners of the day. It was largely of United States origin, considerably influ-enced by German thinking, and can be attributed to a major concern about the purpose and role of both appreciation and depreciation of fixed assets.[4] The lack of legal and accounting guidance in these matters in the last quarter of the nineteenth century and first quarter of the twentieth century were also catalysts for the debate. According to Brief (1976), revaluation of fixed assets was common, depreciation accounting was relatively undeveloped, the realiza-tion principle was not fully recognized prior to World War I, and lawyers did not appear to wish to pronounce on business practices and thereby give guidance to accountants.

The interest in the United States debate petered out in the 1940s largely due to the impact of World War II, was resumed at a very modest level in the 1950s and 1960s (when relatively low rates of inflation prevailed), and

---

[3] Symposium 1930.

[4] There was also at the same time a considerable Dutch contribution based on the work of Limperg (1964). However, because of its inaccessibility, and its isolation from the English-speaking literature, it is difficult to integrate it in this chapter beyond making relevant mention of Limperg's theory at particular points. The sources for these comments have been Mey 1966 and Burgert 1972.

burst into full prominence in the 1970s with double digit inflation. It has not diminished since despite the practical implementation of current cost accounting in several English-speaking countries.[5] It therefore appears pertinent to go back in time to rediscover the early contributions to the debate—first, to acknowledge their significance in the development of financial reporting thought; secondly, to identify the main issues with which they were concerned and to compare them, where relevant, with the issues of today; and, thirdly, to speculate from such an analysis on the reasons why no apparent progress has been achieved in the United States and, to a lesser extent, in the United Kingdom in the resolution of the capital debate. In this way, it is hoped that lessons from the past may be learned in order to avoid lack of progress in the future.

EARLY RECOGNITION OF THE PROBLEM

It can be argued that the earliest accounting practitioners of the modern era recognized the need to maintain the physical asset structure of the reporting entity, and to implement methods of financial accounting which could aid this process. Brief (1976) provides a reminder that, prior to 1875, the practice of replacement accounting (that is, charging the cost of fixed asset replacement against sales revenue in arriving at periodic income) was fairly widespread, and was adopted in place of conventional depreciation policies. Income was therefore determined on a quasi-replacement cost basis with the balance sheet containing outdated and undepreciated historic costs. The replacement costs used for income purposes, however, were those occurring at the time of replacement rather than at the time of reporting. The practice was apparently limited to replaced fixed assets, and its use can be confirmed in the United States railway industry which was governed by the regulations of the Interstate Commerce Commission (which specified the use of replacement accounting).[6]

There was also evidence of revaluation of fixed assets prior to 1875, and an awareness of the danger of distributing any resulting unrealized holding gains.[7] But, gradually, a more conservative approach to accounting was adopted, and historical cost depreciation practices to maintain invested

---

[5] It is interesting to note that the accounting theory of Limperg (1964), which was developed in the 1920s and 1930s, influenced his students sufficiently to go beyond the debating stage, and to implement a system of accounting containing several features of present-day current cost practice—see e.g. Goudeket 1960 and Burgert 1972.

[6] Stockwell 1909.   [7] Brief 1976.

money capital were implemented.[8] Also, at about the same time, a further accounting practice was being advocated—that is, the *appropriation* of amounts from income to reserve (in excess of historical cost depreciation) in order to aid the funding of fixed asset replacements.[9]

Thus, although the conventional depreciation practices of the time may have been relatively primitive (that is, appropriations of income rather than cost allocations), there was an obvious awareness by certain leading accountants of the day that adequate accounting could aid the function of *financing* the reporting entity's physical asset structure. However, a contrary view existed which, despite recognizing the potential financial problem of inadequate depreciation to fund fixed asset replacement, preferred to depreciate historical costs and not to recognize value changes, either because of the danger of overvaluation when prices eventually fell after a period of rising[10] or because the entity was a going concern which was unaffected financially by the recognition of unrealized holding gains—these ultimately being realized at some future date.[11]

The latter historical cost school of thought appeared to prefer the financial capital approach of maintaining the original invested capital. The alternative approaches of replacement accounting and reserve accounting indicated a movement towards physical capital maintenance without abandoning the traditional historical cost system. In addition, a further school of thought was to develop in the early 1920s—balance sheet revaluations being encouraged (usually based on replacement costs) to provide more realistic descriptions of entity financial position, but with the income statement recommended to continue on a historical cost basis, thus not reflecting a maintenance of the revalued position.[12] In this way, realized holding gains were included in the income statement and unrealized holding gains were put to reserve. By contrast, replacement accounting and reserve accounting effectively excluded a certain proportion of realized holding gains from income, and historical cost accounting failed to recognize unrealized holding gains.

These different contributions mark a useful starting-point for the debate on capital and capital maintenance—particularly in the 1920s and 1930s.[13]

---

[8] Ibid.   [9] Dickinson 1904; Cole 1908; Sells 1908.

[10] Knight 1908.   [11] Gower 1919.

[12] Paton 1920, 1922; Rastall 1920; Moss 1923.

[13] By contrast the Dutch debate commenced at about the same time for a somewhat different reason. Limperg (1964) was concerned about changes in thinking about the economic approach to valuation (particularly regarding business decisions based on marginal utility), and preferred an accounting system for management based on the producer. Thus, economic arguments to aid management accounting practice were the basis for the Dutch debate, rather than the more pragmatic accounting issue of how best to account for fixed assets in practice.

They reveal the first major problem facing accountants in this area—that is, the difficulty of separating the *managerial* need to fund the replacement of assets underlying invested capital from the *accounting* need to maintain that capital. This particular problem was first made explicit in the literature by Saliers (1913) but is also to be found in the work of others throughout the 1920s and 1930s—including Jackson (1921); Scott (1929); Paton (1934); and Crandell (1935). At times it is somewhat difficult to distinguish the two functions in the recommendations of these writers, and this is perhaps best evidenced in the words of the accountants concerned.

Bauer produced the following major statement of the problem:

The question therefore arises, is the purpose of management merely to maintain investment in terms of dollars, and to show current costs and profits accordingly, or is it really to keep up the plant and equipment and to maintain the physical productivity of the property?[14]

He obviously identified the managerial task of asset replacement, and linked it with the accounting process of capital maintenance. He therefore appeared to see no need to separate the two functions, and was quite clear in his accounting answer to the managerial question posed—the expected cost of replacement and not historical cost should be matched against sales revenue. He went even further than modern theorists in this respect, appearing to advocate the use of future rather than current replacement costs.

Jackson asked the same question in a much briefer manner: 'Is the purpose of the depreciation charge to maintain the capital investment or is it to replace the physical plant?'[15] It should be noted that the question was asked solely in connection with fixed asset replacement, and this appeared to be the major preoccupation of these early accounting theorists (working capital being usually ignored). Jackson argued that historical cost was the true cost for accounting purposes (without defining the term 'true'), and advocated financial capital maintenance based on historical costs. However, as the above quotation reveals, accounting and managing are completely merged in the question asked.

Rorem was much less confused but arguably no less confusing, fully recognizing the alternative physical capital basis for accounting:

The purpose of writing the appreciated value into the cost of manufacturing is entirely independent of any accounting procedure for insuring the maintenance of physical capital. It is true, that physical capital must be maintained if an enterprise is to continue business operations. It is true, however, that an enterprise must be

[14] Bauer 1919: 414.   [15] Jackson 1921: 83.

considered unprofitable unless its accounts are so handled as to deduct provision for capital maintenance as a cost of business operations. The charge for depreciation is a writing off of values which have already appeared; it is in no sense a provision for expenses which are yet to be incurred.[16]

Rorem then argued for the use of replacement costs for depreciation purposes, criticizing the alternative policy of transfers from income to reserve in addition to historical cost depreciation. He undoubtedly regarded replacement cost accounting as a means of determining the profitability of the entity (the primary aim) while maintaining physical capital (the secondary aim). His paper clearly and logically makes the case for accounting for the physical structure of the entity, separate from the issue of financially managing asset replacements.

The then radical proposals of Rorem contrasted with the continuing support of leading accountants for historical cost accounting supplemented with income appropriations to reserve. Thomas (1916) had suggested the latter approach to preserve the financial solvency of the entity; Rastall (1920) preferred to reserve prudently to avoid overdepreciation; Jackson (1920) believed the use of historical cost depreciation reflected the 'privilege' of using low cost equipment in higher cost times, but thought that additional amounts should be reserved from income; and other similar contributions come from Martin (1927), Scott (1929), and Daniels (1933). Each of these writers appeared to support a financial capital-based approach to income accounting, capital being measured in terms of aggregations of money units comprising historical costs. Some recognized the need also to provide separately for a funding of asset replacement at higher costs by reserve accounting. This approach was well described by Martin:

Such a reserve has the advantage of keeping the attention of the management and the stockholders centered on the real significance of increases in asset values. If they are to continue the business with the physical capital intact they must provide sufficient net earnings to make possible an increase in the money statement of net worth equal to the difference between original cost and replacement cost.[17]

The above quotation is a useful way of summarizing the somewhat confused state of thinking about income accounting and capital maintenance in the 1920s particularly. Financial capital recognition (for example, the money statement of net worth) was a popular approach, coupled with a growing awareness of the need to fund asset replacement and aid this by some form of accounting (for example, transfers to reserve). Managing and preserving the

---

[16] Rorem 1929: 172–3.   [17] Martin, 1927: 123.

physical structure of the reporting entity was therefore a fairly well-known idea; accounting for its maintenance tended to be relatively crude. Also, it must be noted that the physical structure was normally interpreted in a limited way to non-monetary fixed assets—inventory and other assets typically being ignored.

Thus, there appeared to be some confusion in the minds of writers between the financial management function of replacing entity assets, and the financial accounting function of reporting on entity profitability and financial position.[18] It would therefore seem relevant to pursue further the early arguments for accounting to aid management or preserve the physical assets and capital of the entity. To do so, may provide clues as to why the writers concerned had difficulty distinguishing between asset management and capital accounting. To do so is important, for the common cry nowadays from companies is—why do we need current cost accounting when we manage effectively with regard to price changes? As the chairman of one United Kingdom company has put it:

From a management point of view we have all the information we require in our monthly accounting statements to ensure that the full effects of inflation are taken into account in arriving at management decisions and . . . the attached accounts do not provide our management with any additional useful information.[19]

The present United Kingdom current cost accounting provision[20] confuses internal and external accounting needs in its statement of aims, and provides no answer to the above statement.

MANAGERIAL NEEDS AND CAPITAL MAINTENANCE

The replacement of assets appeared to be regarded at the end of the nineteenth century as essentially a matter for good management rather than formal accounting procedures.[21] According to Brief (1976), for example, the question of whether or not to provide for fixed asset depreciation was left very much in the hands of management and the internal rules and regulations of the reporting entity—courts of law gave little or no guidance and the

---

[18] This was not the case with Limperg (1964). His writings make it quite clear that he saw his system of accounting based on replacement values (using a valuation rule of the lower of replacement value and net realizable value) as being primarily for management accounting purposes but also of considerable use for financial accounting. He did not appear to regard it as essential to separate the two functions.

[19] Wedgewood 1981: 3.

[20] Accounting Standards Committee 1980a.

[21] Litherland 1951.

accountancy profession was in its infancy. Thus, the accounting emphasis for income determination purposes arguably included some notion of financial capital maintenance in a great many cases, depreciation procedures being largely ignored and revaluations being fairly common.

This picture of self-regulation undoubtedly must have influenced writers in the 1920s and 1930s who were concerned to ensure that management had sufficient relevant information with which to make adequate funding arrangements for fixed asset replacements. Not unexpectedly, writings occasionally merged the separate issues of internal management information systems with external financial reporting.[22] It is therefore important to read them with care.

The use of replacement accounting and reserve accounting procedures appears to have been a device for reflecting the funding of fixed asset replacements (particularly) without interfering with the then traditional practices of accounting based on historical cost measurements and financial capital maintenance (of original invested capital). However, in the first decades of the twentieth century a number of writers began to advocate the use of replacement costs for internal management information purposes. Paton (1918), for example, argued that managers (and shareholders) needed replacement cost data—to aid the making of management decisions (presumably including asset replacement), and to let shareholders know their rights (presumably referring to the need to disclose total income, including unrealized holding gains).

By 1920, however, Paton (1920) was arguing for the use of replacement cost accounting for management only in order to aid it in preserving physical assets and productive capacity. Canning (1929), while not recommending the use of replacement costs generally for external reporting, believed they might be useful to management for purposes of deciding which goods to buy in the future, and for determining selling prices. Scott (1929), Schmidt (1930), and Wasserman (1931) held relatively similar views on the managerial relevance of replacement costs.

Each of these contributors to the United States literature therefore appears to have had a clear idea of the utility of replacement cost accounting for management purposes, particularly as an aid to funding asset replacement. Some of them also supported its use for external financial reporting, but to a far lesser extent. Occasionally, their recommendations were unclear as to the distinction between internal and external reporting. But it can be concluded that

---

[22] This is especially true of the work of Limperg (1964).

they were reasonably of a single mind with regard to one matter—they did not believe it was essential to account formally for the maintenance of physical capital in order to preserve the physical asset structure of the reporting entity. Instead, they felt that the latter could be aided by reserve transfers of financial capital-based income; and also by an adequate determination of selling prices to be charged to customers. In addition, it should be noted that replacement cost accounting was originally devised as a system of internal management accounting—particularly by Paton (1920).

The above comments contrast sharply with the ideas of the Dutch theorist Limperg (1964). Throughout the 1920s and 1930s he argued for the use of replacement value-based accounting to aid management in the buying and selling activities associated with its products. He defined replacement value as a measure of the sacrifice by the producer when selling his products or using his assets (Limperg's replacement value referred only to replaceable assets, and was the cost at the time of sale or use of what was technically necessary and economically unavoidable to replace the asset concerned). In addition, he argued for the use of replacement value to determine selling prices. However, he did appear to have a firm view regarding physical capital maintenance (without specifically defining or using the term). His definition of income was essentially a physical capital-based one—holding gains being taken to reserve, and holding losses being treated in the same way until the reserve containing aggregate holding gains was exhausted. Any holding losses thereafter were to be written off against income.

This concept of preserving what Limperg described as the 'source of income' was something which he saw as being useful for both internal and external reporting purposes—to aid the analysis of business operations, provide sufficient funds to finance asset replacements, and to prevent over-consumption. He felt that, by such a process of capital maintenance, income could be determined 'without ambiguity and with certitude'—presumably for all its users. Nevertheless, as with that of Paton in the United States, Limperg's system was devised essentially as one of management accounting—although, undoubtedly, he also felt that external interests such as investors could benefit considerably from the reporting of such management-orientated information. Continuing evidence of this belief is provided by the limited but important use of replacement valuing accounting for external reporting by certain Dutch companies.

REPLACEMENT COSTS AND SELLING PRICES

Several writers in the 1920s and 1930s made strong statements on the place of replacement costs in the managerial determination of selling prices of goods and services to customers. Paton (1922), in an all too rare paper on accounting for current assets, claimed that replacement cost was the only price relevant to management as it governed the selling price of a good or service in the long term. Rorem (1929), too, argued that replacement cost accounting was relevant to management because it represented the minimum value established by competition and to be paid when looking forward to the eventual resale of the good or service concerned. For this reason, Rorem went on to argue for the use of replacement costs in external reports because he regarded the difference between replacement cost and historical cost as the provision for capital maintenance which should be treated as a cost of business operations. Daniels (1933) also felt that the customer should be paying for the replacement cost of goods in the long run (in this case, fixed assets), and thus concluded that the entity's pricing policy should result in income which was sufficient to replace fixed assets at higher costs.[23] He believed the function of depreciation, however, was not to provide for physical capital maintenance (recommending instead the funding of replacement by prudent reserving).

The idea of funding asset replacement by passing on increasing costs to the entity's customers, and thereby hopefully preserving its physical structure, was not universally accepted by the writers of the day. Jackson (1920) thought it unfair to ask customers to pay for anything other than the original cost of fixed assets in the case of public utilities, but thought it fair to charge replacement cost to private enterprise customers (so long as the realized difference between replacement cost and historical cost was taken to reserve). The 1930 Symposium on Appreciation[24] produced an even stronger position. It was argued that only historical costs should be passed on to the consumer because of the danger of being priced out of a competitive market, and that what was really needed in this area was good management rather than amendments to traditional accounting. Littleton (1936) argued along similar lines.

Thus, from these writings, it can be concluded that there was a recognition that management had to make decisions concerning the entity's asset

---

[23] It should be noted that these views are compatible with those of Limperg (1964), who believed that, on average, the use of replacement costs to determine selling prices would generate sufficient cash to fund asset replacements.

[24] Symposium 1930.

structure, and that financial information was needed for this purpose. Some writers argued for using replacement costs, and others for historical costs. But it was also apparent that there was no general consensus that the use of the former data in external financial reports could provide a more informed way of describing how the physical structure of the entity had been maintained by management. In other words, there appeared to be a growing awareness in the 1920s and 1930s of the need to use replacement costs (*ex ante*) for management decisions, and the possibility of using them (*ex post*) for external reporting—in both cases, the aim being to reflect the need to maintain the physical asset structure of the entity; the first to demonstrate how to provide sufficient funds to finance replacement and the second to report on the maintenance of the capital representing the replaced and replaceable assets. The common factor in all this seemed to be the physical assets of the entity, and this brought into question the purposes of external financial reporting—what was to be reported and to whom was it to be reported?

AIMS AND USES

The previous two sections have attempted to show that the early accounting theorists were concerned with asset replacement and the management of financial funds to do so. This inevitably raised the question of whether or not these matters should be the subject of a formal accounting in external financial reports. In other words, should external reports reflect such matters as the maintenance of the physical capital of the entity?

Views varied from one extreme to another. Paton (1918) stated that the physical nature of an asset was only important in terms of its influence on value. Bauer (1919) argued that external accounting should reflect the maintenance of the physical productivity of the assets. Jackson (1921) believed that maintenance of original invested costs was essential. Sweeney (1927 and 1930) complained that maintenance of physical capital did not maintain the general purchasing power of capital which gave the entity command over goods and services. And Daniels (1933) and Littleton (1936) felt that the job of accounting was to allocate past costs and not to value. Therefore, some were for financial capital maintenance (in money value or purchasing power terms) and others favoured physical capital maintenance. Few statements were made by these writers as to why these approaches should be the preferred ones from the point of view of the report users.

Daines (1929), for example, wrote of the objectives of accounting (and of current values) mainly in relation to the dividend decision. However, he also felt that users other than investors should be recognized—but made little effort to specify who these users were. Krebs (1930), too, wrote of unspecified users in relation to accounting for asset appreciation but without amplifying the matter. Littleton (1936) preferred to concentrate on uses rather than users, even arguing against the use of financial accounting data for dividends, taxation, and selling price determination.

Other writers clearly identified investors as the main external user group to which income and capital issues could be related—Paton (1920), when arguing for physical capital maintenance, sympathized with reporting on this for management decision purposes only, and not for investors (holding gains not being treated as distributable income); Schmidt (1930) made a similar argument, and defined distributable income as that remaining after maintaining business assets; in a later paper Schmidt (1931) identified distributable income more directly as current operating profit (that is, after full provision for the replacement cost of assets consumed). The Dutch position, too, as expressed by Limperg (1964), despite its management accounting basis, also appeared to concentrate on the owner/investor as the main external user—replacement value arguments being related to the determination of income for consumption or dividend decisions. All in all, however, the coverage of report users and uses by writers advocating change to traditional practice was poor, and resulted in a significant gap in the financial versus physical capital debate. It was at least partly bridged by proponents of the traditional historical cost school of thought.

THE NEED FOR HISTORICAL COST ACCOUNTING

Although the aims of financial reporting in the 1920s and 1930s may have been poorly covered in the literature, several writers were adamant in their view of the nature of the process—that is, it was an attempt to reflect what had actually happened in the reporting entity rather than to hypothesize about what might have occurred under different circumstances and transactions. Canning (1929), for example, argued strongly along these lines—that historical costs were needed to calculate income on past transactions; costs are history and nothing can be done to change them; and fictitious data should not be introduced into accounting. Gower (1919) pleaded for the maintenance of invested capital and the use of historical costs, so long as a going concern could be assumed for the reporting entity. Jackson (1920) pointed out that historical costs had actually been transacted, and that replacement costs depended on some as yet non-existent event. Prudence was given as the main reason for historical cost usage by Mather (1928). Littleton (1928 and 1929) believed income only existed when a sale transaction took place, and that it could not therefore be recognized in the form merely of unrealized asset value changes.

Each of these writers argued against the use of replacement costs, and their main reason appeared to be the need to attempt to reflect in financial reports the income which had been realized through sale transactions. They seemed to regard asset value appreciation as purely fictitious data so long as sale or exchange had not taken place. As previously mentioned, the emphasis was on what had happened. But these arguments were made in relation to external financial reports; several of these writers were at pains to point out the utility of replacement cost accounting for purposes of internal management decisions. In addition, they pinpointed a major problem in income and capital accounting which remains a contemporary issue—that is, whether or not holding gains are income or capital adjustments.

THE NATURE OF HOLDING GAINS

The early accounting theorists in the income and capital debate were fully aware of the nature and possible existence of holding gains and the problems of accounting for them. Initially termed asset appreciation, the holding gain arose as a reporting issue from the 1920s debate concerning asset values, and gained practical importance because of the possibility of distributing unrealized asset value increases as well as realized gains. However, as a result of the debate concerning the maintenance of physical capital generally, and replacement cost depreciation particularly, the holding gain question was extended to include both realized and unrealized elements. It thus reached a status in the early literature akin to that given to it today.

Paton (1918) was one of the earliest writers on holding gains. He called for their inclusion in income (whether realized or unrealized) in order to let shareholders 'know their rights', while preventing balance sheets from being understated (he did not expand on these advocations). However, Paton (1920) soon changed his mind regarding the treatment of holding gains as income—he later argued that they were capital adjustments, thus supporting the physical capital approach and treating holding gains as non-distributable. He gave no reasons for this change of viewpoint.

Jackson (1920) also adopted Paton's latter stance—holding gains in his opinion being funds of the entity belonging to future investors, and thus not to be accounted for until realized. Several years went by following this contribution, until Martin (1927) wrote a paper which relied heavily on the earlier work of Paton. He agreed that holding gains should be recognized and treated as capital adjustments in order to keep managers and investors aware of the historical cost profits required to be retained in order to fund the increased cost of replacing assets.

Two years later Rorem (1929) produced a major paper arguing for the inclusion of at least realized holding gains in income measurements, although he would have required them to be separately disclosed in the income statement. However, he was very unclear as to his views on the distributability of holdings gains—he was fully aware of the need to calculate cost of sales and depreciation on a replacement cost basis in order to provide for the maintenance of physical capital. But he also believed customers should pay for asset replacement increases through increased selling prices. He made no specific comment on distributable income.

Schmidt (1930 and 1931) was more certain in his approach: holding gains are not income; they cannot be distributed because they may not be realized. In this way, he appeared to support physical capital maintenance, although his argument for the use of replacement costs was for management purposes only in the first paper, but appeared to extend to external reports in the second.

Sweeney (1932) also supported the view that holding gains should not be treated as income, being capital adjustments. However, after making general purchasing power adjustments to the holding gain to eliminate the inflationary element, he further advocated the inclusion of real holding gains in the income statement once they had been realized (thus presumably making them available for distributions).

The Dutch view on the treatment of holdings is evidenced in the writings of Limperg (1964) in the 1920s and 1930s. Consistently, he argued that holding gains were not income and should be taken to a non-distributable reserve. This is compatible with a physical capital maintenance approach. Holding losses were also recommended to be charged against the aforementioned reserve so long as there were gains at its credit to cover them. Thereafter, when the reserve was exhausted, Limperg suggested holding losses should reduce income, thereby implying a switch to financial capital maintenance. No particular reason seems to have been forthcoming to explain this apparent inconsistency in his accounting arguments.

In summary, it can therefore be seen that the problem of the treatment of holding gains was well recognized in the early 1900s, and usually debated within the context of writings on income and capital involving aspects of physical capital maintenance. The consensus appeared to be for the recognition of holding gains, usually not as income (generally) or distributable income (particularly). The main reason for this approach appeared to be the need to ensure the maintenance of physical capital by retaining funds to aid the replacement of assets at higher costs. However, the recognition and accounting treatment of holding gains within the context of capital maintenance raises questions concerning the changing structure of the capital to be maintained. The latter problem was recognized by the early accounting theorists, although not necessarily to the extent of providing a feasible solution.

CHANGING ASSET STRUCTURES AND TECHNOLOGIES

Several writers on income and capital matters indicated their awareness of the problem of maintaining capital in physical terms when the nature of the underlying asset structure was changing due to related changes in operating activities and/or technologies. Bauer (1919), for example, when discussing the specific example of accounting for the renewal cost of street cars, wrote of the difficulty of doing so when there was a constantly changing structure of physical assets. He presented this as a problem to be faced by accountants without advocating any particular solution. Martin (1927) also recognized the problem—but merely as one which caused instability in asset valuations, thus making accounting for fixed assets a somewhat more hazardous function than would be the case with a situation of stability. But, again, no solution was prescribed or recommended. Limperg (1964), too, offered no answers, merely suggesting (without definition) that the accounting should allow for 'economic replacement'—implying non-identical replacement. This is confirmed by his definition of replacement value as the technically necessary and economically unavoidable cost of the asset concerned at the time of its sale or use.

Sweeney (1927) was far more forthright in his comments on the matter. Because he recognized there would be a decline in the business need for certain assets as others became more desirable resources for the reporting entity, he disagreed with accounting for physical capital and its maintenance. Instead, he (then) favoured the alternative financial capital approach of applying general price-level adjustments to historical cost data to 'preserve economic power over goods and services'. In other words, he presumably felt that the difficulties associated with changing asset structures were such that the reporting accountant should focus his attention on the more easily identified financial features of capital.

Rorem (1929), on the other hand, took a contrary stance—akin to the one associated with contemporary systems of current cost accounting.[25] Totally committed to the idea of reporting in replacement cost terms, he recognized the problem of technological change, and the problem of obtaining replacement costs for accounting in such circumstances. He therefore suggested that the replacement cost used to value a fixed asset should be adjusted to represent equivalent services to those obtained from the existing asset— that is, similar to the contemporary concept of the modern equivalent asset.[26]

This approach would have been whole-heartedly condemned by Canning (1929). A consistent critic of replacement cost accounting because of its reliance on 'fictitious data' and 'imponderables', he had this to say of asset structure changes:

Outlay cost is a real thing—a fact. So, too, will replacement cost *become* a real thing when it is incurred. But because prices of equipment fluctuate, because there are always many alternative ways of getting service, that is, many kinds of serving agents that will do a given kind of work, and because the amount and kind of service needed in an enterprise change with its selling, as well as with its buying, opportunities— because of all these extremely elusive matters it requires a good deal of positive evidence to show on which side of experienced cost per unit of service a future unit cost is likely to lie.

We do not often see old establishments duplicated in new ones. Cost of reproduction new less an allowance for depreciation may be a good working rule in damage suits; it is absurd as a sole rule of going-concern valuation.[27]

Not surprisingly, Canning preferred to account for capital in financial terms—ideally, those of present value, but practically in terms of a mixture of historical costs and net realizable values (when these could be obtained directly). He was not alone in this respect. Paton (1934) was by then arguing against the use of replacement costs, admitting that historical cost accounting could be the best basis for mainstream accounting purposes, with replacement costs only being reported as supplementary data. One of his reasons for this radical change of heart was the specialist complexity of fixed assets which meant that replacement in the same form as the original asset was impossible.

Thus, the problem of continually changing asset structures was not

---

[25] Accounting Standards Committee 1980*a*.   [26] Accounting Standards Committee 1980*b*.
[27] Canning 1929: 254–5.

unknown in the 1920s and 1930s, although its discussion was limited (mainly to fixed assets), and usually avoided by advocacy of the adoption of some form of financial capital approach for reporting purposes. The support for the latter can be best evidenced by those writings which discussed the need to maintain capital in general purchasing power terms.

GENERAL PURCHASING POWER ACCOUNTING

Financial capital maintenance using general purchasing power techniques gained considerable support during the 1920s and 1930s. Middleditch (1918) provided the impetus for historical cost adjusted data, but paid little direct attention to ideas of capital maintenance (he suggested losses on monetary items—including inventory as such—should be taken to reserve, and implied that purchasing power gains on liabilities should be treated as income). Paton (1918), on the other hand, argued that information ought to reflect specific price changes rather than changes in the general price level.

By 1920, however, Paton's views on general purchasing power accounting were changing.[28] Although favouring replacement cost accounting, he did recognize the difficulty of comparing data at different points of time for income purposes when the general price level was changing. Thus he argued that replacement cost figures should only be used for management purposes. The idea of general purchasing power accounting, however, was not developed further until the work of Sweeney was published in the late 1920s. Indeed, Canning (1929) stated that, although accountants would prefer such a system of accounting, they did not use it because of the lack of data available in time to make the adjustments (that is, presumably general price indices took a considerable time to prepare and publish at that time).

Nevertheless, the work of Sweeney had a considerable influence on income measurement—even if this was not immediate. He did not agree with the maintenance of physical capital in replacement cost accounting and, instead, preferred the maintenance of real capital in order to preserve the reporting entity's economic power over goods and services.[29] In this way, he would adjust historical costs for the general movement in prices, maintaining the outward form of capital (general command over goods) rather than the inner substance (physical assets).[30] By 1931, however, although still roundly

---

[28] Paton 1920.   [29] Sweeney 1927.
[30] Sweeney 1930.

condemning the use of pure historical cost and replacement cost systems, he argued at least that the latter was better than the former.[31]

In 1932, his views regarding replacement costs had changed somewhat.[32] Although his main system was based on general purchasing power, he also recommended the introduction of replacement cost changes in the balance sheet on top of the general price-level-adjusted data—the total holding gains being taken to reserve until realized when the real element was transferred to income. Thus, he preferred to use a replacement cost system which, when combined with general price-level changes, effectively maintained financial capital—only allowing holding gains to be treated as income when realized, and only to the extent of real price changes. This combined approach was also favoured by Schmidt (1931), although he only regarded speculative holding gains as income.

By 1933, Sweeney (1933*b*) regarded all realized and unrealized gains as income, advocating their separation in the income statement. These ideas were developed within the context of a combined replacement cost and general price-level system. Monetary gains and losses appeared in the income statement (a point disagreed with by Jones (1935)), but no calculation was made of liability gains or losses of purchasing power. Fixed asset depreciation was measured in general purchasing power terms, thus emphasizing the financial capital approach. A summation of his ideas appeared in two further papers.[33]

The work of Sweeney in the 1920s and 1930s did much to establish a case for adopting an accounting approach which depended on financial capital maintenance. Indeed, he revealed clearly that it was perfectly possible to do this *and* to use replacement costs—that is, financial capital maintenance and replacement cost accounting are not incompatible.[34] This last point is something which remains a matter of confusion for contemporary accountants (for example, the attempt to maintain physical capital and financial capital in the provisions of the most recent current cost accounting recommendations).[35]

---

[31]   Sweeney 1931.

[32]   Sweeney 1932.

[33]   Sweeney 1934, 1935.

[34]   But his was a lone view—arguably one of the leading replacement cost advocates of the time, Limperg (1964), made no attempt to account for general price-level changes.

[35]   Accounting Standards Committee 1980*a*.

LITTLE SUPPORT FOR SALE VALUES

Sweeney's relatively lone effort in the 1920s and 1930s to promote a financial capital maintenance approach (using general price changes) indicates a possible reluctance to move away from the traditional historical cost-based model. There was also a reluctance to adopt an alternative financial capital strategy which has been consistently and vigorously advocated in more recent times[36]—that is, the use of allocation-free sale values. This reluctance was a deep-seated one, reflecting an unwillingness to account for income before it was realized and a contrary support for the eventual accounting for income as and when it is realized by the entity as a going concern.[37] Paton (1918) was against the use of sale values, believing that to do so was to anticipate income (in a way which he also believed replacement costs did not do—a point which confirms that he regarded holding gains from replacement costs as potential income at that time).

By 1929, however, there were signs of some support for the idea of using sale values for external financial reporting—but only in limited circumstances. Rorem (1929) advocated the use of replacement costs but, following a 'value to the business' rule akin to that seen in most contemporary systems of current cost accounting, suggested the use of net realizable value in circumstances when the latter had fallen below replacement cost. Daines (1929), on the other hand, indicated that sale values might be of use in financial reports, but only to creditors interested in liquidity matters. And Canning (1929) advocated the use of sale values for reporting on assets where valuations could be applied directly to the objects concerned—for example, as in inventory for resale (as did MacNeal (1970)). In fact, so far as these direct valuations were concerned, he indicated merit in reporting historical costs, replacement costs and sale values. His reasons for this approach were less than clear.

Limperg (1964), on the other hand, advocated the occasional use of net realizable values for reporting purposes. His valuation rule was the lower of replacement value and net realizable value, thereby reflecting the sacrifice of the owner of the assets concerned when he sold or used the latter. In addition, he argued that net realizable value, when compared with replacement value, should be the higher of the immediate liquidation value and the sale value on an orderly liquidation. Limperg therefore represented one of the few

---

[36] Chambers 1966; Sterling 1970.   [37] Guthrie 1883; Best 1885.

writers on accounting in the 1920s and 1930s who attempted to use sale values within a mixed value system—somewhat similar to that evidenced in present-day current cost accounting systems.[38]

The above brief commentary reflects a limited attention paid to net realizable value accounting in the 1920s and 1930s, a situation not unlike that of today. It meant that the capital debate centred around historical costs, replacement costs, and purchasing power units.

DEALING WITH PRICE DECREASES

A further problem created by replacement cost accounting and physical capital maintenance is the treatment of price decreases. To treat them in a similar way to price increases results in increasing operating income and decreasing financial capital (due to the setting-off of holding losses against reserves).[39] Arguably, this problem can be resolved by reverting to a financial capital system when prices are falling,[40] But this does not cater for a situation in which some prices are rising and some falling. Brief (1970), when reviewing late nineteenth-century contributions to the income and capital debate, indicated that these early writers were aware of the problem of falling prices, and this is clear from the writings of Best (1885) and Cooper (1888)—capital losses being written off against income for dividend purposes. This awareness was also to be seen in the work of later writers.

Knight (1908), for example, advocated depreciation based on original cost because of the danger of fixed asset values falling. Rastall (1920) pointed out the danger of overstating income by underdepreciating when prices fell. And Sweeney (1930) complained that, if a physical capital maintenance approach were adopted when prices were falling, then the reporting entity's general command over goods would not be maintained (that is, its financial capital in terms of generalized purchasing power would diminish) and, if prices continued to fall, would reduce capital towards zero. This would be no problem so long as the reporting entity continued to invest in and replace assets subject to price decreases. But, as Sweeney indicated, it creates a problem when the entity wishes to diversify into assets subject to different price movements. On the other hand, Daniels (1933) took a pragmatic stance by suggesting that

---

[38] e.g. Accounting Standards Committee 1980a.

[39] See Sterling 1982.

[40] See Lee 1982. Attention should also be paid to the work of Limperg (1964) in this respect. He recommended that holding losses should be written off against income when they exceeded aggregate holding gains taken to reserve.

historical cost depreciation policies should be applied in order to allow for both replacement cost increases and decreases. McCowen (1937) felt that a physical capital system, using replacement costs, should be applied irrespective of prices increasing or decreasing—replacement cost accounting reflecting, in his view, how much the reporting entity's selling prices must be adjusted upwards or downwards. Schmidt (1931) also took this approach of consistently accounting for replacement costs, recommending that operating income be distributable (that is, before deduction of holding losses) on the grounds that the entity did not need such income in order to maintain its operations.[41]

Thus, the 1920s and 1930s witnessed three alternative treatments for falling prices: (1) either revert from a physical capital to a financial capital approach; (2) continue to use original costs as a financial capital basis; or (3) consistently apply physical capital accounting irrespective of the direction of price movements. As the problem has not been specifically covered in the United Kingdom current cost accounting provisions,[42] it can be reasonably stated that the early writings were sensitive to a problem which remains today.

SUMMARY AND CONCLUSIONS

There are many more topics which were debated in the 1920s and 1930s, and which could be analysed in this chapter. For example, Sweeney (1931) recommended that all expenses deducted in arriving at income should be in replacement cost terms if such accounting was adopted; several writers[43] commented on the problem of using current or future replacement costs for assets yet to be replaced; and the feasibility of finding suitable replacement costs was commented on by at least one writer.[44] Space prevents such issues being discussed further, but the following general conclusions can be drawn from the previous sections: first, the early writers were fully aware of the distinction between financial and physical capital and capital maintenance (some favouring one or the other); secondly, much of the discussion centred around the possible use of replacement costs as an alternative to historical cost accounting, although general purchasing power accounting and net realizable value accounting were discussed also; thirdly, there was a confusion in the minds of early writers about the role of external financial reporting, many of

---

[41] Note should be taken, however, of the aforementioned objection of Sweeney.
[42] Accounting Standards Committee 1980*a*.
[43] Bauer 1919; Scott 1929; Paton 1934; Crandell 1935.
[44] Rorem 1929.

the proposals inadequately distinguishing external reporting from internal reporting and asset management; fourthly, the previous point may have arisen because of the relative brevity and lack of detail in external financial reports of the time; fifthly, replacement cost accounting was viewed not merely as a means of maintaining physical capital but also as a means of adequately determining selling prices in times of changing input prices; sixthly, a considerable amount of the debate in the 1920s and 1930s concerned the aims and uses of financial reports; seventhly, the need for historical cost accounting was debated rather than swept aside; and, finally, some of the problems of replacement cost accounting were not only revealed but analysed in detail—for example, holding gains, changing asset structures and technologies, and price decreases.

It would be wrong to suggest that the early writers on income and capital cited in this chapter either adequately recognized and analysed the problems or presented credible solutions. Certainly, there appeared to be little general acceptance by professional accountants and accountancy bodies of the ideas proposed. However, it is disturbing to find the same problems being, at best, debated and, at worst, ignored today in the various alternatives to historical cost accounting. Accountants thus appear to perpetuate problems rather than resolve them, and it is interesting to hypothesize some reasons for this, using the foregoing commentary as a basis:

1. The issue of income and capital measurement is a complex one, involving many problems, and reflecting numerous schools of thought. If a particular system is to be recommended to accountancy practitioners, it is essential that there is an adequate and prior discussion of all relevant matters. The present-day debate over current cost accounting has been fragmented, hasty, and lacking in sustained debate involving all interested parties (including users and preparers).

2. The early contributions to the debate reveal, in the complexities of the various arguments, the need to present the major viewpoint in full in order that accountants, businessmen, and others are fully apprised of all the issues involved. Current cost accounting proposals have failed to do this, concentrating solely on a limited argument to support them.

3. The reasons for the benefits of a particular reporting system must be fully explained and understood if it is to succeed. The early writers tended to concentrate more on technical matters and less on aims and purposes, and thus major confusions arose over the recommendations. Current cost accounting has suffered a similar fate today.

4. Changing circumstances can alter viewpoints and stances, and the early

writers (particularly Paton) were prepared to adapt. This is difficult to handle in a complex area but systems such as current cost accounting must be allowed to change as circumstances dictate. Changing views must never be used as reasons for not changing or for unnecessary doubt regarding the credibility of the system concerned.

5. Finally, given all the problems of attempting to account and report on physical capital, it is of concern to see no attempt made in the early 1900s (or today) to discuss whether or not these problems outweigh the benefits to be gained from an accounting system based on the maintenance of physical capital. The difficulties of defining physical capital, and its changing nature over time, make it a concept with considerable practical problems regarding implementation. The early debate, and the unrest with it in countries such as the United Kingdom, indicate it may remain a matter of conceptual rather than practical significance.

References

Accounting Standards Committee (1980*a*), 'Current Cost Accounting', in *Statement of Standard Accounting Practice 16* (London: Accounting Standards Committee).

—— (1980*b*), *Guidance Notes on SSAP 16 Current Cost Accounting* (London: Accounting Standards Committee).

Australian Society of Accountants and the Institute of Chartered Accountants in Australia (1976, 1978), 'Current Cost Accounting', in *Statement of Provisional Accounting Standards 1.1.* (Melbourne: Australian Society of Accountants and the Institute of Chartered Accountants in Australia).

Bauer, J. (1919), 'Renewal Costs and Business Profits in Relation to Rising Prices', *Journal of Accountancy* (Dec.): 413–19.

Best, J. W. (1985), 'Payment of Dividend Out of Capital', *Accountant* (5 Dec.): 7–10.

Brief, R. P. (1970), 'The Late Nineteenth Century Debate over Depreciation, Capital and Income', *Accountant* (26 Nov.): 737–9.

—— (1976), *Nineteenth Century Capital Accounting and Business Investment* (New York: Arno Press).

Burgert, R. (1972), 'Reservations about "Replacement Value" Accounting in the Netherlands', *Abacus* (Dec.): 111–26.

Canning, J. B. (1929), *The Economics of Accountancy: A Critical Analysis of Accounting Theory* (New York: Ronald Press).

Chambers, R. J. (1966), *Accounting, Evaluation and Economic Behavior* (Englewood Cliffs, NJ: Prentice-Hall).

Cole, W. M. (1908), *Accounts: Their Construction and Interpretation* (Boston: Houghton Mifflin).

Cooper, E. (1888), 'What is Profit of a Company?', *Accountant* (10 Nov.): 740–6.

Crandell, W. T. (1935), 'Income and its Measurement', *Accounting Review* (Dec.): 380–400.

Daines, H. C. (1929), 'The Changing Objectives of Accounting', *Accounting Review* (June): 94–110.

Daniels, M. B. (1933), 'The Valuation of Fixed Assets', *Accounting Review* (Dec.): 302–16.

Dickinson, A. L. (1904), 'Profits of a Corporation', *Financial Record, Lawyers' and Accountants' Manual* (2 Nov.): 38–43.

Financial Accounting Standards Board (1979), 'Financial Reporting and Changing Prices', in *Statement of Financial Accounting Standards 33* (Stamford, Conn.: Financial Accounting Standards Board).

Goudeket, A. (1960), 'An Application of Replacement Value Theory', *Journal of Accountancy* (July): 37–47.

Gower, W. B. (1919), 'Depreciation and Depletion in Relation to Invested Capital', *Journal of Accountancy* (Nov.): 353–68.

Guthrie, E. (1883), 'Depreciation and Sinking Funds', *Accountant* (21 Apr.): 6–10.

Jackson, J. H. (1920), 'Depreciation Policy and True Cost', *Journal of Accountancy* (June): 452–5.

—— (1921), 'Some Problems in Depreciation', *Journal of Accountancy* (Feb.): 81–102.

Jones, R. C. (1935), 'Financial Statements and the Uncertain Dollar', *Journal of Accountancy* (Sept.): 171–97.

Knight, A. (1908), 'Depreciation and Other Reserves', *Journal of Accountancy* (Jan.): 189–200.

Krebs, W. S. (1930), 'Asset Appreciation: Its Economic and Accounting Significance', *Accounting Review* (Mar.): 60–9.

Lee, T. A. (1982), 'Current Cost Accounting and Physical Capital', in K. W. Lemke and R. R. Sterling (eds.), *Maintenance of Capital: Financial versus Physical* (Houston, Tex.: Scholars Book Co.).

Lemke, K. W., and Sterling, R. R. (eds.) (1982), *Maintenance of Capital: Financial versus Physical* (Houston, Tex.: Scholars Book Co.).

Limperg, Th. (1964), *Industrial Economy* (Amsterdam: Collected Works). This is the best available reference to the work of Limperg, and is cited by Burgert.

Litherland, D. A. (1951), 'Fixed Asset Replacement a Half Century Ago', *Accounting Review* (Oct.): 475–80.

Littleton, A. C. (1928), 'What is Profit?', *Accounting Review* (Sept.): 278–88.

—— (1929), 'Value and Price in Accounting', *Accounting Review* (Sept.): 147–54.

—— (1936), 'Contrasting Theories of Profit', *Accounting Review* (Mar.): 10–15.

McCowen, G. B. (1937), 'Replacement Cost of Goods Sold', *Accounting Review* (Sept.): 270–7.

MacNeal, K. (1970), *Truth in Accounting* (Houston, Tex.: Scholars Book Co.).

Martin, O. R. (1927), 'Surplus Arising through Revaluation', *Accounting Review* (June): 111–23.

Mather, C. E. (1928), 'Depreciation and Appreciation of Fixed Assets', *Journal of Accountancy* (Mar.): 185–90.

Mey, A. (1966), 'Theodore Limperg and his Theory of Values and Costs', *Abacus* (Sept.): 3–24.

Middleditch, L. (1918), 'Should Accounts Reflect the Changing Value of the Dollar?', *Journal of Accountancy* (Feb.): 114–20.

Moss, A. G. (1923), 'Treatment of Appreciation of Fixed Assets', *Journal of Accountancy* (Sept.): 161–79.

Paton, W. A. (1918), 'The Significance and Treatment of Appreciation in the Accounts', in G. H. Coons (ed.), *Twentieth Annual Report of the Michigan Academy of Science*, 35–49.

—— (1920), 'Depreciation, Appreciation and Productive Capacity', *Journal of Accountancy* (July): 1–11.

—— (1922), 'Valuation of Inventories', *Journal of Accountancy* (Dec.): 432–50.

—— (1934), 'Aspects of Asset Valuations', *Accounting Review* (June): 122–9.

Rastall, E. S. (1920), 'Depreciation Reserves and Rising Prices', *Journal of Accountancy* (Feb.): 123–6.

Rorem, C. R. (1929), 'Replacement Cost in Accounting Valuation', *Accounting Review* (Sept.): 167–74.

Sallers, E. A. (1913), 'Depreciation Reserves versus Depreciation Funds', *Journal of Accountancy* (Nov.): 358–65.

Schmidt, F. (1930), 'The Importance of Replacement Value', *Accounting Review* (Sept.): 235–42.

—— (1931), 'Is Appreciation Profit?', *Accounting Review* (Dec.): 289–93.

Scott, DR (1929), 'Valuation for Depreciation and the Financing of Replacement', *Accounting Review* (Dec.): 221–6.

Sells, E. W. (1908), *Corporate Management Compared with Government Control* (New York: Press of Safety).

Sterling, R. R. (1970), *Theory of the Measurement of Enterprise Income* (Lawrence, Kan.: University of Kansas Press).

—— (1982), 'Limitations of Physical Capital', in K. W. Lemke and R. R. Sterling (eds.), *Maintenance of Capital: Financial versus Physical* (Houston, Tex.: Scholars Book Co.).

Stockwell, H. G. (1909), 'Depreciation, Renewal and Replacement Accounts', *Journal of Accountancy* (Dec.): 89–103.

Sweeney, H. W. (1927), 'Effects of Inflation on German Accounting', *Journal of Accountancy* (Mar.): 180–91.

—— (1930), 'The Maintenance of Capital', *Accounting Review* (Dec.): 277–87.

—— (1931), 'Stabilised Depreciation', *Accounting Review* (Sept.): 165–78.

—— (1932), 'Stabilised Appreciation', *Accounting Review* (June): 115–21.

—— (1933*a*), 'Capital', *Accounting Review* (Sept.): 185–99.

—— (1933*b*), 'Income', *Accounting Review* (Dec.): 323–35.

Sweeney, H. W. (1934), 'How Inflation Affects Balance Sheets', *Accounting Review* (Dec.): 275–99.

—— (1935), 'The Technique of Stabilised Accounting', *Accounting Review* (June): 185–205.

Symposium (1930), 'What is Appreciation?', *Accounting Review* (Mar.): 1–9.

Thomas, J. L. (1916), 'Depreciation and Valuation', *Journal of Accountancy* (Jan.): 24–33.

Wasserman, M. J. (1931), 'Accounting Practice in France During the Period of Monetary Inflation (1919–1927)', *Accounting Review* (Mar.): 1–32.

Wedgewood Ltd. (1981), *Annual Report 1981*.

POSTSCRIPT: RECYCLING—A HISTORICAL NORM IN ACCOUNTING

I wrote my chapter on the early history of the accounting for capital debate at the beginning of the 1980s. It was a time when the accountancy profession in different parts of the world had prescribed various forms of accounting for price or price-level changes. Typically, such prescriptions followed several years of debate, experimentation, and exposed proposals (see Tweedie and Whittington 1984 for a complete history to 1983). The requirements were usually for supplementary current cost accounting data (e.g. Financial Accounting Standards Board 1979; Accounting Standards Committee 1980). Thus, for more than a decade, the accounting literature was dominated by contributions on a multiplicity of current cost accounting issues. In that context, my chapter was no more than a detailed reflection on the propensity for accountants to recycle debates and issues such as current cost accounting, and on their failures to resolve pressing problems.

Recycling

This conclusion was not new. It had been commented on in various ways by a number of writers (e.g. Brief 1975; Sterling 1975; Lee 1979; and Mumford 1979). And I ended my paper with the prophecy that the debate might remain a matter of conceptual rather than practical significance. Subsequent events have confirmed the accuracy of my forecasting. In the USA, for example, Statement 33 (Financial Accounting Standards Board 1979) met with such resistance from the producers of current cost data that FASB effectively withdrew the requirement in 1986. A similar process occurred in 1985 with

SSAP 16 (Accounting Standards Committee 1980). Thus, the pressure to report on price and price-level changes disappeared in practice, and so too did the research interest.

Deep freeze

Nowadays, it is rare to find any mention in the accounting literature of any aspect of the debate on income and capital determination. Researchers have moved on to other more topical subjects, and the relevant literature appears to be frozen in time—a matter solely for accounting historians. Reporting entities continue to report in historical cost terms, thus avoiding as before the problem of significant price changes. That is, until relatively recently.

Renewed interest

Two matters suggest that the cycling may have restarted. The first relates to the efforts of the research committee of a major professional body (ICAS), and its proposal for a market value-based system (McMonnies 1988). This has led to a UK effort to argue for the utility of current value accounting (Arnold *et al.* 1991), and has influenced thinking in other EC countries as well as US bodies such as the SEC and FEI (see Lee 1992 for a review). The second matter concerns the after-shock of the US Savings and Loan débâcle. There is a growing debate on what is described as *marking to market*—the use of market values to describe reported assets, particularly those of a financial nature (e.g. Wyatt 1991; Macve and Jackson 1991). FASB (1991) has responded with a standard on reporting the market values of financial instruments.

In other words, as a result of events in the economic environment, the issue of price and price-level changes is rearing its head again. As before, the debate is led within the accounting practice community as a result of criticisms of conventional accounting. The academic community is beginning to take interest (e.g. Schwarzbach and Vangermeersch 1991). Time will tell if this will lead to further cyclings of long-lived issues. The lessons of history tell me that we could be pedalling for a long time if that is the case.

References

Accounting Standards Committee (1980), 'Current Cost Accounting', *Statement of Standard Accounting Practice 16* (London: Accounting Standards Committee).

Arnold, J., Boyle, P., Carey, A., Cooper, M., and Wild, K. (1991), *The Future Shape of Financial Reports* (London: Institute of Chartered Accountants in England and Wales and Institute of Chartered Accountants of Scotland).

Brief, R. P. (1975), 'The Accountant's Responsibility in Historical Perspective', *Accounting Review* (Apr.): 285–97.

Financial Accounting Standards Board (1979), 'Financial Reporting and Changing Prices', in *Statement of Financial Accounting Standards 33* (Stamford, Conn.: Financial Accounting Standards Board).

—— (1991), 'Disclosure about Market Value of Financial Instruments', in *Statement of Financial Accounting Standards 107* (Stamford, Conn.: Financial Accounting Standards Board).

Lee, T. A. (1979), 'The Evolution and Revolution of Financial Accounting: A Review Article', *Accounting and Business Research* (Autumn): 209–16.

—— (1992), 'Marking-to-Market: Another Case of Doing "Nothing"?: Observations on the UK Experience', unpublished paper, University of Alabama.

McMonnies, P. N. (1988) (ed.), *Making Corporate Reports Valuable* (London: Kogan Page).

Macve, R., and Jackson, J. (1991), *'Marking to Market': Accounting for Marketable Securities in the Financial Services Industry* (London: ICAEW Research Board).

Mumford, M. (1979), 'The End of a Familiar Inflation Accounting Cycle', *Accounting and Business Research* (Spring): 98–104.

Schwarzbach, H., and Vangermeersch, R. (1991), 'The Current Value Experiences of the Rouse Company, 1973–1989', *Accounting Horizons* (June): 45–54.

Sterling, R. R. (1975), 'Toward a Science of Accounting', *Financial Analysts Journal* (Sept.–Oct.): 28–36.

Tweedie, D. P., and Whittington, G. (1984), *The Debate on Inflation Accounting* (Cambridge: Cambridge University Press).

Wyatt, A. (1991), 'The SEC Says: Mark to Market!', *Accounting Horizons* (Mar.): 80–4.

20 · THE END OF A FAMILIAR INFLATION ACCOUNTING CYCLE

M. J. Mumford

With the modest recommendations of the Hyde Report,[1] persuasive in nature rather than mandatory and clearly a compromise version of earlier statements, we appear to be heading for the end of a five-year cycle of events in British accounting which mirror very closely events which occurred about twenty-five years ago. The similarity is so marked, and the steps so predictable, that they are described below as a blueprint for the next surge of inflation.

Eight stages may be discerned. First there arises an increase in the rate of domestic inflation, accompanied by a fall in stock market prices. Next the profession responds. Then government intervenes, on the grounds that broader social issues are involved than the profession can embrace in its deliberations. Stage four sees the publication of 'radical' studies of accounting techniques, with strong proposals for reform. Not surprisingly, this leads to intense controversy within the profession. A compromise recommendation is put forward, but by this time inflation rates are past their worst (and the stock market has picked up again); and in the final stage, interest in reform dwindles.

These eight stages are described below in more detail, in each case with the events of 1948–54 shown first and labelled '*A*', and with the events of 1973–8 shown beneath and labelled '*B*'.

First published in *Accounting and Business Research* (Spring 1979). Written in April 1978 while the author was working for the United Nations in Nigeria. The views expressed are of course entirely his own.

[1]   Accounting Standards Committee, *Inflation Accounting—an Interim Recommendation* (London: ASC, 4 Nov. 1977).

STAGE I. AN INCREASE IN DOMESTIC INFLATION AND A FALL IN STOCK MARKET PRICES

A. As measured by the percentage rate of change of the Retail Price Index (yearly averages), domestic inflation reached a rate of 6.7 per cent in 1947 and 7.8 per cent in 1948, rates unprecedented in Britain in peacetime this century. Such a phenomenon might well be expected to produce criticism of conventional accounting methods, based upon the use of historic costs for asset measurement and income recording. This may indeed be so, but recent research suggests that falls in stock market prices seem to have a stronger impact upon the profession than rises in the general price level,[2] and in fact the F-T 500 share index showed a fall of 4.0 per cent in 1948. Whichever index may be regarded as the more influential, the conditions appear to have been ripe for some professional reaction.

B. From 1953 to 1968, general price increases were below 5 per cent per annum; but in 1970, 1971, 1972, and 1973 they rose to 6.4, 9.4, 7.1 and 9.3 per cent respectively, and there was a fall in stock market prices of 13.4 per cent in 1973. Once again, such rates of inflation might be expected to evoke criticism of the historical cost convention. Matching current revenues with past costs could produce distorted results, since holding gains could be expected to be material, and historical cost accounting includes all holding gains without separate disclosure in reported income in the period when such income is realized. Some professional reaction was to be expected.

STAGE 2. A REACTION BY THE ACCOUNTING PROFESSION

A. The Economist repeatedly criticized the historical cost convention between 1948 and 1954; the issue was raised for example in an article entitled 'What

---

[2] The argument that professional statements of general accounting principles are responses to falls in stock market prices, both in the UK and in the USA, is made in M. J. Mumford, 'A Crisis Theory of Professional Statements of General Accounting Principles', a paper presented to the Northern Group of the Association of University Teachers of Accounting, Liverpool, Mar. 1977.

The Retail Price Index data were compiled from Table 2 of the Central Statistical Office Statement, *The Internal Purchasing Power of the Pound* (Dec. 1973), with figures for 1973 and 1974 from the CSO *Annual Abstract of Statistics* (1976), Table 449; and for 1975, 1976, and 1977 from the *Monthly Digest of Statistics*, May 1978, Table 17.8. The F-T 500-Share Index data are from the London and Cambridge Economic Bulletin, *The British Economy: Key Statistics, 1900–64*, Table G, with the 1973 and 1974 figures from Table 418 of the 1976 Annual Abstract, and later figures from Table 16.16 of the *Monthly Digest of Statistics*.

are Profits?' published on 12 June 1948, reflecting the concern of business-men and academics alike. Commercial enterprises repeated the complaint that shortage of capital was damaging British industry, and that this shortage was made worse by the assessment of tax upon the basis of historical cost profits rather than current cost figures. Lord Piercy, for example, made much of this point in his Chairman's Statement in the Annual Report of the Industrial and Commercial Finance Corporation published on 12 November 1948. The accounting profession seems to have agreed with the view that taxation should recognize the effects of rising prices, without agreeing that published accounts should similarly treat rising replacement costs as an expense.[3]

The arguments for using replacement costs were not new. In Britain, the work of R. S. Edwards had been widely known since 1938, as was that of F. Sewell Bray. Moreover, two other authors, K. Lacey and Leo T. Little, had published such views widely in the professional press. Influential American writing included H. Sweeney's book, *Stabilized Accounting* published in 1936, which linked American research and earlier European work of the 1920s and 1930s. The mid-1940s was a time of intense controversy over inflation accounting in America, ending with a strong statement in favour of historical cost (similar to the English Institute's N12) in *Accounting Research Bulletin No. 33*, 'Depreciation and High Costs', published by the AICPA Committee on Accounting Procedure in 1947.

In January 1949 the Institute of Chartered Accountants in England and Wales published in its series of *Recommendations on Accounting Principles* its Recommendation N12, 'Rising price levels in relation to accounts'. This briefly reconsidered the alternative options open to accountants in recognizing the effects of rising prices in accounts, and concluded that the basic historical cost method was fundamentally adequate, although directors were recommended to anticipate rising replacement costs by means of appropriations of profit to reserves. This represented the orthodox position.

B. On 17 January 1973 the Accounting Standards Steering Committee published *Exposure Draft No. 8*, 'Accounting for Changing in the Purchasing Power of Money', recommending the use of general price indexation in the

---

[3] This view was expressed by Mr F. R. M. de Paula in a paper at Brighton to a joint meeting of professional accountancy bodies on 18 May 1948, reported in the *Accountant* (5 June 1948), 441–3. An Editorial in the *Accountant* of 27 Mar. 1948, entitled 'Quo Vadis?', asked the question whether or not a 'true and fair view' implied the use of replacement costs, commenting that 'many accountants are preaching this same doctrine' (237). The editorial recognized that the Council of the English Institute did not share this opinion, but held that inflation should only be recognized after striking a profit figure based upon historical costs.

accounts of quoted public companies. While this appears a revolutionary change in thinking as compared with N12, in fact ED8 merely proposed that the information should be published by way of a supplementary statement attached to the main (historical cost) accounts. Moreover, by 1973 the 'current purchasing power' (or 'constant purchasing power') method was quite a familiar idea, having been proposed to the American profession in the AICPA's *Accounting Research Study No. 6*, 'Reporting the Financial Effects of Price-level Changes', as early as October 1963. The same method had been advocated in Britain in 1968 in a paper published by the Research Committee of the English Institute, *Accounting for Stewardship in a Period of Inflation*; and also in an ASSC discussion paper of September 1971, *Inflation and Accounts*. Such a supplementary statement was, then, by no means a revolutionary proposal by the profession in the face of fast rising price levels and a collapse in stock market values. In May 1974, ED8 was adopted substantially unaltered, and under the same title, as *Statement of Standard Accounting Practice No. 7*.

STAGE 3. INTERVENTION BY GOVERNMENT

A. Following the publication of N12 in January 1949, it was announced in the Budget Debate in April 1949 that studies were to be set up on the taxation of profits and income. This was to include a reconsideration of the accounting definition of profits, in view of the case presented by many members of the commercial and industrial community. The Federation of British Industries was prominent amongst these, arguing that taxation was eliminating all real profits: 'it is fundamentally wrong that industry should need to raise fresh capital merely to preserve productive ability'.[4] In the course of the Budget Speech on 16 April 1949, Sir Stafford Cripps stated that: 'There is a number of issues arising out of the present structure of taxation, including the incidence of tax and its effects on risk-bearing, which require further examination. We must continue to look to industry, broadly speaking, for the same total contribution to the national revenue as at present, but within this limitation it may well be that the present arrangements could be modified to enable the burden to be more easily borne. An enquiry covering the whole subject would be a very extensive undertaking. I propose to make a start by taking the technical issues which arise in connection with the computation of

---

[4] *Minutes of Evidence before the Royal Commission on the Taxation of Profits and Income*, Day 4, p. 80, para. 28 (see reference in n. 10 below).

taxable profits.' This would clear the way, he added, for the general enquiry which he hoped to set afoot at a later stage. There is no doubt that the Chancellor had been concerned for some time over the need to raise the level of industrial productivity. He had called upon the TUC and the FBI on 3 September 1948 to undertake 'parallel and co-ordinate action' to this end; and the FBI had set up on 8 September a special committee to advise on action, leading to a 'Memorandum on Taxation and the Shortage of Industrial Capital' published on 30 December 1948.

A committee of enquiry under the Chairmanship of Mr J. Millard Tucker QC was appointed on 17 June 1949 to look into the Taxation of Trading Profits, its findings being published in April 1951. The Royal Commission on the Taxation of Profits and Income was announced on 27 July 1950, and members were appointed on 2 January 1951. The Royal Commission published three reports, in 1953, 1954, and 1955. The accounting profession was invited to present evidence, and the various professional bodies did so. A wide variety of views became immediately apparent. Despite the evident belief of the Council of the English Institute that the assessment of profits for tax purposes could be considered as a problem distinct from the measurement of profits for reporting purposes, the report of the Millard Tucker Committee makes it absolutely clear that the Committee found the controversy over this matter in the profession disturbing. In view of the majority opinion amongst accountants that historical cost needed to be preserved for measuring profits, the Committee would have felt unable to recommend any alternative for tax purposes even if it had felt so inclined.[5]

B. After the publication of ED8 and in the face of strong signs of support for ED8 from the profession and from the Confederation of British Industry, the then Minister of Trade and Industry announced that the government was setting up its own committee to study the problem, under the Chairmanship of Mr F. E. P. Sandilands. The Sandilands Report specifically refers to the relationship between its work and ED8: 'The immediate cause of the setting up of our Committee was the issue by the Accounting Standards Steering Committee (ASSC) on 17 January, 1973 of Exposure Draft 8 "Accounting for changes in the purchasing power of money". This document gave rise to increasing discussion of inflation accounting throughout 1973 and the first part of 1974, and this was intensified by the issue in May 1974 by the professional accounting bodies of the United Kingdom and Ireland of Statement of Standard Accounting Practice No. 7 (SSAP7) with the same

---

[5] *Report of the Committee on the Taxation of Trading Profits* (London: HMSO, Cmd. 8189, Apr. 1951), para. 98.

title. The issue of these two documents by the accounting profession focused attention on the need to show the effects of inflation on the affairs of companies. We found as our work proceeded an increasing interest in the subject in the Press and elsewhere, coupled with a growing belief that reform of accounting conventions was a matter of urgency.' (*Report of the Inflation Accounting Committee*, London, HMSO Cmnd. 6225 (September 1975) para. 7.) 'While acknowledging the valuable contribution to the subject made by the issue of Exposure Draft 8 and SSAP7 we consider that the most fruitful line of development in inflation accounting is a system based on the principles of value accounting, which shows the specific effect of inflation on individual companies. We recommend that a system to be known as Current Value Accounting should be developed.' (Ibid. para. 11.)

Professor Edward Stamp was later to write of 'the rather shabby way in which Mr. Peter Walker went about announcing the formation of the Inflation Accounting Committee, right at the end of the Parliamentary Session, leaving the profession in the dark about his intentions. [And] the fact that the Government, which had been fully consulted about the CPP proposals whilst they were being formulated, suddenly decided to pull the rug from under the feet of the Accounting Standards Steering Committee'.[6] The statement reflects the annoyance and sense of frustration felt by the profession at the intervention of the government, even though this was tempered by optimism in business quarters over the inclusion of taxation in the terms of reference of the Inflation Accounting Committee.[7]

STAGE 4. 'RADICAL' STUDIES OF ACCOUNTING TECHNIQUES

A. Rejection of inflation accounting by the English Institute and by the Millard Tucker Committee came as a severe disappointment to businessmen and accountants within industry and commerce. A series of four articles in *The Economist* over August and September 1951 found a strong response with these accountants, and further strengthened the links already forming between the staff of *The Economist* and prominent members of the Association of Certified and Corporate Accountants. Further studies of inflation accounting were set in train.

[6] Edward Stamp, 'Sandilands: Some Fundamental Flaws', *Accountant's Magazine* (Dec. 1975), reprinted in G. W. Dean and M. C. Wells (eds.) *Current Cost Accounting: Identifying the Issues* (Lancaster: International Centre for Research in Accounting, 1977), 87.

[7] See e.g. the Editorial in *The Economist*, 6 Sept. 1975.

Thus, as a reaction to the publication in 1949 of Recommendation N12, two studies were published in 1952, both prepared under the auspices of professional accountancy bodies in Britain, and both advocating the adoption of current replacement cost accounts. The Institute of Cost and Works Accountants (as it was then known) published what amounted to a manual on the application of replacement costs to the conventional historical cost system, in order to replace historical cost figures with their current equivalents. The Association of Certified (and Corporate) Accountants, through their Taxation and Research Committee, published a more substantial analysis of the principles involved.[8] This was based upon the precept that, before profits could be defined, provision must be made for the maintenance of physical capacity. For this purpose, current replacement costs needed to be used to measure the costs of goods sold and the depreciation of fixed assets. The need to change the basis of taxation was explicitly argued throughout the book, which was drafted under the supervision of a committee consisting half of Certified Accountants and half of members of the Economist Intelligence Unit.

Strong cases were also argued for replacement cost accounts elsewhere in Britain at this time. The 1952 International Congress on Accounting was held in London, and the session on 'Fluctuating Price levels in relation to Accounts' was introduced with a paper by C. Percy Barrowcliff of the Society of Incorporated Accountants and Auditors, advocating (as did most of the papers presented in this session) replacement cost accounting instead of conventional historic cost accounts. Given the mood of the Congress on this matter it can hardly have been a comfortable task for Mr T. B. Robson, the current President of the English Institute, to act as Chairman to this session.

B. 1975 saw the publication of the Sandilands Report,[9] which made 'current cost accounting' its chief recommendation, to be used in place of historic cost accounts in published company accounts. Remarkably, in the previous month (August 1975) the Accounting Standards Steering Committee's own study group on the objectives of published accounts made very closely similar recommendations in *The Corporate Report*, working completely independently. Neither group apparently had foreknowledge of the line of thinking pursued by the other, and there was no common membership. Unfortunately, since neither study includes a bibliography or any appreciable number of

[8] ICWA Research and Technical Committee, *The Accountancy of Changing Prices* (London: ICWA, 1952); ACCA Taxation and Research Committee, *Accounting for Inflation* (London: Gee and Company, 1952).

[9] *The Report of the Inflation Accounting Committee* [the 'Sandilands Report'], 'Inflation Accounting' (London: HMSO, Cmnd. 6225, Sept. 1975).

references, it is hard to identify the ways in which their similar conclusions arose.

Basically the 'current cost accounting' method follows the line of thinking in current replacement cost accounting, but using a concept of 'value' as a capital base in place of 'physical capacity'. The major practical result is that the cost of using obsolete assets is measured not in terms of replacement costs (since replacement in similar form is implausible), but usually in terms of realizable values.

STAGE 5. CONTROVERSY IN THE PROFESSION

A. Following the publication of Recommendation NI2 in 1949, and particularly in view of the setting up of the government's enquiries into the tax system, the professional bodies in Britain embarked upon a series of meetings at which attempts were made to find some common ground. That this proved impossible is abundantly clear from the Report of the Committee on the Taxation of Trading Profits, April 1951, and from the published minutes of evidence before the Royal Commission which followed.[10] Harold Edey of the London School of Economics observed in the *Accountant* on 29 January 1949 that the English Institute was 'lambasted for timidity and for clinging to tradition'. Although his own position was defensive of the English Institute, he referred in the same article to the strength of criticism from *The Economist* and from the *Investor's Chronicle* in both cases in their issue of 15 January 1949. It would appear that the profession was discomfited by the public disagreement between the professional bodies before the Millard Tucker Committee. Soon afterwards an invitation was sent by the English Institute to the other British professional bodies to discuss informally their views on inflation accounting, and a number of meetings took place. Little or no progress was made, however. One such meeting took place on 4 April 1952, and in the following month the English Institute published its Recommendation NI5 which reaffirmed once again its adherence to historical cost accounting. Recommendation NI5 ends with a note on two subsequent meetings which took place between the professional bodies:

All these bodies appointed representatives to meet with representatives of the Council with the object of considering whether there is a practicable and generally acceptable

    [10] *The Report of the Committee on the Taxation of Trading Profits* (London: HMSO, Cmd. 8189, Apr. 1951); *The Report of the Royal Commission on the Taxation of Profits and Income* (London: HMSO, Cmd. 9474, June 1955), and the Minutes of Evidence published simultaneously.

alternative to the existing conception of profit computed on the basis of historical cost. A first meeting was held in November 1952, when Recommendation 15 was discussed and the representatives of the Scottish Institute, the Society and the Association undertook to obtain for consideration at a further meeting the views of their respective Councils. (The representative of the Irish Institute was unable to be present.)

Memoranda submitted on behalf of the Councils of each of the three bodies were considered at a second meeting in December 1953. At the end of this meeting the representatives of the Council stated that they were willing to arrange a further meeting or meetings if the representatives of the other bodies so desired, but as none felt there was any likelihood of general agreement being reached between the various bodies it was decided that the discussions should be regarded as closed.

During these two meetings nothing has emerged which makes it necessary for the time being for the Council to amend or add to the comprehensive review of the subject which is contained in Recommendation 15.

After the meeting in December 1953, it was decided that memoranda should be published separately by the relevant institutions. This took place shortly afterwards, with the publication in *The Accountant* of an editorial on 16 January 1954 objecting strongly to the fact that criticisms were being expressed publicly of the English Institute by other professional accounting bodies. Ironically, it was Gee and Company, publishers of *The Accountant*, who had published the Association's book *Accounting for Inflation* in 1952, upon which the Association's opposition to N15 was based.

B. Controversy in the months after September 1975 was less clearly identified with the various professional bodies. (The Society of Incorporated Accountants and Auditors had in any case been absorbed into the English Institute shortly after 1952; and a measure of co-ordination was being achieved through the Consultative Committee of Accountancy Bodies, set up after a frustrated initiative towards integration in the late 1960s.) Controversy now tended to be between the large professional firms and accountants in business companies in the one camp, and small practitioners in the other. The latter make up a majority of the individual members of the English Institute; and the move by two Chartered Accountants (Messrs Keymer and Haslam) to call an extraordinary meeting of the English Institute in June 1977 to propose a resolution opposing any mandatory form of current cost accounting was successful, despite a vigorous public relations campaign by the Council of the Institute.[11] Even though the profession itself

---

[11] By coincidence, there was also an International Congress on Accounting in 1977, in Munich, as there had been in 1952. However, in the later year, inflation accounting was much less conspicuous on the agenda, despite several official studies on inflation accounting currently in progress, in America, Canada, Australia, and New Zealand as well as in Britain.

was in a state of some turmoil over inflation accounting in 1977, some strong authoritative support for the supplementary information to be supplied about current values was contained in a letter from the Chairman of the Stock Exchange to all listed companies, issued shortly after the suspension of SSAP7 on the publication of the Sandilands Report. This letter asked for information on the current costs of goods sold, on depreciation, and concerning monetary items.

STAGE 6. A COMPROMISE RECOMMENDATION

A. In the face of resolute adherence by the English Institute to historic cost, and adamant demands for full replacement cost accounting by the ACCA and ICWA, the Society of Incorporated Accountants and Auditors took up a modified reform, suggesting that instead of a complete restatement of the profit and loss account and balance sheet, all that was necessary was an additional charge in the income statement to reflect the current replacement costs of goods and of depreciation on fixed assets. This suggestion met with a favourable response in some quarters, and statements from the Councils of the Society and of the Association were duly published, recommending action along these lines.[12]

B. The Keymer/Haslam resolution made it a practical impossibility for the English Institute to proceed with its support for current cost accounting as already embodied in an Exposure Draft (No. 18) of the Accounting Standards Committee of the CCAB.[13] Despite the diplomatic steps which had been taken to restore the dignity of the profession, badly affronted by the setting up of the Sandilands Committee, the joint government/CCAB Inflation Accounting Steering Group, chaired by Mr D. S. Morpeth, was halted in its tracks. A new committee was therefore set up on 27 July 1977, under the Chairmanship of Mr W. Hyde, to prepare a new set of 'interim recommendations' for the Accounting Standards Committee, pending a revised version of ED18 from the IASG. These rapidly appeared, on 4 November 1977, and included proposals for a supplementary statement to be appended to the accounts of companies listed on the Stock Exchange.[14] This statement should show, not a full restatement of the profit and loss account and balance sheet, but merely an amended income statement in which the

---

[12] The Council resolutions were in each case reprinted in the *Accountant*, 16 Jan. 1954.

[13] ASC *Exposure Draft No. 18*, 'Current Cost Accounting' (London: ASC, 30 Nov. 1976).

[14] ASC, *Inflation Accounting—an Interim Recommendation* (n. 1 above).

cost of goods sold and the depreciation of fixed assets shown in the historical cost accounts were both to be augmented by a further adjustment to raise the two charges from historical cost levels to the levels indicated by the use of current costs (as set out in Sandilands and in EDI8). A further adjustment should be made to reduce the effects of these supplementary changes if the company is financed in part by loan capital, this adjustment seeking to reflect the concern expressed by the CCAB that Sandilands failed to show the effects of inflation upon the values of monetary assets and liabilities.[15]

To some extent this compromise version followed the recommendations of the Chairman of the Stock Exchange, in his letter to the Chairmen of listed companies in September 1975. The 'interim recommendations' drafted by the Hyde Committee appear to have less authority than Statements of Standard Accounting Practice, and in any case apply only to quoted companies.

STAGE 7. A REDUCTION IN DOMESTIC INFLATION AND A RECOVERY OF STOCK MARKET PRICES

A. After a peak in the rate of increase of the Retail Price Index in 1951 (9.1 per cent due to the Korean War), inflation rates fell to 6.0 per cent in 1952, and to 1.6 and 1.9 per cent in the following two years. The stock market rose and fell in 1951 and 1952, recovering in 1953 and 1954 with strong rises of 33 and 17 per cent respectively. The crisis conditions had thus passed.

B. The peak rate of increase of 24.2 per cent in 1975 fell below the 16.5 per cent rate of 1976 to a relatively modest rate of 11.8 per cent in 1977. Historically, these rates are extremely high: the 1977 rate is far higher than the rates during the previous 'crisis' period of 1947–52. However, public perception has been altered by its experience of rates, over certain periods, in excess of 30 per cent, so that 10 per cent appears quite modest. The F-T 500 share index, which fell by 13.4 per cent in 1973 and 41.3 per cent in 1974 (a heavier fall than in the 'Great Crash' between 1929 and 1932), rose in 1975 by 25.0 per cent and in 1976 by 19.8 per cent with further gains in 1977.

---

[15] Consultative Committee on Accountancy Bodies, *Initial Reactions to the Report of the Inflation Accounting Committee (the Sandilands Report)* (London: CCAB, 30 Oct. 1975).

STAGE 8. INTEREST IN REFORM DWINDLES

A. Despite some complaints which met the Reports of the Royal Commission on the Taxation of Profits and Income,[16] the profession seems to have had little more to say on the subject of inflation accounting in the years immediately after 1954. Some companies did in fact publish information on the replacement costs of assets (for example, Pilkington Brothers Ltd.); but there was no obligation to do so, and it was not the normal practice. It is noticeable that the submissions to the Jenkins Committee on Company Law (reporting in 1962) included few references to the need for inflation-adjusted accounts, although accounting was one of the headings under which recommendations were specifically sought.

B. It is still a little early to say that the present inflation accounting debate is dying away. However, there are signs of this, despite a rate of inflation which is still higher than the previous peacetime peak this century. (About 13 per cent was recorded in 1940, which is otherwise the only precedent above 10 per cent, even in wartime.)

The Inflation Accounting Steering Group is still in being, but its activities are much less frequently reported in the professional press than was the case in the two years up to July 1977. Two surveys by the Technical Department of the Institute of Cost and Management Accountants report some sympathy for the principles of current cost accounting, but a clear majority of respondents take the view that they do not intend publishing extra information unless disclosure is made mandatory.[17] Granted, some companies have published accounts in accordance with current cost accounting principles. Indeed, the wholly-owned British subsidiary of the American family-controlled Mars confectionery company has published in the UK current cost accounts with no historical cost equivalent; and Arthur Andersen and Co. have given the British company a clean audit report.[18] But it seems unlikely that a substantial number of companies will follow even the Hyde guidelines unless obliged to comply with some mandatory requirement, for example for a Stock Exchange quotation.

---

[16] See e.g. F. L. Clarke, 'CCA: Progress or Regress?', in Dean and Wells, *Current Cost Accounting*, 74.

[17] See the report in *Accountancy Age* (11 Nov. 1977), p. 2. The surveys were carried out in 1977 before the publication of the Hyde recommendations.

[18] Reported in *Accountant's Weekly* (3 Feb. 1978), 3–4.

CONCLUSION

On the evidence presented there do appear to be close similarities between the earlier and the later cycles. There are of course some differences. The time lags are not the same in each case, for one thing. It took three years for the ACCA and ICWA books to be prepared and published, although no doubt some part of this time was due to the attempts taking place between the professional bodies to arrive at a consensus before publication. The two studies published in 1975 were less substantial in that neither supported the arguments with such detailed empirical evidence as the 1952 ACCA study. It is plausible that the debate in the 1970s took place in a more informed environment than that of the 1950s. More had been published on inflation accounting; there were more journals being published, including two widely circulated journals sent free to qualified accountants.[19]

Whether the cycle will indeed be triggered off again by some future surge of inflation or by a fall in stock prices remains to be seen. It is all too likely. Public concern will provoke some sort of professional response, hasty and ill researched. The government will suddenly acknowledge that the problems of inflation accounting, and in particular the effects of inflation upon the tax system, involve value judgements and social effects which go beyond the authority of the profession to resolve. Government intervention will be resented, and attempts to out-flank the Civil Servants (and regain the initiative) will result in the publication of far more radical reforms than the profession would willingly countenance. Controversy will lead to compromise and eventual inaction as the crisis motivating reform becomes less pressing.

There is one particular measure which could effectively break the cycle, namely a programme of research into inflation accounting and its practical implementation (for example its effects upon the existing SSAPs). This the Inflation Accounting Steering Group is at present undertaking. The chances are that these activities will be allowed to decelerate, instead of being sustained and encouraged. On past experience, this would be disastrous; it would be likely to create just the conditions for a repetition of the cycle, perhaps in rather less than twenty years' time.

---

[19] *Accountancy Age* and *Accountant's Weekly*.

POSTSCRIPT

When this article was written, it was not clear how the second 'inflation accounting cycle' from 1970 would end. As the chapter comments:

It is still a little early to say that the present inflation accounting debate is dying away. However, there are signs of this, despite a rate of inflation which is still higher than the previous peacetime peak this century.

In fact, interest did not die away for another six or seven years. By then, ED18 had given way to ED24 and SSAP 16 'Current Cost Accounting', implemented for quoted companies on a trial basis for three years from March 1980, but discontinued in 1984 in the face of disregard by increasing numbers of companies. A further attempt, ED35, was abandoned in the face of controversy. Many auditors of large companies had by this time lost faith in CCA, and inflation rates had fallen.

Looking back fifteen years later, a similar inflation accounting cycle still seems plausible if inflation were to increase at a rate that caused popular alarm. There would be calls for inflation accounting; political pressure for tax reforms would induce government reaction; refinements to the new proposals would produce controversy; and agreement would be difficult before inflation died down again.

Now, however, it is possible to explain some of the stages in more detail, using the concept of reliability. As long as inflation is at a low level, historic cost information is fairly reliable, in two senses. The mean square error of observations about the 'true' mean is small (accountants would record the same figure for a given asset, based on its cost); and the bias arising from understating cost would also be relatively small. But as the rate of inflation grows, the bias error increases, so that it begins to outweigh the observation error from using estimates of hypothetical current market prices rather than more certain historic cost numbers.

Indeed, the author's former enthusiasm for current cost accounting has by now given way to serious doubts about the reliability of the information produced. As Ken Peasnell has pointed out (in private discussions), historical cost may give better information than CCA *even judged by the criteria of the CCA system*. Business people in the 1970s may have formed such a view themselves. The lessons of Oliver Williamson's 'Transaction Cost Economics' makes the problem worse. According to this, the firm only exists to take advantage of certain 'core' assets whose services cannot be bought readily on the market.

These include tangible assets, and also intangibles and human assets such as skilled specialist staff teams. Not only does the conventional balance sheet omit many of these, but most of the core assets that do appear are probably internalized by the firm for the very reason that they do not have identifiable market prices. So to seek 'current costs' for them seems somewhat perverse. Maybe the defeat of current cost accounting was not so disastrous after all.

ACCOUNTING IN CONTEXT

21 · ACCOUNTING IN ITS SOCIAL CONTEXT:TOWARDS A HISTORY OF VALUE ADDED IN THE UNITED KINGDOM

S. Burchell, C. Clubb, and A. G. Hopwood

Accounting is coming to be seen as a social rather than a purely technical phenomenon. The social contexts of the accounting craft are starting to be both recognized and made more problematic. Albeit slowly, the ways in which accounting both emerges from and itself gives rise to the wide contexts in which it operates are starting to be appreciated. Accounting, in turn, also has come to be more actively and explicitly recognized as an instrument for social management and change. Attempts have been made to reform accounting in the name of its social potential. Proposals have been made for accounting to embrace the realm of the social as well as the economic, to objectify, quantify, and thereby give a particular insight into the social functioning of organizations. To this end, attempts have been made to orchestrate social accountings, social reports, social audits, socio-economic statements, social cost–benefit analyses and accountings of the human resource.

However, despite such apparent manifestations of an intertwining of accounting with the social, relatively little is known of the social functioning of the accounting craft (Hopwood 1985). Accounting seemingly remains embedded in the realm of the technical. Although it is now recognized that the social can influence the technical practice of accounting and that that, in turn, can mobilize and change the world of the social, the processes by which these intersections take place have been subject to hardly any investigation.

First published in *Accounting Organizations and Society*, 10/4 (1985). We wish to acknowledge the helpful comments of George Benston, Wai Fong Chua, David Cooper, Jeremy Dent, Dick Hoffman, John Hughes, Janine Nahapiet, and Ted O'Leary. The financial support of the Anglo-German Foundation for the Study of Industrial Society is gratefully appreciated. One of the authors wishes to acknowledge the facilitative and supportive environment provided by the College of Business Administration, Pennsylvania State University, which greatly eased the final writing up of this study.

Accounting has not been explored in the name of its social functioning or potential. The social has been brought into contact with accounting but the intermingling of the two has not been explored. As a result, little is known of how the technical practices of accounting are tethered to the social, of how wider social forces can impinge upon and change accounting, and of how accounting itself functions in the realm of the social, influencing as well as merely reacting to it. For to date the relationship of accounting to the social has tended to be stated and presumed rather than described and analysed.[1]

Recognizing the very significant gap in present understandings, the present discussion merely aims to illustrate and discuss one specific instance of the intertwining of accounting and the social, namely the rise of interest in value added accounting in the United Kingdom during the 1970s. The contours of this event are outlined and an analysis conducted of the wider arenas in which such a form of accounting came to function. Drawing on this analysis, an attempt thereafter is made to explicate some of the implications for an understanding of the emergence of value added accounting in particular and the social functioning of accounting more generally. Initially, however, we discuss some existing understandings of accounting's relationship to the social. Our aim in so doing is to provide a basis for appreciating both the possibilities for and the difficulties of conducting a social investigation of the accounting craft.

ACCOUNTING AND SOCIAL CHANGE

No doubt reflecting the more general concerns of the social responsibility movement (Ackerman and Bauer 1976; Vogel 1978), a literature emerged during the 1970s which concerned itself more or less directly with the impact of social change on accounting (e.g. Bedford 1970; Estes 1973; Gambling 1974; Gordon 1978; Livingstone and Gunn 1974; Vangermeersch 1972). However, although a social challenge to accounting thereby was recognized, most of this literature accepted both the fact of social change and its relevance to accounting, seeking primarily to change and reform accounting in the name of its social context. Despite a proliferation in pleas, suggestions and possibilities for different accountings, very few attempts were made to

---

[1] One noteworthy exception to this tendency has been the work of Tinker. See Tinker 1980, Tinker *et al.* 1982, Tinker 1984, and Neimark and Tinker 1986. Although there are a number of significant differences between the work of Tinker and ourselves, we nevertheless recognize the pioneering attempts he and his colleagues have made to investigate the social origins and functioning of accounting practice. Also see Cooper 1981.

explicate and develop any general description and characterization of the processes involved in the interaction of accounting with its social context. Technical reform took precedence over social understanding once a necessity for change had been stated.

Gilling (1976) was one exception to this tendency. Although he too notes the fact of and argues the necessity for accounting change under the impact of environmental (social and technical) change, Gilling also attempted to provide some understanding of the underlying social and institutional forces at work. His animating concern was the lag that he perceived to have arisen in the adaptation process. Gilling argued that accounting change was lagging behind environmental change as a consequence of the incapacity of the accounting professions to decide, or rather agree, on the appropriate modifications to be made in accounting practice. This immobilization of the agency of accounting change stemmed in turn from the absence of any one dominant point of view on accounting, or of what Gilling termed accounting 'ideology'.[2] Thus the process of adjustment of accounting practice to changes in its environment was blocked not because accounting theory was in some sense inadequate but because of the clash of interests as they were represented by the different accounting ideologies. Each of these alone 'could provide order and direction to accounting endeavour' (p. 70) but each also 'provides little possibility of reconciliation or compromise with other views'. According to Gilling the net effect of this impasse was that both the autonomy and the expertise of the accounting professions were under challenge—there existed a crisis: 'As a result of its failure to react to new environmental circumstances the accounting profession is facing something of a crisis; a crisis in part of public confidence and in part of identity' (Gilling 1976: 64).

Thus within Gilling's framework, accounting appears as something marked off from its environment. With the passage of time, the latter requires the former to change. Accounting thereby is seen to be something that is and certainly should be a reflective phenomenon. As the environment develops or evolves it requires accounting to fulfil different needs. The process of accounting change passes through the accounting professions and depends on

---

[2] Gilling (1976: 69) defined ideology in the following terms: 'All professions have a defining ideology, which in a general sense establishes a pattern of thought and a way of looking at the world for the profession. This pattern of thought defines the activity of the profession, its problems, and appropriate ways of approaching those problems. The behaviour of a profession towards its environment is a matter of perception of that environment. Once an image of that environment has been established, then behaviour will be determined by that image and the frame of reference that it creates. As long as image and perception are appropriate to the real world, behaviour will be appropriate to the real world. If perception does not correspond to the real world, behaviour will be inappropriate and irrelevant.'

their perceptions to determine precisely what adjustment is necessary. These perceptions are, in turn, structured by particular world-views or ideologies which amongst other things are characterized by a number of assumptions concerning the basic properties, purposes, and functions of accounting.[3]

Such a contingent perspective of accounting change is common to most discussions of the topic (see, for example, Bedford 1970; Chambers 1966; Flint 1971). It is however, open to enormous variation in its details, with considerable differences in the specification of the environmental changes to which accounting must respond.[4] Gilling's own specification was not very precise. He argued that the principal environment change in the last forty years has been 'the recognition of the public character of accounting information' (Gilling 1976: 65). This, he continued, had arisen out of public concern over the activities of the business corporation, as evidenced at the time of his writing by the debate over corporate social responsibility. The consequent search by the accounting profession for ways to improve the accuracy and utility of published financial statements resulted in, amongst other things, the creation of institutions for accounting standardization and regulation, themselves a significant new part of the accounting environment.[5] Others have identified the growing power of labour (Barratt Brown 1978; Carlsson et al.

---

[3] Gilling (1976: 69) elaborated his views on the different and conflicting ideologies of accounting in the following way: 'Within accounting there is a latent ideological clash, frequently on issues of topical and lasting concern, between those who support the utilitarian view of accounting with its consequent piecemeal, case-by-case approach to the development of principles and practices, and those who seek to provide a sound, consistent theoretical base, to which all principles and practices can be related. Within those who are theory-orientated there exists further considerable differences of opinion between the current cash equivalents, the value to the owner, and the replacement cost schools of thought. To further cloud the issues there is the clash between those who see accounting as technology and those who see it as policy making.'

[4] Even when there is some agreement over the specification of the environmental change, the significance attached to it may vary. There is, for example, no sense of threat or crisis in Churchill's (1973) comments on the search for corporate social responsibility and the concomitant emergence of a plethora of different social indicators and measurement techniques. There is rather a sense of an opportunity for the expansion of the accounting domain.

[5] Other commentators and theorists would fully agree with Gilling in identifying the emergence of such institutions of accounting regulation as being crucial for the subsequent development of accounting practice. However, different analyses would put the functioning of these bodies in an altogether different light. For Watts and Zimmerman (1978, 1979), for instance, accounting regulation appears as a wasteful and ill-fated maladaption. (Also see Watts 1977.) The search for an agreed set of accounting principles on which to base regulation is doomed to failure because the different accounting ideologies discussed by Gilling mask a mass of necessarily different interests which are rooted in the different positions individuals occupy in the business environment. Further, the accounting standards actually reduce social welfare because of the existence of significant political transactions costs which mean that bureaucrats cannot in general be assumed to act in the public interest. Also see Benston (1969, 1976, 1983). For a different view of the emergence and functioning of these bodies and their interest in and utilization of knowledge, see Hopwood (1984).

1978; Gold *et al.* 1979; Hird 1975), the increasing recognition of consumer rights (Medawar 1978; Vogel 1978), the acknowledgement of significant externalities associated with the conduct of business (Estes 1976; Frankel 1978; Ramanathan 1976) and changing political conceptions of corporate accountability as being amongst the important environmental changes which have influenced or should influence accounting theory and practice. Moreover for Gandhi (1976, 1978), environmental developments were characterized in terms of the emergence of the non-market economy. For him, the significance of this development was that it has increasingly made accounting an inadequate means of rational action given its unidimensional monetary character. Gandhi exhorted accountants to 'come to a collective realization that there is more to performance evaluation than financial indicators' (Gandhi 1978).

The notion of the environment implicit in such contingent theories of accounting change is therefore a diffuse and only partially articulated one. Given the significance attached to accounting being or desirably being a reflective phenomenon, this introduces a large element of indeterminacy into such understandings of accounting change. Whilst imperatives for change are recognized,[6] the means for their explication and influence remain imprecise and relatively unexamined.

A different perspective on accounting change is provided by Wells (1976). In a sense Wells turns the contingency model on its head. He argues that the present crisis in accounting is less a question of a lack of adaption, on the part of accounting, to a changing environment, but more a product of virtually autonomous developments within accounting theory. Basing his analysis on the work of Kuhn (1970), Wells argues that a distinct, identifiable accounting disciplinary matrix emerged for the first time in the 1940s. This disciplinary matrix provided the framework for the work of normal science which subsequently, under the impact of criticism 'by scholars, businessmen and in the courts', brought to light a number of anomalies within the body of accounting theory and it is these anomalies which engendered a crisis. During the 1960s and 1970s, so the argument goes, a series of *ad hoc* attempts were made to deal with the anomalies and criticisms. In part, at least, this resulted in a more general concern for the theoretical basis of accounting which, amongst other things, led to the 1960s being described as the 'golden age in the history of *a priori* research in accounting' (Nelson 1973: 4). However, far from resolving difficulties, these works of high theory instead served to 'highlight the defects of the disciplinary matrix and loosen the grip of tradition'.

---

[6] For a critique of the notion of accounting imperatives see Burchell *et al.* (1980).

As a result there emerged a number of different schools of thought which tended to have different axiomatic starting points and were thus difficult to compare.[7] Each of these schools is in principle a candidate for a new disciplinary matrix, however, and Wells looks forward to the next stage in the development of accounting thought in which, according to Kuhn's schema, there 'will be "an increasing shift in allegiances" in favour of one of the alternatives' (Wells 1976: 480).

Wells' arguments are suggestive of the constitutive capacities of accounting. Rather than simply reflecting the context in which it operates, accounting has a power to influence its own context. Difficulties and disputes within accounting can engender accounting developments and a perception of crisis both internal and external to the specifically accounting domain. Accounting thereby is seen to give rise to developments which shape the context in which it operates. The environment of accounting can become, in part, at least, contingent upon the accountings of it.

In fact both Gilling (1976) and Wells (1976) move towards recognizing the duality of accounting change. For although it is the constitutive capacities of accounting that tend to be stressed by Wells as compared to the reflective capacities which are highlighted in Gilling, both these writers offer some initial insights into a dialectic of accounting (in the case of Wells, accounting *theory*) and its environment. The environment, having previously partly been created by accounting, calls for changes in accounting:

He [Kuhn] argues that the change takes place only after a serious malfunction has occurred in the sense that 'existing institutions (or practices) have ceased adequately to meet the problems posed by an environment that they have in part created'. (Wells 1976: 472)

The interdependency of accounting and its environment results in change being brought about by a process of mutual adaption. Environmental demands lead to changes in accounting practice and changes in accounting practice lead to changes in environmental demands and expectations. (Gilling 1976: 61)

It would appear that however the tale is told, the environment–accounting contingency model cannot avoid tackling the seemingly indeterminate dualistic character of the process of accounting change that it proposes.[8]

---

[7] One important aspect of the differences between the different approaches is that members of competing schools have different views of the phenomena which were the subject of their discipline. In particular, there were represented in the different schools of accounting theory, different conceptions of the business enterprise.

[8] A further discussion of the reflective and constitutive aspects of accounting change is given in Hopwood 1985. Also see Roberts and Scapens 1985.

Our study of value added accounting attempts to cast a little more light on the character of just such an accounting–society interdependence. In our case, however, it would perhaps be better to speak of an accounting–society inter-penetration. In the discussion of value added accounting which follows we have not employed the categories of 'accounting' and 'society' as if they denoted two distinct, mutually exclusive domains. Rather attention has been focused on the specific practices and institutions in which the category 'value added' appeared and functioned and on the contexts and the manner in which it has been mentioned and discussed. It will be seen that the social, or the environment, as it were, passes through accounting. Conversely, accounting ramifies, extends and shapes the social.

THE VALUE ADDED EVENT

The particular object of interest in this chapter is 'the sudden upsurge of interest in value added' (Cameron 1977*b*) that occurred in the United Kingdom during the late 1970s.[9] The general contours of this event appear to be fairly uncontroversial and they therefore compromise the basic facts of the matter. These facts are that the concept 'value added' appeared as an indicator of the value created by the activities of an enterprise in a number of different sites (private companies, newspapers, government bodies, trade unions, employer associations, professional accountancy bodies, etc.), functioning in a number of different practices (financial reporting, payment systems, profit sharing schemes, economic analyses, information disclosure to employees and trade unions, etc.), where before it had been largely absent or, at the most, an object of very limited sectional interest.

The widespread discussion of value added within the ranks of professional accountants commenced with its appearance in *The Corporate Report*, a discussion paper prepared by a working party drawn from the accountancy bodies, which was published by the Accounting Standards Steering Committee (later the Accounting Standards Committee) in August 1975. At least for accountants, this was the official debut of value added.

The Corporate Report recommended, amongst other things, a 'statement of value added, showing how the benefits of the efforts of an enterprise are

---

[9] The discussion in this chapter focuses on value added accounting in the UK. However, at the same time attention also was being given to it in other European countries. See McLeay 1983. For developments in German see Dierkes 1979, Reichmann and Lange 1981, Schreuder 1979 and Ullmann 1979. For the Netherlands see Dijksma and van der Wal 1984. In France interest was expressed in the idea of surplus accounting (see Maitre 1978; Rey 1978: 132–4).

shared between employees, providers of capital, the state and reinvestment' (ASSC 1975: 48). Subsequently a first draft of a consultative document entitled 'Aims and Scope of Company Reports', prepared by the Department of Trade, was issued on 9 June 1976 for comment. This paper, which reads very much as a commentary on *The Corporate Report*, states:

our preliminary view is that the subjects identified in *The Corporate Report* which should be given highest priority for further consideration as candidates for new statutory disclosure requirements are:

(a) Added Value;
(b) Employee Report;
(c) Future Prospects;
(d) Corporate Objectives (*Accountant* (1 July 1976), 13).

When the Government's Green Paper on *The Future of Company Reports* finally appeared in July 1977, one of the legislative proposals contained in it was for a statement of value added (Department of Trade 1977b: 7–8).

This policy debate in the realm of accounting regulation was paralleled by the phenomena of a number of companies using value added statements in their company reports and for reporting to employees. Fourteen companies (out of 300) in the Institute of Chartered Accountants in England and Wales' *Survey of Published Accounts* included value added statements in their annual reports for the year 1975–6 (ICAEW 1978). This figure grew to 67 for 1977/8, 84 for 1978/9, and 90 for 1979/80 before declining to 88 in 1980/1, 77 for 1981/2 and 64 for 1982/3 (ICAEW 1980; Skerratt and Tonkin 1982; Tonkin and Skerratt 1983). Other surveys indicate that more than one-fifth of the largest UK companies produced value added statements in the late 1970s (Gray and Maunders 1980).

The exact incidence of the use of added value in employee reports is unclear, although several commentators mentioned its popularity in this context (e.g. Fanning 1978). It also is of interest to note its use by several winners of the *Accountancy Age* competition for the best employee report, its advocacy for the purposes of explaining company performance to employees by the Engineering Employers' Federation (EEF 1977) and its mention by the Trades Union Congress as a possible performance indicator in the context of a discussion of information disclosure to employees (TUC 1974).

The Engineering Employers' Federation's advocacy of value added was a development of its position as presented in an earlier document, *Business Performance and Industrial Relations: Added Value as an Instrument of Management Discipline*, published by the Federation in 1972. As the title suggests, added value appears in this document as part of a discussion concerned with its use 'as a practical tool of management' rather than simply as a form of presentation of financial information in company and employee reports. The particular area of decision-making in which it was envisaged this 'practical tool' could be brought into play was the one concerned with the utilization of and payment for labour:

The Federation therefore aims to encourage the use of added value as a discipline, so that all managers, with or without experience of accounting practices will appreciate the financial environment within which decisions affecting manpower are taken. (EEF 1972)

In the later 1977 EEF pamphlet the discussion of the applications of value added is taken further. Examination of its uses has shifted from simply describing how it may serve as a guide to management when formulating wages policy to describing how it may be linked more directly to earnings when serving as the basis of a value added incentive payment scheme (VAIPS). Moreover it should be noted that VAIPSs themselves became the focus of considerable interest. It has been estimated that 200–300 companies were operating, or about to operate, added value schemes in 1978 (Woodmansay 1978).

In addition to the above uses of value added as a vehicle for information disclosure and as a basis for determining rewards at the level of the enterprise, the category also has appeared on several occasions in the context of policy discussions concerned with the performance of British industry (Jones 1976, 1978; New 1978). In addition it has been canvassed as the means of reforming company-wide profit-sharing schemes (Cameron 1977a) and appears in stockbroker reports (Vickers da Costa 1979) as a means of facilitating financial performance analysis.

The value added event, as we term it, already has stimulated some research and analytical reflection. In particular, four of the leading UK accountancy bodies—the Institute of Chartered Accountants in England and Wales, the Institute of Chartered Accountants of Scotland, the Institute of Cost and Management Accountants, and the Association of Certified Accountants, commissioned and issued research reports on the subject of value added (respectively, Renshall *et al.* 1979; Morley 1978; Cox 1979; Gray and Maunders 1980). Our concerns, however, are somewhat different from those which motivated and characterize these reports. In each they very largely take for granted 'the sudden upsurge of interest in value added'. Value added is discussed in terms of its possible uses and the principles of measurement and forms of presentation that may be employed. As such, this discussion may be considered to be as much part or continuation of the value added event as it is a reflection on it. In so far as an attempt is made to explain why this event took place, its occurrence is attributed to the phenomenon of social change:

Accountants have reported on profit for many centuries. Why do we now need to report on Value Added as well? One answer is that the Value Added Statement reflects a social change: shareholders have become less powerful and central Government and organized labour have become more powerful. (Morley 1978: 3)

Indeed in the case of value added this is not an uncommon theme (see Pakenham-Walsh 1964; Wilsher 1974; Robertson 1974) and it is precisely our interest in the relation between accounting change and social change that motivates this study of value added.

VALUE ADDED AND THE SOCIAL

On the face of it, the basic facts of the value added event appear clear enough. However, on closer inspection the picture becomes more complex and somewhat enigmatic. To begin with just what is value added? Rutherford (1977) responds to this question by advancing a definition drawn from Ruggles and Ruggles (1965: 50):

The value added by a firm; i.e. the value created by the activities of the firm and its employees, can be measured by the difference between the market value of the goods that have been turned out by the firm and the cost of those goods and materials purchased from other producers. This measure will exclude the contribution made by other producers to the total value of this firm's production, so that it is essentially equal to the market value created by this firm. The value added measure assesses the net contribution made by each firm to the total value of production; by adding up all these contributions, therefore it is possible to arrive at a total for the whole economy.

However, as Rutherford goes on to point out, this definition does not provide a detailed prescription for the *calculation* of value added. Indeed, he has pointed out elsewhere (Rutherford 1978), as have other writers (Vickers da Costa 1979; Morley 1978), that calculative practice is very diverse. The treatment of depreciation varies (McLeay 1983). A great deal of discretion exists as to the treatment of taxation, and so on. Furthermore, this calculative diversity is compounded by the fact that value added statements are presented in a number of different formats (tables, graphs, pie charts, pictures, etc.) which in turn bear a variety of different names ('value added', 'wealth created', 'where the money goes', etc.) (see Fanning 1978). There are clearly very many different value addeds.

Another curious feature emerges on inspecting the purported advantages of using value added. We already have indicated that the uses of value added are multiple—payment systems, company reporting, information disclosure to employees and trade unions, economic analysis, etc. What, however, is only rarely discussed is that the descriptions or specifications of the functioning of value added in any given organizational practice are commonly characterized by a form of duality. Value added is seen as a system of both determination and representation.

In the case of, for example, an incentive payment system (see Bentley Associates 1975; Smith 1978) value added is specified as a clearly defined financial category, the magnitude of which determines, according to certain well-defined calculative procedures, a component of labour income. However, in addition to such a description of a particular system of *determination* there is usually associated a description of a system of *representation*, albeit that the latter is usually thoroughly intertwined with the former. The system of representation is itself composed of two strands. On the one hand, value added, it is argued, represents wealth; to be precise it represents the wealth created in the accounting entity concerned. Furthermore, so the argument goes, this representational property provides a basis for the improved calculation of certain important indices of enterprise performance, namely efficiency and productivity (e.g. Ball 1968). On the other hand, it also is claimed that value added has the property of revealing (or representing) something about the social character of production, something which is occluded by traditional profit and loss accounting. Value added reveals that the wealth created in production is the consequence of the combined efforts of a number of agents who together form a co-operating team: 'Value Added measures the wealth creation which has been built up by the cooperative efforts of shareholders, lenders, workers and the Government' (Morley 1978: 3). It follows, therefore, that value added 'puts profit into proper perspective vis-à-vis the whole enterprise as a collective effort by capital, management and employees' (ASSC 1975: 49). Together these representational properties of value added are presumed to make it a means for both the more rational control of production and the achievement of a more harmonious and co-operative productive endeavour.

Now these expressive properties of value added, properties which provide it with both a technical and a social rationality, create a dilemma. For in order for value added to be able to represent the company as a co-operating

team, the company must first have been constituted as such. On further investigation, however, it transpires that value added is seen as being able to serve
as one means to this end. Value added therefore does not simply represent
the company as a co-operating team, it also is seen as playing a positive role
in the creation of this co-operative harmony. This is a point that was made
very clearly some time before value added became such a widespread object of
interest:

The growth we are interested in is a growth of the national product, growth of the
national product is achieved by making changes which lead to increased production
by business undertakings. This will not be realised until production is seen by managers to be the central purpose of business and until the accounting profession re-
orients its practices to this view. The profit and loss orientations of accounts, and
notably of published accounts, is inimical to the improvement of industrial relations
without which the growth in production desired will be attenuated.

   Although the antagonism between capital and labour has declined in recent years,
the basic division of interest between maximising profits and providing maximum
rewards for labour will continue to afflict industrial relations, unless we cease to see
profits as the objective. (Pakenham-Wash 1964: 268)

In such a context accounting is seen as a means of vision. A change in
accounting implies a change in what is seen and hence a change in action.
Social harmony might therefore not so much be revealed by value added as
constituted by it. We are on the horns of the very dilemma which, as we
already have indicated, is central to the society–accounting contingency
model. On the one hand, it is asserted that value added may be accounted for
by reference to wider changes and shifts in society (see Morley 1978;
Robertson 1974; Wilsher 1974). On the other hand, it now appears that this
same social change might not be independent of the existence of value added.
Value added is thus called upon to provide at least some of its own preconditions.

   Whatever may be the logical problems that arise from the circularity that
characterizes attempts to explain accounting innovations in terms of their
purported roles (also see Burchell *et al.* 1980), it is also important to note that
there does not exist any unanimous agreement over what the roles of value
added are in the first place. The roles we have described above by no means
exhaust the significance of this particular accounting innovation. In respect of
its social rationality—value added as an expression of production as team
production—it has been pointed out by Stolliday and Attwood (1978) that
there is no obvious logical reason why the use of value added should not
serve as a spur to workers in their attempts totally to eliminate the claims of

others in its distribution. In this case value added still functions to reveal a 'truth' about production as teamwork. From yet another standpoint, the use of value added is viewed as a way of 'misleading the workers' in an attempt to gloss 'over the problem of profits' (see Hird 1980; *Labour Research* 1978). In this case value added serves as a device for *mis*representing reality. It presents a picture of a unity of interests in the financial performance of a given business organization, whereas in fact there exists a basic conflict of interests. Value added, it seems, is a distinctly equivocal social indicator.

There is yet another problem concerning the roles of value added and the statuses attributed to them. We have already pointed to calculative diversity as an important feature of the event we are seeking to unravel. Virtually all those writers who comment on it see this calculative diversity as subversive of those very properties that are often deemed to characterize value added:

published statements of value added have, to date, been characterised by ambiguous terminology and by the treatment of items in ways inconsistent with the model of value added, and inconsistent within and between individual statements. The impression received by lay users of SVAs must be one of confusion—together possibly, with a conviction that value added, like profit can be made to mean whatever the accountant wishes it to mean. (Rutherford 1978: 52)

The advantages offered by the Value Added Statement are, however, currently jeopardised by great diversity of practice. (Morley 1978: 141)

Most of those [value-added statements] available seem to be designed to show, often by a 'sales-cake' diagram, how much of the value-added goes to the employees themselves, how much the Government absorbs and how little the shareholder receives. (Vickers da Costa 1979)

Rather than shedding light, reducing conflict, etc. value added statements appear to be equally conducive to confusion, doubt and suspicion. This state of affairs problematizes not only the social rationality of value added but also its technical rationality. Clearly there may be as many productivities and efficiencies as there are added values. Thus value added is always more or less inadequate to its roles and the value added event cannot therefore be viewed simply as either the dawning of economic enlightenment or the expression of a particular social transformation.

The general upshot of this discussion is that the roles of value added do not of themselves provide a very satisfactory explanation of 'the sudden upsurge of interest in value added'. To summarize the argument so far: we encounter logical problems if we attempt to explain the widespread use of value added in terms of its roles; in any case, the precise specification of these roles is controversial; and, finally, the value addeds we actually encounter do not function flawlessly to achieve their appointed end. It is therefore suggested that these roles would be better considered as part of the phenomena to be explained and with this idea in mind it is possible to specify in rather greater detail our object of investigation and certain problems in respect of it which we wish to solve.

To the basic facts of the value added event we now have to add that it was not a sudden and massive outbreak of a single, unambiguous concept of value added that occurred during the 1970s. There occurred instead the widespread discussion and use of a range of very particular, differentiated value addeds. These value addeds vary in definition and form of presentation and they came into the world in association with a number of properties. However historically contingent this association may be, the value addeds that we are interested in do not exist independently of these, their properties—namely the various roles that are imputed to value added and in the name of which it is frequently advanced. Although there is no unanimity in respect of these roles (or rationales), two have tended to predominate in the discussion and debate surrounding value added. It is frequently argued that value added is a superior means of the measurement, and hence pursuit, of wealth, productivity, and efficiency. In addition it is also argued that it is the measure of income appropriate to production seen as a process involving the action of a team of co-operators. Finally, the circularity which is involved when seeking to explain the appearance of value added in terms of its roles coupled with the lack of general agreement over the specification of these roles enables value added to serve as the focus of a widely differentiated field of political interest. The very ambiguity of value added might, in other words, be implicated in its emergence and functioning. Depending on the point at which the circle of reasoning is entered, value added may be seen as a determining factor in the process of social change, a harbinger of social change or a consequence of social change. As Morley (1978: 5–6) has expressed it:

In saying that the Value Added Statement reflects social change one does not necessarily approve of the phenomenon. Indeed, one can distinguish three very different views on this:
  (i) One might report Value Added in order to hurry the change along and to give impetus to the movement of power from capital owners towards labour and central Government.
  (ii) One might report Value Added in order to alert the business community to this change, hoping that it may thereby be reversed.
  (iii) One might report Value Added in the hope that it would help one's new masters to make sensible decisions.

These three attitudes may perhaps explain why Value Added enthusiasts are to be found at both ends of the political spectrum. One encounters both left and right wingers who support this new Statement though their expectations from it differ greatly.

It is precisely this highly differentiated social space within which the value added event took place that is our object of investigation. In what follows we have attempted to discover some of its preconditions—the factors that made possible the the value added event. This work of description and analysis has been carried out by delineating three arenas, or complexes of issues, institutions, bodies of knowledge, practices and actions, within each of which there may be traced a descent—a succession of phases in the trajectory of a social movement. These movements intersected in the 1980s with value added serving as an important element in the triple conjuncture. No doubt arenas other than the ones that we have outlined could be constructed. However the aim of this paper is *not* to provide an exhaustive description of the genesis and development of value added. Such a study would in any case take us back to before the Industrial Revolution and is therefore a task beyond the scope of the present chapter (see, for example, Crum 1982). The aim here is more modest: it is merely to shed a little descriptive and analytical light on the processes of accounting change.

THREE ARENAS

Each of the three arenas discussed below marks out a particular field of operations, namely the explication of standards for corporate financial reporting, the management of the national economy, and the functioning of the system of industrial relations. Within each arena there has been charted the shifting patterns of relations between the various agencies functioning in these fields, e.g. the government, trade unions, the accounting profession, and the changes in their modes of operation and objects of concern, e.g. productivity, strikes, accounting standards. In each case some emphasis is placed on the interest in economic calculation and reporting in general and in value added in particular.

At this stage in the argument the movement in each arena, along with its associated 'problems' and 'solutions', has been handled as if it had a trajectory which was largely independent of those in the other arenas. This is no doubt an oversimplification. Clearly, macro-economic management concerns with payment systems were not without their implications for industrial relations. Conversely, the interest in industrial relations reform was not unrelated to

certain postulated negative consequences of the existing structure of industrial relations for national economic performance. Similarly developments in
accounting standardization were related to both macro-economic issues, not
least in the context of the inflation prevailing in the period, and the management of industrial relations in a time of a perceived growth in the power of
the trade union movement. However the approach which we adopt at this
stage does in our opinion have the merits not only of enabling the field of
social relations in each of the arenas to be analysed more readily, allowing, in
the process, both their autonomies and their interdependencies to be recognized, but also of facilitating an investigation of how issues such as economic
performance and calculation were brought into relation with those of the status of employees and trade unions rather than presuming any *a priori* necessity
for this to happen.[10]

The debate surrounding economic performance and industrial relations
spilled over into a *pre-existing* debate in the area of corporate reporting which
was concerned with determining the appropriate categories, principles, and
forms of presentation and distribution of corporate reports. While our treatment of accounting as a separate domain or arena has been motivated by a
prior commitment not to handle accounting solely in a reductive or reflective
manner, the discussion below goes some way towards indicating in a more
positive fashion not only the components of this domain but also its articula-
tions with other fields of action.

Accounting standards

As we already have observed, value added is characterized by considerable calculative diversity.[11] In a survey of published value added statements it was
concluded that 'It is difficult to capture systematically the degree of diversity
present in the construction of statements of Value Added' (Rutherford
1980). Moreover, such a heterogeneity of practice was seen as problematic
for the roles, rationales, and purposes that value added was seen and mobil-
ized to serve. Rather than promoting efficient, harmonious, productive activ-

---

[10] We would argue that there is after all no obvious way in which notions of efficiency should be
related to those of democracy. The nature of such a relationship has been subject to very little analysis and
investigation, with the two notions inhabiting two distinct orders of discourse, namely those of economic
and political theory. The same point applies to the relationship between the various practices concerned
with the measurement and pursuit of efficiency and those concerned with the representation of interests.

[11] We would not wish to claim that value added is unusual in this respect. Most other key accounting
indicators are subject to a similar ambiguity of definition and diversity of practice. In fact this characteristic of so seemingly an objective phenomenon could provide an interesting perspective for both technical
and social analyses of the accounting craft.

ity, the motley collection of value addeds was seen as subverting the very roles allocated to them precisely as a consequence of their variegated character. Amongst other things, the calculative diversity opened management to the charge of manipulation and bias. In the case of employee newsletters, for example, it was asserted that 'most of those available seem to be designed to show . . . how much of the value added goes to the employees themselves, how much the Government absorbs and how little the shareholder receives' (*Accountant* 1978: 373).

One consequence of the perception that the practice of value added was not adequate to the roles commonly attributed to it was a call for its standardization (Fanning 1979; Vickers da Costa 1979). The relevant agency in this respect was the Accounting Standards Committee. As a result of these and other[12] pressures, four of the accountancy bodies represented on the Accounting Standards Committee commissioned research studies of value added. The reports issued by both the Institute of Chartered Accountants in England and Wales (Renshall *et al.* 1979) and the Institute of Chartered Accountants of Scotland (Morley 1978) conclude in favour of value added reporting but add the caveat that 'Standardisation of practice is a necessary precondition to any formal requirement' (Renshall *et al.* 1979: 38), so as 'to bring comparability to Value Added Statements and so safeguard the confidence of readers in the Statement' (Morley 1978: 141). The study prepared for the Institute of Cost and Management Accountants was notably less enthusiastic and presented value added as just one more addition to the kit-bag of management tools which may be usefully employed in connection with employee payment systems and public relations (Cox 1979). The issue of standardization was not raised in the report. The Association of Certified Accountants' study investigated the information needs of potential users of value added statements and reviewed existing corporate practice in the area before discussing measurement and disclosure policy (Gray and Maunders 1980). Two approaches to the measurement of value added were identified, and although it was stated that 'conceptually it would seem desirable that a consistent approach be adopted one way or the other' (p. 28), it also was argued that value added reporting should be 'placed outside the restrictions established by convention' in order to facilitate its 'imaginative development' according to the decision requirements of its potential users (p. 37).

---

[12] By initiating these research studies at least three of the four accountancy bodies also were responding to the Labour Government's threat of legislation requiring the reporting of value added. Given that the concept was a new part of the official accounting discourse, they were quite strategically investing in enhancing their understanding of the category.

There are two points of note concerning these four research studies. First, although all the reports commented on the sudden growth of interest in value added, an interest which provided the pretext for their discussions, none of them investigated the factors underlying this phenomenon. They all provided some sort of inventory of the various alleged advantages of using value added but none of them asked why these should have been perceived so suddenly or so late in the day. This point is important because if it can be shown that the emergence of value added was deeply implicated in certain wider socio-economic processes peculiar to a particular historical conjuncture, processes which moreover might have imbued value added with a particular historically contingent significance, then under different conditions debating the potential uses and advantages of value added might well be quite irrelevant. The second point relates to the fact that accounting policy in relation to the formulation of financial accounting standards has been fairly narrowly constrained to issues of measurement and forms of presentation. Until recently (Zeff 1978), these problems have been deliberated very largely without reference to the likely implications of introducing particular standards. Indeed, in relation to the American experience, it has been argued that the dominant means of discourse in this domain—those furnished by accounting theory—have served to obscure the political character of the standard setting process and thereby have rendered ineffectual certain procedural reforms and research initiatives aimed at resolving the problem of obtaining agreement on accounting standards (Moonitz 1974; Watts and Zimmerman 1979; Zeff 1978). In this sense it is ironic that the difficulties encountered by the Accounting Standards Committee in its standard setting programme—difficulties which could well have extended to any attempt to standardize value added should that ever have appeared on the agenda—provided an important impetus to the publication of *The Corporate Report* in which value added first entered the ranks of the accountancy profession.

The present arrangements for setting accounting standards in the UK were established at the end of the 1960s in the aftermath of the considerable controversy and debate surrounding a series of company collapses and take-over battles (Zeff 1972). The standards setting programme very quickly ran into trouble, however, not least in relation to its stated aim of narrowing the areas of difference and variety in accounting practice (ICAEW 1969). This was most dramatically exemplified in the case of the inflation accounting debate (Whittington 1983), but the same difficulties also applied to a number of other areas of accounting standardization.

Although initiated to maintain professional control over accounting standardization, the inflation accounting proposals of the then Accounting
Standards Steering Committee quickly engendered such a breadth and intensity of debate that the Conservative Government of the time established a
committee of inquiry in the area—the Sandiland's Committee (1975) (for an
initial analysis of the context see Hopwood *et al.* 1980; Hopwood 1984).
That in itself was perceived by the profession as a threat to the traditional
division of responsibility between the professional bodies and the government concerning the determination of the content and form of presentation
of and the measurement principles employed in corporate reports. The sense
of professional crisis was further intensified by the fact that the committee
was anticipated to report in a not uncritical manner during a new Labour
administration whose opposition Green Paper, *The Community and the Company*
(1974), had also threatened the existing framework of professional self-regulation with its proposals for the setting up of a powerful Companies
Commission for regulating companies and financial institutions.

In anticipation of the report of the Sandilands Committee, the Accounting
Standards Steering Committee established a committee to re-examine 'the
scope and aims of published financial reports in the light of modern needs
and conditions' (ASCC 1975)—something which had until then been
ignored by the standards setters.[13] The committee's findings were published
as *The Corporate Report*. In appraising current reporting practices, *The Corporate
Report* evinces some concern for what it considers to be an overemphasis on
profit and goes on to argue that:

The simplest and most immediate way of putting profit into proper perspective vis-à-
vis the whole enterprise as a collective effort by capital, management and employees
is by the presentation of a statement of value added (that is, sales income less materials and services purchased). Value added is the wealth the reporting entity has been
able to create by its own and its employees efforts. This statement would show how
value added had been used to pay those contributing to its creation. It usefully elabo-
rates on the profit and loss account and in time may come to be regarded as a preferable way of describing performance (ASSC 1975: 49).

In this way value added entered the discourse of accounting policy making.[14]

---

[13] In-depth research had been mentioned as one aspect of the standard setting programme, but no concrete steps had been taken in this area until the establishment of *The Corporate Report* Working Party. For an
insider's comments on the establishment and functioning of this group see Stamp (1985).

[14] One reviewer suggested that further effort be put into tracing the origins of the interest in value
added by *The Corporate Report* Working Party. Our investigations revealed that one of the authors of the present paper might have been influential in this respect! If this is so, it further reinforces our concluding
observations on the non-monolithic and unanticipated nature of accounting change.

Value added was seen as a performance criterion that put employees on a par with other interests in the enterprise. Moreover this claim for an equality of status was reinforced by the stakeholder model adopted in *The Corporate Report*. Where before there only existed the shareholder (Sharp 1971), there now stood a number of stakeholders, each of which is deemed to have 'a reasonable right to information concerning the reporting entity' (ASSC 1975: 17). The employee group constituted one such stakeholder. The report makes the point that 'it is likely that employees will more suitably obtain the information they need by means of special purpose reports at plant or site level' (p. 22). However, it goes on to argue that corporate reports could be used as a check on the reliability of these special purpose documents and could be useful to employees in evaluating managerial efficiency, estimating the future prospects of the entity and of individual establishments within a group.

The merits of value added as an alternative or complementary performance indicator had not been advanced in a vacuum, however. Two very important contextual considerations that should be borne in mind in connection with conditions in the United Kingdom during the second half of the 1970s were the debates, legislation, and practical initiatives concerned with incomes policy and information disclosure to employees and trades unions. Although value added was new to the accounting policy-making arena, it was functioning as a practice in both of these other two contexts.

Macro-economic management

Income policies have been linked to the use of the value added category by a number of writers (Beddoe 1978; Cameron 1978; IDR 1977; Low 1977). In every case the connection has been made via a discussion of value added incentive payment schemes (VAIPSs). VAIPSs are group bonus schemes which are usually operated on a plant basis, thus covering both blue- and white-collar employees. The bonus pool available for distribution to the employees is related to the value added of the plant. This pool may, for example, be determined by a certain agreed percentage of any increase in the value added per pound of payroll costs, over some agreed base figure for this ratio. These schemes came very much to the fore during the period of the 1974–9 Labour Government. With the inception of Stage III of that Government's pay policy in August 1977 there was imposed a 10 per cent limit on wage settlements with the provision for agreements above this level where self-financing productivity deals had been implemented. VAIPSs, which had been introduced into the UK during the 1950s, were already functioning in a number of firms and were strongly advocated by a number of management consultants, are almost by definition self-financing and thus were well placed under Stage III to become more widely adopted.

One of the most important conditions of this particular conjuncture of value added and national incomes policy was that constituted by the practices of government management of the national economy. The 'national economy' as an object of government intervention and 'macro-economic policy' as a domain wherein this intervention is deliberated, planned, and conducted were only constituted in the UK, in the sense that we understand them today, during and immediately after the Second World War (Tomlinson 1981). For a long time this field of action remained very much as it was initially structured by the conditions under which it emerged. This was particularly the case for the problem of productivity. 'Before the war productivity was largely confined to academic discussion', Leyland (1953: 381) observed. 'Today,' he went on to add, 'it is common currency.' Such an interest is not hard to understand. Under conditions of full employment, improving productivity had been the only source of economic growth. It also facilitated the maintenance of an external balance without reducing domestic consumption or investment—both painful exercises with hazardous side-effects for the government of the day. Moreover productivity also provided an indicator for gauging the competitive position of the manufacturing sector—a factor given continuing attention in the UK in the post-war era.[15] In short, productivity growth appeared to be a key to economic success.

While productivity and, more generally, economic efficiency have been continuing concerns of government, as evidenced by agencies such as the National Economic Development Office and earlier, the Anglo-American Productivity Council, neither these bodies nor the means of intervention associated with monetary and fiscal policy afforded governments a very effective purchase on these key economic variables. However, a rather more direct form of intervention has been provided from time to time by government incomes policies. These have been introduced, usually reluctantly and *in extremis*, in order to attempt to resolve one of the central presumed dilemmas of modern demand management, namely how is it possible to reconcile the

[15] In the second half of the 1970s value added was itself increasingly used in political and media discussions of national economic performance and policy (Jones 1976, 1978; New 1978). Indeed productivity tended to be seen as something that was, if not synonymous with value added, at least very closely related to it. From this perspective discussions focused on the need for income policies, increased investment, particularly in 'high value added sectors', and policies on the proportion of value added devoted to industrial research and development. In these ways value added appeared simultaneously to function as a way of describing the economy, elucidating policy problems, and, in the context of VAIPSs, facilitating the solution of the problems so identified.

objectives of price stability and full employment using only the instruments of fiscal and monetary policy. What is interesting here is that productivity growth has reoccurred as an important criterion for judging wage increases throughout the various phases of the post-war history of incomes policies.

Productivity was so emphasized during the incomes policies of 1961 and 1962. The theme re-emerged during the life of the National Board of Prices and Incomes (NBPI) established by the Labour Government in 1965 and wound up on 31 March 1971. The NBPI was assigned the task of examining 'particular cases in order to advise whether or not the behaviour of prices, salaries or other money incomes was in the national interest . . .' (see Fels 1972, ch. 3). 'The national interest' was first specified in the White Paper, *Prices and Incomes Policy*, of April 1965 and was subsequently elaborated and modified in a series of White Papers until 1970. Initially it required that there should be an incomes 'norm', i.e. a maximum percentage by which the wages and salaries of individuals should increase. A figure of 3–3½ per cent per annum was derived from the expected annual rate of growth of productivity per head. In addition certain exceptional circumstances in which increases above the norm were considered justifiable were also defined. Amongst these there was one which allowed for above-norm increases in pay where employees had made a direct contribution towards an increase in productivity. For certain periods during the life of the NBPI there was imposed a zero norm and the exceptional criteria became the only permissible grounds for obtaining an increase in pay. It was under this regime that productivity agreements became very popular. The NBPI's third report on productivity agreements showed that 25 per cent of all workers had been involved in productivity agreements, mainly in 1968 and 1969 (NBPI 1968).

Subsequent investigation of these productivity deals led certain commentators to conclude that many of them were bogus, i.e. 'the productivity increase was mostly that which would have happened in any case; so that what many so-called "productivity bargains" really did was to use this to justify an exceptional wage increase' (Turner 1970: 203). This experience plus the *ad hoc*, piecemeal character of many productivity deals which tended to be self-perpetuating thereafter (Elliott 1978) and, perhaps more importantly, the lack of any mechanism relating the increases in hourly rates paid to the increase in productivity actually achieved were the cause of some concern on the part of both Government and the Confederation of British Industry in the discussions over the arrangements to be brought into effect with the expiry of Stage II of the 1974–9 Labour Government's incomes policy. At that time the Government was keen to build a productivity element into the provisions for Stage III. In this context VAIPSs could be presented as model schemes. They were comprehensive in character and maintained a continuous link between performance and reward. VAIPSs therefore involved the use of a measurement technology that offered the use of a measurement technology that offered a solution to many of the problems that had created difficulties for the NBPI in its attempts to audit the productivity deals of the late 1960s. However, it is important to note that the force of the claims made on behalf of VAIPSs did not rest on these features alone.

In discussions of VAIPSs it is rare to find their merits presented solely in terms of their scope, self-financing character, or measurement technology. In a number of different ways, the point was nearly always made that the effective functioning of these schemes presupposes a number of changes in the intra-organizational relations of the enterprise concerned. Further, it was often made clear that these changes were considered to be of positive value in their own right. The relevant organizational changes were usually discussed in terms of 'information disclosure' and 'participation'. As one leading management consultant in this area put it:

the contribution of Added Value requires:

(a) an open management style that will 'open the books' and welcome the increased questioning that will ensure
(b) a preference for a more participative and less autocratic way of getting results. (Binder, Hamlyn, Fry & Co. 1978: 18).

The underlying reasoning appears to be that given that the relevant unit of performance for determining bonus is a company or plant rather than a single machine, improved performance and hence bonus presupposes co-operation across functions and different activities and occupational groups within functions. This co-operation, so the argument goes, can only be achieved by means of the widespread disclosure of detailed company information which then provides the basis for discussion and agreement on the appropriate action for attempting to improve performance. Thus, in the case of the Bentley plan—a particular British variant of the VAIPS—the scheme 'is initiated through a fully representative employee management council. A structure which will establish employee involvement and participation in a wider range of problems and enable profits, productivity and earnings to be rationally discussed and improved' (Bentley Associates 1975: 12). In one group of companies in which a VAIPS was introduced the scheme in each company in the group was administered by a company consultative council. These bodies included representatives from senior and junior management and from all shop floor departments. Each council was given the details of its company's performance for the preceding month. Council members then reported back on the figures to colleagues in their own sectors (Cameron 1977b; also see Woodmansay 1978: 13). It is interesting to note that although the trade union response to VAIPSs was somewhat guarded it was suggested that if unions did enter such schemes they would require, amongst other things, complete access to all the relevant data (Beddoe 1978).

The positive value of all these changes was generally seen in terms of the improvement in industrial relations that they were said to effect. It was argued that flexible working arrangements would become more likely and employees would become positively motivated to cut costs and improve efficiency. As a result there would be some amelioration in the repeated confrontation between workers and managers over working practices (Marchington 1977; Cameron 1977b). Now it was for very similar reasons that the NBPI was earlier so interested in productivity deals. It has been argued that the 'NBPI's recommendations on pay policy often required changes in the machinery of wage determination; in addition, the incomes policy was often used as a Trojan horse to bring about reforms in collective bargaining institutions' (Fels 1972: 150). The productivity deal was one of the principal means whereby the NBPI sought to supplant the hold of traditional factors in income determination and give practical effect to its own criteria.

However, in the 1970s there occurred a significant change in the character of the discussion surrounding the intra-organizational changes associated with the reform of payment systems. The productivity deals of the NBPI period were discussed wholly in terms of the rhetoric of management control:

genuine productivity agreements, for example, would have very useful side effects, such as improving management by increasing cost-consciousness, by providing new information about performance and information about performance and new methods of assessing it, and by directing attention to the possibility of changing methods of work. Management negotiations were brought into closer touch with unions, and more managers became aware of the implications for industrial relations of technical and financial decisions. The experience of applying the agreements with their provisions on overtime, flexibility, manning and so on often brought a revolution in managerial control over working hours and practices. There were changes in organisation, personnel and the provision of training, and senior and other managers were better informed and organised than before the agreements. (Fels 1972: 133)

While the discussion of VAIPSs during the second half of the 1970s still contained this thread concerned with management control and the efficiency of enterprise operations, it was also conducted according to the rhetoric of employee participation and industrial democracy. Indeed it became possible completely to invert the normal order of presentation and use the issue of industrial democracy as a springboard for advancing the claims of VAIPSs (e.g. Marchington 1977). The significance acquired by and emphasis placed on the participative characteristics of VAIPSs at this time was rooted in a number of parallel developments occurring within the area of industrial relations.

Industrial relations and information disclosure

During the 1960s there commenced a significant shift in the conditions of trade union activity in the UK. The pre-existing voluntary system of 'free collective bargaining' was displaced by a progressively elaborated object of government intervention—an object increasingly overlaid by a network of legal relations and inset with a variety of new institutions concerned with the investigation, regulation, and normalization of industrial relations (see Crouch 1979). This shift was preceded by two events of some interest. In 1961 there commenced the production of a record of unofficial strikes and in 1965 the Labour Government appointed a Royal Commission on Trade Unions and Employers' Associations—the Donovan Commission (Donovan 1968). Thus there occurred the production of a key statistic, to be read a little later as a sign of a 'central defect in British industrial relations' (Crouch 1979: 264). In addition to its work of diagnosis, the Donovan Report contained a clearly articulated conceptual framework which would serve as a means of generating programmes of intervention designed to rectify this 'defect'.

A singular feature of the interventions into industrial relations that occurred during the period of the 1974–9 Labour Government was the degree to which the discussions and debates surrounding them were organized around the theme of industrial democracy (Elliott 1978). Despite its apparent centrality, 'industrial democracy' is an extremely difficult concept to pin down. According to one commentator 'the term "industrial democracy" is incapable of definition' (Kahn-Freund 1977) and Elliott (1978: 6) has noted that:

Despite its central semi-political theme of increasing the role and status of workers in an industrial society, industrial democracy means different things to different people. To some on the far left it is perceived as a path to full workers' control, while for many employers and Conservative politicians, who dislike its political connotations, it should be called simply 'employee participation' and only involve a partnership between employer and employee in making the company and the present social and economic system work more efficiently and productively, without any changes in power relationships.

As for value added itself, it is perhaps precisely *because* of its equivocal character that industrial democracy was able to serve as a key point of articulation between a number of distinct conceptions of enterprise and industrial relations reform. The ambiguity might be required if the concept is to orchestrate the considerable number of positions that can be argued concerning the specification of individual and group interests and their political representations (Pitkin 1967).[16]

An inquiry into industrial democracy chaired by Lord Bullock (Department of Trade 1977*a*) and the enactment of the Employment Protection Act of 1975 were important elements in the programme of industrial relations reform of the 1974–9 Labour Government. However its democratic content may be judged, this programme implied a change in the information economies of private companies. Amongst other things it entailed the creation of new agents and bodies for the receipt and relay of information, new rights of access for certain existing bodies, and the setting up of certain national agencies to oversee and supervise the implementation and functioning of the new provisions. The Employment Protection Act of 1975 gave statutory form to the Advisory, Conciliation and Arbitration Service (ACAS)[17] which was 'charged with the general duty of promoting the improvement of industrial relations'. To this end it was empowered to issue Codes of Practice containing practical guidance for promoting the improvement of industrial relations. A Code of Practice on the disclosure of information to trade unions was issued by ACAS and came into effect on 22 August 1977. The disclosure provisions placed a general duty on an employer to disclose information to representatives of independent recognized trade unions,

---

[16] 'Industrial democracy' may be thought of as functioning in two different ways. First, it is the name attached to particular palpable regimes of industrial democracy. For example, in the name of industrial democracy, the Trades Union Congress advanced a comprehensive set of proposals for developing trade union activity at the level of the economy, industry, company, and the plant (TUC 1974). A rather different set of proposals are to be found in the evidence of the Confederation of British Industry to the Bullock Committee. There is thus a wide range of institutional and procedural arrangements that can lay claim to being democratic. In its second mode of functioning industrial democracy serves as a criterion for critically evaluating given institutions and procedures for their democratic content—the extent to which the arrangements in question may be considered to represent the interests of all the persons concerned. Thus Gospel appraises the provisions of the Employment Protection Act 1975 (Gospel 1976) and the signatories of the minority report take their stand in relation to the majority report of the Bullock Committee (Department of Trade 1977*a*: 175, para. 23).

[17] ACAS was first established on an administrative basis in 1974.

'(a) without which the trade union representatives would be to a material extent impeded in carrying on with him . . . collective bargaining, and (b) which it would be in accordance with good industrial relations practice that he would disclose to them for the purposes of collective bargaining'. Although the Bullock Report did not result in any legislation, parallel developments in the areas of occupational pension schemes (Lucas 1979) and health and safety took some steps towards taking workers into the sphere of management decision-making. The Health and Safety at Work Act was enacted in 1975. It provided for the appointment of employee safety representatives with functions of representation and consultation, workplace inspection and investigation, and rights of access to certain documents and information. As one writer put it: 'For the first time in law, the Regulations have given trade unions decision-making rights in their workplaces' (Stuttard 1979).

It was in this context, in which the relative status of management personnel *vis-à-vis* trade unionists had come under considerable pressure, both in respect of information access and decision-making, that there developed a considerable amount of interest in employee reporting. Popular versions of companies' annual reports to shareholders were prepared in an attempt to make them understandable to employees (Hussey 1978, 1979; Holmes 1977). Around these corporate initiatives there had in turn grown up a parallel literature of prescription and advice emanating from such bodies as the Institute of Personnel Management, the ICAEW, and the CBI. In addition to the use of employee reports, information also was disseminated to employees by means of personal presentations by company chairmen to mass meetings, slide and video presentations, and small group briefing sessions. It was within this area of corporate communication with employees that value added frequently appeared and was discussed as a preferred form of presentation (Hopkins 1975; EEF 1977; Smith 1978; Hilton 1978). The Trades Union Congress, in its statement of policy on industrial democracy, had itself suggested that companies should provide information on value added to their employees (TUC 1974: 33).

One final strand of interest in the industrial democracy debate is that of profit sharing. As a result of undertakings made to the Liberal Party during the formation of the 'Lib-Lab' alliance, profit sharing was encouraged by provisions introduced in the Finance Act 1978 (Elliott 1978). This particular innovation is one that was continued under the Conservative administration which came to power in 1979. The Confederation of British Industry viewed financial participation schemes as a means of obtaining a 'sense of purpose, at least at company level' and 'as a useful contribution to an employee participation programme' (CBI 1978). Of particular interest here are the changes introduced by ICI into its own profit-sharing scheme. This scheme had been running since 1953 and covered nearly 100,000 monthly and weekly paid staff who received an annual profit-related share allocation. In 1976 an ICI working party report proposed that the right of the ICI board to unilaterally fix the annual bonus should be replaced by a formula based on an added value concept (Cameron 1977*a*). This scheme differed from a VAIPS in that it operated at the company level as opposed to the plant level and it was not viewed as a major productivity incentive. The stated objectives were '(1) to help encourage the cooperation and involvement of all employees in improving the business performance of the company; (2) to provide tangible evidence of the unity of interests of employees and stockholders in the continued existence of ICI as a strong and financially viable company; (3) to help focus the interest of the employees towards being part of a more effective company, by being involved as stockholders' (Wellens 1977).

It is perhaps no surprise therefore that VAIPSs having been introduced into the UK during the 1950s and effectively incubated during the 1960s then came into their own in the 1970s. While the topics of information disclosure to employees and economic performance were by no means new (see for example BIM 1957; Searle 1971), the discussion of them took place within and was driven forward by the rhetoric of industrial democracy which tended to place in the foreground the issue of the relative status of economic agents. It is precisely under these conditions, formed by the intersection of a number of different developments in the fields of setting accounting standards, the management of the national economy and the regulation and reform of industrial relations, that profit and its associated connotations could appear as a problem—an 'awkward term'—and value added could establish its claim as an alternative performance indicator.

THE ACCOUNTING CONSTELLATION

Our concern is to discover the preconditions of the social space within which the value added event took place. As we indicated earlier, this particular social space is, amongst other things, characterized by the fact that the discussions concerning efficiency and productivity that took place within it during the second half of the 1970s were extensively intertwined with those concerning employee participation. The language of economic performance was strongly

inflected with that of industrial representation and democracy. In the literature of the period concerned with such enterprise administrative practices as
accounting and payments systems, problems were diagnosed and solutions
proposed according to the terms of a discourse which was organized around
the notions of efficiency and democracy. However, these two ideas function
as a pair of values the commensurability of which is far from clear. Just how
is 'efficiency' to be brought into relation with 'democracy'? One solution to
this problem seemingly was offered by value added. Value added was repeatedly presented as a means of achieving a felicitous combination of participation, if not democracy, and efficiency. Within the network of statements
generated by the efficiency-democracy discourse, value added functioned as
one strategic node or point of interrelation.

Notions of efficiency and participation did not exist as a pair of pre-given,
disembodied categories, however. Nor did the debates and discussions concerning them simply consist of a series of words and statements, lacking any
historical or contextual specification save that of the dates between which
they occurred. In our discussion of the three arenas we have attempted to
outline a three branched genealogy (Foucault 1977) of the specific social
space within which value added appeared and developed. As a consequence of
tracing this genealogy, the space which the value added event occupied is seen
to be comprised of a very particular field of relations which existed between
certain institutions, economic and administrative processes, bodies of knowledge, systems of norms and measurement, and classification techniques. We
have called such a field an accounting constellation. It was in the network of
intersecting practices, processes, and institutions which constituted this constellation that value added was caught and it was this network that governed
how it might function as a calculative, administrative, and discursive practice.
In this latter sense the constellation also operates as a regime—one which
governs the production, distribution, and use of value added statements.
Business organizations themselves appear within this regime as dense concen-
trations of social relations—a chain or archipelago of individual information
economies set into a web of more dispersed, loosely knit relations.

We have described the development of activities along three strands of this
web and how these three strands or arenas together made it possible for a
number of mutually reinforcing interventions to be relayed into the information economies of individual enterprises during the 1970s in the United
Kingdom. These interventions associated with incomes policies and the management of the national economy, company and labour law, and the reform
of industrial relations, accounting regulation and the standardization of

financial reporting, simultaneously affected a number of different aspects of the business enterprise. For example, productivity deals in general and VAIPSs in particular resulted in a significant elaboration of a firm's administrative apparatus. Moreover, this elaboration was aimed at increasing its pervasiveness in order to secure greater unity in the combined action of the component parts of the enterprise. It also has been argued that productivity deals were seen to offer workers the scope for greater involvement and participation in decision-making giving rise to the application of wage-work rules (McKersie and Hunter 1973: 21–3), an implication that was particularly apparent in many of the discourses that were associated with VAIPSs. Overall, therefore, these diverse strategies and interventions together had the possibility to intensify the regime of economic information within an enterprise and to move towards some reconstitution of the patterns of social relations. One interesting index of such an overall change was the widespread concern shown for the general level of financial and commercial literacy. Indeed the disclosure of corporate information to employees was often discussed as if it were part and parcel of an exercise in business education. A shift in the pattern of distribution and consumption of corporate information implied, or at least in this particular case was becoming increasingly associated with, a change in the distribution of the cultural resources commonly associated with the receipt and use of this information.

In many respects the appearance of value added statements in company annual reports was merely the tip of the iceberg in relation to the more general shift which had taken place in and around the enterprise in the processing of information. Although further investigation undoubtedly would provide interesting insights, we have not sought to uncover the precise mechanisms whereby value added was written into *The Corporate Report*, for instance. Instead we have attempted to indicate how it was necessary to speak about value added, to adopt a certain style of discourse, if what was basically a very marginal calculative elaboration of existing accounting practice was to generate such widespread interest and debate. Ours, therefore, is a history of possibilities, an account of how and why value added came to be a significant even if technically marginal accounting elaboration. From our perspective the necessity of talking about value added in a particular way arose as a result of the conditions that made the value added event possible—conditions we wish to encapsulate within our notion of an accounting constellation.

It is this idea of an accounting constellation, along with the processes of its formation, modification, and dissolution which now appears as our prime object of interest. As yet, however, it remains a vague and ill-specified idea.

The series of interconnected observations which follow seek to clarify certain of its more general features.

The specificity of the constellation

It is important to note first of all that the accounting constellation discussed here has been constructed in response to a particular problem concerning the value added event. There is no presupposition whatsoever that it encompasses the field of relations governing the production, distribution and use of all accounting statements. An examination of, for example, the conditions of possibility of the debates surrounding accounting for depreciation, deferred taxation or inflation accounting[18] would no doubt reveal an accounting constellation that only partly coincided with that associated with value added. Indeed, this might also be true if one examined an aspect of the value added event other than the one addressed here, e.g. the appearance of value added in a particular firm.

To so argue for the specificity of a particular accounting constellation does not reduce the significance of our general method of analysis. It is merely to recognize the diverse and changing factors that can intermingle with the processes of accounting change (also see Hopwood 1987). However, although advising caution on the transference of any specific accounting constellation to the domains of other accounting innovations and changes, we nevertheless would seek to argue for the general mode of analysis adopted in the present study, not least in respect of its genealogical emphasis, its mobilizing theoretical and practical concerns, and the very real theoretical cautions which resulted in the use of this approach rather than any other.

---

[18] For some brief but related comments on the emergence and functioning of the inflation accounting debate see Burchell *et al.* 1980 and Hopwood 1984. Inflation accounting occupies some of the same accounting constellation as the value added event, albeit that different aspects are emphasized. Indeed in the accounting standards arena discussions of the two were intertwined at particular junctures in the politics surrounding the processes of accounting regulation. Inflation accounting also was implicated in debates on macro-economic management, although in somewhat different policy arenas than those which explicitly related to value added. (The emphasis was on questions of indexation, albeit a problem that had arisen in the context of incomes policies, and the performance of the manufacturing sector.) Moreover in the context of a wider politics surrounding the techniques for surplus declaration, the inflation accounting debate became intertwined with industrial relations issues. In addition to such partial overlaps, however, other significant arenas also became involved with the development and functioning of inflation accounting, including questions of taxation policy, debates on the relative performance of different sectors of the UK economy, a questioning of the high levels of profitability of financial institutions and discussions and developments within the academic community.

The pursuit of interests and unintended consequences

The accounting constellation as we have described it was very much an *unintended* phenomenon. The field of action that we have outlined in relation to value added was not designed by anyone, and no blueprint for its construction can be found. It was produced as the consequence of the intersection of a great many events, some famous, and, as a consequence, well documented, and others unnoticed and possibly lost to history forever. Most of these events were produced by people with clear views of what they were doing—negotiating a wages settlement; conforming to an Act of Parliament; fighting inflation; seeking information; informing workers of the facts of economic reality—and no thought at all for an accounting constellation. Although there were identifiable causes to that which eventually emerged, they were ones which operated without any reference to certain of their effects.

Admittedly such a view differs from other notions of the interested nature of accounting practice. While, as we have stated, we do not seek to deny the purposive nature of accounting action, we are concerned to emphasize the potential multitude of different actors acting on accounting in purposive ways in an array of different arenas, each having specific, often non-overlapping and sometimes conflicting interests in the accounting practice they are utilizing and only partial knowledge of both its consequences and the resistance that its use will engender (Hindess 1982). Although at any particular moment of time there may be some mobilization of consequences that relates to the interests in the name of which accounting is advanced, in our analysis there is no assumption as to either any functional orchestration of these diverse initiatives or their precise effectivity in realizing the objectives which were stated for them. Accounting may, in other words, be purposive but whether it is purposeful is a matter for detailed and careful investigation across the diverse arenas in which specific accountings can become intertwined.

A non-monolithic constellation

One consequence of being the unintended product of a large number of different purposive actions is that the accounting constellation is non-monolithic in character. Although an accounting constellation may well govern the form of reasoning concerning certain of the decisions confronting enterprise management, such as, for example, the choice of the form of accounting and payment system to be adopted, there still remains considerable scope for conflict and disagreement. It is possible to imagine a situation in which workers and management of a firm are both agreed on the desirability of introducing VAIPS and yet for both sides to violently disagree on virtually all the procedural and organizational details which would effectively constitute the new payment system. In an analogous way, a particular mode of reasoning and institutional milieu can be said to organize the conflictual debates that have occurred in the area of accounting standard setting (Zeff 1978). In the case of value added, we have indicated how a field of action was laid down by the intersection of developments in three distinct arenas—developments which in each case proceeded without reference to certain of the possibilities and consequences of their interaction in mind. One aspect of this meshing of these developments, in fact one of the very ways in which they were articulated with one another, was that certain systems such as VAIPSs and certain categories such as value added functioned as the vehicle for a number of different interests and purposes. They were overdetermined phenomena, equivocality and ambiguity being central to their functioning. Seen in such terms, an accounting constellation is less a system or an entity which is usually understood in relation to some unambiguous governing principle, role or function, than a garbage can (Cohen *et al.* 1972).

Accounting's embeddedness in the organizational and the social

Our model of accounting change is still in many ways a contingency model. We have not suggested or discovered any general theory of accounting change. Everything all depends on the circumstances under which change occurs. There are, however, important differences with the accounting-environment contingency model of change discussed earlier. For a start, we have not attempted to separate out two domains called accounting and the environment and then conduct the analysis in terms of this prior distinction. Instead we have attempted to outline a network of social relations throughout which there may be found in the process of their emergence and functioning a certain class of statements—value added statements, company reports, employee reports, financial statements, statements concerning financial statements, etc. Within this network accounting can be found providing the conditions of existence of certain social relations, such as helping to define the rights, duties, and field of action of certain agents and playing a role in the specification of both organizational boundaries and intra-organizational segments. Accounting, so seen, is intimately implicated in the construction and facilitation of the contexts in which it operates. It cannot be extracted from its environment like an individual organism from its habitat. Of course it is possible to discuss categories such as profit and indeed value added in a general abstract manner without any reference to the law, organizational rules and functioning, and the rights and duties of agents. However, the added values we are interested in, the added values featuring in the value added event, did not exist thus. To attempt to investigate them in such an abstract fashion would be to investigate a different problem. We have been concerned to capture and analyse the way value added exists and functions as an integral part of and inscribed with certain social relations.[19]

The accounting constellation and networks of social relations and organizational practices

We have frequently described the set of social relations pertinent to the emergence and functioning of value added as a network. Our use of this term is very similar to the way in which it is deployed in organizational theory (Aldrich 1979). There the idea of a network of organizations has opened up research perspectives which tend to cut across the organization-environment dichotomy. Interest focuses less on the intra-organizational problems of adaptation to a changing environment than of the properties of a network of inter-organizational relations.

In our analysis the formation of a network of social relations has been described as a means of accounting for the outbreak of value added which during the 1970s characterized financial statements emerging from a wide range of sources. Although we have not analysed the properties of this network in any detail, it is important to note that in certain respects we conceive the accounting constellation rather differently from the way networks are specified in organizational theory. The main components of our network are not individual organizations, but rather particular systems or processes—payments systems, financial reporting systems, information systems. We have

---

[19] In a very different context (that of the emergence of prisons), Patton (1979) similarly noted that 'the abstract machine, however, can only function by means of concrete social machines which give it content'. He elaborated this idea in the following way: 'each concrete social machine is composed of both discursive and non-discursive elements. While the abstract machine only functions through its concrete forms, it is nevertheless that which renders possible the emergence of those concrete social machines. It plays the role of immanent cause, which "selects" a particular machine according to its own design.' In the case of value added the actual historical emergence of the abstract discursive category is so intimately bound up with its social functioning that it is difficult to disentangle the two. In other areas of accounting, however, it might be possible to more readily conduct an analysis of the interrelationship between the discursive and non-discursive components. Inflation accounting comes to mind in this respect.

indicated how these systems are caught up and elaborated in networks of relations existing between various agents, agencies and the systems themselves. Moreover these networks were uncovered by studying developments in three arenas, each of which could be characterized in terms of specific fields of action, and targets and agents of intervention, along with their means of surveillance and intervention and associated bodies of knowledge. The developments within each arena were then seen as involving the formation of relations between particular agents, agencies and administrative practices as a consequence of the various interventions taking place. Finally, the accounting constellation was itself specified as a network by noting the often unintended interdependencies between the processes and the practices in the separate arenas.

In this way we provided an account of the emergence and functioning of value added across a diverse social space with developments in particular fields of action both changing the preconditions for developments elsewhere and enabling or constraining specific innovations to take place. Thus the arena of accounting standard setting was shown not to be independent of developments taking place in the arenas of macro-economic management and the conduct of industrial relations. Although each of these arenas had its own trajectory of change, the notion of a network enabled us to locate the possibilities for their interpenetration and mutually dependent functioning.

We attempted to use such a perspective in order to avoid giving a privileged ontological status to the notion of an organization as a discrete bounded entity with a well-defined interior and exterior. Clearly such notions do exist and certain agents act in their name and are engaged in their fabrication and maintenance. What is important to note, however, is that the conditions of possibility for the actions of organization builders are *not* contained in that which they are attempting to build. An organization can hardly be presupposed as a means for its own (auto-)generation. Aware of such problems, by focusing on certain administrative systems and their position within each of the arenas we have studied, we hope to have indicated how the very substance of organizations is constructed by processes which cut across any single distinction that might be made between organizational members and non-members. In a similar way Litterer (1961; 1963) has indicated how the organizational phenomenon of 'Big Business' (Chandler 1962) was made possible by the emplacement of cost accounting, production, and inventory control systems as joint effects of the systematic management movement.[20]

[20] Unlike Chandler (1962, 1977) who merely provides a rationale for certain organizational forms by reference to general economic developments (railways, markets, etc.), Litterer (and others) describe some

In a similar manner the developments in each of our arenas also amount to the elaboration and development of certain dimensions of those complex entities we call the economy, society, and the environment (see Donzelot 1979). The interventions within the different arenas, which are conducted according to a variety of different principles, single out and privilege certain agents and their means of action. In the process of being used to intervene in the organization, practices for the management of the social and the economic are elaborated and changed. 'The organization' thereby designates a particular site of intersection of practices conducted in the name of the social and the economic, amongst other things. It represents a common nodal point in a number of different networks, each having different objects and means of intervention. And it also represents a site where people in attempting to draw boundaries seek to co-ordinate the actions of those enclosed within them, striving to fashion out of the diverse processes and interventions at work a machine for pursuing certain goals and performing certain functions. Seen in such terms, the organization and society and the economy are not independent realms. Rather than residing without, the social and the economic pass through the organization in the course of their own formation, as we have seen in the case of the value added event.

The mode of investigation

Finally, it is worth making some comments concerning the mode of investigation that we employed. The choice of arenas around which the investigation has been organized was a product of the particular origins and history of a more general inquiry of which this paper is one (unintended) outcome. It was not determined at the beginning on the basis of any general theoretical principles or model. However, the decision to attempt to divide the accounting

---

of the processes and mechanisms at work in the construction of the large bureaucratic firm. The systematic and scientific management movements and the welfare movement were very specific, describable forms of intervention in the enterprise involving very specific agents (engineers, welfare secretaries, foremen) which coalesced around a number of measurement techniques and administrative procedures (cost accounting, inventory and production control systems, measurement of efficiency and personnel turnover) and emerged and functioned under very specific social, political, and economic conditions. These different movements were not unified in their goals and encountered resistance to their attempts to implement their programmes, clashing with one another and with certain of the agents they attempted to (re-)construct (the foreman, the labourer, etc.). As Jenks (1960: 421) has said: 'The contemporary institutionalization of business management developed through the convergence of an indeterminate number of distinct movements of thought and action.' He went on to add: 'Perhaps it would be well to think of several origins for the management movement, each of limited scope but some possible overlap . . .' (p. 427). Such a form of analysis is very consistent with our own.

context into a number of arenas—whatever they might have been—and to consider the process of development within each as *sui generis*, marching to its own drummer, was motivated by a prior theoretical concern to attempt to avoid the problems entailed in adopting an enterprise–environment and/or an accounting–environment model of change.

Having identified three arenas, our mode of investigation was in many ways very similar to those conducted by the authorities—Department of Trade Inspectors—when investigating irregularities in the affairs of a company. The irregularity that we set out to investigate was the outbreak of added value during the second half of the 1970s. How was this phenomenon or event possible? What did it signify? Now Department of Trade Inspectors in their investigations presuppose and attempt to reconstruct the accounting regime—system of bookkeeping, accounting, and internal control—existing in the particular company under investigation. Such a regime must have served as the condition of possibility for the irregularities which precipitated the investigation. We have been concerned with a considerably more widespread and heterogeneous set of phenomena than those normally addressed by Department of Trade Inspectors. However, we have argued that certain features of the value added event were only possible given the existence of a set of conditions—the accounting constellation—which together also comprise a regime of sorts. It is however a regime which no one designed, and is never audited.

The enquiries of the authorities are also of interest because they must of necessity study accounting systems in terms other than the roles or functions, e.g. stewardship, that are commonly attributed to them. It is not enough merely to register the fact of irregularities, errors, and anomalies in the operation of an accounting system. In order to refine and elaborate accounting systems so as to prevent such irregularities occurring again in the future it is necessary to discover the positive determinants of errors and anomalies. How is it that something that is assumed to function as a means of accountability, served instead as a mechanism for financial irregularity? In the case of the value added event we have pointed to the multiplicity of roles attributed to value added statements and commented on the seeming inadequacy of any given statement as to its purported role(s). Our genealogical study of the event attempts to show how certain roles came to be attributed to a number of processes within which value added could be found functioning. We have attempted throughout to avoid making any assumptions concerning the essential or proper functions of accounting practice.

ON EMERGENCE AND DECLINE

Having discussed the nature, significance, and specificity of the constellation which provided the conditions for the value added event, it is now of interest to note that the attention given to value added subsequently waned during the early 1980s. With the election of a new Conservative Government in 1979 the three arenas of the value added constellation were suddenly ruptured and transformed. Different policies were introduced for the management of the national economy. Industrial relations came quite quickly to be seen and conducted in fundamentally different terms. And albeit with a lag, the specification of accounting standards was no longer seen to be subject to so real a possibility of government intervention. In these ways the specific significances which had been attached to value added were no longer salient. With its context so radically changed, the functioning of value added in social relations started to approximate to its technical marginality. Value added started to become a phenomenon of the past.

Although the state of the British economy was still such that economic performance remained a fundamental governmental policy concern, the new administration attempted to deal with this in very different ways. Emphasis was placed on the roles that could be served by monetary policies, financial stringency, and the enhancement of competitive pressures. The level of wage settlements was still seen as problematic, but incomes policies did not enter into the explicit political repertoire. Market pressures in an increasingly high unemployment economy were seen to offer more effective means for income control. Productivity and efficiency also remained important objects of government attention. Here too, however, very different interventionist strategies were used. A re-emergence of the managerial prerogative was seen as being capable of enhancing the efficiency of British industry. Gone were the days when conceptions of co-operation and participation were interwoven into the vocabulary and practice of economic management. Stress was placed on the positive roles that could be played by a re-emphasis of competitive pressures, increased training, the shedding of 'surplus' labour and increased investment, particularly in areas of high technology and capital intensity. Related changes were taking place in the industrial democracy, participation, and the enhancement of worker rights ceased. Indeed efforts were made to repeal or not to enforce legislative rights conveyed by the previous administration. The relevance of a relationship between democracy and efficiency was no longer seen. The vocabulary of change focused on competition, free markets, and the ending of restrictive practices and monopoly powers. Certain economic rather than more widespread social and political rights came to be emphasized. More significance was attached to decisive and entrepreneurial action rather than co-operation and persuasion. Leadership rather than participation was the order of the day.

The accounting profession was slow to recognize the relevance of the changes taking place. The fear of government intervention had been a very deeply felt and widely articulated one. Eventually, however, it came to realize that it was no longer subject to the same intensity of threat. Although still very much concerned with very visible remnants of an era past in the form of inflation accounting, the profession in general and the Accounting Standards Committee in particular started to adjust itself to the new political situation. Representatives of wider industrial and financial constituencies were brought on to the Accounting Standards Committee now that its legitimacy as a protector of the profession from an interventionist State was no longer apparent. New investments were made in the potential legitimizing roles of knowledge (see Hopwood 1984). And the agenda of future areas of standard setting was radically curtailed. Amongst other things, value added was removed from the agenda for future deliberation and action.

The time for value added was no longer. The specific constellation which had resulted in its emergence, significance, and development had been ruptured. The arenas out of which value added had emerged had been subject to significant discontinuities. The social context of value added had mutated. Devoid of its specific social conditions of possibility, value added was little more than a mere technical accounting possibility—perhaps something to be mentioned in the footnotes of accounting texts. The factors that had endowed it with a wider significance and momentum for development had disappeared.

Such a waning of interest in value added was not a new phenomenon, however. Value added also had had a period of temporary significance in the United Kingdom in the late 1940s and early 1950s. Then, as in the mid-1970s, there also was conjoined a considerable interest in employee communication and information disclosure and a concern for the performance of the British economy. It was in this context that value added also appeared in company reporting practices in a way which also completely anticipated the practices of the late 1970s (Burchell *et al.* 1981). Between those two periods there was little if any discussion of value added however.

The immediate backcloth to this earlier, proto-value added event was the Second World War. Wartime mobilization resulted in trade unionists being heavily involved at all levels in the administration of social and economic policy (Pelling 1971). Many of these wartime arrangements continued after the war when the problems of post-war reconstruction and the sudden ending of American 'lend-lease' assistance led to a continued concentration on production and productivity. The winter fuel crisis of 1947 brought things to a head. In response to the Government's call for co-operation, the General Council of the Trades Union Congress urged the reconstitution of the joint production committees in the factories, most of which had faded away after the war. In addition, the issue of wage restraint came very much to the fore. One aspect of this period, as evidenced by the work of the Anglo-American Productivity Council and the contents of *Target*, a Central Office of Information publication, was the extent to which attempts were made to propagate the value of more systematic management practices. What is particularly interesting is that this discussion of enterprise practices was shot through with the imagery of co-operative endeavour. Co-operation and participation were presented as the means of underpinning improved economic performance and were to be secured by the disclosure of information. In the words of a *Target* editorial statement (*Target* 1948):

There is undoubtedly widespread misapprehension among working men and women upon the subject of wages and profits. The points made by the Chancellor of the Exchequer . . . at the recent Trades Union Congress need further elaboration and emphasis. The subject must be dealt with fully and frankly if workers generally are to be satisfied on the issues involved . . . the worker, who suspects that the shareholders are reaping large rewards while he, the man who produces the goods, is denied his dues, should be given the facts. More often than not a full and frank explanation will remove such misconceptions . . . if we are going to stand on our own feet by the time American aid comes to an end—by 1952 at the latest—we must concentrate on productivity . . . if workers can be made to feel that they really are partners in this all-out effort to put this country of ours on its feet again, they are surely entitled to the full facts.

Target functioned as a means of communication between companies on the problems of raising productivity. During the first eight months of its existence it focused on works information schemes before being designated the official means of communication between the Anglo-American Productivity Council and British industry in February 1949. Before this happened readers of the publication were greeted by such headlines as 'Telling workers the facts'; 'Scottish firm tells the workers "what and why"'; 'More firms who say where the money goes'; 'The facts about factory economics'; and even 'Workers had all the facts—up went efficiency'.

Many of the employee communication schemes of companies featured in *Target* were organized around forms of distribution accounting, very reminiscent of the value added statements used later in employee newspapers. Information was presented in order to reveal 'how each pound of revenue . . . is paid out to the various costs of manufacture or remain as profits'. It was at this juncture that value added made its entry in a booklet entitled *Added Value* produced by Metal Box Company Ltd. (written by Sir Robert Barlow, the company's chairman). 'In spite of paper difficulties', a copy of *Added Value* was sent to every man and woman on the weekly staff and to hourly-paid workers in certain long service grades. Its publication was timed to coincide with the issue of the company's 1948 annual report which was sent to every member of each factory's work committee. Writing in the booklet, Sir Robert commented that:

There is . . . a great deal of misconception about profits, or, as they might properly be called, earnings. There is even a danger that they may be regarded as evil in themselves—hence that those who earn them are engaged in anti-social activities.

Writing from the standpoint of productive industry, we say that this is the opposite of truth; that a profit which arises from the efficient working of a worthwhile enterprise is legitimate, desirable and necessary. For the alternative to a profit is a loss, and who, may it be asked, will be the better for that? Not the shareholders, not the employees, not the management, nor the State, for all of these benefit from a profit and would suffer from a loss. Least of all, perhaps, the customer; for no enterprise, operating at a loss, can supply him with what he will need in a market competitive in quality and price.

The object of this booklet is to demonstrate this from facts; to go further and to show that from the operations of an industrial concern there arises an added value which is shared by all. For when a man performs a useful piece of work he creates wealth in its real sense. Once a body of men are actuated to perform their part of a common task in a better than normal way and when from their efforts there flows a continually expanding activity, wealth is created to a considerably increased degree. profit ceases to be, if indeed it ever has been, the dominating motive, and pride in work and an ensuing sense of responsibility takes its place. (Metal Box Company Ltd. 1948)

In the name of such ideas, Metal Box introduced a whole array of strategies and practices to communicate the facts of business life to the workers in order 'to explain the significance of . . . various points, their impact on the company, what the organization as a whole and the men and women who make it work, can do to help'.[21]

---

[21] For a discussion of other related schemes at this time see Burchell *et al.* 1981.

The existence of such a proto-value added enables us to reinforce the point concerning the way the functioning and very existence of accounting categories is conditioned by a complex set of circumstances. It also enables us to emphasize the highly specific and contingent nature of those circumstances. For in the early 1950s, as in the early 1980s, interest in value added was to wane. Again with a different political context and, in this case, the emergence of relative economic prosperity rather than the use of very different policies for the continued management of adversity, the value added constellation was ruptured and subjected to significant discontinuities. The very decline of interest in value added thereby serves to reinforce the theoretical perspective developed in this chapter.

CONCLUSION

We have sought to indicate how the value added event arose out of a complex interplay of institutions, issues, and processes. The study of this particular accounting change has enabled us not only to move towards grounding accounting in the specific social contexts in which it operates but also to raise and discuss what we see to be some important theoretical issues which have to be faced when seeking to understand the social functioning of the accounting craft.

Zeff (1978), albeit in a different way from ourselves, is another who has pointed to the need for such richer and more contextual appreciations of accounting in action. Focusing solely on the setting of accounting standards, he points to the myriad political factors which have intruded in the setting (and subsequent criticism) of standards, factors the impact of which is not registered in the accounting model which has traditionally provided the dominant frame of reference for discussing accounting practices and the reasons for adopting them. Zeff argues that the economic and social consequences of accounting practices 'may no longer be ignored as a substantive issue in the setting of accounting standards' (Zeff 1978) and *inter alia* points to the importance of developing our theoretical resources in order to be able to adequately confront this issue.

Recently there has been developed a theoretical approach to accounting based on the agency model of the firm (Jensen and Meckling 1976) which may be seen as a direct response to the problem articulated by Zeff. This approach has been employed in the analysis of the standard setting process (Watts and Zimmerman 1978), the status and form of accounting theory

(Watts and Zimmerman 1979), and the form of particular accounting procedures (Zimmerman 1979). By way of concluding, it is worthwhile to indicate briefly in what ways the approach we have adopted differs from that of the agency theorists and the associated implications for accounting research.

In general terms the differences between the two approaches can be clearly stated. In the case of the agency theorists, financial statements are viewed as economic goods for which there exists a certain demand and the production of which entails certain costs. The function of financial statements is that of a means of determining the magnitude of certain wealth transfers such as dividends, tax credits, loan payments, management renumeration, and agency costs. Accounting procedures differ in their impact on these wealth transfers, and it is argued that individuals and groups are therefore not indifferent as to the particular procedures used. These individuals and groups calculate the effect on their wealth of using any given procedure and take up positions accordingly—whether it be in an unregulated market for financial statements or in relation to some regulatory agency. We do not doubt that individual agents do attempt to estimate the financial effects of proposed changes in accounting practice as part of their process of decision-making in relation to the choice of accounting procedures. We, however, are more interested in the processes whereby a particular configuration of interest groups, or rather groups with an interest in accounting, comes into existence. The agency theorists only distinguish between such configurations to the extent that they distinguish between regulated and unregulated economies. Clearly state intervention into the economy has been of enormous importance for the development of accounting (see Hopwood *et al.* 1980). This, however, does not mean that it is impossible to construct a more nuanced picture than that which the dichotomy between a regulated and unregulated state allows and, at the same time, study in greater detail the processes of change. Amongst other things we would include amongst these processes those whereby accounting, or particular categories and statements, came to feature within the field of interest of certain agents and the *means* whereby the position of these agents with respect to these novel objects is deliberated and calculated: how was it that value added surfaced within the field of industrial relations and how was it evaluated once it had appeared there?

Thus our focus rests on the processes of change whereas the agency theorists attempt to establish correlations between certain classes of action, such as positions adopted on proposed accounting standards, and estimates of the interests of those adopting the positions. The agency theorists present their model as a self-interest theory whereas we are concerned to discover how self-interests, or particular policy positions, are in fact established—including the role which specific economic calculations and accountings rather than the generality of an economic calculus play in this process. The agency theorists privilege a particular mode of calculating (self-)interests derived from economic theory and a particular role for financial statements. Their analysis presupposes the existence of a meta-accounting which somehow guides rational economic action and their studies seek to explore specific explications and elaborations of such an accounting. Our analysis aims to make no such presumption of a primeval account. Rather than being viewed by us as revelatory of particular administrative and policy-making practices, the role and mode of calculation are instead viewed as functioning discursive components *within* these practices.

We have in this chapter adopted a historical, genealogical approach as a device to avoid the assumption that accounting has some essential role or function. Our working principle in this has been that 'the cause of the origin of a thing and its eventual unity, its actual employment and place in a system of purposes, are worlds apart' (Nietzsche 1969: 77 as quoted in Minson 1980). It has been suggested elsewhere that the organization of our concepts and the philosophical difficulties that arise from them, have to do with their historical origins. When there occurs a transformation of ideas, whatever made the transformation possible leaves its mark on subsequent reasoning. It is as if concepts have memories (Hacking 1981). Indeed the study by Wells of the origins of accounting for overhead costs is written in just such a vein (Wells 1978). In a similar way we have attempted to indicate how the processes underlying the value added event determined the character of discourse bearing the category value added.

References

Aims and Scope of Company Reports (1976), *Accountant* (1 July): 12–14.

Accounting Standards Steering Committee (1978), *The Corporate Report* (London: ASSC).

Ackerman, R., and Bauer, R. (1976), *Corporate Social Responsiveness: The Modern Dilemma* (Englewood Cliffs, NJ: Prentice-Hall).

Aldrich, H. F. (1979), *Organizations and their Environments* (Englewood Cliffs, NJ: Prentice-Hall).

Ball, R. J. (1968), 'The Use of Value Added in Measuring Managerial Efficiency', *Business Ratios* (Summer): 5–11.

Barratt Brown, M. (1978), *Information at Work* (London: Arrow Books).

Beddoe, R. (1978), *Value Added and Payment Systems*, Technical note no. 42 (Oxford: The Trade Union Research Unit, Ruskin College).

Bedford, N. M. (1970), *The Future of Accounting in a Changing Society* (Champaign, Ill.: Stipes).

Benston, G. J. (1969), 'The Value of the SEC's Accounting Disclosure Requirements', *Accounting Review* (July): 515–32.

—— (1976) *Corporate Financial Disclosure in the UK and the USA* (Saxon House).

—— (1983), 'An Analysis of the Role of Accounting Standards for Enhancing Corporate Governance and Social Responsibility', in M. Bromwich and A. G. Hopwood (eds.), *Accounting Standard Setting: An International Perspective* (Farnborough: Pitman).

Bentley Associates (1975), *A Dynamic Pay Policy for Growth* (Brighton: Bentley Associates).

Binder, Hamlyn, Fry & Co. (1978), *Added Value as a Concept* (London: Binder, Hamlyn and Fry).

British Institute of Management (1957), *The Disclosure of Financial Information to Employees* (BIM).

Burchell, S., Clubb, C., and Hopwood, A. (1981), '"A Message from Mars"—and other Reminiscences From the Past', *Accountancy* (Oct.): 96, 98, 100.

—— —— —— Hughes, J., and Nahapiet, J. (1980), 'The Roles of Accounting in Organizations and Society', *Accounting Organizations and Society*, 5–27.

Cameron, S. (1977a), 'Added Value Plan for Distributing ICI's Wealth', *Financial Times* (7 Jan.).

—— (1977b), 'Adding Value to Britain', *Financial Times* (31 May).

—— (1978), 'Breeding a New Type of Productivity Deal', *Financial Times* (3 Apr.).

Carlsson, J., Ehn, P., Erlander, B., Perby, M. L., and Sandberg, Å. (1978), 'Planning and Control from the Perspective of Labour: A Short Presentation of the DEMOS Project', *Accounting, Organizations and Society*, 249–60.

Chambers, R. J. (1966), *Accounting, Evaluation and Economic Behavior* (Englewood Cliffs, NJ: Prentice-Hall).

Chandler, A. D. (1962), *Strategy and Structure* (Cambridge, Mass.: MIT Press).

—— (1977), *The Visible Hand: The Managerial Revolution in American Business* (Cambridge, Mass.: Harvard University Press).

Churchill, N. C. (1973), 'The Accountant's Role in Social Responsibility', in W. F. Stone (ed.), *The Accountant in a Changing Business Environment* (Gainsville, Fla.: University of Florida Press), 14–27.

Cohen, M. D., March, J. G., Olsen, J. P. (1972), 'A Garbage Can Model of Organizational Choice', *Administrative Science Quarterly* (Mar.): 1–25.

Confederation of British Industry (1978), *Financial Participation in Companies: An Introductory Booklet* (London: CBI).

Cooper, D. (1981), 'A Social and Organizational View of Management Accounting', in M. Bromwich and A. G. Hopwood (eds.), *Essays in British Accounting Research* (London: Pitman).

Cox, B. (1979), *Value Added: An Appreciation for the Accountant Concerned with Industry* (London: Heinemann in association with the Institute of Cost and Management Accountants).

Crouch, C. (1979), *The Politics of Industrial Relations* (London: Fontana).

Crum, R. P. (1982), 'Added-Value Taxation: The Roots Run Deep into Colonial and Early America, *Accounting Historians Journal* (Autumn): 25–42.

Department of Trade (1977*a*), *Committee of Inquiry on Industrial Democracy* (Chairman: Lord Bullock) Cmnd. 6706.

—— (1977*b*), *The Future of Company Reports* London: HMSO).

Dierkes, M. (1979), 'Corporate Social Reporting in Germany: Conceptual Developments and Practical Experience', *Accounting, Organizations and Society*, 87–100.

Dijksma, J., and van der Wal, R. (1984), 'Value Added in Dutch Corporate Annual Reports 1980–1982'. Working paper of the Faculteit der Economische Wetenschappen, Erasmus University, Rotterdam.

Donovan, Lord (1968), *Royal Commission on Trade Unions* (Cmnd. 3623, London: HMSO).

Donzelot, J. (1979), *The Policing of Families* (New York: Pantheon).

Elliot, J. (1978), 'The Liberals Make their Point', *Financial Times* (3 Feb.).

Engineering Employers Federation (1972), *Business Performance and Industrial Relations* (Kogan Page).

—— (1977), *Practical Applications of Added Value* (Archway Press).

Estes, R. (1973), *Accounting and Society* (Los Angeles: Melville Publishing Co.)

—— (1976), *Corporate Social Accounting* (New York: John Wiley).

Fanning, D. (1978), 'Banishing Confusion from the Added Value Equation', *Financial Times* (13 Dec.): 11.

Fels, A. (1972), *The British Prices and Incomes Board* (Cambridge: Cambridge University Press).

Flint, D. (1971), 'The Role of the Auditor in Modern Society: An Exploratory Essay', *Accounting and Business Research* (Autumn): 287–93.

Foucault, M. (1977), 'Nietzsche, Genealogy, History', in M. Foucault (ed. by D. F. Bouchard), *Language, Counter-Memory; Practice* (Oxford: Basil Blackwell).

Frankel, M. (1978), *The Social Audit Pollution Handbook* (London: Macmillan).

Gambling, I. (1974), *Societal Accounting* (London: Macmillan).

Gandhi, N. M. (1976), 'The Emergence of the Postindustrial Society and the Future of the Accounting Function', *International Journal of Accounting* (Spring): 33–49.

—— (1978), 'Accounting in a Non Market Economy: A Futuristic Look', in L. A. Gordon (ed.), *Accounting and Corporate Responsibility* (Lawrence, Kan.: University of Kansas).

Gilling, D. M. (1976), 'Accounting and Social Change', *International Journal of Accounting* (Spring): 59–71.

Gold, M., Levie, H. and Moore, R. (1979), *The Shop Stewards' Guide to the Use of Company Information* (Nottingham: Spokesman Books).

Gordon, L. A. (ed.) (1978), *Accounting and Corporate Social Responsibility* (Lawrence, Kan.: University of Kansas).

Gospel, H. (1976), 'Disclosure of Information to Trade Unions', *Industrial Law Journal.*

Gray, S. I., and Maunders, K. T. (1980), *Value Added Reporting: Uses and Measurement* (London: Association of Certified Accountants).

Hacking, I. (1981), 'How Should we do the History of Statistics', *Ideology and Consciousness* (Spring): 15–26.

Hilton, A. (1978), *Employee Reports: How to Communicate Financial Information to Employees* (Cambridge: Woodhead-Faulkner).

Hindess, B. (1982), 'Power, Interests and the Outcomes of Struggles', *Sociology* (Nov.): 498–511.

Hird, C. (1975), *Your Employers' Profits* (Pluto Press).

—— (1980), 'Beware of Added Value', *New Statesman* (4 Aug.).

Holmes, G. (1977), 'How UK Companies Report their Employees', *Accountancy* (Nov.): 64–8.

Hopkins, L. (1975), 'Value Added', *Accountancy Age* (7 Nov.).

Hopwood, A. G. (1984), 'Accounting Research and Accounting Practice: The Ambiguous Relationship Between the Two'. Paper presented to the Conference on New Challenges for Management Research, Leuven, Belgium.

—— (1985), 'The Tale of a Committee that Never Reported: Disagreements on Intertwining Accounting with the Social', *Accounting, Organizations and Society*, 361–77.

—— (1987), 'The Archeology of Accounting Systems', *Accounting, Organizations and Society*, 207–34.

—— Burchell, S., and Clubb, C. (1980), 'The Development of Accounting in its International Context: Past Concerns and Emergent Issues', in A. Roberts (ed.), *A Historical and Contemporary Review of the Development of International Accounting* (Georgia State University).

Hussey, R. (1978), *Employees and the Employment Report—A Research Paper* (London: Touche Ross & Co.).

—— (1979), *Who Reads Employee Reports?* (London: Touche Ross & Co.).

Incomes Data Report (1977), 'New Thoughts on Profit Sharing at ICI', *Report 251* (Feb.): 21.

Institute of Chartered Accountants in England and Wales (ICAEW) (1969), 'Statement of Intent on Accounting Standards in the 1970s', *Accountant* (18 Dec.): 842–3.

—— (1978), *Survey of Published Accounts 1977* (ICAEW).

—— (1980), *Survey of Published Accounts 1979* (ICAEW).

Jenks, L. H. (1960), 'Early Phases of the Management Movement', *Administrative Science Quarterly*, 421–47.

Jensen, M. C., and Meckling, W. H. (1976), 'Theory of the Firm: Managerial Behavior, Agency Costs and Ownership Structure', *Journal of Financial Economics*, 305–60.

Jones, F. C. (1976), *The Economic Ingredients of Industrial Success* (James Clayton Lecture; London: The Institution of Mechanical Engineers).

Jones, F. T. (1978), 'Our Manufacturing Industry—The Missing £100,000 million', *National Westminster Bank Quarterly Review* (May): 8–17.

Kahn-Freud, O. (1977), 'Industrial Democracy', *Industrial Law Journal*, 75–6.

Kuhn, T. (1970), *The Structure of Scientific Revolutions*, 2nd edn. (Chicago: University of Chicago Press).

Labour Party (1974), *The Community and the Company*.

Labour Research (1978), 'Value Added' (Feb.).

Leyland, N. H. (1952), 'Productivity', in G. D. N. Worswick and P. H. Ady, *The British Economy 1945–1950* (Oxford: Clarendon Press).

Litterer, J. (1961), 'Systematic Management: The Search for Order and Integration', *Business History Review*, 461–76.

—— (1963), 'Systematic Management: Design for Organizational Recoupling in American Manufacturing Firms', *Business History Review*, 369–91.

Livingstone, J. I., and Gunn, S. C. (1974), *Accounting for Social Goals: Budgeting and Analysis of Non Market Projects* (London: Harper & Row).

Low, E. (1977), 'Forget Piecework and Develop a Fair Way to Reward Employees', *Accountants Weekly* (6 May): 16–17.

Lucas, R. J. (1979), *Pension Planning within a Major Company: A Case Study of the Negotiation of the British Leyland Pension Plan for Manual Workers* (Oxford: Pergamon Press).

McKersie, R. B., and Hunter, L. C. (1973), *Pay Productivity and Collective Bargaining* (Macmillan).

McLeay, S. (1983), 'Value Added: A Comparative Study', *Accounting, Organizations and Society*, 31–56.

Maitre, P. (1978), 'The Measurement of the Creation and Distribution of Wealth in a Firm by the Method of Surplus Accounts', *Accounting, Organizations and Society*, 227–36.

Marchington, M. P. (1977), 'Worker Participation and Plant-wide Incentive Systems', *Personnel Review* (Summer): 35–8.

Medawar, C. (1978), *The Social Audit Consumer Handbook* (London: Macmillan).

Metal Box Company Limited (1948), *Added Value* (London: Metal Box Company Ltd.).

Minson, J. (1980), 'Strategies for Socialists? Foucault's Conception of Power', *Economy and Society*.

Moonitz, M. (1974), *Obtaining Agreement on Standards in the Accounting Profession*, Studies in Accounting Research No. 8 (Sarasota, Fla.: American Accounting Organization).

Morley, M. F. (1978), *The Value Added Statement* (Gee & Co. for the Institute of Chartered Accountants of Scotland).

National Board for Prices and Incomes (1968), *General Report, August 1967–July 1968* (Cmnd. 3715, London: HMSO).

Neimark, M. D., and Tinker, A. M. (1986), 'The Social Construction of Management Control Systems', *Accounting, Organizations and Society*.

Nelson, C. L. (1973), '*A Priori* Research in Accounting', in N. Dopuch and L. Revsine (eds.), *Accounting Research 1960–1970: A Critical Evaluation* (Champaign, Ill.: Center for International Education and Research in Accounting).

New, C. (1978), 'Factors in Productivity that Should Not be Overlooked', *The Times* (I Feb.).

Nietzsche, F. (1969), *On the Genealogy of Morals*, trans. W. Kaufmann (New York: Vintage Books).

Pakenham-Walsh, A. A. (1964), 'Spanners in the Growth Engine', *Cost Accountant* (July): 260–8.

Patton, P. (1979), 'Of Power and Prisons', in M. Morris and P. Patton (eds.), *Michel Foucault: Power, Truth, Strategy* (Sydney: Feral Publications).

Pelling, A. (1971), *A History of British Trade Unionism* (Harmondsworth: Penguin Books).

Pitkin, H. F. (1967), *The Concept of Representation* (Berkeley, Calif.: University of California Press).

Ramanathan, K. V. (1976), 'Theory of Corporate Social Accounting', *Accounting Review* (July): 516–28.

Reichmann, T., and Lange, C. (1981), 'The Value Added Statement as Part of Corporate Social Reporting', *Management International Review*.

Renshall, M., Allan, R., and Nicholson, K. (1979), *Added Value in External Financial Reporting* (London: Institute of Chartered Accountants in England and Wales).

Rey, F. (1978), *Introduction à la comptabilité sociale: domaines, techniques et applications* (Paris: Entreprise Moderne d'Édition).

Roberts, J., and Scapens, R. (1985) 'Accounting Systems and Systems of Accountability—Understanding Accounting Practices in their Organizational Contexts', *Accounting, Organizations and Society*, 443–56.

Robertson, J. (1974), 'Can we have a Non-Profit Society?', *Sunday Times* (19 May).

Ruggles, R., and Ruggles, N. D. (1965), *National Income Accounts and Income Analysis*, 2nd edn. (New York: McGraw Hill).

Rutherford, B. A. (1977), 'Value Added as a Focus of Attention for Financial Reporting: Some Conceptual Problems', *Accounting and Business Research* (Summer): 215–20.

—— (1978), 'Examining Some Value Added Statements', *Accountancy* (July): 48–52.

—— (1980), 'Published Statements of Value Added: A Survey of Three Year's Experience', *Accounting and Business Review* (Winter): 15–28.

Sandilands Committee (1975), *Inflation, Accounting: Report of the Inflation Accounting Committee* (Cmnd. 6225, London: HMSO).

Schreuder, H. (1979), 'Corporate Social Reporting in the Federal Republic of Germany: An Overview', *Accounting, Organizations and Society*, 109–22.

Searle, G. R. (1971), *The Quest for National Efficiency* (Oxford: Basil Blackwell).

Sharp, K. (1971), 'Accounting Standards After 12 Months', *Accountancy* (May): 239–45.

Skerratt, L. C. I., and Tonkin, D. J. (1982), *Financial Reporting 1982–83: A Survey of U.K. Published Accounts* (London: Institute of Chartered Accountants in England and Wales).

Smith, G. (1978), *Wealth Creation—the Added Value Concept* (London: Institute of Practitioners in Work Study, Organizations and Methods).

Stamp, E. (1985), 'The Politics of Professional Accounting Research: Some Personal Reflections', *Accounting, Organizations and Society*, 111–23.

Stolliday, I., and Attwood, M. (1978), 'Financial Inducement and Productivity Bargaining', *Industrial and Commercial Training*.

Stuttard, G. (1979), 'Industrial Democracy by the Back Door', *Financial Times* (21 Mar.).

Target (1948), 'The Facts About Factory Economics' (Nov.).

Tinker, A. M. (1980), 'Towards a Political Economy of Accounting: An Empirical Illustration of the Cambridge Controversies', *Accounting, Organizations and Society*, 147–60.

—— (1984), 'The Naturalization of Accounting: Social Ideology and the Genesis of Agency Theory'. Working paper, New York University.

—— Merino, B. D., and Neimark, M. D. (1982), 'The Normative Origins of Positive Theories: Ideology and Accounting Thought', *Accounting, Organizations and Society*, 167–200.

Tomlinson, J. (1981), *Problems of British Economic Policy, 1870–1945* (London: Methuen).

Tonkin, D. J., and Skerratt, L. C. L. (1983), *Financial Reporting 1983–84: A Survey of U.K. Published Accounts* (London: Institute of Chartered Accountants in England and Wales).

Trades Union Congress (1974), *Industrial Democracy* (London: TUC).

Turner, H. A. (1970), 'Collective Bargaining and the Eclipse of Incomes Policies: Retrospect, Prospect and Possibilities', *British Journal of Industrial Relations* (July).

Ullman, A. A. (1979), 'Corporate Social Reporting: Political Interests and Conflicts in Germany', *Accounting, Organizations and Society*, 123–33.

Vangermeersch, R. G. J. (1972), *Accounting: Socially Responsible and Socially Relevant* (London: Harper and Row).

Vickers da Costa (1979), *Testing for Success* (London: Mimeo).

Vogel, D. (1978), *Lobbying the Corporation: Citizen Challenges to Business Authority* (New York: Basic Books).

Watts, R. L. (1977), 'Corporate Financial Statements: A Product of the Market and Political Process', *Australian Journal of Management* (Apr.): 53–75.

—— and Zimmerman, J. L. (1979), 'The Demand for the Supply of Accounting Theories: The Market for Excuses', *Accounting Review* (Apr.): 273–305.

Watts, R. L., and Zimmerman, J. L., 'Towards a Positive Theory of the Determination of Accounting Standards', *Accounting Review* (Jan.): 112–34.

Wellens, J. (1977), 'An ICI Experiment in Company-wide Communication', *Industrial and Commercial Training* (July): 271–8.

Wells, M. C. (1976), 'A Revolution in Accounting Thought', *Accounting Review* (July): 471–82.

—— (1978), *Accounting for Common Costs* (International Centre for Accounting Education and Research, University of Illinois).

Whittington, G. (1983), *Inflation Accounting: An Introduction to the Debate* (Cambridge: Cambridge University Press).

Wilsher, P. (1974), 'How do you cut your Profit and Save Prosperity', *Sunday Times* (30 June).

Woodmansay, M. (1978), *Added Value: An Introduction to Productivity Schemes* (London: British Institute of Management).

Zeff, S. A. (1972), *Forging Accounting Principles in Five Countries* (Champaign, Ill.: Stipes).

—— (1978), 'The Rise of Economic Consequences', *Journal of Accountancy* (Dec.).

Zimmerman, J. L. (1979), 'The Cost and Benefits of Cost Allocations', *Accounting Review*, 504–21.

22 · IMPORTING AND EXPORTING ACCOUNTING: THE BRITISH EXPERIENCE

R. H. Parker

Accounting techniques, institutions, and concepts are all capable of being imported and exported from one country to another. The following discussion considers, by way of three case-studies, the British experience of such imports and exports and in particular the way in which the British have imported double-entry bookkeeping (a technique) and have exported professional accountancy (an institution) and a 'true and fair view' (a concept).

The analysis focuses on the British experience for two reasons. First, it is the one with which the writer is most familiar. Secondly, and more importantly, British accounting history is not just of parochial interest. From being, in the sixteenth century, distinctly underdeveloped in mercantile accounting, Britain became in the nineteenth the pioneer of modern professional accountancy. In the twentieth century, however, the United States has become the pace-setter in many aspects of accounting.

The scope of the discussion has been limited as follows. First, there is no consideration of which accounting techniques, institutions, or concepts *ought* to be transferred from one country to another and how this can best be done (Seidler 1969; Needles 1976). There is no assumption that one set of techniques, institutions, or concepts is inherently better than another.

Secondly, countries are taken as a whole, with no attempt to distinguish between early and late adopters of an import. This means that the emphasis is placed on economic rather than sociological variables (cf. Griliches 1971: 266). Thirdly, the analysis is not concerned with imports which may be regarded as choices among accounting policies and analysed as part of a con-

First published in A. Hopwood (ed.), *International Pressures for Accounting Change* (1989). Earlier drafts of this chapter were presented in 1985 at an EIASM workshop on 'Accounting and Culture' at the Free University of Amsterdam, at a number of Australian universities, and at the National University of Singapore. I have benefited greatly from comments received.

tracting process between managers and owners. (The literature in this area is summarized in Watts and Zimmerman 1986.)

The discussion is concerned with the international transfer of accounting technology (AT) in its widest sense. AT differs from physical productive technology in that it is non-proprietary (Taylor and Turley 1985: 3) and more specific to particular countries (Seidler 1969: 36–7).

Each case-study is built around the following questions:

1. What was available for import?
2. Who were the importers and exporters? Were they active or passive?
3. How did the importers find out about the potential import?
4. How did importers and exporters assess the costs and benefits?
5. How, if at all, were imports adapted, i.e. made appropriate to an environment different from that of the exporter?
6. How were problems of terminology dealt with?

DOUBLE-ENTRY BOOKKEEPING

Double-entry bookkeeping is a technique of recording economic events which was evolved by merchants in the Italian city states from the end of the thirteenth century onwards. It is not the only such technique and until about the year 1500 it was not used outside Italy except by Italian merchants who had established branches of their firms in other countries, including England (de Roover 1956).

In principle, techniques are easier to import than institutions or concepts since there are presumably no cultural, social, or political costs or benefits attached to them, but British merchants, the potential importers, did not start to adopt double entry until the sixteenth century.

To adopt a technique one must first find out about it. This was relatively easy since Italian merchants made no attempt to keep double entry a trade secret. On the other hand they were not active exporters. Italian cultural influence was strong throughout Europe, including England, during this period (as the settings of many of Shakespeare's plays attest) but both England and Scotland were influenced more by France and the Low Countries. The main commercial link with continental Europe was Antwerp, the port through which most English exports passed in the sixteenth and seventeenth centuries (Davis 1973).

The ways in which British merchants could obtain a knowledge of double entry can be listed as follows:

1. reading a manuscript or book (*a*) in a language other than English, (*b*) in English;
2. learning from a native teacher in Britain;
3. learning from a foreign merchant or teacher resident in Britain;
4. learning abroad from a foreign merchant or teacher.

There is evidence that all these sources were used. Textbooks on double entry were published in Italy from 1494 (Pacioli's *Summa*) and in the Netherlands, France, and Britain from 1543 onwards. A book which illustrates the way in which knowledge of double entry spread from country to country is Jan Ympyn's *Nieuwe instructie* . . . published in Antwerp in Flemish (Dutch) and French (as the *Nouvelle Instruction* . . .) in 1543 and in London in 1547 (as *A Notable and Very Excellente Woorke* . . .). In his Prologue the author states that his book is based on a translation of a work in Italian by one Juan Paulo di Bianchi. No published work by an author of this name is known and there has been much speculation about the existence of a manuscript which may have been used not only by Ympyn but also by Pacioli (Yamey 1967). Appended to Ympyn's work, unlike Pacioli's or Oldcastle's, is an illustrative set of books which, it has been plausibly suggested, may have been based on Ympyn's own business. The long title of the English version states that the book has been 'Translated with great diligence out of the Italian toung into Dutche, and out of Dutche, into French, and now out of French into Englishe'. It is clear from this (and other similar evidence) that knowledge of double entry was made available throughout sixteenth-century Europe through both books and manuscripts; that these were translated into various languages; and that they often contained illustrative sets of books (the first to do so was an Italian work by Tagliente published in 1525).

For merchants and their apprentices who needed oral as well as written instruction, teachers were available, many of whom were also textbook writers. Sixteenth-century English examples (with the dates of their books in brackets) include Hugh Oldcastle (1543), James Peele (1553, 1569), and John Mellis (1588).

It is also possible that some British merchants learned double entry from foreign merchants or teachers resident in Britain. The earliest double-entry or near double-entry record written up in England which has survived is an account book (1305–8) of the London branch of the Gallerani company of Siena. There is no evidence, however, that the Gallerani had any influence on indigenous English accounting records (Nobes 1982). More interesting in the history of English accounting are the four ledgers (1436–9) bound together in one volume of the London branch of the Borromei, a firm of merchant bankers with its main office in Milan. According to Kats (1926) the textbooks of James Peele have a number of features to be found in the Borromei ledgers but not in Pacioli. Kojima (1980: 63) has suggested that Oldcastle, a citizen and shearman (i.e. draper) acquainted with wool merchants, might have worked in an Italian firm or might have learnt the Italian language or Italian bookkeeping from contacts with Italian merchants. This, while plausible, is, of course, no more than conjecture.

It is possible that many British accountants learned more accounting from practical experience than they learned from books and teachers. The double-entry or near double-entry records of the sixteenth century which have survived suggest that English merchants may have gained such experience overseas (Ramsey 1956). These account books include the ledger of Thomas Howell, a member of the Drapers' Company resident and trading in Spain; the ledger of John Smythe, a leading merchant of Bristol; the journal of Sir Thomas Gresham; the ledger of John Johnson, a merchant of the Staple at Calais (a French port which was an English possession from 1347 to 1558); and ledgers and a journal of Thomas Laurence, a Merchant Adventurer. Howell's ledger was written up in Spain; Smythe also had strong Spanish connections (Vanes 1974). Gresham spent much of his career in the Netherlands. Johnson's business was in Calais; Laurence traded overseas.

One of the earliest English language texts, John Weddington's *A Breffe Instruction* . . . (1567), was even published in Antwerp rather than London. Weddington was an English merchant resident in Antwerp and at one time an agent of Gresham. His book differs in many ways from others of the time and it 'is highly probable that Weddington encountered the particular arrangement of the records, as taught by him in his book, in some business firm or firms in Antwerp' (Yamey 1958: 124).

There is no record of the use of double entry in Scotland before the seventeenth century, the first text on double entry, Colinson's *Idea rationaria*, being published as late as 1683. The books (1696–1707) of the ill-fated Darien Scheme ('The company of Scotland trading to Africa and the Indies') were, it has been said, kept 'in exact concordance with the methods . . . in the school-masters' lesson-books' by a 'clerk who might have been Pacioli himself' (Row Fogo in Brown 1905: 157). In Scotland, textbooks were, of course, readily available from England, but Dutch influence was also important. Colinson had lived and traded in the Netherlands, includes a Dutch quotation in his book, and dedicates it to the 'Lord Conservator of the Priviledges of the Scots Nation in the 17. Provinces of the Netherlands' (Parker 1974).

It is clear from the above that British merchants in the sixteenth and seventeenth centuries had every opportunity to adopt double entry if they wished to do so. In fact it appears that double entry made slow headway and was not in widespread use until the nineteenth century (Yamey 1977: 17). It was only in that century that it ceased to be generally known as the 'Italian method' of bookkeeping: an indication perhaps that the import had been completed.

Such a slow adoption presumably reflects British merchants' assessment of the costs and benefits. It can be argued that Britain's stage of commercial development when double entry was first available for import was such that double entry was not an 'appropriate technique'. At the beginning of the six-teenth century, and for some time afterwards, England and Wales was 'a small poor country with a single-crop economy [wool]' (Kenyon 1978: 15). Scotland was even smaller and poorer. Nearly two centuries later, however (about 1780), London had become the commercial centre of Europe.

There is little direct evidence of how British merchants perceived the bene-fits of double entry. The textbook writers, who, in order to sell their books, were more likely to overestimate than to underestimate, saw double entry as creating order from chaos by providing complete, integrated, and interlocking records within a self-correcting system; better knowledge of, and hence con-trol of, amounts owed and owing and of merchandise; and better profit calcu-lations on individual ventures. They placed little emphasis on profit calculations and measures of wealth related to the whole enterprise (Winjum 1972: 239–40). Yamey (1977: 17) finds little evidence in pre-nineteenth-century British accounting practice of systematic income measurement and asset valuation. Balancing was highly irregular and merchants more usually prepared inventories of their fortunes at irregular intervals. The profit and loss account was used as a place to which detailed but unwanted information could be removed. Winjum (1972, ch. 11) concludes that double entry was valued more for its ability to provide systematic and comprehensive recording than for its ability to provide accurate income determination.

It would appear that most British merchants did not, until the nineteenth century, require much of what double entry had to offer. Orderliness and control were of course worth having but could often be achieved without double entry. Interlocking and self-correcting records not always regarded as worth the effort. Annual profit calculation and asset valuation were of little use in the absence of sophisticated capital markets and income tax collectors, neither of which, so far as most business enterprises were con-cerned, were present until the late nineteenth century. It was only then that the benefits of double entry were generally perceived to exceed the costs.

One problem that any importers of a technique, institution, or concept must face is that of terminology, especially when importer and exporter do not share a common language. The importer has a number of options (Parker 1984: 119). He can treat the foreign words as native words; change them into native words; invent new words in his native language; or use already existing native words. English writers on double entry mainly chose the second option, taking and adapting from Italian such words as journal, folio, capital (replacing stock), cash (replacing money), and bank. It is also possible that the word bookkeeping is an adaptation of the equivalent Dutch word (Parker 1984: 114–16).

What can we conclude about the import of double entry into Britain? Double entry was a technique which reached British merchants without any active exporting on the part of its Italian inventors. It was adopted because of its merits but only to the extent that it was thought to be an appropriate technology and it thus spread only slowly. Although it was close trading ties with the Netherlands that first made British merchants aware of the technique, its Italian origins have left a lasting mark on English accounting terminology.

PROFESSIONAL ACCOUNTANCY

We turn next to professional accountancy. We may note first of all that this is a more difficult import or export than double entry because it is an institution rather than a technique. Acceptance of the existence of self-regulating professional organizations, especially when they act as qualifying associations independent of any government control, implies acceptance of a particular form of economic and social structure.

There was little need for professional accountancy in Britain before the nineteenth century. Previously, accounting was regarded simply as one of the necessary skills of a merchant. In the nineteenth century, however, the growth of large-scale organizations and in particular of the railways, the development of the limited liability company, the high rate of insolvencies, and the introduction of income taxation produced demands for insolvency, auditing, costing, and tax services. These demands led to the emergence of specialist experts who came together to discuss common problems, to distinguish competent and honourable practitioners from incompetent and dishonourable ones, to raise their status, and to protect their material interests. They endeavoured to achieve these aims by formal association (Parker 1986).

The way in which this took place (the 'British model' of professional accountancy) can be deduced from Table 22.1 which lists the numerous professional accountancy bodies established during the period 1853 to 1919. Three characteristics of these bodies may be discerned:

TABLE 22.1 *Accountancy bodies formed in the British Isles: 1853–1919*

1853	Society of Accountants in Edinburgh (royal charter 1854)[a]
1853	Institute of Accountants and Actuaries in Glasgow (royal charter 1855)[a]
1867	Society of Accountants in Aberdeen[a]
1870	Incorporated Society of Liverpool Accountants[b]
1870	Institute of Accountants in London[b]
1871	Manchester Institute of Accountants[b]
1872	Society of Accountants in England[b]
1877	Sheffield Institute of Accountants[b]
1880	Institute of Chartered Accountants in England and Wales
1880	Scottish Institute of Accountants[c]
1885	Society of Accountants and Auditors[d]
1885	Corporate Treasurers' and Accountants' Institute[e]
1888	Institute of Chartered Accountants in Ireland
1891	Corporation of Accountants in Scotland[f]
1903	Institute of Certified Public Accountants[g]
1904	London Association of Accountants[f]
1905	Central Association of Accountants[h]
1919	Institute of Cost and Works Accountants[i]

[a] Merged to form Institute of Chartered Accountants of Scotland, 1951.
[b] Merged to form Institute of Chartered Accountants in England and Wales, 1880.
[c] Absorbed by the Society of Accountants and Auditors, 1899.
[d] Name changed to Society of Incorporated Accountants and Auditors, 1908; to Society of Incorporated Accountants, 1954; integrated into the English, Scottish and Irish Chartered Institutes, 1957.
[e] Name changed to Institute of Municipal Treasurers and Accountants, 1901; to Chartered Institute of Public Finance and Accountancy, 1973.
[f] Amalgamated in 1939 to form the Association of Certified and Corporate Accountants.
[g] Amalgamated in 1941 with the Association of Certified and Corporate Accountants (from 1971 the Association of Certified Accountants and from 1984 the Chartered Association of Certified Accountants).
[h] Absorbed by the Institute of Certified Public Accountants, 1933.
[i] Name changed to Institute of Cost and Management Accountants, 1972; to Chartered Institute of Management Accountants, 1986.

1. Many were formed on a regional basis and there are indeed still three separate Institutes of Chartered Accountants in the British Isles: of Scotland, in England and Wales, and in Ireland (covering both the Republic of Ireland and Northern Ireland).
2. If, in the absence of government regulation, the founders of an associa-

tion are allowed to decide who is to be allowed to join and who is not, those who are excluded are likely to consider themselves harshly treated and to go out and form their own association (which explains the present existence of a Chartered Association of Certified Accountants).

3. Since accountants practise not one technique but a related set of techniques, specialized associations may be formed, as happened with local government accountants in 1885 and cost accountants in 1919.

Professional accountancy can be imported and exported in a variety of ways, which may be listed as follows:

1. The *idea* of professional accountancy is exported, i.e. local accountants form their own association on (*a*) the British model, or (*b*) some other model.
2. British accounting *qualifications* are exported, i.e. local accountants either (*a*) form a local branch of a British body, or (*b*) become full members of a British body, by (i) qualifying in Britain, or (ii) qualifying in their own country.

The combination of British political and economic dominance and of technological advances meant that knowledge of professional accountancy developments in Britain could spread rapidly. By the end of the nineteenth century the British Empire covered Canada, the Australian continent and New Zealand, much of southern, central, east, and west Africa, India, Ceylon, parts of South-East Asia, and numerous islands in the Mediterranean, Caribbean, Atlantic, Indian, and Pacific Oceans. Moreover, Britain's 'informal empire' (Gallagher and Robinson 1953) of overseas trade and investment spread well beyond these, notably to the United States, Argentina, and Brazil. Many 'local accountants' were in fact British accountants (not necessarily members of a formal association) who had emigrated overseas. Steamships and the telegraph gave even remote Australia reliable and fast links with Britain and helped to defeat the 'tyranny of distance' (Blainey 1966, ch. 9).

The formation of associations on the British model, but independent of British bodies, was most common in Canada, Australia, New Zealand, and South Africa, as is demonstrated in Table 22.2. The merits of such associations were expressed by a pioneer accountant in Melbourne, Thomas Brentnall, as follows:

It was gradually borne in upon a few of us that if those who were holding themselves out as public practitioners were to gain the confidence and support of the public, there must be a standard fixed which would connote the possession of the necessary qualifications for this special work. To that end a meeting was held [in Melbourne]

on April 12, 1886, at which thirty practising accountants met to consider the propriety of establishing an 'Association of those having kindred interests in their common
calling, and a desire to place their profession on a higher plane than it had previously
occupied in public esteem'. We knew the position attained by the Institute of
Chartered Accountants in England and Wales, which had been incorporated by
Royal Charter in 1880, by the Society of Accountants and Auditors in 1885, as well
as the three Scottish Institutes which had come into existence some years previously.
With these examples before us, we had no difficulty in arriving at the conclusion that
our object could best be attained by following in their footsteps. (Brentnall 1938:
64).

As we shall see later, the accountants of Melbourne consciously rejected the
alternative of constituting themselves a branch of a British body.

Table 22.2 clearly shows the inheritance of both regionalism (e.g. by 1904
there was a separate professional body in every Australian state) and duplication (e.g. the larger Australian states had more than one body). Later (and
thus not shown in the table), specialized bodies were also formed.

American accountants also formed their own associations but they adapted
the British model to their own needs. The right to practise public accoun-

TABLE **22.2** *Accountancy bodies formed in Canada, Australia, New Zealand, and South Africa:
1880–1904*

1880	The Association of Accountants in Montreal
1883	The Institute of Chartered Accountants of Ontario
1885	The Adelaide Society of Accountants (renamed the Institute of Accountants in South Australia, 1889)
1886	The Chartered Accountants' Association of Manitoba
1887	The Incorporated Institute of Accountants of Victoria (renamed Commonwealth Institute of Accountants, 1921)
1891	The Queensland Institute of Accountants
1894	The Sydney Institute of Public Accountants
1894	The Incorporated Institute of Accountants of New Zealand
1894	The Federal Institute of Accountants and Auditors in the South African Republic (became Transvaal branch of the [British] Society of Accountants and Auditors, 1902)
1895	The Institute of Accountants in Natal
1897	The Tasmanian Institute of Accountants
1898	The New Zealand Accountants' and Auditors' Association
1899	The Corporation of Accountants of Australia (Sydney)
1900	The Institute of Accountants and Auditors of Western Australia
1900	The Society of Accountants and Auditors of Victoria
1900	The Institute of Chartered Accountants of Nova Scotia
1902	The Dominion Association of Chartered Accountants (Canada)
1903	The Institute of Chartered Accountants in South Africa
1904	The Institute of Accountants of British Columbia
1904	The Transvaal Society of Accountants

tancy came to depend upon a licensing authority (normally one of the states) with not all public accountants so certified considering it necessary to join a professional body. Unlike Britain, Canada, and Australia, the United States managed to avoid a multiplicity of competing professional bodies. In the first comprehensive survey of accountancy bodies round the world, made on the occasion of the fiftieth anniversary of the Edinburgh Society of Accountants, Brown (1905: 274) compared the advantages of the two models: 'The American plan prevents more effectively the misuse of the title adopted, while the British insures the benefits of association. There is greater freedom and elasticity under the British system, which is, however, accompanied by some liability to abuse.' Brown could also have pointed out that the British model lends itself more easily to the export of professional qualifications, since the barrier of a home-based licensing authority does not exist (Seidler 1969: 44). British accountants have in fact been active exporters of professional accountancy qualifications. By the 1900s there were about 400 members of British accountancy bodies around the British Empire, forming 6 per cent of a total membership of about 7,000. In round terms 200 of the 400 were in Africa (mainly South Africa) and 100 in Australasia. Of the 400 over 70 per cent were incorporated accountants (Johnson and Caygill 1971).

The attitudes of the various British bodies to accountancy overseas differed in interesting ways. The English Institute insisted that English chartered accountants could only be trained in England and Wales; the Scottish bodies, with their small home base, allowed training in England and Wales as well as in Scotland. The smaller home base also meant a greater migration of Scots CAs not only to England and Wales but also to the Empire and Commonwealth. In the 1900s, 4 per cent of them were located there; in the 1920s, 1940s, and 1960s, 11 per cent (Johnson and Caygill 1971: table I, p. 158); in the 1970s and 1980s, 7 per cent. Unlike certified accountants (see below) they were and are mainly to be found in the 'old' Commonwealth.

The Society of Incorporated Accountants and Auditors, however, kept in second place by the chartered bodies in the United Kingdom, made, under the indefatigable leadership of James Martin, determined efforts to expand through the British Empire. The historian of the Society (Garrett 1961: 14) reports that 'At an early stage the Society claimed for itself a "British Empire" policy.' The success of this varied from country to country.

In Australia it was unsuccessful. A commissioner for Australia (a Mr Charles A. Cooper) appointed in 1886 established a committee in Victoria but was not able to make the Society the nucleus of a nascent profession in

Australia. The first annual report of the Incorporated Institute of Accountants of Victoria (the body of which Brentnall was a founding member) records that 'Mr Cooper's proposals were, after careful consideration, set aside in favour of a local independent body'. Martin was, however, appointed in 1888 as a corresponding member of the Institute in London (Commonwealth Institute of Accountants 1936; 8, 17). Nevertheless Martin complained at the First International Congress of Accountants in St Louis that Australia was 'dominated very largely by the working classes, and the working classes of Australia have nothing in common with professional men, and they brought our efforts to naught' (Official Record 1978: 105). Local practitioners in each colony formed their own accountancy bodies which after many vicissitudes were merged into the Institute of Chartered Accountants in Australia (1928) and the Australian Society of Accountants (1958).

What it failed to do in Australia, the Society was successful in achieving in South Africa (Garrett 1961: 14, 55–9)—perhaps because Martin was able to go to South Africa personally (yet another example of the 'tyranny of distance' so important in Australian history); perhaps because South African governments were not dominated by the working classes; but also perhaps because accountants in Johannesburg 'having regard to the wide ramifications and finance of the mining industry . . . preferred to become part of a British Society with world-wide connexions, rather than remaining members of a body with local limitations' (Garrett 1961: 57). A mining industry also existed in Australia but its links with Britain were rather less. The South African arrangement lasted until the late 1950s.

Apart from Australia and South Africa, the Society established branches in Canada (Montreal, 1905), India (Bombay, 1931; Bengal, 1933), and Central Africa (Salisbury, 1954). A president of the Society, Harry L. Price, has even been claimed as the 'unlikely father' of the present organizational form of chartered accountancy in Canada. It was under Price's chairmanship during the 1908 conference in Atlantic City, New Jersey, of the American Association of Public Accountants that the Dominion Association of Chartered Accountants and the Institute of Chartered Accountants of Ontario were reconciled. The event has a symbolic significance and according to the historian of the Ontario Institute is 'so beautifully and typically Canadian it is hard to imagine how it could be improved' (Creighton 1984: 63).

As the Society became stronger in the United Kingdom, its overseas activities became less important, and it underwent a 'loss of enthusiasm for Empire glory once it had fully established its position at home' (Johnson and Caygill 1971: 159).

By 1957, when the Society merged with the Chartered Institutes, the Association was already playing the leading role in this area which it has retained ever since. Between 1913 and 1967 the Association established branches in South Africa, India, Malaya, Jamaica, Trinidad, Hong Kong, Central Africa, Cyprus, British Guiana, Nigeria, the Bahamas, Canada, and Tanzania (Johnson and Caygill 1971). The Chartered Association, as it has now become, remains the world's largest exporter of accountancy qualifications. Six per cent of the Association's members were in the Commonwealth in the 1920s, rising to 11 per cent in the 1960s and 33 per cent in the 1980s. As already noted, overseas certified accountants, unlike overseas Scots CAs, are to be found in the 'new' Commonwealth rather than the 'old'. The Institute of Cost and Management Accountants has also built up a significant overseas membership in the last two decades (Banyard 1985: 56, 79, 89).

As was the case with incorporated accountants in South Africa, many of the overseas members of the Association are also members of their own local accountancy bodies. It is a measure of the prestige value attaching to a word that most of these are 'chartered' rather than 'certified'. The historian of the English Institute (Howitt 1966: 194–5) noted that 'chartered' bodies had been formed outside the United Kingdom as follows: Canada (1902, earlier in some provinces), Australia (1928, the only one based on a royal charter), Rhodesia (now Zimbabwe) (1928), South Africa (1946, earlier in some provinces), India (1949), Ceylon (now Sri Lanka) (1959), Pakistan (1961), Ghana (1963), Jamaica (1965), and Nigeria (1965). Since that date may be added the Bahamas, Bangladesh, Barbados, and Trinidad and Tobago.

What can we conclude about the British experience as an exporter of the institution of professional accountancy? Professional accountancy was both actively exported and actively imported. On the exporting side, some British bodies have been much more active than others, the difference being explainable in terms of their relative strengths in the home market. On the importing side, the United States actively imported the idea of professional accountancy (but not on the British model); Canada, Australia, and New Zealand actively imported the British model but preferred to form their own local bodies rather than import British accounting qualifications; the countries of the 'new' Commonwealth have been twentieth-century importers of British qualifications and have formed local bodies only recently; South African accountants until the 1950s were willing to hold both local and British qualifications.

How can these differences be explained? The active nineteenth-century importers were in general located in those temperate regions of recent settlement which were recipients of British overseas investment; which had experienced British colonial rule but attained independence or a considerable measure of self-government; and where British cultural influence was strong and the English language dominant.

It is important to note the complex pattern of influences. Professional accountancy on the British model did not simply follow the direction of British investment, which appears to have been a necessary but not a sufficient condition. Thus, the British model was not adopted in those areas (the United States and South America) to which British investment was directed most (see Table 22.3). Nor was it adopted first in those areas where British political power was the strongest but, on the contrary, it succeeded best in those parts of the Empire which had achieved most self-government. In the twentieth century professional accountancy bodies have developed most rapidly after the achievement of independence. Under colonial rule development was sometimes slowed down by, for example, restricting public company audits to members of British bodies (Johnson and Caygill 1971: 170; Kapadia: 1973). On the other hand professional accountancy made little

TABLE 22.3 *Direction of new British portfolio investment 1865–1914*

	%
By continent	
North America	34
South America	17
Asia	14
Europe	13
Australasia	11
Africa	11
	100
By political status	
Independent	59
British Empire	40
Foreign dependencies	1
	100
By climatic-ethnic category	
Temperate regions of recent European settlement	68
Tropics	27
Non-tropical Asia	5
	100

Source: Simon (1967).

headway in areas such as South America where Britain had considerable investments but no political power.

For local professional bodies to develop on the British model, the further factor of strong British cultural influence (as in Australia, New Zealand, Canada, and to a lesser extent South Africa) was needed. British investment alone was not sufficient. 'In neither [the United States nor Argentina]', a distinguished economic historian has concluded, 'did the British create the social structure they encountered. Their [economic] activity aided and abetted the tendencies that were already there' (Jenks 1951: 388). These conclusions can be extended to professional accountancy.

TRUE AND FAIR VIEW

We turn finally to a discussion of an accounting concept, that of a true and fair view. In principle, just as an institution should be more difficult to export or import than a technique, a concept should be more difficult than an institution, since what is being transferred is part of a culture and culture cannot easily be transferred piecemeal. On the other hand, concepts are expressed as forms of words rather than as actions or physical things, so apparent exports or imports may be easier.

The concept of a true and fair view received its first legal formulation in the British Companies Act 1947 but its origins can be traced back to the mid-nineteenth century (Chastney 1975). It represents an amalgam of the previous Acts (see Table 22.4). The provisions of the 1947 Act (reenacted in the 1948 Act) followed the recommendations of the Cohen Committee on Company Law Amendment (1945), which in turn followed the memorandum submitted to it by the Institute of Chartered Accountants in England and Wales.

It is much less easy than in the previous sections of this chapter to state what was available for import, for British accountants have never defined very clearly what a true and fair view is or how to make it operational. An authoritative view of one of the accountant members of the Cohen Committee (Kettle 1950: 117) was that: 'A true and fair view implies that all statutory and other essential information is not only available but is presented in a form in which it can be properly and readily appreciated.' Asked for an explanation by continental Europeans when the Fourth Directive was under discussion in the 1970s, British accountants referred to 'fairness of presentation (i.e. unbiased as between the different users of financial information) and

Table **22.4** *Extracts from British Companies Acts*

1844   'the Directors . . . shall cause . . . a full and fair Balance Sheet to be made up' (s. 35).

1862   'The Auditors shall make a Report to the Members upon the Balance Sheet and Accounts, and in every such Report they shall state whether, in their Opinion, the Balance Sheet is a full and fair Balance Sheet, containing the Particulars required by these Regulations, and properly drawn up so as to exhibit a true and correct View of the State of the Company's Affairs' (para. 94, table A).

1879   (Banking Companies) 'The auditor or auditors . . . shall state whether, in his or their opinion, the balance sheet . . . is a full and fair balance sheet properly drawn up so as to exhibit a true and correct view of the state of the company's affairs, as shown by the books of the company' (s. 7)

1900   'the auditors . . . shall state whether, in their opinion, the balance sheet . . . is properly drawn up so as to exhibit a true and correct view of the state of the company's affairs as shown by the books of the company' (s. 23).

1948   '(1) Every balance sheet of a company shall give a true and fair view of the state of affairs of the company as at the end of its financial year, and every profit and loss account of a company shall give a true and fair view of the profit or loss for the financial year. . . .

(3) . . . the [detailed] requirements of [the 8th Schedule] shall be without prejudice either to the general requirements of subsection (1) of this section or to any other requirements of this Act' (s. 149, re-enacting s. 13, Companies Act 1947).

1985   '(2) The balance sheet shall give a true and fair view of the state of affairs of the company as at the end of the financial year; and the profit and loss account shall give a true and fair view of the profit or loss of the company for the financial year.

(3) Subsection (2) overrides—

(a) the requirements of Schedule 4, and

(b) all other requirements of this Act as to the matters to be included in a company's accounts or in notes to those accounts:

and accordingly the following two subsections have effect.

(4) If the balance sheet or profit and loss account drawn up in accordance with those requirements would not provide sufficient information to comply with subsection (2), any necessary additional information must be provided in that balance sheet or profit and loss account, or in a note to the accounts.

(5) If, owing to special circumstances, in the case of any company, compliance with any such requirement in relation to the balance sheet or profit and loss account would prevent compliance with subsection (2) (even if additional information were provided in accordance with subsection (4)), the directors shall depart from that requirement in preparing the balance sheet or profit and loss account (so far as necessary in order to comply with subsection (2)).

(6) If the directors depart from any such requirement, particulars of the departure, the reasons for it and its effect shall be given in a note to the accounts' (s. 228—re-enactment of s. 149 of 1948 Act as amended by 1981 Act; s. 230 provides similarly for group accounts).

frank[ness] in the recognition of economic substance rather than mere legal form' (Rutteman 1984: 8). One British commentator has concluded that 'True and fair is what you make it' (Chastney 1975: 92).

The potential importers of the concept in the 1950s were those countries which were accustomed, when amending their company legislation, to give great weight to British law, i.e. most of the member countries of the British Commonwealth. Australia may be taken as an example.

The legislation of the Australian States echoed the requirements of United Kingdom legislation fairly closely until the 1970s (NCSC 1984: 8–9). There were originally good reasons for this which were expressed by parliamentarians and lawyers as follows:

Investors at Home [i.e. in the United Kingdom] were shy about investing in a State whose company law they did not understand. (Manifold 1910, quoted Gibson 1971: 48)

uniformity would give to Victoria the guidance of English decisions and English textbooks on the Act would continuously furnish precedents and illustrations. Divergence would mean uncertainty . . . access to a wide range of experience is vital, and . . . this the narrow limits of a small community cannot furnish. (Moore 1934: 182).

These views prevailed into the 1950s and 1960s and the Victorian Act of 1955 and the Uniform Companies Acts based on it all included the phrase 'true and fair view'. The requirement remains in present Australian company law.

By the 1960s, however, the United States was replacing Britain as Australia's main trading partner and source of investment, and knowledge of American accounting was spreading. Australian accountants began to define a true and fair view in an American as well as a British way.

Recommendation on Accounting Principles No. 1 (1963) of the Australian Institute, for example, stated that a true and fair view 'implies appropriate classification and grouping of the items . . . [and] also implies the consistent application of generally accepted principles'. In 1984 the Auditing Standards Board (AuSB) of the Australian Accounting Research Foundation (AARF) issued Statement of Auditing Practice AUP3, 'The Auditor's Report on Financial Statements' (Pound 1984), which sought to introduce a reporting format in which the auditor's opinion was formed and expressed in the context of whether financial statements 'present fairly the financial position and results in accordance with Australian Accounting Standards'.

However, a consultative document of the Australian National Companies and Securities Commission (written by Professor R. G. Walker of the University of New South Wales) rejected suggestions that a true and fair view should be stated to be in accord with generally accepted accounting principles or approved accounting standards and proposed the following addition to the Australian Act:

Without affecting the generality of the meaning of the term, *'true and fair view,'* a 'true and fair view' in relation to accounts or group accounts means a representation which affords those who might reasonably be expected to refer to those accounts (including holders or prospective purchasers of shares, debentures, notes or other interests, and creditors or prospective creditors) information which is relevant to the decisions which may be made by those persons in relation to the purchase, sale or other action in connection with their securities or interests. (NCSC 1984: 3)

The Auditing Standards Board reacted strongly against this recommendation, which it regarded as placing 'an impossible responsibility on accountants, auditors and directors', and recommended instead the phrase 'present fairly . . . in accordance with approved accounting standards and comply with the Companies Code' (Edwards 1985).

Whilst Australian accountants have begun to doubt the wisdom of their import, continental Europeans have been persuaded to write the concept of a true and fair view into their legislation. Table 22.5 shows how the wording of the relevant clause, which at first closely followed German law, was changed during the discussions of the various drafts. The changes were made at the suggestion of the United Kingdom negotiators but at the same time a minute of the Council of Ministers was recorded to the effect that in general following the provisions of the directive would be sufficient to achieve a true and fair view of a company's economic situation (Rutteman 1984: 8).

British accountants were keener to export the concept of a true and fair view than accountants of other EEC member states such as France and Germany were to import it. Whilst British accountants genuinely believe in the importance of the concept and its general applicability, the export took place in order to protect its role in British accounting rather than in the expectation of other countries making radical changes in their own accounting styles. It may be doubted whether a concept developed in a country where the main users of financial statements are investors is appropriate to countries where the main users are government (as tax collectors), creditors, and trade unions. This may not matter, however, if the concept is interpreted in such a way as to fit its new environment.

This is quite likely to happen. In France, for example, there was, before the Fourth Directive, already a requirement for financial statements to be *régulier*

TABLE 22.5 *'True and fair' in the Fourth Directive*

1971 Draft	1. The annual accounts shall comprise the balance sheet, the profit and loss account and the notes on the accounts. These documents shall constitute a composite whole.
	2. The annual accounts shall conform to the principles of regular and proper accounting.
	3. They shall be drawn up clearly and, in the context of the provisions regarding the valuation of assets and liabilities and the lay-out of accounts, shall reflect as accurately as possible the company's assets, liabilities, financial position and results.
1974 Draft	1. (as 1971 Draft)
	2. The annual accounts shall give a true and fair view of the company's assets, liabilities, financial position and results.
	3. They shall be drawn up clearly and in accordance with the provisions of this Directive.
1978 Final	1. (as 1971 Draft)
	2. They shall be drawn up clearly and in accordance with the provisions of this Directive.
	3. The annual accounts shall give a true and fair view of the company's assets, liabilities, financial position and profit or loss.
	4. Where the application of the provisions of this Directive would not be sufficient to give a true and fair view within the meaning of paragraph 3 additional information must be given.
	5. Where in exceptional cases the application of a provision of this Directive is incompatible with the obligation laid down in paragraph 3, that provision must be departed from in order to give a true and fair view within the meaning of paragraph 3. Any such departure must be disclosed in the notes on the accounts together with an explanation of the reasons for it and a statement of its effect on the assets, liabilities, financial position and profit or loss. The Member States may define the exceptional cases in question and lay down the relevant special rules.

Source: Nobes and Parker 1984: 84.

(in accordance with the letter of the regulations) and *sincère* (in accordance with the spirit of the regulations). French law now requires that the statements be not only *réglier et sincère* but also show a true and fair view (*une image fidèle*). What this means has led to considerable debate (Pham 1984), but the most probable result is that the concept will have no effect on the balance sheet and profit and loss account but will lead to additional disclosures in the notes to the accounts (which have assumed a new importance in France as a result of the Directive). It is not expected that German financial statements will change their nature unless the underlying economic and social structures do so first (Busse von Colbe 1984). The general idea of a true and fair view existed in Dutch law before the Fourth Directive, although not in so many words. The law (as now stated in the Civil Code, article 362) has not been substantially changed in this respect and there is, for instance, no explicit reference to a true and fair view in Moret and Limperg's (1984) commentary on the new Dutch legislation on annual reports.

The phrase 'true and fair view' is Britain's contribution to twentieth-century accounting terminology. Those importers for whom English is a native language have not had to translate it. Continental European importers on the other hand have had the task of translating the phrase into their own language (Rutherford 1983). In French a true and fair view becomes *une image fidèle*, in Italian *un quadro fedele*, in Dutch *een getrouw beeld*. German speakers have had difficulty in finding the right translation. The more or less literal *ein getreue Einblick* gave way to *ein den tatsächlichen Verhältnissen entsprechendes Bild*, which may be translated as 'a picture corresponding to actual conditions'.

It is interesting to note that all four languages prefer a 'picture' to a 'view' and (except the 1978 German) express 'true and fair' by one word whose most literal translation is 'faithful'. This at least avoids the British and Australasian discussions about financial statements which are true but not fair. An American accountant unaware of the original English might translate the Continental phrases as 'representational faithfulness' or 'faithful representation'. Whilst it is at first sight surprising that the Continental European countries have accepted such a concept it is clear that what they have really imported is a form of words which they are translating and applying so as not to disturb unduly what already exists. Perhaps this is the fate of all indefinable concepts.

SOME CONCLUSIONS

An analysis of the case-studies presented in the preceding sections suggests two sets of conclusions. First, both exporters and importers must be considered and there is an important distinction between active exporters and importers on the one hand and passive exporters and importers on the other. Secondly, in assessing costs and benefits the position of exporters in their home markets is important, whilst it makes a difference to the importer whether it is a technique, an institution, or a concept that is being imported.

The relationship between exporters and importers can be set out as follows:

A. Active exporter   Active importer
B. Active exporter   Passive importer
C. Passive exporter   Active importer
D. Passive exporter   Passive importer

Clearly, an import and export is likely to take place most quickly and effectively when an active exporter is faced with an active importer (situation A) and is least likely to be quick and effective when a passive exporter is faced with a passive importer (situation D).

Active exporters and importers are those who have made an assessment of the costs and benefits of importing or exporting a technique, institution, or concept, have decided that the benefits outweigh the costs, and are eager to go ahead. Examples of active exporters in this chapter are British accountancy bodies interested in expanding overseas and the United Kingdom negotiators keen to get the EEC to accept the concept of a true and fair view.

Success has for such exporters depended in part upon what importers were willing to accept. British accountancy bodies have regarded the British Empire and Commonwealth as a legitimate market and have used appropriate economic, political, and cultural influence. The more advanced countries politically and economically have, however, preferred, and been able, to set up their own bodies rather than accept membership of British bodies. Continental Europeans have been willing to accept the concept of a true and fair view in the knowledge that they could adapt it to their own needs and also because they could successfully export standardized formats and valuation rules to Britain.

Examples of active importers are the Australian and Canadian accountants of the nineteenth century who formed accountancy bodies on the British model. They were also for a time active importers of British company accounting (including, in the case of Australia, the concept of a true and fair view).

Passive exporters and importers are those who have either not made an assessment of costs and benefits (perhaps through lack of knowledge) or have made the assessment and decided that the costs outweigh the benefits. An example of a passive exporter in this chapter is the early Italian practitioner of double entry. An example of a passive importer is a Continental European negotiator who accepted the British concept of a true and fair view. The three cases studied in this discussion can thus be entered in a matrix shown in Table 22.6.

The position of the exporter in the home market has been seen to be

TABLE **22.6** *Importing and exporting options*

Exporter	Importer	
	Active	Passive
Active	Professional accountancy	True and fair view
Passive	—	Double entry

important both in the spread of professional accountancy throughout the British Empire and Commonwealth and in the export of the true and fair view to Continental Europe. The former would probably have happened anyway, given the existence of active importers, but the latter would not have taken place if British practitioners had not been concerned to make sure that the concept survived in *British* law and practice.

It is easier to import a technique than an institution or a concept. Double entry has spread from Italy not just to Britain but to the whole world. Professional accountancy has spread more selectively. We have already noted Brown's (1905) findings for the United States and for Canada, Australia, South Africa, and New Zealand. In other British colonies Brown found accountants but not, at that date, professional bodies. In Continental Europe he noted the existence of bodies in Italy, Holland (from 1895), and Sweden (from 1899) but found none in any other European country. Where professional accountancy developed late in Europe it did so with more government intervention than in Britain or the United States and the bodies so created are less influential. They have not been created on either the British or American model and can hardly be regarded as imports from the United Kingdom or the United States.

Until recently, the concept of a true and fair view had spread even more selectively than professional accountancy, being confined to the United Kingdom and members of the British Commonwealth such as Australia, New Zealand, Nigeria, and Singapore. It was not found in Canada or the USA. How real its export to Continental Europe will be remains to be seen.

References

Banyard, C. W. (1985), *The Institute of Cost and Management Accountants: A History* (London: The Institute of Cost and Management Accountants).

Blainey, G. (1966), *The Tyranny of Distance* (Melbourne: Sun Books).

Brentnall, T. (1938), *My Memories* (Melbourne: Robertson & Mullins).

Brown, R. (1905), *A History of Accounting and Accountants* (Edinburgh: Jack).

Busse von Colbe, W. (1984), 'A True and Fair View: A German Perspective', in S. J. Gray and A. G. Coenenberg (eds.), *EEC Accounting Harmonisation: Implementation and Impact of the Fourth Directive* (Amsterdam: North-Holland).

Chastney, J. G. (1975), *True and Fair View: History, Meaning and the Impact of the Fourth Directive* (London: Institute of Chartered Accountants in England and Wales).

Commonwealth Institute of Accountants (1936), 'Historical Survey 1886–1936', in *Commonwealth Accountants' Year Book 1936* (Melbourne: Commonwealth Institute of Accountants).

Creighton, P. (1984), *Sum of Yesterdays* (Toronto: Institute of Chartered Accountants of Ontario).

Davis, R. (1973), *English Overseas Trade 1500–1700* (London: Macmillan).

de Roover, R. (1956), 'The Development of Accounting prior to Luca Pacioli According to the Account-Books of Medieval Merchants', in A. C. Littleton and B. S. Yamey, *Studies in the History of Accounting* (London: Sweet & Maxwell).

Edwards, B. (1985), '"True and Fair": Not Just an Academic Debate', *Chartered Accountant in Australia* (Mar.).

Gallagher, J., and Robinson, R. (1953), 'The Imperialism of Free Trade', *Economic History Review*, 2nd ser. 6 (repr. in W. R. Louis (ed.), *Imperialism* (New York: New Viewpoints, 1976)).

Garrett, A. A. (1961), *History of the Society of Incorporated Accountants 1885–1957* (Oxford: Oxford University Press).

Gibson, R. W. (1971), *Disclosure by Australian Companies* (Melbourne: Melbourne University Press).

Griliches, Z. (1971), 'Hybrid Corn and the Economics of Innovation', in N. Rosenberg (ed.), *The Economics of Technological Change* (Harmondsworth: Penguin Books) (1st pub. *Science*, 29 (July 1960)).

Howitt, (Sir) H. G. (1966), *The History of the Institute of Chartered Accountants in England and Wales 1880–1965 and of its Founder Accountancy Bodies 1870–1880* (London: Heinemann).

Jenks, L. H. (1951), 'Britain and American Railway Development', *Journal of Economic History* (Fall).

Johnson, T. J., and Caygill, M. (1971), 'The Development of Accountancy Links in the Commonwealth', *Accounting and Business Research* (Spring).

Kapadia, G. P. (1973), *History of the Accountancy Profession in India* (New Delhi: Institute of Chartered Accountants of India).

Kats, P. (1926), 'Double Entry Book-keeping in England before Hugh Oldcastle', *Accountant*, 74.

Kenyon, J. P. (1978), *Stuart England* (Harmondsworth: Penguin Books).

Kettle, R. (1950), 'Balance Sheets and Accounts under the Companies Act, 1948', in W. T. Baxter, *Studies in Accounting* (London: Sweet & Maxwell).

Kojima, O. (1980), 'James Peele and his Works', essay appended to James Peele, *The Pathe Waye to Perfectnes in th' Accomptes of Debtour and Creditour* (1st pub. 1569).

Moore, W. Harrison (1934), 'A Century of Victorian Law', *Journal of Comparative Legislation and International Law*, 3rd ser. 16.

Moret and Limperg (1984), *New Dutch Legislation on Annual Reports* (Rotterdam).

National Companies and Securities Commission (1984), *'A True and Fair View' and the Reporting Obligations of Directors and Auditors* (Canberra: Australian Government Publishing Service).

Needles, B. E. (1976), 'Implementing a Framework for the International Transfer of Accounting Technology', *International Journal of Accounting* (Fall).

Nobes, C. W. (1982), 'The Gallerani Account Book of 1305–1308', *Accounting Review* (Apr.).

—— and Parker, R. H. (1984), 'The Fourth Directive and the United Kingdom', in S. J. Gray and A. G. Coenenberg, *EEC Accounting Harmonisation: Implementation and Impact of the Fourth Directive.* (Amsterdam: North-Holland).

Official Record of the Proceedings of the Congress of Accountants . . . 1904 (1978) (New York: Arno Press).

Parker, R. H. (1974), 'The First Scottish Book on Accounting: Robert Colinson's *Idea rationaria* (1683)', *Accountant's Magazine* (Sept.).

—— (1984), 'Reckoning, Merchants' Accounts, Bookkeeping, Accounting or Accountancy? The Evidence of the Long Titles of Books on Accounting in English', in B. Carsberg and S. Dev, *External Financial Reporting* (London: Prentice Hall International).

—— (1986), *The Development of the Accountancy Profession in Britain to the Early Twentieth Century* (The Academy of Accounting Historians, Monograph Five).

Pham, D. (1984), 'A True and Fair View: A French Perspective', in S. J. Gray and A. G. Coenenberg (eds.), *EEC Accounting Harmonisation: Implementation and Impact of the Fourth Directive* (Amsterdam: North-Holland).

Pound, G. (1984), 'New Statement of Auditing Practice: AUP 3', *Chartered Accountant in Australia* (May).

Ramsey, P. (1956), 'Some Tudor Merchants' Accounts', in A. C. Littleton and B. S. Yamey, *Studies in the History of Accounting* (London: Sweet & Maxwell).

Rutherford, B. A. (1983), 'Spoilt Beauty: The True and Fair Doctrine in Translation', *AUTA Review* (Spring).

Rutteman, P. (1984), *The EEC Accounting Directives and their Effects* (Cardiff: University College Cardiff Press).

Seidler, L. J. (1969), 'Nationalism and the International Transfer of Accounting Skills', *International Journal of Accounting* (Fall).

Simon, N. (1967), 'The Pattern of New British Portfolio Foreign Investment,

1865–1914', in J. H. Adler, *Capital Movements and Economic Development* (London: Macmillan).

Taylor, P., and Turley, S. (1985), 'The International Transfer of Accounting Technology', University of Manchester Working Paper Series No. 8502.

Vanes, J. (1974) (ed.), *The Ledger of John Smythe 1538–1550* (Bristol: Bristol Record Society's Publications 28).

Watts, R. L., and Zimmerman, J. L. (1986), *Positive Accounting Theory* (Englewood Cliffs, NJ: Prentice-Hall).

Winjum, J. O. (1972), *The Role of Accounting in the Economic Development of England: 1500–1750* (Urbana, Ill.: Centre for International Education and Research in Accounting, University of Illinois).

Yamey, B. S. (1958), 'John Weddington's *A Breffe Instruction*, 1567', *Accounting Research* (Apr. 1958).

—— (1967), 'Fifteenth and Sixteenth Century Manuscripts on the Art of Bookkeeping', *Journal of Accounting Research* (Spring).

—— (1977), 'Some Topics in the History of Financial Accounting in England 1500–1900', in W. T. Baxter and S. Davidson (eds.), *Studies in Accounting* (London: Institute of Chartered Accountants in England and Wales).

23 · THE EVOLUTION OF FINANCIAL REPORTING IN JAPAN: A SHAME CULTURE PERSPECTIVE

T. E. Cooke

Great care must be taken in interpreting the context of developments in Japan, including accounting developments, because there is a substantial Japanese literature both at the popular and the academic levels that tries to emphasize that Japan is unique. This literature is referred to as the *nihonjinron* (literally, discussions of the Japanese). The core of the *nihonjinron* is not that Japan has characteristics different from other nations—since no two countries are identical—but rather that the 'Japanese are incomparably different [and that] the Japanese state of being is preferable [and] superior to what the rest of the world has to offer' (van Wolferen 1989: 264). The danger is that non-Japanese can become convinced that the *nihonjinron* is correct and can, as a consequence, make misinterpretations.

The foundation of the *nihonjinron* is adversarial contrast. Before the eighteenth century the adversary was China but it subsequently changed to the West. For much of the last 130 years the adversary has been the Occident, as though the West is homogeneous, a mistake that does not seem to inhibit the plethora of works which form the *nihonjinron*. Since this chapter is written by someone from the Occident it may offer a slightly different perspective on accounting developments in Japan from those presented by Japanese authors.

A chronological and interpretational approach has been adopted in structuring this paper and a summary of key events in accounting history in Japan is provided in the Appendix. The research method adopted has been based on a literature search that covered Japanese accounting, economic, political,

First published in *Accounting, Business and Financial History*, 1/3 (1991). The author would like to thank Professor M. Kikuya for his assistance and Professor R. H. Parker and the anonymous referees for their helpful comments.

and anthropological history derived from sources written in English, including some translated material. While no original Japanese-language material was consulted, my understanding of Japanese accounting has been enriched by a visit to Japan in 1988.[1] The first section of this chapter defines Japan's shame culture. This is followed by a consideration of early Japanese bookkeeping, the development of double-entry bookkeeping in the context of economic, legal, and cultural developments, the Allied Occupation and the post-war regulatory changes, and the development of two major financial reporting issues, consolidated accounts and segmented financial reports. At the outset it is essential to point out that the shame culture explanation is a partial one since other cultural, economic, and political factors are important to understanding the development process.

JAPAN'S SHAME CULTURE

Since an aspect of this chapter is to consider developments in relation to Japan's 'shame culture' it is important to define this concept. As the concept is controversial and heavily attacked by the *nihonjinron*, some detail must be provided. Benedict (1967) has emphasized the importance of shame rather than guilt in understanding different cultures. The distinction she makes is that a society which 'inculcates absolute standards of morality and relies on men's developing a conscience is a guilt culture by definition' (Benedict 1967: 156). Whereas a man who has sinned can obtain relief by confession and remorse, a man who is shamed cannot unburden himself by contrition. Consequently, 'shame cultures do not provide for confessions, even to the gods. They have ceremonies for good luck rather than expiation' (Benedict 1967: 156). Benedict defines shame as 'a reaction to other people's criticism. A man is shamed either by being openly ridiculed or rejected or by fantasying to himself that he has been made ridiculous. In either case it is a potent sanction. But it requires an audience or at least a man's fantasy of an audience. Guilt does not' (p. 157).

The important distinction that Benedict makes is that the Occidental nations can be classified as guilt cultures whereas Japan is a shame culture.[2] Such a distinction, and other aspects of her analysis, provoked the *nihonjinron*

[1] The author would like to thank the Research Board of the Institute of Chartered Accountants in England and Wales for their financial assistance.
[2] The distinction was made in the first edition of her book published in the US in 1946 when the Americans were trying to understand the psychology of the Japanese in a war situation.

616   *T. E. Cooke*

to make a concerted attack (see e.g. Aida 1972; Sakuta 1967; Doi 1971; Mori 1971). In contrast, there has been support for Benedict's thesis (see e.g. Dale 1986: 182–4).[3]

Having made the distinction between shame and guilt, it is important to consider the term 'culture' in this context. Bennett and Nagai (1953: 407) argue that the term 'culture' is generally accepted to mean 'high-level generalizations about the fundamental "design for living" of a society'. Kroeber and Kluckhohn (1952) identified 164 definitions of culture and Jahoda (1984: 140) has argued that the term is extremely elusive. More recent definitions include Hofstede (1980) and Rohner (1984). Hofstede (1980) defines culture as 'the collective programming of the mind which distinguishes the members of one human group from another' and this definition is useful for the purposes of this paper. The distinction between a shame and a guilt culture is accepted here as part of a number of possible influences on the evolution of financial reporting and the author accepts that a different interpretation and explanation can be developed based on economic motives.

ACCOUNTING DEVELOPMENTS TO 1900

The economic and cultural background

From 1639 the shogun (the generalissimo of the emperor's army and in actuality the overall ruler over Japan other than the emperor's court) cut Japan off from the rest of the world and the country continued to be isolated for a further 200 years. While some changes began towards the end of the Tokugawa period, the Meiji period in 1868 heralded the start of a concerted attempt to catch up and overtake the West, which formed the adversarial model of contrast. Even in the later part of the Tokugawa period Japan had a 'purely preindustrial economy [with an] archaic feudal system of autonomous domains' (Reischauer 1988: 78).

It can be argued that shame was important and the fantasy that Japan might be ridiculed by foreigners because of its feudal backwardness 'produced a literature of reverse identity, which placed all things foreign on a pedestal and demeaned anything smacking of the Orient' (Dale 1986: 176). As Shively (1971: 82) states, 'it is evidently a cultural characteristic of the

[3] Note that the shame–guilt distinction stems in part from the Protestant notion of internal dignity whereas external dignity is emphasized in Confucianism (Dale 1986: 182). However, empirical studies on China (see e.g. Eberhard 1967) have found that guilt rather than shame was an inherent part of their culture.

Japanese to be unusually self-conscious and anxious not to appear ridiculous in the eyes of foreigners'.

It is possible that the feeling of shame and backwardness in relation to the West could have been one of the catalysts. However, while there was a feeling of political, economic, and military inferiority when compared to the West (Reischauer 1988: 78–9), it is undeniable that the dispatch of a substantial US naval fleet, under the command of Commodore M. C. Perry, was significant in forcing the Japanese to allow the Americans into their ports.

An important aspect of this process of catching up was the Iwakura Mission.[4] In November 1871 a large party (in excess of 100 officials) left Japan to visit both Europe and the USA with a view to revising the unequal treaties[5] and to finding out as much as possible about the West (Soviak 1971: 7). When they returned in September 1873 they had realized that the process of catching up with the West would involve 'drastic political, judicial, and social reforms along Western lines, in addition to technological innovation and knowledge of international law. . . . That the Iwakura Mission was one significant factor in the development of modern Japan is unquestionable' (Soviak 1971: 7–8).

One element that the Iwakura Mission was impressed by was the paternal nature of Western business (Soviak 1971: 22). Such a model proved very influential and still forms the basis of modern large-firm organizations in which employees' lives are taken over to a much greater extent than in modern Western corporations. It is the paternal nature of modern Japanese corporations that assists in the process of tying the individual to the corporation and has the effect of ensuring long hours of labour and group pressure to demonstrate loyalty to their employers by not taking the whole of their annual leave entitlement (OECD 1989; Ezzamel, Hoskin, and Macve 1990).[6] Furthermore, the Iwakura Mission was also impressed by the close

---

[4] While other missions have been dispatched from time to time, for example the UK sent a mission to the USA after the Second World War, the Iwakura Mission was of fundamental importance to Japanese development, being more akin to the Eastern European delegations that have recently been sent to the West and Japan. The Mission sought to establish how Japan, the Japanese, and their institutions should change fundamentally to compete with the West.

[5] The unequal treaties, introduced in 1858 following Perry's activities, involved, first, tariff arrangements that the subsequent Meiji regime considered to be too low and, second, the condition that foreigners who broke Japanese laws were not to be dealt with in the Japanese courts but would instead be dealt with by the appropriate consular official. In 1899 the unequal treaties provisions expired after implementation of standards of law acceptable to the West. The new Code contained aspects of English, German, and French as well as Japanese law.

[6] The OECD Economic Survey on Japan (1988/9) points out that the average hours worked in Japan exceeded those worked in the UK and USA by more than 10% and exceeded those of Germany and France by nearly 25%. The Survey also notes that the share of workers having two days off each week was still only 30% in 1988. In addition, paid annual leave taken by Japanese workers was, on average, only 7.5

co-operation between business and government, especially in Germany. Close co-operation or interdependency between parties is a fundamental characteristic of modern Japan.

Introduction of double-entry bookkeeping into Japan

Before 1870 a variety of bookkeeping methods was used by merchants and some of these systems were specific to a particular firm (Ogura 1982; Taketera and Nishikawa 1984). Indeed, traditional methods of bookkeeping continued in use, in certain quarters, even after the introduction of the double-entry method of accounting, and some of those systems were treated as carefully guarded family secrets (Nishikawa 1977: 25–6). Whether or not the indigenous systems proved adequate is open to debate. For example, one leading Japanese authority, Nishikawa (1977: 25), argues that their adequacy is demonstrated by their continued use even after the importation of double-entry bookkeeping, whereas Someya (1989: 75) states that the double-entry method of bookkeeping 'replaced very unsatisfactory traditional methods'. Nishikawa (1977: 25) continues his argument by stating that double-entry spread to the rest of Europe, as a result of Italian trade, because there were few indigenous bookkeeping methods, a situation in stark contrast to that prevailing in Japan. Leading British researchers have reached a different conclusion: 'whilst knowledge of double-entry bookkeeping was available throughout sixteenth century Europe through both books and manuscripts' (Parker 1989: 9), the method was not extensively adopted until the nineteenth century (Yamey 1977: 17).

Parker (1989: 11) argues that slow adoption in Britain was probably a function of the stage of commercial development and that it was not until the rise of the capital markets and income tax collectors that more sophisticated methods of recording transactions were necessary. In Britain, methods of bookkeeping had been used for several centuries based on the requirements of merchants to maintain control and keep order. For Japan, like Britain, somewhat earlier, merchants adopt a method whose net advantages outweigh those of other systems, although inevitably there is resistance to radical change.[7]

---

days per year out of an entitlement of 15 days compared with 20 to 30 days typically taken in the USA and Europe respectively. Furthermore, average regular hours worked per week by Japanese workers were 44 hours in 1988, compared with 36 to 39 hours in Europe, although Japan was only slightly longer than the UK.

[7] Single-entry bookkeeping may be perfectly adequate to record the relatively simple transactions undertaken by merchants on their own but was probably less effective in adequately recording more complicated transactions that developed from increased exposure to international trade and the adoption of corporate organization.

The development of Western business beyond merchanting, to encompass industrial activity, became apparent to Japan in the latter part of the Tokugawa period (1603–1867), and it was in order to advance and compete with its adversary that Japan copied from the West such devices as the limited liability company. The first Japanese companies were established in 1867, the last year of the Tokugawa period, although the procedure was somewhat cumbersome in that special approval was required for each company formation. However, most of these companies failed quickly, because of managerial inexperience and government interference, and in the early Meiji period (1868–1912) the government had to coerce the merchants to form companies (Clark 1979: 30).

Difficulties were encountered at first because the mercantile houses were based on single families with one head whereas corporations required co-operation between houses. However, in

spite of the lack of success of the trading and exchange companies, the Meiji government continued to propagate the idea of a company as a form of business organization with almost missionary zeal. Explanatory pamphlets were published to help promoters of companies, and government aid for a venture was often made conditional on its incorporation. The company was extolled not merely for its financial and administrative advantages but also simply because it was modern and Western. (Clark 1979: 31)

These developments proved very important in the acceptance of double-entry bookkeeping into Japan.

Shimme (1937: 291) states that the first use of double-entry bookkeeping as a technique was in 1865 at the Yokosuka Steel Works, where Suwa Inabanokami, Oguri Kozukenosuke, and French naval accountants introduced Western bookkeeping. With the country embarking on a programme of modernization, which included the importation of European machinery and equipment, 'accounting for business transactions [became] so complicated that the hereditary Japanese system could hardly do justice to the business methods, so considerable impetus was given to the introduction of European accounting methods' (Shimme 1937: 291). Such an observation is consistent with Parker's (1989: 11) analysis of the introduction of double-entry bookkeeping into Britain.

If the cultural and economic environment was ripe for the importation of Western ideas, including double-entry bookkeeping, how was it achieved? As Fujita (1966: 50–1) has noted, Western bookkeeping was introduced further into Japan through the simultaneous importation of books from Britain, France, Germany, Russia, and the USA. Indeed, the whole education system was vulnerable to Western ideas (Shively 1971: 87). In addition to the importation of Western books on bookkeeping, a number of accounting experts—including Vicente Braga from Portugal, Alexander Shand from Britain, and William Whitney from the USA—were invited to train Japanese accountants based on Western models (Fujita 1966: 51). For instance, the Japanese government employed Shand to develop a detailed method of book-keeping for banks based on double-entry bookkeeping. A year later, in 1873, Shand's work (*The Detailed Method of Bank Bookkeeping*) was published by the Ministry of Finance. The system designed by Shand was incorporated into the 1872 National Bank Act which required national banks to:

1. maintain bookkeeping systems;
2. prepare and submit the financial statements to the government and shareholders; and
3. have their financial statements examined by government officers.

In the absence of any other accounting and legal requirements for companies, the National Bank Act was a great influence on other commercial and indus-trial corporations (Fujita 1966: 52).

Probably of even more significance than Shand's work, which assisted the process of the introduction of double-entry bookkeeping, was the translation by Fukuzawa[8] (1835–1901) of the American textbook *Common School Bookkeeping*, which was written by Bryant and Stratton and published in 1871. Fukuzawa argued that existing methods based on single-entry bookkeeping were unsatisfactory and that an understanding of double-entry bookkeeping could help resolve some of these problems. The textbook was used in schools and played a vital role in the acceptance of double-entry bookkeeping in Japan (Someya 1989: 78).

The development of improved accounting systems was associated with the coming of big business. Some of the major businessmen that emerged at that time included Iwasaki of Mitsubishi, Minomura of Mitsui, and Yasuda, whose business activities were encouraged by the government through finan-cial subsidies and materials with the added advantage that profits were tax-free (Clark 1979). In addition, some non-strategic state-owned industries were sold off cheaply during the recession of the 1870s. Entrepreneurs, par-ticularly from the same family, founded companies in several different indus-tries but principally in heavy industry such as engineering, chemicals, iron and steel, and shipbuilding. With common origins and common ownership,

---

[8] Yukichi Fukuzawa was the founder of Keio University and his portrait now appears on the ¥10,000 bank notes.

together with money from the same bank, the core of the *zaibatsu* (financial combines) was formed. The banks received deposits from the public and recycled them in the interests of the group. Throughout this period the financial system was relatively underdeveloped. Even though the Tokyo and Osaka stock exchanges were formed in 1878 they traded almost exclusively in bonds, principally government bonds.

Four main groups developed—Mitsubishi, Mitsui, Sumitomo, and Yasuda—which were characterized by inter-company trading on favourable terms, and these groups continued to benefit from government influence. The structure of each *zaibatsu* was hierarchical, with a central holding company controlled by a founding family. The holding company would own the majority of shares in a number of core companies including the bank, the trust company, trading company, and insurance. Limited liability status as an aspect of modern Western commercial culture was considered to be crucial and clearly assisted the development of the *zaibatsu*. Double-entry bookkeeping was not only considered to be modern but appropriate for complex transactions, often involving the group, that were well beyond the simple methods of record keeping used by the early merchants.

The 1880s saw a considerable reaction against the Westernization of Japan, gaining intellectual support[9] from a new publication, the *Nihonjin*, launched in 1888 with the objective of emphasizing the traditional past. One of the major concerns was a loss of heritage, particularly the social and moral qualities of the Tokugawa period. Paradoxically, this development underlines the determination to match Western economic strength, since such reaction as did occur was confined to aspects of Westernization which were not of direct benefit to Japan in its attempt to compete successfully with its adversary. Economic power was considered to be an essential prerequisite to military power, itself a means of avoiding further shame at the hands of outsiders from the West, and of increasing Japan's standing among its neighbours (reflected by its incursions on to the mainland and wars with China, 1894–5, and Russia, in the early twentieth century).

Legal framework

One factor that hindered the formation and development of companies was the lack of an appropriate legal framework and, consequently, regulation was on an *ad hoc* basis. The determination to improve matters in this area must be

[9] The intellectual support came mainly from Setsurei Miyake, Shigetaka Shiga, Enryo Inoue, and Jugo Sugiura.

attributed, however, not only to the desire to improve economic performance, but also to the fact that the Japanese government gave priority to the revision of the unequal treaties, and success in this respect rested on acceptance by the West that sufficient legal reform had occurred (Shively 1971: 90).

The first draft of the Civil Code in 1878 was rejected as being too close to the French Code, since the Japanese were sensitive to the shame that might accrue from adopting an entire code from a single country. Eventually, in 1898, a draft was accepted which contained elements of French, German, and British law as well as elements of Japanese law. Disagreements between French-trained and English-trained jurists also occurred with the development of the Commercial Code (CC). In 1881 the government tried to resolve the disagreement by employing a German, Hermann Roesler, to draft the Code. Perhaps not surprisingly he used the draft German CC as his foundation (Henderson 1973: 167–9). A version modified by Japanese jurists became law in 1890, demonstrating the country's ability to absorb Western ideas and apply them to different environmental conditions. The CC was substantially amended in 1899 and most notably permitted the formation of joint-stock companies without special arrangements, provided there was a mechanism for dissolution when considered necessary. The Code, which applied to those involved in commercial transactions as a business on their own behalf (i.e. companies), also established the duties of directors and contained four major disclosure articles (190–3) which covered the following areas:

1. preparation of accounting documents (article 190);
2. publicity of accounting documents and annexed specification (article 191);
3. approval of accounting documents and public notice of the balance sheet (article 192);
4. release from liability of directors or auditors (article 193).

The emphasis of the CC was on the provision of information for creditors rather than shareholders, reflecting the European continental influence in its drafting (Choi and Hiramatsu 1987: 35).

Preference for German codified law rather than French law arose, not just to break the deadlock between rival-trained jurists, but also because of the substantial influence of Germany in the development of Japanese authoritarian institutions. Not only had Hirobumi Ito, a senior bureaucrat, been part of the Iwakura Mission but he also spent considerable time in 1882 in Austria and Germany, 'from where he telegraphed a request for the appointment of three advisors, recommended by Bismarck, to come to Japan to aid in drafting political reforms' (Shively 1971: 84). Furthermore, it was the Iwakura Mission that made contact with the eminent German scholars Rudolf von Gneist and Lorenz von Stein, who proved so influential with the élite of the Meiji government (Soviak 1971: 12).

ACCOUNTING DEVELOPMENTS: 1900 TO 1948

While there were minor changes to the CC in 1911 and 1923 it was not until the 1930s that important modifications were made, when a series of laws, ordinances, and plans were passed to try to ensure that the economy was strong enough to fulfil the war aspirations of the military. The main aim of these initiatives was to introduce some degree of uniformity in reporting that would enhance national planning.

It is likely that developments in Germany had been influential in the path pursued by Japan. In the 1930s German ministers, including the Minister of Justice, considered the main aim of the accountancy profession to be to assist the economy and increase efficiency (Matz 1982: 81). The German system of standardized accounting 'represents in some respects an extreme solution—complete national uniformity enforced from above. . . . To some extent, at least, it may be said to owe its origin to the desire to consolidate control by government and party organisations for reasons of public economy and fiscal considerations, rather than to further the interests of the individual undertaking' (Singer 1982: 9–10).

Working Rules for Preparing Financial Statements were issued in 1934 by the Temporary Industrial Rationalization Bureau with the aim of providing guidance to those preparing financial statements as well as assisting national planning. This was an important development because it represented a break from the legalistic approach to financial reporting towards consistency and uniformity. Jurists were not responsible for the drafting of these rules but instead academic accountants were very influential. As a consequence, although there was still a preference for 'things German', the academics took a rather broader approach and considered aspects of Anglo-Saxon accounting and in particular the works of Dicksee and Hatfield (McKinnon 1986). The Working Rules were supported further by the *Manual for Preparing Financial Statements in the Factories of Munitions for the Navy* and the *Working Rules for Preparing Financial Statements in the Factories of Munitions for the Army*. Both manuals were issued in 1940.

Central planning was increased further during the inter-war period and of particular importance was the issuance in 1941 of *Tentative Standards for Financial Statements of Manufacturing Companies*. The *Tentative Standards*, issued by the Uniform Financial Statements Council of the Central Planning Board, were aimed at enhancing macro-economic control by the provision of specific information on pricing and production policies, rather than integrating standards with the CC. The standards represented a statement of standardized accounting rather than a set of accounting standards (Fujita 1968: 124). Such 'standardization aimed first at easing the depression, and later at unifying the military state in preparation for war' (Someya 1989: 80).

ACCOUNTING DEVELOPMENTS SINCE 1948

The Allied occupation

The driving influence behind the Occupation Forces was the USA, who sought to democratize Japan. Since the Japanese were unaccustomed to investing on the Stock Exchange the USA considered it essential to provide some level of investor protection, not least because it wished to distribute the shares of the *zaibatsu* (financial combines). Thus, the interests of shareholders were considered for the first time to be as important as those of creditors.

The USA disbanded the Temporary Industrial Rationalization Bureau and the Planning Board but retained the CC, which continued to be controlled by the Ministry of Justice. However, the Occupation Forces recognized deficiencies in the CC, particularly with respect to the extent of information disclosure for investors. Consequently, the CC was revised in 1947, 1948, 1949, and twice in 1950. The 1950 amendments changed certain provisions which related to the role of auditors, the rights and duties of shareholders, the general meeting, and the individual shareholder (McKinnon 1986: 180).

In addition to modifying the CC, the Occupation Forces introduced a completely new system of regulation, based essentially on that prevailing in the USA. This involved the formation of the Securities Exchange Commission in 1948, the introduction of the Securities and Exchange Law 1949 (promulgated first in 1947 and subsequently amended in 1948 and 1950), the formation of the Japanese Institute of Certified Public Accountants in 1949, the formation of the Investigation Committee on Business Accounting Systems in 1949, and the establishment of the Tax Bureau and National Tax Administration Agency in 1950.

Other than the dissolution of the Securities Exchange Commission in 1953, the regulatory system introduced by the USA still exists. It is possible that shame was a factor in ensuring that the country did not return to the pre-war regulatory framework. Since the Japanese had been defeated in the war they may have believed that they had a lot to learn from their adversaries, particularly the USA.

A summary of the regulatory framework is provided in Fig. 23.I. An important aspect is the dual nature of financial reporting applicable to listed corporations. All companies must prepare a corporate report that complies at least with the regulations of the CC, for which the Ministry of Justice is responsible, and these documents are sent to shareholders. In addition, all listed corporations must prepare a second set of accounts that must comply, at the very least, with the requirements of the Securities and Exchange Law (SEL), for which the Ministry of Finance is responsible. These reports are rarely sent to shareholders but they may be scrutinized at head office or at the relevant stock exchange and they may be purchased at government publication centres. While the profits reported in the two sets of accounts will be the same, the extent of disclosure of information in the SEL accounts is much greater than that in the annual reports prepared in accordance with the CC. Nevertheless, the fact that there are two sets of accounts involves considerable financial reporting costs.

Another important point is that the Japanese cultural characteristic of interdependency rather than independency is apparent in the regulatory framework governing financial reporting and this is highlighted in Fig. 23.1 by horizontal lines. The role of each of these important organizations will be considered separately.

The post-war regulatory framework

Fig. 23.I presents a summary of the major institutions involved in the regulatory framework which has governed financial reporting in Japan since 1945. The Securities and Exchange Commission, which was abolished shortly after the departure of the Occupation Forces in 1952, however, does not appear in the figure due to its short lifespan. The institutions which remain important today are considered in more detail below.

The Securities Exchange Commission (SEC) and the Securities and Exchange Law (SEL). The SEC and the SEL, introduced in Japan in 1947, were based on the Securities Exchange Commission and the Securities and Exchange Act in the USA. The USA considered that these elements of control were essential

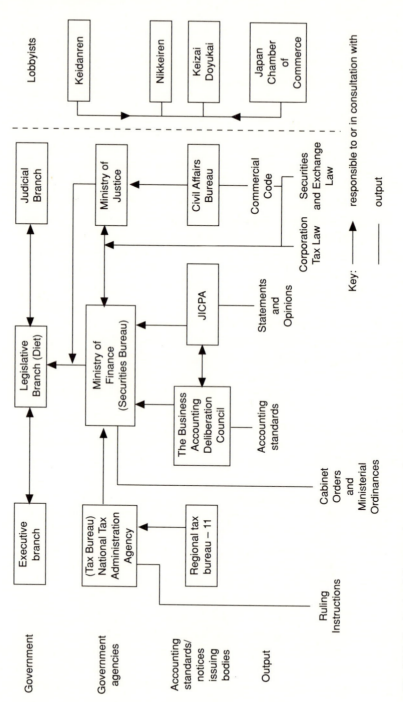

Fig. 23.1 Institutional framework governing financial reporting in Japan

aspects of the democratization programme. This programme involved the liquidation of the *zaibatsu* holding companies and the distribution of their shares to the public, thereby creating the middle class that Japan had lacked in its feudal society. However, within a few months of the departure of the Allied Forces in 1953 the SEC had been abolished and its role transferred to the Securities (Finance) Bureau of the Ministry of Finance (effective from I August 1953). Thus, within a very short period of time a regulatory body, independent of government, had been fundamentally changed.

The introduction of the SEL was a major change in the orientation of corporate financial reporting, since disclosures were orientated to general investors. The original purpose of the Act was: 'to permit and facilitate fair issuance and transfer procedures, as well as other transactions in securities and to provide for the orderly exchange of securities to make possible a rational administration of the national economy, in addition to protecting the investors' (article I).

The Japanese Institute of Certified Public Accountants (JICPA). Organization among professional accountants first occurred in Japan in 1907 (probably as a reaction to the requirements of the CC), although the first formal body of accountants was not established until 1927 by the Registered Accountants Law. However, such was the economic significance of the *zaibatsu* that outside shareholders were of little consequence and there was little pressure to introduce the concept of independent external audit of financial statements at that time.

The Occupation Forces considered the registered accountants body to be inadequate for the new regulatory environment (Fujita 1966: 67) and as a result the Registered Accountants Law was repealed and replaced by the Certified Public Accountants Law (CPAL) 1948. JICPA was formed the following year as a voluntary body and in 1953 the Institute became incorporated under the Civil Code. However, both the profession and the professional body were of little importance until 1966, when the CPAL was amended to make it compulsory for all CPAs to be members. Note that this is akin to the situation that exists in the UK, but differs from that in the USA, where CPAs do not have to be members of the AICPA.

One of the reasons for the introduction of the CPAL was a feeling that the Japanese profession was not as competent as those of its adversaries and therefore it is possible that a feeling of shame necessitated something being done so that the status of a Japanese CPA became as high as that of a US CPA. As the JICPA itself states (1987: I), 'the CPAL was designed to ensure the quality of professional accountants at a level of competence comparable with the United States, the United Kingdom, etc. As a result, the Law requires that Japanese accountants be as comparable in status with Japanese lawyers.'

JICPA has no authority to issue accounting standards, that role being given to the Business Accounting Deliberation Council. In essence the JICPA offers a sort of administrative guidance in the form of statements, opinions, or working rules. Such guidance is not backed by law but, as with its UK counterpart, the JICPA has authority over its members.

Note that, in reality, the accounting profession is effectively controlled by the bureaucracy. Not only does the Ministry of Finance have authority over BADC and therefore controls the issuance of accounting standards, but the Ministry also influences the examination pass rate of the CPA qualification. Pass rates at the final examination are often in single figures, making it extremely difficult to qualify, and thereby the professional body is kept well under control. As a consequence, there were only 8,662 CPAs as at 1 March 1990 compared with 322,135 CPAs (August 1990) in the USA and approximately 165,000 in the UK. In addition to these restrictions, competition between CPA firms is controlled by Codes of Professional Ethics which have established fee schedules and limitations on advertising.

The Investigation Committee on Business Accounting Systems (ICBAS) (now the Business Accounting Deliberation Council (BADC)). Due to the lack of detail and variety of practices in Japanese accounting, the Occupation Forces established the ICBAS of the Economic Stabilization Board in 1948. The following year ICBAS issued the *Working Rules for Preparing Financial Statements and the Business Accounting Principles*, which were based on *A Statement of Accounting Principles* written by Sanders, Hatfield, and Moore (1938) for the American Institute of Certified Public Accountants (McKinnon, 1986). US influence continued with the issuance of a *Tentative Statement of Auditing Standards* in 1950.

In July 1952 the government changed the role of ICBAS away from its independent structure to become, in effect, part of the Ministry of Finance. Thus, within a short period of time both the SEC and the ICBAS had become part of the government machinery, the bureaucracy (Cooke and Kikuya 1992).

ICBAS was renamed the Business Accounting Standards Deliberation Council in 1950 and then the Ministry of Finance changed its name to the Business Accounting Deliberation Council (BADC) in 1952 with the role of sole originator of accounting standards in Japan. Like all Japanese deliberation councils, BADC acts as an advisory body to the Ministry. Membership of BADC comes from business, academe, the professional accounting communities, as well as the Ministry of Finance itself (JICPA 1987: 13). Indeed, the Ministry has to approve the appointment of all members of the Council.

The role of *Business Accounting Principles* issued by ICBAS in 1949 was three-fold:

1. accounting conventions should be followed, even if they are not covered by Ministerial Ordinance, because they are considered to be 'fair and proper';
2. CPAs should follow such standards in the audit of financial statements under the Securities and Exchange Law and the requirements of the Certified Public Accountants Law;
3. accounting standards should be given full consideration in any amendments to the law affecting financial statements, e.g. the CC or tax law.

The purpose of this statement on financial accounting standards is to provide a guide to the establishment of generally accepted accounting principles which should be adhered to by all business enterprises. The *Principles* consist of three main sections, covering general principles, income statement principles, and balance sheet principles. The general principles provide a summary of the seven key principles which in essence are as follows:

1. financial accounts should provide a true and fair report of the financial position of the company and its operational results;
2. financial accounts should be based on accurate accounting records in accordance with the principles of orderly bookkeeping;[10]
3. capital surplus and earned surplus should be separately disclosed;
4. the financial statements should incorporate accounting which should not mislead users;
5. accounting principles and practices should be consistently applied and only changed if there is good reason;
6. a prudent approach to accounting should be adopted in providing for possible unfavourable effects upon the financial condition of a business enterprise;
7. accounts should be prepared on a consistent basis in accordance with the accounting records and facts and not with regard to the purpose, e.g. tax accounting, credit rating, etc., or the user of the financial statements, e.g. shareholders, creditors, tax authorities.

Tax Bureau and National Tax Administration Agency (NTAA). The introduction of the Tax Bureau and NTAA to the regulatory system in 1950 was the

[10] Note that 'principles of orderly bookkeeping' is a German phrase.

result of recommendations of the Shoup Committee, which in turn were based on tax theory in the USA. One important aspect, which still prevails today, was the introduction of a dual system of tax returns that encourage good bookkeeping and honest self-assessment (Peat Marwick 1986). Privileged taxpayers (blue tax returns) receive additional tax deductions—particularly in the areas of losses, research and development, and accelerated depreciation—and the authorities can only adjust tax assessments for errors in the books of account and records (Cooke and Kikuya 1992).

In order to obtain tax relief for provisions and reserves they must be incorporated into the financial statements. As a result, deferred taxation is rarely practised, although permanent and timing differences do occur. Tax law is based on the Corporation Tax Law, the Income Tax Law, and the Special Taxation Measures Law. The latter provides the government with special measures considered necessary to achieve its social and economic goals.

The power to tax and make people responsible for payment is vested in the Diet (the Japanese parliament) as provided by the Japanese Constitution. Proposed legislation is drafted by the Tax Bureau, which is part of the Ministry of Finance. The actual administration of the tax laws rests with the NTAA, which is part of the Ministry of Finance (McKinnon 1986). The Ministry issues regulations and rules called Cabinet Orders or Ministerial Ordinances which in effect implement the national tax laws. The director of NTAA issues ruling instructions or directives to the regional tax bureaux, with the aim of ensuring uniformity in the interpretation of tax law. However, as with all legal matters, definitive interpretation rests with the courts.

Ministry of Justice. The Ministry of Justice has been influential in the setting of minimum levels of disclosure in the annual reports of Japanese companies, particularly since the inception of the 1899 CC.

The underlying objective of financial statements prepared in accordance with CC requirements is to protect creditors and current investors. Accordingly, disclosures as to the availability of earnings for dividend distributions, creditworthiness and earning power are of prime importance. The emphasis is on proper presentation of the Company's financial position and results of operations in accordance with law. (JICPA 1984: 4–5)

Emphasis is placed on financial position, although a statement of changes in financial position has never been a requirement of the CC. In contrast, a cash flow statement is required under the SEL.

Ministry of Finance. This Ministry is probably the most important body which influences accounting in Japan, particularly with regard to listed corporations, a position gained since the Second World War. Previously, the Ministry of Justice had been the most influential, since it administered financial reporting based on the CC of 1899 and as subsequently amended. Consequently, the Ministry of Justice has an important role which had been well established before the imposition of a new regulatory environment by the USA.

The imposed regulatory environment gave the Ministry of Finance new powers which elevated it to its predominant position. The purpose of reporting under the SEL is 'adequate and appropriate disclosure for the protection of general investors' (JICPA 1984: 38). While reporting under the SEL is mainly limited to listed companies, such corporations represent a significant proportion of economic activity. The Ministry of Finance must be kept informed, not only through disclosures at the time of issuing securities by a registration statement for which Ministry approval must be obtained by the issuing corporation, but also by continuous disclosure. The form and content of the registration statement and securities report are prescribed by the Ministry of Finance Ordinance.

Since both the form and content of the financial statements prepared under the SEL are more detailed than under the CC, there has been considerable uneasiness between the two Ministries. Furthermore, there are, at times, contradictions between the SEL and the CC. In addition, the SEL accounts must be filed with the Ministry of Finance. Control over BADC and the Tax Bureau and the NTAA, together with effective control over JICPA, places the Ministry of Finance in a particularly strong position. Discussions have taken place between the two Ministries to reconcile some of the differences between accounting standards and the CC. While conflict was common in the 1950s and 1960s the two Ministries now enjoy a stable relationship based on mutual distrust. Indeed, amendments to the CC in 1990 bring the laws closer together.

Civil Affairs Bureau (CAB). The CAB is part of the Ministry of Justice and is responsible for the Legal Affairs Bureau and the District Legal Affairs Bureau. It is the responsibility of the CAB to draft both laws and Ministerial Ordinances which relate to commercial or civil matters. Consequently, it is the responsibility of this bureau to draft both amendments to the CC and Ministerial Ordinances.

Lobbyists. The four major business lobbyists in descending order of importance are Keidanren, Nikkeiren, the Keizai Doyukai, and the Japan Chamber of Commerce and Industry. Keidanren is a powerful body of major industrialists particularly automobile manufacturers, shipbuilders, iron and steel, petrol companies, the chemical industry, as well as trading companies. So powerful and influential is this employers' organization that the chief of Keidanren is often referred to as the 'prime minister of business' (van Wolferen 1989: 354).

Keidanren, effectively the forerunner of the post-war ruling party, the Liberal Democrats, emerged as a result of the demise of the *zaibatsu* which allowed the large industrial federations to develop. Keidanren is brought within the political system by regular consultation with the most important ministries. Furthermore, Keidanren is able to appoint members to BADC in order to ensure that the interests of its federation are protected. While this organization has been influential in determining changes in accounting principles it does not always get its own way. For example, Keidanren has never been in favour of extending the nature and scope of the audit function. Despite such opposition, the 1974 amendment to the CC involved an extension of the scope of audit and consequently an increase in responsibility for auditors.

The other lobbying bodies pale into insignificance when compared with Keidanren. For example, Nikkeiren, the Japan Federation of Employers' Association, was set up by 'business bureaucrats formerly in the forefront of wartime industrial organisations, for the specific purpose of combating the labour movement' (van Wolferen 1989: 68). The organization has been successful in lobbying for changes in the national education curriculum as well as influencing business policy. The Keizai Doyukai, Committee for Economic Development, 'has provided a forum in which elite zaikai members can formulate a theoretical basis for business policies; it attracted attention in the mid-1950s with proposals for a Japanese style "reformed capitalism"' (van Wolferen 1989: 34). Keizai Doyukai has emphasized the need for economic mobilization and the interplay between corporations, effectively public institutions, and the administration: objectives heavily influenced by German economic and political development. Furthermore, Keizai Doyukai has consistently taken a national interest point of view in which profit may not be consistent with that objective. As in all these lobbying organizations, former bureaucrats serve in senior positions, not least because of their good connections. The Japan Chamber of Commerce and Industry, the last of the four lobbyists, protects the interests of small businesses. It is important to realize that these lobbying organizations are not independent of each other but interdependent. Consequently, each organization can influence accounting by lobbying the most effective body. For example, the Chamber of Commerce and Industry may try to protect the interests of its members by lobbying Keidanren, which has direct access to the appropriate regulatory authority.

Financial reporting issues

The two major issues that have resulted in a substantial amount of criticism about Japanese financial reporting in the USA involve consolidated accounts and segmental reporting. While consolidated accounts became mandatory from 1977 for Japanese corporations that issue securities to the public, these reports represent supplementary statements to the Japanese corporate reports and not the main accounts.

A second financial reporting issue that has caused some controversy involves segmental reporting. Japanese corporations with a listing in the USA have been able to claim an exemption from the disclosure requirements on segmental reporting in the Securities and Exchange Act filing. As a result, up until 1990 the English-version accounts of Japanese corporations that had an independent audit report invariably had a 'subject to' paragraph which highlighted the omission of segment information.

The development of consolidated financial reports

During the 1960s there were several cases where a large number of investors sustained losses as a result of profit manipulation or window dressing through subsidiary companies, which might have come to light if consolidated accounts had been prepared. In particular, the bankruptcy of Sanyo Special Steel Ltd. in 1965 led to considerable criticism of accounting practices in Japan. This is, in fact, not that unusual since Japan is used to a relatively high level of bankruptcies (van Wolferen 1989: 47). However, the case of Sanyo Steel did receive more public criticism than many previous cases. 'The strength of the public outcry, based on the social and political ramifications and the potential of fraudulent reporting to prejudice the operations of the Japanese securities markets, created intense pressure on Diet and the Ministry of Finance to improve corporate disclosure under the Securities Exchange Law' (McKinnon and Harrison 1985: 210–11).

As a result, the Japanese stock exchanges began in 1970 to delist the shares of companies which issued fraudulent financial statements (JICPA 1987: 47). There was also concern about the level of bankruptcies, and consequently the quality of information disclosed, arising from the oil crisis of 1973. Furthermore, companies were merging during periods of high economic growth to form larger groups. These factors increased pressure on government, in particular, to bring Japanese financial reporting up to standards of Anglo-Saxon accounting which required the publication of group accounts.

Another factor of considerable importance, which stimulated the development of consolidated accounts in Japan, was the growth of international corporations. In the early 1960s the entry of Japanese corporations on to the New York Stock Exchange was barred by the USA since their accounts were based on the parent company only. In fact the first listing of a Japanese corporation on the New York Stock Exchange did not occur until 1970. McKinnon and Harrison (1985: 211) highlight the feeling of shame by pointing out that 'the Ministry of Finance came to perceive that Japan's parent-only financial statements carried relatively low international status'.

In addition, US corporations and the US government lobbied the Japanese government to allow US corporations to be listed in Japan and file consolidated accounts. The Japanese government agreed to this and in 1973 foreign shares were listed on the Tokyo Stock Exchange for the first time. Three US corporations obtained a quotation on the Tokyo Stock Exchange on 18 December 1973 (CITICORP, Dow Chemical, First Chicago Corp.), but it was not until 1976 that a non-US firm (ROBECO NV) obtained a listing. At 31 December 1988 there were 112 foreign corporations listed on the Tokyo Stock Exchange of which nearly 60 per cent were from the USA and a further 16 per cent from the UK. Consequently, the feeling by the Japanese that their financial statements were not well regarded by foreigners (possibly shame), in particular by the USA, was an important factor in the development of consolidated accounts in Japan.

The various pressures for change led the Ministry of Finance to ask the BADC to consider the introduction of consolidation accounting closely, and in 1975 it published the *Accounting Principles for Consolidated Financial Statements*. The Ministry of Finance itself issued the *Regulations Concerning Consolidated Financial Statements* in 1976 and the related interpretative rules in 1977. Consequently, consolidated financial statements became a requirement for listed companies for the financial year beginning on or after 1 April 1977. An important point is that consolidated accounts need be prepared only by corporations reporting under the SEL and even then the consolidated accounts are supplementary to the main set of accounts which are still prepared on an individual basis only. This represents another example of the Japanization of a foreign concept. For a detailed discussion of events in the formulation of the consolidation ordinances see McKinnon (1986) and McKinnon and Harrison (1985).

The development of segmental reporting in Japan

The issue of segmental information is allied to that of consolidation accounting since there is a loss of underlying detail in consolidated financial reports. To compensate in part for the loss in detail, generally accepted US accounting principles require segmental information concerning the company's operations in different industries, its foreign operations, and its export sales. Rather more general provisions had existed in Companies Acts and stock exchange requirements in the UK for many years, but SSAP 25 (1990) now requires more extensive segmental disclosure for accounting periods beginning on or after I July 1990.

Despite the requirements in the USA, foreign issuers of securities have been able to claim an exemption from such disclosure requirements in the Securities and Exchange Act filing with the US Securities and Exchange Commission. As a result, the accounts of Japanese corporations, prepared for the international reader, that have an independent audit report invariably have a 'subject to' paragraph which highlights the omission of segmental information. Thus, there is a conflict of two concepts: shame leads to disclosure of the required information whereas the desire for corporate secrecy encourages resistance to disclosure and the latter concept initially prevailed (Aida 1972; Ballon *et al.* 1976; Someya 1989).

Due to external pressure from the USA, engendering a feeling of shame that the audit reports of major Japanese corporations receive qualified audit reports in the USA, and are therefore somehow inferior to those of US companies, BADC has recently issued requirements to disclose segmental information. From April 1990 Japanese corporations must disclose operating profit and sales for each business segment and turnover for each geographical segment. However, a survey of 196 Japanese First Section corporations (response rate 69 per cent) by Nihon Keizai Shimbun (in *World Accounting Report*, May 1990) found that only 37 per cent considered such disclosures to be beneficial to investors, whereas 55 per cent did not welcome the requirements as they will increase disclosure costs and/or reveal confidential information.

SUMMARY

It is possible that the shame of being inferior to foreigners was a potent force for 'catching up and overtaking' (the slogan 'oituke, oikose!' was used) the Occident, which formed the model of adversarial contrast. After 200 years of isolation during the Tokugawa period the country was ready and willing to import and, where necessary, modify Western culture as well as goods. The feeling of backwardness in relation to the West was emphasized by the vulnerability of Japan to military intimidation such as that by Commodore Perry.

The Iwakura Mission was very impressed by the paternal nature of some of the companies in the West and this formed the model of large-firm development in Japan. Companies developed in Japan in the second half of the nineteenth century and more complex trading arrangements, along with the willingness to accept Western ideas, led to the importation of double-entry bookkeeping which began to replace the single-entry bookkeeping that had been used by the merchant traders, a situation similar to that which occurred in the UK.

While there was a reaction in the 1880s to the wholesale importation of Western culture, mainly because the moral and social qualities of the Tokugawa period appeared to be threatened, the development of modern corporations which used double-entry bookkeeping to record their increasingly complex transactions was driven inexorably forward. However, it was not until the end of the nineteenth century that the CC gave companies their legal status. The Code also introduced disclosure requirements which included the publication of financial statements. Codified law was introduced since this could be achieved relatively quickly to demonstrate to the West that legal reform had occurred. Furthermore, German law and political institutions were adopted because of the symmetry between the needs of the Japanese oligarchs and Germany's authoritarian structure.

Developments in accounting in the first forty-five years of the twentieth century were dominated by the requirements of the military for information prepared on a consistent basis. The Allied Occupation of Japan at the end of the Second World War was dominated by the USA. As part of the democratization programme for Japan the Allied Forces tried to break up the *zaibatsu*, which were considered to have assisted greatly in the war effort. Since the shares of the *zaibatsu* were to be distributed to shareholders the USA introduced a new regulatory framework modelled on that prevailing in the USA to ensure that the disclosure needs of shareholders were met.

The imposed regulatory framework remains largely intact, although power has been concentrated further in the bureaucracy and considerable interdependency between institutions exists. Furthermore, the Allied Forces' hope that a thriving independent accounting profession would develop has not materialized, since the number entering the profession is effectively controlled by the Ministry of Finance and the issuance of accounting standards is controlled likewise. Another aspect of importance is that Keidanren, which represents the large corporations, is very influential over the Ministry of Finance, thereby making it difficult for a thriving independent profession to develop.

Perhaps a factor of some importance is Japan's shame culture, which would not allow the country to return to its pre-war regulatory framework. Furthermore, criticism by the USA concerning consolidated accounts and segmental reporting has had the desired effect as far as Japan's adversary is concerned.

APPENDIX: CHRONOLOGY OF ACCOUNTING IN JAPAN[11]

1865   Double-entry bookkeeping used by French naval accountant at the Yokosuka Steel Works.

1868   [Meiji Restoration.]

1871   V. E. Braga employed, by the government, as a chief accountant at the mint established in Osaka.

1873   The first book in Japanese on Western bookkeeping published by Y. Fukuzawa.

        A. A. Shand's treatise, *Ginko Boki Seiho (The Detailed Method of Bank Bookkeeping)* published by the Ministry of Finance.

1875   W. G. Whitney engaged as a teacher of accounting at the first commercial college.

1890   The first Commercial Code promulgated.

1899   The Commercial Code amended.

        The Income Tax Law (including Corporation Tax provisions) promulgated.

1907   First group of professional accountants formed.

1911   The Commercial Code revised.

1923   The Commercial Code revised.

1927   The Registered Public Accountants Law promulgated.

1934   Working Rules for Financial Statements issued by the Ministry of Commerce and Industry.

1938   The Commercial Code revised.

1940   *Working Rules for the Preparation of Financial Statements in Munitions Factories for the Navy*, issued by the Ministry of Navy; . . . *for the Army*, issued by the Ministry of Army.

        The Corporation Tax Law independently promulgated.

---

[11]   For a more detailed chronology see Cooke and Kikuya 1992.

1941   *Tentative Standards for Manufacturing Companies' Balance Sheets, Profit and Loss Accounts and Inventories* issued by the Planning Bureau.

1947   The Securities Exchange Commission (SEC) established.
Instructions on the Preparation of Financial Statements for Industrial and Commercial Companies issued by general headquarters of the Occupation Forces.
Anti-Monopoly Law promulgated.
Full revision to the Corporation Tax Law.
The Securities and Exchange Law promulgated.

1948   The Securities and Exchange Law established.
The Investigation Committee on Business Accounting Systems of the Economic Stabilization Board, later to be known as the Business Accounting Standards Deliberation Council (BASDC), established.
The Registered Public Accountants Law superseded by the Certified Public Accountants Law.

1949   The *Business Accounting Principles and Working Rules for Financial Statements* issued by the Investigation Committee on Business Accounting Systems.
First Report of the Shoup Committee on the restructuring of the Japanese taxation system issued.
The Japanese Institute of Certified Public Accountants established.

1950   The Corporation Tax Law amended.
The Commercial Code revised.
The Securities and Exchange Law amended.
Second Report of the Shoup Committee issued.
Regulation Concerning Terms, Formats and Preparation Methods of Financial Statements (Regulation Concerning Financial Statements) issued by the SEC.
Auditing Standards and Auditing Working Rules for the Preparation of Audit Report issued by the BASDC.

1951   *Working Rules on Audit Certification* issued by the SEC.
Audits by CPAs under Securities and Exchange Law commenced.
The Certified Tax Accountants Law promulgated.

1952   The Japanese Federation of Certified Tax Accountants established.
The administration of the BASDC transferred to the Ministry of Finance and renamed the Business Accounting Deliberation Council (BADC).

1953   The SEC abolished and the administration of the Securities and Exchange Law transferred to the Finance (Securities) Bureau of the Ministry of Finance.

1956   *Auditing Standards, Auditing Working Rules for the Preparation of Audit Reports* amended and *Auditing Working Rules for the Reporting of Audit Reports* issued by BADC.

1957   The Special Tax Measures Law promulgated.

1962   The Commercial Code revised.
Cost Accounting Standards issued by BADC.

1963   Revision to the *Business Accounting Principles*.

1965   Full revision of the Corporation Tax Law.
       [Bankruptcy of Sanyo Special Steel.]
1966   *Provisional Opinion on Consolidated Financial Statements* issued by BADC.
       The Certified Public Accountants Law amended.
       Ordinance on Audit Corporations issued by the Ministry of Finance.
       Opinion on the Reconciliation of the Tax Law and the Business Accounting Principles issued
       by BADC.
1967   Revision to the Corporation Tax Law.
       Title of Registered Public Accountant abolished.
       Opinion on Consolidated Financial Statements issued by BADC.
1971   The Securities and Exchange Law revised.
1973   *Ordinance on the Disclosure of Financial Position* issued by the Ministry of Finance.
1974   The Commercial Code revised (Law Concerning the Special Case of
       Commercial Code for Audit of Kabushiki-Kaisha issued).
       Audit by independent external auditor under the Commercial Code began.
1975   The Securities and Exchange Law revised.
       Accounting Principles for Consolidated Financial Statements issued by BADC.
1976   *Ordinances concerning Consolidated Financial Statements Regulations* issued by the
       Ministry of Finance.
       Auditing Working Rules for Preparation and Reporting of Audit Reports amended.
1977   *Opinion on Interim Financial Statements Included in Semi-annual Reports* issued by BADC.
       Audits of interim financial statements by CPAs begun.
1978   First disclosure of consolidated financial statements.
1979   *Accounting Standards for Foreign Currency Transactions, etc.* issued by BADC.
1980   *Opinion on Disclosure of Financial Information of Price-Level Changes* issued by
       BADC.
       Revision to the Certified Tax Accountants Law.
1981   Revision to the Commercial Code (including the Special Case Law in 1974).
       The Securities and Exchange Law revised.
1982   Revision to the *Business Accounting Principles.*
       Revision to *Note to Accounting Principles for Consolidated Financial Statements.*
       Ordinance on Audit Reports of Large-Sized Companies issued by the Ministry of
       Justice.
1983   Mandatory application of the equity method under the Securities and
       Exchange Law.
       Revision to the Certified Public Accountants Law.
       Revision to *Accounting Standards for Foreign Currency Transactions, etc.*
1985   Revision to the Securities and Exchange Law.
1987   Revision to *Ordinance Concerning Consolidated Financial Statements Regulations.*
       Survey Results on the Disclosure of Segmental Information issued by BADC.
1988   *Opinion on the Disclosure of Segmental Information* issued by BADC.
       Revision to the Securities and Exchange Law.

1989   Revision to Ordinance of the Securities and Exchange Law and the related ordinances (regulation on insider dealing).
Revision to *Auditing Working Rules for Preparation of Audit Reports.*

References

Aida, Y. (1972), *Nihonjin no ishiki kozo* (Tokyo: Kodansha Gendai Shinsho).

Ballon, R. J., Tomita, I., and Usami, H. (1976), *Financial Reporting in Japan* (Tokyo: Kodansha International).

Benedict, R. (1967), *The Chrysanthemum and the Sword* (London: Routledge & Kegan Paul).

Bennett, J. W., and Nagai, M. (1953), 'The Japan Critique of the Methodology of Benedict's *The Chrysanthemum and the Sword*', *American Anthropologist*, 55.

Choi, F. D. S., and Hiramatsu K. (1987), *Accounting and Financial Reporting in Japan* (Wokingham: Van Nostrand Reinhold).

Clark, R. G. (1979), *The Japanese Company* (Princeton, NJ: Princeton University Press).

Cooke, T. E., and Kikuya, M. (1992), *Financial Reporting in Japan: Regulation, Practice and Environment* (Oxford: Blackwell).

Dale, P. N. (1986), *The Myth of Japanese Uniqueness* (London: Routledge).

Doi, T. (1971), *'Amae' no kozo* (Tokyo: Kobundo).

Eberhard, W. (1967), *Guilt and Sin in Traditional China* (Berkeley, Calif.: California University Press).

Ezzamel, M., Hoskin, K., and Macve, R. (1990), 'Managing it All by Numbers: A Review of Johnson and Kaplan's *Relevance Lost*', *Accounting and Business Research* (Spring): 153–66.

Fujita, Y. (1966), 'The Evolution of Financial Reporting in Japan', *International Journal of Accounting*, 2: 49–75.

—— (1968), 'An Analysis of the Development and Nature of Accounting Principles in Japan'. Department of Accountancy, University of Illinois: unpublished doctoral thesis.

Henderson, D. F. (1973), *Foreign Enterprise in Japan, Law and Politics* (Chapel Hill, NC: University of North Carolina Press).

Hofstede, G. H. (1980), *Culture's Consequences: International Differences in Work-Related Values* (Beverly Hills, Calif.: Sage Publications).

Jahoda, G. (1984), 'Do we Need a Concept of Culture?', *Journal of Cross-Cultural Psychology* (June), 139–51.

Japanese Institute of Certified Public Accountants (JICPA) (1984), *Corporate Disclosure in Japan: Reporting* (Tokyo: JICPA).

—— (1987), *Corporate Disclosure in Japan: Overview* (Tokyo: JICPA).

Kroeber, A. L., and Kluckhohn, C. (1952), *Culture: A Critical Review of Concepts and Definitions* (Cambridge, Mass.: Harvard University Press).

McKinnon, J. L. (1986), *The Historical Development and Operational Form of Corporate Reporting Regulation in Japan* (New York: Garland Publishing).

—— and Harrison, G. L. (1985), 'Cultural Influence on Corporate and Governmental Policy Determination in Japan', *Journal of Accounting and Public Policy*, 4: 201–33.

Matz, A. (1982), 'Accounting as a Tool for Economy in German Business', in H. W. Singer (ed.), *Standardized Accountancy in Germany* (New York: Garland Publishing).

Mori, M. (1971), *'Na' to 'haji' no bunka* (Tokyo: Kodansha Gendai Shinsho).

Nishikawa, K. (1977), 'The Introduction of Western Bookkeeping into Japan', *Accounting Historians Journal* (Spring), 25–36.

Organization for Economic Co-operation and Development (1989), *Economic Surveys: Japan* (Paris: OECD).

Ogura, E. (1982), 'The Nakai Family's Bookkeeping System', *Accounting and Business Research* (Spring): 148–52.

Parker, R. H. (1989), 'Importing and Exporting Accounting: The British Experience', in A. G. Hopwood (ed.), *International Pressures for Accounting Change* (London: ICAEW).

Peat Marwick (1986), *Taxation in Japan* (Tokyo: Peat Marwick).

Reischauer, E. O. (1988), *The Japanese Today: Change and Continuity* (Cambridge, Mass.: Belknap Press).

Rohner, R. P. (1984), 'Towards a Conception of Culture for Cross-cultural Psychology', *Journal of Cross-Cultural Psychology* (June): 111–38.

Sakuta, K. (1967), *Haji no bunka saiko* (Tokyo: Chikuma Shobo).

Shimme, S. (1937), 'Introduction to Double-Entry Bookkeeping in Japan', *Accounting Review* (Sept.): 290–5.

Shively, D. H. (1971), 'The Japanization of the Middle Meiji', in D. H. Shiveley (ed.), *Tradition and Modernization in Japanese Culture* (Princeton, NJ: Princeton University Press).

Singer, H. W. (1982), *Standardized Accountancy in Germany* (New York: Garland Publishing).

Someya, K. (1989), 'Accounting "Revolutions" in Japan', *Accounting Historians Journal* (June): 75–86.

Soviak, E. (1971), 'On the Nature of Western Progress: The Journal of the Iwakura Embassy', in D. H. Shiveley (ed.), *Tradition and Modernization in Japanese Culture* (Princeton, NJ: Princeton University Press).

Taketera, S., and Nishikawa, N. (1984), 'Genesis of Divisional Management and Accounting Systems in the House of Mitsui, 1710–1730', *Accounting Historians Journal* (Spring): 141–9.

van Wolferen, K. (1989), *The Enigma of Japanese Power* (London: Macmillan).

Yamey, B. S. (1977), 'Some Topics in the History of Financial Accounting in England 1500–1900', in W. T. Baxter and S. Davidson (eds.), *Studies in Accounting* (London: ICAEW).

INDEX